VOLUME 63

SCREEN WORLD™

The Films of 2011

BARRY MONUSH

SCREEN WORLD
Volume 62 Copyright © 2012 by Barry Monush
Executive publisher, Ben Hodges

Published in 2012 by Theatre World Media
Distributed by Applause Theatre & Cinema Books
An Imprint of Hal Leonard Corporation
7777 West Bluemound Road
Milwaukee, WI 53213

Trade Book Division Editorial Offices
33 Plymouth Street, Montclair, NJ 07042

Printed in the United States of America
Book design by Tony Meisel

ISBN 978-1-55783-952-7
ISSN 1545–9020

theatreworld.com

To Barbra Streisand

A strikingly unique personality who, shortly after entering show business, rose to the very top to become one of the most acclaimed, popular and famous entertainment figures of her time; and has since then continued to capture the public imagination as a peerless vocalist, a superb actress, and an accomplished director-producer-writer-composer.

FILMS: *Funny Girl* (1968; Academy Award winner for Best Actress); *Hello, Dolly!* (1969); *On a Clear Day You Can See Forever* (1970); *The Owl and the Pussycat* (1970); *What's Up, Doc?* (1972); *Up the Sandbox* (1972); *The Way We Were* (1973; Academy Award nomination); *For Pete's Sake* (1974); *Funny Lady* (1975); *A Star is Born* (1976; also executive producer, song writer; Academy Award winner for Best Song: "Evergreen – Love Theme from 'A Star is Born'"); *The Main Event* (1979; also producer, music producer); *All Night Long* (1981); *Yentl* (1983; also director, co-writer, and producer); *Nuts* (1987; also producer, composer); *Listen Up: The Lives of Quincy Jones* (1990); *The Prince of Tides* (1991; also director and producer; Academy Award nomination as producer); *The Mirror Has Two Faces* (1996; also director, producer, song writer, and music producer; Academy Award nomination as song writer: "I've Finally Found Someone"); *Meet the Fockers* (2004); *Little Fockers* (2010); *The Guilt Trip* (2012).

CONTENTS

Silence was Golden

In case you were keeping track, there were, by my count, a mere 807 movies that opened in the United States in 2011. No, that's not a misprint. Unless you're an extreme addict (and we know you're out there), there's a good chance that the number of films you saw in a theater during that calendar year didn't quite match that staggering figure. With all that competition out there vying for screens (and most of them barely getting a run beyond a week), you had to do something pretty special to stand out from the pack. French director-writer Michel Hazanavicius managed to do just that by giving us a charming Hollywood story that was not only in black and white but silent! Audacity gets you points, certainly, but the fact that this film was so delightfully done was what really made it click, causing a stir among the critics and then managing to win over enough skeptical audiences that it wound up with a $44 million gross in the U.S. True, it was no box office threat to Harry Potter, but getting a sizable portion of today's public to patronize a silent movie was nothing to sneeze at. And it won the Best Picture Oscar, too, giving the only previous silent winner, *Wings*, some company after 84 years!

Another Oscar very deservedly went to Christopher Plummer, giving one of the great performances of the year and possibly his best ever, as a newly out-of-the-closet senior citizen facing his final months, in the sublime *Beginners*. His victory made him the oldest-ever performer to take home the trophy, while Meryl Streep broke her own record for nominations, bringing the already impressive total up to 17. As icing on the cake she actually won this time, for her uncanny portrayal of Margaret Thatcher in *The Iron Lady*, her 3rd Oscar and first win in 29 years. Less well known than these two acting legends but no less superb was the Academy's Supporting Actress winner, Octavia Spencer, for her sharp and sassy portrayal of a vengeful domestic in *The Help*, an outstanding adaptation of one of the best-loved recent best sellers and one of the rare recent movies to make a killing at the turnstiles that didn't depend on special effects.

Special effects *were* in evidence in *Harry Potter and the Deathly Hallows Part 2*, the 8th and final chapter of the 21st century cinema's great fantasy saga, one that stayed on track, remembered to emphasize the humanity as well as the whimsical, and kept fans pleased throughout its entire run. Another of this ilk that was good fun, *Captain America*, proved to be the best of the pre-*Avengers* comic book-based adventures. Among the animated features that pleased were the off-the-wall western spoof *Rango* (another Oscar winner) and one of the rare Yule-themed movies of recent years to not grate on one's nerves, *Arthur Christmas*. If the Muppets (not to mention Mickey Rooney thrown in for maximum nostalgic impact!) being back on the big screen wasn't reason enough to feel good about the year at the movies consider some other highpoints:

Steven Soderbergh presented a terrifying what-if scenario about near-annihilation (with an all-star cast to give it an added kick) in *Contagion*; Ed Helms presided over a band of affable misfits in *Cedar Rapids*; *Dolphin Tale* told an inspiring true story for family audiences without insulting anyone's intelligence; the touchy subject of illegal immigration was humanized in *A Better Life*; Robert Redford presented a fascinating chapter of history in *The Conspirator*, about the trial of the Lincoln assassination participants; Liam Neeson gave us some more Europe-based kick-ass action in *Unknown*; Glenn Close, in fine form, hid from the world as a meek cross-dresser in the sad tale of *Albert Nobbs*; Martin Sheen reached a career peak as a man literally following in the footsteps of his late son in *The Way*; Simon Pegg and Nick Frost gleefully kidded the world of sci-fi geeks in *Paul*; Michelle Williams and Kenneth Branagh managed to capture the essence of two of our greatest stars in the always intriguing *My Week with Marilyn*; Graham Greene's excellent novel *Brighton Rock*, already expertly adapted in the 1940s, actually got a second top-notch filming; *The Ides of March* proved to be the sort of whip-smart political melodrama we could use more of these days; director Clint Eastwood and star Leonardo DiCaprio probed the complex life of one of America's most controversial gay figures in *J. Edgar*; Matthew McConaughey found a suitable role as an unscrupulous shyster in *The Lincoln Lawyer*; Paul Rudd went the stoner route with surprisingly pleasing results in *Our Idiot Brother*; Steven Spielberg delivered two satisfying entertainments of extreme opposites, the stirring anti-war drama *War Horse* and one of the better motion-capture efforts, *The Adventures of Tintin*; one of modern cinema's treasures, Woody Allen, delivered once again and even cultivated his first substantial audience in a while with *Midnight in Paris*; *The Descendants* was a marvelous teaming of one of our most thoughtful actors, George Clooney, and one of our most astute current filmmakers, Alexander Payne; Britain's *Attack the Block* was a clever combination of street punks and aliens, with just the right balance of humor and suspense; *Margin Call* was a topical and gripping exposé of the precarious nature of big business, with a fine cast given the sort of meaty roles and brainy dialogue actors crave; *Win Win* was another prime showcase for the ever-dependable Paul Giamatti; Brad Pitt nailed the role of a hot shot baseball coach in *Moneyball*; and Martin Scorsese presented a visually stunning and affectionate tribute to the movies in *Hugo*.

But if the good titles seeped through against all odds, consider this: Two of the finest performances last year were those given by Freddie Highmore and Ving Rhames in the long-overdue adaptation of the play *Master Harold ... and the Boys*. And yet, who beyond a handful of curious spectators even managed to see it? Awaiting distribution for an extended period of time, chalking up a few token screenings, and then being unceremoniously dumped on the DVD market, this is a prime example of how some of today's better work goes unseen, unremarked upon, unappreciated. Maybe if we put the brakes on the number of movies flooding the market for their all-too brief visits, week after week, maybe more attention could be given to the worthy ones otherwise doomed to slip through the cracks. It's something to consider. But in the meantime, we'll take the gems we can find, silent or otherwise.

– Barry Monush

ACKNOWLEDGMENTS

Abramorama, Anchor Bay, Anthology Film Archives, Apparition, Balcony Releasing CBS Films, Benjamin Barrett, The Cinema Guild, Cinema Libre, Columbia Pictures, DreamWorks, Brian Durnin, E1 Entertainment, Film Forum, First Independent Pictures, First Look, First Run Features, Focus Features, Fox Searchlight, Freestyle Releasing, Ben Hodges, IFC Films, International Film Circuit, Tim Johnson, Marybeth Keating, Kino International, Koch Lorber Films, Lionsgate, Tom Lynch, MGM, Magnolia Films, Anthony Meisel, Miramax Films, Music Box Films, New Line Cinema, New Yorker Films, Oscilloscope, Overture Films, Paladin, Paramount Pictures, Paramount Vantage, Regent/here!, Roadside Attractions, Rogue Pictures, Screen Gems, Screen Media, Seventh Art Releasing, Samuel Goldwyn Films, James Sheridan, Sony Pictures Classics, Strand Releasing, Summit Entertainment, TLA Releasing, TriStar, Truly Indie, Twentieth Century Fox, United Artists, Universal Pictures, Variance Films, Walt Disney Pictures, Warner Bros., The Weinstein Company

DOMESTIC FILMS A

2011 Releases / January 1–December 31

PHIL OCHS: THERE BUT FOR FORTUNE

(FIRST RUN FEATURES) Producers, Michael Cohl, Kenneth Bowser, Michael Ochs; Executive Producer, Elliot Abbott; Co-Producers, Lizzy McGlynn, Brian MacDonald, Michael Farrell, Sage Scully; Director/Screenplay, Kenneth Bowser: Photography, Jarred Alterman, Jacob Cohl, Zev Greenfield, Rob Humphreys, Tom Kaufman, Jefferson Miller, Nick August Perna, Trevor Smith; Music, Phil Ochs; Editor, Pamela Scott Arnold; a 2 Lefts Don't Make a Right Productions in association with Barking Dog Productions; Dolby; Color/Black and white; HD; Not rated; 98 minutes; Release date: January 5, 2011. Documentary on folk singer Phil Ochs.

WITH
Joan Baez, Jello Biafra, Billy Bragg, François De Menil, Deni Frand, Arthur Gorson, Tom Hayden, Judy Henske, Christopher Hitchens, Jac Holzman, Paul Krassner, Larry Marks, Lincoln Mayorga, Jerry Moss, Alice Ochs, Meegan Ochs, Michael Ochs, Van Dyke Parks, Sean Penn, Ed Sanders, Pete Seeger, Larry "Ratso" Sloman, Lucian Truscott IV, Peter Yarrow

Phil Ochs © First Run Features

Phil Ochs

Nicolas Cage, Ron Perlman

Stephen Campbell Moore
© Rogue Pictures

SEASON OF THE WITCH

(ROGUE) Producers, Charles Roven, Alex Gartner; Executive Producers, Ryan Kavanaugh, Alan G. Glazer, Steve Alexander, Tom Karnowski, Tucker Tooley; Director, Dominic Sena; Screenplay, Bragi Schut; Photography, Amir Mokri; Designer, Uli Hanisch; Costumes, Carlo Poggioli; Music, Atli Örvarsson; Editors, Mark Helfrich, Dan Zimmerman; Special Effects Supervisor, Paul Stephenson; Casting, Elaine Grainger; an Atlas Entertainment and Relativity Media production; Dolby; Super 35 Widescreen; Technicolor; Rated PG-13; 95 minutes; Release date: January 7, 2011

CAST
Behmen von Bleibruck	**Nicolas Cage**
Felson	**Ron Perlman**
Debelzaq	**Stephen Campbell Moore**
The Girl	**Claire Foy**
Hagamar	**Stephen Graham**
Johann Eckhart	**Ulrich Thomsen**
Kay von Wollenbarth	**Robert Sheehan**
Cardinal D'Ambroise	**Christopher Lee**

Kevin Rees (Dying Monk), Andrew Hefler (Jail Bailiff), Fernanda Dorogi (Givaudon, Old Woman), Rebekah Kennedy (Peasant Turk Girl), Matt Devere (Sergeant in Arms), Róbert Bánlaki (Livery Boy), Barna Illyés (Cardinal's Priest), Kevin Killebrew (Voice of Demon), Simone Kirby (Midwife), Elen Rhys (Peasant Girl), Nick Sidi (Priest), Rory MacCann (Soldier Commander), Nicola Sloane (Spinster), Brían F. O'Byrne (Grandmaster), Ada Michelle Loridans (Mila), Lisa Marie Dupree (Tavern Girl), Gergely Horpácsi, László Imre, Norbert Kovács, Zsolt Magyari (Soldiers)

Turning their back on the Crusades, a pair of warriors are taken prisoner in a plague-infested village where its inhabitants hope to break the curse of a woman they are certain is a witch.

Channing Tatum © Universal Studios

Kevin James, Vince Vaughn

THE DILEMMA

(UNIVERSAL) Producers, Brian Grazer, Ron Howard, Vince Vaughn; Executive Producers, Todd Hallowell, Victoria Vaughn, Kim Roth; Director, Ron Howard; Screenplay, Allan Loeb; Photography, Salvatore Totino; Designer, Daniel Clancy; Costumes, Daniel Orlandi; Music, Hans Zimmer, Lorne Balfe; Music Supervisor, Alexandra Patsavas; Editors, Mike Hill, Dan Hanley; Casting, Jane Jenkins, Janet Hirshenson; an Imagine Entertainment presentation in association with Spyglass Entertainment of a Brian Grazer/Wild West Picture Show production; Dolby; Color; Super 35 Widescreen; Rated PG-13; 111 minutes; Release date: January 14, 2011

CAST

Ronny Valentine	**Vince Vaughn**
Nick Brannen	**Kevin James**
Beth	**Jennifer Connelly**
Geneva	**Winona Ryder**
Zip	**Channing Tatum**
Susan Warner	**Queen Latifah**
Diane Popovich	**Amy Morton**
Thomas Fern	**Chelcie Ross**

Eduardo N. Martinez (Felix), Rance Howard (Burt), Clint Howard (Herbert Trimpy), Guy Van Swearingen (Saul), Troy West (Dr. Rosenstone), Laura Whyte (Sue), Grace Rex (Cousin Betty), Mike McNamara (Cousin James), Rebecca Spence (Jackie), Tim Rhoze (Charles), Madison Dirks, Michael Patrick Thornton, Mimi Sagadin (B&V Workers), Sandy Marshall (Medic at Gardens), Talulah Riley (Concept Car Spokesmodel), William Smillie (Poissonier), Jillian Burfete, Katie Korby (Restaurant Servers), Catherine Bruzzini (Restaurant Patron), Laura Cooper (Waitress), Mariko Hayashi-Hall (Vietnamese Parlor Owner), Cheryl Hamada (Vietnamese Parlor Worker), Gary Houston (Camera Clerk), Wendy George (Store Clerk), Keith Kupferer, Kevin Bigley, Christina Anthony (Bank Customers), Philip Rayburn Smith (Gilbert), Elaine Robinson (Mom), Noah Jerome Schwartz (Son), Chante Linwood (El Train Patron), Kielor Roebrts (Diane's Son), Benjamin Toby Mullinkosson, Nick Brade, Michael Trnka (Skate Rats), Karen Aldridge (Receptionist), Gene Honda (Shoot the Puck Announcer), Heidi Johanningmeier (Shoot the Puck Girl), Brennan Buhl (Shoot the Puck Guy), William M. Connor (Disgruntled Fan), Christopher Meister, Charlie Hilbrant (Concession Stand Customers)

Ronny Valentine wrestles with the dilemma of whether or not to tell his best friend Nick Brannen that he has seen Nick's wife cheating with another man.

Winona Ryder, Jennifer Connelly, Kevin James, Vince Vaughn

Christoph Waltz

Cameron Diaz, Seth Rogen

THE GREEN HORNET

(COLUMBIA) Producer, Neal H. Moritz; Executive Producers, Seth Rogen, Evan Goldberg, Michael Grillo, Ori Marmur, George W. Trendle, Jr.; Director, Michel Gondry; Screenplay, Seth Rogen, Evan Goldberg; Based on the radio series created by George W. Trendle; Photography, John Schwartzman; Designer, Owen Paterson; Costumes, Kym Barrett; Music, James Newton Howard; Editor, Michael Tronick; Visual Effects Supervisor, Jamie Dixon; Stunts, Vic Armstrong; Casting, Francine Maisler; an Original Film production; Dolby; Panavision; Deluxe color; 3D; Rated PG-13; 119 minutes; Release date: January 14, 2011

CAST
Britt Reid (The Green Hornet)	**Seth Rogen**
Kato	**Jay Chou**
Lenore Case	**Cameron Diaz**
James Reid	**Tom Wilkinson**
Chudnofsky	**Christoph Waltz**
D.A. Frank Scanlon	**David Harbour**
Mike Axford	**Edward James Olmos**
Popeye	**Jamie Harris**
Chili	**Chad Coleman**
Tupper	**Edward Furlong**

Jill Remez, Joe O'Connor, Morgan Rusler (*Daily Sentinel* Reporters), Joshua Chandler Erenberg (Young Britt), Analeigh Tipton (Ana Lee), Taylor Cole (Limo Girl), Robert Clotworthy (Politician), Jamison Yang (City Hall Reporter), Michael Holden (Funeral Businessman), Irene White (Maid), Gary Davis, Billy Mayo (Police Officers), Brandon Rudat, Beverly Brooks, Lu Parker (TV Anchors), Diane Mizota (TV Reporter, Reid Estate), Theodore Bressman (Daniel Vertlieb, Dead Reporter), Dave Rickley (Archive Reporter), Dina Mamedova (Russian Aftermath Reporter), Tanner Gill (SWAT Leader), George Fisher (Chauffeur), Daniel Arrias, Eddie Perez (Drug Dealers), Bryan Thompson, Reuben Langdon (Crackheads), Ameer Alexander (Armenian Gang Boss), Alexandra Lord, Christy Petersen (Pool Girls), Frederick C. Ruiz (Club Bouncer), Keith Adams, Dennis Keiffer, Travon Magee, Dave Powledge, Jerry Trimble (Chudnofsky's Gang), James Franco (Danny Cleer)

The hedonistic son of a Los Angeles newspaper tycoon decides to put his wastrel ways behind him and fight crime after his father dies under mysterious circumstances.

Jay Chou, Seth Rogen

EVERY DAY

(IMAGE) Producer, Miranda Bailey, Matt Leutwyler; Co-Producer, Amanda Marshall; Executive Producer, Sam Hoffman; Director/Screenplay, Richard Levine; Photography, Nancy Schreiber; Designer, Adam Stockhausen; Costumes, Ane Crabtree; Music, Jeanine Tesori; Editor, Pam Wise; Casting, Kerry Barden, Paul Schnee; a Cold Iron Pictures and Image Entertainment presentation of an Ambush Entertainment production; Dolby; Color; Rated R; 93 minutes; Release date: January 14, 2011

CAST
Ned	**Liev Schreiber**
Jeannie	**Helen Hunt**
Robin	**Carla Gugino**
Garrett	**Eddie Izzard**
Ernie	**Brian Dennehy**
Jonah	**Ezra Miller**
Ethan	**Skyler Fortgang**
Brian	**David Harbour**

Tilky Jones (Ian), Chris Beetem (Eric), Daniel Yelsky (Callen), Matt Kempner (Gabe), Stan Carp, George Riddle (Old Men), Albert M. Chan (Dr. Lee), Sabrina Hahn (Ashley), Kahan James (Matt), Daniel Farcher (Kirk), June Miller (Anita Roosin), Michael H. Ingram (Mitch).

A television writer, failing to produce material for a show he doesn't like, becomes even more stressed when his wife's cranky, ailing father is forced to move in with them.

Brian Dennehy, Helen Hunt © Image Entertainment

Liev Schreiber, Ezra Miller, Skyler Fortgang, Helen Hunt

Karen Young, Reed Birney © Twelve Thirty Prods.

Portia Reiners, Jonathan Groff

TWELVE THIRTY

(TWELVE THIRTY PRODS.) Producer, Dan Satorius; Director/Screenplay, Jeff Lipsky; Photography, Ruben O'Malley; Designer, Stacia Allen; Costumes, Amy Bradshaw; Editor, Sara Corrigan; Casting, Julie Schubert; Dolby; Color; Not rated; 120 minutes; Release date: January 14, 2011

CAST
Martin	**Reed Birney**
Jeff	**Jonathan Groff**
Maura	**Mamie Gummer**
Mel	**Portia Reiners**
Vivien	**Karen Young**

Halley Feiffer (Irina), Rebecca Schull (Katherine), Barbara Barrie (Eve), Kirby Mitchell (Mr. Levinson), Fred Berman (Chris), Juliette Monaco (Drunken Friend), Anne Ackerman (Cashier).

Jeff takes an interest in his co-worker Mel, experiencing sexual intimacy not only with her but the girl's sister and mother as well.

NO STRINGS ATTACHED

(PARAMOUNT) Producer, Ivan Reitman, Joe Medjuck, Jeffrey Clifford; Executive Producers, Roger Birnbaum, Gary Barber, Jonathan Glickman, Natalie Portman, Tom Pollock; Co-Executive Producer, Lisa Bruce; Director, Ivan Reitman; Screenplay, Elizabeth Meriwether; Story, Mike Samonek, Elizabeth Meriwether; Photography, Rogier Stoffers; Designer, Ida Random; Costumes, Julie Weiss; Music, John Debney; Editor, Dana E. Glauberman; Casting, Joanna Colbert, Richard Mento; a Cold Spring Pictures, Spyglass Entertainment presentation of a Montecito Picture Company production; Dolby; Super 35 Widescreen; Deluxe color; Rated R; 108 minutes; Release date: January 21, 2011

Ashton Kutcher, Mindy Kaling, Natalie Portman, Greta Gerwig

CAST

Emma Kurtzman	**Natalie Portman**
Adam Franklin	**Ashton Kutcher**
Alvin	**Kevin Kline**
Dr. Metzner	**Cary Elwes**
Patrice	**Greta Gerwig**
Lucy	**Lake Bell**
Katie	**Olivia Thirlby**
Wallace	**Chris 'Ludacris' Bridges**
Eli	**Jake Johnson**

Mindy Kaling (Shira), Talia Balsam (Sandra Kurtzman), Ophelia Lovibond (Vanessa), Guy Branum (Guy), Ben Lawson (Sam), Jennifer Irwin (Megan), Adhir Kalyan (Kevin), Brian Dierker (Bones), Abby Elliott (Joy), Vedette Lim (Lisa), Gary David Goldberg (Emma's Relative), Armen Weitzman (Taxi Driver), T. Shaun Russell (LACMA Guard), Nealla Gordon (Lydia), Seth Morris (Man with Dog), Nasim Pedrad, Elizabeth Meriwether (Writers), Mollee Gray (Sari), Derek Ferguson (Benji), Matthew Moy (Chuck), Tyne Stecklein (Victoria), Kym Connor (Stage Mom), Renna Bartlett (Stage Assistant Director), Jennifer Hamilton (On Camera Choreographer), Krystal Ellsworth, Kim Marko Germar, Megan Honore, Nicholas Lanzisera, Moira 'Anjolie' Marfori, Dalphe Morantus, Katrina Katie Norman, Heather Phillips, Britt Stewart, Paula Van Oppen, William T. Loftis, Casey 'KC' Monnie, Jason Williams (Secret High Dancers), Hugo Chakrabongse, John Gerald Barclay (Bar Group), Tom Tangen, Tim Matheson (Eli's Dads), Ben Lautman (Rabbi), Joshua Allen Andreacola, Milton Greenberg (Boys at Wake), Rachel McDermott (STK Waitress), Robert Trapp (Mini-Golfer), Rachael Markarian, Kherington Payne (Frat Party Dancers), Dylan Hayes (Young Adam), Stefanie Scott (Young Emma), Ivan Reitman (TV Director)

Jake Johnson, Chris Bridges, Abby Elliott, Ashton Kutcher

Emma and Adam try to keep their relationship on a strictly sexual level without the unwanted stress of falling in love.

Kevin Kline, Ashton Kutcher

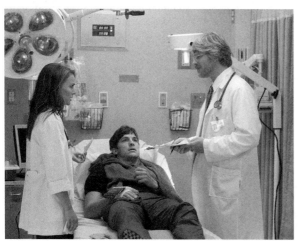

Natalie Portman, Ashton Kutcher, Cary Elwes © Paramount Pictures

THE MECHANIC

(CBS FILMS) Producers, David Winkler, Bill Chartoff, Rene Besson; Executive Producers, Irwin Winkler, Robert Chartoff, Avi Lerner, Danny Dimbort, Trevor Short, Boaz Davidson; Co-Producers, Matthew Leonetti Jr., Jib Polhemus; Director, Simon West; Screenplay, Richard Wenk, Lewis John Carlino; Story, Lewis John Carlino; Photography, Eric Schmidt; Designer, Richard Lassalle; Costumes, Christopher Lawrence; Music, Mark Isham; Editors, Todd E. Miller, T.G. Herrington; Visual Effects Supervisor, Glenn Neufeld; Stunts, Noon Orsatti; Casting, Amanda Mackey, Cathy Sandrich Gelfond; a Millennium Films presentation of a Chartoff Winkler Prod. and Nu Image production; Dolby; Super 35 Widescreen; Technicolor; Rated R; 93 minutes; Release date: January 28, 2011

Jason Statham, Ben Foster

Ben Foster, Jason Statham

CAST

Arthur Bishop	**Jason Statham**
Steve McKenna	**Ben Foster**
Harry McKenna	**Donald Sutherland**
Dean	**Tony Goldwyn**
Burke	**Jeff Chase**
Sarah	**Mini Anden**
Jorge Lara	**James Logan**
Lara's Guard	**Eddie Fernandez**
Car Jacker	**Joshua Bridgewater**
Vaughn	**John McConnell**
Kelly	**Christa Campbell**

Joel Davis (Husband), Mark Anthony Nutter (Mr. Finch), Ardy Brent Carlson (Bell Hop), Lara Grice (Mrs. Finch), Lance Nichols (Henry), J.D. Evermore (Gun Runner), Ada Michelle Loridans (Finch's Daughter), Linnzi Zaorski (Jazz Club Singer), Dawn Neufeld, Molly Rosenblatt (News Reporters), Bill Scharpf (Dean's Driver), John Teague (Ney), David Leitch (Sebastian), Jennifer Ortega, LaTeace Towns-Cuellar (Lara's Girls), Paul Abraham (Shuttle Driver), David Dahlgren (Dr. X), Stuart Greer (Ralph), Katarzyna Wolejnio (Maria), Larrel France (Vaughn's Intern), Danny Cosmo (Peasant), Derek Schreck (Security Guard), Choop ('Arthur' the Dog)

After his mentor is killed, hit man Arthur Bishop reluctantly agrees to teach the man's son to become a trained assassin. Remake of the 1972 UA film that starred Charles Bronson and Jan-Michael Vincent.

Jason Statham

Mini Anden © CBS Films

Juno Temple, Thomas Dekkker

Juno Temple, Thomas Dekker, Haley Bennett

Thomas Dekker, Haley Bennett, Roxane Mesquida

KABOOM

(SUNDANCE SELECTS) Producers, Andrea Sperling, Gregg Araki; Executive Producers, Sébastien K. Lemercier, Pascal Caucheteux, Jonathan Schwartz; Co-Producer, Pavlina Hatoupis; Associate Producer, Beau J. Genot; Director/Screenplay/Editor, Gregg Araki; Photography, Sandra Valde-Hansen; Designer, Todd Fjelsted; Costumes, Trayce Gigi Field; Music, Robin Guthrie, Ulrich Schnauss, Mark Peters, Vivek Maddala; Music Supervisor, Tiffany Anders; Casting, Johanna Ray, Jenny Jue; a Why Not U.S. productions/Desperate Pictures presentation in association with Wild Bunch and Super Crispy; American-French; Dolby; Widescreen; Color; Not rated; 86 minutes; Release date: January 28, 2011

CAST
Smith	**Thomas Dekker**
Stella	**Haley Bennett**
Thor	**Chris Zylka**
Lorelei	**Roxane Mesquida**
London	**Juno Temple**
Rex	**Andy Fischer-Price**
Red-Haired Girl	**Nicole LaLiberte**
Hunter	**Jason Olive**

James Duval (The Messiah), Brennan Mejia (Oliver), Kelly Lynch (Nicole), Carlo Mendez (Milo), Christine Nguyen (Freshman Bimbo), Michael James Spall (Smith's Dad)

After consuming some hallucinogenic cookies, college freshman Smith is convinced that he witnessed the murder of a mysterious red-haired girl who has been entering his dreams.

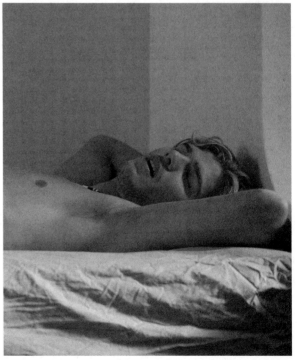

Chris Zylka

THE RITE

(NEW LINE CINEMA/WB) Producers, Beau Flynn, Tripp Vinson; Executive Producers, Richard Brenner, Merideth Finn, Robert Bernacchi; Co-Producers, Christy Fletcher, Emma Parry, Mark Tuohy; Director, Mikael Håfström; Screenplay, Michael Petroni; Suggested by the book by Matt Baglio; Photography, Ben Davis; Designer, Andrew Laws; Costumes, Carlo Poggioli; Music, Alex Heffes; Editor, David Rosenbloom; Visual Effects Supervisor, Marc Kolbe; Casting, Deborah Aquila, Tricia Wood; a Contrafilm production; a New Line Cinema presentation; Distributed by Warner Bros.; Dolby; Panavision; Deluxe Color; Rated PG-13; 114 minutes; Release date: January 28, 2011

CAST
Father Lucas Trevant	**Anthony Hopkins**
Michael Kovak	**Colin O'Donoghue**
Angeline	**Alice Braga**
Father Xavier	**Ciarán Hinds**
Father Matthew	**Toby Jones**
Istvan Kovak	**Rutger Hauer**
Rosaria	**Marta Gastini**
Aunt Andria	**Maria Grazia Cucinotta**
Francesca	**Arianna Veronesi**
Vincenzo	**Andrea Calligari**
Eddie	**Chris Marquette**
Nina	**Torrey DeVitto**

Ben Cheetham (Young Michael), Marija Karan (Sandra), Rosa Pianeta (Woman in Exorcism Video), Giampiero Ingrassia (Doctor), Rosario Tedesco (Police Officer), Cecilia Dazzi (Nurse), Attila Bardóczy (Xavier's Secretary), Nadia Kibout (Ethnic Nun), Anita Pititto (Vatican Nun), Sándor Baranyai (Concierge), Fabiola Balestriere (Young Girl), Anikó Vincze (Katalin Kovak)

A young priest questioning his faith is sent to Rome to study exorcism, where his close encounters with victims possessed by Satan turn his beliefs around.

Anthony Hopkins © New Line Cinema

Leighton Meester, Minka Kelly © Screen Gems

THE ROOMMATE

(SCREEN GEMS) Producers, Doug Davison, Roy Lee; Executive Producers, Beau Marks, Sonny Mallhi; Director, Christian E. Christiansen; Screenplay, Sonny Mallhi; Photography, Phil Parmet; Designer, Jon Gary Steele; Costumes, Maya Lieberman; Music, John Frizzell; Music Supervisor, Michael Friedman; Editor, Randy Bricker; Casting, Lindsey Hayes Kroeger; a Vertigo Entertainment production; Dolby; Panavision; Deluxe color; Rated PG-13; 91 minutes; Release date: February 4, 2011

CAST
Rebecca Evans	**Leighton Meester**
Sara Matthews	**Minka Kelly**
Stephen	**Cam Gigandet**
Tracy Morgan	**Aly Michalka**
Irene	**Danneel Harris**
Alison Evans	**Frances Fisher**
Jeff Evans	**Tomas Arana**
Professor Roberts	**Billy Zane**

Nina Dobrev (Maria), Matt Lanter (Jason), Katerina Graham (Kim Johnson), Johannes Raassina, Cameron Fisher Brousseau, Evan Michael Brown (Band Members), Alex Meraz (Frat Boy), Jerrika Hinton (Shiana), Jennifer Cadena (Dorm R.A.), Adam Saunders (Handsome Guy), Cory Tucker (Club Bartender), Will McFadden, Munda Razooki (Club Guys), Ryan Doom (Rick), Carrie Finklea (Marina, Bookstore Girl), Andrej Nagy (Older Designer), Ashleigh Falls (Make-Up Girl), Jacqueline Mazarella (Professor), Nathan Parsons (Coffee Shop Cashier), Elena Franklin, Lauren Storm (Maria's Girlfriends), Stacy Barnhisel (Librarian), Cherilyn Wilson (Frat Party Girl), G.O. Parsons (Mocha Kid), Brian David Miller (Frat Bouncer), Jake Perry (Slacker Co-Worker), Cayla Korven (Tracy's Friend), Shirley Norris (Kate), Nick Bylsma (Hunter)

An unhinged college freshman becomes dangerously obsessed with her new roommate.

JUST GO WITH IT

(COLUMBIA) Producers, Adam Sandler, Jack Giarraputo, Heather Parry; Executive Producers, Barry Bernardi, Tim Herlihy, Allen Covert, Steve Koren; Director, Dennis Dugan; Screenplay, Allan Loeb, Timothy Dowling; Based on *Cactus Flower* screenplay by I.A.L. Diamond, from the stage play by Abe Burrows, based upon the French play *Fleur de cactus* by Pierre Barillet and Jean-Pierre Gredy; Photography, Theo Van de Sande; Designer, Perry Andelin Blake; Costumes, Ellen Lutter; Music, Rupert Gregson-Williams; Music Supervisors, Michael Dilbeck, Brooks Arthur, Kevin Grady; Editor, Tom Costain; a Happy Madison production; Dolby; Deluxe Color; Rated PG-13; 117 minutes; Release date: February 11, 2011

CAST
Danny Maccabee	**Adam Sandler**
Katherine Murphy	**Jennifer Aniston**
Devlin Adams	**Nicole Kidman**
Eddie	**Nick Swardson**
Palmer	**Brooklyn Decker**
Maggie/Kiki Dee	**Bailee Madison**

Griffin Gluck (Michael/Bart), Dave Matthews (Ian Maxtone Jones), Kevin Nealon (Adon), Rachel Dratch (Kirsten Brant), Allen Covert (Soul Patch), Dan Patrick (Tanner Patrick), Minka Kelly (Joanna Damon), Jackie Sandler (Veruca), Rakefet Abergel (Patricia), Dana Min Goodman, Julia Wolov, Colby Kline, Jana Sandler (Bridesmaids), Jonathan Loughran, Peter Dante (Pick Up Guys), Michael Laskin (Mr. Maccabee), Carol Ann Susi (Mrs. Maccabee), Gene Pompa (Delivery Guy), Mario Joyner (Henderson), Keegan Michael Key (Ernesto), Heidi Montag (Adon's Wife), Andy Roddick (Good Looking Guy on Plane), Jillian Nelson (Young College Girl), Elena Satine (Christine), Lilian Tapia (Rosa), Azer Greco (Silas), Lori Heuring (Salesgirl), Darrin Lackey (Waiter), Julie Dixon Jackson (Mrs. Harrington), Branscombe Richmond (Bartender), Aaron Zachary Philips (Fat Kid), Jessica Jade Andres (Teenage Girl at Dive Restaurant), Kent Avenido (Guy at Dive Restaurant), Rachel Specter (Lisa Hammond), Tia Van Berg (Scary Woman), Todd Sherry (Check-In Clerk), Brendon Eggertsen (Ariel), Andrew Tomoso (Rope Bridge Guy), Lila Titone, Sadie Sandler, Sunny Sandler (Hawaiian Family at Rope Bridge), Lorna Scott (Big Country), Newton DeLeon (Diner at Dive Restaurant), Teresa Ann Zantua (Hawaiian Rosa), Roger Parham-Brown (Pizza Hut Janitor), Tom Dill (Coach Dill), Vanessa Villalovos (Saleswoman), Cort Rogers (Tripping Kid), Sharon Ferguson (Pregnant Woman at McFunnigans), Sheroum Kim (Waitress), Jevon Scott, Brandon Force, Samuel Nims, Elijah Scholer (Sailors)

A womanizing plastic surgeon who uses a fake wedding ring to keep him from commitments suddenly realizes he must come up with a faux "wife" when he meets a girl he wants to marry. Remake of the 1969 film *Cactus Flower* (Columbia) that starred Walter Matthau, Ingrid Bergman, and Goldie Hawn.

Bailee Madison, Adam Sandler, Griffin Gluck

Jennifer Aniston, Adam Sandler

Nick Swardson, Jennifer Aniston

Brooklyn Decker © Columbia Pictures

Channing Tatum, Mark Strong, Jamie Bell

Tahar Rahim, Jamie Bell, Channing Tatum © Focus Features

THE EAGLE

(FOCUS) Producer, Duncan Kenworthy; Executive Producers, Tessa Ross, Miles Ketley, Charles Moore; Co-Producer, Caroline Hewitt; Director, Kevin MacDonald; Screenplay, Jeremy Brock; Based on the novel *The Eagle of the Ninth* by Rosemary Sutcliff; Photography, Anthony Dod Mantle; Designer, Michael Carlin; Costumes, Michael O'Connor; Music, Atli Örvarsson; Editor, Justine Wright; Casting, Jina Jay; a Duncan Kenworthy production, presented in association with Film4; American-British; Dolby; Super 35 Widescreen; Deluxe color; Rated PG-13; 114 minutes; Release date: February 11, 2011

CAST
Marcus Aquila	**Channing Tatum**
Esca	**Jamie Bell**
Uncle Aquila	**Donald Sutherland**
Guern	**Mark Strong**
Seal Prince	**Tahar Rahim**
Lutorius	**Denis O'Hare**
Galba	**Paul Ritter**
Paulus	**Zsolt László**
Cassius	**Julian Lewis Jones**
Flavius Aquila	**Aladár Laklóth**
Young Marcus	**Bence Gerö**
Cradoc	**Douglas Henshall**
Stephanos	**James Hayes**
Claudius	**Dakin Matthews**

Pip Carter (Placidus), István Göz (Cohort Centurion), Marcell Miklós, Bálint Magyar, Ferenc Pataki (Fort Legionaries), Bálint Antal (Young Legionary), Lukács Bicskey (Druid), András Faragó (Captain of the Gladiators), Simon Paisley Day (Surgeon), Ben O'Brien (Milecastle Guard), Róbert Bánlaki (Young Rogue Warrior), Brian Gleeson, Jon Campling (Travellers), Thomas Henry (Seal Boy), Ned Dennehy (Seal Chief, The Horned One), Ralph Aiken, Granville Saxton, Walter Van Dyke (Patricians)

In the year 120 A.D., centurion Marcus Aquila journeys with his slave Esca into Northern Britain in hopes of retrieving the Roman Empire's symbolic golden Eagle that had been lost along with his father's Ninth Legion.

Jamie Bell

Donald Sutherland

Anne Heche, Ed Helms, Mike O'Malley © Fox Searchlight

Anne Heche, John C. Reilly, Ed Helms, Isiah Whitlock Jr.

CEDAR RAPIDS

(FOX SEARCHLIGHT) Producers, Jim Burke, Alexander Payne, Jim Taylor; Executive Producer, Ed Helms; Co-Producer, Brian Bell; Director, Miguel Arteta; Screenplay, Phil Johnston; Photography, Chuy Chavez; Designer, Doug Meerdink; Costumes, Hope Hanafin; Music, Christophe Beck; Music Supervisor, Margaret Yen; Editor, Eric Kissack; Casting, Joanna Colbert, Richard Mento, Meredith Tucker; an Ad Hominem Enterprises production; Dolby; Deluxe color; Rated R; 87 minutes; Release date: February 11, 2011

CAST

Tim Lippe	**Ed Helms**
Dean Ziegler	**John C. Reilly**
Joan Ostrowski-Fox	**Anne Heche**
Ronald Wilkes	**Isiah Whitlock Jr.**
Bill Krogstad	**Stephen Root**
Orin Helgesson	**Kurtwood Smith**
Bree	**Alia Shawkat**
Roger Lemke	**Thomas Lennon**
Gary	**Rob Corddry**
Mike Pyle	**Mike O'Malley**
Macy Vanderhei	**Sigourney Weaver**

Inga R. Wilson (Gwen Lemke), Mike Birbiglia (Trent), Seth Morris (Uncle Ken), Christopher Lemon, Sudhi Rajagopal (Rock Climbing Dudes), Chris DiAngelo (Kurt Gambsky), Lindsey Alexandra Hartley (Pam Gambsky), Welker White (Dione Krogstad), John Djurovski (Bartender), Charlie H. Sanders (TSA Agent), Craig Janos (Jack Nicholson Impersonator), Tracey Maloney (Flight Attendant), Steve Blackwood (Lindy), Carl Harry Carlson (Older Man), Kenneth H. Wood (Waiter), Lise Lacasse (Lila), James Howard Carr (Swarthy Man), David Rhoads (Ball Pit Judge), Bruce Griffin (Photographer), Teresa Yenque (Maid), Helen-Jean Arthur (Church Lady), Michael Tuba Heatherton (Plate Spinner), Leisa Pulido (Talent Show MC), Ed Jewett (Bearded Dude), Zackary Hamlin (Clem), Kimberly Moncrieff (Small Woman), Linda Riker (Small Woman's Friend), Michael Buie (Brian Early), Roz Music (Lady), Loit A. Maripuu, Bruce Lawson (Customers), Ian Minicuci (Perry, Man in Wheelchair), Penny Gibbs (ASMI Representative), Victor Pytko (Merle Huss), Sandy Gittleson (Sherri Fahrenkrug), Richard L. Fox (Hotel Employee), John F. McCormick (Dad), Joanne McGee (Mom), Hayley Zeccardi (Daughter)

A straight-laced insurance salesman starts learning to relax and let loose during a business trip to Cedar Rapids, Iowa.

Ed Helms

Isiah Whitlock Jr., Mike O'Malley, Ed Helms

GNOMEO & JULIET

(WALT DISNEY STUDIOS) Producers, Baker Bloodworth, Steve Hamilton Shaw, David Furnish; Executive Producer, Elton John; Co-Producer, Igor Khait; Director, Kelly Asbury; Screenplay, Andy Riley, Kevin Cecil, Mark Burton, Emily Cook, Kathy Greenberg, Steve Hamilton Shaw, Kelly Asbury; Story, Rob Sprackling, John R. Smith, Andy Riley, Kevin Cecil, Kelly Asbury, Steve Hamilton Shaw; Based on an original screenplay by Rob Sprackling and John R. Smith, from the play *Romeo & Juliet* by William Shakespeare; Designer/Art Director, Karen deJong; Music, James Newton Howard, Chris Bacon; Songs, Elton John, Bernie Taupin; Editor, Catherine Apple; Character Designer, Gary Dunn; Casting, Gail Stevens; a Walt Disnay Studios Motion Pictures release of a Touchstone Pictures presentation of a Rocket Pictures production; American-British; Dolby; Deluxe color; 3D; Rated G; 84 minutes; Release date: February 11, 2011

Gnomeo, Juliet, Featherstone

VOICE CAST

Gnomeo	**James McAvoy**
Juliet	**Emily Blunt**
Nanette	**Ashley Jensen**
Lord Redbrick	**Michael Caine**
Benny	**Matt Lucas**
Featherstone	**Jim Cummings**
Lady Bluebury	**Maggie Smith**
Tybalt	**Jason Statham**
Fawn	**Ozzy Osbourne**
Paris	**Stephen Merchant**

Patrick Stewart (Bill Shakespeare), Julie Walters (Miss Montague), Hulk Hogan (Terrafirminator), Kelly Asbury (Red Good Gnomes), Richard Wilson (Mr. Capulet), Dolly Parton (Dolly Gnome), Julia Brams (Stone Fish), James Daniel Wilson (Fishing Gnome), Tim Bentinck (Conjoined Gnome Left), Julio Bonet (Mankini Gnome), Neil McCaul (Conjoined Gnome Right), Maurissa Horwitz (Call Me Doll)

A pair of garden gnomes in the neighboring homes of Miss Montague and Mr. Capulet defy their warring tribes and fall in love.

Nanette, Juliet, Paris

Gnomeo, Lady Bluebury

Lord Redbrick © Walt Disney Studios

JUSTIN BIEBER: NEVER SAY NEVER

(PARAMOUNT) Producers, Scooter Braun, Justin Bieber, Antonio "L.A." Reid, Usher Raymond IV, Dan Cutforth, Jane Lipsitz; Executive Producers, David Nicksay, Randy Phillips, Doug Merrifield; Co-Producer, Jonathan McHugh; Director, Jon M. Chu; Photography, Reed Smoot; Music, Deborah Lurie; Editors, Avi Youabian, Jay Cassidy, Jillian Moul; a Scooter Braun Films and L.A. Reid Media production in association with AEG Live; Dolby; Color; DV; 3D; Rated G; 105 minutes; Release date: February 11, 2011. Documentary on teen singer Justin Bieber

WITH

Justin Bieber, Christopher Abad, Melvin Baldwin, Jeremy Bieber, Boyz II Men, Scooter Braun, Miley Cyrus, Bruce Dale, Diane Dale, Ryan Good, Kenny Hamilton, Bernard Harvey, Taylor James, Reginald Jones, Daniel Kanter, Allison Kaye, Sean Kingston, Delfin Lazaroii, Ludacris, Pattie Mallette, Dominic Manuel, Thomas Martin, Carin Morris, Randy Phillips, L.A. Reid, Jaden Smith, Mama Jan Smith, Snoop Dogg, Scrappy Stassen, Micah Tolentino, Usher; and Marvin Millora, Anthony Carr, Anis Cheurfa, Nicholas DeMoura, Aja George, Antonio Hudnell, Raymond Mora, Jeremy Marinas, Jonathan "Legacy" Perez, Straphanio "Shonnie" Solomon, Michael Vargas (Dancers)

Justin Bieber, Usher

Justin Bieber

Justin Bieber, Jaden Smith

Justin Bieber © Paramount/Scooter Braun Films

Pattie Mallette, Justin Bieber

Alex Pettyfer, Dianna Agron © DreamWorks Pictures

Callan McAuliffe, Alex Pettyfer

I AM NUMBER FOUR

(DREAMWORKS/TOUCHSTONE) Producer, Michael Bay; Executive Producers, David Valdes, Chris Bender, J.C. Spink; Director, D.J. Caruso; Screenplay, Alfred Gough, Miles Millar, Marti Noxon; Based on the novel by Pittacus Lore; Photography, Guillermo Navarro; Designer, Tom Southwell; Costumes, Marie-Sylvie Deveau; Music, Trevor Rabin; Editors, Jim Page, Vince Filippone; Visual Effects & Animation, Industrial Light & Magic; Casting, Deborah Aquilla, Tricia Wood; a DreamWorks Pictures and Reliance Big Entertainment presentation of a Bay Films production; Dolby; Deluxe color; PG-13; 109 minutes; Release date: February 18, 2011

CAST
John Smith	**Alex Pettyfer**
Henri	**Timothy Olyphant**
Number Six	**Teresa Palmer**
Sarah Hart	**Dianna Agron**
Sam	**Callan McAuliffe**
Mogadorian Commander	**Kevin Durand**
Mark James	**Jake Abel**
Sheriff James	**Jeff Hochendoner**
Kevin	**Patrick Sebes**
Number 3	**Greg Townley**
Number 3's Guardian	**Reuben Langdon**
Nicole	**Emily Wickersham**

Molly McGinnis (Receptionist), Brian Howe (Frank), Andy Owen (Bret), Sophia Caruso (Girl on Street), Charles Carroll (Sam's Stepdad), L. Derek Leonidoff (Mr. Berhman), Garrett M. Brown (Principal Simms), Sabrina de Matteo (Physics Teacher), Cooper Thornton (Sarah's Dad), Judith Hoag (Sarah's Mom), Jack Walz (Sarah's Brother), Bill Laing (Demented Farmer), Beau Mirchoff (Drew), Cody Johns (Kern), Isabella Robbins (Teen at Party)

An extra-terrestrial arrives on Earth in hopes of escaping from the Mogadorians who have already eliminated three of his eight fellow fugitives.

Timothy Olyphant, Alex Pettyfer

Teresa Palmer

Hayden Christensen

Jacob Latimore, Thandie Newton © Magnet Releasing

VANISHING ON 7TH STREET

(MAGNET) Producers, Norton Herrick, Celine Rattray, Tove Christensen; Executive Producers, Elayne Herrick, Michael Herrick, Peter Graves, Lawrence Mattis, Kelly McCormick, Ken Hirsch, Nick Quested; Co-Producers, Pam Hirsch, Peter Pastorelli, Riva Marker; Director, Brad Anderson; Screenplay, Anthony Jaswinski; Photography, Uta Briesewitz; Designer, Stephen Beatrice; Costumes, Danielle Hollowell; Music, Lucas Vidal; Editor, Jeffrey Wolf; Visual Effects Supervisor, John Bair; Casting, Matthew Lessall; a Herrick Entertainment presentation of a Mandalay Vision production, in association with Circle of Confusion and Forest Park Pictures; Dolby; Color; Rated R; 91 minutes; Release date: February 18, 2011

CAST
Luke	**Hayden Christensen**
Paul	**John Leguizamo**
Rosemary	**Thandie Newton**
James	**Jacob Latimore**
Briana	**Taylor Groothuis**

Jordon Trovillion (Concession Girl), Arthur Cartwright (Security Guard), Neal Huff (Chicago Reporter), Hugh Maguire (Patient), Erin Nicole Brolley (Paige), Stephen Clark, Carolyn Clifford-Taylor (TV Anchors), Larry Fessenden (Bike Messenger), Nick Yu (Chinese Reporter)

After a power outage causes most of the population of Detroit to vanish, a small group of strangers take refuge in a bar where they hope to survive the darkness.

BIG MOMMAS: LIKE FATHER, LIKE SON

(20TH CENTURY FOX) Producers, David T. Friendly, Michael Green; Executive Producers, Martin Lawrence, Jeffrey Kwatinetz, Jeremiah Samuels, Arnon Milchan; Director, John Whitesell; Screenplay, Matthew Fogel; Story, Don Rhymer, Matthew Fogel; Based on characters created by Darryl Quarles; Photography, Anthony B. Richmond; Designer, Meghan C. Rogers; Costumes, Leah Katznelson; Music, David Newman; Music Supervisors, Dave Jordan, Jojo Villanueva; Editor, Priscilla Nedd Friendly; Prosthetic Makeup Design, Wesley Wofford; Casting, Kim Taylor-Coleman; a Regency Enterprises presentation of a New Regency/Friendly Films/Runteldat Entertainment/The Collective production; Dolby; Super 35 Widescreen; Color; Rated PG-13; 107 minutes; Release date: February 18, 2011

CAST
Malcolm Turner (Big Momma)	**Martin Lawrence**
Trent Pierce (Charmaine)	**Brandon T. Jackson**
Haley Robinson	**Jessica Lucas**
Mia	**Michelle Ang**
Jasmine	**Portia Doubleday**
Chirkoff	**Tony Curran**
Isabelle	**Emily Rios**
Gail	**Ana Ortiz**

Henri Lubatti (Vlad), Lorenzo Pisoni (Dmitri), Marc John Jefferies (Rembrandt), Brandon Gill (Scratch), Zack Mines (Delanté), Trey Lindsey (TJ), Ken Jeong (Mailman), Max Casella (Canetti), Susan Walters (Mall Mother), Sherri Shepherd (Beverly Townsend), Susan Griffiths, Brianne Gould, Dawntavia Bullard (Cafeteria Girls), Mari Morrow (Ms. Mercier), Susie Spear Purcell (Art Teacher), Lily Chambers, Jasmine Burke (Drama Queens), Juliet Kim (Quad Student), Brian Lafontaine (Crawford), Jazmia Battle, Christiani Pitts (Divas), Ramsey Luke (FBI Agent), Faizon Love (Kurtis Kool)

Joined by his rebellious teen stepson, detective Malcolm Turner goes undercover disguised as a corpulent house mother at a girl's school in order to retrieve a valuable flash drive with information incriminating a powerful Russian mobster. Third in the Fox series, following *Big Momma's House* (2000) and *Big Momma's House 2* (2006).

Brandon T. Jackson, Martin Lawrence © 20th Century Fox

Owen Wilson, Jenna Fischer, Jason Sudeikis, Christina Applegate

Kristin Carey, Owen Wilson, Jason Sudeikis © New Line Cinema

Stephen Merchant, Larry Joe Campbell, Jason Sudeikis, Owen Wilson

Christina Applegate, Tyler Hoechlin, Jenna Fischer, Bruce Thomas

HALL PASS

(NEW LINE CINEMA/WB) Producers, Bradley Thomas, Charles B. Wessler, Peter Farrelly, Bobby Farrelly; Executive Producers, Toby Emmerich, Richard Brener, Merideth Finn, Marc S. Fischer; Co-Producers, Mark Charpentier, John Rickard; Directors, Peter Farrelly, Bobby Farrelly; Screenplay, Pete Jones, Peter Farrelly, Kevin Barnett, Bobby Farrelly; Story, Pete Jones; Photography, Matthew F. Leonetti; Designer, Arlan Jay Vetter; Costumes, Denise Wingate; Music Supervisors, Tom Wolfe, Manish Raval; Editor, Sam Seig; Casting, Rick Montgomery; a Conundrum Entertainment production presented by New Line Cinema; Distributed by Warner Bros.; Dolby; Super 35 Widescreen; Fotokem Color; Rated R; 105 minutes; Release date: February 25, 2011

CAST
Rick	**Owen Wilson**
Fred	**Jason Sudeikis**
Maggie	**Jenna Fischer**
Grace	**Christina Applegate**

Nicky Whelan (Leigh), Richard Jenkins (Coakley), Stephen Merchant (Gary), Larry Joe Campbell (Hog-Head), Bruce Thomas (Rick Coleman), Tyler Hoechlin (Gerry), Derek Waters (Brent), Alexandra Daddario (Paige), Rob Moran (Ed Long), Lauren Bowles (Britney), Christa Campbell (Emma), Macsen Lintz (Gunnar), Kristin Carey (Aunt Meg), Joy Behar (Dr. Lucy), Carly Craig (Nicotine Patch Girl), Kaliko Kauahi (Chief), Landon T. Riddle (Ed's Son), Halli-Gray Beasley (Ed's Daughter), J.B. Smoove (Flats), Vanessa Angel (Missy), Andrew Wilson (Larry Bohac), Alyssa Milano (Mandy), Danny Murphy (Boshane), Al Wisne (Clyde), Mike Meldman (Himself), Susan Sandberg (Doctor), Dwight Evans (Maggie's Father), Shannon Leade (20-Something Woman), Gus G. Williams (Bouncer), Gordon Danniels (Golf Ranger), Jamie Lee (Dry Clean Korean Lady), Quynh Thi Le (Young Korean Wmoan), Robert Flaherty (Awards Dinner Bartender), Matt Fairbairn (Harold Goldberg), Doris Morgado, Maria Duarte (Latino Women), Thaddues Rahming, Rich Brown (Naked Guys), Jeff Norton, Terry Mullany (Lake Cops), Brian Mone (Honorable Judge William Mone), Taylor Treadwell (Emma, Young Bride), Craig X. Scott (Older Gunnar), Kathryn Kim (Another Korean Woman), Richard Melton (Burly Cop), Eddie Barbanell (Coach Eddie), Romy Wang, Suki Frick, Soon Yup Han (Women Golfers), Ezra Neo Dierking (Party Boy), Bo Burnham (Bartender), Mike Cerrone (Driver Cop), Zen Gesner (Passenger Cop), Kristyl Dawn Tift (Gary's Wife), Daniel Greene, Patricia French (Officers), Bob Weekes (Bar Manager), Stella Barrow, Willie Barrow, Jikker Barrow, Ron Brown (Stella Bass Band), Meredith Oliver Oglesby, Candice Ozechowski, Lee Anne Freeman, Christina Avalos (Bar Patrons), Igor Vovkovinskiy (Johnny's Hideaway Tall Stud), Chloe Snyder (Stootfish Babe), Kathy Griffin (Herself), Anna Byers (Backyard BBQ Friend), Wen Yann Shih (Asian Woman), Tom Choi (Asian Husband), Juan Qian (Elderly Asian Woman), Jesse Farrelly (Witness on Roof)

Worried that their husbands' straying eyes might lead to a rift in their marriages, Maggie and Grace grant them one week off to go sow their wild oats.

DRIVE ANGRY

(SUMMIT) Producers, Michael DeLuca, Rene Besson; Executive Producers, Adam Fields, Joe Gatta, Avi Lerner, Danny Dimbort, Trevor Short, Boaz Davidson, John Thompson; Co-Producer, Ed Cathell III; Director, Patrick Lussier; Screenplay, Todd Farmer, Patrick Lussier; Photography, Brian Pearson; Designer, Nathan Amondson; Costumes, Mary E. McLeod; Music, Michael Wandmacher; Editors, Patrick Lussier, Devin C. Lussier; Visual Effects Supervisor, Glenn Neufeld; Stunts, Johnny Martin; Casting, Nancy Nayor; a Millennium Films presentation of a Michael DeLuca production and a Nu Image production in association with Saturn Films; Dolby; 3D; Technicolor; Rated R; 104 minutes; Release date: February 25, 2011

CAST
John Milton	**Nicolas Cage**
Piper	**Amber Heard**
The Accountant	**William Fichtner**
Jonah King	**Billy Burke**
Webster	**David Morse**

Todd Farmer (Frank Raimi), Christa Campbell (Mona), Charlotte Ross (Candy), Tom Atkins (Cap), Jack McGee (Fat Lou), Katy Mixon (Norma Jean), Wanetah Walmsley (American Indian Mother), Robin McGee (Guy with Camera Phone), Fabian C. Moreno (Latino Busboy), Edrick Browne (Rookie), Marc Macaulay (Sarge), Pruitt Taylor Vince (Roy), Julius Washington (Uniformed Officer), Jamie Teer (Babysitter), Bryan Massey, Timothy Walter (Troopers), Kent Jude Bernard, Brent Henry (Teens), Gerry May, Sherri Talley (News Reporters), Arianne Martin (Milton's Daughter, Older), Con Schell (Fucking Driver), Nick Gomez (Fucking Middle), Joe Chrest (Fucking Passenger), Oakley Lehman (Cultist with Iron Pipe), Thirl R. Haston (Cultist with Sickle), Jake Brake (Cultist with Machete), Tim J. Smith (Cultist with Hatchet), Jeff Dashnaw (Cowboy with Cattle Prod), Tim Trella (Cultist with Sledge), James Hébert (Man in Leather Jacket), Kenneth Wayne Bradley (Man in Wig), Kendrick Hudson (Burly Dude), Michael Papajohn (Tattooed Guy), April Littlejohn (Business Woman), Henry M. Kingi (Thin Old Man), Simona Williams (Lady in Leopard Skin), Shelby Swatek (Truck Driving Woman)

John Milton escapes from hell to track down and kill the men who murdered his daughter and captured his grandchild.

David Morse, Nicolas Cage © Summit Entertainment

Jerry McDaniel

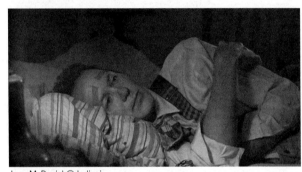
Jerry McDaniel © Indiepix

EVERYTHING STRANGE AND NEW

(INDIEPIX) Producers, Laura Techera Francia, A.D. Liano; Executive Producer, Stephen Bannatyne; Director/Screenplay/Photography, Frazer Bradshaw; Art Director, Corey Weinstein; Music, Dan Plonsey, Kent Sparling; Editors, Frazer Bradshaw, Jesse Spencer; a Lucky Hat Entertainment production; Dolby; Color; Not rated; 84 minutes; Release date: February 25, 2011

CAST
Wayne	**Jerry McDaniel**
Beth	**Beth Lisick**
Manny	**Luis Saguar**
Leo	**Rigo Chacon Jr.**

Diana Tenese (Gena), Oliver McDaniel, Finnegan McDaniel (Kids), Eric Reid (Benny), Jered Daniel (Lyle), David Rodriguez (Robert), Susie Wise (Sara), Hanna Kerns (Benny's Wife), Dexter Kerns (Benny's Kid), Abdullah Hussain (Convenience Store Clerk), Andreas Schnell (Construction Worker), Christopher Galdes, PJ Hand (Drug Dealers), Amoni Riggin, Aryanna Riggin, Gus Crews, Hattie Bradshaw, Justin Riggin, Katherine Rodriguez, Rahsaan Jones, Ronin Jones, Sabrina Rodriguez, Saife Ragh (Birthday Party Kids)

Reflecting on his life, a construction worker wonders why he has not received the fulfillment from his wife and kids that others seem to have from their families.

Anthony Mackie, Matt Damon

John Slattery, Matt Damon, Anthony Ruivivar

Matt Damon, Emily Blunt
© Universal Studios

THE ADJUSTMENT BUREAU

(UNIVERSAL) Producers, Michael Hackett, George Nolfi, Bill Carraro, Chris Moore; Executive Producer, Isa Dick Hackett, Jonathan Gordon; Co-Producer, Joel Viertel; Director/Screenplay, George Nolfi; Based on the short story "Adjustment Team" by Philip K. Dick; Photography, John Toll; Designer, Kevin Thompson; Costumes, Kasia Walicka Maimone; Music, Thomas Newman; Editor, Jay Rabinowitz; Visual Effects Supervisor, Mark Russell; Casting, Amanda Mackey, Cathy Sandrich-Gelfond; a Media Rights Capital presentation of a Gambit Pictures production in association with Electric Shepherd Productions; Dolby; Super 35 Widescreen; Technicolor; Rated PG-13; 104 minutes; Release date: March 4, 2011

CAST
David Norris	**Matt Damon**
Elise Sellas	**Emily Blunt**
Harry Mitchell	**Anthony Mackie**
Richardson	**John Slattery**
Charlie Traynor	**Michael Kelly**
Thompson	**Terence Stamp**

Lisa Thoreson, Florence Kastriner (Suburban Moms), Phyllis MacBryde, Natalie E. Carter (Suburban Neigbors), Chuck Scarborough, Jon Stewart, Mayor Michael R. Bloomberg, James Carville, Mary Matalin, Betty Liu, Daniel Bazile (Themselves), Capt. Gregory P. Hitchen (U.S. Coast Guard Officer), Darrell James LeNormand (Upstate Farmer), Kar, RJ Konner (Political Consultants), Susan D. Michaels (Reporter), Gregory Lay (Albert, Campaign Aide), Lauren Hodges (Robyn, Campaign Aide), Amanda Mason Warren (Senior Campaign Aide), Anthony Ruivivar (McCrady), Sandhi Santini, Laurie Dawn (Norris Supporters), Christine Lucas (Christine, Charlie's Assistant), Jim Edward Gately (Man in Madison Square Park), Don Hewitt Sr. (Bus Driver), Venida Evans, Kyoko Bruguera, David Gregoire (Bus Passengers), Julie Hays (Susan, RSR Receptionist), Fabrizio Brienza (Miller), David Bishins (Burdensky), Kate Nowlin, Rob Yang (Junior Partners), Jennifer Ehle (Brooklyn Ice House Bartender), Johnny Cicco (Johnny from Red Hook), Pedro Pascal (Maitre D' Paul De Santo), Michael Boyne (New Leaf Waiter), Sarah Bradford (New Leaf Waitress), Pete Epstein (Taxi Driver), Brian Haley (Police Officer Maes), Kirsty Meares (Police Sergeant), Laura Kenley (Lora, Orivela's Waitress), Jessica Lee Keller (Lauren , Elise's Best Friend), Donnie Keshawarz (Donaldson), Kieran Campion (Donaldson's Aide), Sandi Carroll (Orthopedic Surgeon), Shane McRae (Adrian Troussant, Elise's Fiancé), Meghan Andrews (Cedar Lake Receptionist), Sandra Berrios (Court Registrar), David Alan Basche, Joel de la Fuente, Mike DiSalvo (Thompson's Aides), Dina Cataldi (DMV Clerk), Paul DiPaola (Courthouse Security Officer), Jason Kravits (New Yorker in Courthouse Lobby), Peter Jay Fernandez (County Clerk), Lawrence Leritz (Court Officer), Peter Benson, LeRoy McClain, Brit Whittle, Wayne Scott Miller, Lorenzo Pisoni, Bart Wilder (Bureau Headquarters Staff)

A mysterious group of men inform failed politician David Norris that he must avoid making further contact with the woman he met and was smitten with, as it will alter the already designated path of both their lives.

Terence Stamp, Matt Damon

Michael Biehn © Rogue Pictures

Anna Faris, Chris Pratt

TAKE ME HOME TONIGHT

(ROGUE) Producers, Ryan Kavanaugh, Jim Whitaker, Sarah Bowen; Executive Producers, Topher Grace, Gordon Kaywin, Dany Wolf, Tucker Tooley; Director, Michael Dowse; Screenplay, Jackie Filgo, Jeff Filgo; Based on a story by Topher Grace and Gordon Kaywin; Photography, Terry Stacey; Designer, William Arnold; Costumes, Carol Oditz; Music, Trevor Horn; Editor, Lee Haxall; a Rogue and Imagine Entertainment presentation in association with Relativity Media; Dolby; Super 35 Widescreen; Color; Rated R; 97 minutes; Release date: March 4, 2011

CAST
Matt Franklin	**Topher Grace**
Wendy Franklin	**Anna Faris**
Barry Nathan	**Dan Fogler**
Tori Frederking	**Teresa Palmer**
Kyle Masterson	**Chris Pratt**
Bill Franklin	**Michael Biehn**
Libby Franklin	**Jeanie Hackett**
Shelly	**Lucy Punch**
Ashley	**Michelle Trachtenberg**
Carlos	**Demetri Martin**

Michael Ian Black (Pete Bering), Bob Odenkirk (Mike), Angie Everhart (Trish Anderson), Jay Jablonski (Benji), Edwin Hodge (Bryce), Candace Kroslak (Ally), Nathalie Kelley (Beth), Wade Allain-Marcus (Broder), Robert Hoffman (Tyler "Dance Machine" Jones), Ryan Bittle (Rick Herrington), Bruce Nelson (Office Frank Johnson), Seth Gabel (Brent), James Sharpe (Steven), Erin Eisenhower (Tyler's Girlfriend), Kimberly Dearing (Betsy), Clement von Franckenstein (Frances Triebverbrecher), Jennifer Sommerfield (Martina), Kyle Gonnell (D.J. Rubik's 3), Dustin Leighton (That Loser Who Always Shows up at the Party with a Guitar), Richard Meek (Arnold), Megan Mieduch (Betsy's Friend), Meghan Stansfield (Claire), Diana Newton (Popular Girl), Alicia de la Vega (D.I.N.K.), Joe Jones (Jake), Michael Rolland (Party Guy), Josh Smith (Rocker Dude), David Vincent Merenda (Drunk Guy), Annie Boon (Crying Girl), Dany Wolf, Wil Daly, Roxanne Lauren Knouse, Richie Keen (Guests at Banker Party), Darla Haun (Record Store Manager), Chien Yang (Korean Man), Ginnifer Goodwin (Banky)

Grad student Matt Franklin decides to take charge of his listless life by pursuing the seemingly unobtainable girl whom he has pined for since the 10th grade.

Michelle Trachtenberg, Dan Fogler

Topher Grace, Teresa Palmer

BEASTLY

(CBS FILMS) Producer, Susan Cartsonis; Executive Producer, Michael Flynn; Director/Screenplay, Daniel Barnz; Based on the novel by Alex Flinn; Photography, Mandy Walker; Designer, Rusty Smith; Costumes, Suttirat Larlarb; Music, Marcelo Zarvos; Music Supervisor, Linda Cohen; Editor, Thomas J. Nordberg; Special Makeup Effects and Prosthetics, Tony Gardner; Casting, Sarah Halley Finn; a Storefront Pictures production; Dolby; Super 35 Widescreen; Color; Rated PG-13; 86 minutes; Release date: March 4, 2011

CAST
Kyle Kingson	**Alex Pettyfer**
Lindy	**Vanessa Hudgens**
Kendra	**Mary-Kate Olsen**
Sloan	**Dakota Johnson**
Rob	**Peter Krause**
Zola	**LisaGay Hamilton**
Will	**Neil Patrick Harris**

Erik Knudsen (Trey), David Francis (Dr. Davis), Gio Perez (Victor), Roc LaFortune (Lindy's Father), Miguel Mendoza (Victor's Brother), Steve Godin (Junkie), Julie Dretzin (Rob's Assistant), Justin Bradley (Student), Karl Graboshas (Teacher), Jonathan Dubsky (Student at Green Party), Rhiannon Moller-Trotter (Halloween Partygoer)

An arrogant, narcissistic high schooler is punished by a Goth girl who turns him ugly with the understanding that he can only change back to his former handsome self if he can get someone to love him in his hideous state.

Alex Pettyfer, Neil Patrick Harris © CBS Films

Alex Pettyfer, Vanessa Hudgens

Michael Algieri, Josh Radnor © Anchor Bay

Josh Radnor, Kate Mara

HAPPYTHANKYOUMOREPLEASE

(ANCHOR BAY) Producers, Benji Kohn, Chris Papavasiliou, Austin Stark, Jesse Hara; Executive Producers, Glenn Williamson, Peter Sterling, Bingo Gubelmann; Director/Screenplay, Josh Radnor; Photography, Seamus Tierney; Designer, Jade Healy; Costumes, Sarah Beers; Music, Jaymay; Music Supervisor, Andy Gowan; Editor, Michael Miller; Casting, Suzanne Smith Crowley, Jessica Kelly; a Paper Street Films & Tom Sawyer Entertainment in association with Back Lot Pictures presentation; Dolby; HD Widescreen; Color; Rated R; 99 minutes; Release date: March 4, 2011

CAST
Sam Wexler	**Josh Radnor**
Annie	**Malin Akerman**
Mississippi	**Kate Mara**
Mary Catherine	**Zoe Kazan**
Charlie	**Pablo Schreiber**

Tony Hale (Sam #2), Peter Scanavino (Ira), Michael Algieri (Rasheen), Richard Jenkins (Paul Gertmanian), Bram Barouh (Spencer), Dana Barron (The Gynecologist), Sunah Bilsted (Receptionist), Jimmy Gary Jr. (Police Officer), Marna Kohn (Melissa), Laith Nakli (MTA Worker), Katharine Powell (Girl Leaving Apartment), Maria Elena Ramirez (Jill), Mary Ann Urbano (Social Worker), Fay Wolf (Beth)

A young boy, separated from his family on the subway, is befriended by a struggling writer.

MAKING THE BOYS

(FIRST RUN FEATURES) Producers, Crayton Robey, Douglas Tirola, Susan Bedusa; Co-Producers, Miguel Camnitzer, Jack Morrissey; Executive Producer, Bill Condon; Director, Crayton Robey; Photography, Charles Poekel; Music, Lucian Piane; Editors, Robert Greene, Seth Hurlbert; a 4th Row Films production; Color; Not rated; 90 minutes; Release date: March 11, 2011. Documentary on Mart Crowley's landmark 1968 play about gay lives, *The Boys in the Band*, and the varied reactions to it from members of the gay community.

WITH

Edward Albee, Joe Allen, Matt Baney, David Carter, Candis Cayne, Andy Cohen, Mart Crowley, Michael Cunningham, Dominick Dunne, David Ehrenstein, William Friedkin, Peter Harvey, Aarion Hicklin, Jerry Hoose, Cheyenne Jackson, Page Johnson, Charles Kaiser, Curtis Kelly, Jush Kilmer-Purcell, Ed Koch, Norm Korpi, Larry Kramer, Carson Kressley, Tony Kushner, Charles Ledslie, Laurence Luckinbill, Terrence McNally, Michael Musto, Patrick Pacheo, Gilbert Parker, George Rondo, David Rothenberg, Paul Rudnick, Dan Savage, Marc Shaiman, Christian Siriano, Andy Tobias, Tree, Stephen Tropiano, Robert Wagner, Peter White, Scott Wittman, Robert Woodworth

Embeth Davidtz, Edie Falco

Kathryn Erbe, Elias Koteas
© Screen Media

Mart Crowley © First Run Features

Mart Crowley

3 BACKYARDS

(SCREEN MEDIA) Producers, Rocco Caruso, Amy Durning, Eric Mendelsohn; Executive Producer, Fred Berner; Co-Producers, Jennifer Grausman, Bogdan George Apetri, Atilla Salih Yucer, Liz Manne; Director/Screenplay, Eric Mendelsohn; Photography, Kasper Tuxen; Designer, Markus Kirschner; Costumes, Suzanne McCabe, Susan Carrano; Music, Michael Nicholas; Editors, Morgan Faust, Jeffrey K. Miller; Casting, Lynn Kressel, Kevin Kuffa; a Caruso/Mendelsohn production in association with Fred Berner Films; Dolby; Deluxe color; Rated R; 87 minutes; Release date: March 11, 2011

CAST
The Actress	**Embeth Davidtz**
Peggy	**Edie Falco**
John	**Elias Koteas**
Christina	**Rachel Resheff**
John's Wife	**Kathryn Erbe**
Big Man	**Wesley Broulik**

Danai Gurira (Woman in Blue Dress), Dana Eskelson (Debbie), Randi Kaplan (Jill), Peyton List (Emily), Ann Arvia (Matron), Jessica Bernard (Young Woman), Nicole Brending (Frazzled Housewife), Nick Diamantis (Young Guy), Tasha Guevara, Catrina Ganey (Mothers), Mahadeo Shivraj, Edward Hajj (Bellhops), Pam La Testa (Waitress), Alicia Masten (Peggy's Daughter), Susan McBrien (Woman), Louise Millmann (Teacher), Cory Nichols (Peggy's Son), Antonio Ortiz (Juan), Victor Pagan (Man on Street), Ron Phillips (Christina's Father), Jeremy Rishe (Desk Clerk), Jamel Rodriguez (Mechanic), Kathy Searle (Ticket Agent), Sándor Técsy (Gus), Paul Urcioli (Peggy's Husband), LeRoy Wilson Jr. (Cop), Frank Zinghini (Hotel Concierge), Joe Cipoletti, John Monteleone (Janitors), Judy Ross (Natalie)

A trio of stories exploring the complicated lives of some diverse Long Islanders: a couple whose unhappy marriage causes the husband to seek refuge in a motel; a housewife who seizes her chance to spend time with the famous actress who lives nearby; and a young girl who stumbles upon an abusive neighbor.

Ray Stevenson

Val Kilmer © Anchor Bay

Brian Balzerini, Christopher Walken

KILL THE IRISHMAN

(ANCHOR BAY) Producers, Al Corley, Bart Rosenblatt, Eugene Musso, Tommy Reid; Executive Producers, Jonathan Dana, Tara Reid, Peter Miller, Rick Porrello, Arthur Sarkissian; Co-Producers, Kim Olsen, John Leonetti, George Perez, Jeremy Walters; Director, Jonathan Hensleigh; Screenplay, Jonathan Hensleigh, Jeremy Walters; Based on the book *To Kill the Irishman* by Rick Porrello; Photography, Karl Walter Lindenlaub; Designer, Patrizia Von Brandenstein; Costumes, Melissa Bruning; Music, Patrick Cassidy; Music Supervisor, John Bissell; Visual Effects Supervisor, Chris Ervin; Casting, Mary Vernieu, JC Cantu; a Code Entertainment production, a Dundee Entertainment production; Dolby; Color; HD; Rated R; 106 minutes; Release date: March 11, 2011

CAST
Danny Greene	**Ray Stevenson**
John Nardi	**Vincent D'Onofrio**
Joe Manditski	**Val Kilmer**
Shondor Birns	**Christopher Walken**
Joan Madigan	**Linda Cardellini**

Fionnula Flanagan (Grace O'Keefe), Jason Butler Harner (Art Sneperger), Vinnie Jones (Keith Ritson), Paul Sorvino (Tony Salerno), Marcus Thomas (William "Billy" McComber), Robert Davi (Ray Ferritto), Bob Gunton (Jerry Merke), Tony Lo Bianco (Jack Licavoli), Steven R. Schirripa (Mike Frato), Mike Starr (Leo "Lips" Moceri), Vinny Vella (Frank Brancato), Tony Darrow (Mikey Mendarolo), Laura Ramsey (Ellie O'Hara), Brian Balzerini (Valet), Cody Christian (Young Danny Greene), Dante Wildern (Young Billy McComber), Sean O'Reilly (Tony Lupero), Vincent Rogo Angelini (Vic Centauro), Grant Krause (Tommy Sinito), Jeff Chase (Joe Buka), Jim Porterfield (Stan Gilroy), Nina Kircher (Merke's Secretary), Loren Bass (Macleish), Richard Jewell (Agent Mike Malloy), John Seibert (Steve Marshak), Greg Trzaskoma (Theatrical Grille Bartender), John Hawkinson (Det. Podorski), Jimmy Doom (Biker Bill), Lise Lacasse (Mrs. Shaughnessy), Arthur Cartwright (Leg Breaker), Joey Albright (Garbage Man), Walter Lindsey Jr. (Furniture Mover), Douglas Minckiewicz (Kevin McKiernan), Robert Skrok (Brendan Calhoun), Ruth Crawford (Mrs. Birns), Steven Goldsmith (Martin), Renell White (Billy Cox), Jeff Wolfe (Undercover Cop), John Duffey Leo (Geoffrey Greene), Al Corley (TV Reporter), Michael Brian Ogden (Julius), Trevor Callaghan (Cleveland Kid)

The true story of how former Cleveland longshoreman Danny Greene became a union organizer whose defiance of the Mafia led to an all-out mob war.

Vincent D'Onofrio

Michelle Rodriguez

BATTLE LOS ANGELES

Michael Peña, Joey King, Aaron Eckhart

(COLUMBIA) Producer, Neal H. Moritz, Ori Marmur; Executive Producers, Jeffrey Chernov, David Greenblatt; Director, Jonathan Liebesman; Screenplay, Chris Bertolini; Photography, Lukas Ettlin; Designer, Peter Wenham; Costumes, Sanja Milkovic Hays; Music, Brian Tyler; Editor, Christian Wagner; Visual Effects Supervisor, Everett Burrell; an Original Film production, presented in association with Relativity Media; Dolby; Super 35 Widescreen; Deluxe color; Rated PG-13; 117 minutes; Release date: March 11, 2011

CAST
Sgt. Michael Nantz	**Aaron Eckhart**
TSgt. Elena Santos	**Michelle Rodriguez**
2nd Lt. William Martinez	**Ramon Rodriguez**
Michele	**Bridget Moynahan**
Cpl. Kevin Harris	**Ne-Yo**
Joe Rincon	**Michael Peña**
Cpl. Scott Grayston	**Lucas Till**
Cpl. Jason Lockett	**Cory Hardrict**
Cpl. Nick Stavrou	**Gino Anthony Pesi**
LCpl. Steven Mottola	**James Hiroyuki Liao**
Pfc. Shaun Lenihan	**Noel Fisher**

Adetokumboh M'Cormack (Corpsman Jibril Adukwu), Bryce Cass (Hector Rincon), Neil Brown Jr. (LCpl. Richard Guerrero), Taylor Handley (LCpl. Corey Simmons), Joey King (Kirsten), Kenneth Brown Jr. (Cpl. Richard Oswald), Jadin Gould (Amy), Joe Chrest (1st Sgt. John Roy), E. Roger Mitchell (Company Captain), Rus Blackwell (Lt. Col. K.N. Ritchie), Susie Abromeit (Amanda), Brandi Coleman (Cherise), Elizabeth L. Keener (Kathy Martinez), Jessica Heap (Jessy), David Jensen (Psychiatrist), Stacey Turner, Tom Hillmann (Reporters on TV), Lena Clark (Kristy), Jamie Norwood (Flower Shop Employee), Todd Cochran (Command Hangar Marine), Nzinga Blake (Adukwu's Sister), Taryn Southern (Reporter on Beach), Jim Dever (Sgt. Major), Will Rothhaar (Cpl. Lee Imlay), Jim Parrack (LCpl. Peter Kerns)

The marines launch a full-scale defensive against a deadly alien attack that is causing untold chaos and destruction in Los Angeles.

© Columbia Pictures

Billy Burke, Julie Christie, Virginia Madsen

Gary Oldman, Lukas Haas © Warner Bros.

Shauna Kain, Amanda Seyfried

Max Irons, Shiloh Fernandez

RED RIDING HOOD

(WARNER BROS.) Producers, Jennifer Davisson Killoran, Leonardo DiCaprio, Julie Yorn; Executive Producers, Jim Rowe, Michael Ireland, Catherine Hardwicke; Director, Catherine Hardwicke; Screenplay, David Leslie Johnson; Photography, Mandy Walker; Designer, Tom Sanders; Costumes, Cindy Evans; Music, Brian Reitzell; Editor, Nancy Richardson; Visual Effects Supervisor, Jeffrey A. Okun; Visual Effects, Rhythm & Hues Studios; Stunts, Andy Cheng, Scott Nicholson; Casting, Ronna Kress; an Appian Way production; American-Canadian; Dolby; Super 35 Widescreen; Technicolor; Rated PG-13; 99 minutes; Release date: March 11, 2011

CAST

Valerie	**Amanda Seyfried**
Solomon	**Gary Oldman**
Cesaire	**Billy Burke**
Peter	**Shiloh Fernandez**
Henry	**Max Irons**
Suzette	**Virginia Madsen**
Father Auguste	**Lukas Haas**
Grandmother	**Julie Christie**
Roxanne	**Shauna Kain**
The Reeve	**Michael Hogan**
Captain	**Adrian Holmes**
Claude	**Cole Heppell**

Christine Willes (Madame Lazar), Michael Shanks (Adrien Lazar), Kacey Rohl (Prudence), Carmen Lavigne (Rose), Don Thompson (Tavern Owner), Matt Ward (Captain's Brother), Megan Charpentier (Young Valerie), Dj Greenburg (Young Peter), Jennifer Halley (Marguerite), Alexandria Maillot (Lucie), Archie Rice (Wolf Voice), Bella King, Olivia Steele-Falconer (Solomon's Daughters), Alexander Pesusich (Man in Wolf Costume), Jordan Becker (Woodcutter), James Michalopoulos, Darren Shahlavi, Dalias Blake, Michael Adamthwaite, Lauro Chartrand, Brad Kelly, Paul Wu, Gavin Buhr, Samuel Smith (Solomon's Soldiers), Che Pritchard, Kaitlyn McCready, Michelle C. Smith, Sarah Elgart (Dancers)

Villagers ravaged by wolf attacks are informed by a newly arrived lycanthropy expert that there is a werewolf among them causing the destruction.

Gribble, Milo

Gribble, Milo

Ki © Walt Disney Pictures

MARS NEEDS MOMS

(WALT DISNEY PICTURES) Producers, Robert Zemeckis, Jack Rapke, Steve Starkey, Steven Boyd; Director, Simon Wells; Screenplay, Simon Wells, Wendy Wells; Based on the book by Berkeley Breathed; Photography, Robert Presley; Designer, Doug Chiang; Music, John Powell; Editor, Wayne Wahrman; Animation Supervisor, Huck Wirtz; Visual Effects Supervisor, Kevin Baillie; an Imagemovers Digital presentation; Dolby; 3D; Technicolor; Rated PG; 88 minutes; Release date: March 11, 2011

CAST
Milo	**Seth Green**
Gribble	**Dan Fogler**
Mom	**Joan Cusack**
Ki	**Elisabeth Harnois**
Supervisor	**Mindy Sterling**
Wingnut	**Kevin Cahoon**
Dad	**Tom Everett Scott**

Jacquie Barnbrook, Matthew Henerson, Adam Jennings, Stephen Kearin, Amber Gainey Meade, Aaron Rapke, Julene Renee, Kirsten Severson, Matthew Wolf (Martians), Raymond Ochoa, Robert Ochoa, Ryan Ochoa, Meredith Wells, Teagan Wells, Gavin Bryson Thompson (Martian Hatchlings), Marianne Bennett, Jo McGinley, Daniel James O'Conner, Edi Patterson (Voice Performers), Seth Dusky (Milo's Voice)

A nine-year-old boy constantly at odds with his mom comes to her rescue when she is kidnapped by Martians who hope to download her disciplinary tactics for their own species.

Milo's Mom

BILL CUNNINGHAM NEW YORK

(ZEITGEIST) Producer, Philip Gefter; Director, Richard Press; Photography, Tony Cenicola, Richard Press; Editor, Ryan Denmark; Title Design and Photo Animation, Keira Alexandra; The New York Times and First Thought Films presentation; Stereo; Color; Digitial; Not rated; 84 minutes; Release date: March 16, 2011. Documentary on *New York Times* photographer Bill Cunningham.

WITH:
Bill Cunningham, Editta Sherman, Patrick McDonald, Harold Koda, John Kurdewan, Carmen Dell' Orefice, Annette de la Renta, Anna Wintour, Iris Apfel, Shail Upadhya, Kim Hastreiter, Annie Flanders, Josef Astor, Toni "Suzette" Cimino, Thelma Golden, Tom Wolfe, Kenny Kenny, Anna Piaggi, Didier Grumbach, Michael Kors, Brooke Astor, Lesley Vinson

Cara Seymour, Lou Taylor Pucci © Roadside Attractions

Lou Taylor Pucci, J.K. Simmons

Bill Cunningham

THE MUSIC NEVER STOPPED

(ROADSIDE ATTRACTIONS) Producers, Julie W. Noll, Jim Kohlberg, Peter Newman, Greg Johnson; Executive Producers, Neal Moritz, Brad Luff; Co-Producer, George Paaswell; Associate Producers, Kate Edgar, Wendy Smith; Director, Jim Kohlberg; Screenplay, Gwyn Lurie, Gary Marks; Based upon the essay *The Last Hippie* by Oliver Sacks; Photography, Steve Kazmierski; Designer, Jennifer Dehghan; Costumes, Jacki Roach; Music, Paul Cantelon; Music Producer, Susan Jacobs; Editor, Keith Reamer; Casting, Antonia Dauphin; an Essential Pictures production in association with Peter Newman/Interal Productions; Dolby; Technicolor; DV-to-35mm; Rated PG; 105 minutes; release date: March 18, 2011

CAST
Henry Sawyer	**J.K. Simmons**
Gabriel Sawyer	**Lou Taylor Pucci**
Helen Sawyer	**Cara Seymour**
Dianne Daley	**Julia Ormond**
Tamara	**Tammy Blanchard**

Mia Maestro (Celia), Scott Adsit (Dr. Biscow), James Urbaniak (Mike Tappin), Peggy Gormley (Florence), Max Antisell (Young Gabriel), Ryan Karels (Bernie the Hermit), Josh Segarra (Mark Ferris), Phil Bender (Jerry Garcia), Buzz Roddy (Bill Kreutzman), Ethan Hambvurg (Phil Lesh), Mark Greenberg (Mickey Hart), Martin Moran (Minister), Erica Berg (College Representative), Rich Campbell (Bob Weir), Matthew J. McCarthy (Carl the Cafeteria Worker), Lance Rubin (Rocker Dude), Paul Sigrist (Brent Mydland), Rashad Edwards (Police Officer), Xander Johnson (Weed), Wade Mylius (Political Activist), Jesse Roche (Steve), James Eason (Hippie Vendor)

Henry Sawyer reconnects with his long absent son who because of brain damage has had all intervening memory since the 1960s erased.

Bill Cunningham © Zeitgeist Films

PAUL

(UNIVERSAL) Producers, Nira Park, Tim Bevan, Eric Fellner; Executive Producers, Liza Chasin, Debra Hayward, Natascha Wharton, Robert Graf; Director, Greg Mottola; Screenplay, Simon Pegg, Nick Frost; Photography, Lawrence Sher; Designer, Jefferson Sage; Costumes, Nancy Steiner; Music, David Arnold; Editor, Chris Dickens; Special Effects Supervisor, Larz Anderson; Puppet Effects Creator, Mike Elizalde; Animation Supervisor, Anders J.L. Beer; Visual Effects, Double Negative; Casting, Jo Edna Boldin, Allison Jones; a Working Title production in association with Big Talk Pictures, presented in association with Relativity Media; Dolby; Super 35 Widescreen; Technicolor; Rated R; 104 minutes; Release date: March 18, 2011

CAST
Graeme Willy	**Simon Pegg**
Clive Gollings	**Nick Frost**
Agent Lorenzo Zoil	**Jason Bateman**
Ruth Buggs	**Kristen Wiig**
Haggard	**Bill Hader**
Tara Walton	**Blythe Danner**
Moses Buggs	**John Carroll Lynch**
The Big Guy	**Sigourney Weaver**
Voice of Paul	**Seth Rogen**
O'Reilly	**Joe Lo Truglio**
Adam Shadowchild	**Jeffrey Tambor**
Pat Stevens	**Jane Lynch**

David Koechner (Gus), Jesse Plemons (Jake), Mia Stallard (Young Tara), Jeremy Owen (Sword Vendor), David House (Security Guard), Jennifer Granger (Adam Shadowchild Fan), Nelson Ascencio (Jorge), Mark Sivertsen (State Trooper), Joe Berryman (Gas Station Attendant), Steven Spielberg (Himself – Voice), Syd Masters, Gary Roller, Oliver O'Shea, Lonnie Otha-Mayer, Will Veitch (Band Members), Michael Miller (Police Officer), Lori Dillen (Robed Woman), J. Todd Anderson (Comic Store Clerk), Brett Michael Jones (Keith Nash), Diego Deane (Fireworks Store Clerk)

While touring the U.S.A.'s notable extra-terrestrial sites, two British sci-fi enthusiasts find themselves giving a lift to an aggressive, foul-mouthed alien, anxious to finally get back to his home planet after being stranded on Earth for years.

Kristen Wiig, Paul, Nick Frost, Simon Pegg, Blythe Danner

Simon Pegg, Kristen Wiig, Nick Frost, Paul © Universal Studios

Sigourney Weaver

Joe Lo Truglio, Bill Hader, Jason Bateman

Amy Ryan, Paul Giamatti, Burt Young, Bobby Cannavale, Alex Shaffer

Bobby Cannavale, Paul Giamatti

Paul Giamatti, Alex Shaffer © Fox Searchlight

WIN WIN

(FOX SEARCHLIGHT) Producers, Mary Jane Skalski, Michael London, Lisa Maria Falcone, Tom McCarthy; Executive Producers, Lori Keith Douglas, Tom Heller; Director/Screenplay, Tom McCarthy; Story, Tom McCarthy, Joe Tiboni; Photography, Oliver Bokelberg; Designer, John Paino; Costumes, Melissa Toth; Music, Lyle Workman; Music Supervisor, Mary Ramos; Editor, Tom McArdle; Casting, Kerry Barden, Paul Schnee; a Groundswell/Next Wednesday production, presented in association with Everest Entertainment; Dolby; Technicolor; Rated R; 106 minutes; Release date: March 18, 2011

CAST

Mike Flaherty	**Paul Giamatti**
Jackie Flaherty	**Amy Ryan**
Terry Delfino	**Bobby Cannavale**
Stephen Vigman	**Jeffrey Tambor**
Leo Poplar	**Burt Young**
Cindy	**Melanie Lynskey**
Kyle	**Alex Shaffer**
Eleanor	**Margo Martindale**
Stemler	**David Thompson**
Jimmy Reed	**Mike DiLiello**
Shelly	**Nina Arianda**
Gina Flaherty	**Marcia Haufrecht**
Judge Lee	**Sharon Wilkins**
Abby	**Clare Foley**
Stella	**Penelope Kindred, Sophie Kindred**
Stuart Thatcher	**Tim Ransom**
BH Coach	**Nicholas Somers**

Jacqueline Brogan, Marceline Hugot (Women Jogging), Michael Goodwin (Regional Ref), Earl Baker Jr. (Staff Member), Edmund Ikeda (Frank), Joseph Tiboni (Steve Deluca, Principal), Edwin Thompson (Ref), Pam Levine (Church Soloist), Darren C. Goldstein (Sheffield Coach), Michael D. Davey (Referee), Ann M. Hayes (Betty), Rudy Lanzillotta III (Kenny Randall), Christopher Lantz (Kyle's Regional Opponent), Ryan Arnel (Carol's Match #1 Opponent), Kevin Antero (Kyle's Match #1 Opponent), Chris Sarro (Zack Lowenstein's Match #4), Dante Porrazzo (Stemler's Match #4 Masked Opponent), Lilly (Frank's Cat); The New Providence Team: Dariusz Uczkowski (Zack Lowenstein), Chris Federlin (Thomlinson), Nicholas Labarbera (Korsic), Nicholas Lopez (Anthony Pizzno), Quinn Knauer (Kurt Vetner), Austin Ward (Peter Molter), Jonathan Anderson (Feeney), Delon Richards (Dean Stol), Chris Loew (Paul Bell, a.k.a. Pill), Dean Shmuely (Rew), John Goncalves (Carlos)

A disillusioned attorney volunteers to coach a high school wrestling team where he discovers a young athlete with great potential.

Bobby Cannavale, Jeffrey Tambor, Paul Giamatti

Robert De Niro, Bradley Cooper

Bradley Cooper, Andrew Howard

Bradley Cooper, Abbie Cornish

LIMITLESS

(RELATIVITY) Producers, Leslie Dixon, Scott Kroopf, Ryan Kavanaugh; Executive Producers, Tucker Tooley, Bradley Cooper, Jason Felts; Co-Producer, Kenneth Halsband; Line Producer, Patty Long; Director, Neil Burger; Screenplay, Leslie Dixon; Based on the novel *The Dark Fields* by Alan Glynn; Photography, Jo Willems; Designer, Patrizia von Brandenstein; Costumes, Jenny Gering; Music, Paul Leonard-Morgan; Music Supervisors, Happy Walters, Season Kent; Editors, Naomi Geraghty, Tracy Adams; Casting, Douglas Aibel; a Rogue Production, a Many Rivers/Boy of the Year Production in association with Intermedia Film, presented in association with Virgin Produced; Dolby; Super 35 Widescreen; Technicolor; HD; Rated PG-13; 105 minutes; Release date: March 18, 2011

CAST

Eddie Morra	**Bradley Cooper**
Carl Van Loon	**Robert De Niro**
Lindy	**Abbie Cornish**
Gennady	**Andrew Howard**
Melissa	**Anna Friel**
Vernon	**Johnny Whitworth**
Man in Tan Coat	**Tomas Arana**
Pierce	**Robert John Burke**
Kevin Doyle	**Darren Goldstein**
Morris Brandt	**Ned Eisenberg**

T.V. Carpio (Valerie), Richard Bekins (Hank Atwood), Patricia Kalember (Mrs. Atwood), Cindy Katz (Marla Sutton), Brian A. Wilson (Detective), Rebecca Dayan (Rebecca), Ann Marie Green (Financial Newscaster), Damali Mason, Chris McMullin (Cops), Meg McCrossen (Assistant), Tom Bloom (Dunham), Nina Hodoruk (Realtor), Tom Teti (Tailor), Stephanie Humphrey (TV News Reporter), Joe McCarthy, Peter Pryor (Day Traders), Daniel Breaker (Campaign Manager), Dave Droxler (Technician), Luisina Quarleri (Italian Hostess), Piper Brown (Girl Skater), Simon MacLean (Father Skater), Saxon Palmer, Stephen Sable (Businessmen), Caroline Maria Winberg (Maria), Damaris Lewis (Beautiful Black Woman), Martha Ann Talman (Van Loon's Assistant), Robert Bizik (Coffee Shop Owner), Hugh Douglas, Howard Strong (Poker Players), Arlette de Alba (Passenger), Eddie Fernandez (Gennady Thug), Ray Siegle (Gennady Blind Thug), Nicolas le Guern, Richard Miller, Violeta Silva, Anna Parkinson, Laurence Roscoe (Friends at Beach)

A struggling writer finds his life changing for the better when he begins taking a pill that allows him to use 100% of his brain power.

Anna Friel © Relativity Media

THE LINCOLN LAWYER

(LIONSGATE) Producers, Sidney Kimmel, Richard Wright, Scott Steindorff, Tom Rosenberg, Gary Lucchesi; Executive Producers, Eric Reid, David Kern, Bruce Toll; Director, Brad Furman; Screenplay, John Romano; Based on the novel by Michael Connelly; Photography, Lukas Ettlin; Designer, Charisse Cardenas; Costumes, Erin Benach; Music, John Frizzell; Editor, Jeff McEvoy; Casting, Tricia Wood, Deborah Aquila; a Lakeshore Entertainment and Lionsgate production in association with Sidney Kimmel Entertainment and Stone Village Pictures, presented with Lakeshore Entertainment; Dolby; Deluxe color; Rated R; 118 minutes; Release date: March 18, 2011

CAST
Mick Haller	**Matthew McConaughey**
Maggie McPherson	**Marisa Tomei**
Louis Roulet	**Ryan Phillippe**
Frank Levin	**William H. Macy**
Ted Minton	**Josh Lucas**
Val Valenzuela	**John Leguizamo**
Jesus Martinez	**Michael Peña**
Cecil Dobbs	**Bob Gunton**
Mary Windsor	**Frances Fisher**
Det. Lankford	**Bryan Cranston**

Trace Adkins (Eddie Vogel), Laurence Mason (Earl), Margarita Levieva (Reggie Campo), Pell James (Lorna), Shea Whigham (DJ Corliss), Katherine Moennig (Gloria), Michael Paré (Det. Kurlen), Michaela Conlin (Det. Sobel), Mackenzie Aladjem (Hayley Haller), Reggie Baker (Judge Fullbright), Javier Grajeda (Bailiff Reynaldo), David Castro (Harold Casey), Conor O'Farrell (Judge Orton Powell), Charlie Hirsch (Prosecutor), Roland Feliciano (Biker), Jeffrey Cole (Van Nuys Judge), Andrew Staes (Maggie's Co-Counsel), Donnie Smith (Sticks), Erin Carufel (Leslie Faire), Sam Upton (Officer Maxwell), Matthew Moreno, L. Emille Thomas (Officers), Kate Mulligan (Minton's Secretary), Melanie Molnar (Junior Prosecutor), Stephanie Mace (Diner Waitress), Yari Deleon (Donna Renteira), Christian George (San Quentin Guard), Randy Mulkey (Bartender), Scott Wood (L.A. Rehab Guard), Earl Carroll (Court Clerk), Melanie Benz (Assistant D.A.), Eric Etebari (Charles Talbot), Sharyn Bamber (Court Stenographer), Edwin Dunn, Eric Huus, Rick Filkins (Golfers)

A smooth-talking LA lawyer, used to defending a lower degree of client, is enlisted to try the case of a well-to-do Beverly Hills millionaire accused of the attempted rape and murder of a prostitute.

Bob Gunton, Ryan Phillippe, Matthew McConaughey, William H. Macy

Marisa Tomei, Matthew McConaughey © Lionsgate

John Leguizamo, Matthew McConaughey

Michael Peña, Matthew McConaughey

SUCKER PUNCH

(WARNER BROS.) Producers, Deborah Snyder, Zack Snyder; Executive Producers, Thomas Tull, Wesley Coller, Jon Jashni, Chris deFaria, Jim Rowe, William Fay; Director/Story, Zack Snyder; Screenplay, Zack Snyder, Steve Shibuya; Photography, Larry Fong; Designer, Rick Carter; Costumes, Michael Wilkinson; Music, Tyler Bates, Marius De Vries; Editor, William Hoy; Special Makeup Effects, Quantum Creation FX; Special Effects Coordinator, Joel Whist; Visual Effects, MPC, Pixomondo, Animal Logic, Pixomondo, Prime Focus, Digiscope; a Cruel and Unusual production, presented in association with Legendary Pictures; Dolby; Super 35 Widescreen; Technicolor; Rated PG-13; 109 minutes; Release date: March 25, 2011

Abbie Cornish, Jena Malone, Emily Browning, Scott Glenn, Vanessa Hudgens, Jamie Chung

CAST

Babydoll	**Emily Browning**
Sweet Pea	**Abbie Cornish**
Rocket	**Jena Malone**
Blondie	**Vanessa Hudgens**
Amber	**Jamie Chung**
Dr. Vera Gorski	**Carla Gugino**
Blue Jones	**Oscar Isaac**
High Roller/Doctor	**Jon Hamm**
Wise Man	**Scott Glenn**

Richard Cetrone (CJ), Gerard Plunkett (Stepfather), Malcolm Scott (The Cook), Ron Selmour (Danforth), AC Peterson (Mayor/Lighter Orderly), Revard Dufresne (Big Boss Thug/Orderly #3), Kelora Clingwall (Babydoll's Mother), Frederique De Raucourt (Babydoll's Sister), Monique Ganderton, Lee Tomaschefski (Lobotomy Nurses/High Roller Girls), Eli Snyder, Cainan Wiebe, Danny Bristol (Tommy Soldiers), Brad Kelly, Peter Bryant (Guards/ Chauffeurs), Patrick Sabongui (Earl), John R. Taylor (Grim Doctor), Chris Nowland (Cemetery Cop), Christine Willes (Reception Nurse/Designer), Gina Garenkooper (Bitter Clipboard Nurse), Michael Adamthwaite, Phillip Mitchell (State Troopers), Ian Tracey, Sean Campbell (Police Officers), Arassay Reyes, Danielle Benton, Caitlin Goguen, Maiko Miyauchi, Paula Giroday, Louise Hradsky, Juliana Semenova, Allie Bertram, Vicky Lambert, Caroline Torti, Chantal Hunt, Carla Catherwood, Stephanie Sy, Kathryn Schellenberg, Geneen Gorgiev, Annie Au, Tia Haraga, Hailley Caulfield, Daniela Dib (Dancers), Jeff Dimitriou ("Emilio" Gangster Dancer), John Howard, Thomas Fornataro, Antoine Baby Harry Calaway, G! Force, Nii Nortey Engmann (Band Members), Gary Hecker (Special Creature Vocals)

Sent to a mental institution in order to receive a lobotomy, Babydoll retreats into a fantastical world where she and some of her fellow inmates fight various creatures in an effort to retrieve five valuable items that can help them break free of their prison.

Jon Hamm © Warner Bros.

Jena Malone, Abbie Cornish, Vanessa Hudgens

Carla Gugino, Oscar Isaac

DIARY OF A WIMPY KID: RODRICK RULES

(20TH CENTURY FOX) Producers, Nina Jacobson, Brad Simpson; Executive Producer, Jeff Kinney; Co-Producer, Ethan Smith; Director, David Bowers; Screenplay, Gabe Sachs, Jeff Judah; Based upon the book by Jeff Kinney; Photography, Jack Green; Designer, Brent Thomas; Costumes, Tish Monaghan; Music, Edward Shearmur; Music Supervisor, Julia Michels; Editor, Troy Takaki; Visual Effects and Animation, Custom Film Effects; Casting, Ronna Kress, Coreen Mayrs, Heike Brandstatter; a Fox 2000 Pictures presentation of a Color Force production; Dolby; Super 35 Widescreen; Deluxe color; Rated PG; 99 minutes; Release date: March 25, 2011

Peyton List, Zachary Gordon, Robert Capron, Karan Brar

Zachary Gordon, Laine MacNeil

Robert Capron, Zachary Gordon

CAST

Greg Heffley	**Zachary Gordon**
Rodrick Heffley	**Devon Bostick**
Susan Heffley	**Rachael Harris**
Rowley Jefferson	**Robert Capron**
Frank Heffley	**Steve Zahn**
Holly Hills	**Peyton List**
Patty Farrell	**Laine MacNeil**
Fregley	**Grayson Russell**
Chirag Gupta	**Karan Brar**

Connor Fielding, Owen Fielding (Manny Heffley), Terence Kelly (Grandpa), Fran Kranz (Bill Walter), Bryce Hodgson (Ben Segal), Andrew McNee (Coach Malone), John Shaw (Mr. Draybick), Alfred E. Humphreys (Rowley's Dad), Teryl Rothery (Mrs. Kohan), Serge Houde (Mr. Salz), Dalila Bela (Taylor Pringle), Jakob Davies (Scotty), Maple Batalia (Melissa), Melissa Roxburgh (Rachel), Jeff Kinney (Holly's Dad), Alec Williows (Minister), Sean Mathieson (Mean Skater Dude), Belita Moreno (Mrs. Norton), Elysia Rotaru (Ingrid, Girl in *The Foot*), Ben Hollingsworth (Terence, Man in *The Foot*), Michelle Harrison (Wealthy Woman), Kevin Kazakoff (Wealthy Man), Graeme Duffy (Emcee), Christopher De-Schuster (Chris the Bass Player), Samantha Page (Shelley), Ava Hughes (Marley), Jake D. Smith (Archie Kelly), Owen Best (Bryce Anderson), Spencer Drever (Harry Gilberston), Michael Strusievici (Crying Boy), Conner Ingram (Young Rodrick), Mark Brandon, Dawn Chubai (News Anchors), Brenda Anderson (Mrs. Fiorkowski), Doreen Ramus (Mrs. Cabbage), Betty Phillips (Mrs. Evesham), Tae Helgeth (Mrs. Tan), Sheila Paterson (Mrs. Bingham), Monica Marko (Mrs. Anholtz), Darcy Michael, Manoj Sood, Angela Moore, Nancy Ebert (Convenience Store Customers)

7th grader Greg Heffley must cope not only with the angst of school life but with his ever-tormenting older brother and an unrequited crush on Holly Hills.
Sequel to the 2010 Fox film *Diary of a Wimpy Kid*, with most of the principals repeating their roles.

Zachary Gordon, Devon Bostick © 20th Century Fox

Nick Thurston, Leslie Murphy

Geoffrey Wigdor, Nick Thurston

WHITE IRISH DRINKERS

(SCREEN MEDIA) Producers, John Gray, Melissa Jo Peltier, Paul Bernard, James Scura; Director/Screenplay, John Gray; Photography, Seamus Tierney; Designer, Tommaso Ortino; Costumes, Nicole Capasso; Music, Mark Snow; Editor, Neil Mandelberg; Casting, Russell Boast; an Ovington Ave Prods. in association with Bernard/Scura Productions presentation; Color; Rated R; 109 minutes; Release date: March 25, 2011

CAST
Brian Leary	**Nick Thurston**
Danny Leary	**Geoffrey Wigdor**
Margaret Leary	**Karen Allen**
Patrick Leary	**Stephen Lang**
Whitey	**Peter Riegert**
Shauna Friel	**Leslie Murphy**

Zachary Booth (Todd McKay), Robbie Collier Sublett (Ray Stone), Michael Drayer (Dennis Gleason), Henry Zebrowski (Jerry Flanagan), Ken Jennings (Jimmy Cheeks), Regan Mizrahi (Little Brian), Anthony Amorim (Little Danny), Jonathan Dwyer (Lawyer), Lizzy Grant (Diane), Jimmy Palumbo (Jimmy)

Teenager Brian Leary hopes to escape from his increasingly frustrating life at home and find an outlet for his artistic ambitions, while his older brother is certain that scoring some cash in a robbery will be their ticket out of there.

TRUST

(MILLENNIUM FILMS) Producers, David Schwimmer, Robert Greenhut, Heidi Jo Markel, Tom Hodges, Ed Cathell III, Dana Golomb; Executive Producers, Avi Lerner, Danny Dimbort, Trevor Short, Boaz Davidson, John Thompson; Director, David Schwimmer; Screenplay, Andy Bellin, Robert Festinger; Photography, Andrzej Sekula; Designer, Michael Shaw; Costumes, Ellen Lutter; Music, Nathan Larson; Editor, Douglas Crise; Casting, Mary Vernieu, Lindsay Graham; a Nu Image production, a Dark Harbor production; Dolby; Super 35 Widescreen; Technicolor; Rated R; 106 minutes; Release date: April 1, 2011

CAST
Will Cameron	**Clive Owen**
Lynn Cameron	**Catherine Keener**
Annie Cameron	**Liana Liberato**
Agent Doug Tate	**Jason Clarke**
Al Hart	**Noah Emmerich**
Gail Friedman	**Viola Davis**

Chris Henry Coffey (Charlie/Graham Weston), Brandon Molale (Volleyball Coach), Noah Crawford (Tyler Martel), Jordan Trovillion (Waitress), Sarab Kamoo (Officer Gomez), Garrett Ryan (Marcus Weston), Zanny Laird (Serena Edmonds), Laura Niemi (Susanna), Milica Govich (Ms. Worley), Tristan Peach (Charlie), Robert Axelrod (Gun Salesman), Spencer Curnutt (Peter), Inga R. Wilson (Aunt Nicole), Aislinn DeButch (Katie), Jennifer Kincer (Charlie's Mom), Olivia Wickline (Louise), Zoe Levin (Brittany), Yolanda Mendoza (Tanya), Shenell Randall (Alexa), Ruth Crawford (Grandma Susan), Marty Bufalini (Grandpa Cal), Mary Murphy (Teacher), Sandro Carotti (Italian Teacher), Jared Conrad (Cell Phone Student), Lise Lacasse (Passing Nurse), Anthonia Kitchen (Security Officer), Joe Sikora (Rob Moscone), Julia Glander (Sandra Van Dorsey), Lauren Hirte (Becky), DJ Coburger (Child Predator), Brooke Bayless (Bikini Woman), Cassi Fitch (Sally Moscone), Lili Kaufman (Apple Woman), Miles A. Robinson, Deanna Fakhouri, Martin Malota, Jamal Johnson (FBI), Jay Siegel (Tour Guide), Nathan Zylich (Will's Co-Worker), Pamela Washington (Ad Agency Lady)

The Cameron family is shattered when their 14-year-old daughter Annie is raped after meeting up with an Internet hookup she believed was someone closer to her own age.

Clive Owen, Catherine Keener © Millennium Films

E.B. © Universal Studios

Gary Cole, Elizabeth Perkins

James Marsden

HOP

(UNIVERSAL) Producers, Chris Meledandri, Michele Imperato Stabile; Executive Producer, John Cohen; Director, Tim Hall; Screenplay, Cinco Paul, Ken Daurio, Brian Lynch; Story, Cinco Paul, Ken Daurio; Photography, Peter Lyons Collister; Designer, Richard Holland; Costumes, Alexandra Welker; Music, Christopher Lennertz; Music Supervisor, Julianne Jordan; Editors, Peter S. Elliot, Gregory Perler; a Illumination Entertainment production in association with Relativity Media; Dolby; Color; Rated PG; 95 minutes; Release date: April 1, 2011

CAST

Fred O'Hare	**James Marsden**
Sam O'Hare	**Kaley Cuoco**
Henry O'Hare	**Gary Cole**
Bonnie O'Hare	**Elizabeth Perkins**
Alex O'Hare	**Tiffany Espensen**
Himself	**David Hasselhoff**

Chelsea Handler (Mrs. Beck), Dustin Ybarra (Cody), Carlease Burke (Receptionist), Veronica Alicino (Waitress), Blind Boys of Alabama (Themselves), Coleton Ray (Young Fred), Greg Lewis (Performer), Mark Riccardi (Security Guard), Cici Lau (Chinese Woman), Jayden Lund (Another Parent), Christian Long (Production Assistant), Nick Drago (Dancer), David Goldsmith (Warm-Up Guy)

VOICE CAST

E.B./Production Assistant	**Russell Brand**
Carlos/Phil	**Hank Azaria**
E.B.'s Dad	**Hugh Laurie**
Young E.B.	**Django Marsh**
Voice at Playboy Mansion	**Hugh Hefner**

The next rabbit in line to become the Easter Bunny decides he'd much rather be a rock 'n' roll drummer and heads for L.A. to achieve his goal.

Carlos, E.B.'s Dad

SOURCE CODE

(SUMMIT) Producers, Mark Gordon, Philippe Rousselet, Jordan Wynn; Executive Producers, Hawk Koch, Jeb Brody, Fabrice Gianfermi; Co-Producers, Stuart Fenegan, Tracy Underwood; Director, Duncan Jones; Screenplay, Ben Ripley; Photography, Don Burgess; Designer, Barry Chusid; Costumes, Renée April; Music, Chris Bacon; Editor, Paul Hirsch; Special Effects Supervisor, Ryal Cosgrove; Stunts, Stéphane Lefebvre, Patrick Kerton, Michael Scherer; Casting, John Papsidera; a Vendôme Pictures presentation of a Mark Gordon Company production; Dolby; Deluxe Color; Rated PG-13; 93 minutes; Release date: April 1, 2011

Jake Gyllenhaal

CAST

Capt. Colter Stevens	**Jake Gyllenhaal**
Christina Warren	**Michelle Monaghan**
Colleen Goodwin	**Vera Farmiga**
Dr. Rutledge	**Jeffrey Wright**
Derek Frost	**Michael Arden**
Hazmi	**Cas Anvar**
Max Denoff	**Russell Peters**
George Troxel	**Brent Skagford**
Gold Watch Executive	**Craig Thomas**
Conductor	**Gordon Masten**
Nurse	**Susan Bain**
Coffee Mug Lady	**Paula Jean Hixson**
Minister Sudoku	**Lincoln Ward**

Kyle Gatehouse (College Student), Albert Kwan (Soda Can Guy), Anne Day-Jones (Office Manager), Clarice Byrne (Secretary), James A. Woods (Aviator Glasses Guy), Joe Cobden (Lab Technician), Tom Tammi (CNN Anchor), Matt Holland (Lock Tech), Jasson Finney (M.P.), Kyle Allatt (Aide), Frédérick De Grandpré (Sean Fentress Reflection), Pierre Leblanc (Train Official), Scott Bakula (Voice of Colter's Father)

Jake Gyllenhaal, Michelle Monaghan

Captain Stevens is placed aboard a commuter train with an experimental implant that allows him to relive the last eight minutes of someone else's life, in hopes of finding out who detonated a bomb aboard the train.

Vera Farmiga, Jeffrey Wright © Summit Entertainment

Michael Arden, Jake Gyllenhaal

Patrick Wilson, Ty Simpkins, Rose Byrne

Rose Byrne, Patrick Wilson

Leigh Whannell, Lin Shaye

INSIDIOUS

(FILMDISTRICT) Producers, Jason Blum, Steven Schneider, Oren Peli; Executive Producer, Brian Kavanaugh-Jones; Co-Producers, Aaron Sims, John R. Leonetti; Director, James Wan; Screenplay, Leigh Whannell; Photography, John A. Leonetti, David M. Brewer; Designer, Aaron Sims; Costumes, Kristin M. Burke; Music, Joseph Bishara; Editors, James Wan, Kirk Morri; Visual Effects, Spy; Special Effects Coordinator, Bart Dion; Special Makeup Effects, Fractured FX; Casting, Annie McCarthy, Kellie Gesell; an Alliance Films and IM Global presentation of a Haunted Movies production, presented in association with Stage 6 Films; Dolby; Super 35 Widescreen; Color; Rated PG-13; 101 minutes; Release date: April 1, 2011

CAST
Josh Lambert	**Patrick Wilson**
Renai Lambert	**Rose Byrne**
Dalton Lambert	**Ty Simpkins**
Foster Lambert	**Andrew Astor**
Elise Rainier	**Lin Shaye**
Specs	**Leigh Whannell**
Tucker	**Angus Sampson**
Lorraine Lambert	**Barbara Hershey**

Corbett Tuck (Nurse Adelle/Doll Girl #2), Heather Tocquigny (Nurse Kelly), Ruben Pla (Dr. Sercarz), John Henry Binder (Father Martin), Joseph Bishara (Lipstick-Face Demon), Philip Friedman (Old Woman), J. LaRose (Long Haired Fiend), Kelly Devoto (Doll Girl #1)

After their son falls into a coma, Josh and Renai Lambert come to the realization that his condition is a direct result of the boy being possessed by evil spirits.

© FilmDistrict

Geraldine James, Russell Brand, Jennifer Garner, Nick Nolte, Leslie Hendrix
© Warner Bros.

Russell Brand, Greta Gerwig

Russell Brand, Luis Guzmán

ARTHUR

(WARNER BROS.) Producers, Larry Brezner, Kevin McCormick, Chris Bender, Michael Tadross; Executive Producers, Scott Kroopf, J.C. Spink, Russell Brand, Nik Linnen; Director, Jason Winer; Screenplay, Peter Baynham; Story, Steve Gordon; Photography, Uta Briesewitz; Designer, Sarah Knowles; Music, Theodore Shapiro; Music Supervisors, Dave Jordan, Jojo Villanueva; Editor, Brent White; Casting, Juliet Polcsa; a Kevin McCormick/MBST Entertainment/Benderspink production; Dolby; Technicolor; Rated PG-13;110 minutes; Release date: April 8, 2011

CAST
Arthur Bach	**Russell Brand**
Hobson	**Helen Mirren**
Naomi Quinn	**Greta Gerwig**
Susan Johnson	**Jennifer Garner**
Vivienne Bach	**Geraldine James**
Bitterman	**Luis Guzmán**
Burt Johnson	**Nick Nolte**
Tiffany	**Christina Calph**
Office Kaplan	**Murphy Guyer**

José Ramón Rosario (Employment Clerk), John Hodgman (Candy Store Manager), Scott Adsit (Gummy Bear Man), Evander Holyfield (Boxing Trainer), Peter Van Wagner (Naomi's Dad), Robert Clohessy (Veteran Cop), Ed Herbstman (Rookie Cop), Jared Parker (Wedding Kid), Tom Toner (Wedding Priest), Richard Bekins (Chancellor), Matt Malloy (Spoon Guy), Nigel Barker (Photographer), Tuffy Questell (Tito), Sara Chase, Ali Reza Farahnakian, Kimberly Pauley (Journalists), Brian McElhaney (College Student), Charlie Hewson (Receptionist/Best Man), Peter Brouwer (Auctioneer), Saul Stein (Officer #2), Stink Fisher (Foreman), Debbie Lee Jones (Kissed Woman), Pascal Yen-Pfister (Maitre D'), Dylan Clark Marshall (Boy on Tour), Steve Rosen (Grand Central Waiter), Leslie Hendrix (Alice Johnson), George Feaster (James), Ed Jewett (Group Leader), John Carrafa (Choreographer), Jennifer Eisenhower (Maid of Honor), Sean G. Tarjyoto (Bookstore Clerk), Pamela Holden Stewart (Librarian), Tori Feinstein, Jackson Nicoll, Caden Draper, Jase Draper (Library Kids)

A childishly hedonistic multi-milionaire is told he will be disinherited unless he agrees to marry the daughter of another wealthy family.
Remake of the 1981 Orion film that starred Dudley Moore, Liza Minnelli, and John Gielgud.

Russell Brand, Helen Mirren

SUPER

(IFC FILMS) Producers, Ted Hope, Miranda Bailey; Executive Producers, Rainn Wilson, Lampton Enochs, Matt Leutwyler; Co-Producer, Amanda Marshall; Director/Screenplay, James Gunn; Photography, Steve Gainer; Designer, William Elliot; Costumes, Mary Matthews; Music, Tyler Bates; Editor, Cara Silverman; Visual Effects Supervisor, Louis Morin; Casting, Ryan Glorioso; a Cold Iron Pictures presentation of a This is That, Ambush Entertainment production; American-British; Dolby; Color; HD; Not rated; 96 minutes; Release date: April 1, 2011

CAST
Frank Darbo (The Crimson Bolt)	**Rainn Wilson**
Libby (Boltie)	**Ellen Page**
Sarah Helgeland	**Liv Tyler**
Jacques	**Kevin Bacon**
The Holy Avenger	**Nathan Fillion**
Det. John Felkner	**Gregg Henry**

Michael Rooker (Abe), Andre Royo (Hamilton), William Katt (Sgt. Fitzgibbon), Rob Zombie (Voice of God), Sean Gunn (Toby), Stephen Blackehart (Quill), Don Mac (Mr. Range), Linda Cardellini (Pet Store Employee), Gerardo Davilla (Cop), Grant Goodman (Young Frank), Paul T. Taylor (Frank Sr.), Connor Day (Teenage Frank), James Gunn (Demonswill), Mikaela Hoover (Holly), Nick Holmes (Jim), Matt Moore (Jesus/Guy in Line), Steve Agee (Comic Book Store Jerk), Laurel Whitsett (Librarian), James Lentzsch, Nate Rubin (Teen Passengers), Edrick Browne (Nathaniel), Danny Cosmo (Purse-Snatcher), Krystal Mayo (Wheelchair Woman), Russell Towery (Chickenhawk), Mario Jimenez Jr. (Chicken), Jonathan Winkler (Transvestite), Mollie Milligan (Sarah's Sister), Gerry May (Newscaster), Valentine Miele (Line Butter), Michelle Gunn (Line Butter's Girlfriend), Darcel Moreno (Waitress), Greg Ingram (Long-Haired Hood), Lindsay Soileau (Libby's Friend), Brandon Belknap (Christian), Zach Gilford (Jerry), Lloyd Kaufman (911 Man), Tim Smith (Range's Technician), Mark De Alessandro (Thug Jumped on by Boltie), Cole McKay (Thug Set on Fire), Dominick LaBlanca (Thug #1), John W. Lawson (Thug Missing Arms)

After his wife is stolen away by a sleazy drug-dealer, fry cook Frank Darbo turns himself into a costumed vigilante super hero.

Rainn Wilson © IFC Films

Paul Dano

Shirley Henderson, Zoe Kazan, Michelle Williams © Oscilloscope

MEEK'S CUTOFF

(OSCILLOSCOPE) Producers, Neil Kopp, Anish Savjani, Elizabeth Cuthrell, David Urrutia; Executive Producers, Todd Haynes, Phil Morrison, Rajen Savjani, Andrew Pope, Steven Tuttleman, Mike S. Ryan; Director/Editor, Kelly Reichardt; Screenplay, Jon Raymond; Photography, Christopher Blauvelt; Designer, David Doernberg; Costumes, Vicki Farrell; Music, Jeff Grace; Casting, Laura Rosenthal; an Evenstar Films, Filmscience, Harmony/Primitive Nerd production; Dolby ; Deluxe Color; Rated PG; 101 minutes; Release date: April 8, 2011

CAST
Emily Tetherow	**Michelle Williams**
Stephen Meek	**Bruce Greenwood**
Soloman Tetherow	**Will Patton**
Millie Gately	**Zoe Kazan**
Thomas Gately	**Paul Dano**
Glory White	**Shirley Henderson**
William White	**Neal Huff**
Jimmy White	**Tommy Nelson**
The Indian	**Rod Rondeaux**

Three families journeying by covered wagon to the Willamette Valley find themselves in danger of perishing when they choose to take a shortcut and end up lost.

MEET MONICA VELOUR

(ANCHOR BAY) Producers, Gary Gilbert, Jordan Horowitz; Co-Producer, Shauna Bogetz; Line Producer, Michael R. Williams; Director/Screenplay, Keith Bearden; Photography, Masanobu Takayanagi; Designer, Lou A. Trabbie, III; Costumes, Rebecca Bentjen; Music, Andrew Hollander; Music Supervisor, Season Kent; Editor, Naomi Geraghty; Casting, Kerry Barden, Paul Schnee; a Gilbert Films production; Dolby; Panavision; Deluxe color; Rated R; 98 minutes; Release date: April 8, 2011

CAST
Monica Velour	**Kim Cattrall**
Tobe	**Dustin Ingram**
Pop Pop	**Brian Dennehy**
Amanda	**Jee Young Han**
Kenny	**Daniel Yelsky**
Claude	**Keith David**

Sam McMurray (Ronnie), Elizabeth Wright Shapiro (Snickers), Jamie Tisdale (Young Monica), Tony Cox (Petting Zoo Club Owner), Henry Yuk (Amanda's Dad), Lauren Mae Shafer (Punk Girl), Peter Carey (Cop), Greg Trzaskoma (Biker Guy #1), Anna Li Egan (Cambodian Neighbor), Kevin Scollin (Commencement Speaker), John W. Lawson (Fireworks Salesman), Jay Malack (Porn Producer), Chris Dendrinos, Michael Force, Steve Holiday (Frat Boys), My-Ishia Cason-Brown (Jazelle), Dan Pesta (Dork Fudgepacker), Ric Carver (Frankenbooty Juggler), Nicole "Jade" Barley (Uta), Jason Waugh (Frankenbooty Burgermeister), Nicole Stober (Greta), Kathleen Moore (Store Owner), Benjamin Ralph Brennan (Bandito)

Finding out that his favorite '80s porn star is making a rare live appearance, a socially inept teen treks hundred of miles to see her.

Dustin Ingram © Anchor Bay

James Franco, Zooey Deschanel, Danny McBride © Universal Studios

YOUR HIGHNESS

(UNIVERSAL) Producer, Scott Stuber; Executive Producers, Danny McBride, Andrew Z. Davis, Jonathan Mone, Mark Huffam; Director, David Gordon Green; Screenplay, Danny R. McBride, Ben Best; Photography, Tim Orr; Designer, Mark Tildesley; Costumes, Hazel Webb-Crozier; Music, Steve Jablonsky; Editor, Craig Alpert; Visual Effects Supervisor, Mike McGee; Stunts, Paul Herbert; Casting, Gail Stevens; a Stuber Pictures production; Dolby; Panavision; Color; Rated R; 102 minutes; Release date: April 8, 2011

CAST
Thadeous	**Danny McBride**
Fabious	**James Franco**
Isabel	**Natalie Portman**
Belladonna	**Zooey Deschanel**
Courtney	**Rasmus Hardiker**
Leezar	**Justin Theroux**
Julie	**Toby Jones**
King Tallious	**Charles Dance**

Damian Lewis (Boremont), Simon Farnaby (Manious the Bold), Deobia Oparei (Thundarian), B.J. Hogg (Royal Advisor), Matyelok Gibbs, Angela Pleasence, Anna Barry (Mothers), Amber Anderson (Maiden), Stuart Loveridge (Skinny Prisoner), John Fricker (Marteetee), Rupert Davis (2nd Knight), Julian Rhind-Tutt (Warlock), Mario Torres (Great Wize Wizard), Noah Huntley (Head Knight), Ben Wright (Dastardly), Susie Kelly, Roma Tomelty, Brigid Erin Bates, Eilish Doran, Rene Greig (Hooded Witches), Kiran Shah (Tiniest One), Simon Cohen (The Barbarian), Graham Hughes (Dwarf King), Zhaidarbek Kunguzhinov, Nurlan Altaev (Brothers Mein), David Garrick (Daronius the Swift), Caroline Grace-Cassidy (Handmaiden), Elle Liberachi (Bridesmaid), Dorian Dixon, Darren Thompson, David Thompson (Trolls), Brian Steele (Minotaur), Ben Willbond (Ranger), Phil Holden (Dwarf Executioner), Chris Burke, Sinead Burke (Dwarves), Tobias Winter (Timotay Dungeon Master), Paige Tyler (Pale-Skinned Beauty), Rhian Sugden, Amii Grove, Madison Welch (Forest Women), Iga Wyrwal (Regina), Charles Shaughnessy (Narrator/Soul of the Maze)

Spoiled Prince Thadeous gets his chance to prove himself when his brother Fabious' bride-to-be is kidnapped by the wicked Leezar, and the two siblings embark upon a quest to rescue her and vanquish evil.

Dennis Quaid, Helen Hunt, Anna Sophia Robb

Dennis Quaid, AnnaSophia Robb, Helen Hunt © TriStar Pictures

SOUL SURFER

(TRISTAR) Producers, David Zelon, Douglas Schwartz, Dutch Hofstetter, David Brookwell, Sean McNamara; Executive Producers, David Tice, Dominic Ianno; Director, Sean McNamara; Screenplay, Sean McNamara, Deborah Schwartz, Douglas Schwartz, Michael Berk; Screen Story, Sean McNamara, Deborah Schwartz, Douglas Schwartz, Michael Berk, Matt R. Allen, Caleb Wilson, Brad Gann; Based on the book by Bethany Hamilton, Sheyrl Berk, Rick Bundschuh; Photography, John R. Leonetti; Designer, Rusty Smith; Costumes, Kathe James; Music, Marco Beltrami; Music Supervisor, Julia Michels; Editor, Jeff W. Canavan; Casting, Joey Paul Jensen; a Filmdistrict and Enticing Entertainment presentation in association with Island Film Group and Affirm Films of a Brookwell McNamara Entertainment, Lifes a Beach Entertainment and Mandalay Vision production; Dolby; Super 35 Widescreen; Color; Rated PG; 106 minutes; Release date: April 8, 2011

CAST

Bethany Hamilton	**AnnaSophia Robb**
Tom Hamilton	**Dennis Quaid**
Cheri Hamilton	**Helen Hunt**
Holt Blanchard	**Kevin Sorbo**
Sarah Hill	**Carrie Underwood**
Noah Hamilton	**Ross Thomas**
Alana Blanchard	**Lorraine Nicholson**
Keoki	**Cody Gomes**
Byron	**Jeremy Sumpter**
Dr. David Rovinsky	**Craig T. Nelson**

Sonya Balmores Chung (Malina Burch), Chris Brochu (Timmy Hamilton), Branscombe Richmond (Ben Aipa), Titus Kinimaka (Titus), John Philbin (Fuel TV Reporter), Tahini Bartolome (Girl at Foodland), Bridget Tully (Mother at Foodland), Christie Brooke (National Surf Bethany Fan #1), David Chokachi (Paramedic), Kelly Crean (Vicky, Front Yard Reporter), Yasmin Dar (Transworld Surf Reporter #1), Faith Fay (Media Gnat Lani Lane), John Mitchell Fultz (Keoki's Friend), Kim Morgan Greene (Patsy Lee Brown), Dutch Hofstetter (Brandon), Tiffany Hofstetter (Rosemary), Mark Kubr (ESPN Reporter), Wesley Mann (Calvin), Joshua Margulies (Halloween Party Surfer), Sean Patrick McNamara (Rip Curl Executive), Arlene Newman-Van Asperen (Cydney Blanchard), Kaleo Relator (Boom), Patrick Richwood (Todd), Edward Seid (Cameraman), David Stanfield (Nationals Lead Surf Commentator), Beau Hodge (Nationals Surf Announcer #2), Shelley Trotter, Kimberly-Rose Wolter (Nurses), Irie Driscoll (Ukulele Girl), Dylan Slater (Turtle Bay Open Announcer), Cayla Moore, Moon Otteman (Surfer Girls), David Tice (Contest Official), Michael Coots (Photoshoot Photographer), Kaipo Guerrero, Rocky Canon (H.I. Regionals Surf Announcers), Mark Kubr (ESPN Reporter), Bailey Nagy (Surfer Olivia Jenner), Leilani Gryde (Surfer Zoe Madsen), Kristen Steiner (Surfer Kaila Kahani)

The true story of how Bethany Hamilton overcame a horrific accident to return to the world of surfing.

AnnaSophia Robb, Carrie Underwood

Alexis Bledel

Colm Meaney © Roadside Attractions

THE CONSPIRATOR

(ROADSIDE ATTRACTIONS) Producers, Robert Redford, Greg Shapiro, Bill Holderman, Brian Falk, Robert Stone; Executive Producers, Joe Ricketts, Jeremiah Samuels, Webster Stone; Director, Robert Redford; Screenplay, James Solomon; Story, James Solomon, Gregory Bernstein; Photography, Newton Thomas Sigel; Designer, Kalina Ivanov; Costumes, Louise Frogley; Music, Mark Isham; Editor, Craig McKay; Casting, Avy Kaufman; a production of The American Film Company in association with Wildwood Enterprises; Dolby; Super 35 Widescreen; Deluxe Color; Rated PG-13; 123 minutes; Release date: April 15, 2011

CAST
Frederick Aiken	**James McAvoy**
Mary Surratt	**Robin Wright**
Edwin Stanton	**Kevin Kline**
Anna Surratt	**Evan Rachel Wood**
Joseph Holt	**Danny Huston**
Nicholas Baker	**Justin Long**
David Hunter	**Colm Meaney**
Reverdy Johnson	**Tom Wilkinson**
John Surratt	**Johnny Simmons**
Sarah Weston	**Alexis Bledel**
Lewis Payne	**Norman Reedus**
John Wilkes Booth	**Toby Kebbell**
John Lloyd	**Stephen Root**
Judge Wylie	**John Cullum**
Louis Weichmann	**Jonathan Groff**
William Hamilton	**James Badge Dale**
George Atzerodt	**John Michael Weatherly**
David Herold	**Marcus Hester**
Major Smith	**Chris Bauer**
Hartranft	**Jim True-Frost**
Captain Cottingham	**Shea Whigham**
Father Walter	**David Andrews**
Edman Spangler	**James Kirk Sparks**
General Howe	**John Curran**
General Harris	**Robert C. Trevelier**
Lieutenant	**Brian F. Durkin**
Stanton's Officer	**Cullen Moss**
Asa Trenchard	**Jason Hatfield**
Mrs. Mountchessington	**Kathleen Hogan**
Abraham Lincoln	**Gerald Bestrom**

Marshell Canney (Mary Todd Lincoln), Andy Martin (Major Rathbone), Dean Mumford (Plainclothes Major), Dennis Clark (Andrew Johnson), Tom Nelson (Senior Officer), Brandon Carroll (Stretcher Bearer), Lori Beth Edgeman, Amy Tipton (Guests), Beau Turpin (Boarding House Guard), Glenn R. Wilder (Secretary Seward), Brian Duffy (Frederick Seward), Richard Deloach (Seward's Servant), Lindsey Lambrakos (Fanny Seward), Cal Johnson (Army Sergeant), Chris Eckles (Stanton's Aide), Kevin Nichols (Douglas), Walter Bankson (Paperboy), Peter Bannon (Toastmaster), Travis Sprayberry (Petersen House Boarder), John Bankson (Alexander Gardner), Lance Miles, Adam Porter (Cell Guards)

The true story of how Mary Surratt was put on trial for her peripheral involvement with the men who conspired to assassinate Abraham Lincoln.

Evan Rachel Wood

Kevin Kline

Robin Wright

Robin Wright, James McAvoy

Toby Kebbell

James McAvoy, Tom Wilkinson

James McAvoy, Justin Long

Linda, Blu

RIO

(20TH CENTURY FOX) Producers, Bruce Anderson, John C. Donkin; Executive Producer, Chris Wedge; Director, Carlos Saldanha; Screenplay, Don Rhymer, Joshua Sternin, Jeffrey Ventimilia, Sam Harper; Story, Carlos Saldhana, Earl Richey Jones, Todd Jones; Photography, Renato Falcao; Music, John Powell; Editor, Harry Hitner; Supervising Animator, Galen Tan Chu; Art Director, Thomas Cardone; Head of Story, Karen Disher; CG Supervisor, Robert V. Calvaleri; Casting, Christian Kaplan; a 20th Century Fox Animation presentation of a Blue Sky Studios production; Dolby; Deluxe color; 3D; Rated G; 96 minutes; Release date: April 15, 2011

VOICE CAST

Blu	**Jesse Eisenberg**
Jewel	**Anne Hathaway**
Nigel	**Jemaine Clement**
Linda	**Leslie Mann**
Luiz	**Tracy Morgan**
Pedro	**will.i.am**
Tulio/Soccer Announcer	**Rodrigo Santoro**
Rafael	**George Lopez**
Nico	**Jamie Foxx**
Chloe, The Goose	**Wanda Sykes**
Alice, The Other Goose	**Jane Lynch**

Karen Disher (Mother Bird), Jason Fricchione (Truck Driver), Sofia Scarpa Saldanha (Young Linda), Kelly Keaton (Bookstore Customer/Tourist), Gracinha Leporace (Dr. Barbosa), Phil Miler (Aviary Intern/Waiter), Bernardo de Paula (Sylvio/Kipo), Carlos Saldana (2nd Waiter), Renato D'Angelo (Police Officer), Carlos Ponce (Marcel, Lead Smuggler), Jeff Garcia (Tipa, Heavy Smuggler/Bat), Davi Vieira (Armando, Tall Smuggler), Jake T. Austin (Fernando), Tom Wilson (Trapped Bird/Screaming Hang Glider), Cindy Slattery (Neurotic Bird), Justine Warwick (Scaredy Bird), Bebel Gilberto (Eva), Judah Friedlander (Tourist), Francisco Ramos (Lead Marmoset), Tim Nordquist (Other Hang Glider), Miriam Wallen (Green Bird), Carlos de Oliveira (Gate Guard), Sergio Mendes (Samba School Director), Ester Dean (Boy in Gondola)

A blue macaw, captured by bird smugglers and taken from his home in the Brazilian rainforest, ends up in Moose Lake, Minnesota, where he becomes the prized pet of a woman who is unaware that he may be the last of his species.

This film received an Oscar nomination for original song ("Real in Rio").

Blu, Jewel

Tulio © 20th Century Fox

Pedro, Nico, Jewel, Blu

SCREAM 4

(DIMENSION) Producers, Kevin Williamson, Iya Labunka, Wes Craven; Executive Producers, Bob Weinstein, Harvey Weinstein, Ron Schmidt, Ehren Kruger, Matthew Stein, Cathy Konrad, Marianne Maddalena; Co-Producer, Carly Feingold; Director, Wes Craven; Screenplay, Kevin Williamson, based on characters created by him; Photography, Peter Deming; Designer, Adam Stockhausen; Costumes, Debra McGuire; Music, Marco Beltrami; Music Supervisor, Liza Richardson; Editor, Peter McNulty; Casting, Avy Kaufman, Nancy Nayor; an Outerbanks Entertainment production, presented in association with Corvus Corax; Distributed by Miramax; Dolby; Panavision; Technicolor; Rated R; 111 minutes; Release date: April 15, 2011

CAST
Dewey Riley	**David Arquette**
Sidney Prescott	**Neve Campbell**
Gale Weathers-Riley	**Courteney Cox**
Jill Roberts	**Emma Roberts**
Kirby Reed	**Hayden Panettiere**

Anthony Anderson (Deputy Perkins), Alison Brie (Rebecca Walters), Adam Brody (Deputy Hoss), Rory Culkin (Charlie Walker), Marielle Jaffe (Olivia Morris), Erik Knudsen (Robbie Mercer), Mary McDonnell (Aunt Kate), Marley Shelton (Deputy Hicks), Nico Tortorella (Trevor Sheldon), Lucy Hale (Sherrie), Roger Jackson (The Voice), Shenae Grimes (Trudie), Dane Farwell (Ghostface), Anna Paquin (Rachel), Kristen Bell (Chloe), Brittany Robertson (Marnie Cooper), Aimee Teegarden (Jenny Randall), Nancy O'Dell (TV Host), Justin Brandt (Film Geek), Gordon Michaels (Deputy Jenkins), John Lepard (Mr. Baker), Julia Ho, Kim Adams, Devin Scillian, Glenda Lewis, William Spencer, Tim Doty, Peter Carey (Reporters), Mark Aaron Buerkle (Dr. Orth), Alex Punch (Cocky Student),

Returning to town to publicize her book about surviving the gruesome killings that disrupted the community more than a decade ago, Sidney Prescott is shocked to learn that a possible copycat killer is on the loose. Previous entries in the *Scream* series were released in 1996, 1997, and 2000.

Alison Brie, Marley Shelton, Adam Brody, Neve Campbell, Courteney Cox, David Arquette, Anthony Anderson © Dimension Films

Taylor Schilling, Matthew Marsden © Rocky Mountain Pictures

ATLAS SHRUGGED: PART 1

(ROCKY MOUNTAIN PICTURES) Producers, Harmon Kaslow, John Aglialoro; Executive Producers, Mike Marvin, Howard Baldwin, Karen Baldwin, Ed Snider; Line Producer, Bruce Wayne Gillies; Director, Paul Johansson; Screenplay, Brian Patrick O'Toole, John Aglialoro; Based on the novel *Atlas Shrugged* by Ayn Rand; Photography, Ross Berryman; Designer, John Mott; Costumes, Jennifer L. Soulages; Music, Elia Cmiral; Editors, Jim Flynn, Sherril Schlesinger; Casting, Ronnie Yeskel, Sharon Howard-Field; a Harmon Kaslow & John Aglialoro Prods. production; Dolby; Color; Rated PG-13; 97 minutes; Release date: April 15, 2011

CAST
Dagny Taggart	**Taylor Schilling**
Henry Rearden	**Grant Bowler**
James Taggart	**Matthew Marsden**
Eddie Willers	**Edi Gathegi**
Ellis Wyatt	**Graham Beckel**
Francisco D'Anconia	**Jsu Garcia**
Orren Boyle	**Jon Polito**
Wesley Mouch	**Michael Lerner**

Rebecca Wisocky (Lillian Rearden), Neill Barry (Phillip Rearden), Paul Johansson (John Galt), Michael O'Keefe (Hugh Akston), Patrick Fischler (Paul Larkin), Armin Shimerman (Dr. Potter), Ethan Cohn (Owen Kellogg), Geoff Pierson (Midas Mulligan), Christina Pickles (Mother Rearden), Craig Tsuyumine, Annabelle Gurwitch, January Walsh (Reporters), Navid Negahban (Dr. Robert Stadler), Joel McKinnon Miller (Herbert Mowen), Frank Cassavetes (Bum), Olivia Presley (Waitress), Daisy McCrackin (Clerk), Sylva Kelegian (Ivy Starnes), Mel Fair, Mandy June Turpin, Kim Swennen, Jan Morris, Christopher Mur (Newscasters), Rob Brownstein (Eugene Lawson), Matt O'Toole (Brenden Brady), Dave Goryl (Jay Knight), Mercedes Connor (Cherryl Brooks), Nikki Klecha (Gwen Ives), Jack Milo (Richard McNamara), Maia Tarin (Joy), Jeff Cockey, Travis Seaborn (Bartenders), Katherine M. O'Connor, Christopher Karl Johnson (Senators at Press Conference), Steven Chester Prince (Engineer)

Railroad tycoon Dagny Taggart hopes to transform the nation's econmy with her new formula for a stronger, lighter form of steel.

Robert Pattinson, Tai

Robert Pattinson, Reese Witherspoon, Uggie, Tai

WATER FOR ELEPHANTS

(20TH CENTURY FOX) Producers, Gil Netter, Erwin Stoff, Andrew R. Tennenbaum; Executive Producer, Kevin Halloran; Director, Francis Lawrence; Screenplay, Richard LaGravenese, based upon the novel by Sara Gruen; Photography, Rodrigo Prieto; Designer, Jack Fisk; Costumes, Jacqueline West; Music, James Newton Howard; Music Supervisor, Alexandra Patsavas; Editor, Alan Edward Bell; Casting, Denise Chamian; a Fox 2000 Pictures presentation of a 3 Arts Entertainment/Gil Netter/Flashpoint Entertainment production; Dolby; Panavision; Color; Rated PG-13; 121 minutes; Release date: April 22, 2011

CAST
Marlena Rosenbluth	**Reese Witherspoon**
Jacob Jankowski	**Robert Pattinson**
August Rosenbluth	**Christoph Waltz**
Charlie	**Paul Schneider**
Camel	**Jim Norton**
Old Jacob	**Hal Holbrook**

Mark Povinelli ("Kinko," Walter), Richard Brake (Grady), Stephen Monroe Taylor (Wade), Ken Foree (Earl), Scott MacDonald (Blackie), James Frain (Rosie's Caretaker), Sam Anderson (Mr. Hyde), John Aylward (Mr. Erwin), Brad Greenquist (Mr. Robinson), Tim Guinee (Diamond Joe), Donna W. Scott (Barbara), E.E. Bell (Cecil the Barker), Kyle Jordan (Russ), Aleksandra Kaniak (Mrs. Jankowski), Ilia Volok (Mr. Jankowski), Bruce Gray (Proctor), Jim Jansen (Dean Wilkins), James Keane (Chaplain), Ivo Nandi (Grocer), Karynn Moore (Catherine Hale), Andrew Connolly (Weehawken Officer), Doug McDougal (Big Top Band Leader), Tracy Phillips (Nell, Coochie Girl), Rowan O'Hara (Stampede Girl), Tai (Rosie), Uggie (Queenie), Ice (Silver Star), Major (Rex), Sita Acevedo, Danny Castle, Michael Coronas, Aloysia Gavré, Chobi Gyorgy, David Hunt, George Landkas-Coronas, Kerren McKeeman, Rebecca Ostroff, Bianca Sapetto, Katia Sereno, Vladimir Sizov, Russ Stark, Sebastien Stella, Lee-Anne Telford, Dreya Weber (Circus Performers), Tara Ferguson, Shannon Freyer, Kelsey McNamee, Molly O'Neill (Showgirls), Aryiel Hartman, Michelle LaVon (Coochie Girls), Mark Barnett, Kacie Borrowman, Rob Crites, Kelly Erickson, Derrick Gilday, Jonathan Moore, Mary Newman, Brad Potts, Dalmacio Pueblos, Gabriel Ramos-Gomez, Jackie Zane (Sideshow), Aaron Bloom, Chris Grabher, Eddie Medrano, Stephen Simon, Jon Weiss, Tom Weymouth (Clowns)

After his parents are killed in a car accident, young veterinarian student Jacob Jankowski starts life anew by joining a traveling circus.

Christoph Waltz, Reese Witherspoon © 20th Century Fox

Reese Witherspoon, Robert Pattinson

POM WONDERFUL PRESENTS
THE GREATEST MOVIE EVER SOLD

(SONY CLASSICS) Producers, Keith Calder, Jeremy Chilnick, Abbie Hurewitz, Morgan Spurlock, Jessica Wu; Co-Producer, Jonathan McHugh; Director, Morgan Spurlock; Screenplay, Jeremy Chilnick, Morgan Spurlock; Photography, Daniel Marracino; Music, Jon Spurney; Music Supervisor, Jonathan McHugh; Editor, Thomas M. Vogt; a Snoot Entertainment/Warrior Poets production, in association with Stage 6 Films; Color; HD; Rated PG-13; 86 minutes; Release date: April 22, 2011.Documentary filmmaker Morgan Spurlock explores the rampant degree of advertising and product placement in motion pictures by setting out to ensure that his film is financed entirely by product placement.

WITH
Morgan Spurlock, J.J. Abrams, Peter Berg, Paul Brennan, Noam Chomsky, Jimmy Kimmel, Rick Kurnit, Mark Crispin Miller, Ralph Nader, Brett Ratner, Antonio Reid, Quentin Tarantino, Donald Trump, John Wells

Morgan Spurlock © Sony Pictures Classics

Morgan Spurlock, Ralph Nader

Connor Paolo © Dark Sky Films

STAKE LAND

(DARK SKY FILMS) Producers, Derek Curl, Adam Folk, Peter Phok, Brent Kunkle, Larry Fessenden; Executive Producers, Malik B. Ali, Badie Ali, Hazma Ali, Greg Newman; Director/Editor, Jim Mickle; Screenplay, Nick Damici, Jim Mickle; Photography, Ryan Samul; Designer, Daniel R. Kersting; Costumes, Elisabeth Vastola; Music, Jeff Grace; Special Effects Makeup, Brian Spears, Peter Gerner; Casting, Sig De Miguel, Stephen Vincent; a Glass Eye Pix production in association with Off Hollywood Pictures and Belladonna Productions; Dolby; Widescreen; Color; HD; Not rated; 96 minutes; Release date: April 22, 2011

CAST
Mister	**Nick Damici**
Martin	**Connor Paolo**
Belle	**Danielle Harris**
Sister	**Kelly McGillis**
Willie	**Sean Nelson**
Jebedia Loven	**Michael Cerveris**

Bonnie Dennison (Peggy), Chance Kelly (Officer Harley), Adam Scarimbolo (Kevin), Marianne Hagan (Dr. Foley), Eilis Cahill (Scamp), Traci Hovel (Martin's Mother), Stuart Rudin (Pops the Barber), Lou Sumrall (Brotherhood Man), Jean Brassard (Benoit, End of Days Speaker), Adam Folk (Soldier Crier), Vonia Arslanian (Dark Haired Bartender), Jim Mickle, Graham Reznick (Local Radio Voices), Gregory Jones (Martin's Father), Tim House (Sheriff), Phyllis Bash (Phyllis), James Godwin (Barn Vamp), Heather Robb (Screwdriver Vamp), Larry Fessenden (Roadhouse Bartender), Angelique Biasutto (Little Girl Victim), Lou Sumrall (Brotherhood Man), Phyllis Bash (Mama), Jackson McCord, Seamus Boyle, Danny Mefford, Anastasia Neimann, Mike Jensen, Jacques Roy, Mona Lessnick, Brian Spears, Grant McCord, B. Beddoe, Lizz Morhaim, Bryce Burke, Shawn Snow, Emily Cain, Jack Walker, Asa Liebmann (Vamps)

In a post-apocalyptic world in which most of the human race has been turned into ravenous vampires, a hardened vampire hunter takes a teen under his wing to teach him how to fend for himself as they make their way towards what they hope will be a safer destination.

Tyler Perry's MADEA'S BIG HAPPY FAMILY

(LIONSGATE) Producers, Tyler Perry, Reuben Cannon, Roger M. Bobb; Executive Producers, Ozzie Areu, Joseph P. Genier, Michael Paseornek; Director/Screenplay, Tyler Perry, based on his play; Photography, Toyomichi Kurita; Designer, Ina Mayhew; Costumes, Keith G. Lewis; Music, Aaron Zigman; Music Supervisor, Joel C. High; Editor, Maysie Hoy; Casting, Kim Williams; a Tyler Perry Studios/ Lionsgate/Reuben Cannon production; Dolby; Deluxe color; Rated PG-13; 106 minutes; Release date: April 22, 2011

CAST
Madea/Joe	**Tyler Perry**
Shirley	**Loretta Devine**
Byron	**Shad "Bow Wow" Moss**
Mr. Brown	**David Mann**
Aunt Bam	**Cassi Davis**
Kimberly	**Shannon Kane**
Calvin	**Isaiah Mustafa**
Tammy	**Natalie Desselle Reid**

Rodney Perry (Harold), Tamela J. Mann (Cora), Teyana Taylor (Sabrina), Lauren London (Renee), Stevie Wash Jr. (H.J.), Nicholas Milton (Will), Benjamin "LB" Aiken (C.J.), Philip Anthony-Rodriguez (Dr. Evans), Maury Povich (Himself), Stephen Caudill (Policeman), Chandra Currelley (Sister Laura), Palmer Williams Jr. (Manager), Yakini Horn (Worker), James Farster (Clerk), Ron Grant (Pastor Jackson), Cindy L. Jefferson (Nanny), Mark E. Swinton (Choir Leader), Ronnie Garrett (Bandleader), Cheryl Pepsii Riley, Crystal Collins, Dequina Moore, Tamar Davis, Danny Clay, Brandi Milton, Jeffrey Lewis, Zuri Craig, Kislyck "Kissy" Halsey, Kristal Daynell Murphy, Dave Tolliver, Kenneth "Mistro" Lowe, Tim Stylez, Monica Lisa Stevenson, Eugene Clarence Brown Jr. (Choir)

Shirley hopes to break the news of her terminal cancer during a family get-together, in which her relatives try to sort out their own problems.

Sita and Her Cubs

Loretta Devine, Cassi Davis © Lionsgate

Isaiah Mustafa, Shannon Kane

© Walt Disney Studios

AFRICAN CATS

(WALT DISNEY STUDIOS) Producers, Keith Scholey, Alix Tidmarsh; Executive Producer, Don Hahn; Directors, Keith Scholey, Alastair Fothergill; Screenplay, Keith Scholey, John Truby; Story, Keith Scholey, Owen Newman; Photography, Owen Newman, Sophie Darlington; Music, Nicholas Hooper; Editor, Martin Elsbury; Narrator, Samuel L. Jackson; a Disneynature presentation; Dolby; Deluxe color; Rated G; 89 minutes; Release date: April 22, 2011. Documentary follows the stories of Sita, a cheetah and her newborn cubs, and Mara, a female lion cub and her pride.

Yin Chang, Jared Kusnitz

DeVaughn Nixon, Cameron Monaghan, Nolan A. Sotillo

Aimee Teegarden, Thomas McDonell © Walt Disney Pictures

Kylie Bunbury, DeVaughn Nixon

PROM

(WALT DISNEY PICTURES) Producers, Ted Griffin, Justin Springer; Executive Producer, Sean Bailey, Samson Mucke; Director, Joe Nussbaum; Screenplay, Katie Welch; Photography, Byron Shah; Designer, Mark White; Costumes, Shoshana Rubin; Music, Deborah Lurie; Music Supervisor, Jojo Villanueva; Editor, Jeffrey M. Werner; Casting, Marcia Ross, Gail Goldberg; a Rickshaw production; Dolby; Deluxe color; Rated PG; 103 minutes; Release date: April 29, 2011

CAST
Nova Prescott	**Aimee Teegarden**
Jesse Richter	**Thomas McDonell**
Tyler Barso	**DeVaughn Nixon**
Jordan Lundley	**Kylie Bunbury**
Simone Daniels	**Danielle Campbell**
Mei Kwan	**Yin Chang**
Justin Wexler	**Jared Kusnitz**
Lucas Arnaz	**Nolan A. Sotillo**

Cameron Monaghan (Corey Doyle), Joe Adler (Rolo), Janelle Ortiz (Ali Gomez), Jonathan Keltz (Brandon Roberts), Nicholas Braun (Lloyd Taylor), Raini Rodriguez (Tess Torres), Christine Elise McCarthy (Sandra Richter), Robbie Tucker (Charlie Richter), Dean Norris (Frank Prescott), Faith Ford (Kitty Prescott), Amy Pietz (Corey's Mom), Jere Burns (Principal Dunnan), Aimee-Lynn Chadwick (Rachel), Allie Trimm (Betsy), Madison Riley (Kristen), Rocco Nugent (Anton), Ivy Malone (Alice), Blair Fowler (Leah), Carlease Burke (Rhoda Wainwright), Chloe Little (Janel Lundley), Kristopher Higgins (Derek), Tahlena Chikami (Molly), Laura Miranda (Anna), Trevor Peterson (Logan), Benjamin P. Scott (Nick), Riley Voelkel (Claire), Gabriela Banus (Sofia), Karyn Nesbit (Hannah), Britney Bailey (Julia), Sierra Autumn Kane (Lindsay), Emil Beheshti (Mr. Freni), David Dustin Kenyon (Janitor), Marcuis W. Harris (Fireman), Sharon Omi (Teacher), Kofi Siriboe (Max)

Various high school teens prepare with differing degrees of anticipation for the senior prom.

Orlando Bloom, Juliette Lewis © Maya Films

SYMPATHY FOR DELICIOUS

(MAYA) Producers, Andrea Sperling, Scott Prisand, Matthew Weaver, Christopher Thornton, Mark Ruffalo; Executive Producers, Dean M. Leavitt, Gina Resnick, Marcelo Paladini, Robert Stein, Michael Roban, Barry Habib, Joanne Jacobson; Co-Producer, Andrew F. Renzi; Director, Mark Ruffalo; Screenplay, Christopher Thornton; Photography, Chris Norr; Designer, Michael Grasley; Costumes, Erin Benach; Music, The Besnard Lakes; Music Supervisor, Howard Paar; Editor, Pete Beaudreau; Casting, Heidi Levitt; a Corner Store Entertainment presentation in association with Super Crispy Entertainment; Dolby; Techniscope; Deluxe Color; Not rated; 96 minutes; Release date: April 29, 2011

CAST
"Delicious" Dean O'Dwyer	**Christopher Thornton**
Father Joe	**Mark Ruffalo**
Ariel Lee	**Juliette Lewis**
Rene Faubacher	**Noah Emmerich**
Father Bill Rohn	**James Karen**
Healer	**John Carroll Lynch**
Nina Hogue	**Laura Linney**
The Stain	**Orlando Bloom**

Stephen Mendillo (Angry Drunk Harry), Dov Tiefenbach (Oogie), Jason Hiller (Church Organist), Michael Spady (Mute Brute), Niko Nicotera (Rasha), Deantoni Parks (Chuck), Sandra Seacat (Mrs. Matilda), Willie Macc (Pretty Boy Willie), Daniel Escobar (Hector), Timothy McNeil (Ryan Webster), Millisa Skoro (Melissa), Karen Jin Beck (DJ Shy), Laurel Stri (Laura), Tiffany T. Tynes ("Sasha" Groupie), Valeri Ross (Judge), George W. Scott (Jerry), Marnie Alexenburg (Paramedic), Tara Stewart (Lupus Woman), Lydia Blanco (Boy's Mother), Hipe Le (Volunteer), Louis Mendoza (Maria Leceta), Sylvia St. James (Homeless Woman), Shaun Duke (Dr. Zaheedi), Bonnie McNeil (Mrs. Zaheedi)

An aspiring musician, whose promising career is destroyed after he is paralyzed in an accident, discovers that he has the ability to heal others who are suffering, but not himself.

THAT'S WHAT I AM

(GOLDWYN) Producers, Mike Pavone, Denise Chamian; Co-Producer, Nancy Hirami; Line Producer, Todd Lewis; Director/ Screenplay, Mike Pavone; Photography, Kenneth Zunder; Designer, Raymond Pumilia; Costumes, Claire Breaux; Music, James Raymond; Music Supervisor, Matt Kierscht; Editor, Marc Pollon; Casting, Denise Chamian Casting; a WWE Studios presentation; Dolby; Fotokem color; Rated PG; 101 minutes; Release date: April 29, 2011

CAST
Mr. Simon	**Ed Harris**
Sherri Nichol	**Molly Parker**
Principal Kelner	**Amy Madigan**
Andy Nichol	**Chase Ellison**
Ed Freel	**Randy Orton**
Jim Nichol	**Daniel Roebuck**

Mia Rose Frampton (Mary Clear), Cameron Stewart (Carl Freel), Daniel Yelsky (Norman Grunmeyer), Alexander Walters (Big G), Camille Bourgeois (Jason Freel), Jordan Reynolds (Ricky Brown), Sean Cunningham (Jimmy Tadlock), Taylor Faye Ruffin (Doris Gebben), Brett Lapeyrouse (Bruce Modak), Renwick D. Scott II (Dan Rainier), Cassidy Smith (Janice Conkel), Sarah Celano (Karen "Cootie" Connor), Raymond Diamond (Myron Stort), Vanessa Cloke (Irene Freel), Geraldine Singer (Mrs. Cranby), Dalton Zachary Mitchell (Sam Nolan), Holly Settoon (Barbara Foss), Joe Chrest (Mr. Clear), Alex Hardee (Stan Geyer), Greg Kinnear (Narrator)

During the 1960s, 12-year-old Andy Nichol finds himself learning lessons in tolerance when he is reluctantly partnered for a class project with an outcast student, while one of his teachers faces his own decisions when he is accused of being gay.

Ed Harris, Amy Madigan © Samuel Goldwyn Films

Mia Rose Frampton, Chase Ellison

Paul Walker, Tyrese Gibson, Don Omar, Sung Kang, Ludacris, Jordana Brewster, Gal Gadot, Vin Diesel

Paul Walker, Jordana Brewster

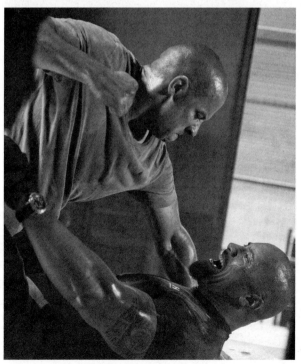

Paul Walker, Vin Diesel

FAST FIVE

(UNIVERSAL) Producers, Neal H. Moritz, Vin Diesel, Michael Fottrell; Executive Producer, Amanda Lewis; Director, Justin Lin; Screenplay, Chris Morgan; Based on characters created by Gary Scott Thompson; Photography, Stephen F. Windon; Designer, Peter Wenham; Costumes, Sanja Milkovic Hays; Music, Brian Tyler; Editors, Christian Wagner, Kelly Matsumoto, Fred Raskin; Special Effects Supervisor, R. Bruce Steinheimer; Supervising Stunt Coordinator, Mike Gunther; Casting, Debra Zane; an Original Film/One Race Films production; Dolby; Panavision; Color; Rated PG-13; 130 minutes; Release date: April 29, 2011

CAST
Dominic Toretto	**Vin Diesel**
Brian O'Conner	**Paul Walker**
Mia Toretto	**Jordana Brewster**
Roman Pearce	**Tyrese Gibson**
Tej Parker	**Chris "Ludacris" Bridges**
Vince	**Matt Schulze**
Han Lue	**Sung Kang**
Gisele Harabo	**Gal Gadot**
Tego Leo	**Tego Calderon**
Rico Santos	**Don Omar**
Hernan Reyes	**Joaquim de Almeida**
Luke Hobbs	**Dwayne Johnson**

Elsa Pataky (Elena Neves), Michael Irby (Zizi), Fernando F. Chien (Wilkes), Alimi Ballard (Fusco), Yorgo Constantine (Chato), Geoff Meed (Macroy), Joseph Melendez (Chief of Police Alemeida), Jeirmarie Osorio (Rosa), Mark Hicks (Capa), Esteban Cueto (Berto), Corey Eubanks (Lanzo), Luis Da Silva Jr. (Diogo), Luis Gonzaga (Cash House Door Guard), Carlos Sanchez (Evidence Technician), Ben Blankenship (Lead DEA Agent), Pedro García (Conductor), Arturo Gaskins (Croupier), Jay Jackson, Arlene Santana (Field Reporters), Kent Shocknek, Sharon Tay, Andy Rosa Adler (News Anchors), Eva Mendes (Monica Fuentes)

After escaping from a Rio drug lord, Dominic and Brian recruit their street-racing gang to rob him of $11 million. Fifth in the Universal series following: *The Fast and the Furious* (2001), *2 Fast 2 Furious* (2003), *The Fast and the Furious: Tokyo Drift* (2006), and *Fast & Furious* (2009).

Vin Diesel, Dwayne Johnson © Universal Studios

THOR

(PARAMOUNT) Producer, Kevin Feige; Executive Producers, Patricia Whitcher, Louis D'Esposito, Alan Fine, Stan Lee, David Maisel; Co-Producers, Craig Kyle, Victoria Alonso; Director, Kenneth Branagh; Screenplay, Ashley Edward Miller, Zack Stentz, Don Payne; Story, J. Michael Straczynski, Mark Protosevich; Based on the Marvel comic book by Stan Lee, Larry Lieber, Jack Kirby; Photography, Haris Zambarloukos; Designer, Bo Welch; Costumes, Alexandra Byrne; Music, Patrick Doyle; Music Supervisor, Dave Jordan; Editor, Paul Rubell; Visual Effects Supervisor, Wesley Sewell; Special Visual Effects and Digital Animation, Digital Domain; Second Unit Director, Vic Armstrong, Casting, Randi Hiller, Sarah Halley Finn; a Marvel Studios production; Dolby; Panavision; 3D; Deluxe color; Rated PG-13 ; 114 minutes; Release date: May 6, 2011

Tom Hiddleston, Chris Hemsworth

CAST

Thor	**Chris Hemsworth**
Jane Foster	**Natalie Portman**
Loki	**Tom Hiddleston**
Odin	**Anthony Hopkins**
Dr. Erik Selvig	**Stellan Skarsgård**
Darcy Lewis	**Kat Dennings**
Agent Coulson	**Clark Gregg**
King Laufey	**Colm Feore**
Heimdall	**Idris Elba**
Volstagg	**Ray Stevenson**
Hogun	**Tadanobu Asano**
Fandral	**Joshua Dallas**
Sif	**Jaimie Alexander**
Frigga	**Rene Russo**
Isabel Alvarez	**Adriana Barraza**
Agent Sitwell	**Maximiliano Hernandez**
Frost Giant Captain	**Richard Cetrone**
Frost Giant Sentry	**Darren Kendrick**
Frost Giant Hailstrum	**Josh Coxx**
Frost Giant Brute	**Justice Jesse Smith**
Frost Giant Grundroth	**Joseph Gatt**
Frost Giant Raze	**Luke Massy**
Einherjar Guard	**Matthew Ducey**
Einherjar Guard	**Jason Camp**
Agent Delancey	**Buddy Sosthand**
Techie	**Blake Silver**
Agent Jackson	**Jamie McShane**
Agent Garrett	**Dale Godboldo**
Agent Cale	**Patrick O'Brien Dempsey**
Clint Barton (Hawkeye)	**Jeremy Renner**
Nick Fury	**Samuel L. Jackson**

Rene Russo

Jim Palmer (SHIELD Guard), Seth Coltan, J. Michael Straczynski, Ryan Schaefer (Townies), Matt Battaglia (Pete), Stan Lee (Stan the Man), Joel McCrary (Drunk Townie), Isaac Kappy (Pet Store Clerk), Juliet Lopez (Admission Nurse), Rob Mars (Orderly), Carrie Lazar (Viking Mother), Harley Graham (Viking Child), Alexander Wright (Viking Elder), Hilary Pringle, Shawn-Caulin Young, Kinsey McLean, Kelly Hawthorne (Vikings), Dakota Goyo (Young Thor), Ted Allpress (Young Loki)

Cast out of Asgard for disobeying his father, Thor, the God of Thunder, ends up banished to Earth thereby allowing his scheming brother Loki to try to take the throne.

Natalie Portman, Kat Dennings

Tadanobu Asano, Joshua Dallas, Ray Stevenson

Chris Hemsworth, Anthony Hopkins

Stellan Skarsgård

Jaimie Alexander

Idris Elba © Paramount Pictures

Jodie Foster, Mel Gibson

Jennifer Lawrence, Anton Yelchin © Summit Entertainment

Jodie Foster, Riley Thomas Stewart, Anton Yelchin

THE BEAVER

(SUMMIT) Producers, Steve Golin, Keith Redmon, Ann Ruark; Executive Producers, Jeff Skoll, Mohammed Mubarak Al Mazrouei, Paul Green, Jonathan King; Director, Jodie Foster; Screenplay, Kyle Killen; Photography, Hagen Bogdanski; Designer, Mark Friedberg; Costumes, Susan Lyall; Music, Marcelo Zarvos; Music Supervisor, Alexandra Patsavas; Editor, Lynzee Klingman; Casting, Avy Kaufman; a Participant Media presentation in association with Imagenation Abu Dhabi of an Anonymous Content production; Dolby; Deluxe color; Rated PG-13; 91 minutes; Release date: May 6, 2011

CAST
Walter Black	**Mel Gibson**
Meredith Black	**Jodie Foster**
Porter Black	**Anton Yelchin**
Norah	**Jennifer Lawrence**
Henry Black	**Riley Thomas Stewart**
Vice President	**Cherry Jones**
Norah's Mom	**Kelly Coffield Park**
Jared	**Zachary Booth**
Volunteer Dad	**Jeff Corbett**
Hector	**Michael Rivera**
Skeptical Man	**Baylen Thomas**
Man	**Sam Breslin Wright**

Kris Arnold (Waiter), Elizabeth Kaledin (Reporter), Matt Lauer, Jon Stewart, Terry Gross (Themselves), Folake Olowofoyeku, Lorna Pruce (Nurses), Bill Massof (Prosthetic Technician)

A man sinking deep into clinical depression discovers that the only way he can try to communicate with others is by speaking through a beaver hand puppet that he has found in a trash dumpster.

Riley Thomas Stewart, Mel Gibson

THERE BE DRAGONS

(SAMUEL GOLDWYN) Producers, Igancio Gómez-Sancha, Roland Joffé, Guy J. Louthan, Ignacio Núñez; Co-Executive Producers, Damaso Ezpeleta, Andrew Cullen, Rusty Lemorande; Director/Screenplay, Roland Joffé; Photography, Gabriel Beristain; Designer, Eugenio Zanetti; Costumes, Yvonne Blake; Music, Stephen Warbeck; Editor, Richard Nord; Stunts, Rocky Taylor, Richard Cruz; Special Effects Supervisors, Eduardo Puga, Pau Costa; Makeup, Michele Burke; Casting, Amy Hubbard, Jon Hubbard, Ros Hubbard; a Mount Santa Fe presentation; American-Argentine-Spanish; Dolby; Super 35 Widescreen; Technicolor; Rated PG-13; 122 minutes; American release date: May 6, 2011

CAST
Josemaria Escrivá	**Charlie Cox**
Manolo Torres	**Wes Bentley**
Roberto Torres	**Dougray Scott**
Oriol	**Rodrigo Santiago**
Honorio Soto	**Derek Jacobi**
Ildiko	**Olga Kurylenko**
Pedro Casciano	**Unax Ugalde**

Geraldine Chaplin (Abileyza), Charles Dance (Monsignor Solano), Pablo Lapadula (Isidoro), Rusty Lemorande (Father Lazaro), Golshifteh Farahani (Leila), Ana Torrent (Dolores), Alfonso Bassave (Jiménez), Jordi Mollá (José), Alejandro Casaseca (Jaime), Yaiza Guimaré (Pilar), Jan Cornet (Ortiz), Lily Cole (Aline), Lito Cruz (Burly Man), Michael Feast (Vicar General), Robert Blythe (Archishop of Valencia), Dolores Reynals (Carmen), Christian J. Giardino (The Snpier), Carlos Kaspar (Italo), Carlos Leal (Jorge), Juan Cruz (Young Josemaria), Kevin Schiele (Diego), Zoe Trilnick (Young Carmen), Felipe Agote (Young Manolo), Pedro Nicolás Merlo (Alvaro del Portillo), Juan Diego Montoya (Ignasi)

The true story of Josemaria Escrivá and the founding of the Opus Dei religious movement.

Charlie Cox © Samuel Goldwyn Films

Wes Bentley

Keira Knightley, Guillaume Canet © Tribeca Films

Keira Knightley, Sam Worthington

LAST NIGHT

(TRIBECA) Producer, Nick Wechsler, Massy Tadjedin, Sidonie Dumas; Executive Producers, Christophe Riandee, Buddy Enright; Co-Producer, Satsuki Mitchell; Director/Screenplay, Massy Tadjedin; Photography, Peter Deming; Designer, Tim Grimes; Costumes, Ann Roth; Music, Clint Mansell; Music Supervisor, Randall Poster; Editor, Susan E. Morse; Casting, Laray Mayfield; a Nick Wechsler/Westbourne/Gaumont production; American-Canadian-French; Dolby; Panavision; Color; Rated R; 92 minutes; Release date: May 6, 2011

CAST
Joanna Reed	**Keira Knightley**
Michael Reed	**Sam Worthington**
Alex Mann	**Guillaume Canet**
Laura	**Eva Mendes**
Truman	**Griffin Dunne**
Andy	**Daniel Eric Gold**

Scott Adsit (Stuart), Stephanie Romanov (Sandra), Anson Mount (Neal), Stephen Mailer, John Treacy Egan (Clients), Justine Cotsonas (Maggie), Karen Pittman (Caroline), Jon Norman Schneider (Server), Chriselle Almeida (Hostess), Zach Poole (Waiter), Rae Ritke (Barbara), Christian Lorentzen (Fred), William Clemente (Front Desk Clerk)

Worried that her husband's intimacy with a colleague suggests an affair going on or one about to happen, Joanna finds herself facing the possibility of an extra-marital fling when she is visited by a former lover who admits to still having feelings for her.

JUMPING THE BROOM

(TRISTAR) Producers, T.D. Jakes, Tracey E. Edmonds, Curtis Wallace, Elizabeth Hunter, Glendon Palmer; Co-Producer/Director, Salim Akil; Screenplay, Elizabeth Hunter, Arlene Gibbs; Story, Elizabeth Hunter; Photography, Anastas Michos; Designer, Doug McCullough; Costumes, Martha Curry; Music, Edward Shearmur; Editor, Terilyn A. Shropshire; Casting, Tracy Byrd; a T.D. Jakes/Our Stories Films production, presented in association with Stage 6 Films; Dolby; Deluxe color; Rated PG-13; 112 minutes; Release date: May 6, 2011

Tenika Davis, Paula Patton, Meagan Good

CAST

Mrs. Watson	**Angela Bassett**
Sabrina Watson	**Paula Patton**
Jason Taylor	**Laz Alonso**
Mrs. Taylor	**Loretta Devine**
Blythe	**Meagan Good**
Shonda	**Tasha Smith**
Amy	**Julie Bowen**
Malcolm	**DeRay Davis**
Aunt Geneva	**Valarie Pettiford**
Willie Earl	**Mike Epps**
Ricky	**Pooch Hall**
Sebastian	**Romeo Miller**
Mr. Watson	**Brian Stokes Mitchell**

Gary Dourdan (Chef), T.D. Jakes (Rev. James), El DeBarge (Singer), Tenika Davis (Lauren), Vera Cudjoe (Mabel), Will Lemay (Bobby), Laura Kohoot (Amanda), Marguerite McNeil (Mrs. O'Neal)

Class conflicts erupt between the families of well-to-do Sabrina Watson and working class Jason Taylor when the two decide to marry.

Brian Stokes Mitchell, Angela Bassett

Loretta Devine, Paula Patton © TriStar Pictures

Brian Stokes Mitchell, DeRay Davis, Laz Alonso, Romeo Miller, Paula Patton, Mike Epps, Loretta Devine

John Krasinski, Steve Howey

John Krasinski, Ginnifer Goodwin, Kate Hudson, Colin Egglesfield

SOMETHING BORROWED

(WARNER BROS.) Producers, Hilary Swank, Molly Mickler Smith, Broderick Johnson, Andrew A. Kosove, Aaron Lubin, Pamela Schein Murphy; Executive Producer, Ellen H. Schwartz; Co-Producers, Yolanda T. Cochran, Steven P. Wegner; Director, Luke Greenfield; Screenplay, Jennie Snyder Urman; Based on the novel by Emily Giffin; Photography, Charles Minsky; Designer, Jane Musky; Costumes, Gary Jones; Music, Alex Wurman; Music Supervisors, Dave Jordan, Jojo Villanueva; Editor, John Axelrad; Casting, Mandy Sherman, Sari Knight; an Alcon Entertainment presentation of a 2S Films production, a Wild Ocean Films production; Dolby; Super 35 Widescreen; Technicolor; Rated PG-13; 112 minutes; Release date: May 6, 2011

CAST
Rachel	**Ginnifer Goodwin**
Darcy	**Kate Hudson**
Dex Thaler	**Colin Egglesfield**
Ethan	**John Krasinski**
Marcus	**Steve Howey**
Claire	**Ashley Williams**
Dexter Thaler Sr.	**Geoff Pierson**
Bridget Thaler	**Jill Eikenberry**
Professor Zigman	**Jonathan Epstein**
Bridal Consultant	**Leia Thompson**
June	**Sarah Baldwin**
Marcus's Dad	**Mark La Mura**
Salesgirl	**Lindsay Ryan**

Kirsten Day (Pretty Brunette), Christopher Peuler (Husband), Herb Lieberz, Jimmy Palumbo (Cabbies), Mary O'Rouke (Fallen Angel), Marina Hirschfeld (Club Girl), Tim Dunavant (Bartender), Noel Poyner (NYU Law Student), P.T. Walkely (Lead Singer), Scott Hollingsworth, Nicky Kulund, Jared Schlemovitz (Band Members), Peyton List (Young Darcy)

Rachel, who has for years accepted her backseat role in the life of her overbearing best friend Darcy, finds herself in a sticky situation when she begins having an affair with the man Darcy is set to marry.

Kate Hudson, Ginnifer Goodwin © Warner Bros.

Ashley Williams

Ellie Kemper, Melissa McCarthy, Wendi McLendon-Covey

Rebel Wilson, Matt Lucas, Kristen Wiig © Universal Studios

Melissa McCarthy, Ellie Kemper, Rose Byrne, Wendi McLendon-Covey, Maya Rudolph, Kristen Wiig

BRIDESMAIDS

(UNIVERSAL) Producers, Judd Apatow, Clayton Townsend, Barry Mendel; Executive Producer/Director, Paul Feig; Screenplay/Co-Producers, Annie Mumolo, Kristen Wiig; Photography, Robert Yeoman; Designer, Jefferson Sage; Costumes, Leesa Evans; Music, Michael Andrews; Music Supervisor, Jonathan Karp; Editors, William Kerr, Mike Sale; Casting, Allison Jones;an Apatow production, presented in association with Relativity Media; Dolby; Super 35 Widescreen; Color; Rated R; 125 minutes; Release date: May 13, 2011

CAST

Annie Walker	**Kristen Wiig**
Lillian	**Maya Rudolph**
Helen Harris	**Rose Byrne**
Rita	**Wendi McLendon-Covey**
Becca	**Ellie Kemper**
Megan	**Melissa McCarthy**
Officer Nathan Rhodes	**Chris O'Dowd**
Judy, Annie's Mom	**Jill Clayburgh**
Brynn	**Rebel Wilson**
Gil	**Matt Lucas**
Don Cholodecki	**Michael Hitchcock**
Air Marshal John	**Ben Falcone**
Lillian's Dad	**Franklyn Ajaye**
Kevin	**Greg Tuculescu**
Dougie	**Tim Heidecker**
Bill Cozbi	**Richard Riehle**
Nervous Woman on Plane	**Annie Mumolo**
Rodney, Boot Camp Instructor	**Terry Crews**
Whitney	**Jessica St. Clair**
Kahlua	**Kali Hawk**
Minister	**Jimmy Brogan**
Oscar the Security Guard	**Joseph A. Nunez**
Annie's Mistaken Husband	**Steve Bannos**
Annie's Mistaken Fella	**Hugh Dane**
Lillian's Mom	**Lynne Marie Stewart**
Helen's Husband	**Andy Buckley**
Ted	**Jon Hamm**

Tom Yi, Elaine Kao (Jewelry Store Couple), Molly Buffington (Helen's Stepdaughter), Matt Bennett (Helen's Stepson), Nancy Carell (Helen's Tennis Partner), Melanie Hutsell (Annie's Tennis Partner), Eloy Casados (Churra Chi Waiter), Dana Powell (Flight Attendant Claire), Mitch Silpa (Flight Attendant Steve), Angelica Acedo (Fligth Attendant in Coach), Mia Rose Frampton (13-Year-old Girl in Jewelry Store), Joel Madison (13-Year-Old Girl's Father), R.F. Daley (Butler), Jordan Black (Horseman), David Hoffman (Doorman at Shower), Jillian Bell, Ariance Price (Girls at Shower), Frederik Hamel (Shower Waiter), Carnie Wilson, Chynna Phillips, Wendy Wilson (Wilson Phillips), Paul Feig (Wedding Guest)

As her own life begins to unravel, Annie is asked to be her best friend Lillian's maid of honor at her upcoming wedding, leading to all sorts of mishaps.

This film received Oscar nominations for supporting actress (Melissa McCarthy) and original screenplay.

Kristen Wiig

Maya Rudolph, Kristen Wiig

Kristen Wiig, Annie Mumolo

Kristen Wiig, Chris O'Dowd

Jill Clayburgh, Kristen Wiig

Jon Hamm

EVERYTHING MUST GO

(LIONSGATE/ROADSIDE ATTRACTIONS) Producers, Marty Bowen, Wyck Godfrey; Executive Producers, Scott Lumpkin, Martin Bowen, Bill Hallman, Marc Erlbaum, J. Andrew Greenblatt; Co-Executive Producers, Peter Fruchtman, Jerry Fruchtman, Jody Simon; Director/Screenplay, Dan Rush; Based on the short story "Why Don't You Dance" by Raymond Carver; Photography, Michael Barrett; Designer, Kara Lindstrom; Costumes, Mark Bridges; Music, David Torn; Music Supervisor, Margaret Yen; Editor, Sandra Adair; Casting, Joanna Colbert, Richard Mento; a Temple Hill Entertainment presentation in association with CowTown Cinema Ventures and Nationlight EMG; Dolby; Panavision; Deluxe Color; Rated R; 96 minutes; Release date: May 13, 2011

Laura Dern, Will Ferrell

CAST
Nick Halsey	**Will Ferrell**
Kenny Loftus	**Christopher C.J. Wallace**
Samantha	**Rebecca Hall**
Frank Garcia	**Michael Peña**
Kitty	**Rosalie Michaels**
Elliot	**Stephen Root**
Delilah	**Laura Dern**
Gary	**Glenn Howerton**
Shopper	**Argos MacCallum**
Driver (Repo Guy)	**Todd Bryant**
Hipster	**Jason Spisak**
Liquor Store Clerk	**Narinder Singh**

Tyler Johnstone (Big Teenager), Kyle Sharkey (Lanky Teenager), Scottt Takeda (Bank Manager), Matthew Dearing (Jacket Buyer), Leeann Dearing (Girlfriend), Chris Cook (Samantha's Husband), Andy McDermott (Cop), Lance Gray (Blender Guy)

Returning home after being fired, Nick Halsey is dismayed to discover that his wife has left him, changed the locks, and tossed his belongings on the front law. Defiantly, and with no prospects in site, Nick simply takes up residence right there in the yard.

Rebecca Hall © Lionsgate

Will Ferrell, Christopher C.J. Wallace

Will Ferrell

Cam Gigandet © Screen Gems

Maggie Q

Paul Bettany

PRIEST

(SCREEN GEMS) Producers, Michael De Luca, Joshua Donen, Mitchell Peck; Executive Producers, Glenn S. Gainor, Steven H. Galloway, Stu Levy; Director, Scott Stewart; Screenplay, Cory Goodman; Based on the graphic novel series by Min-Woo Hyung; Photography, Don Burgess; Designer, Richard Bridgland Fitzgerald; Costumes, Ha Nguyen; Music, Christopher Young; Editor, Lisa Zeno Churgin; Visual Effects Supervisor, Jonathan Rothbart; Stunts, Lance Gilbert; a Michael De Luca Productions/Stars Road Entertainment production in association with Tokyopop; Dolby; Panavision; Deluxe color; 3D; Rated PG-13; 87 minutes; Release date: May 13, 2011

CAST
Priest	**Paul Bettany**
Black Hat	**Karl Urban**
Hicks	**Cam Gigandet**
Priestess	**Maggie Q**
Lucy Pace	**Lily Collins**
Salesman	**Brad Dourif**
Owen Pace	**Stephen Moyer**
Monsignor Orelas	**Christopher Plummer**
Monsignor Chamberlain	**Alan Dale**
Shannon Pace	**Mädchen Amick**

Jacob Hopkins (Boy), Dave Florek (Crocker), Joel Polinsky (Dr. Tomlin), Josh Wingate, Jon Braver, Casey Pieretti, Theo Kypri, John Griffin, David Backhaus, Roger Stoneburner, David Bianchi (Familiars), Tanoai Reed (Brave Priest), Arnold Chon (Strong Priest), Henry Kingi, Jr. (Bold Priest), Austin Prester (Flashback Priest), Marilyn Brett (Woman), Kanin Howell (Husband), Julie Mond (Wife), Michael D. Nye (Station Master), Raynor Scheine (Minister), Kevin T. McCarthy (English Speaking Preacher), Boyuen Lou (Chinese Speaking Vendor), Anthony Azizi (Farsi Speaking Preacher), Pramod Kumar (Hindi Speaking Vendor), Lafayette R. Dorsey Sr. (Clergy Trooper)

In the post-apocalyptic future, a legendary warrior priest breaks his vow to remain in hiding when his niece is abducted by a murderous pack of vampires.

Christopher Plummer

Devin Brochu, Natalie Portman, Joseph Gordon-Levitt

Devin Brochu, Natalie Portman

Joseph Gordon-Levitt

Natalie Portman © Wrekin Hill Entertainment

HESHER

(WREKIN HILL) Producers, Lucy Cooper, Matthew Weaver, Scott Prisand, Natalie Portman, Spencer Susser, Johnny Lin, Win Sheridan; Executive Producers, Jonathan Weisgal, Wayne Chang, Annette Savitch, Aleen Keshishian, Scot Armstrong, Ravi Nandan, Marc Bell, Michael Roban, Jerry Fruchtman, Peter Fruchtman, Ian Fruchtman, Scott Kluge; Co-Producers, Aaron Downing, Jeff Davis, Tom Pellegrini; Director, Spencer Susser; Screenplay, Spencer Susser, David Michod; Story, Brian Charles Frank; Photography, Morgan Pierre Susser; Designer, Laura Fox; Costumes, April Napier; Music, Francois Tetaz; Editors, Michael McCusker, Spencer Susser; Casting, Kim Davis, Justin Baddeley; a Newmarket Films, Neca Films, Corner Store Entertainment presentation of The Last Picture Company production with Handsomecharlie Films in association with American Work Inc. and DRO Entertainment in association with Dreamengine Entertainment and Catchplay; Dolby; Widescreen; FotoKem Color; DV; Rated R; 100 minutes; Release date: May 13, 2011

CAST
Hesher	**Joseph Gordon-Levitt**
Paul Forney	**Rainn Wilson**
Nicole	**Natalie Portman**
T.J. Forney	**Devin Brochu**
Madeleine Forney	**Piper Laurie**
Larry, Salvage Yard Boss	**John Carroll Lynch**
Dustin	**Brendan Hill**
Mom	**Monica Staggs**
Funeral Director	**Frank Collison**
Coleen Bolder	**Audrey Wasilewski**
Jack Bolder	**Lyle Kanouse**

Allan Graf (Security Guard), Paul Bates (Mr. Elsberry), Ralph P. Martin (Tow Truck Driver), Milt Kogan (Doctor), Helen Slayton-Hughes (Mrs. Rosowski), Van Epperson (Rearended Driver), Barry Sigismondi (Cop at House), Mary Elizabeth Barrett (Meryl), Brian Lally (Sheriff Cuvin), Rafael J. Noble (Mario, Foreman), Tim Davis (Tony, Mechanic), Richard Susser (Booking Officer), William Jones (Waiter)

A noxious, scraggly drifter takes up residence in the garage of the home of young T.J. who, along with his dad, has been left numb by the recent death of his mother in a car accident.

PIRATES OF THE CARIBBEAN: ON STRANGER TIDES

(WALT DISNEY PICTURES) Producer, Jerry Bruckheimer; Executive Producers, Mike Stenson, Chad Oman, John DeLuca, Ted Elliott, Terry Rossio, Barry Waldman; Director, Rob Marshall; Screen Story and Screenplay, Ted Elliott, Terry Rossio; Suugested by the novel *On Stranger Tides* by Tom Powers; Based characters created by Ted Elliott, Terry Rossio, Stuart Beattie, Jay Wolpert and on Disney's *Pirates of the Caribbean* theme park ride; Photography, Darisuz Wolski; Designer, John Myhre; Costumes, Penny Rose; Music, Hans Zimmer; Editors, David Brenner, Wyatt Smith; Special Effects Supervisor, Charles Gibson; Visual Effects, Industrial Light & Magic; Casting, Francine Maisler, Kathy Driscoll-Mohler, Susie Figgis, Lucy Bevan; a Jerry Bruckheimer Films presentation; Dolby; Deluxe color; 3D; Rated PG-13; 136 minutes; Release date: May 20, 2011

CAST
Jack Sparrow **Johnny Depp**
Angelica Teach **Penélope Cruz**
Barbossa **Geoffrey Rush**
Blackbeard **Ian McShane**
Joshamee Gibbs **Kevin McNally**
Philip **Sam Claflin**
Syrena **Astrid Bergès-Frisbey**
Scrum **Stephen Graham**
King George **Richard Griffiths**

Keith Richards (Capt. Teague), Greg Ellis (Groves), Damian O'Hare (Gillette), Óscar Jaenada (The Spaniard), Anton Lesser (Lord John Carteret), Roger Allam (Prime Minister Henry Pelham), Judi Dench (Society Lady), Christopher Fairbank (Ezekiel), Paul Bazely (Salaman), Bronson Webb (Cook), Richard Thomson (Derrick), Yuki Matsuzaki (Garheng), Robbie Kay (Cabin Boy), Steve Evets (Purser), Ian Mercer (Quartermaster), Deobia Oparei (Gunner), Gemma Ward (Tamara – First Mermaid), Sebastian Armesto (King Ferdinand VI), Juan Carlos Vellido (Spanish Sea Captain), Tristan Laurence Perez (Spanish Fisherman), Norberto Morán (Spanish Castaway), Gerard Monaco (Spanish Officer), Tyrone Lopez (Spanish Soldier), Luke Roberts (Captain of the Guard), Daniel Ings (Guard), Emilia Jones (English Girl), Patrick Kennedy (English Father), Jody Halse (Jailor), Clifford Rose (Bailiff), Paul Hunter (Foreman), Jorgelina Guadalupe Airaldi, Brea Berrett, Sanya Hughes, Daphne Joy, Antoinette Nikprelaj (Mermaids), Derek Mears (Master-at-Arms), Danny Le Boyer (Yeoman), Kit Barrie (Courtroom Wench), Steve Morphew (Courtroom Heckler), Alan Utley-Moore (Justice Smith)

Jack Sparrow's ex-lover kidnaps him and ferries him aboard a pirate ship commanded by her father, Blackbeard, in hopes that he will help them locate the Fountain of Youth. Fourth entry in the Walt Disney Pictures *Pirates of the Caribbean* series following *The Curse of the Black Pearl* (2003), *Dead Man's Chest* (2006), and *At World's End* (2007), all of which starred Johnny Depp.

Penélope Cruz, Johnny Depp, Ian McShane © Walt Disney Pictures

Robbie Kay, Deobia Oparei

Keith Richards
Sam Claflin, Astrid Bergès-Frisbey

KUNG FU PANDA 2

(DREAMWORKS/PARAMOUNT) Producer, Melissa Cobb; Director, Jennifer Yuh Nelson; Co-Producers, Jonathan Aibel, Glenn Berger, Suzanne Burgy; Screenplay, Jonathan Aibel, Glenn Berger; Designer, Raymond Zibach; Art Director, Tang K. Heng; Music, Hans Zimmer, John Powell; Editor, Clare Knight; Supervising Animator/Fight Choreographer, Rudolphe Guenoden; Head of Character Animation, Dan Wagner; Head of Story, Philip Crave; Visual Effects Supervisor, Alex Parkinson; Casting, Leslee Feldman; a DreamWorks Animation SKG presentation; Dolby; Widescreen; Technicolor; 3D; Rated PG; 91 minutes; Release date: May 26, 2011

CAST
Po	**Jack Black**
Tigress	**Angelina Jolie**
Shifu	**Dustin Hoffman**
Lord Shen	**Gary Oldman**
Monkey	**Jackie Chan**
Mantis	**Seth Rogen**
Viper	**Lucy Liu**

David Cross (Crane), James Hong (Mr. Ping), Michelle Yeoh (Soothsayer), Jean-Claude Van Damme (Master Croc), Victor Garber (Master Thundering Rhino), Dennis Haysbert (Master Storming Ox), Danny McBride (Wolf Boss), Paul Mazursky (Musician Bunny), Michael Patrick Bell, (Gorilla Guard #1), Jason Bertsch (Antelope Driver), Michael DeMaio (Happy Bunny), Joseph Izzo, Maury Sterling, Shane Glick (Wolf Soldiers), Lena Golia (Pig Fan/Bunny), April Hong (Mop Bunny), Alexandra Jourden (Bunny Fan), Stephen Kearin (Musician Pig/Awesome Pig), Liam Knight (Baby Po), Dan O'Connor (Stain Pig/Wolf Soldier #2), Romy Rosemont (Pig Mother), Jeremy Shipp (Dumpling Bunny), Fred Tatasciore (Panda Dad/Gorilla Guard #2), Lauren Tom (Market Sheep), Conrad Vernon (Boar)

Dragon Warrior Po and his fellow kung fu masters must fight the nefarious Lord Shen who hopes to use a secret weapon to conquer China. Sequel to the 2008 DreamWorks film.

This film received an Oscar nomination for animated feature.

Po

Po, Wolf Boss © DreamWorks Pictures

Monkey, Po, Tigress

Monkey, Crane, Po, Shifu, Tigress, Viper

Bradley Cooper, Zach Galifianakis, Ed Helms © Warner Bros.

THE HANGOVER PART II

(WARNER BROS.) Producers, Todd Phillips, Dan Goldberg; Executive Producers, Thomas Tull, Scott Budnick, Chris Bender, J.C. Spink; Director, Todd Phillips; Screenplay, Craig Mazin, Scot Armstrong, Todd Phillips; Photography, Lawrence Sher; Designer, Bill Brzeski; Costumes, Louise Mingenbach; Music, Christophe Beck; Editors, Debra Neil-Fisher, Mike Sale; Casting, Justine Baddeley, Kim Davis-Wagner; a Green Hat Films production, presented in association with Legendary Pictures; Dolby; Super 35 Widescreen; Color; Rated R; 102 minutes; Release date: May 26, 2011

CAST
Phil	**Bradley Cooper**
Stu	**Ed Helms**
Alan	**Zach Galifianakis**
Doug	**Justin Bartha**
Mr. Chow	**Ken Jeong**
Kingsley	**Paul Giamatti**

Mike Tyson (Himself), Jeffrey Tambor (Sid Garner), Mason Lee (Teddy), Jamie Chung (Lauren), Sasha Barrese (Tracy), Gillian Vigman (Stephanie), Aroon Seeboonruang (Monk), Nirut Sirichanya (Fohn), Yasmin Lee (Kimmy), Nick Cassavetes (Tattoo Joe), Sondra Currie (Linda Garner), Schnitmunt Busarakamwong (Grand Wizard), Bryan Callen (Samir), Brody Stevens (Kingsley Guy), Nimit Lusameepong (Desk Officer), Michael Berry Jr. (Vladi), Andrew Howard (Nikolai), Danai Thiengdham (Cell Block Officer), Thana Srisuke (Fighting Monk), Pairot Noiply (Shouting Man), Penpak Sirikul (Joi), Sanita Jai-Ua, Chanicha Shindejanichakul (Hostesses), Vithaya Pansringarm (Minister), Kim Lee (Dancer), Palakorn Chaiklang, Palakorn Gunjina, Pongastorn Sawadchatchawan, Kaweewit Chaikaew, PureWatanabe, Rattana Janprasit, Jetsada Yuktabutra (Ska Rangers), Tanner Maguire (Phil – 12 years old), William A. Johnson (Stu – 12 years old), Aedin Mincks (Alan - 12 years old), Dylan Boyack (Doug – 12 years old), William Jiang (Chow – 12 years old), Lynne Kidder (Woman at Restaurant), Crystal (Drug Dealing Monkey), Todd Phillips (Mr. Creepy)

On the eve of Stu's wedding, he and his pals must scower through Bangkok in hopes of locating the bride's missing brother. Sequel to the 2009 Warner Bros. film.

HELLO LONESOME

(BODEGA STUDIOS) Producer/Director/Screenplay/Photography, Adam Reid; Executive Producers, David Gioiella, Mark Littman; Music, Ted Gannon, Jones Street Station; Editor, Scott Rankin; Casting, Brette Goldstein; a Flycollar Films production in association with Northern Lights; Color; DV; Not rated; 92 minutes; Release date: May 27, 2011

CAST
Debby	**Sabrina Lloyd**
Gary	**James Urbaniak**
Eleanor	**Lynn Cohen**
Bill	**Harry Chase**
Gordon	**Nate Smith**
Omar	**Kamel Boutros**

Cathy Trien (Tabitha), Dave K. Williams (Dean), Traci Hovel (Trish)

Three stories: a lonely voiceover artist befriends his deliveryman; having lost her license, an elderly widow turns to her young neighbor for aide; a couple meet online and fall in love.

Sabrina Lloyd, Nate Smith

Harry Chase, Kamel Boutros © Bodega Studios

Brad Pitt, Hunter McCracken

Brad Pitt

Sean Penn

Jessica Chastain, Tye Sheridan

Laramie Eppler, Jessica Chastain, Hunter McCracken

Brad Pitt

Tye Sheridan, Jessica Chastain, Laramie Eppler

Sean Penn

THE TREE OF LIFE

(FOX SEARCHLIGHT) Producers, Sarah Green, Bill Pohlad, Brad Pitt, Dede Gardner, Grant Hill; Executive Producer, Donald Rosenfeld; Co-Producer, Nicolas Gonda; Co-Executive Producers, Steve Schwartz, Paula Mae Schwartz; Director/Screenplay, Terrence Malick; Photography, Emmanuel Lubezki; Designer, Jack Fisk; Costumes, Jacqueline West; Music, Alexandre Desplat; Editor, Mark Yoshikawa; Supervisor, Casting, Francine Maisler, Vicky Boone; a River Road Entertainment presentation; Dolby; Deluxe color; Rated PG-13; 139 minutes; Release date: May 27, 2011

CAST

Mr. O'Brien	**Brad Pitt**
Jack O'Brien	**Sean Penn**
Mrs. O'Brien	**Jessica Chastain**
Young Jack	**Hunter McCracken**
R.L. O'Brien	**Laramie Eppler**
Steve O'Brien	**Tye Sheridan**
Grandmother	**Fiona Shaw**
Guide	**Jessica Fuselier**
Mr. Reynolds	**Nicolas Gonda**
Architect	**Will Wallace**
Father Haynes	**Kelly Koonce**
Robert	**Bryce Boudoin**
Jimmy	**Jimmy Donaldson**
Cayler	**Kameron Vaughn**
Harry Bates	**Cole Cockburn**
George Walsh	**Dustin Allen**
Jo Bates	**Brayden Whisenhunt**
Jack's Wife	**Joanna Going**
Messenger	**Irene Bedard**
Jack at 2	**Finnegan Williams**
Jack at 5	**Michael Koeth**
R.L. at 2	**John Howell**
Samantha	**Samantha Martinez**
Mrs. Kimball	**Savannah Welch**
Mrs. Stone	**Tamara Jolaine**
Beth	**Julia M. Smith**
Rue	**Anne Nabors**
Uncle Ray	**Jackson Hurst**
Elisa	**Crystal Mantecon**

Christopher Ryan (Prisoner), Tyler Thomas (Tyler Stone), Michael Showers (Mr. Brown), Kim Whalen (Mrs. Brown), Margaret Ann Hoard (Jane), Wally Welch (Clergyman), Hudson Long (Mr. Bagley), Michael Dixon (Dusty Walsh), William Hardy (Jack's Work Colleague), Tommy Hollis (Tommy), Cooper Franklin Sutherland (Robert #2), John Cyrier (Bi-Plane Pilot), Erma Lee Alexander (Erma), Nicholas Yedinak (Nicholas Swimmer)

Seeking answers to life's meaning, Jack O'Brien looks back on his Midwestern upbringing during the 1950s and his complicated relationship with his demanding father.

This film received Oscar nominations for picture, director, and cinematography.

Laramie Eppler, Brad Pitt © Fox Searchlight

X-MEN: FIRST CLASS

(20TH CENTURY FOX) Producers, Lauren Shuler Donner, Simon Kinberg, Gregory Goodman, Bryan Singer; Executive Producers, Stan Lee, Tarquin Pack, Josh McLaglen; Director, Matthew Vaughn; Screenplay, Ashley Edward Miller, Zack Stentz, Jane Goldman, Matthew Vaughn; Story, Sheldon Turner, Bryan Singer; Photography, John Mathieson; Designer, Chris Seagers; Costumes, Sammy Sheldon; Music, Henry Jackman; Editors, Lee Smith, Eddie Hamilton; Visual Effects Designer, John Dykstra; Visual Effects Producer, Denise Davis; Casting (UK), Lucinda Syson, (US) Roger Mussenden, Jeremy Rich; a Bad Hat Harry/Donners' Company production, presented in association with Marvel Entertainment; Dolby; Panavision; Deluxe color; Rated PG-13; 132 minutes; Release date: June 3, 2011

CAST
Charles Xavier	**James McAvoy**
Erik Lensherr/Magneto	**Michael Fassbender**
Moira MacTaggert	**Rose Byrne**
Raven/Mystique	**Jennifer Lawrence**
Emma Frost	**January Jones**
Hank McCoy/Beast	**Nicholas Hoult**
Man in Black Suit	**Oliver Platt**
Azazel	**Jason Flemyng**
Alex Summers/Havok	**Lucas Till**
Armando Muñoz/Darwin	**Edi Gathegi**
Sebastian Shaw	**Kevin Bacon**
Sean Cassidy/Banshee	**Caleb Landry Jones**
Angel Salvadore	**Zoë Kravitz**
CIA Director McCone	**Matt Craven**
Janos Quested/Riptide	**Álex González**
Russian General	**Rade Sherbedgia**
Col. Hendry	**Glenn Morshower**
Charles Xavier (12 years)	**Laurence Belcher**
Young Erik	**Bill Milner**
Mrs. Xavier	**Beth Goddard**
US General	**James Remar**
Secretary of State	**Ray Wise**
Soviet Captain	**Olek Krupa**
Communications Officer	**Brendan Fehr**
Captain	**Michael Ironside**
XO	**Jason Beghe**
Men in Black Suits Agents	**Tony Curran, Randall Batinkoff**

Morgan Lily (Young Raven, 10 years), Corey Johnson (Chief Warden), Demetri Goritsas (Levene), Don Creech (William Stryker), Ludger Pistor (1st German/Pig Farmer), Wilfried Hochholdinger (2nd German/Tailor), Greg Kolpakchi, Andrei Zayats (Russian Soldiers), Michael Medeiros (Political Officer), Yuri Naumkin (Soviet Fire Control), Gene Farber (Soviet Radioman), David Agranov (Soviet NCO), Katrine De Candole (Swiss Receptionist), James Faulkner (Swiss Bank Manager), Éva Magyar (Edie Lensherr), Annabelle Wallis (Co-Ed), Juan Herrera (Airport Worker), Greg Savage (Coastguard), Jarid Faubel (US Fire Control Officer), Gregory Cox (Dr. Leigh), Josh Cohen (Junior Agent), David Crow (Weasley Agent), Kieran Patrick Campbell (Little Boy), Sasha Pieterse (Teenage Girl), Veniamin Manzyuk (Lt. Commander), Peter Stark, Leonard Redlich (Storm Troopers), Carlos Peres (German Bartender), Sean Brown (Russian Chopper Pilot), Neil Fingleton, Marios (Russian General's Bodyguards), Greg Nikoloff (Mr. Lensherr, Erik's Dad), Arthur Darbinyan (Aral Sea Captain), Hugh Jackman (Logan/Wolverine), Rebecca Romijn (Mystique – Older)

Given the power of telepathy, Charles Xavier makes it his mission to round-up as many other outcasts who have been bestowed with special gifts, in an effort to use their powers for the good of mankind, while Erik Lensherr uses his ability to manipulate metal as a way of exacting revenge on the Nazi officer who killed his mother. Fifth film in the Fox series following *X-Men* (2000), *X2* (2003), *X-Men: The Last Stand* (2006), and *X-Men Origins: Wolverine* (2009).

Caleb Landry Jones, Michael Fassbender, Jennifer Lawrence, Rose Byrne, Nicholas Hoult, James McAvoy, Lucas Till

Michael Fassbender, James McAvoy

James McAvoy, Michael Fassbender

January Jones

January Jones, Kevin Bacon

Michael Fassbender

Kevin Bacon, January Jones

James McAvoy, Jennifer Lawrence, Michael Fassbender, Nicholas Hoult
© Twentieth Century Fox

Jennifer Lawrence, Nicholas Hoult

Christopher Plummer, Cosmo, Ewan McGregor

Mélanie Laurent, Ewan McGregor

Ewan McGregor, Mélanie Laurent

Christopher Plummer, Ewan McGregor

Ewan McGregor, Cosmo © Focus Features

Christopher Plummer, Ewan McGregor

BEGINNERS

(FOCUS) Producers, Leslie Urdang, Dean Vanech, Miranda de Pencier, Jay Van Hoy, Lars Knudsen; Co-Producers, Fran Giblin, Geoff Linville; Director/Screenplay, Mike Mills; Photography, Kasper Tuxen; Designer, Shane Valentino; Costumes, Jennifer Johnson; Music, Roger Neill, David Palmer, Brian Reitzell; Music Supervisor, Robin Urdang; Editor, Olivier Bugge Coutte; Casting, Courtney Bright, Nicole Daniels; an Olympus Pictures presentation in association with Parts & Labor; Dolby; Color; Rated R; 105 minutes; Release date: June 3, 2011

Christopher Plummer

CAST

Oliver Fields	**Ewan McGregor**
Hal Fields	**Christopher Plummer**
Anna	**Mélanie Laurent**
Andy	**Goran Visnjic**
Elliot	**Kai Lennox**
Georgia Fields	**Mary Page Keller**
Young Oliver	**Keegan Boos**
Shauna	**China Shavers**
Liz	**Melissa Tang**
Party Person	**Amanda Payton**
Green Witch	**Luke Diliberto**
Magician	**Lou Taylor Pucci**
Record Company Rep	**Jennifer Lauren**
Juan	**Reynaldo Pacheco**
Dr. Long	**Jodi Long**
Dr. Wright	**Bruce French**
ICU Nurses	**Leslie Shea, Lana Young**
Hal's Priest	**Michael Chieffo**
Secretary	**Jennifer Hasty**
1978 Museum Staff	**Rodney Saulsberry**
1978 Fancy Woman	**June Sanders**
1978 Older Woman	**Catherine McGoohan**
Terse Nurse	**Terry Walters**
Nice Nurse	**Algerita Lewis**
Strict Nurse	**Regina Redwing**
Home Nurse #1	**Sunday Burke**
Hal Look-Alike	**Patrick L. Birkett**
Skating Rink Manager	**Sabera Wise**
Brian	**Rafael J. Noble**
Robert	**Jose Yenque**
Arthur	**Cosmo**

Goran Visnjic, Christopher Plummer

Bambadjan Bamba, Hana Hwang, Samuel T. Ritter (The Sads), T.G. Cody, Patrick Scott, Tom Suckhasem, Charles Valentino, Seth Walker, Michael Wilhelms (The Primetimers)

Oliver Fields looks back on when his 75-year-old father suddenly declared he was gay and then made up for the years he wasted leading a heterosexual life.

2011 Academy Award winner for Best Supporting Actor (Christopher Plummer).

Christopher Plummer

Dan Castellaneta, Kyle Chandler

Zack Mills, Kyle Chandler

Elle Fanning, Ron Eldard, Joel Courtney

Zack Mills, Elle Fanning, Ryan Lee, Joel Courtney, Gabriel Basso

Gabriel Basso, Ryan Lee, Joel Courtney, Riley Griffiths

Richard T. Jones, Joel Courtney (back to camera), Noah Emmerich, Ryan Lee (back to camera)

Joel Courtney

Kyle Chandler, Noah Emmerich © Paramount Pictures

SUPER 8

(PARAMOUNT) Producers, Steven Spielberg, J.J. Abrams, Bryan Burk; Executive Producer, Guy Riedel; Director/Screenplay, J.J. Abrams; Photography, Larry Fong; Designer, Martin Whist; Costumes, Ha Nguyen; Music, Michael Giacchino; Editors, Mary Jo Markey, Maryann Brandon; Visual Effects Producer, Chantal Feghali; Visual Effects & Animation, Industrial Light & Magic; Casting, April Webster, Alyssa Weisberg; an Amblin Entertainment/Bad Robot production; Dolby; Panavision; Deluxe color; Rated PG-13; 112 minutes; Release date: June 10, 2011

CAST

Jackson Lamb	**Kyle Chandler**
Alice Dainard	**Elle Fanning**
Joe Lamb	**Joel Courtney**
Martin	**Gabriel Basso**
Nelec	**Noah Emmerich**
Louis Dainard	**Ron Eldard**
Charles	**Riley Griffiths**
Cary	**Ryan Lee**
Preston	**Zach Mills**
Mrs. Kaznyk	**Jessica Tuck**
Mr. Kaznyk	**Joel McKinnon Miller**
Jen Kazynk	**AJ Michalka**
Dr. Woodward	**Glynn Turman**
Cooper	**Bruce Greenwood**
Izzy	**Dan Castellaneta**
Deputy Rosko	**Michael Hitchcock**
Kaznyk Twins	**Andrew Miller, Jakob Miller**
Benji Kaznyk	**Jade Griffiths**
Peg Kaznyk	**Britt Flatmo**
Overmyer	**Richard T. Jones**
Lydia Connor, Channel 14 News	**Amanda Foreman**
Donny	**David Gallagher**
Sheriff Pruitt	**Brett Rice**
Deputy Crawford	**Michael Giacchino**
Breen	**Beau Knapp**
Edie	**Dale Dickey**
Mr. Blakely	**Jack Axelrod**
Deputy Milner	**Ben Gavin**
Deputy Skadde	**Jay Scully**
Deputy Tally	**James Hebert**

Thomas F. Duffy (Rooney), Teri Clark Linden (Mrs. Babbit), Tom Quinn (Mr. McCandless), Kate Yerves (Woman in Office), Caitriona Balfe (Elizabeth Lamb), Koa Melvin (Baby Joe), Tom Williams (Flame Thrower), Bingo O'Malley (Mr. Harkin), Tony Guma (Sgt. Walters), Robert B. Quiroz (Boy in EVAC), Jason Brooks (Air Force Security), Tim Griffin (Commando), Marco Sanchez (Hernandez), Emerson Brooks (Military Bus Driver), Jonathan Dixon (Airman Nevil), Patrick St. Esprit (Weapons Commander), Greg Grunberg (Sitcom Actor), Katie Lowes (Tina)

A group of kids shooting an amateur 8mm movie inadvertently capture footage of a trainwreck which unleashes an alien force.

Kyle Chandler, Joel Courtney, Elle Fanning, Ron Eldard

JUDY MOODY AND THE NOT BUMMER SUMMER

(RELATIVITY) Producers, Sarah Siegel-Magness, Gary Magness; Executive Producers, Bobbi Sue Luther, Andrew Sugerman, Ryan Kavanaugh, Tucker Tooley; Director, John Schultz; Screenplay, Kathy Waugh, Megan McDonald; based on the *Judy Moody* book series by Megan McDonald; Photography, Shawn Maurer; Designer, Cynthia Charette; Costumes, Mary Jane Fort; Music, Richard Gibbs; Editor, John Pace III; Casting, Julie Ashton; a Smokewood Entertainment production; Dolby; Deluxe color; Rated PG; 91 minutes; Release date: June 10, 2011

CAST
Aunt Opal	**Heather Graham**
Judy Moody	**Jordana Beatty**
Frank	**Preston Bailey**
Stink	**Parris Mosteller**
Dad	**Kristoffer Winters**
Rocky	**Garrett Ryan**
Mr. Todd	**Jaleel White**

Ashley Boettcher (Jessica Finch), Taylar Hender (Amy), Cameron Boyce (Hunter/Werewolf), Jenica Bergere (Rocky's Mom), Janet Varney (Mom), Jackson Odell (Zeke), Doug MacMillan (Bigfoot Eyewitness), Dean Cameron (Animated Reporter), Ashley Jackson (Maddy), Pedro Shanahan (Ride Attendant), Jenn Korbee (Newscaster), Robert Costanzo (Herb), Sharon Sachs (Rose), Cable Magness (Bouncy House Boy), Frank Caronna (Surf Instructor), Norwood Cheek (Vampire Ticket Seller), Bobbie Sue Luther (Young Woman), Camryn Magness (Zombie Cheerleader), James McManus (Zombie Movie Narrator), Brian Palermo (Zombie), Megan Franich (Ivy the Ticket Taker), Richare Riehle (Ringmaster), Tails & Tux (Mouse), Rainbow (Blue & Gold Macaw)

Judy Moody's boredom over how to spend her summer break is solved by the arrival of her eccentric aunt.

Heather Graham, Jordana Beatty © Relativity Media

Preston Bailey, Jordana Beatty

Cliff De Young, Mallory Culbert © Monterey Media

Mallory Culbert, Michael Bigham

ROAD TO NOWHERE

(MONTEREY MEDIA) Producers, Monte Hellman, Steven Gaydos, Melissa Hellman; Executive Producers, Thomas Nelson, June Nelson; Director, Monte Hellman; Screenplay, Steven Gaydos; Photography, Josep M. Civit; Designer, Laurie Post; Costumes, Chelsea Staebell; Music, Tom Russell; Music Supervisor, Anastasia Brown; Editor, Celine Amesion; Visual Effects Supervisor, Robert Skotak; an Entertainment One presentation; Color; HD; Rated R; 121 minutes; Release date; June 10, 2011

CAST
Cary Stewart/Rafe Tachen	**Cliff De Young**
Laurel Graham/Velam Duran	**Shannyn Sossamon**
Mitchell Haven	**Tygh Runyan**
Bruno Brotherton	**Waylon Payne**
Nathalie Post	**Dominique Swain**

Michael Bigham (Joe Watts), Mallory Culbert (Mallory), Lathan McKay (Erik), Gregory Rentis (Editor), Fabio Testi (Nestor Duran), Rob Kolar (Steve Gales), John Diehl (Bobby Billings), Bonnie Pointer, Peter Bart (Themselves), Nic Paul (Johnny Laidlaw), Larry Lerner (Larry), Araceli Lemos (Araceli), Sarah Dorsey (Sarah)

As a young filmmaker struggles to shoot a movie based on a true crime, he becomes increasingly obsessed with his leading lady.

Mark Strong

Tomar-Re, Kilowog, Ryan Reynolds © Warner Bros.

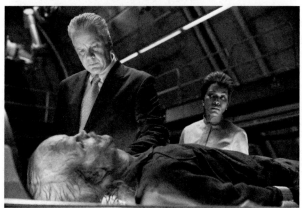

Peter Sarsgaard, Tim Robbins, Angela Bassett

GREEN LANTERN

(WARNER BROS.) Producers, Donald De Line, Greg Berlanti; Executive Producers, Herbert W. Gains, Andrew Haas; Director, Martin Campbell; Screenplay, Greg Berlanti, Michael Green, Marc Guggenheim, Michael Goldenberg; Screen Story, Greg Berlanti, Michael Green, Marc Guggenheim; Based upon characters appearing in comic books published by DC Comics; Photography, Dion Beebe; Designer, Grant Major; Costumes, Ngila Dickson; Music, James Newton Howard; Editor, Stuart Baird; Visual Effects Supervisors, Jim Berney, Kent Houston, Karen Goulekas, John "DJ" DesJardin; Visual Effects, Sony Pictures Imageworks, Peerless Camera Co., Rising Sun Pictures, Pixomondo, Digiscope, Hydraulx, Pixel Playground, MPC; Stunts, Gary Powell; Casting, Pam Dixon Mickelsen; a De Line Pictures production; Dolby; Panavision; Technicolor; 3D; Rated PG-13; 114 minutes; Release date: June 17, 2011

CAST
Hal Jordan (Green Lantern)	**Ryan Reynolds**
Carol Ferris	**Blake Lively**
Hector Hammond	**Peter Sarsgaard**
Sinestro	**Mark Strong**
Dr. Amanda Waller	**Angela Bassett**
Senator Hammond	**Tim Robbins**
Abin Sur	**Temuera Morrison**
Carl Ferris	**Jay O. Sanders**
Martin Jordan	**Jon Tenney**
Tom Kalmaku	**Taika Waititi**
Voice of Parallax	**Clancy Brown**
Voice of Kilowog	**Michael Clarke Duncan**
Voice of Tomar-Re	**Geoffrey Rush**

Jenna Craig (Young Carol), Mike Doyle (Jack Jordan), Gattlin Griffith (Young Hal), Nick Jandl (Jim Jordan), Dylan James (Jason Jordan), Leanne Cochran (Janice Jordan), Deke Anderson (4 Star General Caven), Lena Clark (Senator's Assistant), Ritchie Montgomery (Bunker Doctor), Marcela Duarte Fonseca (Beautiful Girl), Kenneth Brown Jr., Silas Cooper (Avionics Techs), Dane Rhodes (Ferris Security Guard), Melanie Hebert (News Reporter at F-35 Crash), LaTonya Norton (News Reporter #1), Rick Seafross (2 Star General), Michael Jamorski (Football Jock), Laura Cayouette, Bernard Hocke (Party Guests), Douglas M. Griffin, Armando Leduc (DEO Agents), Griff Furst, Garrett Hines (UCav Operators), Warren Burton, Salome Jens (Guardians), Warren P. Munster (Bartender), Tony Owens (Singer), Tiffany Morgan (Mom), Sharon Morris (Bus Driver), Lance E. Nichols (Cop), Jeff Wolfe (Bob Banks)

Fighter pilot Hal Jordan is bequeathed a ring that enables him to become a part of the Green Lantern Corps and help fight the evil Parallax from destroying the universe.

Ryan Reynolds

Jim Carrey

Jim Carrey, Angela Lansbury

Carla Gugino, Maxwell Perry Cotton, Madeline Carroll, Jim Carrey

MR. POPPER'S PENGUINS

(20TH CENTURY FOX) Producer, John Davis; Executive Producers, Jessica Tuchinsky, Mark Waters, Derek Dauchy, Joel Gotler; Co-Producer, Jonathan Filley; Director, Mark Waters; Screenplay, Sean Anders, John Morris, Jared Stern; Based upon the novel by Richard Atwater and Florence Atwater; Photography, Florian Ballhaus; Designer, Stuart Wurtzel; Costumes, Ann Roth; Music, Rolfe Kent; Editor, Bruce Green; Visual Effects and Animation, Rhythm & Hues Studio; Stunts, G.A. Aguilar, Stephen Pope, Blaise Corrigan; Penguin Expert, W. Scott Drieschman; Casting, Marci Liroff, Kathleen Chopin; a Davis Entertainment Company production; Dolby; Color; Rated PG; 94 minutes; Release date: June 17, 2011

CAST
Mr. Popper	**Jim Carrey**
Amanda	**Carla Gugino**
Mrs. Van Gundy	**Angela Lansbury**
Pippi	**Ophelia Lovibond**
Janie	**Madeline Carroll**
Nat Jones	**Clark Gregg**
Mr. Gremmins	**Jeffrey Tambor**
Kent	**David Krumholtz**
Franklin	**Philip Baker Hall**
Billy	**Maxwell Perry Cotton**

James Tupper (Rick), Dominic Chianese (Reader), William C. Mitchell (Yates), Kelli Barrett (Tommy's Mom), Dylan Clark Marshall (Young Tommy Popper), Brian T. Delaney (Voice of Young Tom Popper, Sr.), Elaine Kussack (Gremmin's Secretary), Harlin C. Kearsley (Town Car Driver), Desmin Borges (Daryl), Lee Moore (Reginald), Dominic Colon (Tito), Jeff Lima (Freddy), Frank Ciornei (Klaus), J.R. Horne (Arnold), Matthew Wolf (Voice of Artic Friend), Andrew Stewart-Jones (Animal Control Guy), James Chen (Fish & Game Officer), Rafael Osorio (Marine & Waterfowl Officer), Curtis Shumaker (Sanitation Officer), Joe D'Onofrio (Random Man on Street), Olga Merediz (Nanny), Betsy Aidem (Tavern Hostess), Angel L. Caban (Fishmonger), Chris Beetem (Young Developer), Charles L. Campbell (Voice of Old Tom Popper, Sr.), Daniel Stewart Sherman (Zoo Security Guard), Mike Massimino (Cop #1), Charlie Semine (Quint, Cop #2)

A self-involved businessman's life changes for the better when he inherits six penguins.

Jim Carrey © Twentieth Century Fox

THE ART OF GETTING BY

(FOX SEARCHLIGHT) formerly *Homework*; Producers, P. Jennifer Dana, Gia Walsh, Kara Baker, Darren Goldberg; Executive Producers, Andrew Levitas, David Sweeney, Henry Pincus, Patrick Baker, Nick Quested, Gretchen McGowan, Jonathan Gray, Anthony Gudas; Director/ Screenplay, Gavin Wiesen; Photography, Ben Kutchins; Designer, Kelly McGehee; Costumes, Erika Munro; Music, Alec Puro; Music Supervisor, Linda Cohen; Editor, Mollie Goldstein; Casting, Laura Rosenthal; a Gigi Films and Goldcrest Films International presentation of a Mint Pictures/Atlantic Pictures production in association with Island Bound Productions; Dolby; Super 35 Widescreen; Technicolor; Rated PG-13; 84 minutes; Release date: June 17, 2011

CAST
George Zinavoy	**Freddie Highmore**
Sally Howe	**Emma Roberts**
Dustin	**Michael Angarano**
Vivian Sargent	**Rita Wilson**
Principal Martinson	**Blair Underwood**
Ms. Herman	**Alicia Silverstone**
Charlotte Howe	**Elizabeth Reaser**
Jack Sargent	**Sam Robards**
Zoe Rubenstein	**Sasha Spielberg**
Will Sharpe	**Marcus Carl Franklin**

Ann Dowd (Mrs. Grimes), Maya Ri Sanchez (Cynthia), Ann Harada (Mrs. Dougherty), Jarlath Conroy (Harris McElroy), Andrew Levitas (Javier), Dan Leonard (Nick), Sophie Curtis (Chastity)

A Manhattan high schooler who hasn't the slightest inkling to do homework because of his discontentment, is slowly brought out of his shell by a girl who is intrigued by his non-conformist attitude.

Freddie Highmore, Emma Roberts

Emma Roberts, Michael Angarano

Blair Underwood

Emma Roberts, Freddie Highmore © Fox Searchlight

PAGE ONE: INSIDE THE NEW YORK TIMES

(MAGNOLIA) Producers, Josh Braun, David Hand, Alan Oxman, Adam Schlesinger, Kate Novack, Andrew Rossi; Executive Producers, Daniel Stern, Daniel Pine; Associate Producers, Keith Hamlin, Luke Henry; Director, Andrew Rossi; Screenplay, Kate Novack, Andrew Rossi; Photography, Andrew Rossi; Music, Paul Brill, Killer Tracks; Editors, Chad Beck, Christopher Branca, Sarah Devorkin; a Participant Media and History Films presentation; Dolby; Color; Rated R; 88 minutes; Release date: June 17, 2011. Documentary on how the *New York Times* is dealing with upheaval in journalism and how readers get their news in the age of increasingly changing technology.

WITH

Ken Auletta, Tim Arango, Dean Baquet, Carla Baranauckas, Carl Bernstein, Katherine Bouton, Susan Chira, David Carr, John Carr, Susan Chira, Noam Cohen, Dennis Crowley, Nick Denton, Sarah Ellison, Ian Fisher, Bruce Headlam, Michael Hirschorn, Larry Ingrassia, Jeff Jarvis, Alex S. Jones, Joseph Kahn, Bill Keller, Brian Lam, Nick Lemann, Rick Lyman, James McQuivey, Seth Mnookin, Markos Moulitsas, Richard Pérez-Peña, Claiborne Ray, David Remnick, Andrew Ross Sorkin, Clay Shirky, Shane Smith, Paul Steiger, Brian Stelter, Charles Strum, Gay Talese, Katrina vanden Heuvel, Jimmy Wales, Evan Williams

David Carr, Bruce Headlam

© Magnolia Pictures

Buck Brannaman

Buck Brannaman © Sundance Selects

BUCK

(SUNDANCE SELECTS) Producer, Julie Goldman; Executive Producer/Director, Cindy Meehl; Co-Executive Producer/ Creative Consultant, Andrea Meditch; Line Producer, Alice Henty; Associate Producer, Sofia Santana; Photography, Guy Mossman, Luke Geissbühler; Music, David Robbins; Music Supervisor, Liz Gallacher; Editor, Toby Shimin; a Cedar Creek Productions presentation in association with Motto Pictures and Back Allie Films; Color; HD; Rated PG; 88 minutes; Release date: June 17, 2011 Documentary on horse trainer Buck Brannaman.

WITH

Buck Brannaman, Mary Brannaman, Reata Brannaman, Tina Cornish, Johnny France, Bibb Frazier, Dan Gunter, Shayne Jackson, Gary Myers, Robert Redford, Betsy Shirley, Betty Staley, Gwynn Turnbull Weaver, Nevada Watt, Annette Venteicher, Paige Morris, Bill Seaton, Britt Long, Julie Hueftle

Cameron Diaz

Cameron Diaz, Jason Segel, Justin Timberlake

BAD TEACHER

(COLUMBIA) Producers, Jimmy Miler, David Householter; Executive Producers, Georgia Kacandes, Jake Kasdan, Lee Eisenberg, Gene Stupnitsky; Director, Jake Kasdan; Screenplay, Gene Stupnitsky, Lee Eisenberg; Photography, Alar Kivilo; Designer, Jefferson Sage; Costumes, Debra McGuire; Music, Michael Andrews; Music Supervisors, Manish Raval, Tom Wolfe; Editor, Tara Timpone; Casting, Amy McIntyre Britt, Anya Colloff; a Mosaic production; Dolby; Deluxe color; Rated R; 92 minutes; Release date: June 24, 2011

CAST

Elizabeth Halsey	**Cameron Diaz**
Amy Squirrel	**Lucy Punch**
Russell Gettis	**Jason Segel**
Scott Delacorte	**Justin Timberlake**
Lynn Davies	**Phyllis Smith**
Principal Wally Snur	**John Michael Higgins**
Sandy Pinkus	**Dave 'Gruber' Allen**
Ms. Pavicic	**Jillian Armenante**
Garrett Tiara	**Matthew J. Evans**
Sasha Abernathy	**Kaitlyn Dever**
Chase Rubin-Rossi	**Kathryn Newton**

Igal Ben Yair (Arkady), Aja Bair (Devon), Andra Nechita (Gaby), Noah Munck (Tristan), Finneas O'Connell (Spencer, Twilight), Daniel Castro (Rodrigo, Acne Kid), Adrian Kali Turner (Shawn), Eric Stonestreet (Kirk), Thomas Lennon (Carl Halabi), Paul Bates (School Superintendent), Jeff Judah (Janitor), Nat Faxon (Mark), Stephanie Faracy (Mrs. Pubich), David Paymer (Dr. Vogel), Alanna Ubach (Angela), Christine Smith (Danni), Paul Feig (Dad at Carwash), Deirdre Lovejoy (Sasha's Mother), Melvin Mar (Teacher, Bathroom), Rose Abdoo (School Secretary), Jerry Lambert (Morgan's Dad), Jennifer Irwin (Chase's Mom), Christopher Rockwell (Chase's Dad), David Doty (Armando the Homeless Guy), Molly Shannon (Melody, Garrett's Mom), Rick Overton (Philip), Danny Trap (Cowboy at Palace), Matt Besser (Abraham Lincoln, Tour Guide), Lee Eisenberg (Blacksmith, Re-Enactor), Bruno Gioiello (Police Officer), Jordan Van Vranken (Crying Girl)

Dumped by her fiancé, foul-mouthed, unorthodox teacher Elizabeth Halsey makes it her goal to land a rich, handsome substitute.

Cameron Diaz, Phyllis Smith

Cameron Diaz, Lucy Punch © Columbia Pictures

Carlos Linares, Demián Bichir

Bobby Soto, José Julián, Chelsea Rendon

Demián Bichir, José Julián

Joaquin Cosio, Demián Bichir © Summit Entertainment

A BETTER LIFE

(SUMMIT) Producers, Paul Junger Witt, Christian McLaughlin, Chris Weitz, Jami Gertz, Stacey Lubliner; Executive Producer, Tony Thomas; Co-Producer, Laura Greenlee; Director, Chris Weitz; Screenplay, Eric Eason; Story, Roger L. Simon; Photography, Javier Aguirresarobe; Designer, Melissa Stewart; Costumes, Elaine Montalvo; Music, Alexandre Desplat; Music Supervisor, Alexandra Patasvas; Editor, Peter Lambert; Casting, Joseph Middleton, Carla Hool; a Witt-Thomas/ Depth of Field production in association with McLaughlin Films; presented in association with Lime Orchard Productions; Dolby; Color; Rated PG-13; 98 minutes; Release date: June 24, 2011

CAST

Carlos Galindo	**Demián Bichir**
Luis Galdino	**José Julián**
Anita	**Dolores Heredia**
Blasco Martinez	**Joaquín Cosio**
Mrs. Donnely	**Nancy Lenehan**
Juvie Officer	**Tim Griffin**
Ramon	**Gabriel Chavarria**
Facundo	**Bobby Soto**
Ruthie Valdez	**Chelsea Rendon**
Santiago	**Carlos Linares**
Linda	**Isabella Rae Thomas**
Bella	**Isabella Balajadia**
Gigi	**Giselle Nieto**

Eddie "Piolín" Sotelo (Himself), Trampas Thompson (School Security Officer), Valorie Hubbard (School Secretary), Robert Peters (Truck Driver), Richard Cabral (Marcelo Valdez), Luis A. Colocio, Ray Moreno (Ruthie's Uncles), Yelyna De Leon (Ruthie's Mother), Rolando Molina (Jesus), Taide Acosta (Young Woman), Joe Renteria (Bearded Man), Isidro Vallin (Payaso), Magi Avila (Shot Girl), Henry Ambriz (Mexican Singer), Miguel Alejandro Gaxiola, Jorge Arturo Gaxiola (Voz de Mando Singers), Robert Renedros (Busboy), Charles Currier (Auto Mart Security Guard), Marlon Correa (Prison Guard), Adrian Mojica (Police Officer), Todd Felix (Gabe Wettenal), Eddie Martinez (Rey), Jason Medwin, Tom Schanley (ICE Officer), Abraham Chaidez (Coyote)

Determined to make a better life for his teenage son, illegal Mexican immigrant Carlos Galindo purchases a truck so that he can continue to work at his landscaping jobs, only to have a series of unfortunate events throw his life into turmoil.

This film received an Oscar nomination for actor (Demián Bichir).

Acer, Siddeley, Lightning McQueen, Mater, Finn McMissile

CARS 2

(WALT DISNEY STUDIOS) Producer, Denise Ream; Director, John Lasseter; Co-Director, Brad Lewis; Associate Producer, Mark Nielsen; Screenplay, Ben Queen; Original Story, John Lasseter, Brad Lewis, Dan Fogelman; Photography, Sharon Calahan, Jeremy Lasky; Music, Michael Giacchino; Designer, Harley Jessup; Story Supervisor, Nathan Stanton; Editor, Stephen Schaffer; Supervising Animators, Shawn Krause, Dave Mullins; Character Supervisors, Sajan Skaria, Robert Moyer; Effects Supervisor, Gary Bruins; Casting, Kevin Reher, Natalie Lyon; a Walt Disney Pictures presentation of a Pixar Animation Studios production; Dolby; Widescreen; Deluxe color; 3D; Rated G; 107 minutes; Release date: June 24, 2011

VOICE CAST
Lightning McQueen	**Owen Wilson**
Mater	**Larry the Cable Guy**
Finn McMissile	**Michael Caine**
Holley Shiftwell	**Emily Mortimer**
Sally	**Bonnie Hunt**
Luigi	**Tony Shalhoub**
Ramone	**Cheech Marin**
Siddeley/Leland Turbo	**Jason Isaacs**
Grem	**Joe Mantegna**
Acer	**Peter Jacobson**
Professor Z	**Thomas Kretschmann**
Guido	**Guido Quaroni**
Fillmore/Combat Ship	**Lloyd Sherr**
Sarge	**Paul Dooley**
Mack	**John Ratzenberger**

Jenifer Lewis (Flo), Michael Wallis (Sheriff), Katherine Helmond (Lizzie), John Turturro (Francesco Bernoulli), Franco Nero (Uncle Topolino), Vanessa Redgrave (The Queen/Mama Topolino), Eddie Izzard (Sir Miles Axelrod), Bruce Campbell (Rod 'Torque" Redline), Brent Musburger (Brent Mustangburger), Darrell Waltrip (Darrell Cartrip), David Hobbs (David Hobbscap), Patrick Walker (Mel Dorado), Jeff Garlin (Otis), Michael Michelis (Tomber), Teresa Gallagher (Mater's Computer), Stanley Townsend (Victor Hugo/Vladimir Trunkov/Ivan the Tow Truck), Velibor Topic (Alexander Hugo), Sig Hansen (Crabby), John Mainieri (J. Curby Gremlin), Brad Lewis (Tubbs Pacer), Jeff Gordon (Jeff Gorvette), Lewis Hamilton (Lewis Hamilton), Edie McClurg (Minny), Richard Kind (Van), John Lasseter (John Lassetire)

Racecar Lightning McQueen and his buddy, tow truck Mater, decide to compete in the first-ever World Grand Prix, in hopes of being proclaimed the world's fastest car. Sequel to the 2006 Disney/Pixar film.

Finn McMissile

Professor Z

Holley Shitfwell © Disney/Pixar

TRANSFORMERS: DARK OF THE MOON

(PARAMOUNT) Producers, Don Murphy, Tom DeSanto, Lorenzo di Bonaventura, Ian Bryce; Executive Producers, Steven Spielberg, Michael Bay, Brian Goldner, Mark Vahradian; Director, Michael Bay; Screenplay, Ehren Kruger; Based on Hasbro's Transformers action figures; Photography, Amir Mokri; Designer, Nigel Phelps; Costumes, Deborah L. Scott; Music, Steve Jablonsky; Editors, Roger Barton, William Goldenberg, Joel Negron; Visual Effects & Animation, Industrial Light & Magic; a di Bonaventura Pictures production, a Tom DeSanto/Don Murphy production, presented in association with Hasbro; Dolby; Panavision; 3D; Deluxe color; Rated PG-13; 154 minutes; Release date: June 29, 2011

Bumblebee

CAST

Sam Witwicky	**Shia LaBeouf**
Lennox	**Josh Duhamel**
Simmons	**John Turturro**
Epps	**Tyrese Gibson**
Carly Spencer	**Rosie Huntington-Whiteley**
Dylan	**Patrick Dempsey**
Bruce Brazos	**John Malkovich**
Mearing	**Frances McDormand**

Kevin Dunn (Ron Witwicky), Julie White (Judy Witwicky), Ken Jeong (Jerry Wang), Alan Tudyk (Dutch), Glenn Morshower (Gen. Morshower), Lester Speight (Eddie), Rich Hutchman (Engineer), Buzz Aldrin, Bill O'Reilly (Themselves), Ravil Isyanov (Voshkod); *Lennox Team:* Dustin Dennard (Lieutenant), Markiss McFadden (Baby Face), Nick Bickle (Chapman), Ajay James (Atroui), Brett Lynch (Phelps), Chris A. Robinson (Bruno), Scott C. Roe (Nelson), James Weston III (Tuens), Brian Call (Taggart); *Epps Team:* Aaron Garrido (Mongo), Mikal A. Vega (Hooch), Kenneth Sheard (Marc L), Josh Kelly (Stone); Keiko Agena (Mearing's Aide), LaMonica Garrett (Morshower's Aide), Yasen Peyankov (Voshkod Associate), Brett Stimely (President Kennedy), John Tobin (President Nixon), Drew Pillsbury (Defense Secretary McNamara), Patrick Panhurst (Director of NASA); *1969:* Larry Clarke (NASA Scientist), Tom Virtue, Thomas Crawford, Kevin Sizemore (Black Ops NASA Technicians), Alan Pietruszewski (NASA Mission Controller), Michael Daniel Cassady (NASA Launch Technician), Peter B. Murnik (Tracking Station Supervisor), Don Jeanes (Neil Armstrong), Cory Tucker (Buzz Aldrin); Lindsey Ginter, David St. James (Old NASA Scientists), Mitch Bromwell (NASA Technician), Elya Baskin (Cosmonaut Dimitri), Eugene Alper (Cosmonaut Yuri), Inna Korobkina (Russian Lady), Zoran Radanovich (Russian Bouncer), Kathleen Gati (Russian Bartender), Annie O'Donnell (Human Resources Lady), Chris Sheffield (Pimply Corporate Kid), Ken Takemoto (Japanese Executive), Michael Loeffelholz (Executive Interviewer), Mindy Sterling (Insurance Agent), Stephen Monroe Taylor, Andy Daly, Derek Miller (Mailroom Workers), Scott Krinsky (Accuretta Executive), Katherine Sigismund, Maile Flanagan (Acccuretta Workers), Darren O'Hare (Berated Scientist), Jack Axelrod (Simmons Tileman), Rich Hutchman (Engineer), Meredith Monroe (Engineer's Wife), Charlotte Labadie (Engineer's Daughter), Christian Baha (Dylan's Executive), Jennifer Williams, Danielle Fornarelli (Dylan's Assistant), Danny McCarthy, John Turk, Peter A. Kelly (NEST Guards), Mark Golden, Sean Murphy, Scott Paulson, Luis Echagarruga (SEALs), Iqbal Theba (UN Secretary General), Anthony Azizi (Lt. Sulimani), Sammy Sheik (Lt. Faraj), John S. McAfee (GPS Tracking Coordinator), Bonecrusher the Mastiff (Bones the Mastiff); *VOICES:* Peter Cullen (Optimus Prime), Hugo Weaving (Megatron), Leonard Nimoy (Sentinel Prime), Jess Harnell (Ironhide), Charlie Andler (Starscream), Robert Foxworth (Ratchet), James Remar (Sideswpie), Francesco Quinn (Dino), George Coe (Que/Wheeljack), Tom Kenny (Wheelie), Reno Wilson (Brains), Frank Welker (Shockwave/Soundwave), Ron Bottitta (Roadbuster/Amp), John Di Maggio (Leadfoot/Target), Keith Szarabajka (Laserbeak), Greg Berg (Igor)

John Malkovich, Shia LaBeouf

Optimus Prime © Paramount Pictures

Yet another clash between the Autobots and the Decepticons threatens to destroy the Earth. Previous entries in the series were *Transformers* (2007) and *Transformers: Revenge of the Fallen* (2009).

This film received Oscar nominations for visual effects, sound mixing, and sound editing.

Rosie Huntington-Whiteley, Patrick Dempsey

Tom Hanks, George Takei © Universal Studios

Cedric the Entertainer, Tom Hanks, Taraji P. Henson

LARRY CROWNE

(UNIVERSAL) Producers, Tom Hanks, Gary Goetzman; Executive Producers, Philippe Rousselot, Steven Shareshian, Jed Brody, Fabrice Gianfermi, David Coatsworth; Co-Producer, Katterli Frauenfelder; Director, Tom Hanks; Screenplay, Tom Hanks, Nia Vardalos; Photography, Philippe Rousselot; Designer, Victor Kempster; Costumes, Albert Wolsky; Music, James Newton Howard; Editor, Alan Cody; Casting, Jeanne McCarthy; a Vendôme Pictures presentation of a Playtone production; Dolby; Color; Rated PG-13; 99 minutes; Release date: July 1, 2011

CAST
Larry Crowne	**Tom Hanks**
Mercedes Tainot	**Julia Roberts**
Dean Tainot	**Bryan Cranston**
Lamar	**Cedric the Entertainer**
B'Ella	**Taraji P. Henson**
Talia Francesco	**Gugu Mbatha-Raw**
Dell Gordo	**Wilmer Valderrama**
Frances	**Pam Grier**
Wilma Q. Gammelgaard	**Rita Wilson**
Dr. Ed Matsutani	**George Takei**
Samantha	**Sarah Mahoney**

Roxana Ortega (Alvarez), Randall Park (Trainee Wong), Brady Rubin (Dorothy Genkos), Alex Quijano, Tina Huang, E-Kan Soong, Tarina Pouncy (Team Leaders), Sy Richardson (Avery), Julie Wagner (Vacuum Shopper), Rob Riggle (Jack Strang), Erin Underwood (Mom with Baby), Dale Dye (Cox), Barry Sobel (Cubby), Claudia Stedelin (Vicky Hurley), Bob Stephenson (Andrews), Holmes Osborne (Dave Busik), Tom Budge (Stan), Rami Malek (Steve Dibiasi), Malcolm Barrett (Dave Mack), Grace Gummer (Natalie Calimeris), Maria Canals-Barrera (Lala Pinedo), A.B. Fofana (Chester), Sarah Levy (Eli), Julia Cho (Tori), Chad Smathers (Michael), David L. Murphy (Bud), Carly Reeves (Sal), Ian Gomez (Frank), Nia Vardalos (Map Genie Voice), Herbert Siguenza (Raul), Ricardo Salinas (Nick), Richard J. Montoya (Carlos), Joshua Bitton (Officer Baker), Jon Seda (Officer Diamond), Jack Milo (Neighbor with Dog), Chet Hanks (Pizza Delivery Boy), Biff Henderson (Cappy), Melissa Christine (Tabitha)

After being fired from his long-time position, Larry Crowne decides to improve his life by taking a public-speaking class, presided over by a cynical instructor who has lost her passion for teaching.

Julia Roberts, Tom Hanks, Rami Malek

Gugu Mbatha-Raw, Wilmer Valderrama

Bridger Zadina, Jacob Wysocki, John C. Reilly © ATO

Bridger Zadina, Jacob Wysocki

TERRI

(ATO) Producers, Alison Dickey, Hunter Gray, Lynette Howell, Alex Orlovsky; Executive Producers, Johnathan Dorfman, Temple Fennell, Sarah Lash, Cameron Brodie, Tyler Brodie, Dawn Cullen Jonas, David Guy Levy, Jacob Pechenik; Director, Azazel Jacobs; Screenplay, Patrick Dewitt; Co-Producer, Chris Stinson; Photography, Tobias Datum; Designer, Matt Luem; Costumes, Diaz; Music, Mandy Hoffman; Editor, Darrin Navarro; Casting, Nicole Arbusto, Joy Dickson; a Verisimilitude production in association with Silverwood Films, Periscope Entertainment, Knowmore; Dolby; Deluxe color; Rated R; 105 minutes; Release date: July 1, 2011

CAST
Terri	**Jacob Wysocki**
Mr. Fitzgerald	**John C. Riley**
Uncle James	**Creed Bratton**
Heather Miles	**Olivia Crocicchia**
Chad Markson	**Bridger Zadina**
Mr. Flemisch	**Tim Heidecker**
Dirty Jack	**Justin Prentice**

Mary Anne McGarry (Ms. Hamish), Curtiss Frisle (Sex Ed), Tara Karsian (Mrs. Davidson), Diane Louise Salinger (Mrs. Vick), Lisa Hoover (Waitress), Jenna Gavigan (Samantha Goode), Jessica D. Stone (Rachel #1), Jamie Lee Redmon (Rachel#2), Robert Towers (Priest), Eddie Pepitone (Joe Hollywood), Josh "The Ponceman" Perry (Marcus Bloom), Melanie Abramoff (Amy), Nelson Mashita (Custodian), Jeffrey Noah Silcock (Donny Washburn), Nate Sanchez, Francisco "Kico" Pedrasa (Teenagers), Logan Holladay (Student on Rope)

An overweight teen misfit forms a bond with a vice principal, who hopes to break through to the boy and other such outcasts at the school.

MONTE CARLO

(20TH CENTURY FOX) Producers, Denise Di Novi, Alison Greenspan, Nicole Kidman, Arnon Milchan; Executive Producers, Stan Wlodkowski, Deborah Schindler, Forest Whitaker, Per Saari; Director, Thomas Bezucha; Screenplay, Thomas Bezucha, April Blair, Maria Maggenti; Story, Kelly Bowe; Based on the novel *Headhunters* by Jules Bass; Photography, Jonathan Brown; Designer, Hugo Lucyzc-Wyhowski; Costumes, Shay Cunliffe; Music, Michael Giacchino; Music Supervisor, Liza Richardson; Editor, Jeffrey Ford; Casting, Deborah Aquila, Tricia Wood; a Fox 2000 Pictures and Regency Enterprises presentation of a Di Novi Pictures production; Dolby; Deluxe color; Rated PG; 108 minutes; Release date: July 1, 2011

CAST
Grace Bennett/ Cordelia Winthrop Scott	**Selena Gomez**
Emma Perkins	**Katie Cassidy**
Meg Kelly	**Leighton Meester**
Owen Andrews	**Cory Monteith**
Pam Bennett-Kelly	**Andie MacDowell**
Robert Kelly	**Brett Cullen**
Riley	**Luke Bracey**

Amanda Fairbanks-Hynes (Amanda), Pierre Boulanger (Theo Marchand), Catherine Tate (Alicia Winthrop Scott), Valérie Lemercier (Madame Valerie), Joe Camp III (Carl at Diner), Franck de la Personne (Manager at Grand Belle), Máté Haumann (Concierge at Grand Belle), István Göz (Doorman at Grand Belle), Attila Árpa (Security at Grand Belle), Joël Lefrançois (Manager at Le Petite Sommeil), Virág Bárány (Maid at Le Petite Sommeil), Shay Cunliffe (Cashier at Eiffel Tower), Barna Illyés, Dániel Mogács, Gábor Nagypál (Paparazzi), Matt Devere (Steward on Jet), Christophe Malavoy (Bernard Marchand), Giulio Berruti (Prince Domenico da Silvano), Bruno Abraham-Kremer (Police Captain), Arnaud Aldigé (Bellhop at Hotel de Paris), Antal Leisen (Room Service at Hotel de Paris), Richard Rifkin, Sophie Care Thompson (Auction Bidders), George Mendel (Auction Announcer), Séverine Vasselin (Waitress on Yacht), Vilma Szécsi (Flower Market Woman), Ben O'Brien (Strolling Policeman), Bernadette Kis (Touring Architect, Romania), Éva Magyar (School Director, Romania)

Grace and her friends' Paris trip takes on an all-new level of glamour when Grace poses as a visiting British heiress and is suddenly given the royal treatment.

Leighton Meester, Selena Gomez, Katie Cassidy © Twentieth Century Fox

Charlie Day, Jennifer Aniston

Donald Sutherland, Colin Farrell, Jason Sudeikis

Jason Bateman, Kevin Spacey

Jason Bateman, Jason Sudeikis, Charlie Day, Jamie Foxx

HORRIBLE BOSSES

(NEW LINE/WARNER BROS.) Producers, Brett Ratner, Jay Stern; Executive Producers, Toby Emmerich, Richard Brener, Michael Disco, Samuel J. Brown, Diana Pokorny; Co-Producers, John Rickard, John Cheng; Director, Seth Gordon; Screenplay, Michael Markowitz, John Francis Daley, Jonathan Goldstein; Story, Michael Markowitz; Photography, David Hennings; Designer, Shepherd Frankel; Costumes, Carol Ramsey; Music, Christopher Lennertz; Music Supervisor, Dana Sano; Editor, Peter Teschner; Casting, Lisa Beach, Sarah Katzman; a New Line Cinema presentation of a Rat Entertainment production; Dolby; Panavision; Deluxe color; Rated R; 98 minutes; Release date: July 8, 2011

CAST

Nick Hendricks	**Jason Bateman**
Dale Arbus	**Charlie Day**
Kurt Buckman	**Jason Sudeikis**
Dr. Julia Harris, D.D.S.	**Jennifer Aniston**
Bobby Pellitt	**Colin Farrell**
Dave Harken	**Kevin Spacey**
Jack Pellitt	**Donald Sutherland**
Dean "Motherfucker" Jones	**Jamie Foxx**
Rhonda Harken	**Julie Bowen**
Stacy	**Lindsay Sloane**
Margie Emerman	**Celia Finkelstein**
Hank Preston	**Scott Rosendall**
Wet Work Man	**Ioan Gruffudd**
Lou Sherman	**Bob Newhart**

Brian George (Voice of Amanand), P.J. Byrne (Kenny Sommerfeld), Steve Wiebe (Thomas, Head of Security), Michael Albala (Mr. Anderton), Jennifer Hasty, Reginald Ballard, George Back, Barry Livingston (Kurt's Co-Workers), Meghan Markle (Jamie), John Francis Daley (Carter), Dave Sheridan (Bartender, Bradford's Bar), Chad L. Coleman (Bartender, Dive Bar), Diana Toshiko, Carla Maria Cadotte (Bobby's Girls), Peter Breitmayer (Pharmacist), Isaiah Mustafa (Officer Wilkens), Wendell Pierce (Det. Hagan), Ron White (Det. Samson), Jimm Giannini, Dawn Frances (Harken Party Guests), Andrew Lukich (Cop #1), Seth Gordon (Voice of Ralph Peterberg)

Tired of the abuse they receive from their respective bosses, three friends plot to have them murdered.

ZOOKEEPER

(COLUMBIA/MGM) Producers, Todd Garner, Kevin James, Adam Sandler, Jack Giarraputo, Walt Becker; Executive Producers, Barry Bernardi, Jeff Sussman, Charles Newirth, Jennfier Eatz; Director, Frank Coraci; Screenplay, Nick Bakay, Rock Reuben, Kevin James, Jay Scherick, David Ronn; Story, Jay Scherick, David Ronn; Photography, Michael Barrett; Designer, Kirk M. Petruccelli; Costumes, Mona May; Music , Rupert Gregson-Williams; Music Supervisor, Michael Dilbeck; Editor, Scott Hill; Visual Effects Supervisor, Peter G. Travers; Special Visual Effects, Sony Pictures Imageworks Inc.; Animatronic Character Effects Designers/Creators, Alec Gillis, Tom Woodruff, Jr.; Casting, Kim Davis, Justine Baddeley; Stunts, Jeff Gibson; a Broken Road/Hey Eddie/Happy Madison production; Dolby; Panavision; Deluxe color; Rated PG; 103 minutes; Release date: July 8, 2011

CAST
Griffin Keyes	**Kevin James**
Kate	**Rosario Dawson**
Stephanie	**Leslie Bibb**
Venom	**Ken Jeong**
Shane	**Donnie Wahlberg**
Voices:	
Bernie the Gorilla	**Nick Nolte**
Donald the Monkey	**Adam Sandler**
Joe the Lion	**Sylvester Stallone**
Janet the Lioness	**Cher**
Barry the Elephant	**Judd Apatow**
Jerome the Bear	**Jon Favreau**
Bruce the Bear	**Faizon Love**
Mollie the Giraffe	**Maya Rudolph**
Sebastian the Wolf	**Bas Rutten**
Frog	**Don Rickles**
Crow	**Jim Breuer**
Ostrich	**Richie Minervini**

and: Joe Rogan (Gale), Nat Faxon (Dave), Steffiana De La Cruz (Robin), Nick Bakay (Franky), Jackie Sandler (TGIF Waitress), Nick Turturro (Manny), Thomas Gottschalk (Jurgen), Brandon Keener (Nimer), Robin Bakay (Rebecca), Gary Valentine (Pizza Guy), Tanner Blaze (Little Boy at Zoo), Tim Gage (Bike Guy), Gino Falsetto (Valet), Etienne Deneault (Acrobat), Katrina Begin (Secretary at TGIF), Matthew R. Staley (Glenn), Michael Burton (Car Customer), Todd Zeile (High Roller), Mookie Barker (Grandfather), Tara Giordano (Shana), Daniel Guire, Mark DellaGrotte (Salesmen), Ellen Colton (Shane's Mother), Barry Bernardi (Cab Driver), Juston McKinney (Upscale Restaurant Manager), Bart (Jerome the Bear), Honey Bump (Bruce the Bear)

A forlorn zookeeper, still suffering after being dumped by his girlfriend, receives advice on love and dating from the animals at the zoo.

Ken Jeong, Kevin James, Rosario Dawson

Kevin James, Leslie Bibb

Barry the Elephant, Kevin James

Bernie the Gorilla, Kevin James © Columbia/MGM

BEATS RHYMES & LIFE:
THE TRAVELS OF A TRIBE CALLED QUEST

(SONY CLASSICS) Producers, Edward Parks, Frank Mele, Michael Rapaport, Eric Matthies, Robert Benavides, Debra Koffler, ATCQ; Co-Producers, Justin Alvarado Brown, Erika Williams; Director/Screenplay, Michael Rapaport; Photography, Robert Benavides; Music, Madlib; Editor, Lenny Mesina; a Rival Pictures/State Street Films Pictures production; Dolby; Color; DV; Rated R; 97 minutes; Release date: July 8, 2011. Documentary on the hip-hop group A Tribe Called Quest.

WITH
Q-Tip, Phife Dawg, Ali Shaheed Mohammed, Jarobi White, Adam Yauch, Mike D, Adam Horovitz, Pharrell Williams, DJ Red Alert, Prince Paul, Large Professor, Pete Rock, Barry Weiss, Common, Mary J. Blige, Amir 'Questlove' Thompson, Andreas Titus, Angela Martibez, Barbara Esmilla, Robert Garcia, Cheryl Taylor, Ludacris, Violatest, Deisha Head Taylor, Drea Smith, Doc McKinney, Rashied Lonnie Lyn, Dexter Mills, Mos Def, Jerry Tineo, Kelvin Mercer, Kenny 'the Jet' Smith, Lester Fernandez, Paul Huston, Michael Small, Monie Love, Nathaniel Hall, Robert Power, Tariq Trotter, Walter Cummings, DJ Maseo, W.P. Mitchell, Too $hort, Skeff Anselm, The Beatnuts, Danny Boy, Teddy Tedd and Special K of Awesome 2, Consequence, Phesto D., Dave, De La Soul, DJ Lethal, 9th Winder, Dres, Everlast, Jungle Brothers, Ghostface Killah, Talib Kweli, Opio, Prince Paul, A-Plus, Posdnus, Freddy Rodriguez, Dante Ross, Jim Swaffield, Tajai, Chang Weisberg, Michael Rapaport

Q-Tip, Phife Dawn, Ali Shaheed Mohammed, Jarobi White

Common

Questlove © Sony Classics

Sholem Aleichem © Intl. Film Circuit

SHOLEM ALEICHEM:
LAUGHING IN THE DARKNESS

(INTERNATIONAL FILM CIRCUIT) Producer/ Director/Screenplay, Joseph Dorman; Photography, Edward Marritz; Narrator, Alan Rosenberg; Music, John Zorn; Editors, Aaron Kuhn, Kenneth Levis, Amanda Zinoman; a Riverside Films production; Dolby; Color/Black and white; Not rated; 93 minutes; Release date: July 8, 2011. Documentary on writer Sholem Aleichem's importance in the Jewish community

WITH
Mendy Cahan, Bel Kaufman, Hillel Halkin, Sheldon Harnick, Aaron Lansky, Dan Miron, Avram Nowersztern, David Roskies, Michael Stanislawski, Ruth Wisse; and Peter Riegert (Tevye), Rachel Dratch (Sheyne Sheyndl/Stepmother), Jason Kravits (Menachem Mendl), Daniel Lerman (Motl the Cantor's Son)

Gringotts Dragon

Daniel Radcliffe, Warwick Davis

Alan Rickman

HARRY POTTER AND THE DEATHLY HALLOWS PART 2

(WARNER BROS.) Producers, David Heyman, David Barron, J.K. Rowling; Executive Producer, Lionel Wigram; Co-Producers, John Trehy, Tim Lewis; Director, David Yates; Screenplay, Steve Kloves; Based on the novel by J.K. Rowling; Photography, Eduardo Serra; Designer, Stuart Craig; Costumes, Jany Temime; Music, Alexandre Desplat; Editor, Mark Day; Visual Effects Supervisors, Tim Burke, Chris Shaw, John Moffatt; Special Make-up Effects, Nick Dudman; Casting, Fiona Weir; a Heyday Films production; Dolby; Panavision; Techincolor; 3D; Rated PG-13; 131 minutes; Release date: July 15, 2011

CAST

Harry Potter	**Daniel Radcliffe**
Ron Weasley	**Rupert Grint**
Hermione Granger	**Emma Watson**
Bellatrix Lestrange	**Helena Bonham Carter**
Rubeus Hagrid	**Robbie Coltrane**
Griphook/Professor Filius Flitwick	**Warwick Davis**
Lord Voldemort	**Ralph Fiennes**
Professor Albus Dumbledore	**Michael Gambon**
Aberforth Dumbledore	**Ciarán Hinds**
Lucius Malfoy	**Jason Isaacs**
Narcissa Malfoy	**Helen McCrory**
Professor Severus Snape	**Alan Rickman**
Professor Minerva McGonagall	**Maggie Smith**
Molly Weasley	**Julie Walters**
Draco Malfoy	**Tom Felton**
Neville Longbottom	**Matthew Lewis**
Luna Lovegood	**Evanna Lynch**
Ginny Weasley	**Bonnie Wright**
Argus Filch	**David Bradley**
Professor Horace Slughorn	**Jim Broadbent**
Kingsley Shacklebolt	**George Harris**
Ollivander	**John Hurt**
Madam Pomfrey	**Gemma Jones**
Helena Ravenclaw	**Kelly Macdonald**
Professor Pomona Sprout	**Miriam Margolyes**
Sirius Black	**Gary Oldman**
Wormtail	**Timothy Spall**
Nymphadora Tonks	**Natalia Tena**
Remus Lupin	**David Thewlis**
Professor Sybil Trelawney	**Emma Thompson**
Arthur Weasley	**Mark Williams**
Bill Weasley	**Domhnall Gleeson**
Lavender Brown	**Jessie Cave**
Cho Chang	**Katie Leung**
Seamus Finnigan	**Devon Murray**
Fred Weasley	**James Phelps**
George Weasley	**Oliver Phelps**
Fleur Delacour	**Clémence Poésy**

Graham Duff, Penelope McGhie, Peter G. Reed, Judith Sharp, Emil Hostina, Bob Yves van Hellenberg Hubar, Granville Saxton, Tony Kirwood, Ashley McGuire (Death Eaters), Anthony Allgood (Gringotts Guard), Rusty Goffe (Aged Gringotts Goblin), Jon Key (Bogrod), Ian Peck, Benn Northover (Hogsmede Death Eaters), Hebe Beardsall (Ariana Dumbledore), Afshan Azad (Padma Patil), Isabella Laughland (Leanne), Anna Shaffer (Romilda Vane), Georgina Leonidas (Katie Bell), Freddie Stroma (Cormac McLaggen), Alfie Enoch (Dean Thomas), William Melling (Nigel), Sian Grace Phillips (Screaming Girl), Ralph Ineson (Amycus Carrow), Suzanne Toase (Alecto Carrow), Scarlett Byrne (Pansy Parkinson), Josh Herdman (Gregory Goyle), Louis Cordice (Blaise Zabini), Amber Evans, Ruby Evans (Twins), Chris Rankin (Percy Weasley), Guy Henry (Pius Thicknesse), Nick

Moran (Scabior), Phil Wright, Gary Sayer, Tony Adkins (Giants), Dave Legeno (Fenrir Greyback), Ellie Darcey-Alden (Young Lily Potter), Ariella Paradise (Young Petunia Dursley), Benedict Clarke (Young Severus Snape), Leslie Phillips (Voice of the Sorting Hat), Alfie McIlwain (Young James Potter), Rohan Gotobed (Young Sirius Black), Geraldine Sommerville (Lily Potter), Adrian Rawlins (James Potter), Toby Papworth (Baby Harry Potter), Arthur Bowen (Albus Severus Potter, 19 Years Later), Daphne de Beistegui (Lily Potter, 19 Years Later), William Dunn (James Sirius Potter, 19 Years Later), Jade Gordon (Astoria Malfoy, 19 Years Later), Bertie Gilbert (Scorpius Malfoy, 19 Years Later), Helena Barlow (Rose Weasley, 19 Years Later), Ryan Turner (Hugo Weasley, 19 Years Later)

Harry Potter and his friends Hermione and Ron continue to search for the Horcruxes that will hopefully destroy Voldemort as the evil wizard unleashes his army of Death Eaters upon the Hogwarts School. Final installment in the Warner Bros. series following: *Harry Potter and the Sorcerer's Stone* (2001), *Harry Potter and the Chamber of Secrets* (2002), *Harry Potter and the Prisoner of Azkaban* (2004), *Harry Potter and the Goblet of Fire* (2005), *Harry Potter and the Order of the Phoenix* (2007), *Harry Potter and the Half-Blood Prince* (2009), and *Harry Potter and the Deathly Hallows Part 1* (2010).

This film received Oscar nominations for art direction, visual effects, and makeup.

Daniel Radcliffe, Maggie Smith © Warner Bros.

Ciarán Hinds, Rupert Grint, Emma Watson

Rupert Grint, Helena Bonham Carter

James Phelps, Rupert Grint, Chris Rankin, Emma Watson, Julie Walters, George Harris

Jason Isaacs, Helen McCrory, Tom Felton

WINNIE THE POOH

(WALT DISNEY STUDIOS) Producers, Peter Del Vecho, Clark Spencer; Executive Producer, John Lasseter; Directors, Stephen Anderson, Don Hall; Story, Stephen Anderson, Clio Chiang, Don Dougherty, Don Hall, Kendelle Hoyer, Brian Kesinger, Nicole Mitchell, Jeremy Spears; Based on the *Winnie the Pooh* books by A.A. Milne and E.H. Shepard; Music, Henry Jackman; Songs, Kristen Anderson-Lopez, Robert Lopez; Title Song, Richard M. Sherman, Robert B. Sherman/peformed by Zooey Deschanel; Music Supervisor, Tom MacDougall; Visual Effects Supervisor, Kyle Odermatt; Editor, Lisa Linder Silver; Casting, Jaime Sparer Roberts; a Walt Disney Pictures presentation; Dolby; Deluxe color; Rated G; 69 minutes; Release date: July 15, 2011

VOICE CAST
Narrator	**John Cleese**
Winnie the Pooh/Tigger	**Jim Cummings**
Eeyore	**Bud Luckey**
Owl	**Craig Ferguson**
Christopher Robin	**Jack Boulter**
Piglet	**Travis Oates**
Kanga	**Kristen Anderson-Lopez**
Roo	**Wyatt Dean Hall**
Rabbit	**Tom Kenny**
Backson	**Huell Howser**

Winnie the Pooh and his pals mistakenly believe that Christopher Robin has been abducted by a fearsome monster called Backson.

Piglet (top); Kanga, Roo, Owl, Tigger, Winnie the Pooh, Eeyore, Rabbit © Walt Disney Studios

Joyce McKinney

Joyce McKinney (right) © Sundance Selects

TABLOID

(SUNDANCE SELECTS) Producers, Julie Bilson Ahlberg, Mark Lipson; Executive Producers, Robert Fernandez, Errol Morris, Angus Wall; Director, Errol Morris; Photography, Robert Chappell; Designer, Steve Hardie; Music, John Kusiak; Editor, Grant Surmi; Graphics, Rob Feng, Jeremy Landman; an Air Loom Enterprises & Moxie Pictures presentation; Dolby; Color/Black and white; Widescreen; HD/16mm/VHS/DigiBeta; Rated R; 88 minutes; Release date: July 15, 2011. Documentary about former beauty queen Joyce McKinney's involvement in the 1978 Kirk Anderson kidnapping.

WITH
Joyce McKinney, Kent Gavin, Dr. Jin Han Hong, Jackson Shaw, Peter Tory, Troy Williams

Patricia Clarkson, Mila Kunis

FRIENDS WITH BENEFITS

(SCREEN GEMS) Producers, Martin Shafer, Liz Glotzer, Jerry Zucker, Janet Zucker, Will Gluck; Executive Producer, Glenn S. Gainor; Director, Will Gluck; Screenplay, Keith Merryman, David A. Newman, Will Gluck; Story, Harley Peyton, Keith Merryman, David A. Newman; Photography, Michael Grady; Designer, Marcia Hinds; Costumes, Renee Ehrlich Kalfus; Music Supervisor, Wende Crowley; Editor, Tia Nolan; Casting, Lisa Miller Katz; a Castle Rock Entertainment/Zucker/ Olive Bridge Entertainment production; Dolby; Panavision; Deluxe color; Rated R; 110 minutes; Release date: July 22, 2011

CAST

Dylan Harper	**Justin Timberlake**
Jamie Rellis	**Mila Kunis**
Lorna	**Patricia Clarkson**
Annie Harper	**Jenna Elfman**
Parker	**Bryan Greenberg**
Mr. Harper	**Richard Jenkins**
Tommy Bollinger	**Woody Harrelson**
Sam	**Nolan Gould**
Quincy	**Andy Samberg**
Himself	**Shaun White**
Kayla	**Emma Stone**
Brice	**Jason Segel**
Maddison	**Rashida Jones**

Andrew Fleming (Driver), Catherine Reitman (Co-Worker), Courtney Henggeler (Flight Attendant), Masi Oka (Darin Arturo Morena), Tiya Sircar (Hostess), Christopher T. Wood (Ira Ungerleider), Lili Mirojnick (Laura), Rupak Ginn (Co-Worker, LA), Duane Shepard Sr. (Older Man), Chike Johnson (Taxi Driver), Angelique Cabral (Pam Niborski), Lance Kerfuffle (Security Guard), Jerry Ying (Photographer), Jerry Hyman (Caricaturist), Nick Lee (Dylan's Neighbor), Jason Sung Lee (Dylan's Friend), Michael Morris (Carriage Driver), Brooklyn McLinn (Policeman), Timothy Bish, LaJon Dantzler, Angel Feliciano, Laura Fremont, Nicole Guidetti, Alicia Mazepa, Mayumi Miguel, Jermaine Montell, Joanna Numata, Danielle Polanco, Wes Pope, Steven Rosa, Seth Stewart, Deanna Walters, Adam Zotovich (Dancers)

Not interested in starting up a romantic relationship, Dylan and Jamie decide to treat one another strictly as sex partners, hoping that it does not disrupt their friendship.

Jenna Elfman, Justin Timberlake, Mila Kunis

Richard Jenkins, Woody Harrelson, Justin Timberlake

Chris Evans, Sebastian Stan

Chris Evans, Hayley Atwell

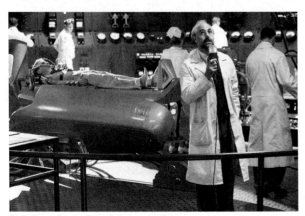

Chris Evans, Stanley Tucci © Paramount Pictures

Chris Evans

Chris Evans

Dominic Cooper, Chris Evans

CAPTAIN AMERICA: The First Avenger

(PARAMOUNT) Producer, Kevin Feige; Executive Producers, Louis D'Esposito, Joe Johnston, Nigel Gostelow; Alan Fine, Stan Lee, David Maisel; Director, Joe Johnston; Screenplay, Christopher Markus, Stephen McFeely; Based on the Marvel comic by Joe Simon and Jack Kirby; Photography, Shelly Johnson; Designer, Rich Heinrichs; Costumes, Anna B. Sheppard; Music, Alan Silvestri; Music Supervisor, Dave Jordan; Editors, Jeffrey Ford, Robert Dalva; Co-Producers, Stephen Broussard, Victoria Alonso; Visual Effects Supervisor, Christopher Townsend; Special Effects Supervisor, Paul Corbould; Visual Effects and Animation, Double Negative; Stunts, Steve Dent; a Marvel Entertainment presentation of a Marvel Studios production; Dolby; Panavision; 3D; Color; Rated PG-13; 124 minutes; Release date: July 22, 2011

Hayley Atwell

CAST

Steve Rogers/Captain America	**Chris Evans**
Colonel Chester Phillips	**Tommy Lee Jones**
Johann Schmidt/The Red Skull	**Hugo Weaving**
Peggy Carter	**Hayley Atwell**
James Buchanan "Bucky" Barnes	**Sebastian Stan**
Howard Stark	**Dominic Cooper**
Dr. Arnim Zola	**Toby Jones**
Timothy "Dum Dum" Dugan	**Neal McDonough**
Gabe Jones	**Derek Luke**
Jim Morita	**Kenneth Choi**
Heinz Kruger	**Richard Armitage**
James Montgomery Falsworth	**JJ Feild**
Jacques Dernier	**Bruno Ricci**
Dr. Abraham Erskine	**Stanley Tucci**
Nick Fury	**Samuel L. Jackson**
Gilmore Hodge	**Lex Shrapnel**
Senator Brandt	**Michael Brandon**
Brandt's Aide	**Martin T. Sherman**
Pvt. Lorraine	**Natalie Dormer**
Search Team Leader	**Oscar Pearce**

William Hope (SHIELD Lieutenant), Nicholas Pinnock (SHIELD Tech), Marek Oravec (Jan), David Bradley (Tower Keeper), Leander Deeny (Steve Rogers Double/Barman), Sam Hoare (Nervous Recruit), Simon Kunz (4F Doctor), Kieran O'Connor (Loud Jerk), Jenna-Louise Coleman (Connie), Sophie Colquhoun (Bonnie), Doug Cockle (Young Doctor), Ben Batt (Enlistment Office MP), Mollie Fitzgerald (Stark Girl), Damon Driver (Sgt. Duffy), David McKail (Johann Schmidt's Artist), Amanda Walker (Antique Store Owner), Richard Freeman (SSR Doctor), Katherine Press (Project Rebirth Nurse), Sergio Corvino (Kruger's Aide), Marcello Walton, Vincent Montuel (Undercover Bums), Fabrizio Santino (Kruger's Driver), Maxwell Newman (Boy at Dock), Anatole Taubman (Roeder), Jan Pohl (Hutter), Erich Redman (Schneider), Rosanna Hoult, Naomi Slights, Kirsty Mather (The Star Spangled Singers), Megan Sanderson, Darren Simpson (Kids in USO Audience), Fernanda Toker (Newsstand Mom), Laura Haddock (Autograph Seeker), James Payton ("Adolph Hitler"), Ronan Raferty, Nick Hendrix, Luke Allen-Gale, Jack Gordon (Army Hecklers), Ben Uttley (HYDRA Guard/HYDRA Pilot), Kevin Millington (Stark's Engineer), Patrick Monckeberg (Manager Velt), Peter Stark (HYDRA Lieutenant), Amanda Righetti (SHIELD Agent), Stan Lee (Man at Ceremony)

Hugo Weaving

Eager to serve his country during World War II, scrawny Steve Rogers agrees to participate in an experimental program to turn him into a Super-Soldier.

Tommy Lee Jones, Hayley Atwell, Chris Evans

THE MYTH OF THE AMERICAN SLEEPOVER

(SUNDANCE SELECTS) Producer, Adele Romanski; Executive Producer, Michael Ferris Gibson; Director/Screenplay, David Robert Mitchell; Photography, James Laxton; Designer, Jeanine A. Nicholas; Music, Kyle Newmaster, William Ryan Fritch; Editor, Julio C. Perez IV; a Roman Spring Pictures presentation; Color; Not rated; 93 minutes; Release date: July 22, 2011

CAST
Maggie	**Claire Sloma**
Rob Salvati	**Marlon Morton**
Claudia	**Amanda Bauer**
Scott Holland	**Brett Jacobsen**
Ady Abbey	**Nikita Ramsey**
Anna Abbey	**Jade Ramsey**
Beth	**Annette DeNoyer**

Wyatt McCallum (Marcus), Mary Wardell (Jen Holland), Doug Diedrich (Steven), Dane Jones (Emma), Shayla Curran (Janelle Ramsey), Christopher Simon (Sean Barber), Madi Oritz (Avalina Height), Stephen Francis (Cameron Nichols), Drew Machak (Andy), Amy Seimetz (Julie), Kathleen McEneaney (Katie Parke), Olivia Coté (Mandy), Danny Agar (Tom Higgins), Amelia Anderson (Pam), Mai Hlee Xiong (Susan), Hannah Nelson (Redhead Girl), Gino Raona (Jeff), Lauren Romanowski (Laurie), Marnie Lewbel (Rob's Mother), Laura Ortiz (Avalina's Mother), Kimberly Lilly, Claire R. Call (Dancers), Shelley Fager-Bajorek (Dance Instructor), Walter McCarthy (Drunk Kid), Peter Flannery II (Drunk Kid's Friend), Josh Hartkorn (Annoying Kid), Diane B. LaRue (University Faculty Woman), Tiffany Bowery, Paris Bowery (Make-out Maze Girls)

On the last night of summer before the start of school, four teens and their friends cross paths as they bask in their final evening of "freedom."

Marlon Morton, Wyatt McCallum © Sundance Selects

Brit Marling, William Mapother © Fox Searchlight

ANOTHER EARTH

(FOX SEARCHLIGHT) Producers, Hunter Gray, Mike Cahill, Brit Marling, Nicholas Shumaker; Executive Producers, Tyler Brodie, Paul Mezey; Director/Photography/Editor, Mike Cahill; Screenplay, Mike Cahill, Brit Marling; Designer, Darsi Monaco; Costumes, Aileen Diana; Music, Fall on Your Sword; Visual Effects Supervisors, Adam Fanton, Darren Fanton; Casting, James Calleri, Paul Davis; an Artists Public Domain presentation; Dolby; Color; HD; Rated PG-13; 92 minutes; Release date: July 22, 2011

CAST
Rhoda Williams	**Brit Marling**
John Burroughs	**William Mapother**
Alex	**Matthew-Lee Erlbach**
Maya Burroughs	**Meggan Lennon**
Amos Burroughs	**AJ Diana**
Kim Williams	**Jordan Baker**
Robert Williams	**Flint Beverage**
Jeff Williams	**Robin Lord Taylor**

DJ Flava, Dr. Richard Berendzen (Themselves), Bruce Colbert, Paul Mezey, Ana Valle, Jeffrey Goldenberg, Joseph Bove (Symposium Speakers), Shannon Maliff, Stephanie Le Blanc, Jasmine Andrade, Kara Tweedie (High School Girls), Rupert Reid (Keith Harding), Natalie Carter (Career Counselor), Kumar Pallana (Purdeep), Ana Kayne (Claire), Yuval Segal (Television Reporter), Diane Ciesla (Dr. Joan Tallis), Robert Phillips, Rich Habersham (Radio Reporters), Hollyce Phillips (Television Anchor), Luis Vega (Federico), Jennfier Jaramillo (Nurse), Ari Gold (Conspiracy Theorist), Steve "Major" Giammaria (Television Interviewer), Rebecca Price (Keith Harding's Secretary)

Released from prison after killing two people in a car accident while intoxicated, a shattered Rhoda Williams hopes to attone for her crime by being chosen to visit Earth 2, an alternate planet that offers the possibility of a new life.

Ron Liebman, Lesley Ann Warren, Daniel Yelsky, Jenna Fischer
© Freestyle Releasing

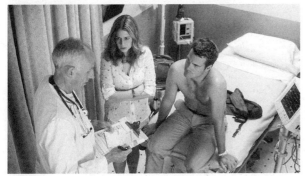

Jenna Fischer, Chris O'Donnell

A LITTLE HELP

(FREESTYLE) Producers, Dena Hysell, Joe Gressis, Michael J. Weithorn; Line Producer, Sirad Balducci; Associate Producer, Glen Trotner; Director/Screenplay, Michael J. Weithorn; Photography, Thomas M. Harting; Designer, Kelly McGehee; Costumes, Jenny Gering; Music, Austin Wintory; Editor, Joe Gressis; Casting, Rick Pagano, Russell Boast; a Secret Handshake Entertainment presentation; Dolby; Color; HD-to-DigiBeta; Rated R; 109 minutes; Release date: July 22, 2011

CAST
Laura	**Jenna Fischer**
Bob	**Chris O'Donnell**
Mel Kaminsky	**Kim Coates**
Joan	**Lesley Ann Warren**
Kathy Helms	**Brooke Smith**
Nancy Feldman	**Aida Turturro**
Warren	**Ron Leibman**
Dennis	**Daniel Yelsky**

Rob Benedict (Paul), Nadia Dajani (Angela Behar), Sam McMurray (Big Bad Dan), Arden Myrin (Ms. Gallagher), Lynn Cohen (Mrs. Cosolito), Shari Albert (Rhonda), Dion DiMucci (Himself), Sarah Wilson (Amanda), Michelle Hurst (Eileen), Gracie Lawrence (Gracie), Jim Florentine (Brian), Joy Suprano (Julie), Zach Page (Kyle), Sara Kapner (Wendy), Miles Williams (Christopher), Mark Vincent (Garage Mechanic), Elaine Kussack (Sara), Markus Goldberg (Birthday Party Guest), Brandon Perler (Noah), Carla Briscoe (Kristen)

A Long Island dental hygienist struggles to cope with her increasingly stressful life, including her angry 12-year-old son, her possibly philandering husband, and her critical parents.

THE FUTURE

(ROADSIDE ATTRACTIONS) Producers, Gina Kwon, Roman Paul, Gerhard Meixner; Executive Producer, Sue Bruce-Smith; Co-Producer, Chris Stinson; Director/Screenplay, Miranda July; Photography, Nikolai von Graevenitz; Designer, Elliott Hostetter; Costumes, Christie Wittenborn; Music, Jon Brion; Music Supervisor, Margaret Yen; Editor, Andrew Bird; Casting, Jeanne McCarthy, Nicole Abellera; a Razor Films, GNK Productions and Film4 presentation in association with The Match Factory and Haut et Court with the support of Medienboard Berlin-Brandenburg and Filmförderungsanstalt; American-German; Dolby; Color; Rated R; 91 minutes; Release date: July 29, 2011

CAST
Sophie/Voice of Paw-Paw	**Miranda July**
Jason	**Hamish Linklater**
Marshall	**David Warshofsky**
Gabriella	**Isabella Acres**
Joe/Voice of the Moon	**Joe Putterlik**
Dr. Straus	**Kathleen Gati**

Angela Trimbur (Dance Studio Receptionist), Mary Passeri (Animal Shelter Receptionist), Clement von Franckenstein (Alain First Solicitation), Tonita Castro (Second Solicitation), Diana Sandoval (Neighbor Woman), Mark Atteberry (Tree by Tree Canvasser), Frank Langley (T-Shirt Puppeteer), Erinn K. Williams (Tammy), Oona Mekas (Sasha), Ryker Baloun (Barry at 3), Olivia Thiering (Carrie at 3), Taylor Cosgrove Scofield (Barry at 10), Sara Rodier (Carrie at 10), Brittney Hewitt (Carrie at 15), Matthew Dunn (Barry at 15), Bru Muller (Barry at 35), Aubree Knecht (Carrie at 35), Samantha Milazzo (Jayleen), Andy Forrest (Last Solicitation)

After adopting a stray cat, a couple unsure about the direction their lives are going decide to quit their jobs and follow different paths.

Miranda July, Hamish Linklater

Miranda July
© Roadside Attractions

Steve Carell, Julianne Moore

Marisa Tomei

Steve Carell, Analeigh Tipton © Warner Bros.

Ryan Gosling, Emma Stone

Josh Groban, Emma Stone

Steve Carell, Jonah Bobo, Joey King

Kevin Bacon, John Carroll Lynch, Ryan Gosling, Steve Carell

Liza Lapira, Emma Stone

CRAZY, STUPID, LOVE.

(WARNER BROS.) Producers, Steve Carell, Denise Di Novi; Executive Producers, David A. Siegel, Vance DeGeneres, Charlie Hartsock; Directors, Glenn Ficarra, John Requa; Screenplay, Dan Fogelman; Photography, Andrew Dunn; Designer, William Arnold; Costumes, Dayna Pink; Music, Christophe Beck, Nick Urata; Editor, Lee Haxall; Casting, Mindy Marin; a Carousel production, a Di Novi Pictures production; Dolby; Super 35 Widescreen; Technicolor; Rated PG-13; 118 minutes; Release date: July 29, 2011

CAST
Cal Weaver	**Steve Carell**
Jacob Palmer	**Ryan Gosling**
Emily Weaver	**Julianne Moore**
Hannah	**Emma Stone**
Kate Taffety	**Marisa Tomei**
David Lindhagen	**Kevin Bacon**
Robbie Weaver	**Jonah Bobo**
Richard	**Josh Groban**
Molly Weaver	**Joey King**

Liza Lapira (Liz), Beth Littleford (Claire Riley), John Carroll Lynch (Bernie Riley), Analeigh Tipton (Jessica Riley), Mekia Cox (Hip Hairdresser, a.k.a. Tiffany), Julianna Guill (Madison), Zayne Emory (Robbie's Friend, Eric), Crystal Reed (Amy Johnson), Joanne Brooks (Waitress for Cal and Kate), Reggie Lee (Officer Huang), Caitlin Thompson (Taylor), Karolina Wydra (Jordyn), Tracy Mulholland (Megan), Katerina Mikailenko (Stephanie), Janine Barris (Heather), Jenny Mollen (Lisa), Charlie Hartsock (Sad Sack), Algerita Lewis (Robbie's Principal), Wendy Worthington (Woman Who Gives Cal Tour), Dan Butler (Cal's Boss), Tiara Parker (Gabby), Laurel Coppock (Sophia), Rasika Mathur (Emily's Assistant), Joshua Sternlicht, Jasen Salvatore, Michael Long, Dillon Neaman, J-Ray Hochfield, Janae Nicole Caudillo, Heather La Bella (Bartenders), Christopher Darga, Rich Hutchman, Richard Horvitz (Lowe's Salesmen), Lauren Stone (Mail Clerk), Megan James, Rebecca Flinn, Billy Atchison, Ehrin Marlow, David Orosz, Camille Abelow (Hannah's Colleagues), Maija Polsley (Jacob's Date), Christian Pitre (Waitress with Check), Georgia Hurd, Lisa Brown, Tingting Yu (Jacob's Girls), Ami Haruna (Ami), Jessica Diz (Olivia), Tania Wagner (Tania), Georgia Treantafelles (Georgia), Holly Daniels (Assistant Principal), Raena Cassidy (Raena)

After his wife announces that they are breaking up, Cal finds himself back in the singles scene where he receives dating advice from an ultra-confident ladies' man.

Steve Carell, Caitlin Thompson, Ryan Gosling

COWBOYS & ALIENS

(UNIVERSAL/DREAMWORKS) Producers, Brian Grazer, Ron Howard, Alex Kurtzman, Roberto Orci, Scott Mitchell Rosenberg; Executive Producers, Steven Spielberg, Jon Favreau, Denis L. Stewart, Bobby Cohen, Randy Greenberg, Ryan Kavanaugh; Director, Jon Favreau; Screenplay, Roberto Orci, Alex Kurtzman, Damon Lindelof, Mark Fergus, Hawk Ostby; Screen Story, Mark Fergus, Hawk Ostby, Steve Oedekerk; Based on Plantinum Studios' comic book *Cowboys and Aliens* by Scott Mitchell Rosenberg; Photography, Matthew Libatique; Designer, Scott Chambliss; Costumes, Mary Zophres; Music, Harry Gregson-Williams; Editor, Dan Lebental; Alien Character and Effects Designer, Legacy Effects; Special Effects Supervisor, Dan Sudick; Visual Effects Supervisor, Roger Guyett; Visual Effects, Industrial Light & Magic, the Embassy Visual Effects, Ghost VFX, Fuel VFX, Shade FX, the Garage VFX; Casting, Sarah Halley Finn; a Universal Pictures/DreamWorks/Reliance Entertainment presentation in association with Relativity Media of an Imagine Entertainment, K/O Paper Products, Fairview Entertainment, Platinum Studios production; Dolby; Panavision; Deluxe Color; Rated PG-13; 118 minutes; Release date: July 29, 2011

Daniel Craig, Harrison Ford

CAST

Jake Lonergan	**Daniel Craig**
Woodrow Dolarhyde	**Harrison Ford**
Ella Swenson	**Olivia Wilde**
Doc	**Sam Rockwell**
Nat Colorado	**Adam Beach**
Percy Dolarhyde	**Paul Dano**
Emmett Taggart	**Noah Ringer**
Sheriff John Taggart	**Keith Carradine**
Meacham	**Clancy Brown**
Alice	**Abigail Spencer**
Wes Claiborne	**Buck Taylor**
Jed Parker	**Chris Browning**
Maria	**Ana de la Reguera**
Hunt	**Walton Goggins**
Pat Dolan	**David O'Hara**
Black Knife	**Raoul Trujillo**
Luke Claiborne	**Matthew Taylor**
Mose Claiborne	**Cooper Taylor**
Deputy	**Brian Duffy**
Charlie Lyle	**Brendan Wayne**
Ed	**Gavin Grazer**
Roy Murphy	**Toby Huss**
Little Mickey	**Wyatt Russell**
Greavey	**Kenny Call**
Bronc	**Julio Cesar Cedillo**
Red	**Troy Gilbert**
Bull McCade	**Chad Randall**

Ana de la Reguera, Sam Rockwell

Jimmy Jatho (Saloon Patron), Garret James Noel (Gang Member), Scout Hendrickson (Jake's Gang Member), David Midthunder, Moses Brings Plenty (Apache Warriors), Phillip Pike, Calum Blaylock (Apache Singers), Paul Ortega (Medicine Man), David Chee, Robyn Simmons, Simon Choneska, Nathaniel Chee, Vonda Tso, Lariat Geronimo, Freddy Apache, Oliver Enjady (Apache Dancers), Hoyle Osborne (Pianist), Rex Rideout (Fiddler)

Jake Lonergan arrives in town sporting a mysterious braclet which appears to be the only weapon that can battle an unexpected alien attack in which several townspeople are taken captive.

Harrison Ford, Sam Rockwell

Daniel Craig

Olivia Wilde

Harrison Ford © Universal/DreamWorks

Sam Rockwell, Adam Beach, Paul Dano

Daniel Craig, Harrison Ford

Brainy, Papa, Clumsy, Gutsy, Smurfette © Columbia Pictures

Neil Patrick Harris, Jayma Mays

Hank Azaria, Mr. Kinkle

THE SMURFS

(COLUMBIA) Producer, Jordan Kerner; Executive Producers, Ezra Swerdlow, Ben Haber, Paul Neesan; Director, Raja Gosnell; Screenplay, J. David Stem, David N. Weiss, Jay Scherick, David Ronn; Story, J. David Stem, David N. Weiss; based on the characters and works of Peyo; Photography, Phil Méheux; Designer, Bill Boes; Costumes, Rita Ryack; Music, Heitor Pereira; Editor, Sabrina Plisco; Visual Effects Supervisor, Richard R. Hoover; Casting, David Rubin, Richard Hicks; a Sony Pictures Animation presentation of a Kerner Entertainment Company production; Dolby; Deluxe Color; 3D; Rated PG; 103 minutes; Release date: July 29, 2011

CAST
Gargamel	**Hank Azaria**
Patrick Winslow	**Neil Patrick Harris**
Grace Winslow	**Jayma Mays**
Odile	**Sofia Vergara**
Henri	**Tim Gunn**

Smurf Voices:
Papa	**Jonathan Winters**
Gutsy	**Alan Cumming**
Smurfette	**Katy Perry**
Brainy	**Fred Armisen**
Grouchy	**George Lopez**
Clumsy	**Anton Yelchin**
Greedy	**Kenan Thompson**

Madison McKinley, Meg Phillips (Models), Julie Chang, Roger Clark (Newscasters), Mark Doherty (Bluetooth Businessman), Minglie Chen (Young Woman), Sean Kenin (Guy in Plaid Shirt), Victor Pagan (Bum), Mahadeo Shivraj (Cabbie), Adria Baratta (Anjelou Employee), Paula Pizzi (Odile's Mother), Andrew Sellon (Waiter), Julianna Rigoglioso (Little Sister), Daria Rae Figlo (Blonde Sister), Bradley Gosnell (Toy Salesperson), Heidi Armbruster, Finnerty Steeves (Toy Store Parents), John Speredakos (Parent with Girls), Skai Jackson (Kicking Girl), Alex Hall, Eric Redgate (Skateboard Kids), Jojo Gonzalez (FAO Custodian), Scotty Dillin, Tyree M. Simpson (Cops), Sean Ringgold (Inmate Bubba), Mario D'Leon (Bubba's Inmate Friend), Liz Smith, Tom Colicchio, Michael Musto, Joan Rivers, Olivia Palermo, Julia T. Enescu, Lauren Waggoner (Party Guests), Mr. Krinkle (Azrael), Hank (Elway); *Additonal Voices*: Jeff Foxworthy (Handy), John Oliver (Vanity), Wolfgang Puck (Chef), Gary Basaraba (Hefty), Paul Reubens (Jokey), B.J. Novak (Baker), Tom Kane (Narrator Smurf), John Kassir (Crazy Smurf), Joel McCrary (Farmer), Frank Welker (Azrael)

When the wicked Gargamel chases the Smurfs out of their village, the tiny blue people end up in the middle of New York City.

Neil Patrick Harris, Clumsy, Brainy, Smurfette, Gutsy, Papa

THE INTERRUPTERS

(THE CINEMA GUILD) Producers, Alex Kotlowitz, Steve James; Executive Producers, Justine Nagan, Gordon Quinn, Tedd Leifer, Paul Taylor; Co-Producer, Zak Piper; Director/Photography, Steve James; Inspired by the *New York Times* magazine article by Alex Kotlowitz; Music, Joshua Abrams; Music Supervisor, Linda Cohen; Editors, Aaron Wickenden, Steve James; a Kartemquin Films presentation for WGBH/Frontline and The Independent Television Service (ITVS) in association with Rise Films; Color; HD; Not rated; 125 minutes; Release date: July 29, 2011. Documentary on CeaseFire, a group of Chicago activists who attempt to intervene in street fights in an effort to find a peaceful resolution for the antagonists.

WITH
Eddie Bocanegra, Ameena Matthews, Cobe Williams, Tio Hardiman, Gary Slutkin, Toya Batey, Earl Sawyer

Cobe Williams © The Cinema Guild

Ameena Matthews

Tio Hardiman,
Eddie Bocanegra

Jessie Wiseman, Evan Glodell © Oscilloscope

BELLFLOWER

(OSCILLOSCOPE) Producers, Vincent Grashaw, Evan Glodell; Executive Producers, Brian Thomas Evans, Josh Kelling, Byron Yee; Co-Producers, Paul Edwardson, Lenny Powell, Joel Hodge, Chelsea St. John, Jonathan Keevil, Jet Kauffman; Director/Screenplay, Evan Glodell; Photography, Joel Hodge; Music, Jonathan Keevil; Editors, Evan Glodell, Joel Hodge, Jonathan Keevil, Vincent Grashaw; a Coatwolf Production; Dolby; Color; Rated R; 105 minutes; Release date: August 5, 2011

CAST
Woodrow	**Evan Glodell**
Milly	**Jessie Wiseman**
Aiden	**Tyler Dawson**
Courtney	**Rebekah Brandes**
Mike	**Vincent Grashaw**
Elliot	**Zack Kraus**
Sarah	**Keghan Hurst**

Alexandra Boylan (Caitlin, Mad Dog's Waitress), Bradshaw Pruitt (Mad Dog's Bartender), Brian Thomas Evans (Dirty Trucker), Britta Jacobellis (Neighbor with Dogs), Ceaser Flores (Scary Man at Party), Chris Snyder (Tattoo Guy), Dan Dulle (Motorcycle Owner), Jon Huck (Himself), Jet Kauffman (Feisty Girl), Josh Kelling (Fancy Waiter), Ken Bailey (Homicide Detective), Mark Nihem (Liquor Store Clerk), Joel Hodge (Man Peeing in Bathroom)

An aimless and possibly unhinged young man finds himself falling in love with a charismatic woman, thereby triggering an increasingly volatile and violent series of events.

Ryan Reynolds, Jason Bateman, Leslie Mann © Universal Studios

THE CHANGE-UP

(UNIVERSAL) Producers, David Dobkin, Neal H. Moritz; Executive Producers, Joe Caracciolo Jr., Ori Marmur, Jeff Kleeman, Jonathon Komack Martin; Director, David Dobkin; Screenplay, Jon Lucas, Scott Moore; Photography, Eric Edwards; Designer, Barry Robison; Costumes, Betsy Heimann; Music, John Debney; Editors, Lee Haxall, Greg Hayden; an Original Film/Big Kid Pictures production, presented in association with Relativity Media; Dolby; Super 35 Widescreen; Color; Rated R; 112 minutes; Release date: August 5, 2011

CAST
Mitch Planko	**Ryan Reynolds**
Dave Lockwood	**Jason Bateman**
Jamie Lockwood	**Leslie Mann**
Sabrina McArdle	**Olivia Wilde**
Mitch's Dad	**Alan Arkin**

Mircea Monroe (Tatiana), Gregory Itzin (Flemming Steel), Ned Schmidtke (Ted Norton), Lo Ming (Ken Kinkabe), Sydney Rouviere (Cara Lockwood), Dax Griffin (Blow-Dried Goon), Andrea Moore (Sophia), Matthew Cornwell (Parks Foreman), Craig Bierko (Valtan), Taaffe O'Connell (Mona), Fred Stoller (Movie Set PA), Faith Alhadeff (Nicolette Peters), Luke Bain (Peter Lockwood), Lauren Bain (Sarah Lockwood), Jamie Renell (Lawyer), Kenny Alfonso (Businessman at Sonsie Café), Joe Knezevich (Amalgamated Exec), TJ Hassan (Kinkabe Lawyer), Matthew Stanton (PA), Gabe Wood (Neighbor), Cooper Gore (Neighbor's Kid), Ed Ackerman (Victor), Jeanine Jackson (Carla Nelson), Vickie Eng (Erin Walsh), Amber Seyer (Beautiful Woman), Anna Colwell (Cute Girl in Elevator), Steven Dean Davis, Adam Boyer Matthew Rimmer (Tattoo Artists), Suzanne Arkin (Pamela), Patricia French (Dave's Secretary), Jeanette Miller (Grandma Taylor), Greg Savage (Construction Worker), Bailey Anne Borders (Babysitter), Ken DeLozier (Minister), Anton Mertens, Paul Barlow Jr., Anthony Breed, Gary Babiarz (Amalgamated Attorneys), Jeremy Lippman (Construction Worker), Dimitrius Pulido (Greased-Up Lorno Guy), Clay Chamberlin (Boom Operator), Blake Goza (First AD), Ryter Shay Cannon (Tommy), Arin Logan (Sexy Girl in Bar), Martha Bird Knighton (Old Lady), Lindsey Blackwell (Little Girl), Michael Beasley, Clay Edmond Kraski (Security Guards)

An uptight married lawyer and his irresponsible womanizing friend make a passing wish to swap lives and find themselves inhabiting each other's bodies.

Harmony Santana, Esai Morales

GUN HILL ROAD

(MOTION FILM GROUP) Producers, Ron Simons, Michelle-Anne M. Small; Co-Producer, Nick Huston; Executive Producers, Ron Simons, Esai Morales; Director/Screenplay, Rashaad Ernesto Green; Photography, Daniel Patterson; Designer, Maya Sigel; Costumes, Elisabeth Vastola; Music, Enrique Feldman, Stefan Swanson; Editor, Sara Corrigan; Casting, Sig De Miguel, Stephen Vincent; a Simonsays Entertainment production in association with A Small Production Co.; Color; HD; Rated R; 86 minutes; Release date: August 5, 2011

CAST
Enrique	**Esai Morales**
Angela	**Judy Reyes**
Michael/Vanessa	**Harmony Santana**
Fernando	**Robin de Jesus**
Tico	**Franky G**

Felix Solis (Pete), Flaco Navaja (Danny), Isiah Whitlock Jr. (Thompson), Miriam Colon (Gloria), Vincent Laresca (Hector), Tyrone Brown (Chris), Robert Prescott (Mr. Donovan), Shirley Rumierk (Jeanette), Vanessa Aspillaga (Karina), Gleendilys Inoa (Samantha), Caridad "La Bruja" De La Luz (MC), Ty Jones, Reinaldo Marcus Green (Prison Guards), Alex Kurz, Paul Mauriello, Emiliano Styles, Courtney S. Bunbury (Prisoners), J.W. Cortes (Police Officer), Anthony Grasso (Chef), Dennis Leonard Johnson (Antoine), Adel L. Morales (Manny), Karina Casiano (Magdalena), Robert Salzman (Sugar), Ceez Liive (Jai), Barbie Crawford (Tatiana), Ron Simons (Manager), Joe Urban (Cigar Chomping Militiaman)

Enrique returns to his family after a three year stretch in prison and must confront his feelings over his son's cross-dressing lifestyle.

Esai Morales, Judy Reyes © Motion Film Group

Freida Pinto, James Franco

Caesar and the Apes

Tom Felton

David Oyelowo © Twentieth Century Fox

RISE OF THE PLANET OF THE APES

(20TH CENTURY FOX) Producers, Peter Chernin, Dylan Clark, Rick Jaffa, Amanda Silver; Executive Producer, Thomas M. Hammel; Director, Rupert Wyatt; Screenplay, Rick Jaffa, Amanda Silver; Photography, Andrew Lesnie; Designer, Claude Paré; Costumes, Renée April; Music, Patrick Doyle; Editors, Conrad Buff, Mark Goldblatt; Special Effects Coordinator, Tony Lazarowich; Makeup Effects, WCT Prods., Bill Terzakis; Stunts, Mike Mitchell, Terry Notary; Casting, Debra Zane, Coreen Mayrs, Heike Brandstatter; a Chernin Entertainment production; Dolby; Panavision; Deluxe color; Rated PG-13; 105 minutes; Release date: August 5, 2011

CAST
Will Rodman	**James Franco**
Caroline Aranha	**Freida Pinto**
Charles Rodman	**John Lithgow**
John Landon	**Brian Cox**
Dodge Landon	**Tom Felton**
Steven Jacobs	**David Oyelowo**
Caesar	**Andy Serkis**

Tyler Labine (Robert Franklin), Jamie Harris (Rodney), David Hewlett (Hunsiker), Ty Olsson (Chief John Hamil), Madison Bell (Alice Hunsiker), Makena Joy (Teen Alice), Kevin O'Grady, Sean Tyson (Animal Control Officers), Jack Kuris (Boy in Muir Woods), Kyle Riefsnyder, Anthony McRae (CHPs), Jeb Beach (Dad in Muir Woods), Jesse Reid (Donnie Thompson), BJ Harrison (Dottie), Leah Gibson, Tracy Spiridakos (Party Girls), Ivan Wanis Ruiz, Trevor Carroll (Handlers at Lab), Chelah Horsdal (Irena), Ryan Booth (South Side Commander), Gordon Douglas Myren (Local Guy), Elizabeth Weinstein (Mom in Muir Woods), Meredith Canby (New Aide), Javier Caballero Cano (Newspaper Dad), Peter Bundic, Dylan Nouri (Newspaper Boys), Derek Morrison, Dean Redman, Hector Johnson (Security Guards), David Richmond-Peck, Adrian Hough, Evans Johnson (Board Members), Joey Roche (Todd Hunisker), Riel Hahn (Zoo Guide), Michael Kopsa (Jerk Driver), Steve Lawlor, Chris Shields, Sandy Robson (SFPDs), Mike Dupud (Northside Officer), Stacey Schmidt (Jogger), Willy Miles (Guy with Newspaper), Adrian Hein (Sharp Shooter), Karin Konoval (Maurice/Court Clerk), Terry Notary (Rocket/Bright Eyes), Richard Ridings (Buck), Chris Gordon (Koba), Devyn Dalton (Cornelia), Jay Caputo (Alpha)

After genetic experimentation produces an ape of unusual intelligence, the chimp rallies other apes to conquer the human race. Prequel to the *Planet of the Apes* (20th, 1968, 2001).

This film received an Oscar nomination for visual effects.

Emma Stone

Jessica Chastain © Walt Disney Studios

THE HELP

(WALT DISNEY STUDIOS) Producers, Brunson Green, Chris Columbus, Michael Barnathan; Executive Producers, Mark Radcliffe, Tate Taylor, L. Dean Jones Jr., Nate Berkus, Jennifer Blum, John Norris, Jeff Skoll, Mohamed Mubarak Al-Mazrouei; Director/Screenplay, Tate Taylor; Based on the novel by Kathryn Stockett; Photography, Stephen Goldblatt; Designer, Mark Ricker; Costumes, Sharen Davis; Music, Thomas Newman; Editor, Hughes Winborne; Casting, Kerry Barden, Paul Schnee; a DreamWorks Pictures and Reliance Entertainment presentation in association with Participant Media and Imagenation Abu Dhabi of a 1492 Pictures/Harbinger Pictures production; Dolby; Deluxe color; Rated PG-13; 146 minutes; Release date: August 10, 2011

CAST

Eugenia "Skeeter" Phelan	**Emma Stone**
Aibileen Clark	**Viola Davis**
Hilly Holbrook	**Bryce Dallas Howard**
Minny Jackson	**Octavia Spencer**
Celia Foote	**Jessica Chastain**
Elizabeth Leefolt	**Ahna O'Reilly**
Charlotte Phelan	**Allison Janney**
Jolene French	**Anna Camp**
Mae Mobley	**Eleanor Henry, Emma Henry**
Stuart Whitworth	**Chris Lowell**
Constantine Jefferson	**Cicely Tyson**
Johnny Foote	**Mike Vogel**
Missus Walters	**Sissy Spacek**
Robert Phelan	**Brian Kerwin**
Carlton Phelan	**Wes Chatham**
Yule Mae Davis	**Aunjanue Ellis**
William Hollbrook	**Ted Welch**
Raleigh Leefolt	**Shane McRae**
Pascagoula	**Roslyn Ruff**
Gretchen	**Tarra Riggs**
Mr. Blackly	**Leslie Jordan**
Elaine Stein	**Mary Steenburgen**
Rebecca	**Tiffany Brouwer**
Cora	**Carol Sutton**
Callie	**Millicent Bolton**
Mary Beth Caldwell	**Ashley Johnson**

Ritchie Montgomery (Bus Driver), Don Brock (White Bus Passenger), Florence "Flo" Roach, Sheerene Whitfield (Maids), Nelsan Ellis (Henry the Waiter), David Oyelowo (Preacher Green), LaChanze (Rachel), Dana Ivey (Gracie Higginbotham), Becky Fly (Woman in Grocery), Cleta E. Ellington (Donna the Receptionist), Henry Carpenter (Jameso), John Taylor (Missus Walters' Date), Charles Cooper, Diana Cooper (Tire Winners at Ballroom), Coyt Bailey (Party Guest #3), Wade Cottonfield (Lead Singer of Band), Kelsey Scott (Sugar Jackson), Amy Beckwith, Sloane Fair, Anna Jennings, Lauren Miller, Elizabeth Smith, Mary Taylor Killebrew, Kathryn Ursy, Steffany Ward (Bridge Club)

In 1963 Jackson, Mississippi, a privileged young woman decides to write a book on the domestic situation, asking several of the black women who virtually raised the children of the white employers what it feels like to be treated as inferiors despite their importance in these households.

2011 Academy Award winner for Best Supporting Actress (Octavia Spencer).

This film received additional Oscar nominations for picture, actress (Viola Davis), and supporting actress (Jessica Chastain).

Bryce Dallas Howard, Sissy Spacek, Octavia Spencer

Emma Stone, Octavia Spencer, Viola Davis

Ahna O'Reilly, Emma Stone (back to camera), Bryce Dallas Howard, Anna Camp, Viola Davis

Jessica Chastain, Octavia Spencer

Viola Davis, Octavia Spencer

Viola Davis, Octavia Spencer

30 MINUTES OR LESS

(COLUMBIA) Producers, Stuart Cornfeld, Ben Stiller, Jeremy Kramer; Executive Producers, Monica Levinson, Brian Levy; Director, Ruben Fleischer; Screenplay, Michael Diliberti; Story, Michael Diliberti, Matthew Sullivan; Photography, Jess Hall; Designer, Maher Ahmad; Costumes, Christie Wittenborn; Music, Ludwig Göransson; Editor, Alan Baumgarten; Stunts, Ricky LeFevour, Tom Lowell; Visual Effects Supervisor, Paul Linden; Casting, Jeanne McCarthy, Nicole Abellera; a Red Hour production, presented in association with Media Rights Capital; Dolby; Panavision; Deluxe color; Rated R; 82 minutes; Release date: August 12, 2011

Dilshad Vadsaria

CAST

Nick	**Jesse Eisenberg**
Dwayne	**Danny McBride**
Chet	**Aziz Ansari**
Travis	**Nick Swardson**
Kate	**Dilshad Vadsaria**
Chango	**Michael Peña**
Juicy	**Bianca Kajlich**
The Major	**Fred Ward**
15 Year Olds	**Sam Johnston, Jack Foley**
Chet's Date	**Elizabeth Wright Shapiro**
Pizza Boss	**Brett Gelman**
Rodney	**Paul Tierney**

Staci Lynn Fletcher (Family Dollar Cashier), Gary Brichetto (Mr. Fisher), Ilyssa Fradin (Mom), Grace Heemstra (Daughter), Torey Adkins (Big Guy), Rebecca Cox (Sandra), Rick Irwin (Bank Manager), Sam Tedesco (Security Guard), Wayne Bibbs (Bank Customer), Jamaal Hines (Cop Outside Bank), Joseph Lyman (Alley Cop), David Fleischer (Bus Passenger #4), Lucas Fleischer (Random Local), Matthew Sullivan (Random Tanning Guy)

In need of $100,000 to pay a hit man to kill his wealthy father, Dwayne kidnaps hapless pizza delivery boy Nick and straps a bomb to his chest, forcing him to rob a bank or face annihilation.

Danny McBride, Nick Swardson © Columbia Pictures

Michael Peña

Aziz Ansari, Jesse Eisenberg

Romola Garai, Jim Sturgess

Jim Sturgess, Patricia Clarkson © Focus Features

Anne Hathaway, Jim Sturgess

ONE DAY

(FOCUS) Producer, Nina Jacobson; Executive Producer, Tessa Ross; Co-Producer, Jane Frazer; Director, Lone Scherfig; Screenplay, David Nicholls, based on his novel; Photography, Benoît Delhomme; Designer, Mark Tildesley; Costumes, Odile Dicks-Mireaux; Music, Rachel Portman; Music Supervisor, Karen Elliott; Editor, Barney Pilling; Casting, Lucy Bevan; a Random House Films presentation in association with Film4 of a Color Force production; American-British; Dolby; Super 35 Widescreen; Deluxe color; Rated PG-13; 108 minutes; American release date: August 19, 2011

CAST

Emma	**Anne Hathaway**
Dexter	**Jim Sturgess**
Alison	**Patricia Clarkson**
Steven	**Ken Stott**
Sylvie	**Romola Garai**
Ian	**Rafe Spall**
Callum	**Tom Mison**
Tilly	**Jodie Whittaker**
Suki	**Georgia King**
Mrs. Cope	**Diana Kent**
Mr. Cope	**James Laurenson**
Murray Cope	**Matthew Beard**
Samuel Cope	**Toby Regbo**

Tim Key (Customer), Joséphine de La Baume (Marie), Heida Reed (Ingrid), Amanda Fairbanks-Hynes (Tara), Gil Alma (Waiter), David Ajala (Floor Manager), Ukweli Roach (Rapper), Lorna Gayle (Mrs. Major), Clara Paget (Cocktail Waitress), Matt Berry (Aaron), Tom Arnold (Colin), Eden Mengelgrein (Jasmine, 2001), Kayla Mengelgrein (Jasmine, 2001), Sienna Poppy-Rodgers (Teenager at Eurostar), Sébastien Dupuis (Jean-Pierre), Maisie Fishbourne (Jasmine, 2005), Phoebe Fox (Nightclub Girl), Emilia Jones (Jasmine, 2007 and 2011), Joanna Ampil (Waitress)

The unpredictable, on-again-off-again relationship of Emma and Dexter is charted over the course of twenty-years according to what took place on a single date, July 15th.

Jim Sturgess

Toni Collette, Imogen Poots, Anton Yelchin

David Tennant © Walt Disney Studios

Colin Farrell

FRIGHT NIGHT

(WALT DISNEY STUDIOS) Producers, Michael De Luca, Alison Rosenzweig; Executive Producers, Ray Angelic, Josh Bratman, Michael Gaeta, Lloyd Miller; Director, Craig Gillespie; Screenplay, Marti Noxon; Based on the film directed and written by Tom Holland; Story, Tom Holland; Photography, Javier Aguirresarobe; Designer, Richard Bridgland Fitzgerald; Costumes, Susan Matheson; Music, Ramin Djawadi; Music Supervisor, Dana Sano; Editor, Tatiana S. Riegel; Special Effects Coordinator, Larz Anderson; Special Makeup Designer, Howard Berger, Greg Nicotero; Stunts, Robert F. Brown; Casting, Allison Jones; a DreamWorks Pictures and Reliance Entertainment presentation of a Michael De Luca and Gaeta/Rosenzweig production; Dolby; Deluxe color; 3D; Rated R; 106 minutes; Release date: August 19, 2011

CAST
Charley Brewster	**Anton Yelchin**
Jerry	**Colin Farrell**
Jane Brewster	**Toni Collette**
Peter Vincent	**David Tennant**
Amy	**Imogen Poots**
Ed Lee	**Christopher Mintz-Plasse**
Mark	**Dave Franco**
Ben	**Reid Ewing**
Adam	**Will Denton**
Ginger	**Sandra Vergara**

Emily Montague (Doris), Chris Sarandon (Jay Dee), Grace Phipps (Bee), Chelsea Tavares (Cara), Lisa Loeb (Victoria), Brian Huskey (Rick), Arron Shiver, Rick Ortega (Cops), Charlie Brown (Doctor), Mike Miller (Store Guy), Marya Beauvais (Mrs. Granada), Rebekah Wiggins (Passing Nurse), Kent Kirkpatrick (Teacher), Eb Lottimer (Adam's Dad), Liezl Carstens, Laura Aidan, Alma Sisneros (Show Nymphs), Jerry Angelo (Guy on Dance Floor), Kevin Christopher Brown, Jesse Pickett (Jerry's House Cops), William H. Burton (Hulking Man), Paula Francis, Dave Courvoisier (Newscasters), Tait Fletcher (Nightclub Security Guy), Bruce Holmes (Pyro Guy), Lovie Johnson (D.J.), Christopher Ranney (Guard)

Suburban teenager Charley Brewster starts to suspect that his mysterious new neighbor is a vampire. Remake of the 1985 Columbia film that starred William Ragsdale, Chris Sarandon, Roddy McDowall, and Stephen Geoffreys.

Anton Yelchin, Christopher Mintz-Plasse

AMIGO

(VARIANCE) Producer, Maggie Renzi; Co-Producers, Mario Ontal, Joel Torre; Director/Screenplay/Editor, John Sayles; Photography, Lee Briones-Meily; Designer, Rodell Cruz; Costumes, Gino Gonzales; Music, Mason Daring; Casting, Ronnie Lazaro, Debra Zane; an Anarchists' Convention presentation; Dolby; Color; Not rated; 128 minutes; Release date: August 19, 2011

CAST
Rafael	**Joel Torre**
Lt. Compton	**Garret Dillahunt**
Col. Hardacre	**Chris Cooper**
Zeke Whatley	**DJ Qualls**
Corazón	**Rio Locsin**
Simón	**Ronnie Lazaro**
Policarpio	**Bembol Roco**
Padre Hidalgo	**Yul Vazquéz**
Gil	**Dane DeHaan**
Locsin	**Art Acuña**

Lucas Neff (Shanker), James Parks (Sgt. Runnels), Stephen Taylor (Pvt. Bates), Bill Tangradi (Dutch), Irma Adlawan (Josefa), John Arcilla (Nenong), Pen Medina (Albay), Brian Lee Franklin (Cpl. Lynch), Spanky Manikan (Tuba Joe), Jemi Paretas (Zuniga), Joe Gruta (Hilario), Raul Manikan (Felix), Ermie Concepcion (Dolores), Merlin Bonning (Creighton), Miguel Faustman (Capt. Narvaez), Raul Morit (Chief), Will Boddington (Soldier)

During the Philippine-American War of 1900, the mayor of a small village faces a complex situation when he is asked by a U.S. garrison to help them hunt down a band of Filipino guerillas, one of whom is the mayor's brother.

Rio Locsin

DJ Qualls

Chris Cooper © Variance Films

Dane DeHaan, Yul Vazquéz, Brian Lee Franklin

Jason Momoa, Rachel Nichols © Lionsate

CONAN THE BARBARIAN

(LIONSGATE) Producers, Fredrik Malmberg, Boaz Davidson, Joe Gatta, Danny Lerner, John Baldecchi, Les Weldon, Henry Winterstern; Executive Producers, Eda Kowan, John Sacchi, Michael Paseornek, Jason Constantine, Avi Lerner, Danny Dimbort, Trevor Short, Frederick Fierst, George Furla; Director, Marcus Nispel; Screenplay, Thomas Dean Donnelly, Joshua Oppenheimer , Sean Hood; Based on the character of Conan as originally created by Robert E. Howard; Photography, Thomas Kloss; Designer, Chris August; Costumes, Wendy Partridge; Music, Tyler Bates; Editor, Ken Blackwell; Casting, Kerry Barden, Paul Schnee; Stunts, David Leitch, Noon Orsatti; Fight Coorindator, Jonathan Eusebio; a Millennium Films production in association with Emmett Furla productions; Dolby; Super 35 Widescreen; Color; 3D; Rated R; 112 minutes; Release date: August 19, 2011

CAST
Conan	**Jason Momoa**
Khalar Zym	**Stephen Lang**
Tamara	**Rachel Nichols**
Corin	**Ron Perlman**
Marique	**Rose McGowan**
Ukafa	**Bob Sapp**

Leo Howard (Young Conan), Steven O'Donnell (Lucius), Nonso Anozie (Artus), Raad Rawi (Fassir), Laila Rouass (Fialla), Saïd Taghmaoui (Ela-Shan), Milton Welsh (Remo), Borislav Iliev (Wild Man), Nathan Jones (Akhun), Diana Lubenova (Cheren), Alina Puscau (Lara), Ioan Karamfilov (Donal), Raicho Vasilev, Stanimir Stamatov (City Guards), Nikolai Stanoev (Lieutenant), Ivana Staneva (Young Marique), Zlatka Raikova (Slavegirl), Anton Trendafilov (Xaltotun), Aysun Aptulova (Sacrificial Victim), Daniel Rashev (Acolyte Priest), Jackson Spidell, Guilermo Grispo, Radolsav Parvanov (Picts), Teodora Duhovnikova, Shelly Varod (Student Nuns), Tezdjan Ahmedova, Uliana Vin, Yoana Temelkova, Nadia Konakchieva, Petya Milluseva, Ruslana Kaneva, Gloria Petkova, Zdravka Krastenyakova (Nuns), Stanislav Pishtalov (Cimmerian Elder – Uran), Velimir Velev (Prison Clerk), Zhaidarbek Kunguzhinov, Eric Laciste, Brian Andrew Mendoza, Nuo Sun, Kim Do (Monks), Bashar Rahal (Quarter Master), Gisella Marengo (Maliva), Yoana Petrova (Young Marique), Vladimir Vladimirov (Den Barman), Samuel Hargrave (Horse Warrior), Katarzyna Wolejnio (Valeria), David Mason Chlopecki (Pirate), Alexandrina Vladova, Guarguina Ilieva (Belly Dancers), Stefka Berova (Mama), Vangelitsa Karadjova, Blagovesta Cakova, Svetlana Vasileva, Zornitsa Stoicheva, Zhenia Zheleva, Nikol Vasileva, Adriana Kalcheva (Topless Wenches), Morgan Freeman (Narrator)

Conan must save the great nations of Hyboria from an encroaching reign of evil.

SPY KIDS: ALL THE TIME IN THE WORLD IN 4D

(DIMENSION) Producers, Robert Rodriguez, Elizabeth Avellán; Executive Producers, Bob Weinstein, Harvey Weinstein; Co-Producers, Rebecca Rodriguez, George Huang; Director/Screenplay, Robert Rodriguez; Photography, Robert Rodriguez, Jimmy Lindsey; Designer, Steve Joyner; Costumes, Nina Proctor; Music, Robert Rodriguez, Carl Thiel; Editor, Dan Zimmerman; Special Effects Coordinator, Steve Davison; Stereoscopy, Rob Nederhorst; Casting, Mary Vernieu, JC Cantu; a Troublemaker Studios production; Dolby; Deluxe color; 3D; Aroma-Scope; Rated PG; 89 minutes; Release date: August 19, 2011

CAST
Marissa Wilson	**Jessica Alba**
Wilbur Wilson	**Joel McHale**
Rebecca Wilson	**Rowan Blanchard**
Cecil Wilson	**Mason Cook**
Danger D'Amo/Time Keeper/Tick Tock	**Jeremy Piven**
Carmen Cortez	**Alexa Vega**
Juni Cortez	**Daryl Sabara**

Belle Solorzano, Genny Solorzano (Spy Baby), Ricky Gervais (Voice of Argonaut), Chuck Cureau (News Anchor), Jett Good (Young Danger), Albert Im (Head Scientist), Danny Trejo (Uncle Machete), Jonathan Breck (Wilbur's Boss), Wray Crawford (Editor/Cameraman), Elmo (Argonaut), Al "Train" Diaz, Angela Lanza (OSS Agents), Chad Guerrero (Henchman in Van), Marci Madison (Agent Fine), Roger Edwards (OSS Agent Adams), Antonio Banderas (Gregorio Cortez)

Former spy Marissa Wilson must spring back into action in order to keep the villainous Time Keeper from speeding up time and bringing forth the apocalypse. Fourth entry in the Dimension Films series following *Spy Kids* (2001), *Spy Kids 2: The Island of Lost Dreams* (2002), and *Spy Kids 3-D: Game Over* (2003).

Jeremy Piven, Jessica Alba © Dimension Films

RED STATE

(SMODCAST PICTURES) Producer, Jonathan Gordon; Executive Producers, Elyse Seiden, Nhaelan McMillan, Victor Choy, Jason Clark, Philip Elway, Shea Kammer; Director/Screenplay/ Editor, Kevin Smith; Photography, David Klein; Designer, Cabot McMullen; Costumes, Beth Pasternak; Casting, Deborah Aquila, Tricia Wood; a Harvey Boys presentation and production; Dolby; Color; HD; Not rated; 88 minutes; Release date: August 19, 2011 (following several single, select city engagements, beginning on March 5, 2011)

CAST
Abin Cooper	**Michael Parks**
Joseph Keenan	**John Goodman**
Sara	**Melissa Leo**
Jarod	**Kyle Gallner**
Travis	**Michael Angarano**
Billy-Ray	**Nicholas Braun**
Sheriff Wynan	**Stephen Root**

Kerry Bishé (Cheyenne), Betty Aberlin (Abigail), Deborah Aquila (Mrs. Vasquez), Ronnie Connell (Randy), Kaylee DeFer (Dana), Joey Figueroa (Route 9 Friend), Anna Gunn (Travis' Mother), Matt Jones (Deputy Pete), John Lacy (Travis' Father), Catherine McCord (News Reporter), Alexa Nikolas (Jesse), Cooper Thornton (Plastic Wrap Man), Ralph Garman (Caleb), Molly Livingston (Fiona May), James Parks (Mordechai), Haley Ramm (Maggie), Jennifer Schwalbach (Esther), Elizabeth Tripp (Melanie), Kevin Alejandro (Harry, the Tactical Agent), Marc Blucas (ATF Sniper), Patrick Fischler (Agent Hammond), Kevin Pollak (ASAC Brooks), David Marciano (Agent Eccles), Damian Young (Agent Carol)

Three teenagers, who have witnessed a local sheriff in a compromising position with another man, then run afoul of a homophobic, murderous backwoods preacher.

Michael Parks © Smodcast Pictures

Michael Angarano, Kyle Gallner, Nicholas Braun

Guy Pearce © FilmDistrict

DON'T BE AFRAID OF THE DARK

(FILMDISTRICT) Producers, Guillermo del Toro, Mark Johnson; Executive Producers, Stephen Jones, William Horberg, Tom Williams; Director, Troy Nixey; Screenplay, Guillermo del Toro, Matthew Robbins; Based on the teleplay by Nigel McKeand; Photography, Oliver Stapleton; Designer, Roger Ford; Costumes, Wendy Chuck; Music, Marco Beltrami, Buck Sanders; Editor, Jill Bilcock; Special Effects Supervisor, Angelo Sahin; Creature Designers, Chet Zar, Mike Elizalde, Keith Thompson; Stunts, Chris Anderson; Casting, Mary Vernieu, Venus Kanani; a Miramax and Guillermo del Toro presentation in association with FilmDistrict of a Necropia/Gran Via production; American-Australian-Mexican; Dolby; Deluxe color; Rated R; 99 minutes; Release date: August 26, 2011

CAST
Kim Raphael	**Katie Holmes**
Alex Hurst	**Guy Pearce**
Sally Hurst	**Bailee Madison**
Harris	**Jack Thompson**
Blackwood	**Garry McDonald**
Housekeeper	**Edwina Ritchard**
Mrs. Underhill	**Julia Blake**
Psychiatrist	**Nicholas Bell**
Charles Jacoby	**Alan Dale**
Evelyn Jacoby	**Trudy Hellier**
Bill	**Terry Kenwrick**

Bruce Gleeson (Buggy Driver), Carolyn Shakespeare-Allen (Airport Cart Driver), David Tocci (Workman), Lance Drisdale (Policeman), Libby Gott (Nurse), James Mackay (Librarian), Emelia Burns (Caterer); Grant Piro, Todd MacDonald, Angus Smallwood, Dylan Young, Guillermo del Toro, Abbe Holmes (Creature Voices)

After her father and his girlfriend move into a house on which they are doing extensive restoration, young Sally encounters deadly creatures who reside in the basement furnace.
Remake of a 1973 ABC television movie that starred Kim Darby and Jim Hutton.

OUR IDIOT BROTHER

(WEINSTEIN CO.) Producers, Anthony Bregman, Marc Turtletaub, Peter Saraf; Executive Producers, Jesse Peretz, Caroline Jaczko, Stefanie Azpiazu, John Hodges, Aleen Keshishian; Director, Jesse Peretz; Screenplay, Evgenia Peretz, David Schisgall; Story, Evgenia Peretz, David Schisgall, Jesse Peretz; Photography, Yaron Orbach; Designer, Inbal Weinberg; Costumes, Christopher Peterson; Music, Nathan Larson, Eric D. Johnson; Music Supervisor, Susan Jacobs; Editors, Andrew Mondshein, Jacob Craycroft; Casting, Jeanne McCarthy; a Big Beach/Likely Story production, presented in association with Yuk Films; Dolby; Deluxe Color; Rated R; 90 minutes; Release date: August 26, 2011

Janet Montgomery, Paul Rudd

CAST

Ned Rochlin	**Paul Rudd**
Miranda	**Elizabeth Banks**
Natalie	**Zooey Deschanel**
Liz	**Emily Mortimer**
Dylan	**Steve Coogan**
Christian	**Hugh Dancy**
Janet	**Kathryn Hahn**
Cindy	**Rashida Jones**
Ilene	**Shirley Knight**
Billy	**T.J. Miller**
River	**Matthew Mindler**
Jeremy	**Adam Scott**

Nick Sullivan (Customer), Francesca Papalia (Sadie), Bob Stephenson (Officer Washburn), Peter Hermann (Terry), Kelly Briter (Girl with Jeremy), Sterling Brown (Officer Omar Coleman), Kayla Squiteri, Summer Squiteri (Echo), Lydia Haug (Tatiana), Gina Artese (Ballerina), Silvestre Rasuk (Conflicted Kid on Train), Andrew Secunda (Curious Man on Train), Janet Montgomery (Lady Arabella Galloway), Wrenn Schmidt (Beth Phillips), Kathy Fitzgerald (Velma), Adi Hanash (Paramedic), Nikki E. Walker (Cop), Marceline Hugot (Judy), Camille Bright, Teja Frank (Destiny's House Girls), Alexia Rasmussen (Chloe), Lucas Near-Verbrugghe (Max), Polly Draper (Ellen), Neal Lerner (Darren), James Biberi (Gus), Katie Aselton (Amy)

Paul Rudd, Elizabeth Banks

Following his split with his girlfriend and his release from jail, affably dimwitted Ned Rochlin becomes a constant presence in the lives of his three sisters, all of whom are experiencing their own problems.

Matthew Mindler, Steve Coogan, Emily Mortimer © Weinstein Co.

Rashida Jones, Zooey Deschanel

Jesse Borrego, Amandla Stenberg © TriStar Pictures

Jordi Mollà

Michael Vartan

COLOMBIANA

(TRISTAR) Producers, Luc Besson, Ariel Zeitoun; Line Producer, Ajoz Films; Director, Olivier Megaton; Screenplay, Luc Besson, Robert Mark Kamen; Photography, Romain Lacourbas; Designer, Patrick Durand; Costumes, Olivier Beriot; Music, Nathaniel Mechaly; Editor, Camille Delamarre; Fight Coordinator, Alain Figlarz; Casting, Meagan Lewis; a Stage 6 Films presentation of a Europacorp, TF1 Films Production, Grive Productions with the participation of Canal+ and Cinecinema production; American-French; Dolby; Super 35 Widescreen; Color; Rated PG-13; 107 minutes; Release date: August 26, 2011

CAST

Cataleya Restrepo	**Zoe Saldana**
Marco	**Jordi Mollà**
Special Agent James Ross	**Lennie James**
Cat – 10	**Amandla Stenberg**
Danny Delanay	**Michael Vartan**
Emilio Restrepo	**Cliff Curtis**
Don Luis	**Beto Benites**
Fabio Restrepo	**Jesse Borrego**
Alicia	**Cynthia Addai-Robinson**

Angel Garnica (Pepe), Ofelia Medina (Mama), Callum Blue (Steven Richard), Sam Douglas (William Woodgard), Graham McTavish (Head Marshal Warren), Charles Maquignon (Sgt. Bill Attwood), Affif Ben Badra (Genarro Rizzo), David Clark (Marshal), Billy Slaughter (Ryan), Nikea Gamby-Turner (Shari), Andrea Helene (Principal), John McConnell (Smith), Sébastien Press, Mark De Alessandro, Pablo Vinos Zelaya (SWAT), Max Martini (Agent Robert Williams), Tony Dalton, Julian Sedgwick (American Embassy), Julien Muller (Doyle), Guillermo Rios (Emilio's Man), Luis Toscano (Fabio's Man), Javier Escobar (Marco's Gun Man), Michael Showers, Wesley Cannon (Cops), Doug Rao (Michael Shino), Reem Kherici, Julie Nicolet (Nymphettes), Stéphane Orsolani (Guy, 6th Floor), Steve Herson (Ticket Agent), Richard Zeringue (Bureaucrat), Stephan Brodziak (Tech FBI), William Raymond (FBI Operator), Alfredo Gonzales (Old Man, Gardener), Alejandro Peraza (Head Bodyguard), Donald Marshall (William's Servant), Mylène Pilutik (CIA Girl), Silas Cooper (Customs Officer), Ariane Brodier (Alexa Milshinova), Donagh Gordon (FBI Mailman), Benoît Lavelatte (Thug)

Cataleya becomes a deadly assassin in order to extract revenge on the drug lord and his cohorts who killed her parents when she was a child.

Zoe Saldana

Dagmara Dominczyk, Vera Farmiga

Boyd Holbrook, Taissa Farmiga, Flynn Hawkey

HIGHER GROUND

(SONY CLASSICS) Producers, Claude Dal Farra, Renn Hawkey, Carly Hugo, Matt Parker, Jon Rubinstein; Executive Producers, Lauren Munsch, Brice Dal Farra, Jonathan Burkhart, Carolyn S. Briggs, Tim Metcalfe; Director, Vera Farmiga; Screenplay, Carolyn S. Briggs, Tim Metcalfe; Based on the memoir *This Dark World* by Carolyn S. Briggs; Photography, Michael McDonough; Designer, Sharon Lomofsky; Costumes, Amela Baksic; Music, Alec Puro; Editor, Colleen Sharp; Casting, Kerry Barden, Paul Schnee; a Strategic Motion Ventures presentation of a BCDF Pictures production in association with Authentic Management Projects, The Group Entertainment and Ruminant Films; Dolby; Color; Rated R; 109 minutes; Release date: August 26, 2011

CAST
Corinne Walker	**Vera Farmiga**
Pastor Bill	**Norbert Leo Butz**
Annika	**Dagmara Dominczyk**
CW Walker	**John Hawkes**
Pastor Bud	**Bill Irwin**
Ethan Miller	**Joshua Leonard**
Luke	**Ebon Moss-Bachrach**
Kathleen Walker	**Donna Murphy**
Teenage Corinne Walker	**Taissa Farmiga**
Teenage Ethan Miller	**Boyd Holbrook**
Ned	**Michael Chernus**

McKenzie Turner (Young Corinne Walker), Matthew Dubas (Salesman), Taylor Schwencke (Young Wendy Walker), Jillian Lindig (Mrs. Tuttle), Alden Rosakranse (Tim), James Noon (Kirk), Kaitlyn Rae King (Teenage Wendy Walker), Brandon Boyer (Mike), Harrison Basch, Noah Bowman (Renegades), Booker James Winter (Biology Teacher), Gene DeWitt (Gene), Flynn Hawkey (Baby Abigail), Warren Haynes (Warren), Luella Roche (Younger Abigail Miller), Sarah Banks (Younger Lily Miller), Barbara Tuttle (Deborah), Molly Hawkey (Molly), Joe Leary (Joe), Frank Goodyear (Voice of Dr. Frank Barnes), Reagan Leonard (Hope), Charles Glaser (Woody), Lucy Owen (Joanne), Nina Arianda (Wendy), Joseph Sinagra (Cop), Sarah Little (Older Abigail Miller), Zoe Pipa (Older Lily Miller), Mathew Biltonen (Gabe Miller), Sonia T. Gittens (Nurse), Eli Rubinstein (Seven Year Old Boy), Amy Helm (Amy), Machan Taylor (Machan), Jorgen Jorgenson (Jorgen), Tom Cherwin (Man in Counseling Office), Laurel S. Andretta (Woman in Counseling Office), Karen Keefe (Receptionist), Jack Gilpin (Dr. Adams), Oliver Wood (Oliver), Sean Mahon (Liam), Natalie Thomas (Liam's Wife), Terry McKenna (Pawn Shop Worker), Deborah Hedwall (Faye)

After spending much of her life as a devoted evangelical Christian, Corinne begins to question her faith and the restrictions her church imposes upon women.

Donna Murphy © Sony Pictures Classics

Sean Mahon, Vera Farmiga

THE DEBT

(FOCUS/MIRAMAX) Producers, Matthew Vaughn, Kris Thykier, Eduardo Rossoff, Eitan Evan; Co-Producer, Mairi Bett; Executive Producer, Tarquin Pack; Director, John Madden; Screenplay, Matthew Vaughn, Jane Goldman, Peter Straughan; Based on the film *Ha-Hov* written by Assaf Bernstein & Ido Rosenblum; Photography, Ben Davis; Designer, Jim Clay; Costumes, Natalie Ward; Music, Thomas Newman; Editor, Alexander Berner; Casting, Michelle Guish; a Marv Films production; Dolby; Super 35 Widescreen; Technicolor; Rated R; 113 minutes; Release date: August 31, 2011

CAST
Tev Aviv 1997
Rachel Singer	**Helen Mirren**
Stephan Gold	**Tom Wilkinson**
David Peretz	**Ciarán Hinds**
Sarah Gold	**Romi Aboulafia**

Tomer Ben David (Sarah's Husband), Ohev Ben David (Sarah's Son), Jonathan Uziel (Mossad Agent), Elana Kivity Davenport (Publisher), Eli Zohar (Stephan's Driver), Irén Bordán (Seminar Moderator)

Ciarán Hinds, Helen Mirren

Berlin 1965
Young Rachel	**Jessica Chastain**
Young Stephan	**Marton Csokas**
Young David	**Sam Worthington**
Doktor Bernhardt/Dieter Vogel	**Jesper Christensen**
Frau Bernhardt/Nurse	**Brigitte Kren**

Bálint Merán (Man on Tram), Christian Strasser (Station Guard), Alexander Fennon (Postal Worker), István Betz (Train Driver), Alexander Jagsch (Border Guard)

Tel Aviv 1970: András Szurdi (Soldier), Melinda Korcsog (Young Sarah), Nitzan Sharron, Adar Beck (Party Guests); *Ukraine 1997*: Kátya Tompos (Newspaper Receptionist), József Rácz (Kátya's Boyfriend), István Göz (Yuri Tiov), Igor Vovk (Babenko Registrar), Morris Perry (Ivan Schevchuk), Erika Szórádi (Babenko Nurse)

In 1997, a pair of former Mossad secret agents must face the truth about a much-heralded mission they had supposedly accomplished back in the mid-1960s, when they were assigned to track down a deadly Nazi war criminal. Remake of the 2007 Israeli film, *Ha-Hov* (*The Debt*).

Jessica Chastain, Marton Csokas, Sam Worthington

Helen Mirren, Tom Wilkinson © Focus Features

Marton Csokas, Sam Worthington

SEVEN DAYS IN UTOPIA

(VISION ENTERTAINMENT) Producers, Mark G. Mathis, Jason Michael Berman; Executive Producers, David L. Cook, Jess Stainbrook, Joseph Coors Jr., Ray C. Davis, Robert A. Innamorati, Rick Jackson, Phil Myers, Ken Herfurth, Lucas Black, Robert Carliner, Mary Vernieu, Lou Waters; Co-Producers, Susan Kirr, Kwesi Collisson; Director, Matthew Dean Russell; Screenplay, David L. Cook, Rob Levine, Matthew Dean Russell, Sandra Thrift; Based on the novel *Golf's Sacred Journey: Seven Days at the Links of Utopia* by David L. Cook; Photography, M. David Mullen; Designer, Clark Hunter; Costumes, Molly Maginnis, Amy Maner; Music, Klaus Badelt, Christopher Carmichael; Editor, Robert Komatsu; Casting, Mary Vernieu, Lindsay Graham; a Utopia Films LLC production in association with Prospect Park Pictures; Dolby; Super 35 Widescreen; FotoKem Color; Rated G; 96 minutes; Release date: September 2, 2011

CAST
Luke Chisholm	**Lucas Black**
Johnny Crawford	**Robert Duvall**
Sarah	**Deborah Ann Woll**
Lily	**Melissa Leo**
Jake	**Brian Geraghty**
Mabel	**Kathy Baker**

Robert Bear (Chuck), Madison Burge (Hannah Chisholm), Kim de Patri, Richard Dillard (Golfers), Jerry Ferrara (Joe Buckner), Sarah Jayne Jensen (Maggie Swanson), Josh Painting (Duane), Ezra Proch (Young Luke Chisholm), Joseph Lyle Taylor (Martin Chisholm), Sally Vahle (Mary Chisholm), Destiny Soria (Golf Fan), Brad Coleman (Patron)

After a meltdown on the course, professional golfer Luke Chisholm receives advice and coaching on how to improve his game through the tutelage of mysterious rancher Johnny Crawford.

Melissa Leo, Lucas Black, Robert Duvall, Kathy Baker, Deborah Ann Woll

Lucas Black, Robert Duvall
© Vision Entertainment

Leslie Bibb, Jason Sudeikis © Goldwyn Films

A GOOD OLD FASHIONED ORGY

(GOLDWYN) Producer, James D. Stern; Executive Producers, Ram Bergman, Brian Etting, Christopher Petzel, Douglas E. Hansen; Line Producer, George Parra; Directors/Screenplay, Alex Gregory, Peter Huyck; Photography, John Thomas; Designer, Alan Hook; Costumes, Leah Katznelson; Music, Jonathan Sadoff; Music Supervisor, Peymon Maskan; Editors, Patrick J. Don Vito, Anita Brandt-Burgoyne; Casting, Susie Farris; a Stage 6 Films presentation in association with the Aura Film Partnership and Fierce Entertainment of an Endgame Entertainment production; Dolby; Super 35 Widescreen; Color; Rated R; 95 minutes; Release date: September 2, 2011

CAST
Eric Keppler	**Jason Sudeikis**
Kelly	**Leslie Bibb**
Alison Lobel	**Lake Bell**
Sue Plummer	**Michelle Borth**
Adam Richman	**Nick Kroll**
Mike McCrudden	**Tyler Labine**
Willow Talbot	**Angela Sarafyan**

Lindsay Sloane (Laura LaCarubba), Martin Starr (Doug Duquez), Lucy Punch (Kate), Will Forte (Glenn), Rhys Coiro (Marcus), Kelly Haas (Ice Cream Girl), Michael Harding (Mr. Weber), Jan Harrelson (Emcee), Bob Hungerford (Farmer), Peter Huyck (Pete), Reiko Kaneshiro (Cherie), David Koechner (Vic George), Andrea Powell (Cop), Dee Dee Rescher (Ellen), Lin Shaye (Dody Henderson), Jon Stafford (Fred), Rick Warner (Deacon), Nick Weber (Golfer), Barbara Weetman (Mrs. Weber), Don Johnson (Jerry Keppler)

Worried that his father selling his Hamptons home means that eternal adolescent Eric can no longer host his wild parties, he talks his friends into coming together for one last bash, in which they all promise to go beyond the limit where sex is concerned.

Edward Gelbinovich, Stefanie Y. Hong, Griffin Newman, Ezra Miller, Zoë Kravitz

Ezra Miller, Zoë Kravitz © Tribeca Film

BEWARE THE GONZO

(TRIBECA FILM) Producers, Craig Cohen, Israel Wolfson, Matthew Weaver; Executive Producers, Jenny Fritz, Scott Prisand; Director/ Screenplay, Bryan Goluboff; Photography, Richard Rutkowski; Designer, Maya Sigel; Costumes, Amela Baksic; Music, The Mod; Editor, Colleen Sharp; Casting, Susan Shopmaker; a Cornerstore Entertainment presentation of a Ridiculous Upside production; Color; Not rated; 95 minutes; Release date: September 9, 2011

CAST
Eddie 'Gonzo' Gilman	**Ezra Miller**
Evie Wallace	**Zoë Kravitz**
Gavin Reilly	**Jesse McCartney**
Cafeteria Guy	**Judah Friedlander**
Principal Roy	**James Urbaniak**
Diane Gilman	**Amy Sidaris**
Arthur Gilman	**Campbell Scott**

Stefanie Y. Hong (Ming Na), Griffin Newman ('Horny' Rob Becker), Edward Gelbinovich (Scott Marshall Schneeman), Marc John Jefferies (Stone), Noah Fleiss (Ryan), Lucy DeVito (Marlene), Tyrone Brown (Johnny Rock), Dustin Ybarra (The Ripper), Steven Kaplan (Kevin), Julia Weldon, Celia Au (Gender Benders), Whitney Vance (Kat), Chris McKinney (Evie's Father), Conor Leslie (Amy), Tyler Johnson (Josh), Colby Minifie (Melanie), Matthew Shear (Dave Melnick), Jordan Price (Julie), Alice Blythe (Isabel), Peter Brensinger (Perv), Andrew Katz (Unabomber), Rafe Scobey-Thal (Rebel #1), Danton Stone (AP History Teacher), Lynn Chandhok (Science Teacher)

After his article on bullying is butchered by the editor of the school paper, an angry student launches his own publication in order to give a voice to the misfits and other under-valued teens.

LAUGH AT MY PAIN

(AMC) Producer, Jeff Clanagan; Supervising Producer, Jeff Atlas; Executive Producers, Kevin Hart, Dave Becky; Co-Producer, Quincy Newell; Director, Leslie Small; Co-Director, Kevin Hart; Special Segment Director, Tim Story; Screenplay, Kevin Hart, Harry Ratchford, Joey Wells; Photography, Ken Glassing; Designer, Bruce Ryan; Music Supervisors, Dylan Berry, Jake Belnick; Editors, A.J. Dickerson, Spencer Averick; a Hartbeat Productions and CodeBlack Entertainment in association with The Usual Suspects Productions and Comedy Central presentation; Color; Rated R; 89 minutes; Release date: September 9, 2011. Comedian Kevin Hart in concert
WITH
Kevin Hart, Na'im Lynn

Kevin Hart © AMC

Tom Hardy

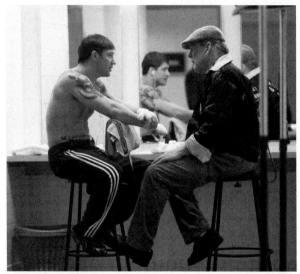

Tom Hardy, Nick Nolte

Tom Hardy, Nick Nolte

WARRIOR

(LIONSGATE) Producers, Gavin O'Connor, Greg O'Connor; Executive Producers, Michael Paseornek, Lisa Ellzey, David Mimran, Jordan Schur, John J. Kelly; Co-Producers, Anthony Tambakis, Jamie Marshall, Josh Fagin; Director, Gavin O'Connor; Screenplay, Gavin O'Connor, Anthony Tambakis, Cliff Dorfman; Story, Gavin O'Connor, Cliff Dorfman; Photography, Masanobu Takayanagi; Designer, Dan Leigh; Costumes, Abigail Murray; Music, Mark Isham; Music Supervisor, Brian Ross; Editors, John Gilroy, Sean Albertson, Matt Chessé, Aaron Marshall; Stunts/Fight Choreographer, JJ "Loco" Perry; Casting, Randi Hiller; a Mimran Schur Pictures presentation of a Lionsgate and Mimran Schur Pictures production, a Solaris Entertainment and Filmtribe production; Dolby; Panavision; Deluxe color; Rated PG-13; 140 minutes; Release date: September 9, 2011

CAST

Brendan Conlon	**Joel Edgerton**
Tommy Conlon	**Tom Hardy**
Paddy Conlon	**Nick Nolte**
Tess Conlon	**Jennifer Morrison**
Frank Grillo	**Frank Campana**
Principal Zito	**Kevin Dunn**
Colt Boyd	**Maximiliano Hernandez**
Themselves	**Bryan Callen, Sam Sheridan, Dan "Punkass" Caldwell, Timothy "Skyskrape" Katz, Josh Rosenthal, Jonathan Matthew Anik, Rashad Evans, Stephan Bonnar, Michelle Dawn Mooney**
Fenroy	**Fernando Funan Chien**
Mark Bradford	**Jake McLaughlin**
Pilar Fernandez	**Vanessa Martinez**
Stephon	**Denzel Whitaker**
Tito	**Carlos Mlranda**
Nash	**Nick Lehane**
KC	**Laura Kenley**
Emily Conlon	**Capri Thomas**
Rosie Conlon	**Lexi Cowan**
Dan Taylor	**Noah Emmerich**
J.J. Riley's Assistant	**Julia Sotckstad**
Koba	**Kurt Angle**
Pete "Mad Dog" Grimes	**Erik Apple**
Orlando "Midnight" Lee	**Anthony Johnson**
Karl Kruller	**Nate Marquardt**
Marcos Santos	**Roan Cameiro**
Francisco Barbosa	**Daniel Stevens**
Sun Chu	**Anthony Nanakornpanom**
Diego Santana	**Hans Marrerp**
Houston Greggs	**Yves Edwards**
Yosi	**Amir Perets**

Anthony Tambakis (Sparta Official), Jimmy Cvetic (Tender Trap Promoter), Jace Jeanes (Mike "The Mutilator" Moore), Jake Digman (Tender Trap Announcer), Richard Fike (Tender Trap Referee), Andre Mason (Midnight Corner Man), James Houk (State Official), Aaron R. Kleiber, Raymond Rowe, Lambert R. Strayer, Roman Vasylyshyn (Koba Entourage), Tim Bickel (A.V. Simers), Jack Fischer (Platoon Sergeant), Jeff Hochendoner, Armon York (Marine MPs), Adam Christian Stanley, James Dreussi (Marines), Kevin P. Hanley (Inspector), Tammy Townsend (Zito's Wife), Etta Cox (Zito's Secretary), Sandy Notaro (Diner Waitress), Francesca Ortenzio (Concierge), Jaime Sinue Aguirre (Manny), Tracy Campbell (Desk Girl), Thomas McCue (Taxi Cab Driver)

Former marine Tommy Conlon enslists the aide of his estranged father to train for the Sparta mixed martial arts competition, while Tommy's brother, Brendan, a former-fighter-turned teacher, returns to the ring in hopes of settling some financial debts.

This film received an Oscar nomination for supporting actor (Nick Nolte).

Nick Nolte

Tom Hardy, Joel Edgerton

Kurt Angle

Joel Edgerton, Frank Grillo

Jennifer Morrison © Lionsgate

Jennifer Morrison, Joel Edgerton

Gwyneth Paltrow

Jude Law

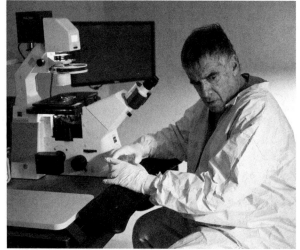

Elliott Gould

Kate Winslet, Larry Clark

Anna Jacoby-Heron, Matt Damon

Sanaa Lathan © Warner Bros.

Chin Han, Marion Cotillard

Bryan Cranston, Laurence Fisburne, Jennifer Ehle

Jennifer Ehle, Demetri Martin

CONTAGION

(WARNER BROS.) Producers, Michael Shamberg, Stacey Sher, Gregory Jacobs; Executive Producers, Jeff Skoll, Michael Polaire, Jonathan King; Director, Steven Soderbergh; Screenplay, Scott Z. Burns; Photography, Peter Andrews; Designer, Howard Cummings; Costumes, Louise Frogley; Music, Cliff Martinez; Editor, Stephen Mirrione; Casting, Carmen Cuba; a Double Feature Films/Gregory Jacobs production, presented in association with Participant Media and Imagenation Abu Dhabi; Dolby; Technicolor; Rated PG-13; 106 minutes; Release date: September 9, 2011

CAST

Dr. Leonora Orantes	**Marion Cotillard**
Mitch Emhoff	**Matt Damon**
Dr. Ellis Cheever	**Laurence Fishburne**
Alan Krumwiede	**Jude Law**
Beth Emhoff	**Gwyneth Paltrow**
Dr. Erin Mears	**Kate Winslet**
RADM Lyle Haggerty	**Bryan Cranston**
Dr. Ally Hextall	**Jennifer Ehle**
Aubrey Cheever	**Sanaa Lathan**
Roger	**John Hawkes**
Dr. David Eisenberg	**Demetri Martin**
Dr. Ian Sussman	**Elliott Gould**
Dave	**Larry Clarke**
Jory Emhoff	**Anna Jacoby-Heron**
Li Fai	**Chui Tien You**
Li Fai's Sister	**Josie Ho**
Irina	**Daria Strokous**
Clark Marrow	**Griffin Kane**
Japanese Bus Man	**Yoshiaki Kobayashi**
Lorraine Vasquez	**Monique Gabriela Curnen**
School Nurse	**Teri McEvoy**
Damian Leopold	**Armin Rohde**
Dennis French	**Enrico Colantoni**

Sue Redman, Teri Campbell (ER Nurses), Stef Tovar (Dr. Arrington), Mary Jo Faraci (Social Worker), Grace Rex (Carrie Anne), Joseph Anthony Foronda (WHO Official), Phillip James Brannon (Paramedic), Rebecca Spence (Jon Neal's Wife), David Lively (Minnesota Medical Examiner), Andrew White (Assistant Medical Examiner), Ira Blumen, MD (Helpful Doctor), Scott Stangland, Jimmy Chung, Rick Uecker, Tara Mallen (Minnesota Health), John Hines, Joshua Weinstein, Sarah Charipar, Mark Czoske (AIMM Employees), Dan Aho (Aaron Barnes), Chin Han (Sun Feng), Hee-Wan Kwon (Japanese Official), Phil Tang, Robert Chi (Village Men), Blair Robertson (Sussman's Assistant), Randy Lowell (Hedge Fund Man in Park), Pete Sack (TV Anchor), Brian J. O'Donnell (Andrew), Kwok Wah Wong, Sau Ming Raymond Tsang (Chinese Health Officials), Jim Ortlieb (Funeral Director), Annabel Armour (Beth's Mother), Kara Zediker (Elizabeth Nygaard), Joshua Pollock (Coughing Man), Laura T. Fisher (Sick Lady), Peter A. Kelly (National Guardsman), Marty Beth Dolan (Nun), Jason Babinsky (Shivering Man), Howie Johnson (Morgue Worker), Sanjay Gupta, MD (Himself), Thomas Gebbia (Man with Megaphone), Dan Flannery (Hextall's Father), Dan Sanders-Joyce (Home Invasion Thug), Joshua Seiden (Anthony), Kam Tong Wong (Chef), Steven Soderbergh (Voice of John Neal)

Returning from a business trip to Hong Kong, Beth Emhoff soon succumbs to a mysterious disease, which is only the beginning of a series of similar deaths that trigger a world wide contagion.

I DON'T KNOW HOW SHE DOES IT

(WEINSTEIN CO.) Producer, Donna Gigliotti; Executive Producers, Bob Weinstein, Harvey Weinstein, Kelly Carmichael, Aline Brosh McKenna, Scott Ferguson, Ben Silverman; Co-Producer, Allison Pearson; Director, Douglas McGrath; Screenplay, Aline Brosh McKenna; Based upon the novel by Allison Pearson; Photography, Stuart Dryburgh; Designer, Santo Loquasto; Costumes, Renée Ehrlich Kalfus; Music, Aaron Zigman; Casting, Douglas Aibel; Dolby; Color; Rated PG-13; 89 minutes; Release date: September 16, 2011

CAST
Kate Reddy	**Sarah Jessica Parker**
Jack Abelhammer	**Pierce Brosnan**
Richard Reddy	**Greg Kinnear**
Allison Henderson	**Christina Hendricks**
Clark Cooper	**Kelsey Grammer**
Chris Bunce	**Seth Meyers**
Momo Hahn	**Olivia Munn**
Marla Reddy	**Jane Curtin**

Mark Blum (Lew Reddy), Busy Philipps (Wendy Best), Sarah Shahi (Janine LoPietro), Jessica Szohr (Paula), Emma Rayne Lyle (Emily Reddy), Julius Goldberg, Theodore Goldberg (Ben Reddy), James Murtaugh (Roger Harcourt), Mika Brzezinski (Herself), Eugenia Yuan (Jack's Receptionist), Joseph Amato (I/T Guy), Michelle Hurst (Nurse), Beth Fowler (Clark's Secretary), Michael Hogan (Bowling Alley Clerk), Marceline Hugot (Beth), Steve Routman (Marcus), Raymond McAnally (Roy), Katie Jyde Lewars (Organic Mom), Robbie Sublett (Dad), Natalie Gold (Young Mother with Cell Phone), Lorna Pruce (Woman in Bowling Alley), Jacob Alexander (Towncar Driver)

Financial executive Kate Reddy gives the outward impression of "having it all," while actually struggling to cope with the pressures of business and family.

Sarah Jessica Parker, Pierce Brosnan © Weinstein Co.

Sarah Jessica Parker, Greg Kinnear

Mia Wasikowska, Henry Hopper

Henry Hopper, Ryo Kase © Sony Pictures Classics

RESTLESS

(SONY CLASSICS) Producers, Brian Grazer, Ron Howard, Bryce Dallas Howard, Gus Van Sant; Executive Producers, David Allen Cress, Eric Black, Michael Sugar, Sarah Bowen, Erica Huggins; Director, Gus Van Sant; Screenplay, Jason Lew; Photography, Harris Savides; Designer, Anne Ross; Costumes, Danny Glicker; Music, Danny Elfman; Editor, Elliot Graham; an Imagine Entertainment presentation of a Brian Grazer production; Dolby; Deluxe color; Rated PG-13; 91 minutes; Release date: September 16, 2011

CAST
Enoch Brae	**Henry Hopper**
Annabel Cotton	**Mia Wasikowska**
Hiroshi Takahashi	**Ryo Kase**
Elizabeth Cotton	**Schuyler Fisk**
Rachel Cotton	**Lusia Strus**
Mabel	**Jane Adams**
Edward	**Paul Parson**
Minister	**Thomas Lauderdale**

Christopher D. Harder (Funeral Director), Morgan Lee (Driver), Kenneth L. Peterson (CT Technician), William Eggleston (X-Ray Technician), Chin Han (Dr. Lee), John Goodwin (Nurse Goodwin), Kelleen Crawford (Nurse Laura), Meg Chamberlain (Suzette), Sotirios Bakouros (Ian), Victor Morris (Joseph), Strider Schmidt (Screaming Boy), Colton Lasater (Ozzie), Jesse Henderson (Alger), Liz Osthus (Eulogist), Garland Lyons (Police Officer), De Ann Marie Odom (Enoch's Nurse), Frank Etxaniz (Frank), Kyle Leatherberry (Orderly)

An emotionally troubled young man finds himself falling in love with a girl facing a terminal illness.

James Woods

James Marsden, Laz Alonso © Screen Gems

Drew Powell, Alexander Skarsgård

James Marsden, Kate Bosworth

STRAW DOGS

(SCREEN GEMS) Producer, Marc Frydman; Executive Producers, Beau Marks, Gilbert Dumontet; Director/Screenplay, Rod Lurie; Based on the screenplay by David Zelag Goodman and Sam Peckinpah and on the novel *The Siege of Trencher's Farm* by Gordon Williams; Photography, Alik Sakharov; Designer, Tony Fanning; Costumes, Lynn Falconer; Music, Larry Groupé; Editor, Sarah Boyd; Special Effects Supervisor, John J. Lynch; Stunts, Mic Rodgers; Casting, Sharon Bialy, Sherry Thomas; a Battleplan production; Dolby; Super 35 Widescreen; Deluxe color; Rated R; 110 minutes; Release date: September 16, 2011

CAST
David Sumner	**James Marsden**
Amy Sumner	**Kate Bosworth**
Charlie	**Alexander Skarsgård**
Tom Heddon ("Coach")	**James Woods**
Jeremy Niles	**Dominic Purcell**
Norman	**Rhys Coiro**
Chris	**Billy Lush**
Sheriff John Burke	**Laz Alonso**
Janice Heddon	**Willa Holland**
Daniel Niles	**Walton Goggins**
Coach Milkens	**Anson Mount**
Bic	**Drew Powell**
Abby	**Kristen Shaw**

Megan Adelle (Melissa), Jessica Cook (Helen), Randall Newsome (Blackie), Tim Smith (Larry), Richard Folmer (Pastor), Wanetah Walmsley (Kristen), Clyde Heun (Referee), Rod Lurie (Logger #1), Kelly Holleman (Beauty Queen), Grayson Capps, Tommy MacLuckie, Josh Kerin, John Milham (Band Members), Kristin Kelly (Teenager at BBQ)

A mild-mannered screenwriter and his wife return to her redneck Southern town to live, only to encounter a simmering hostility from her ex-boyfriend and several of the locals who want to give the outsiders a hard time. Remake of the 1971 Cinerama-ABC film that starred Dustin Hoffman and Susan George.

Oscar Isaac, Ryan Gosling

Albert Brooks, Ryan Gosling

Ryan Gosling © FilmDistrict

DRIVE

(FILMDISTRICT) Producers, Marc Platt, Adam Siegel, Gigi Pritzker, Michel Litvak, John Palermo; Executive Producers, David Lancaster, Gary Michael Walters, Bill Lischak, Linda McDonough, Jeffrey Stott, Peter Schlessel; Director, Nicholas Winding Refn; Screenplay, Hossein Amini; Based on the novel by James Sallis; Photography, Newton Thomas Sigel; Designer, Beth Mickle; Costumes, Erin Benach; Music, Cliff Martinez; Editor, Mat Newman; Casting, Mindy Marin; a Marc Platt/Motel Movies production, presented in association with Bold Films and Oddlot Entertainment; Dolby; Widescreen; Fotokem Color; Rated R; 100 minutes; Release date; September 16, 2011

CAST

Driver	**Ryan Gosling**
Irene	**Carey Mulligan**
Shannon	**Bryan Cranston**
Bernie Rose	**Albert Brooks**
Standard	**Oscar Isaac**
Blanche	**Christina Hendricks**
Nino	**Ron Perlman**
Benicio	**Kaden Leos**
Tan Suit	**Jeff Wolfe**
Cook	**James Biberi**
Doc	**Russ Tamblyn**
Chauffeur	**Joey Bucaro**
Young Woman	**Tiara Parker**
Hitmen	**Tim Trella, Jimmy Hart**
Waitress	**Tina Huang**
Stripper	**Andy San Dimas**
Bearded Redneck	**John Pyper-Ferguson**
Masked Men	**Craig Baxley Jr., Kenny Richards**
Assistant Directors	**Joe Pingue, Dieter H. Busch**
Caterer	**Chris Muto**
Newscaster	**Rachel Dik**
Waiter	**Cesar Garcia**
Movie Star	**Steve Knoll**
Movie Star's Girlfriend	**Mara LaFontaine**
Police Officer	**Teonee Thrash**
Basketball Announcer	**Ralph Lawler**

A movie stunt driver, who supplements his income by driving getaway cars for criminals, is plunged into a seemingly inescapable quandary after an unexpected turn of events causes disaster at one of his jobs.

This film received an Oscar nomination for sound editing.

Tim Trella, Ryan Gosling

Ryan Gosling

Carey Mulligan

Ron Perlman

Christina Hendricks

Bryan Cranston

DOLPHIN TALE

(WARNER BROTHERS) Producers, Andrew A. Kosove, Broderick Johnson, Richard Ingber; Executive Producers, Robert Engelman, Steven P. Wegner; Co-Producers, Yolanda T. Cochran, David Yates; Director, Charles Martin Smith; Screenplay, Karen Janszen, Noam Dromi; Photography, Karl Walter Lindenlaub; Designer, Michael Corenblith; Costumes, Hope Hanafin; Music, Mark Isham; Music Supervisor, Deva Anderson; Editor, Harvey Rosenstock; Visual Effects Supervisor, Robert Munroe; Stunts/Marine Coordinator, Ricou Browning, Jr.; an Alcon Entertainment presentation; Dolby; Technicolor; 3D; Rated PG; 113 minutes; Release date: September 23, 2011

CAST

Dr. Clay Haskett	**Harry Connick, Jr.**
Lorraine Nelson	**Ashley Judd**
Sawyer Nelson	**Nathan Gamble**
Reed Haskett	**Kris Kristofferson**
Hazel Haskett	**Cozi Zuehlsdorff**
Dr. Cameron McCarthy	**Morgan Freeman**
Kyle Connellan	**Austin Stowell**
Gloria Forrest	**Frances Sternhagen**
Phoebe	**Austin Highsmith**
Kat	**Betsy Landin**
Rebecca	**Juliana Harkavy**
Brittany	**Megan Lozicki**
Philip J. Hordern	**Tom Nowicki**
Max Connellan	**Jim Fitzpatrick**
Alyce Connellan	**Kim Ostrenko**
Donovan Peck	**Michael Roark**
Fisherman	**Richard Libertini**
Herself	**Winter**
Mr. Doyle	**Ray McKinnon**
Sandra Sinclair	**Ashley White**
Coach Vansky	**Rus Blackwell**
Board Member Fitch	**Marc Macaulay**
Board Member Marx	**Jennifer De Castroverde**
Board Member Christina	**Denise Durette**
Virginia	**Vivian Ruiz**
Little Girl in Wheelchair	**Laila Harris**
Little Girl's Mother	**Stacy Ann Rose**
Veteran Tim	**Kurt Yaeger**
Veteran Mike	**Mike Maki**
Prosthetic Consultant	**Mike Pniewski**
Bullies	**Nicholas Turner Martin, Carlos Guerrero Jr.**
Kyle's Friend	**Paul Amadi**
Hordern Grandchild	**Charlotte Connick**

The true story of how an injured dolphin required her tail to be amputated, which led to a special prosthetic device being fashioned to help her swim again.

Nathan Gamble, Winter © Warner Bros.

Nathan Gamble, Cozi Zuehlsdorff, Kris Kristofferson

Juliana Harkavy, Nathan Gamble, Austin Highsmith, Cozi Zuehlsdorff, Harry Connick, Jr.

Ashley Judd

Nathan Gamble, Morgan Freeman, Austin Highsmith, Cozi Zuehlsdorff, Harry Connick Jr.

Nathan Gamble, Harry Connick, Jr.

Winter

Nathan Gamble, Austin Stowell

Nathan Gamble

Brad Pitt, Jonah Hill

Brad Pitt

Chris Pratt

Brad Pitt

Brad Pitt © Columbia Pictures

Brad Pitt, Kerris Dorsey

MONEYBALL

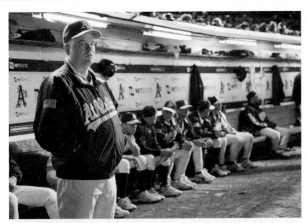

Philip Seymour Hoffman

Jonah Hill

(COLUMBIA) Producers, Michael De Luca, Rachael Horovitz, Brad Pitt; Executive Producers, Scott Rudin, Andrew Karsch, Sidney Kimmel, Mark Bakshi; Director, Bennett Miller; Screenplay, Steven Zaillian, Aaron Sorkin; Story, Stan Chervin; Based on the book *Moneyball: The Art of Winning an Unfair Game* by Michael Lewis; Photography, Wally Pfister; Designer, Jess Gonchor; Costumes, Kasia Walicka Maimone; Music, Mychael Danna; Editor, Christopher Tellefsen; Baseball Coordinator, Michael Fisher; Casting, Francine Maisler; a Scott Rudin/Michael De Luca/Rachael Horovitz production; Dolby; Deluxe color; Rated PG-13; 133 minutes; Release date: September 23, 2011

CAST

Billy Beane	**Brad Pitt**
Peter Brand	**Jonah Hill**
Art Howe	**Philip Seymour Hoffman**
Sharon	**Robin Wright**
Scott Hatteberg	**Chris Pratt**
David Justice	**Stephen Bishop**
Mark Shapiro	**Reed Diamond**
Ron Washington	**Brent Jennings**
Grady Fuson	**Ken Medlock**
Elizabeth Hatteberg	**Tammy Blanchard**
John Poloni	**Jack McGee**
Pittaro	**Vyto Ruginis**
Matt Keough	**Nick Searcy**
Ron Hopkins	**Glenn Morshower**
Chad Bradford	**Casey Bond**
Jeremy Giambi	**Nick Porrazzo**
Casey Beane	**Kerris Dorsey**
John Henry	**Arliss Howard**
Young Billy	**Reed Thompson**
Billy's Dad	**James Shanklin**
Billy's Mom	**Diane Behrens**
Suzanne – Billy's Secretary	**Takayo Fischer**

Derrin Ebert (Mike Magnante), Miguel Mendoza (Ricardo Rincon), Adrian Bellani (Carlos Peña), Tom Gamboa (Scout Martinez), Barry Moss (Scout Barry), Artie Harris (Scout Artie), Bob Bishop (Scout Bob), George Vranau (Scout George), Phil Pote (Scout Pote), Art Ortiz (Eric Chavez), Royce Clayton (Miguel Tejada), Marvin Horn (Terrence Long), Brent Dohling (Mark Ellis), Ken Rudulph, Lisa Guerrero (Reporters), Christopher Dehau Lee (Eric Kubota), Joe Satriani (Himself), Simon James (Voos), Greg Papa (Game Announcer), Bob Costas, Tim McCarver (Sports Announcers), Eddie Frierson (Call-In Radio Host), Glen Kupier (Oakland A's Announcer), Joe Provost (Oakland A's Security Guard), John Cole (Young Jongewaard), Jake Wilson (Sabatini), Robert P. Macaluso (Coach Bob), Keith Middlebrook (Coach Parker), Damon Farmar (Shapiro's Advisor), Michael Gillespie (Ken Macha), Chad Kreuter (Rick Peterson), Blake Pike (John), Robert Ninfo (Eric Byrnes), Gary Johnson (Jermaine Dye), Corey Vanderhook (Ramon Hernandez), Melvin Perdue (Ray Durham), Ari Zagaris (Jim Mecir), Jonathan Stein (Seymour), Madeleine G. Hall (Hatteberg's Daughter), Holly Pitrago (Shapiro's Assistant), Ken Korach (Radio Color Commentator), Julie Wagner, Ken Colquit (Clubhouse Reporters), Eric Winzenried (PR Guy), Richard Padilla (Umpire – Game 20), Ed Montague (Umpire – Indians), Jack Knight (Umpire – 1984), Patrick Riley (Umpire – 1989), Phil Benson (1st Base Umpire), Joyce Guy (Flight Attendant), George Thomas (Security Guard #2), Chris McGarry (Ed Wade)

Having lost his star players, Oakland A's coach Billy Beane teams with a Yale economics specialist to rebuild his team.

This film received Oscar nominations for picture, actor (Brad Pitt), supporting actor (Jonah Hill), adapted screenplay, film editing, and sound mixing.

Brad Pitt

MACHINE GUN PREACHER

(RELATIVITY) Producers, Robbie Brenner, Gary Safady, Deborah Giarratana, Craig Chapman, Marc Forster; Executive Producers, Myles Nestel, Louise Rosner-Meyer, Brad Simpson; Director, Marc Forster; Screenplay, Jason Keller; Photography, Roberto Schaefer; Designer, Philip Messina; Costumes, Frank L. Fleming; Music, Asche & Spencer; Editor, Matt Chessé; Casting, Kerry Barden, Paul Schnee; a Safady Entertainment, Apparatus GG Filmz production in association with 1984 P.D.C. MPower Pictures ITS Captial and Merlina Entertainment, presented in association with Virgin Produced; Dolby; Hawk Scope Widescreen; color; Rated R; 127 minutes; Release date: September 23, 2011

CAST
Sam Childers	**Gerard Butler**
Lynn Childers	**Michelle Monaghan**
Daisy	**Kathy Baker**
Donnie	**Michael Shannon**
Paige	**Madeline Carroll**
Deng	**Souleymane Sy Savane**

Grant Krause (Billy, Contractor), Reavis Graham (Pastor Krause), Peter Carey (Bill Wallace), Barbara Coven (Shannon Wallace), Misty Mills (Biker Chick), Nicole Sobchack (Bartender), Sidi Henderson (Shaved Head), Mike Litaker (Drifter), Judy Stepanian (Employment Woman), Peter Tocco (Mechanic), Inga Wilson (Mrs. Shields), Bruce Bennett (Pastor Relling), Brett Wagner (Ben Hobbs, Biker), Ava Schroeder (Hobb's Daughter), Sean Patrick Leonard (Crackhead), Amanda Carlson (Paige's Friend), David Whitesell (Customs Officer), Matthew Boucher (Mover), Richard Goteri (Pawnshop Owner), Claudia Rodgers (Suc, Volunteer), Michele DeSelms (Newscaster), Rhema Voraritskul (Child Singer), Janet L. Miller (Church Pianist), Paul Lang (Prison Clerk), Percy Matsemela (Nineteen), Ronnie Nyakale (AJ), Mduduzi Mabaso (Marco), Fana Mokoena (John Garang), Junior Magale (William), Abena Ayivor (Betty), Warona Seane (Rose), Sophie 'Mer' Ayang (Betty's Helper), Ruley Madriagi, Chris Agwai, Makhaola Ndebele, Mandla Gaduka (SPLA Soldiers), Jacob Ayuel (SPLA Dinka Soldier), Khutso Thobejane (Matak), Tshepiso Chanke (Cleo), Nompumeleo Khumalo (Poppy), Tinah Mnumzana (William's Mother), Themba Ndaba (William's Father), Kgosi Modisane (Christopher at 12 years old), Leonard Mahore, Sphelele Mzimela (LRA Walking Soldiers), Warren Masemola, Wandile Molebatsi (LRA Commanders), Festo Ayume Sanya (Village Man #1), Anthony Bishop (Dan), Jerry Mofokeng (Administrator), Xolile Gama, Khulu Skenjana (Adult Rebels), Nande Myamya (Alice), Aristotle Bashengezi (Alice's Brother), Zithulele 'Zele' Masondo (Alice's Sister), Mulweli Muofhe (Anthony), Masasa Mbangeni (Lip-less Woman), Jan Rust Maloney, Marianee Boshof (Doctors), Robert Kuloba (Acholi Refugee), , Tau Maserumule (LRA Soldier), Sicelo Sithole (LRA Leader at Bridge), Wandile Mdandla, Sebo Moabelo (Child Rebels at Bridge)

The true story of how ex-con Sam Childers turned to religion and journeyed to Sudan to help rescue children from the carnage of war.

Souleymane Sy Savane, Gerard Butler © Relativity Media

Mark Kassen, Chris Evans © Millennium Pictures

PUNCTURE

(MILLENNIUM) Producers/Directors, Adam Kassen, Mark Kassen; Executive Producers, Paul Danziger, Rod De Llano, Craig Cohen, Jeffrey Gou, Joan Huang; Screenplay, Chris Lopata; Story, Ela Their, Paul Danziger; Photography, Helge Gerull; Designer, Christopher Stull; Costumes, Kari Perkins; Music, Ryan Ross Smith; Editor, Chip Smith; Casting, Nicole Daniels, Courtney Bright; a Like Minded Pictures presentation in association with Cherry Sky Films; Dolby; Color; Rated R; 99 minutes; Release date: September 23, 2011

CAST
Mike Weiss	**Chris Evans**
Paul Danziger	**Mark Kassen**
Jeffrey Dancort	**Marshall Bell**
Nathaniel Price	**Brett Cullen**
Daryl King	**Jesse L. Martin**
Nurse Vicky Rogers	**Vinessa Shaw**

Roxanna Hope (Sylvia), Michael Biehn (Red), Kate Burton (Senator O'Reilly), Erinn Allison (Kim Danziger), Tess Parker (Jaime Weiss), Justin Anderson (Skateboard Kid), Jack Lee (Mr. Clean), Brittney Karbowski (Suzie, Blonde Student), Mark Lanier (Himself), Danae Ayala (Nicole Morris), Troy Hogan (Pete Downing), Claire Risoli (Karen Baker), Jennifer Blanc (Stephany), Matt Hill (Street Dealer), Phil Fisher (Bartender), Austin Stowell (ER Medic), Amelia Jeffries (Rita King), Shelley Calene-Black, Werner Richmond (Hospital Administators), David Maldonado (ER Doctor), Craig Nigh (Senator's Chief Aide), Linda Lorelle Gregory (Denise Starks), Samuel Romero (Neck Brace), Anthony Solomon (Thug), Bo Johnson (Fire Chief), Davi Jay (EMS Captain), Cheryl Tanner (ER Doctor), Susan O'Rourke (News Reporter), Bob Boudreaux (Network Reporter), Deanna Brochin (Tiffany), David Born (Judge Black), Patrick Henning (Court Clerk), Barry Stiles (Shipping Manager), Julin Jean (Candy), Katie Stuckey (Nurse), Bill Ross (Dan Jones), Jim Lawrence (Purchasing Officer), Shondra Marie (Administrator – Pink Blouse), Adam Kassen (Young Doctor), Ruth Garcia (Pierced Mexican Woman), Pineapple Tangaroa (Large Samoan), Luke Waterson (David, 6 years), Sophia Boisvert (Kia, 9 years), Paris Smith (Kia, 12 years), Max Maisonneuve (David, 9 years), Weldon Renfro (Shoeshine Guy), Steve Garris (Waiter), Marty Fleck (Well-Dressed Lawyer), Morgane Slemp (Nurse), Jake Messinger (Doctor)

A drug addicted lawyer and his more responsible partner decide to take on a case involving an ER nurse who has been pricked by a contaminated needle while at work.

Clive Owen © Open Road Films

Yvonne Strahovski, Jason Statham

Jason Statham

KILLER ELITE

(OPEN ROAD FILMS) Producers, Sigurjon Sighvatsson, Steven Chasman, Michael Boughen, Tony Winley; Executive Producer, Christopher Mapp, Matthew Street, David Whealy, Peter D. Graves; Director, Gary McKendry; Screenplay, Matt Sherring; Inspired by the book *The Feather Men* by Sir Ranulph Fiennes; Photography, Simon Duggan; Designer, Michelle McGahey; Costumes, Katherine Milne, Aude Bronson-Howard; Music, Johnny Klimek, Reinhold Heil; Editor, John Gilbert; Casting, Leigh Pickford, Maura Fay Casting; an Omnilab Media presentation of an Ambience Entertainment production in association with Current Entertainment and Sighvatsson Films, Film Victoria and the Wales Creative IP Fund; American-Australian; Dolby; Super 35 Widescreen; Deluxe Color; Rated R; 105 minutes; Release date: September 23, 2011

CAST
Danny	**Jason Statham**
Spike	**Clive Owen**
Hunter	**Robert De Niro**
Davies	**Dominic Purcell**
Meier	**Aden Young**
Anne	**Yvonne Strahovski**
Martin	**Ben Mendelsohn**
Sheikh Amr	**Rodney Afif**
Agent	**Adewale Akinnuoye-Agbaje**
MI6 Man	**David Whiteley**
Pennock	**Matthew Nable**
Harris	**Lachy Hulme**
Bakhait	**Firass Dirani**

Nick Tate (Commander B), Bille Brown (Colonel Fitz), Stewart Morritt (Campbell), Grant Bowler (Cregg), Michael Dorman (Jake), Daniel Roberts (McCann), Rodney Afif (Sheikh Amr), Jamie McDowell (Diane), Dion Mills (Fiennes), Andrew Stehlin (Dutchy), Simon Armstrong (Gowling), Richard Elfyn (Porter), Chris Anderson (Finn), Brendan Charleson (Bazza), Sandy Greenwood (Harris' Girlfriend), Boris Brkic (Justice), Riley Evans (Joey), Sofia Nikitina (Donna), Tim Hughes (Major D), Tony Porter (Colonel Z), Michael Carman (The Don), Jack Llewellyn (Soldier #1), Huw Garmon, Barry Stones (Sergeants), Salim Fayad (Karim Bux), Sharbel Sukkar (Bakhait Guard), Melissa Martin (Woman in Office), Stephen Phillips (Local), Kristy Barnes-Cullen (Supply Room Nurse), Kate Neilson (Air Hostess), Ray Tiernan (Footman), Zane Dirani (Hussain), Mohamed Dirani (Salim), Michael Dirani (Ali), Emily Jordan (Exotic Woman), Grahame Mapp, Sue Mapp (Airline Passengers), Blake O'Leary, Cody Faull (Car Kids)

When his former partner is kidnapped by an Omani sheikh, hitman Danny agrees to help the despotic ruler eliminate those responsible for killing his sons.

Robert De Niro, Jason Statham

Lily Collins, Taylor Lautner

Alfred Molina, Taylor Lautner

Taylor Lautner, Sigourney Weaver

ABDUCTION

(LIONSGATE) Producers, Doug Davison, Ellen Goldsmith-Vein, Lee Stollman, Roy Lee, Dan Lautner, Pat Crowley; Executive Producers, Jeremy Bell, Gabriel Mason, Anthony Katagas, Allison Shearmur, Wolfgang Hammer; Director, John Singleton; Screenplay, Shawn Christensen; Photography, Peter Menzies Jr.; Designer, Keith Brian Burns; Costumes, Ruth Carter; Music, Edward Shearmur; Music Supervisor, Tracy McKnight; Editor, Bruce Cannon; Special Effects Coordinator, Drew Jiritano; Stunts, Brad Martin; Casting, Joseph Middleton; a GothamGroup/Vertigo Entertainment/Quick Six Entertainment production, a Lionsgate production in association with Mango Films; Dolby; Deluxe color; Rated PG-13; 106 minutes; Release date: September 23, 2011

CAST
Nathan	**Taylor Lautner**
Karen	**Lily Collins**
Burton	**Alfred Molina**
Kevin	**Jason Isaacs**
Mara	**Maria Bello**
Dr. Bennett	**Sigourney Weaver**
Gilly	**Denzel Whitaker**
Kozlow	**Michael Nyqvist**
Gregory	**Richard Cetrone**
Tom Shealy	**Victor Slezak**
Mr. Miles	**Roger Guenveur Smith**
Burns	**Antonique Smith**

Jake Andolina (CIA Man), Oriah Acima Andrews (Riah), Ken Arnold (Thermal), Steve Blass (Game Announcer), Derek Burnell (Hot Dog Vendor), Ben Cain (Driver), Holly Scott Cavanaugh (Mrs. Murphy), Radick Cembrzynski (Kozlow's Tech), Mike Clark (News Reporter), Jack Erdie (Short Sleeves), Rita Gregory (Nurse), Tim Griffin (Red Flannel), Nathan Hollabaugh (Cop), Mike Lee (Tech), James Liebro (Stadium Usher), Frank Lloyd (Brighton Beach #2), Christopher Mahoney (Caretaker), Emily Peachey (Girl), William Peltz (Jake), Elisabeth Rohm (Woman, Lorna), Nickola Shreli (Alek), Antonique Smith (Burns), Adam Stanley (CIA SWAT Leader), Art Terry (Amtrak Security Guard), Ilia Volok (Sweater), Cherokee Walker (Helicopter Pilot), Allen Williamson (Billy), Dermot Mulroney (Martin Price)

After finding his image on a missing persons' website, Nathan's parents are killed, prompting him and his neighbor to flee in hopes of finding out his true identity and why the CIA and an underworld boss are after him.

Taylor Lautner © Lionsgate

DREAM HOUSE

(UNIVERSAL) Producers, James G. Robinson, David Robinson, Daniel Bobker, Ehren Kruger; Executive Producers, Rick Nicita, Mike Drake; Director, Jim Sheridan; Screenplay, David Loucka; Photography, Caleb Deschanel; Designer, Carol Spier; Costumes, Delphine White; Music, John Debney; Music Supervisor, Dave Jordan; Editor, Glen Scantlebury; Visual Effects Supervisors, Dion Hatch, Marc Kolbe; Casting, Avy Kaufman; a James G. Robinson presentation of a Morgan Creek production, a Bobker/Kruger Films production; Dolby; Super 35 Widescreen; Deluxe color; Rated PG-13; 92 minutes; Release date: September 30, 2011

CAST
Will Atenton	**Daniel Craig**
Ann Patterson	**Naomi Watts**
Libby	**Rachel Weisz**
Jack Patterson	**Marton Csokas**
Dr. Greeley	**Jane Alexander**
Boyce	**Elias Koteas**
Trish	**Taylor Geare**
Dee Dee	**Claire Astin Geare**

Rachel Fox (Chloe Patterson), Brian Murray (Dr. Medlin), Bernadette Quigley (Heather Keeler), Sarah Gadon (Cindi), Gregory Smith (Artie), Mark Wilson (Capt. Conklin), David Huband (Officer Nelson), Martin Roach (Tommy), Jean Yoon (New Editor), Lynne Griffin (Sadie), Jonathan Potts (Tony Ferguson), Marlee Otto (Young Author), Nigel Henry, Bryon Mumford (Author's Assistants/Guards), Joe Pingue (Martin), Ryan Blakely (Harkness Client), Karen Glave (Harkness Receptionist), David Fox (Building Inspector)

Will Atenton's hopes of settling into a comfortable suburban house in order to write a novel are disrupted by a series of unexplainable events that lead him to believe that something supernatural is taking place and that all is not what it appears to be.

Claire Astin Geare, Daniel Craig, Rachel Weisz © Universal Studios

Ari Graynor, Anna Faris, Kate Simses © Twentieth Century Fox

WHAT'S YOUR NUMBER?

(20TH CENTURY FOX) Producers, Beau Flynn, Tripp Vinson; Executive Producers, Arnon Milchan, Anna Faris, Nan Morales; Director, Mark Mylod; Screenplay, Gabrielle Allan, Jennifer Crittenden; Based on the book *20 Times a Lady* by Karyn Bosnak; Photography, J. Michael Muro; Designer, Jon Billington; Costumes, Amy Westcott; Music, Aaron Zigman; Music Supervisor, Julia Michels; Editor, Julie Monroe; Casting, Kathleen Chopin; a Regency Enterprises presentation of a New Regency/Contrafilm production; Dolby; Super 35 Widescreen; Deluxe color; Rated R; 106 minutes; Release date: September 30, 2011

CAST
Ally Darling	**Anna Faris**
Colin Shea	**Chris Evans**
Daisy Darling	**Ari Graynor**
Roger the Boss	**Joel McHale**
Mr. Darling	**Ed Begley, Jr.**
Ava Darling	**Blythe Danner**

Oliver Jackson-Cohen (Eddie Vogel), Heather Burns (Eileen), Eliza Coupe (Sheila), Kate Simses (Katie), Tika Sumpter (Jamie), Jacquelyn Doucette (Sheila's Mom), Zachary Quinto (Boyfriend Rick), Chris Pratt (Disgusting Donald), Anthony Mackie (Tom Piper), Denise Vasi (Cara), Sondra James (Plant Lady), Jason Bowen (Brad), Danielle Perry (Melissa), Tyler Peck (Gene), Mike Vogel (Dave Hansen), Martin Freeman (Simon), Andy Samberg (Gerry Perry), Nadine Jacobson (14 Year Old Ally), Colby Parsons (14 Year Old Jake), Thomas Lennon (Dr. Barrett Ingold), Lonnie Farmer (Maitre D' at Italian Restaurant), Ivana Milicevic (Jacinda), Dave Annable (Jake Adams), Aziz Ansari (Jay), Ed Jewett (Kevin), Bronwen Booth (Officiant at Wedding), Ben Hanson (Security Guard at Wedding), Elio Lo Russo (Accordion Player), Dale Place (Man at Library), Alyana Barbosa, Molly Goldfarb, Jackson Walsh, Henry J. Grabowski (Kids), Aaron C. Belyea, Carl Alleyne, Damon Carter, Jaime Galarza Jr., Johan Narsjo, Penni Layne, Steve Bankuti, Larry Jackson (Daisy's Band Members), Eli T. Scheer, Jon Bistline, Eliot Hunt, Shawn Marquis (Colin's Band Members), Onur Dilise, Ann Dillon, Emily Wolf, Robin Ryczek (Quartet Members), Andy Favreau (Matt)

Realizing it is time to stop sleeping around and settle down, Ally Darling decides to track down all the men she dated in hopes of finding one with whom she can hit it off again.

50/50

(SUMMIT) Producers, Evan Goldberg, Seth Rogen, Ben Karlin; Executive Producers, Nathan Kahane, Will Reiser; Line Producer, Shawn Williamson; Co-Producers, Nicole Brown, Kelli Konop, Tendo Nagenda; Director, Jonathan Levine; Screenplay, Will Reiser; Photography, Terry Stacey; Designer, Annie Spitz; Costumes, Carla Hetland; Music, Michael Giacchino; Music Supervisors, Jim Black, Gabe Hilfer; Editor, Zene Baker; Casting, Francine Maisler; a Point Grey production, presented in association with Mandate Pictures; Dolby; Technicolor; Rated R; 100 minutes; Release date: September 30, 2011

Anna Kendrick, Joseph Gordon-Levitt

CAST
Adam Lerner	**Joseph Gordon-Levitt**
Kyle	**Seth Rogen**
Katherine	**Anna Kendrick**
Rachael	**Bryce Dallas Howard**
Diane	**Anjelica Huston**
Richard	**Serge Houde**
Dr. Ross	**Andrew Airlie**
Mitch	**Matt Frewer**
Alan	**Philip Baker Hall**
Dr. Walderson	**Donna Yamamoto**
Susan	**Sugar Lyn Beard**

Yee Jee Tso (Dr. Lee), Sarah Smyth (Jenny), Peter Kelamis (Phil), Jessica Parker Kennedy (Jackie), Daniel Bacon (Dr. Phillips), P. Lynn Johnson (Bernie), Laura Bertram (Claire), Matty Finochio (Ted), Luisa D'Oliveira (Agabelle Loogenburgen), Veena Sood (Nurse Stewart), Jason Vaisvila (Cute Guy with Dreads), Brent Sheppard (Minister), Marie Avgeropoulos (Allison), Adrian McMorran (Bartender), Stephanie Belding (Friendly Nurse), Andrea Brooks (Attractive Woman #2), Ryan W. Smith (Joe), Karen van Blankenstein (Nurse Scott), William "Bigsleeps" Stewart (George), Bonnie Bolivar (Elderly Chemo Patient), Beatrice Ilg (Pretty Girl), Chilton Crane (Mother on the Bus), Amitai Marmorstein (Young Person on the Bus), Lauren A. Miller (Bodie), Will Reiser (Greg), Richard C. Burton (Thom the Patient), Neil Corbett (Hospital Tech), Karolina Anna Sabat, Christopher De Schuster (Art Gallery Patrons), Susan McLellan (Bar Girl), Marlow the Wonderdog (Himself), Denver, William (Skeletor)

Young Adam Lerner faces a 50/50 chance of survival when he is diagnosed with cancer.

Joseph Gordon-Levitt, Seth Rogen

Anjelica Huston © Summit Entertainment

Bryce Dallas Howard, Joseph Gordon-Levitt

Michael Shannon, Tova Stewart

Michael Shannon

Michael Shannon © Sony Pictures Classics

TAKE SHELTER

(SONY CLASSICS) Producers, Tyler Davidson, Sophia Lin; Executive Producers, Sarah Green, Brian Kavanaugh-Jones, Colin Strause, Greg Strause, Richard Rothfeld, Chris Perot, Christos Konstantakopoulos; Director/Screenplay, Jeff Nichols; Photography, Adam Stone; Designer, Chad Keith; Costumes, Karen Malecki; Music, David Wingo; Editor, Parke Gregg; Casting, Lillian Pyles; a Hydraulx Entertainment, REI Capital and Grove Hill Productions presentation of a Strange Matter Films production; Dolby; Color; Rated R; 120 minutes; Release date: September 30, 2011

CAST
Curtis LaForche	**Michael Shannon**
Samantha LaForche	**Jessica Chastain**
Dewart	**Shea Whigham**
Nat	**Katy Mixon**
Sarah	**Kathy Baker**
Hannah LaForche	**Tova Stewart**
Kyle	**Ray McKinnon**
Kendra	**LisaGay Hamilton**
Jim	**Robert Longstreet**
Cammie	**Natasha Randall**
Russell	**Ron Kennard**
Lewis	**Scott Knisley**

Heather Caldwell (Special Ed Teacher), Sheila Hullihen (Woman in Road), John Kloock (Man in Road), Marianna Alacchi (Bargain Hunter), Jacque Jovic (News Anchor), Bob Maines (Walter Jacobs), Charles Moore (Man at Window), Pete Ferry (Melvin), Molly McGinnis (Janine), Angie Marino-Smith (Kathryn), Isabelle Smith (Sue), Tina Stump (Nurse), Ken Strunk (Doctor Shannan), Maryanne Nagel (Insurance Agent), Hailee Dickens (Pharmacist), Guy Van Swearingen (Myers), William Alexander (EMT), Joanna Tyler (Attendant), Stuart Greer (Army-Navy Dave), Jake Lockwood (Andy), Kim Hendrickson (Customer), Bart Flynn (Dave), Nick Koesters (Rich), Jeffrey Grover (Psychiatrist)

Struggling to provide for his wife and daughter, Curtis LaForche begins having terrifying dreams of an encroaching, apocalyptic storm.

Jessica Chastain, Tova Stewart

Sarah Steele, Anna Paquin, Matthew Broderick © Fox Searchlight

MARGARET

(FOX SEARCHLIGHT) Producers, Sydney Pollack, Gary Gilbert, Scott Rudin; Executive Producer, Anthony Minghella; Director/Screenplay, Kenneth Lonergan; Photography, Ryszard Lenczewski; Designer, Dan Leigh; Costumes, Melissa Toth; Music, Nico Muhly; Editor, Anne McCabe; Casting, Douglas Aibel; a Gilbert Films presentation of a Camelot Pictures/Mirage Enterprises/Scott Rudin production; Dolby; Technicolor; Rated R; 149 minutes; Release date: September 30, 2011

CAST
Lisa Cohen	**Anna Paquin**
Joan	**J. Smith-Cameron**
Ramon	**Jean Reno**
Emily	**Jeannie Berlin**
Monica Patterson	**Allison Janney**
John	**Matthew Broderick**
Paul	**Kieran Culkin**
Maretti	**Mark Ruffalo**
Mr. Aaron	**Matt Damon**

Sarah Steele (Becky), John Gallagher, Jr. (Darren), Cyrus Hernstadt (Curtis), Stephen Adly Guirgis (Mitchell), Betsy Aidem (Abigail), Adam Rose (Anthony), Nick Grodin (Matthew), Jonathan Hadary (Deutsch), Josh Hamilton (Victor), Rosemarie DeWitt (Mrs. Maretti), Glenn Fleshler, Stephen Conrad Moore (Men), Gio Perez (Kid), Jake O'Connor (David), David Mazzucchi (Lionel), Jerry Matz (Mr. Klein), Kevin Carroll (Mr. Lewis), Hina Abdullah (Angie), Olivia Thirlby (Monica), Kenneth Lonergan (Karl), Enid Graham (Bonnie), Brittany Underwood (Leslie), T. Scott Cunningham (Gary), Michael Ealy (Dave the Lawyer), Renée Fleming, Susan Graham (Opera Singers), Adam LeFevre (Rob), Krysten Ritter (Salesgirl), Matthew Bush (Kurt), Anna Berger, Rose Arrick (Neighborhood Ladies), Pippin Parker (Opera Fan), Stephanie Cannon (Mourner), Kevin Geer (AIG Detective #2), Kelly Wolf (Annette), Johann Carlo (Neighbor), Carlo Alban (Rodrigo), Christine Goerke (Opera Singer "Norma"), Liza Colón-Zayas (Nurse), Yves Abel ("Hoffman" Conductor)

A New York high school student, certain that she has inadvertently played a part in a traffic accident that claimed a woman's life, sets out to atone for her actions, only to face opposition at every turn.

DIRTY GIRL

(WEINSTEIN CO.) Producers, Rob Paris, Jana Edelbaum, Rachel Cohen; Executive Producers, Ed Hart, Joan Huang, Robert Bevan, Samantha Horley, Cyril Mégret, Christine Vachon, Daniel Crown, Bob Weinstein, Harvey Weinstein; Director/Screenplay, Abe Sylvia; Photography, Steve Gainer; Designer, Alan E. Muraoka; Costumes, Mary Claire Hannan; Music, Jeff Toyne; Music Supervisor, Linda Cohen; Editor, Jonathan Lucas; Casting, Eyde Belasco; an Ideal Partners and Hart/Lunsford Pictures presentation in association with Cherry Sky Films and The Salt Company of a Paris Films, Inc. production; Dolby; Color; Rated R; 90 minutes; Release date: October 7, 2011

CAST
Danielle	**Juno Temple**
Sue-Ann	**Milla Jovovich**
Ray	**William H. Macy**
Peggy	**Mary Steenburgen**
Joseph	**Dwight Yoakam**
Clarke	**Jeremy Dozier**

Zach Lasry (Brad), Jonathan Slavin (Mr. Potter), Marcella Lentz-Pope (Tonya), William Horwich (Tim), Gary Grubbs (Principal Mulray), Deborah Theaker (Mrs. Hatcher), Natalie Amenula (Benita), David Petruzzi (Bobby), Vivian Smallwood (Shellie the Neighbor), Jack Kehler (Dr. Shelby), Reiley McClendon (Mike), Nate Hartley (Charlie), Madison Meyer (Mindy), Pat Healy (Billy), Rob Boltin (Peter), Brent Briscoe (Officer Perry), Jim Cody Williams (Big Biker Dude), Nicholas D'Agosto (Joel), Frank Clem (Gas Station Attendant), Grady Lee Richmond (Strip Club Manager), Andrew Ableson (Jade), P.D. Mani (Taxi Driver), Maeve Quinlan (Janet), Tim McGraw (Danny), Elsie Fisher (Tiffany), Juliane Godfrey, Alexandra Harding, Miriam McSpadden, Alexandra Nicandros, Carolyn Oler, Brittni Ping, Marylyn Sohlberg, Katrina Williams (Perpetual Motion), Melissa Manchester (Piano Playing Teacher)

Slutty Danielle takes to the road with ostracized, closeted Clarke in hopes of finding her dead-beat father.

Juno Temple, Jeremy Dozier © Weinstein Co.

Martin Sheen, James Nesbitt, Deborah Kara Unger, Yorick van Wageningen

Martin Sheen, Emilio Estevez

Martin Sheen © Producers Distribution Agency

Martin Sheen

THE WAY

(PRODUCERS DISTRIBUTION AGENCY/ARC ENTERTAINMENT) Producers, Emilio Estevez, David Alexanian, Julio Fernandez; Executive Producers, John Sloss, Trevor Drinkwater, Julio Fernandez, Alberto Marini, Stewart Till, Janet Templeton, Ramon Gerard Estevez; Co-Producer, Lisa Niedenthal; Director/ Screenplay, Emilio Estevez; Story, Emilio Estevez, and selected stories from *Off the Road: A Modern-Day Walk Down the Pilgrim's Route* by Jack Hitt; Photography, Juanmi Azpiroz; Designer, Victor Molero; Costumes, Tatiana Hernandez; Music, Tyler Bates; Music Supervisor, Dondi Bastone; Editors, Raul Davalos, Richard Chew; Casting, Mary Vernieu, J.C. Cantu; a Producers Distribution Ageny and Arc Entertainment in association with Eleventy One presentation of an Elixir Films production; Dolby; Technicolor; Rated PG-13; 123 minutes; Release date: October 7, 2011

CAST
Tom Avery	**Martin Sheen**
Daniel Avery	**Emilio Estevez**
Sarah	**Deborah Kara Unger**
Jack	**James Nesbitt**
Captain Henri	**Tchéky Karyo**
Joost	**Yorick van Wageningen**
Phil	**Spencer Garrett**
Angélica	**Ángela Molina**
Jean	**Carlos Leal**
Pilgrim	**Nacho Estévez**
Roger	**David Alexanian**
Ishmael	**Antonio Gil**
Father Frank	**Matt Clark**

Simón Andreu (Don Santiago), Santi Prego (Miguel), Eusebio Lázaro (Ramón), Joan Diez (Carlo), Alfonso Delgado (Penitente #1),, Romy Baskerville (Eunice), William Holden (Cal), Joe Torrenueva (Father Sandoval), Stéphane Dausse (French Mortician), Patxi Pérez (Waiter), Anthony Von Seck (Seta Playing Pilgrim), José Luis Molina, José Javier Ruiz (Policemen), Omar Muñoz (Gypsy Boy), Coro el Encuento Burgos (Gypsy Singers), Alfonso Delgado, Victor Motero, Manu Calvo (Penitentes), Milagros Alcade Díez, Maximiano Benito Nebreda (El Molino Innkeepers)

Learning that his son has been killed while hoping to trek along the historic path to the Cathedral de Santiago, conservative Tom Avery makes the unexpected decision to honor his offfspring by taking the walk himself.

THE IDES OF MARCH

(COLUMBIA) Producers, Grant Heslov, George Clooney, Brian Oliver; Executive Producers, Leonardo DiCaprio, Stephen Pevner, Nigel Sinclair, Guy East, Todd Thompson, Nina Wolarsky, Jennifer Killoran, Barbara A. Hall; Co-Producer, Beau Willimon; Director, George Clooney; Screenplay, George Clooney, Grant Heslov, Beau Willimon; Based on the play *Farragut North* by Beau Willimon; Photography, Phedon Papamichael; Designer, Sharon Seymour; Costumes, Louise Frogley; Music, Alexandre Desplat; Music Supervisor, Linda Cohen; Casting, Ellen Chenoweth; a Cross Creek Pictures presentation in association with Exclusive Media Group and Crystal City Entertainment of a Smokehouse/Appian Way production; Dolby; Super 35 Widescreen; Deluxe color; Rated R; 100 minutes; Release date: October 7, 2011

Ryan Gosling

CAST

Stephen Meyers	**Ryan Gosling**
Governor Mike Morris	**George Clooney**
Paul Zara	**Philip Seymour Hoffman**
Tom Duffy	**Paul Giamatti**
Molly Stearns	**Evan Rachel Wood**
Ida Horowicz	**Marisa Tomei**
Senator Thompson	**Jeffrey Wright**
Ben Harpen	**Max Minghella**
Cindy Morris	**Jennifer Ehle**
Jack Stearns	**Gregory Itzin**
Senator Pullman	**Michael Mantell**
Mike	**Yuriy Sardarov**
Jenny	**Bella Ivory**
Sue	**Maya Sayre**
Campaign Editor	**Danny Mooney**
Advance Guy	**John Manfredi**
Piano Player	**Robert Mervak**
Security Guard	**Fabio Polanco**
Janitor	**Frank Jones, Jr.**
Head First Bartender	**Peter Harpen**
Stage Manager	**Rohn Thomas**
Director	**David McConnell**
Sound Man	**Mark Stacey White**
Students	**Lauren Wainwright, Kris Reilly**
Pullman Staffer	**Michael D. Ellison**
Clinic Nurse	**Leslie McCurdy**
Jill	**Hayley Meyers**
Beth	**Talia Akiva**

Rob Braun, Rachel Maddow, Chris Matthews, Charlie Rose (Themselves), Deb Dixon (Local Anchor), Neal Anthony Rubin, Loretta Higgins (Reporters), Joe Dinda (Joe the Staffer), John Repulski (Organist), Cherie Bowman (Air Tran Ticket Agent)

Evan Rachel Wood, Ryan Gosling

In the days leading up to the Ohio presidential primary, candidate Mike Morris' campaign press secretary finds himself uncovering a political scandal.

This film received an Oscar nomination for adapted screenplay.

Marisa Tomei, Ryan Gosling

George Clooney, Jeffrey Wright, Jennifer Ehle, Talia Akiva

Ryan Gosling, Max Minghella © Columbia Pictures

Ryan Gosling

Ryan Gosling, Paul Giamatti

Philip Seymour Hoffman, Ryan Gosling

George Clooney

Dakota Goyo, Hugh Jackman

Evangeline Lilly, Hugh Jackman

Karl Yune, Olga Fonda © Walt Disney Studios

REAL STEEL

(WALT DISNEY STUDIOS) Producers, Don Murphy, Susan Montford, Shawn Levy; Executive Producers, Jack Rapke, Robert Zemekis, Steve Starkey, Steven Spielberg, Josh McLaglen, Mary McLaglen; Co-Producer, Rick Benattar; Director, Shawn Levy; Screenplay, John Gatins; Story, Dan Gilroy, Jeremy Leven; Based on the short story "Steel" by Richard Matheson; Photography, Mauro Fiore; Designer, Tom Meyer; Costumes, Marlene Stewart; Music, Danny Elfman; Editor, Dean Zimmerman; Stunts, Garrett Warren; Animatronic Supervisor, John Rosengrant; Live-Action Animatronic and Robotic Effects, Legacy FX; Special Effects Supervisor, Joey DiGaetano; Casting, David Rubin, Richard Hicks; a DreamWorks Pictures and Reliance Entertainment presentation of a 21 Laps/Montford Murphy production; Dolby; Widescreen; Deluxe Color; Rated PG-13; 126 minutes; Release date: October 7, 2011

CAST

Charlie Kenton	**Hugh Jackman**
Max Kenton	**Dakota Goyo**
Bailey Tallet	**Evangeline Lilly**
Finn	**Anthony Mackie**
Ricky	**Kevin Durand**
Deborah Barnes	**Hope Davis**
Marvin Barnes	**James Rebhorn**
Tak Mashido	**Karl Yune**
Farra Lemkova	**Olga Fonda**

John Gatins (Kingpin), Sophie Levy (Big Sister), Tess Levy (Little Sister), Charlie Levy (Littlest Sister), Gregory Sims (Bill Panner), Torey Adkins (Large Texan Man), Tom Carlson, John Hawkinson (San Leandro Gentlemen), David Alan Basche, Phil LaMarr (ESPN Boxing Commentators), David Herbst, Julian Gant (Starblaze Area Reporters), Ken Alter (Virgin America Spectrum Ring Announcer), Leilani Barrett (Virgin America Spectrum Ref), Eric Gutman (WRB Promoter), Nicholas Yu (Twin Cities Corner Tech), D.B. Dickerson (Twin Cities Controller), Peter Carey (Bing Arena Announcer), Dan Lemieux (Bing Arena Ref), Richard Goteri (Older Gentleman), Tim Holmes (Blacktop Controller), Ricky Wayne Robinson, Jr. (Underground Promoter), Taris Tyler (Robot Promoter), Kevin Dorman (Atom Performance Capture), John Manfredi (Sergei Lemkova), Jeff Caponigro (Bailey's Dad), Michael Patrick Carmody (Axelrod Handler)

In the future when only machines are permitted to box, a down on his luck ex-fighter, given temporary custody of his estranged son, hopes to return to the big time and possibly reunite with his boy by training a robot to become a champion in the ring.

This film received an Oscar nomination for visual effects.

Atom, Zeus

THE BIG YEAR

(20TH CENTURY FOX) Producers, Karen Rosenfelt, Stuart Cornfeld, Curtis Hanson; Executive Producers, Carol Fenelon, Ben Stiller, Jeremy Kramer; Director, David Frankel; Screenplay, Howard Franklin; Inspired by the book by Mark Obmascik; Photography, Lawrence Sher; Designer, Brent Thomas; Costumes, Monique Prudhomme; Co-Producer, Brad Van Arragon; Music, Theodore Shapiro; Music Supervisor, Julia Michels; Editor, Mark Livolsi; Casting, Margery Simkin; a Fox 2000 Pictures presentation of a Red Hour Films/Deuce Three/Sunswept Entertainment production; Dolby; Panavision; Deluxe color; Rated PG; 101 minutes; Release date: October 14, 2011

Steve Martin © Twentieth Century Fox

CAST
Stu Preissler	**Steve Martin**
Brad Harris	**Jack Black**
Kenny Bostick	**Owen Wilson**
Raymond Harris	**Brian Dennehy**
Annie Auklet	**Anjelica Huston**
Ellie	**Rashida Jones**
Jessica	**Rosamund Pike**
Brenda Harris	**Dianne Wiest**
Edith Preissler	**JoBeth Williams**

Anthony Anderson (Bill Clemont), Corbin Bernsen (Gil Gordon), Barry Shabaka Henley (Dr. Neil Kramer), Joel McHale (Barry Loomis), Tim Blake Nelson (Fuchs), Jim Parsons (Crane), Kevin Pollak (Jim Gittelson), Nate Torrence (Ted Simkin), Steven R. Weber (Rick McIntire), Zahf Paroo (Prasad), John Cleese (Historical Montage Narrator), Paul Campbell (Tony), Cindy Busby (Susie), Greg Kean (Computer Birder), Eva Allan (Birder's Daughter), Bill Dow (Dr. Paul Elkin), Calum Worthy (Colin Debs), June Squibb (Old Lady), Craig Bockhorn (Lawyer), Joey Aresco (Frank Falucci), Ryan Caltagirone (Frank Jr.), Al Roker (New York Weatherman), Christopher Mann (Security Guard), Jan Bos (Local Newsman – High Island), Kate Gajdosik (Local Newswoman – High Island), William Samples (British Tourist), Scott Patey (Birder – High Island), Marci T. House (Troop Leader), Michael Bean (Waiter), Chris Redman (Scott), Devon Weigel (Karen), Andrew Wilson (Mike Shin), Gabrielle Rose (Mary Swit), Doreen Ramus (CB Announcer), Terence Kelly (Pete Shackelford), Steve Darling (Anchorage Weatherman), Jon Frankel (Anchorage Anchorman), David Lewis (Lanky Birder), Kathy Dugray (Motel Manager), Jesse Moss (Darren), Morgan Brayton (Ferry Ticket Seller), Sheelah Megill (Nurse), Veena Sood (Nurse Katie), DeeJay Jackson (Parking Attendant), Calvin Lee (Chinese Waiter), Tshering Garie (Chinese Waitress)

Steve Martin, Jack Black

Brad Harris and Stu Preissler set out to spot a record number of birds in hopes of dethroning the champion birder, Kenny Bostick, and win "the big year" competition.

Tim Blake Nelson, Jack Black, Rashida Jones

Owen Wilson, Steve Martin, Jack Black

TEXAS KILLING FIELDS

(ANCHOR BAY) Producers, Michael Mann, Michael Jaffe; Executive Producers, Bill Block, Paul Hanson, Justin Thomson, Anthony J.A. Bryan Jr., Ethan Smith, John Friedberg, Michael Ohoven; Director, Ami Canaan Mann; Screenplay/Associate Producer, Donald F. Ferrarone; Photography, Stuart Dryburgh; Designer, Aran Redmann; Costumes, Christopher Lawrence; Music, Dickon Hinchcliffe; Editor, Cindy Mollo; Casting, Bonnie Timmermann, Kerry Barden, Paul Schnee; a Blue Light Block/Hanson Watley Entertainment production in association with Infinity Media; Dolby; Technicolor; Rated R; 105 minutes; Release date: October 14, 2011

CAST
Mike Souder	**Sam Worthington**
Brian Heigh	**Jeffrey Dean Morgan**
Ann Sliger	**Chloë Grace Moretz**
Pam Stall	**Jessica Chastain**
Rule	**Jason Clarke**
Gwen Heigh	**Annabeth Gish**
Rhino	**Stephen Graham**
Lucie Sliger	**Sheryl Lee**

Corie Berkemeyer (Shauna Kittredge), Trenton Ryan Perez (White Kid), Maureen A. Brennan (Mrs. Kittredge), Tony Bentley (Capt. Bender), Becky Fly (Neighbor), James Hébert (Eugene), John Neisler (DPS Officer), Deneen Tyler (Lady Worm), Samantha Beaulieu (Sheila), Kelvin Payton, Ron Flagge (Congregation), Jon Eyez (Levon), Joseph Meissner (Uniformed Cop), Russell M. Haeuser (Foreman), Joe Chrest (Salter), Tom Druilhet (Uniformed Officer #1), Tatelyn Ione Galentine (Jump Rope Girl), Donna Duplantier (Riba), Jade Radford, Cassidy Smith (Shelter Girls), Leanne Cochran (Lila), Leah Elizabeth Sanchez (Lila's Daughter), Jen Kober (911 Operator), Ryan Reinike (911 Supervisor), Wayne Ferrara (Canine Officer), Lyle Brocato (Jim), Kerry Cahill (Carla Romer), Kirk Bovill (Boyfriend), Jason Mitchell (7-Eleven Cashier), Leonre Banks (Haddie), Coryn Cunningham (Elizabeth Heigh), Sean Cunningham (Billy Heigh), Seth Cunningham (Tim Heigh), Brayden Turner-Iuso (Young Boy), Anastasia Boissier (Girl at Vigil), Richard "Doc" Whitney (Constable Rankin), Brian Duffy (Flannel Shirt Poacher), Brittney Diez (Store Clerk), Mark Adam, John A. Stassi (Surveillance Detectives), Jim Chimento (Radio Operator), David Presley (Medic), Tom E. Proctor (Poacher #2)

In a small Texas town, two detectives investigate the brutal serial killings perpetrated by a maniac who has been dumping his mutilated victims in a nearby marsh.

Jessica Chastain © Anchor Bay

Willem Dafoe, Julia Roberts © Senator Entertainment

Hayden Panettiere, Cayden Boyd

FIREFLIES IN THE GARDEN

(SENATOR ENTERTAINMENT) Producers, Marco Weber, Vanessa Coifman, Sukee Chew, Philip Rose; Executive Producers, Jere Hausfater, Milton Liu; Director/Screenplay, Dennis Lee; Photography, Danny Moder; Designer, Robert Pearson; Costumes, Kelle Kutsugeras; Music, Jane Antonia Cornish; Editors, Dede Allen, Robert Brakey; Casting, Ferne Cassel; a Kulture Machine presented of a Marco Weber production; European Premiere: 2008; Dolby; CinemaScope; Color; Rated R; 98 minutes; Release date: October 14, 2011

CAST
Michael Taylor	**Ryan Reynolds**
Charles Taylor	**Willem Dafoe**
Jane Lawrence	**Emily Watson**
Kelly Hanson	**Carrie Anne Moss**
Lisa Taylor	**Julia Roberts**
Addison Wesley	**Ioan Gruffudd**
Young Michael	**Cayden Boyd**

Hayden Panettierre (Young Jane), Shannon Lucio (Ryne Taylor), George Newbern (Jimmy Lawrence), Chase Ellison (Christopher Lawrence), Brooklynn Proulx (Leslie Lawrence), Diane Perella (Flight Attendant), Natalie Karp (Social Worker), Rev. John Stennfeld (Rev. Byers), Phillip Rose (Papi), Babs George (Nana), Frank Ertl (Morgan Duncan), Grady McCardell (Officer #1)

A writer examines his troubled relationship with his cruel father by turning his memories of a tortured past into a novel.

Kenny Wormald, Miles Teller

Julianne Hough, Kenny Wormald © Paramount Pictures

FOOTLOOSE

(PARAMOUNT) Producers, Craig Zadan, Neil Meron, Dylan Sellers, Brad Weston; Executive Producers, Timothy M. Bourne, Gary Barber, Roger Birnbaum, Jonathan Glickman; Director, Craig Brewer; Screenplay, Dean Pitchford, Craig Brewer; Story, Dean Pitchford; Photography, Amelia Vincent; Designer, Jon Gary Steele; Costumes, Laura Jean Shannon; Music, Deborah Lurie; Editor, Billy Fox; Choreographer, Jamal Sims; Casting, Laray Mayfield, Julie Schubert; a Spyglass Entertainment presentation of a Dylan Sellers, Zadan/Meron, Weston Pictures production, presented with MTV Films; Dolby; Super 35 Widescreen; Color; Rated PG-13; 113 minutes; Release date: October 14, 2011

CAST
Ren MacCormack	**Kenny Wormald**
Ariel Moore	**Julianne Hough**
Rev. Shaw Moore	**Dennis Quaid**
Vi Moore	**Andie MacDowell**
Willard	**Miles Teller**
Wes Warnicker	**Ray McKinnon**
Chuck Cranston	**Patrick John Flueger**
Rusty	**Ziah Colon**
Lulu Warnicker	**Kim Dickens**
Woody	**Ser'Darius Blain**
Andy Beamis	**L. Warren Young**
Roger Dunbar	**Brett Rice**

Maggie Jones (Amy Warnicker), Jayson Smith (Officer Herb), Mary-Charles Jones (Sarah Warnicker), Enisha Brewster (Etta), Josh Warren (Rich), Corey Flaspoehler (Russell), Anessa Ramsey (Caroline), Jason Ferguson (Travis), Frank Hoyt Taylor (Mr. Parker), Claude Phillips (Claude), Clay Chappell, Tony Vaughn, Staley Colvert, Daniel Burnley, Jack Davidson, Alisa Pettit (Councilpersons), Tracy Goode (Judge), Clayton Landey (Coach Guerntz), John Still (Track Official), Brian Durkin (Big Cowboy), Amber Wallace (Instructor), Sandra Lafferty (Mrs. Allyson), D. Dylan Schettina (Drive-in Bus Boy), Blair Jasin (Bobby), Jasmine Cook, Reece Thomas, Ivey Lowe, Anna Marie Dobbins (Car Accident Victims), Kevin Renard Fisher (Woody's Cousin), Andrew Ruark (Cotton Gin Worker), Travis Young (Big Bubba), Jamal Sims (Kegger D.J.)

Ren MacCormack moves to a small Tennessee town where dancing has been forbidden, a rule he hopes to defy in an effort to show the adult population how important it is for teens to cut loose. Remake of the 1984 Paramount film that starred Kevin Bacon, Lori Singer, John Lithgow, and Dianne Wiest.

Andie MacDowell, Kenny Wormald, Dennis Quaid

Kenny Wormald, Julianne Hough

Adewale Akinnuoye-Agbaje, Joel Edgerton

Mary Elizabeth Winstead © Universal Studios

THE THING

(UNIVERSAL) Producers, Marc Abraham, Eric Newman; Executive Producer, J. Miles Dale; Director, Matthijs van Heijningen; Screenplay, Eric Heisserer; Based on the story "Who Goes There?" by John W. Campbell, Jr.; Photography, Michel Abramowicz; Designer, Sean Haworth; Costumes, Luis Sequeira; Music, Marco Beltrami; Editors, Julian Clarke, Peter Boyle; Visual Effects Supervisor, Jesper Kjölsrud; Visual Effects, Image Engine; Stunts, Rick Forsayeth; Casting, Denise Chamian, Angela Demo; a Morgan Creek Productions presentation of a Strike Entertainment production; Dolby; Panavision; Color; Rated R; 103 minutes; Release date: October 14, 2011

CAST
Kate Lloyd	**Mary Elizabeth Winstead**
Sam Carter	**Joel Edgerton**
Dr. Sander Halvorson	**Ulrich Thomsen**
Adam Finch	**Eric Christian Olsen**
Derek Jameson	**Adewale Akinnuoye-Agbaje**
Griggs	**Paul Braunstein**
Edvard Wolner	**Trond Espen Seim**

Kim Bubbs (Juliette), Jørgen Langhelle (Lars), Jan Gunnar Røise (Olav), Stig Henrik Hoff (Peder), Kristofer Hivju (Jonas), Jo Adrian Haavind (Henrik), Carsten Bjørnlund (Karl), Jonathan Lloyd Walker (Colin), Ole Martin Aune Nilsen (Matias, Heli Pilot), Michael Brown (Security Guard)

A mysterious organism discovered in Antarctica manages to hide itself within the bodies of its victims, causing havoc at a remote outpost. Previous versions of the story were released in 1951 and 1982.

FATHER OF INVENTION

(ANCHOR BAY) Producers, Jonathan D. Krane, Ken Barbet, Jason Sciavicco, Dana Brunetti, Kevin Spacey, Kia Jam; Executive Producers, Stephan Jacobs, Sergei Bespalov, Mark Manuel, Jordan Yospe, Gary Raskin, Jared Ian Goldman, Rita Benson LeBlanc, David Bergstein, Ron Tutor; Director, Trent Cooper; Screenplay, Jonathan D. Krane, Trent Cooper; Photography, Steve Tedlin; Designer, Joseph T. Garrity; Costumes, Johanna Argan, Molly Elizabeth Grundman; Music, Nick Urata, Music Sueprvisor, Mary Ramos; Editor, Heather Pearsons; Casting, Mary Vernieu, Venus Kanani; a K Jam Media presentation of a Sunrise Films, Jonathan Krane Motion Picture Organization, K Jam Media, Horizon Entertainment production in association with Trigger Street Prods.; Dolby; HD; Widescreen; Color; Rated PG-13; 93 minutes; Release date: October 14, 2011

CAST
Robert Axle	**Kevin Spacey**
Claire Axle	**Camilla Belle**
Phoebe	**Heather Graham**
Troy Coangelo	**Johnny Knoxville**
Donna	**Anna Anissimova**
Steven Leslie	**John Stamos**

Red West (Sam Bergman), Michael Rosenbaum (Eddie the Ex), Danny Comden (Matt James), Jack McGee (Parole Officer), Craig Robinson (Jerry King), Virginia Madsen (Lorraine), Marc Macaulay (General Store Clerk), Morgan Saylor (Young Claire, 12), Karen Livers (Maria), Zacharias Foppe (Customer at Familymary), George Cooper (Handball Kid), Lara Grice (Mom at Park), Suehyla El-Attar (Shop Girl), Sofia Spadoni (Lily), Julia Lashae (Lily's Mother), Marel Medina (Stock Boy), Jason Davis (Neil), Kristen Shaw (Bank Teller), Walt Elder (Harold), Audra Marie (Business Man's Date), Joe Nemmers (Business Man), Rhoda Griffis (Penny Camp), Brett Rice (Howard Camp), Randy Austin (Security Guard), Mary-Charles Jones (Young Claire, 6), Tina Parker (Steak), Sam Best (Mailbox Patron), Mary Elizabeth Cobb (Sheila), Leon Gisclair (Andre), Carol Sutton (Bingo Caller), Kim Holden (News Anchor), Tiffany Morgan (Mother on Infomercial)

Following a stint in prison, gadget inventor Robert Axle hopes to repair his damaged relationship with his daughter.

Heather Graham, Kevin Spacey © Anchor Bay

OKA!

(DADA FILMS) Producers, James Bruce, Lavinia Currier; Co-Producer, Norbert Bogbeyate; Co-Executive Producer, Isaach De Bankolé; Director, Lavinia Currier; Screenplay, Louis Sarno, Lavinia Currier, Suzanne Stroh; Based on Louis Sarno's memoir *Thoughts before Vanishing from the Face of the Earth*; Photography, Conrad W. Hall; Designer, Alexandre Vivet; Costumes, Cora Currier, Delphi Squires; Music, Chris Berry, with the Musicians of Yandombe; Editors, Kristina Boden, Nic Gaster; Casting, Lisa Hamil; a Roland Films in association with James Bruce Productions presentation; Dolby; Color; Not rated; 106 minutes; Release date: October 14, 2011

CAST
Larry Whitman	**Kris Marshall**
Bassoun	**Isaach De Bankolé**
Sataka	**Mapumba**
Mr. Yi	**Will Yun Lee**
Makombe	**Mbombi**
Ekadi	**Essandia**
Dr. Maguire	**Peter Riegert**
Lydia Blake	**Haviland Morris**

Sebastian Beacon (Derek), Jakob Von Eichel (Jurgen), Mbombi (Makombe), Tete (Simboki), Mokule (Bienvenu), Singha (Singha), Gana (Eloba), Julian (Likiti), Mekeke (Mekeke), Gbanda (Bobanjo), Michael McCleary (Boy in Museum), Waterlily Lee (Waterlily), Dieu Donnet (Kirikiri), Albert Oyoma (Police Chief), Mobila (Flute Player), Pascal (Man with Gifts), Evaris (Barnaby), Greg Fawcett (Logger in Truck), Samson (Restaurant Owner), Naqui (Bicycle Messenger), Mekupa (Lalo)

The true story of how an American ethno-musicologist lived among Central Africa's Bayakay pygmies for 25 years.

Kris Marshall © Dada Films

Dan Byrd

Richard Jenkins © AMC Independent

NORMAN

(AMC INDEPENDENT) Producers, Jonathan Segal, Hawk Koch, Dan Keston: Executive Producers, Rich Cowan, Kim Blackburn, Bob Bowen; Co-Producer, Sarah Platt; Director, Jonathan Segal; Screenplay, Talton Wingate; Photography, Darren Genet; Designer, Vincent Defelice; Costumes, Lisa Caryl; Music, Andrew Bird; Music Supervisor, Peymon Maskan; Editor, Robert Hoffman; Casting, Nike Imoru, Jennifer L. Smith; a Camelot Entertainment presentation of a Grand Dream LLC in association with North by Northwest Entertainment and Ivy Road Productions presentation of a Tempest Ridge Entertainment production; Dolby; Color; Rated R; 99 minutes; Release date: October 21, 2011

CAST
Norman Long	**Dan Byrd**
Emily Parrish	**Emily VanCamp**
Doug Long	**Richard Jenkins**
Mr. Angelo	**Adam Goldberg**
James	**Billy Lush**
Helen Black	**Camille Mana**

Jesse Head (Bradley), John Aylward (Robert Bessent), Sewell Whitney (Dr. Malloy), Bobbi Kotula (Mom), Kevin Partridge (Steve), Jeff Rosick (Frank), Jery Sciarrio (Principal Harbuck), Trent Sweeney (Young Norman)

A sardonic, misfit teen, dealing with the death of his mother in a car accident and his father's fatal illness, places himself in an uncomfortable position when he lies about his own health, claiming to be the one dying of cancer.

Jeremy Irons

Zachary Quinto

Paul Bettany

Zachary Quinto, Penn Badgley

Zachary Quinto

Simon Baker

Kevin Spacey

Penn Badgley, Zachary Quinto, Paul Bettany

MARGIN CALL

(LIONSGATE/ROADSIDE ATTRACTIONS) Producers, Michael Benaroya, Neal Dodson, Zachary Quinto, Robert Ogden Barnum, Corey Moosa, Joe Jenckes; Executive Producers, Joshua Blum, Kirk D'Amico, Randy Manis, Anthony Gudas, Michael Corso, Rose Ganguzza, Cassian Elwes, Laura Rister; Co-Producer, Anna Gerb; Line Producer, Susan Leber; Director/Screenplay, J.C. Chandor; Photography, Frank DeMarco; Designer, John Paino; Costumes, Caroline Duncan; Music, Nathan Larson; Editor, Pete Beaudreau; Casting, Bernard Telsey, Tiffany Little Canfield; Myriad Pictures and Benaroya Pictures presentation of a Before the Door production in association with Washington Square Films, Sakonnet Capital Partners and Untitled Entertainment; Dolby Color; Rated R; 106 minutes; Release date: October 21, 2011

CAST
Sam Rogers	**Kevin Spacey**
Will Emerson	**Paul Bettany**
John Tuld	**Jeremy Irons**
Peter Sullivan	**Zachary Quinto**
Seth Bregman	**Penn Badgley**
Jared Cohen	**Simon Baker**
Mary Rogers	**Mary McDonnell**
Sarah Robertson	**Demi Moore**
Eric Dale	**Stanley Tucci**
Ramesh Shah	**Aasif Mandvi**
Heather Burke	**Ashley Williams**
Lauren Bratberg	**Susan Blackwell**
Executive Assistant	**Maria Dizzia**
Security Guard	**Jimmy Palumbo**
Louis Carmelo	**Al Sapienza**
Timothy Singh	**Peter Y. Kim**
Lucy	**Grace Gummer**
Coffee Guy	**Oberon K. Adjepong**

A major investment firm faces possible destruction as its key players attempt to avert disaster during the first 24-hours of the 2008 financial crisis.

This film received an Oscar nomination for original screenplay.

Stanley Tucci

Demi Moore, Simon Baker © Lionsgate/Roadside Attractions

Logan Lerman, Gabriella Wilde, Carsten Norgaard

Orlando Bloom, Milla Jovovich

Ray Stevenson, Matthew Macfadyen, Luke Evans, Logan Lerman

Christoph Waltz, Freddie Fox © Summit Entertainment

THE THREE MUSKETEERS

(SUMMIT) Producers, Jeremy Bolt, Paul W.S. Anderson, Robert Kulzer; Executive Producer, Martin Moszkowicz; Executive Producer in Charge of Production, Christine Rothe; Line Producer, Siliva Tollmann; Co-Producers, Manuel Malle, Rory Gilmartin; Director, Paul W.S. Anderson; Screenplay, Alex Litvak, Andrew Davies; Based upon the novel by Alexandre Dumas; Photography, Glen MacPherson; Designer, Paul Denham Austerberry; Costumes, Pierre-Yves Gayraud; Music, Paul Haslinger; Editor, Alexander Berner; Visual Effects Supervisor, Dennis Beraradi; Digital Visual Effects, Mr. X Inc.; Casting, Suzanne M. Smith; a Constantin Film presentation of a Constantin Film/Impact Pictures production in co-production with NEF Productions and New Legacy Film; American-German-French-British; Dolby; Color; 3D; Widescreen; Rated PG-13; 110 minutes; Release date: October 21, 2011

CAST
D'Artagnan	**Logan Lerman**
Milady de Winter	**Milla Jovovich**
Athos	**Matthew Macfadyen**
Porthos	**Ray Stevenson**
Aramis	**Luke Evans**
Rochefort	**Mads Mikkelsen**
Duke of Buckingham	**Orlando Bloom**
Cardinal Richelieu	**Christoph Waltz**
Constance	**Gabriella Wilde**
Planchet	**James Corden**
Queen Anne	**Juno Temple**
King Louis XIII	**Freddie Fox**
Cagliostro	**Til Schweiger**

Helen George (Blonde), Christian Oliver (Venetian Nobleman), Markus Brandl (Sergeant, Venetian Guard), Dexter Fletcher (D'Artagnan's Father), Jane Perry (D'Artagnan's Mother), Andy Gatherhood (Drunk), Ben Moor (Tailor), Susanne Wolff (Cougar), Carsten Norgaard (Jussac), Isaiah Michalski (Boy), Nina Eichinger (Lady in Waiting), Max Cane (Beefeater Sergeant), Gode Benedix (Helmsman), Hannes Wegener (Crewman #1), Iain McKee (Spengler), Horst Kiss, Gudrun Meinke, Victoria Koestler, Yvonne Pajonowski (Crowd Members), Florian Brückner (Rochefort's Replacement)

Three swordsmen join up with a young, aspiring hero to thwart a plan to overthrow France's king. Previous versions of the novel include those made in 1935 (RKO, Walter Abel), 1948 (MGM, Gene Kelly), 1974 (20th, Michael York), and 1993 (Disney; Chris O'Donnell).

MARTHA MARCY MAY MARLENE

(FOX SEARCHLIGHT) Producers, Josh Mond, Antonio Campos, Chris Maybach, Patrick Cunningham; Executive Producers, Ted Hope, Matt Palmieri, Saerom Kim, Saemi Kim, Alexander Schepsman; Director/Screenplay, Sean Durkin; Photography, Jody Lee Lipes; Designer, Chad Keith; Costumes, David Tabbert; Music, Saunder Jurriaans, Danny Bensi; Editor, Zac Stuart-Pontier; Casting, Susan Shopmaker, Randi Glass; a Maybach Cunningham and FilmHaven Entertainment presentation of a Borderline Films production in association with This is That; Dolby; Super 35 Widescreen; Technicolor; Rated R; 101 minutes; Release date: October 21, 2011

CAST
Martha	**Elizabeth Olsen**
Max	**Christopher Abbott**
Watts	**Brady Corbet**
Ted	**Hugh Dancy**
Katie	**Maria Dizzia**
Sarah	**Julia Garner**
Patrick	**John Hawkes**
Zoe	**Louisa Krause**
Lucy	**Sarah Paulson**

Adam Thompson (Bartender), Allen McCullough (Man in Home #2), Lauren Molina, Louisa Braden Johnson, Tobias Segal (Cult Members), Gregg Burton (Man in Home #1)

A disoriented teenager who has dropped out of sight for an extended period of time moves in with her sister and her husband who are unaware that the girl has just spent time as part of a dangerous, backwoods cult.

Elizabeth Olsen, Sarah Paulson

Elizabeth Olsen

John Hawkes © Fox Searchlight

John Hawkes, Elizabeth Olsen, Louisa Krause, Christopher Abbott

BEING ELMO: A PUPPETEER'S JOURNEY

(SUBMARINE DELUXE) Producers, Constance Marks, James Miller, Corinne LaPook; Director, Constance Marks; Co-Director, Philip Shane; Screenplay/Editors, Philip Shane, Justin Weinstein; Photography, James Miller; Music, Joel Goodman; Animation, Magnetic Dreams Animation Studio; Narrator, Whoopi Goldberg; a Constance Marks Productions presentation; Color; Not rated; 85 minutes; Release date: October 21, 2011. Documentary on puppeteer Kevin Clash and how he achieved his goal of working on *Sesame Street*.

WITH
Kevin Clash, Bill Barretta, Fran Brill, Joan Ganz Cooney, Whoopi Goldberg, Rosie O'Donnell, Frank Oz, Martin P. Robinson, Caroll Spinney

Kevin Clash, Elmo

Elmo

Kevin Clash

Marley Shelton, Carla Gugino © Freestyle Releasing

THE MIGHTY MACS

(FREESTYLE) Producers, Whitney Springer, Tim Chambers; Executive Producers, Vince Curran, John Chambers, Thomas Karl, Bud S. Smith, Pat Croce; Director/Screenplay, Tim Chambers; Story, Tim Chambers, Anthony L. Gargano; Photography, Chuck Cohen; Designer, Tim Galvin; Costumes, Teresa Binder Westby; Music, William Ross; Editor, M. Scott Smith; Casting, Adrienne Stern; an Alexandra Grace Curran presentation in association with Pat Croce and Ocean Avenue Entertainment of a Quaker Media production; Dolby; Color; Rated G; 98 minutes; Release date: October 21, 2011

CAST
Cathy Rush	**Carla Gugino**
Mother St. John	**Ellen Burstyn**
Sister Sunday	**Marley Shelton**
Ed Rush	**David Boreanaz**
Mary Margaret O'Malley	**Lauren Bittner**

Katie Hayek (Trish Sharkey), Meghan Sabia (Jen Galentino), Margaret Anne Florence (Rosemary Keenan), Phyllis Somerville (Sister Sister), Jesse Draper (Mrs. Ballard), Kim Blair (Lizanne Caufield), Kathy Romano (Flight Attendant), Kate Nowlin (Colleen McCann), Malachy McCourt (Monsignor), Taylor Steel (Mimi Malone), Tony Luke Jr. (Salvatore Galentino), Christopher Mann (Julius Moore), Ward Horton (Frankie Sharkey), Lauren Karl (Kelly MacDougal), Brooke Geiger (Mrs. Kincade), Gina Allegro (Rosemont Coach), Marianne Bonner (Sister Sarge), Steven J. Klaszky, Sonny Vellozzi, Mark Schroeder (Scorekeepers), Vale Anoai (College Student in Church), Jodie Lynne McClintock (Sister Thomas), Ryan Windish (Monsignor Assistant), Mary Ellen Driscoll (Assistant Coach, Mississippi State), Tisha Tinsman (Rita Galentino), Brandon Hannan (Tony Galentino), Bianca Brunson (Gayle Moore), Ryan Tygh (Sporting Goods Stock Boy), William R. Johnson (LaSalle Athletic Director), John Peakes (Harry McHale), Kendal Ridgeway (Marian Sharkey), Chuck Schanamann (Charlie Malone), Josh Green (Cowboy), Tess Roney (Joanne Caufield), Erin Mosher (Mrs. Sullivan), Mike Burns (Young Priest)

The true story of how Cathy Rush helped turn the Immaculata College girl's basketball team into one of the champions in women's sports.

Chloe Csengery, Jessica Tyler Brown © Paramount Pictures

PARANORMAL ACTIVITY 3

(PARAMOUNT) Producers, Jason Blum, Oren Peli, Steven Schneider; Executive Producer, Akiva Goldsman; Directors, Henry Joost, Ariel Schulman; Screenplay, Christopher Landon; Based on the original film *Paranormal Activity* directed and written by Oren Peli; Photography, Magdelena Gorka; Designer, Jennifer Spence; Costumes, Leah Butler; Editor, Gregory Plotkin; Casting, Terri Taylor; a Blumhouse/Solana Films/Room 101 production; Dolby: Color; Rated R; 81 minutes; Release date: October 21, 2011

CAST
Dennis	**Chris Smith**
Katie	**Katie Featherston**
Kristi Rey	**Sprague Grayden**
Julie	**Lauren Bittner**
Young Katie	**Chloe Csengery**
Young Kristi	**Jessica Tyler Brown**

Dustin Ingram (Randy Rosen), Brian Boland (Daniel Rey), Marilyn Alex, Jackie Benoit, Jody Carter, Maria Olsen, Karen Teliha (Creepy Ladies), Jessica Berger, Saige Gernhauser, Asher Rowland, Hayden Sosa (Kids), Johanna Braddy (Lisa), Bailey Brown (Bailey), Paitoon Cheng (Ida), Meredith Eaton (Woman), Hallie Foote (Grandma Lois), Bonita Friedericy (Dorothy Wolfe), Eddie Medrano (Party Magician), Jackson Prieto, William Prieto (Hunters), Rebecca Delgado Smith (Crying Bridesmaid), Tucker Brown (Tucker)

Videotapes left behind by Kristi's sister reveal unusual supernatural events recorded when they were children. Third in the *Paranormal Acivity* series, the two previous entries having been released in 2009 and 2010.

THE DOUBLE

(IMAGE ENTERTAINMENT) Producers, Ashok Amritraj, Patrick Aiello, Derek Haas, Andrew Deane; Executive Producers, Mohamed Al Mazrouei, Edward Borgerding; Co-Producers, Stefan Brunner, Manu Gargi; Director, Michael Brandt; Screenplay, Michael Brandt, Derek Haas; Photography, Jeffrey L. Kimball; Designer, Giles Masters; Costumes, Aggie Guerard Rodgers; Music, John Debney; Editor, Steven Mirkovich; Visual Effects Supervisors, Sean Findley, Troy Morgan; Casting, Kelly Wagner; a Hyde Park Entertainment presentation in association with Imagenation Abu Dhabi, an Ashok Amritraj production in association with Brandt/Haas Productions; Dolby; Super 35 Widescreen; Deluxe color; Rated PG-13; 98 minutes; Release date: October 28, 2011

CAST
Paul Shepherdson	**Richard Gere**
Ben Geary	**Topher Grace**
Tom Highland	**Martin Sheen**
Brutus	**Stephen Moyer**
Natalie Geary	**Odette Yustman**

Stana Katic (Amber), Chris Marquette (Oliver), Tamer Hassan (Bozlovski), Nicole Forester (Molly), Ivan Fedorov (The Scrounger), Jeffrey Pierce (Agent Weaver), Jimmy Ortega (Coyote), Yuriy Sardarov (Leo), Ed Kelly (Senator Darden), Larry Gilliard Jr. (Agent Burton), Mike Kraft (FBI Director Roger Bell), Ellca McKeon Maltby (Lucy), Randy Flagler (Martin Miller), Darcy Leutzinger (Vlad), Maxfield Lund (Doctor), Andy Manning (EMT), Dan Lemieux (Russian Military Officer), Ele Bardha (American Man), Nina Kircher (Russian Woman), Devin Scillian (Newscaster), Jimmy Rhoades (CIA Officer), Hugh Maguire (Senator Morris Friedman), Jamie Ridge (French Woman), Sonja Crosby (Employee), David Shakelford (Security Guard), Isaac Ellis, Matt McColm (Guards), Frank Fileti (Bumped Pedestrian)

Retired CIA Agent Paul Shepherdson is called back to duty to investigate the murder of a U.S. senator, a crime that looks like the work of an infamous Russian spy whom Shepherdson claims to have already killed.

Topher Grace, Richard Gere © Image Entertainment

ANONYMOUS

(COLUMBIA) Producers, Roland Emmerich, Larry Franco, Robert Leger; Executive Producers, Volker Engel, Marc Weigert, John Orloff; Co-Producers, Charlie Woebcken, Christoph Fisser, Henning Molfenter, Kiristin Winkler; Director, Roland Emmerich; Screenplay, John Orloff; Photography, Anna J. Foerster; Designer, Sebastian Krawinkel; Costumes, Lisy Christl; Music, Thomas Wander, Harald Kloser; Editor, Peter R. Adam; Visual Effects Supervisors, Volker Engel, Marc Weigert; Casting, Leo Davis, Lissy Holm; American-German; a Centropolis Entertainment production in association with Studio Babelsberg, presented in association with Relativity Media; Dolby; Widescreen; Deluxe color; Rated PG-13; 130 minutes; Release date: October 28, 2011

Rafe Spall

CAST

Earl of Oxford	**Rhys Ifans**
Queen Elizabeth I	**Vanessa Redgrave**
Ben Jonson	**Sebastian Armesto**
William Shakespeare	**Rafe Spall**
William Cecil	**David Thewlis**
Robert Cecil	**Edward Hogg**
Earl of Southampton	**Xavier Samuel**
Earl of Essex	**Sam Reid**
Young Earl of Oxford	**Jamie Campbell Bower**
Young Queen Elizabeth I	**Joely Richardson**
Francesco	**Paolo De Vita**
Christopher Marlowe	**Trystan Gravelle**
Thomas Dekker	**Robert Emms**
Thomas Nashe	**Tony Way**
Captain Richard Pole	**Julian Bleach**
Prologue	**Derek Jacobi**
Spencer	**Alex Hassell**
Heminge	**James Garnon**
Condell	**Mark Rylance**
Pope	**Jasper Britton**
Sly	**Michael Brown**
Interrogator	**Ned Dennehy**
Philip Henslowe	**John Keogh**
Richard Burbage	**Lloyd Hutchinson**

Vicky Krieps (Bessie Vavasour), Helen Baxendale (Anne De Vere), Paula Schramm (Bridget De Vere), Amy Kwolek (Young Anne De Vere), Luke Taylor (Boy Earl of Oxford), Isaiah Michalski (Boy Robert Cecil), Timo Huber (Boy Earl of Southampton), Richard Durden (Archbishop),Shaun Lawton (Footman), Detlef Bothe (John De Vere), James Clyde (King James I), Christian Sengewald (Cecil's Spy Servant), Jean-Loup Fourure (Monsieur Beaulieu), Victoria Gabrysch (Buxom Lady), Axel Sichrovsky (Essex General), Katrin Pollitt, Patricia Grove (Ladies-in-Waiting), Laura Lo Zito (Selling Maid), Gode Benedix (Groundling), Nic Romm (Usher), Henry Lloyd-Hughes (Bear Baiter), Patrick Diemling (Oxford's Servant), Patrick Heyn (Oxford's Doctor), Nino Sandow (Stage Manager, New York), Craig Salisbury (Dwarf/Puck), Rainer Guldener (Quince), Trystan Pütter (Bottom), André Kaczmarczyk (Titania), Jonas Hämmerle (Child Oberon), Leonard Kinzinger (Child Titania), Mike Maas (Pole's Commander), Christian Leonard, Christian Banzhaf, Victor Calero, Martin Engler, Alfred Hartung, Oliver Kube, Christian Ludwig, Oliver Rickenbacher, Claudius von Stolzmann (Stage Players: Shakespeare Company)

A speculative drama that presents the idea that William Shakespeare did *not* write the classic plays that bear his name, but was instead merely a front for the Earl of Oxford.

This film received an Oscar nomination for costume design.

Jamie Campbell Bower, Joely Richardson

Sebastian Armesto

Rafe Spall

Vanessa Redgrave, Rhys Ifans

Xavier Samuel, Sam Reid

David Thewlis, Joely Richardson

Vanessa Redgrave © Columbia Pictures
Rhys Ifans

Amanda Seyfried © Twentieth Century Fox

Vincent Kartheiser, Justin Timberlake, Amanda Seyfried

Justin Timberlake, Amanda Seyfried

IN TIME

(20TH CENTURY FOX) Producers, Andrew Niccol, Eric Newman, Marc Abraham; Executive Producers, Arnon Milchan, Andrew Z. Davis, Kristel Laiblin, Amy Israel; Director/Screenplay, Andrew Niccol; Photography, Roger Deakins; Designer, Alex McDowell; Costumes, Colleen Atwood; Music, Craig Armstrong; Editor, Zach Staenberg; Special Effects Supervisor, Matt Sweeney; Visual Effects Supervisor, Ellen Somers; Stunts, David Leitch; Casting, Denise Chamian; a Regency Enterprises presentation of a New Regency/Strike Entertainment production; Dolby; Widescreen; Deluxe color; Rated PG-13; 109 minutes; Release date: October 28, 2011

CAST
Will Salas	**Justin Timberlake**
Sylvia Weis	**Amanda Seyfried**
Raymond Leon	**Cillian Murphy**
Philippe Weis	**Vincent Kartheiser**
Rachel Salas	**Olivia Wilde**
Henry Hamilton	**Matt Bomer**
Borel	**Johnny Galecki**
Fortis	**Alex Pettyfer**
Moser	**Matt O'Leary**

Collins Pennie (Timekeeper Jaeger), Toby Hemingway (Timekeeper Kors), Shyloh Oostwald (Maya), Colin McGurk (Citizen), Will Harris (Ulysse), Michael William Freeman (Nardin), Jesse Lee Soffer (Webb), Aaron Perilo (Bell), Nick Lashaway (Ekman), William Peltz (Pierre), Ray Santiago (Victa), Zuleyka Silver (Pasha), Laura Ashley Samuels (Sagita), Brendan Miller (Kolber), LaMonde Byrd (Minuetman Rado), Paul David Story (Minuteman Roth), Yaya DaCosta (Greta), Maximilian Osinski (Louis), Blake Sheldon (Man at Door), Melissa Ordway (Leila), Abhi Sinha (Ross), Ethan Peck (Constantin), Germano Sardinha (Carlo), Korrina Rico (Hotel Clerk), Emma Fitzpatrick (Kara), Seema Lazar (Timekeeper Ellini), Adam Jamal Craig (Girard), Andreas Wigand (Milus), Bella Heathcote (Michele Weis), Sasha Pivovarova (Clara), Luis Chávez (Ernest), August Emerson (Levi), Cathy Baron (Ruby), Kris Lemche (Markus), Sterling Sulieman (Franck), Rachel Roberts (Carrera), Christiann Castellanos (Jasmine), Jeff Staron (Oris), Drew James (Thomas), Swen Temmel (Breitling), Jessica Parker Kennedy (Eduoarda), Trevor O'Brien (Nomos), Faye Kingslee (Timekeeper Jean), Kristopher Higgins (Timekeeper Dent)

In a parallel world where a person's remaining time is measured by a life-expectancy timer embedded in their arm, Will Salas finds himself unexpectedly inheriting 100-plus years given him by a suicide.

Cillian Murphy

LIKE CRAZY

(PARAMOUNT VANTAGE) Producers, Jonathan Schwartz, Andrea Sperling; Executive Producers, Zygi Wilf, Audrey Wilf, Steven Rales, Mark Roybal; Co-Producers, Brian Buckland, Marius Markevicius; Director, Drake Doremus; Screenplay, Drake Doremus, Ben York Jones; Photography, John Gulesarian; Designer, Katie Byron; Costumes, Mairi Chisholm; Music, Dustin O'Halloran; Music Supervisor, Tiffany Anders; Editor, Jonathan Alberts; Casting, Eyde Belasco; an Indian Paintbrush presentation of a Super Crispy Entertainment, Jonathan Schwartz/Andrea Sperling production; Dolby; Color; Rated PG-13; 89 minutes; Release date: October 28, 2011

CAST
Jacob	**Anton Yelchin**
Anna	**Felicity Jones**
Sam	**Jennifer Lawrence**
Simon	**Charlie Bewley**
Jackie	**Alex Kingston**
Bernard	**Oliver Muirhead**
Liz	**Finola Hughes**
Mike Appletree	**Chris Messina**
Ross	**Ben York Jones**
Elliot	**Jamie Thomas King**

Amanda Carlin (American Consulate Woman), Barry Sabath (Professor), Keeley Hazell (Sabrina), Kayla Barr (College Roommate), James Messer (Delivery Man), Natalie Blair (Natalie), Robert Pike Daniel (Court Clerk), Jimmy Tamborello, Meredith Landman, David Foster (Figurine Band Members), Iris Taylor Cameron, Michael Lovett, Eddie El Masri (Customs Officials), Stephen Young, Callie Beckmann (Ticketing Agents), Michael Hyatt (Customs Agent), Julian Stone (Voice of Harry), Eric Satterberg, John Weselcouch, Michael Reilly, David Cuddy (Jacob's Friends), Katie Wallack (Alex), Julia Montague, Jason King (Kissing Couple), Jo Victoria Russell, Vickie Moss (Girls in Market), Dermot Canavan (Janitor)

After falling in love, Los Angeles students Anna and Jacob face an uncertain future when her visa expires and she is exported back to England.

Jennifer Lawrence

Felicity Jones, Anton Yelchin © Paramount Vantage

Charlie Bewley

Anton Yelchin, Felicity Jones

THE RUM DIARY

(FILMDISTRICT) Producers, Johnny Depp, Christi Dembrowski, Anthony Ruhlen, Robert Kravis, Tim Headington, Graham King; Executive Producers, Patrick McCormick, George Tobia, Bill Shively, A.J. Dix, Greg Shapiro, Colin Vaines; Co-Producer, Peter Kohn; Director/ Screenplay, Bruce Robinson; Based on the novel by Hunter S. Thompson; Photography, Dariusz Wolski; Designer, Chris Seagers; Costumes, Colleen Atwood; Music, Christopher Young; Editor, Carol Littleton; Casting, Denise Chamian; a GK Films, Infinitum Nihil, Film Engine production; Dolby; Deluxe Color; Rated R; 120 minutes; Release date: October 28, 2011

Giovanni Ribisi, Michael Rispoli

CAST
Paul Kemp	**Johnny Depp**
Sanderson	**Aaron Eckhart**
Sala	**Michael Rispoli**
Chenault	**Amber Heard**
Lotterman	**Richard Jenkins**
Moberg	**Giovanni Ribisi**
Segarra	**Amaury Nolasco**
Donovan	**Marshall Bell**
Mr. Zimburger	**Bill Smitrovich**
Wolsley	**Julian Holloway**
Mrs. Zimburger	**Karen Austin**

Bruno Irizarry (Lazar), Enzo Cilenti (Digby), Aaron Lustig (Monk), Tisuby González (Rosy), Natalia Rivera (Chenault's Friend), Julio Ramos (Intruder), Rafa Alvarez (Taxi Driver), Sasha Merced (Café Girl), Eduardo Cortés (Café Patron), Karimah Westbrook (Papa Nebo), Guillermo Valedon (Xanadu Maitre d'), William Charlton (Hotel Waiter), Javier Grajeda (Judge), Miguel Angel Reyes (El Monstruo's Trainer), Terrance Harkless (Man in Hat), Andy Umberger (Mr. Green), Armando Perez (Policeman), Bill Chott (Bowling Champ), Gavin Houston (Sailor), Lisa Robins (Bowling Champ Wife), Noel Delgado (Night Club Dancer), Alejandro Carpio (Morell), Jaime "Jimmy" Navarro (Hubert), Carlos Alberto Lopez (Union Leader), Jimmy Ortega (Cop on Fire), José Coriano (Drunk), Angel Nolasco (Segarra's Daddy), Javier Ortiz Cortés, Jorge Antares (Union Leaders), Aurelio Lima, Luis Gonzaga (Intruder Sidekicks), Randy Jacobs (Hound Dog Taylor), Edgar Lebrón Landrau (Bouncer), Eric Colón (Cock Fight Referee), Dan Kalal (Party Guest)

Richard Jenkins © FilmDistrict

An American journalist takes a job at a local newspaper in Puerto Rico where between drinking binges he finds himself being empolyed by an American businessman who hopes to cover up a shady real-estate deal.

Amber Heard, Johnny Depp

Johnny Depp, Aaron Eckhart

Kitty Softpaws, Puss in Boots

Puss in Boots

PUSS IN BOOTS

(PARAMOUNT/DREAMWORKS) Producers, Joe M. Aguilar, Latifa Ouaou; Executive Producers, Andrew Adamson, Guillermo del Toro, Michelle Raimo; Co-Executive Producer, John H. Williams; Director, Chris Miller; Screenplay, Tom Wheeler; Story, Brian Lynch, Will Davies, Tom Wheeler; Designer, Guillaume Aretos; Music, Henry Jackman; Editor, Eric Dapkewicz; Head of Layout, Gil Zimmerman; Visual Effects Supervisor, Ken Bielenberg; Head of Character Animation, Fabio Lignini; Head of Story, Bob Persichetti; Character Designer, Patrick Mate; a DreamWorks Animation presentation; Dolby; Widescreen; Technicolor; 3D; Rated PG; 90 minutes; Release date: October 28, 2011

VOICE CAST

Puss in Boots	**Antonio Banderas**
Kitty Softpaws	**Salma Hayek**
Humpty Alexander Dumpty	**Zach Galifianakis**
Jack	**Billy Bob Thornton**
Jill	**Amy Sedaris**
Imelda	**Constance Marie**
Moustache Man/Comandante	**Guillermo del Toro**
Bounty Hunter	**Rich Dietl**
Luis	**Ryan Crego**
Raoul/Soldier	**Conrad Vernon**
Bar Thief	**Tom McGrath**
Giuseppe	**Bob Joles**

Tom Wheeler (Bartender/Hotel Owner/Mean Boy/Wagon Driver/Rodrigo), Latifa Ouaou (Crazy Woman/Mean Girl/Milk Lady/Little Boy), Robert Persichetti Jr. (Ohhh Cat), Chris Miller (Little Boy Blue/Friar Miller/Prison Guard/Manual/Rafael), Jessica Schulte Jones (Estella Maria), Mike Mitchell (Andy Beanstalk), Nina Barry (Ivana/Charo)

Puss in Boots reluctantly reteams with Humpty Dumpty to steal some magic beans from Jack and Jill, which hopefully will lead to gold with which they can repay some debts from a past incident that left Puss's reputation in tatters.

This film received an Oscar nomination for animated feature.

Jill, Jack

Puss in Boots, Humpty Dumpty © DreamWorks

Michael Peña, Casey Affleck, Ben Stiller, Judd Hirsch

Ben Stiller, Eddie Murphy

Téa Leoni, Alan Alda

TOWER HEIST

(UNIVERSAL) Producers, Brian Grazer, Eddie Murphy, Kim Roth; Executive Producers, Bill Carraro, Karen Kehela Sherwood; Director, Brett Ratner; Screenplay, Ted Griffin, Jeff Nathanson; Story, Adam Cooper, Bill Collage, Ted Griffin; Photography, Dante Spinotti; Designer, Krist Zea; Costumes, Sarah Edwards; Music, Christophe Beck; Editor, Mark Helfrich; Visual Effects Supervisor, Mark Russell; Stunts, Jery Hewitt; Casting, Kathleen Chopin; an Imagine Entertainment presentation in association with Relativity Media of a Brian Grazer production; Dolby; Panavision; Deluxe Color; Rated PG-13; 104 minutes; Release date: November 4, 2011

CAST
Josh Kovaks	**Ben Stiller**
Slide	**Eddie Murphy**
Charlie	**Casey Affleck**
Arthur Shaw	**Alan Alda**
Mr. Fitzhugh	**Matthew Broderick**
Lester	**Stephen McKinley Henderson**
Mr. Simon	**Judd Hirsch**
Special Agent Claire Denham	**Téa Leoni**
Enrique Dev'Reaux	**Michael Peña**
Odessa	**Gabourey Sidibe**
Miss Iovenko	**Nina Arianda**
Rose	**Marcia Jean Kurtz**
Manuel	**Juan Carlos Hernández**
Special Agent Danszk	**Harry O'Reilly**
Marty Klein, Esq.	**Peter Van Wagner**
Director Mazin	**Zeljko Ivanek**
Radio Host	**Lynne Rossetto Kasper**
NASDAQ News Reporter	**Annika Pergament**
Kwan	**Clem Cheung**
Judge Ramos	**Robert Downey, Sr.**
Mr. Hightower's Mistress	**Kate Upton**
Mrs. Jin	**Marilyn Kim**
Rita	**Judianny Compres**
Tower Security	**Omar Nicodemo**
Mr. Newhouse	**Allie Woods Jr.**
Huang	**Johnny Tran**
Sasha	**Jessica Szohr**
Mrs. Cronan	**Jan Owen**
News Reporter	**Dylan Ratigan**
Special Agent Huggins	**James Colby**

Max Russell Pratts, Nathan Malnik, Spencer Malnik, Jarod Malnik, Julie Vilanova, Cynthia Patsos (Kids in Lobby), Monika Plocienniczak (TV News Reporter), Edward Noone (Special Agent), Frank Pesce (Riker's Prison Guard), Annie Park (Girl in Mall), Christina Calph (Victoria's Secret Saleswoman), Kevin Pariseau (Swarovski Jewelry Salesman), Desmin Borges (Modell's Sneaker Salesman), Brian Distance, Village, Les Papp II, Michael Stratton (Tower Security Officers), Christopher Arocho Rivaro (Doorman), Craig Castaldo (Radioman), Dwight "Heavy D" Myers (Courthouse Guard), Veronika Korvin (Maid), Robert Clohessy (Parade Cop), Lucky Park (Lucy the Dog), Robert Christian, Mark Philip Patrick, Paul Hickert, Kelvin Davis, Christopher Breslin (Arresting Special Agents), Ty Jones, Ted Lochwyn (Shaw's Prison Guards), Madison Knopp (Charlie and Sasha's Baby), Troy Hall (Delivery Man), Julie T. Pham (Huang's Wife), Bojun Wang (Huang's Son), Juanita Howard (Mr. Newhouse's Wife), Bob Roseman (Josh's Prison Guard), Joan Rivers, Kanye West, Matt Lauer (Themselves)

Discovering that fat cat billionaire Arthur Shaw has absconded with the pensions of the staff of the luxury tower where he resides, building manager Josh Kovaks plots to steal millions from the embezzler with a motley crew of would-be thieves.

Matthew Broderick, Ben Stiller, Michael Peña (back to camera), Eddie Murphy, Casey Affleck (back to camera)

Ben Stiller, Téa Leoni © Universal Studios

Gabourey Sidibe, Ben Stiller

Michael Peña, Matthew Broderick, Casey Affleck, Stephen McKinley Henderson, Gabourey Sidibe

Ben Stiller, Matthew Broderick, Michael Peña, Casey Affleck, Eddie Murphy

Alan Alda, Ben Stiller

Channing Tatum, James Ransome

Al Pacino © Anchor Bay

THE SON OF NO ONE

(ANCHOR BAY) Producers, John Thompson, Holly Wiersma, Dito Montiel; Executive Producers, Cassian Elwes, Trudie Styler, Alex Francis, Jake Pushinsky, Richard Rionda, Del Castro, Patricia Eberle, Avi Lerner, Danny Dimbort, Trevor Short, Boaz Davidson; Director/Screenplay, Dito Montiel; Photography, Benoit Delhomme; Designer, Beth Mickle; Costumes, Sandra Hernandez; Music, David Wittman, Jonathan Elias; Editor, Jake Pushinsky; an Anchor Bay Films and Millennium Films presentation of a Nu Image production; Dolby; Super 35 Widescreen; Color; Rated R; 91 minutes; Release date: November 4, 2011

CAST
Jonathan "Milk" White	**Channing Tatum**
Det. Charles Stanford	**Al Pacino**
Vincent Carter (Adult)	**Tracy Morgan**
Kerry White	**Katie Holmes**
Capt. Marion Mathers	**Ray Liotta**
Loren Bridges	**Juliette Binoche**
Officer Thomas Prudenti	**James Ransone**

Ursula Parker (Charlotte "Charlie" White), Brian Gilbert (Young Vinny Carter), Jake Cherry (Young Jonathan White), Simone Jones (Young Vicky), Lemon Anderson (Geronimo), Roger Guenveur Smith (Hanky), Michael Rivera (Dominican Nada Puerto Rican), Sean Cregan (Martinez), Karen Christie-Ward (Olive Oil), Peter Tambakis (Dispatcher Numnuts), Marilyn Dobrin (Grandma White), Decorte Snipes (Adult Vicky), Craig Walker (Other Cop), Johnnie Mae (Vinny's Mother), Oberon K.A. Adjepong (Vinny's Mother's Boyfriend), Malik Cherry, Tevon Flemming (Kids), Tony Vasquez (Hector J. Uhuyes), Pat Kiernan, Gisella Marengo (News Reporters), Ralph Rodriguez (Sientate Rodriguez), George James (Grandpa), Paul "The Reverend" Poplawski (Officer Pregnant Bitch), Michelle Walnum (News Reporter Walnum's Voice), Iesha Richardson (Top Floor Aisha), Dito Montiel (Vomit Bum)

A cop finds himself uncovering more corruption than he can imagine when he is assigned to re-open a double-homicide case in his former Queens neighborhood.

IN THE FAMILY

(IN THE FAMILY PRODS.) Producers, Andrew van den Houten, Robert Tonino, Patrick Wang; Director/Screenplay, Patrick Wang; Photography, Frank Barrera; Designer, John El Manahi; Costumes, Michael Bevins; Music, Chip Taylor, Andy Wagner; Editor, Elwaldo Baptiste; Casting, Cindi Rush; Dolby; Technicolor; HD-to-35mm; Not rated; 169 minutes; Release date: November 4, 2011

CAST
Joey Williams	**Patrick Wang**
Cody Hines	**Trevor St. John**
Chip Hines	**Sebastian Brodziak**
Paul Hawks	**Brian Murray**
Eileen Robey	**Kelly McAndrew**
Dave Robey	**Peter Hermann**

Park Overall (Sally Hines), Susan Kellermann (Marge Hawks), Elaine Bromka (Gloria), Zoe Winters (Helen), Eisa Davis (Anne Carter), Chip Taylor (Darryl Hines), Eugene Brell (Jefferson Robinson), Lisa Altomare (Betsy), Conan McCarty (Ed), Harriet D. Foy (Sharon), Zachary Sayle (Brent), Georgie DeNoto (Dennis), Jake Juliette Allen-Angelo (Erin), Cole Savitz-Vogel (Blake Robey), Gina Tognoni (Nurse Jackson), Kit Flanagan (Nurse Edwards), Gregory Jones (Dr. Sills), Julia Motyka (Rebecca Hines), Bill Mootos (Sam), Christopher Graves (Landscape Architect), Jake Mosser (Police Officer), Santana Pruitt (Jamie Carter), Matthew Boston (Charles Grant), Michael Scott King (Security Guard), Christina Hogue (Cheryl), Marsha Waterbury (Court Reporter)

Following the death of his lover in a car accident, Joey Williams must fight for the custody of their six year old son.

Sebastian Brodziak, Patrick Wang © In the Family Prods.

Patrick Wang, Sebastian Brodziak, Trevor St. John

John Cho, Neil Patrick Harris, Kal Penn

Tom Lennon, John Cho, Kal Penn, Amir Blumenfeld © New Line Cinema

John Cho, Kal Penn

A VERY HAROLD & KUMAR 3D CHRISTMAS

(NEW LINE CINEMA/WB) Producer, Greg Shapiro; Executive Producers, Nathan Kahane, Nicole Brown, Richard Brener, Michael Disco, Samuel J. Brown; Director, Todd Strauss-Schulson; Screenplay, Jon Hurwitz, Hayden Schlossberg, based on their characters; Photography, Michael Barrett; Designer, Rusty Smith; Costumes, Mary Claire Hannan; Music, William Ross; Music Supervisor, John Bissell; Editor, Eric Kissack; Co-Producers, Jon Hurwitz, Hayden Schlossberg, Kelli Konop, Jonathan McCoy; Casting, Jeanne McCarthy, Nicole Abellera; Choreographer, Courtney Miller; Stop Motion Animation Sequence, House Special; a Kingsgate Films production, presented in association with Mandate Pictures; Distributed by Warner Bros. Pictures; Dolby; Fotokem color; 3D; Rated R; 90 minutes; Release date: November 4, 2011

CAST

Harold Lee	**John Cho**
Kumar Patel	**Kal Penn**
Himself	**Neil Patrick Harris**
Adrian	**Amir Blumenfeld**
Maria	**Paula Garcés**
Vanessa	**Danneel Harris**
Todd	**Tom Lennon**
Mr. Perez	**Danny Trejo**
Sergei Katsov	**Elias Koteas**

Patton Oswalt (Mall Santa), Richard Riehle (Santa Claus), Jordan Hinson (Mary), John Hoogenakker (Gustav), Jake Johnson (Jesus), Yasen Peyankov (Yuri), David Burtka (Himself), Isabella Gielniak (Caren), Austin Bickel (Kid in Line), Inga Wilson (Mom in Line), Bobby Lee (Kenneth Park), Marvin Cruz (Timo Perez), Allyson Lengers (Wafflebot Kid), Eric Kissack (Wafflebot Voice), Shirley Benyas (Nana Perez), Esteban Cruz (Pepe Perez), Ashley Coss, Chloe Coss, Hannah Coss (Ava), RZA (Lamar), Da'Vone McDonald (Latrell), Tyler Nelson, Tom Kruszewski, Steven A. Clark (Teens), Bennett Saltzman (Boris), Hilary Anderson (Hot Teeange Girl), Eddie Kaye Thomas (Rosenberg), David Krumholtz (Goldstein), Tristan Canning (Noah), David Rife (White Castle Employee), Dave Davies (Church Security Guard), Gabriella Dilone (Inez Perez), Dana DeLorenzo (Becca the P.A.), Brett Gelman (TV Director), Melissa Ordway (Gracie), Dan Levy (Reporter), Ripper Brown (St. Peter), Evan Mann, Gareth Reynolds (Heaven's Bartenders), Cassie Keller, Chernise Yvette Taylor (Topless Angels), Megan Agrusa, Bobby Amamizu, Christine Babini, Ashley Cinq-Mars, Michelle DiTerlizzi, Marisa Dorchock, Jenelle Engleson, Aundrea Fant, Jessie Lauryn Foutz, Brittany Ashley Freeth, Erin Gales, Alicia Gilley-Kingsley, Sarah Alice Hurbert-Burns, Annika Inhat, Brandon Koepsell, Jessica Lamarre, Martimiano Nito Larioza, Kandis Mak, Marcy McCusker, Cortney Millar, Lindsey Oleary, Rachel Omell, Taylor Peters, Jessica Provencher, Katie Reese, Lindsey Tuer, Florencer Vinger, Shawn Lee Vitale (Dancers)

When his father-in-law's prize Christmas tree goes up in flames, Harold reluctantly agrees to join his former buddy Kumar on a trip to New York City to find the perfect replacement, with a good degree of partying on the side.

Previous films in the series starring John Cho, Kal Penn, and Neil Patrick Harris are *Harold & Kumar Go to White Castle* (2004) and *Harold & Kumar Escape from Guantanamo Bay* (2008).

Patton Oswalt, Kal Penn

Leonardo DiCaprio, Naomi Watts

Leonardo DiCaprio, Judi Dench

Josh Lucas

J. EDGAR

(WARNER BROS.) Producers, Clint Eastwood, Brian Grazer, Robert Lorenz; Executive Producers, Tim Moore, Erica Huggins; Director/Music, Clint Eastwood; Screenplay, Dustin Lance Black; Photography, Tom Stern; Designer, James J. Murakami; Costumes, Deborah Hopper; Editors, Joel Cox, Gary D. Roach; Visual Effects Supervisor, Michael Owens; Prosthetic Makeup for DiCaprio, Sian Grigg; Casting, Fiona Weir; an Imagine Entertainment production, a Malpaso production; Dolby; Panavision; Technicolor; Rated R; 136 minutes; Release date: November 9, 2011

CAST

J. Edgar Hoover	**Leonardo DiCaprio**
Helen Gandy	**Naomi Watts**
Clyde Tolson	**Armie Hammer**
Charles Lindbergh	**Josh Lucas**
Annie Hoover	**Judi Dench**
Harlan Fiske Stone	**Ken Howard**
Robert Kennedy	**Jeffrey Donovan**
Colonel Schwarzkopf	**Dermot Mulroney**
Albert Osborne	**Denis O'Hare**
Lela Rogers	**Lea Thompson**
Robert Irwin	**Josh Hamilton**
Mitchell Palmer	**Geoff Pierson**
Roberta Dixon Palmer	**Cheryl Lawson**
Palmer's Daughter	**Kaitlyn Dever**
Inspector	**Brady Matthews**
Dwight Eisenhower	**Gunner Wright**
Franklin Roosevelt	**David A. Cooper**
Agent Smith	**Ed Westwick**
Head Secretary	**Kelly Lester**
Edgar's Father	**Jack Donner**
Hoover as a Child	**Dylan Burns**

Jordan Bridges (Labor Dept. Lawyer), Jack Axelrod (Caminetti), Josh Stamberg (Agent Stokes), Jessica Hecht (Emma Goldman), Michael James Faradie (Bureau Agent, 1919), Christian Clemenson (Inspector Schell), Billy Smith (Secret Service Officer), Michael Rady (Agent Jones), Scot Carlisle (Agent Williams), Geoff Stults (Raymond Caffrey), Sadie Calvano (Edgar's Niece), Allen Nabors (Agent Appel), Ryan McPartlin (Lawrence Richey), William Bebow (Mr. Walters), Joseph Culliton (Credit Director), Scott Johnston (Tailor), Tom Archdeacon (Gangster), Mike Vaughn (Balding Agent), Miles Fisher (Agent Garrison), Stephen F. Schmidt (NJ Officer), Zach Grenier (John Condon), Johnny Cicco (Young Agent), Damon Herriman (Bruno Hauptmann), Kahil Dotay (Elmer Irey), Lea Coco (Agent Sisk), Scott C. Roe (Wiretap Agent), Ernest Harden Jr. (James Crawford, Hoover's Driver), Roberta Bassin (Roosevelt's Secretary), Steve Monroe (Restaurant Host), Christopher Lee Philips (William), Sean Murphy (Truck Driver), Stephen Root (Arthur Koehler), Gary Werntz (Attorney General), David Clennon (Senator Friendly), Michael O'Neill (Senator McKellar), Eric Larkin (Fred Hunter), Manu Intriaymi (Alvin Karpis), Eric Frentzel (William Mahan), Michael Klinger (Harry Brunette), Shaun Daley (Radical), Evan Charest (Reporter), Emily Alyn Lind (Shirley Temple), Kyle Eastwood, Joe Bagg, Kye Palmer, Jason Harnell (Stork Club Band), Michael Gladis (Stork Club Owner), Jamie LaBarber (Ginger Rogers), Amanda Schull (Anita Colby), Craig Zucchero (Man at the Counter), Gregory Hoyt (Agent One), Jeff Cockey (Agent Two), Gerald Downey (FBI Agent), Brennan Coulter (Newspaper Boy), Jenny Phagan (Baker's Wife), Tom Christensen (Theater Cashier), Chris Caputo (Bronx Baker), Austin Basis (Bank Teller), Adam Driver (Walter Lyle), Shannon McClain (African American Woman), Eric Matheny (Doctor), Ary Katz (Agent Owens), Duncan Hood (Radio Announcer), Aaron Lazar (Prosecutor Wilentz), Ernest Heinz (Jury Foreman), Teresa Hegji (Hauptmann's Wife), Thomas Langston (Young Boy), Robert Fleet (Edgar's Mother's Doctor), Joe Keyes (Edgar's Brother), Christopher Shyer (Richard Nixon), Maxine Weldon (Hoover's Maid), Larkin Campbell (H.R. Haldeman), Mark Thomason (Nixon Aide)

The true story of how J. Edgar Hoover became one of the most powerful men in America by heading the Federal Bureau of Investigation for nearly 50 years.

Leonardo DiCaprio, Armie Hammer

Leonardo DiCaprio

Jeffrey Donovan

Leonardo DiCaprio, Ed Westwick

Damon Herriman, Leonardo DiCaprio © Warner Bros.

Leonardo DiCaprio, Armie Hammer

IMMORTALS

(RELATIVITY MEDIA) Producers, Gianni Nunnari, Mark Canton, Ryan Kavanaugh; Executive Producers, Tucker Tooley, Jeff Waxman, Tommy Turtle, Jason Felts; Co-Executive Producers, Craig Flores, Robbie Brenner, Rene Rigal; Co-Producer, Kenneth Halsband; Director, Tarsem Singh Dhandwar; Screenplay, Charles Parlapanides, Vlas Parlapanides; Photography, Brendan Galvin; Designer, Tom Foden; Costumes, Eiko Ishioka; Music, Trevor Morris; Music Supervisors, Happy Walters, Bob Bowen; Color Designer, Lionel Kopp; Editor, Stuart Levy; Visual Effects Supervisor, Raymond Gieringer; 3D Creator, Prime Focus; Casting, Joseph Middleton; Stunts, Arthur Malesci, Marc Désourdy; Fight Coordinator, Jean Frenette; a Mark Canton, Gianni Nunnari production; Dolby; Technicolor; 3D; Rated R; 110 minutes; Release date: November 11, 2011

Mickey Rourke

CAST

Theseus	**Henry Cavill**
King Hyperion	**Mickey Rourke**
Stavros	**Stephen Dorff**
Phaedra	**Freida Pinto**
Zeus	**Luke Evans**
Old Man	**John Hurt**
Lysander	**Joseph Morgan**
Aethra	**Anne Day-Jones**
The Monk	**Greg Bryk**
Dareios	**Alan Van Sprang**
Helios	**Peter Stebbings**

Daniel Sharman (Aries), Isabel Lucas (Athena), Kellan Lutz (Poseidon), Steve Byers (Heracles), Stephen McHattie (Cassander), Matthew G. Taylor (Mondragon, King's Guard), Romano Orzari (Icarus), Cory Sevier (Apollo), Conrad Pla (The Jailer), Neil Napier (Beast Handler), Tyrone Benskin (Hoplite Captain), Abdul Ayoola (Kerkyon – Guard), Dylan Scott Smith (Stephanos), Robert Naylor (Young Theseus), Mercedes Leggett, Kaniehtiio Horn, Ayisha Issa (High Priestesses), Jason Cavalier (Heraklion Watchman), Danny Blanco Hall (Archon), Robert Maillet (Minotaur), Alain Chanoine (Checkpoint Gatekeeper), Edward Yankie (Checkpoint Soldier), Gage Munroe (Acamas), Aron Tomori (Young Lysander), Marcello Bezina (Village Father), Roc LaFortune (Hoplite General), Jade Larocque, Charlie Duret (Young Virgins), Alisha Nagarsheth (Young Phaedra), Makayla Jade McManus-Leggett, Madison McAleer, Zelia Mouana-Bankouezi (Young Priestesses), André Kasper Kolstad (Little Boy), Tyler Hynes (Slave), Carlo Mestroni (Holy Man), Chantal Simard (Lysander's Mother), Brent Skagford (Hoplite Sentry), Kevin Kelsall, Patrick Sabongui (Hoplite Soldiers), Samuel Platel (Heraklion #1), Lise Sita, Francis LaFreniere (Villagers), Shyrelle Yates, John Churchill, Austin Beauchamp (Village Children), Jimmy Duperval (Soldier)

Theseus is called on by the gods to put a stop to the vengeful Hyperion who hopes to defeat the immortals with a powerful weapon called the Epirus Bow.

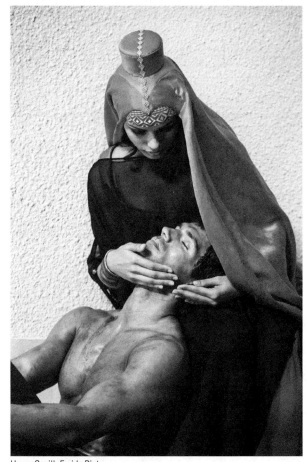

Henry Cavill, Freida Pinto

Stephen Dorff © Relativity Media

Adam Sandler, Adam Sandler

Rohan Chand, Katie Holmes, Elodie Tougne

Adam Sandler, Al Pacino © Columbia Pictures

JACK AND JILL

(COLUMBIA) Producers, Adam Sandler, Jack Giarraputo, Todd Garner; Executive Producers, Barry Bernardi, Bettina Viviano, Allen Covert, Steve Koren, Robert Smigel, Tim Herlihy; Director, Dennis Dugan; Screenplay, Steve Koren, Adam Sandler; Story, Ben Zook; Photography, Dean Cundey; Designer, Perry Andelin Blake; Costumes, Ellen Lutter; Music, Rupert Gregson-Williams, Waddy Wachtel; Music Supervisors, Michael Dilbeck, Brooks Arthur, Kevin Grady; Editor, Tom Costain; Casting, Roger Mussenden, Jeremy Rich; a Happy Madison/Broken Road production; Dolby; Deluxe color; Rated PG; 90 minutes; Release date: November 11, 2011

CAST
Jack Sadelstein/Jill Sadelstein	**Adam Sandler**
Himself	**Al Pacino**
Erin Sadelstein	**Katie Holmes**
Sofia Sadelstein	**Elodie Tougne**
Gary Sadelstein	**Rohan Chand**
Felipe/Felipe's Grandma	**Eugenio Derbez**
Monica	**David Spade**
Todd	**Nick Swardson**

Tim Meadows (Office Worker), Allen Covert(Otto), Norm MacDonald (Funbucket),Geoff Pierson (Carter Simmons), Valerie Mahaffey (Bitsy Simmons), Gary Valentine (Dallas), Dana Carvey (Scraggly Puppeteer), Gad Elmaleh (Xavier), Vince Offer (Shaw-Wow Guy), Regis Philbin, Dan Patrick, Shaquille O'Neal, Drew Carey, John McEnroe, Christie Brinkley, Michael Irvin, Bill Romanowski, Jared Fogle, Billy Blanks, Bruce Jenner, Johnny Depp (Themselves), Jackie Seiden (Tracy), Sadie Sandler, Sunny Sandler (Little Girls on Ship), Georgia Hatzis (Carol), Jonathan Loughran (Monica's Boyfriend), Peter Dante (Carol's Boyfriend), J.D. Donaruma (Tracy's Boyfriend), Tyler Spindel (Coco's Waiter), Owen Benjamin, Christopher Titone (Angry Moviegoers), John Farley (Mort the Hot Dog Vendor), Dennis Dugan (Al Pacino's Standby), Robert C. Lopez (Jose), Jalen Testerman (Jose Jr.), Simrin Player (Josephina), Gerardo Beltran (Felipe's Brother), Kadyr Gutierrez (Soccer Player #1), Virginia Louise Smith (Actress/Queen Elizabeth), Daniel Silverberg (Stage Manager), Richard Kline, Donald Agnelli (Theatergoers), Pepe Balderrama (Spanish Valet), Luis Fernandez-Gil (Italian Cruise Ship Director), Ruben Rabasa (Bathroom Attendant), Nick Gillie (Dunkin' Donuts Customer), Andy Goldenberg, Marisa Field (Dunkin' Donuts Employees), George Gray (*The Price is Right* Announcer), Manuela Arbeláez, Gwendolyn Osborne, Rachel Reynolds (*The Price is Right* Showcase Girls), Anna Mathias (*The Price is Right* Contestant), Robert Harvey (Fan), Lawrence Tanter (Lakers PA Announcer), Rob Schneider (Alan), Santiago Segura (Eduardo), Eric Lamonsoff, Schmeric Lamonsoff, Kara Pacitto, Katelyn Pacitto, Rafael Feldman, Yan Feldman, David Power, Larry Power, Logan Raskin, Roger Raskin, Erica Green, Lina Green, Tiana Madry, Tiara Madry, January Welsh, Marissa Welsh, Gary Lane, Larry Lane, Dingani Beza, Zondwayo Beza, Robbn Jammer Steel, Ronn Slammer Steel, Patty Palmer, Diane Palmer, Alex Burkart, Nathan L. Burkart, Richard Harris, Ronald Harris, Rachel Rife, Rebekah Rife, Elijah Gipson, Elleah Gipson, Katie Cockrell, Kellie Cockrell, Joel Harold, Joseph Harold, Alexis Stier, Megan Stier, Albert Pugliese,Gregory Pugliese, Jordan Tindall, Lance Tindall, Miles Tindall (Documentary Twins)

When Jack's obnoxious twin sister Jill comes to visit, he takes advantage of the crush Al Pacino has on his sibling in order to get the famous actor to do a commercial for him.

George Clooney, Shailene Woodley

George Clooney, Shailene Woodley, Amara Miller

George Clooney

Beau Bridges, George Clooney

Shailene Woodley, George Clooney, Amara Miller, Nick Krause

Nick Krause, Amara Miller, Shailene Woodley, George Clooney
© Fox Searchlight

THE DESCENDANTS

(FOX SEARCHLIGHT) Producers, Jim Burke, Alexander Payne, Jim Taylor; Director, Alexander Payne; Screenplay, Alexander Payne, Nat Faxon, Jim Rash; Based on the novel by Kaui Hart Hemmings; Photography, Phedon Papamichael; Designer, Jane Ann Stewart; Costumes, Wendy Chuck; Music Supervisor, Dondi Bastone; Editor, Kevin Tent; Co-Producer, George Parra; Casting, John Jackson; an Ad Hominem Enterprises production; Dolby; Super 35 Widescreen; Deluxe color; Rated R; 115 minutes; Release date: November 16, 2011

Shailene Woodley, George Clooney, Barbara Lee Southern, Robert Forster

CAST
Matt King	**George Clooney**
Alexandra King	**Shailene Woodley**
Cousin Hugh	**Beau Bridges**
Scott Thorson	**Robert Forster**
Julie Speer	**Judy Greer**
Brian Speer	**Matthew Lillard**
Sid	**Nick Krause**
Scottie King	**Amara Miller**
Kai Mitchell	**Mary Birdsong**
Mark Mitchell	**Rob Huebel**
Elizabeth King	**Patricia Hastie**
Scottie's Teacher	**Grace A. Cruz**
School Counselor	**Kim Gennaula**
Barb Higgins	**Karen Kuioka Hironaga**
Lani Higgins	**Carmen Kaichi**
Matt's Secretary Noe	**Kaui Hart Hemmings**
Cousin Ralph	**Matt Corboy**
Cousin Hal	**Matt Esecson**
Cousin Milo	**Michael Ontkean**
Cousin Stan	**Stanton Johnston**
Cousin Six	**Jonathan McManus**
Cousin Wink	**Hugh Foster**
Cousin Connie	**Tiare R. Finney**
Cousin Dave	**Tom McTigue**
Dr. Johnston	**Milt Kogan**
Troy Cook	**Laird Hamilton**
Dorm Supervisor	**Aileen "Boo" Arnold**
Alex's Roommate	**Esther Kang**
Alex's Drunken Friend	**Melissa Kim**
Alice "Tutu" Thorson	**Barbara Lee Southern**
Reina	**Celia Kenney**
Buzz	**Matt Reese**
Hotel Clerk	**Zoel Turnbull**
Grief Counselor	**Linda Rose Herman**
Barry Thorson	**Scott Michael Morgan**
Tahiti Nui Singers (Kanack Attack)	**Darryl K. Gonzales, Koko Kanealii, Romey "Keola" Yokotake**

Shailene Woodley, Nick Krause

Matt King must re-examine his life and his relationship with his two young daughters when his wife ends up in a coma following a boating accident.

2011 Academy Award winner for Best Adapted Screenplay.

This film received additional Oscar nominations for picture, actor (George Clooney), director, and film editing.

Judy Greer, Matthew Lillard

BREAKING DAWN – PART 1

(SUMMIT) Producers, Wyck Godfrey, Karen Rosenfelt, Stephenie Meyer; Executive Producers, Marty Bowen, Greg Mooradian, Mark Morgan, Guy Oseary; Co-Producer, Bill Bannerman; Director, Bill Condon; Screenplay, Melissa Rosenberg; Based on the novel *Breaking Dawn* by Stephenie Meyer; Photography, Guillermo Navarro; Designer, Richard Sherman; Costumes, Michael Wilkinson; Music, Carter Burwell; Music Supervisor, Alexandra Patsavas; Editor, Virginia Katz; Visual Effects Designer and Supervisor, John Bruno; Casting, Debra Zane; a Temple Hill production in association with Sunswept Entertainment; Dolby; Super 35 Widescreen; Color; Rated PG-13; 117 minutes; Release date: November 18, 2011

Robert Pattinson, Kristen Stewart

CAST

Bella Swan	**Kristen Stewart**
Edward Cullen	**Robert Pattinson**
Jacob Black	**Taylor Lautner**
Charlie Swan	**Billy Burke**
Dr. Carlisle Cullen	**Peter Facinelli**
Esme Cullen	**Elizabeth Reaser**
Emmett Cullen	**Kellan Lutz**
Rosalie Hale	**Nikki Reed**
Jasper Hale	**Jackson Rathbone**
Alice Cullen	**Ashley Greene**
Aro	**Michael Sheen**
Jessica	**Anna Kendrick**
Renée	**Sarah Clarke**
Eleazar Denali	**Christian Camargo**
Billy	**Gil Birmingham**
Leah	**Julia Jones**
Seth	**Booboo Stewart**
Carmen Denali	**Mía Maestro**
Kate Denali	**Casey LaBow**
Irina Denali	**Maggie Grace**
Tanya Denali	**MyAnna Buring**
Phil Dwyer	**Ty Olsson**
Angela	**Christian Serratos**
Eric Yorkie	**Justin Chon**
Mike Newton	**Michael Welch**
Marcus	**Christopher Heyerdahl**
Caius	**Jamie Campbell Bower**
Minister Weber	**Angelo Renai**
Sue Clearwater	**Alex Rice**
Embry	**Kiowa Gordon**
Quil	**Tyson Houseman**
Sam Uley	**Chaske Spencer**
Jared	**Bronson Pelletier**
Paul	**Alex Meraz**
Emily	**Tinsel Korey**
Rachel	**Tanaya Beatty**
Claire	**Sienna Joseph**
Kaure	**Carolina Virguez**
Gustavo	**Sebastião Lemos**

Kellan Lutz, Nikki Reed

Christian Sloan, James Pizzinato, Ian Harmon, Gabriel Carter, Kavinda Dissanayake (Unsavory People), Paul Becker, Stephanie Moseley (Dancers), Kimani Ray Smith (Near-Miss Husband), Tora Hylands (Near-Miss Wife), Mackenzie Foy (Renesmee), Ali Faulkner (Bianca), Charlie Bewley (Demetri), Daniel Cudmore (Felix), Stephenie Meyer (Wedding Guest)

Bella Swan at last decides to marry her vampire lover Edward Cullen, which leads to her tumultuous pregnancy. Fourth in the Summit *Twilight* saga following *Twilight* (2008), *New Moon* (2009), and *Eclipse* (2010).

Ashley Greene, Jackson Rathbone, Elizabeth Reaser, Peter Facinelli

Nikki Reed, Taylor Lautner © Summit Entertainment

Elizabeth Reaser, Maggie Grace, Casey LaBow, MyAnna Buring

Booboo Stewart, Julia Jones

Robert Pattinson, Kristen Stewart

Mia Maestro, Christian Camargo

Taylor Lautner

Bo, Erik, Mumble, Atticus

Will the Krill, Bill the Krill © Warner Bros.

HAPPY FEET TWO

(WARNER BROS.) Producers, Doug Mitchell, George Miller, Bill Miller; Executive Producers, Chris DeFaria, Philip Hearnshaw, Graham Burke, Bruce Berman; Director, George Miller; Screenplay, George Miller, Gary Eck, Warren Coleman, Paul Livingston; Animation Director, Rob Coleman; Co-Directors, David Peers, Gary Eck; Music/Songs, John Powell; Editor, Christian Gazal; Designer, David Nelson; Photography, David Peers, David Dulac; Choreographers, Wade Robson, Dein Perry, Kate Wormald; Dancing & Choreography of Mumble, Savion Glover; Casting, Kristy Carlson; a Kennedy Miller Mitchell production with Dr. D. Studios, presented in association with Village Roadshow Pictures; Dolby; Technicolor; 3D; Rated PG; 100 minutes; Release date: November 18, 2011

VOICE CAST
Mumble	**Elijah Wood**
Lovelace/Ramon	**Robin Williams**
The Mighty Sven	**Hank Azaria**
Gloria	**Pink**
Will the Krill	**Brad Pitt**
Bill the Krill	**Matt Damon**

Sofia Vergara (Carmen), Common (Seymour), Hugo Weaving (Noah the Elder), Richard Carter (Bryan the Beachmaster), Magda Szubanski (Miss Viola), Anthony LaPaglia (The Alpha Skua), Benjamin "Lil P-Nut" Flores, Jr. (Atticus), Carlos Alazraqui (Nestor), Lombardo Boyar (Raul), Jeff Garcia (Rinaldo), Johnny Sanchez III (Lombardo), Ava Acres (Erik), Meibh Campbell (Bo), Lee Perry (Wayne the Challenger/Eggbert/Leopard Seal/Francesco), Jai Sloper, Oscar Beard (Weaner Pups), Danny Mann (Brokebeak)

Mumble is surprised to discover that his son Erik does not want to dance as do the other penguins but instead has ambitions to fly. Sequel to the 2006 Warner Bros. film.

ANOTHER HAPPY DAY

(PHASE 4 FILMS) Producers, Celine Rattray, Todd Traina, Johnny Lin, Michael Nardelli, Salli Newman, Pamela Fielder, Ellen Barkin; Executive Producers, Elana Krausz, Eric Nyari, Bill Brady, Caroline Kaplan, William T. Conway, Cynthia Coury, Sean McEwen, Peter Crane, Tom Costa, Berry Meyerowitz, Lawrence Greenberg, Jonathan Lieberman; Director/Screenplay, Sam Levinson; Photography, Ivan Strasburg; Designer, Michael Grasley; Costumes, Stacey Battat; Music, Olafur Arnalds; Editor, Ray Hubley; Casting, Cindy Tolan; a Mandalay Vision and Phase 4 Films presentation of aTaggart Productions, Princess Pictures, Cineric Inc. Filmula Entertainment, New Mexico Media Partners LLC, Red Rover Films LLC, Prop Blast Films production; Dolby; Color; Rated R; 119 minutes; Release date: November 18, 2011

CAST
Lynn	**Ellen Barkin**
Eliot	**Ezra Miller**
Doris	**Ellen Burstyn**
Patty	**Demi Moore**
Paul	**Thomas Haden Church**
Alice	**Kate Bosworth**
Joe	**George Kennedy**
Lee	**Jeffrey DeMunn**

Michael Nardelli (Dylan), Daniel Yelsky (Ben), Siobhan Fallon Hogan (Bonnie), Diana Scarwid (Donna), Eamon O'Rouke (Brandon), Lola Kirke (Charlie), David Hirsch (Tommy), Geoffrey Beauchamp (Ted), Laura Coover (Heather), Willy Vlasic (Taylor), Sean Rogers (Bobby), Patrick McDade (Father O'Grady), Brian Anthony Wilson (Jason – EMT#1), Christopher Lee Philips (Dr. Stanwick), Jack Hoffman (Carpenter Fred), Dan Usaj (Young Bartender), April Rogalski (Bridesmaid), Lila Vivi (Flower Girl), Jimmie Roach (DJ), Corrin Barnett (DJ Assistant)

Family tensions erupt when Lynn returns to her parents' Annapolis estate for the wedding of her estranged son.

Ellen Burstyn, George Kennedy, Thomas Haden Church © Phase 4 Films

Ben Foster, Woody Harrelson © Millennium Entertainment

Woody Harrelson

Brie Larson, Woody Harrelson

Robin Wright

RAMPART

(MILLENNIUM) Producers, Lawrence Inglee, Clark Peterson, Ben Foster, Ken Kao; Executive Producers, Michael DeFranco, Lila Yacoub, Mark Gordon, Paul Currie, Garrett Kelleher; Co-Producer, Luca Borghese; Director, Oren Moverman; Screenplay, James Ellroy, Oren Moverman; Photography, Bobby Bukowski; Designer, David Wasco; Costumes, Catherine George; Music, Dickon Hinchcliffe; Music Supervisor, Jim Black; Editor, Jay Rabinowitz; Casting, Laura Rosenthal, Rachel Tenner; a Lightstream Pictures presentation of a Waypoint Entertainment production in association with The Third Mind Pictures; Dolby; Widescreen; Fotokem Color; Rated R; 108 minutes; Release date: November 23, 2011

CAST

Dave Brown	**Woody Harrelson**
Linda Fentress	**Robin Wright**
Joan Confrey	**Sigourney Weaver**
Kyle Timkins	**Ice Cube**
Hartshorn	**Ned Beatty**
Bill Blago	**Steve Buscemi**
Barbara	**Cynthia Nixon**
Catherine	**Anne Heche**
Helen Brown	**Brie Larson**
Margaret Brown	**Sammy Boyarsky**
General Terry	**Ben Foster**

Audra McDonald (Sarah), Jon Bernthal (Dan Morone), Jon Foster (Michael Whittaker), Robert Wisdom (Captain), Don Creech (Head Shark Lawyer), Stella Schnabel (Jane), Matt McTighe (Young Detective), Chuti Tiu (Shark Lawyer #1), Leonard Kelly-Young (Cal Woodward), Sophie Kargman (Josephine), Deadlee (Pharmacy Punk), Tim Russ, Bryan Rasmussen (Command Staff), Dominic Flores (Latino Detective), Ruben Garfias (Pharmacy Security Guard), Billy Hough (Piano Player), Keith Woulard (Shondell Parmallee), Harriet Sansom Harris (Stacy Cranston), Ashley Thompson (Captain's Daughter), Angelita Macias, Assieh Ghassemi (Flamenco Dancers), Mike Deldicobo (Singer), Borisolv Solakov (Guitar Player), Francis Capra (Seize Chasco), Jim O'Hagen (Hotel Concierge), William Paul Clark (Barbara's Boyfriend)

A bigoted, arrogant, corrupt L.A. cop, already suspected of overstepping the line in the past, faces further trouble when he is caught on camera roughing up a suspect.

Beaker, Sam the Eagle, Dr. Bunsen Honeydew

Pepe the Prawn, Miss Piggy

Statler, Waldorf

Walter, Kermit

Swedish Chef, Chickens

Kermit, Amy Adams, Walter, Jason Segel, Rowlf

Floyd, Fozzie Bear, Lew Zealand, Janice, Swedish Chef, Camilla, Dr. Bunsen Honeydew, Gonzo, Scooter, Beaker, Dr. Teeth © Walt Disney Pictures

Chris Cooper, Uncle Deadly, Bobo the Bear

Jason Segel, Amy Adams, Walter, Kermit, Fozzie Bear

THE MUPPETS

(WALT DISNEY PICTURES) Producers, David Hoberman, Todd Lieberman; Executive Producers, Jason Segel, Nicholas Stoller, John G. Scotti, Martin G. Baker; Director, James Bobin; Screenplay, Jason Segel, Nicholas Stoller; Photography, Don Burgess; Designer, Steve Saklad; Costumes, Rahel Afiley; Editor, James Thomas; Music, Christophe Beck; Choreographer, Michael Rooney; Visual Effects Supervisor & Producer, Janet Muswell Hamilton; Pupeteer Captain, Bill Barretta; Casting, Marcia Ross, Gail Goldberg; a Walt Disney Pictures presentation; Dolby; Deluxe color; Rated PG; 103 minutes; Release date: November 23, 2011

CAST
Gary	**Jason Segel**
Mary	**Amy Adams**
Tex Richman	**Chris Cooper**
Veronica Martin, CDE Executive	**Rashida Jones**
Kermit/Beaker/Statler/Rizzo/ Link Hogthrob/Newsman	**Steve Whitmire**
Miss Piggy/Fozzie Bear/Animal/ Sam Eagle/Marvin Suggs	**Eric Jacobson**
Gonzo/Dr. Bunsen Honeydew/ Zoot/Beauregard/Waldorf/ Kermit Moopet	**Dave Goelz**
Swedish Chef/Rowlf/Dr. Teeth/ Pepe the Prawn/Bob/ Fozzie Moopet/Whatnot Farmer/Muppet Gary	**Bill Barretta**
Scooter/Janice/Miss Poogy/ Wayne	**David Rudman**
Sgt. Floyd Pepper/Camilla/ Sweetums/80's Robot/Lew Zealand/Uncle Deadly/Rowlf Moopet/Crazy Harry	**Matt Vogel**
Walter	**Peter Linz**
Tour Guide	**Alan Arkin**
Grandfather	**Bill Cobbs**
Hobo Joe	**Zach Galifianakis**
"Punch Teacher" Host	**Ken Jeong**
Human Walter	**Jim Parsons**
Postman	**Eddie Pepitone**
Moderator	**Kristen Schaal**
Greeter	**Sarah Silverman**
Miss Piggy's Secretary	**Emily Blunt**
Themselves	**Jack Black, James Carville, Leslie Feist, Whoopi Goldberg, Selena Gomez, Dave Grohl, Neil Patrick Harris, Judd Hirsch, John Krasinski, Rico Rodriguez, Mickey Rooney**

Raymond Ma (Elderly Asian Man), Shu Lan Tuan (Elderly Asian Woman), Donald Glover (Junior CDE Executive), Jonathan Palmer, Don Yanan (Reporters), Eddie "Piolin" Sotelo, Dahlia Waingort, Michael Albala (TV Executives), Julia Marie Franzese ("Punch Teacher" Kid), Gunnar Smith (Gary age 6), Connor Gallagher (Gary age 9), Justin Marco (Gary age 13), Cameron Kasal, Justin Tinucci, Alex Long (Laughing Kids), Aria Noelle Curzon (Waitress)

Dismayed to discover that the Muppets' old theater is about to be destroyed by an unscrupulous oil tycoon, Walter and Gary round up the Muppets in hopes of putting on a benefit show and raising money to save their heritage.

2011 Academy Award winner for Best Original Song ("Man or Muppet").

HUGO

(PARAMOUNT) Producers, Graham King, Tim Headington, Martin Scorsese, Johnny Depp; Executive Producers, Emma Tillinger Koskoff, David Crockett, Georgia Kacandes, Christi Dembrowski, Barbara DeFina; Director, Martin Scorsese; Screenplay, John Logan; Based on the book *The Invention of Hugo Cabret* by Brian Selznick; Photography, Robert Richardson; Designer, Dante Ferretti; Costumes, Sandy Powell; Music, Howard Shore; Music Supervisor, Randall Poster; Editor, Thelma Schoonmaker; Visual Effects Supervisor, Rob Legato; Casting, Ellen Lewis; a GK Films/Infinitum Nihil production; Dolby; Color; 3D; Rated PG; 126 minutes; Release date: November 23, 2011

Asa Butterfield

CAST

Georges Méliès	**Ben Kingsley**
Gustave, Station Inspector	**Sacha Baron Cohen**
Hugo Cabret	**Asa Butterfield**
Isabelle	**Chloë Grace Moretz**
Uncle Claude	**Ray Winstone**
Lisette	**Emily Mortimer**
Monsieur Labisse	**Christopher Lee**
Mama Jeanne	**Helen McCrory**
Rene Tabard	**Michael Stuhlbarg**
Madame Emilie	**Frances de la Tour**
Monsieur Frick	**Richard Griffiths**
Hugo's Father	**Jude Law**
Policeman	**Kevin Eldon**
Young Tabard	**Gulliver McGrath**
Street Kid	**Shaun Aylward**
Django Reinhardt	**Emil Lager**
Theatre Manager	**Angus Barnett**
Camera Technician	**Edmund Kingsley**
Train Engineer	**Max Wrottesley**
Train Engineer Assistant	**Marco Aponte**
Salvador Dali	**Ben Addis**
James Joyce	**Robert Gill**
Young Tabard's Brother	**Ed Sanders**
Circus Barkers	**Terence Frisch, Max Cane**
Gendarmes	**Frank Bourke, Stephen Box**
Photographer	**Martin Scorsese**
Café Waitress	**Ilona Cheshire**
Children at Café	**Francesca Scorsese, Emily Surgent, Lily Carlson**
Arabian Knights	**Frederick Warder, Christos Lawson, Tomos James**
Eager Student	**Brian Selznick**

Christopher Lee, Asa Butterfield

An orphaned boy, living in a Paris train station, unlocks the secret past of an elderly toy seller when he goes in search of parts to fix the mechanical man left behind by his late father.

2011 Academy Award winner for Best Cinematography, Best Art Direction, Best Visual Effects, Best Sound Mixing, and Best Sound Editing.

This film received additional Oscar nominations for picture, director, adapted screenplay, costume design, film editing, and original score.

Asa Butterfield, Jude Law

Emily Mortimer © Paramount Pictures

Asa Butterfield, Chloë Grace Moretz

Asa Butterfield, Chloë Grace Moretz

Sacha Baron Cohen

Asa Butterfield, Ben Kingsley

Robert De Niro, Halle Berry

Zac Efron, Michelle Pfeiffer

Hector Elizondo, Hilary Swank

NEW YEAR'S EVE

(NEW LINE CINEMA/WB) Producers, Mike Karz, Wayne Rice, Garry Marshall; Executive Producers, Toby Emmerich, Samuel J. Brown, Michael Disco, Josie Rosen, Diana Pokorny; Director, Garry Marshall; Screenplay, Katherine Fugate; Photography, Charles Minsky; Designer, Mark Friedberg; Costumes, Gary Jones; Music, John Debney; Music Supervisor, Julianne Jordan; Editor, Michael Tronick; Casting, Amanda Mackey, Cathy Sandrich Gelfond; a Wayne Rice/Karz Entertainment production; Distributed by Warner Bros.; Dolby; Technicolor; Rated PG-13; 118 minutes; Release date: December 9, 2011

CAST
Resolution Tour
Ingrid   **Michelle Pfeiffer**
Paul   **Zac Efron**
Charlotte Marshall-Fricker (Caring Teenage Girl), Fiona Choi (Balinese Woman), Mary Marguerite Kean (Pet Adoption Clerk), Michael Mandell (Murray), Patrick Reale (Times Square Cop), John Lithgow (Ingrid's Boss)

Hospital Story
Stan Harris   **Robert De Niro**
Nurse Aimee   **Halle Berry**
Cary Elwes (Stan's Doctor), Alyssa Milano (Nurse Mindy), Common (Soldier), Barbara Marshall (Head Nurse Helen)

Maternity Ward
Tess Byrne   **Jessica Biel**
Griffin Byrne   **Seth Meyers**
Grace Schwab   **Sarah Paulson**
James Schwab   **Til Schweiger**
Carla Gugino (Spiritual Dr. Morriset), Amber Bela Muse (Nurse Risa), Peter Allen Vogt (Male Nurse), Ross Ryman (Pedicab Driver), Kal Parekh (Obstetrician)

Jensen & Laura's Story
Laura   **Katherine Heigl**
Jensen   **Jon Bon Jovi**
Ava   **Sofia Vergara**
Russell Peters (Chef Sunil), Serena Poon (Chef Ming), Sarge (Monty)

Elevator
Randy   **Ashton Kutcher**
Elise   **Lea Michele**
Jim Belushi (Building Super), Lillian Lifflander (Mrs. Lifflander),

Mother & Daughter
Kim   **Sarah Jessica Parker**
Hailey   **Abigail Breslin**
Jake T. Austin (Seth), Mara Davi (Mika), Jaclyn Miller (Choreographer), Cassidy Reiff (Piper), Nat Wolff (Walter), Kendra Jain (Kelly), Julia Randall (Julia), Christian Fortune (Cody), Tatyana Disla (Tatyana), Chealy Phoung (Chealy), Marvin Braverman (Vendor Marvin), Alexandra Guthy (Screaming Rocker Girl), Denise Violante (Cop Denise), Katherine McNamara (Lily Bowman), Norman Bukofzer (Newark Commuter), Beth Kennedy (Piper's Mom)

Ahern Party
Sam   **Josh Duhamel**
Groom Rory   **Joey McIntyre**
Bride Tish   **Jackie Seiden**
Mrs. Rose Ahern   **Cherry Jones**
Sean O'Bryan (Pastor Edwin), Larry Miller (Harley), Jack McGee (Grandpa Jed), Yeardley Smith (Maude), Benjamin McGowan (Logan), Jon-Christian Costable (Duncan), Juliette Allen-Angelo (Sadie), Penny Marshall (Herself), Drena

De Niro (Ahern Waitress), Vanessa I. Mendoza (Leopard Print Girl), Christine Lakin (Waitress Alyssa), Sandra Taylor (Patty), Shea Curry (Wendy), Earl Rose (Pianist), Johnny DeBrito (Party Guest), Samuel E. Mitchell (Penny's Dance Partner), Amar'e Stoudemire (Party Dancer)

Times Square

Claire Morgan	**Hilary Swank**
Brendan	**Chris "Ludacris" Bridges**
Kominsky	**Hector Elizondo**

Kathleen Marshall (Stage Manager Charlotte), Joey Sorge (Radio Reporter Arthur), Rob Nagle (Officer Nolan), Matt Walker (Engineer Douglas), Wedil David (Reporter Christina), David Valcin (Reporter Murphy), Stephanie Fabian (Reporter Lupe), Patrick Collins (Reporter Fadda), Pat Battle (Reporter Pat Battle), Tom Hines (Announcer Brady Finley), Greg Wilson (Wade the Aide), Anna Aimee White (Ginger Adams), Sam Marshall (Crowd Surfing Kid), Susan Silver (Bunny Friedberg), Emily Moss Wilson (Crazy Jensen Fan), Bob Weston (Jensen Concert Police), Lucy Woodward, Stephanie Alexander (Backup Singers), Nicole Michele Sobchack, Anna Kulinova (Kissing Revelers), Rylie J. Neale (Kissing Cop), Lily Marshall-Fricker (Reveler Lucy Camille), Lori Marshall (Reveler Ms. Camille), Matthew Broderick (Mr. Buellerton), Ryan Seacrest, Mayor Michael Bloomberg (Themselves)

Several intertwining stories unfold among various New Yorkers as they wait to ring in the New Year.

Abigail Breslin, Sarah Jessica Parker

Josh Duhamel, Cherry Jones

Sofia Vergara, Katherine Heigl

Til Schweiger © New Line Cinema

Chris "Ludacris" Bridges

Ashton Kutcher

Seth Meyers

Jon Bon Jovi, Lea Michele

Charlize Theron

Charlize Theron, Patrick Wilson, Elizabeth Reaser

Charlize Theron, Richard Bekins, Jill Eikenberry

Patton Oswalt, Collette Wolfe © Paramount Pictures

YOUNG ADULT

(PARAMOUNT) Producers, Lianne Halfon, Russell Smith, Diablo Cody, Mason Novick, Jason Reitman; Executive Producers, Nathan Kahane, John Malkovich, Steven Rales, Helen Estabrook; Line Producer, Brian Bell; Director, Jason Reitman; Screenplay, Diablo Cody; Photography, Eric Steelberg; Designer, Kevin Thompson; Costumes, David Robinson; Music, Rolfe Kent; Music Supervisor, Linda Cohen; Editor, Dana E. Glauberman; Casting, Suzanne Smith Crowley, Jessica Kelly; a Mandate Pictures presentation of a Mr. Mudd production in association with Right of Way Films and Denver & Delilah Films; Dolby; Deluxe color; Rated R; 93 minutes; Release date: December 9, 2011

CAST
Mavis Gary	**Charlize Theron**
Matt Freehauf	**Patton Oswalt**
Buddy Slade	**Patrick Wilson**
Beth Slade	**Elizabeth Reaser**
Sandra Freehauf	**Collette Wolfe**
Hedda Gary	**Jill Eikenberry**
David Gary	**Richard Bekins**
Jan	**Mary Beth Hurt**
Mary Ellen Trantowski	**Kate Nowlin**
Nipple Confusion	**Jenny Dare Paulin, Rebecca Hart**
Front Desk Girl	**Louisa Krause**
Sales Lady	**Elizabeth Ward Land**
Book Associate	**Brian McElhaney**

Hettienne Park (Vicki), John Forest (Wheelchair Mike), Rightor Doyle (Babysitter), Brady Smith (Date Man), Timothy Young (Champions Server), Erin Darke, Jee Young Han (Teen Employees), Ella Rae Peck, Aleisha Lanae Allen (Girls), Matt Wilson (Teenage Clerk), Orlagh Cassidy (Party Guest), Charles Techman (Parking Attendant), Emily Meade (Denny's Waitress), Neil Hellegers (Young Dad), Michael Nathanson (Champions Greeter), J.K. Simmons (Mavis' Publisher)

A self-absorbed young adult novelist returns to her home town with the goal of stealing her old flame away from his wife and child.

Jonah Hill

Kevin Hernandez, Jonah Hill © Twentieth Century Fox

Landry Bender, Jonah Hill

Landry Bender, Kevin Hernandez, Max Records, Jonah Hill

THE SITTER

(20TH CENTURY FOX) Producer, Michael De Luca; Executive Producers, Jonah Hill, Donald J. Lee Jr., Lisa Muskat, Josh Bratman; Director, David Gordon Green; Screenplay, Brian Gatewood, Alessandro Tanaka; Photography, Tim Orr; Designer, Richard A. Wright; Costumes, Leah Katznelson; Music, David Wingo, Jeff McIlwain; Music Supervisor, Mark Wike; Editor, Craig Alpert; Casting, Alexa L. Fogel; a Michael De Luca/Rough House Pictures production; Dolby; Super 35 Widescreen; Deluxe color; Rated R; 81 minutes; Release date: December 9, 2011

CAST
Noah Griffith	**Jonah Hill**
Slater	**Max Records**
Marisa Lewis	**Ari Graynor**
Julio	**J.B. Smoove**
Karl	**Sam Rockwell**
Blithe	**Landry Bender**
Rodrigo	**Kevin Hernandez**
Roxanne	**Kylie Bunbury**

Erin Daniels (Mrs. Pedulla), D.W. Moffett (Dr. Pedulla), Jessica Hecht (Sandy Griffith), Bruce Altman (Jim Griffith), Cliff "Method Man" Smith (Jacolby), Sean Patrick Doyle (Garv), Alex Wolff (Clayton), Jack Krizmanich (Ricky Fontaine), Grace Aronds, Jane Aronds (Twins), Lou Carbonneau (Maitre'D), Alysia Joy Powell (Kid City Employee), Ernie Anastos (News Anchor), Dari Alexander Williams (News Broadcaster #2), Samira Wiley (Tina), Sammuel Soifer (Benji Gillespie), Kevin Townley (Valet), Trevor Zhou (Asian Fish Monger), Wendy Hoopes (Bethany), Peg Stegmeyer (Piano Player), Ethan Davis (Ashton Griffith), Reggie A. Green (Soul Baby), Nick Sandow (Officer Frank), Nicky Katt (Officer Petite), Eddie Rouse (Lounge Singer), Henry Kwan, Michael G. Chin (Asian Men), Gracie Bea Lawrence (Wendy Sapperstein), Jackie Hoffman (Mrs. Sapperstein), Jonathan Forte (Guy on Subway Platform), Mark Moynahan (Dr. Stevens), Greg Wall, Zevy Zions, Jordan Hirsch, Jonathan Peretz, Anthony Pompa, David Hirsch (Bat Mitzvah Band), Angel Picard-Ami (Ricky Fontaine's Girlfriend)

When reluctant babysitter Noah Griffith has a chance to get some action at a New York party, he drags his three young charges into the city with him for a night of rowdy and unexpected action.

CORMAN'S WORLD: EXPLOITS OF A HOLLYWOOD REBEL

(ANCHOR BAY) Producers, Alex Stapleton, Jeffrey Frey, Izabela Frank, Mickey Barold, Stone Douglass; Executive Producers, Molly Thompson, Robert DeBitetto, Robert Sharenow, Jared Moshe, Rich Lim, Joshua Ray Levin, Antonio Von Hildebrand, Polly Platt, Taylor Matrene; Director/Screenplay, Alex Stapleton; Photography, Patrick Simpson; Music, Air; Music Supervisor, Margaret Yen; Editors, Victor Livingston, Philip Owen; an A&E IndieFilms presentation of a Far Hills Pictures/Stick N Stone Production in association with Gallant Films; Color/Black and white; HD; Rated R; 95 minutes; Release date: December 16, 2011. Documentary on the career of exploitation filmmaker Roger Corman.

WITH

Roger Corman, Paul W.S. Anderson, Allan Arkush, Eric Balfour, Peter Bogdanovich, Bob Burns, David Carradine, Gene Corman, Julie Corman, Joe Dante, Jonathan Demme, Robert De Niro, Bruce Dern, Frances Doel, Peter Fonda, Pam Grier, Jonathan Haze, George Hickenlooper, Ron Howard, Gale Ann Hurd, Irvin Kershner, Todd McCarthy, Dick Miller, Jack Nicholson, Polly Platt, Eli Roth, John Sayles, Martin Scorsese, William Shatner, Tom Sherak, Penelope Spheeris, Quentin Tarantino, Gary Tunnicliffe, Mary Woronov, Jim Wynorski

Roger Corman

Roger Corman © Anchor Bay

Eleanor, Theodore © Twentieth Century Fox

Alvin, Jason Lee

ALVIN AND THE CHIPMUNKS: CHIPWRECKED

(20TH CENTURY FOX) Producers, Janice Karman, Ross Bagdasarian; Executive Producers, Karen Rosenfelt, Arnon Milchan, Neil Machlis, Steve Waterman; Director, Mike Mitchell; Screenplay, Jonathan Aibel, Glenn Berger; Based on the characters Alvin and the Chipmunks created by Ross Bagdasarian, and the Chipettes created by Janice Karman; Photography, Thomas Ackerman; Designer, Richard Holland; Costumes, Alexandra Welker; Music, Mark Mothersbaugh; Music Supervisor, Julia Michels; Editor, Peter Amundson; Animation Supervisor, Kevin Johnson; Casting, Allison Jones; a Fox 2000 Pictures and Regency Enterprises presentation; Dolby; Deluxe color; Rated G; 87 minutes; Release date: December 16, 2011

CAST

Dave	**Jason Lee**
Ian	**David Cross**
Zoe	**Jenny Slate**
Voice of Alvin	**Justin Long**
Voice of Simon	**Matthew Gray Gubler**
Voice of Theodore	**Jesse McCartney**

Amy Poehler (Voice of Eleanor), Anna Faris (Voice of Jeanette), Christina Applegate (Voice of Brittany), Alan Tudyk (Voice of Simone), Michael Northey (Hawaiian Shirt Guy), Sophia Aguiar, Lauren Gottlieb, Tera Perez (Club Women), Andy Buckley (Captain Correlli), Chad Krowchuk (Waiter), Luisa D'Oliveira (Tessa), Tucker Albrizzi (Tucker, Kite Kid), Nelson Wong (Casino Guy), Michael Karman (Excursion Clerk), Amber-Rochelle DeMarco, Marcela Caceres, Natalie Sutcliffe (Damsels), Ian Harmon (Monster), Phyllis Smith (Flight Attendant)

During a cruise, Alvin and the Chipmunks accidentally find themselves overboard and stranded on a deserted island. Third in the 20th Century Fox series following *Alvin and the Chipmunks* (2007) and *Alvin and the Chipmunks: The Squeakquel* (2009), with Jason Lee and David Cross repeating their roles.

Noomi Rapace, Robert Downey Jr., Jude Law © Warner Bros.

Robert Downey Jr., Jude Law, Kelly Reilly

SHERLOCK HOLMES: A GAME OF SHADOWS

(WARNER BROS.) Producers, Joel Silver, Lionel Wigram, Susan Downey, Dan Lin; Executive Producers, Bruce Berman, Steve Clark-Hall; Director, Guy Ritchie; Screenplay, Michele Mulroney, Kieran Mulroney; Photography, Philippe Rousselot; Designer, Sarah Greenwood; Costumes, Jenny Beavan; Music, Hans Zimmer; Editor, James Herbert; Casting, Reg Porescout-Edgerton; a Silver Pictures production in association with Wigram Productions; Dolby; Super 35 Widescreen; Color; Rated PG-13; 128 minutes; Release date: December 16, 2011

CAST

Sherlock Holmes	**Robert Downey, Jr.**
Dr. John Watson	**Jude Law**
Madam Simza Heron	**Noomi Rapace**
Irene Adler	**Rachel McAdams**
Professor James Moriarty	**Jared Harris**
Mycroft Holmes	**Stephen Fry**
Colonel Sebastian Moran	**Paul Anderson**
Mary Watson	**Kelly Reilly**
Mrs. Hudson	**Geraldine James**
Inspector Lestrade	**Eddie Marsan**

William Houston (Constable Clark), Wolf Kahler (Dr. Hoffmanstahl), Iain Mitchell (Auctioneer), Jack Laskey (Carruthers), Patricia Slater, Karima Adebibe (Shush Club Maitre D's), Richard Cunningham (Businessman), Marcus Shakesheff (Hashisheen), Mark Sheals (Cock Fight Referee), George Taylor (University Student), Michael Webber (Vicar), Mike Grady (Train Conductor), Alexandre Carril, Victor Carril (Twins), Thorston Manderlay (Alfred Meinhard), Affif Ben Badra (Tamas), Daniel Naprous (Marko), Lancelot Weaver (Stefan), Vladimir Furdik (Andrzej), Jacques Senet Larson, Nicolas Senet Larson, Sebastian Senet Larson (Gypsy Kids), Alexander Devrient, Fatima Adoum (Gypsies), Stanley Kaye (Stanley), Thierry Neuvic (Claude Ravache), Martin Nelson (Commendatore), Mark Llewelyn-Evans (Don Giovanni), Anthony Inglis (Conductor), Ian Wilson-Pope (Leporello), Pamela Hay (Elvira), Laurence Dobiesz (Servant), Peter Stark, Roman Jankovic (German Officers), Frederick Ruth (Ballroom Attendant), Carsten Hayes (Ballroom Photographer), Jonathan Christie, James McNeill (Diplomats), Laurentiu Possa (Rene Heron), Maitland Chandler (Banker), Joe Egan (Big Joe), Clive Russell (Captain Tanner)

Sherlock Holmes must stop the nefarious Professor Moriarty from carrying out his scheme of plotting terrorist campaigns in an effort to cause war throughout Europe. Second entry in WB's Robert Downey Jr.-Jude Law series, following *Sherlock Holmes* (2009).

Jack Laskey, Stephen Fry

Tom Cruise

Simon Pegg, Tom Cruise

MISSION: IMPOSSIBLE - GHOST PROTOCOL

(PARAMOUNT) Producers, Tom Cruise, J.J. Abrams, Bryan Burk; Executive Producers, Jeffrey Chernov, David Ellison, Paul Schwake, Dana Goldberg; Director, Brad Bird; Screenplay, Josh Applebaum, André Nemec; Based on the television series created by Bruce Geller; Photography, Robert Elswit; Designer, Jim Bissell; Costumes, Michael Kaplan; Music, Michael Giacchino; *Mission: Impossible Theme* by Lalo Schifrin; Editor, Paul Hirsch; Visual Effects Supervisor, John Knoll; Visual Effects and Animation, Industrial Light & Magic; Casting, April Webster, Alyssa Weisberg; Stunts, Gregg Smrz; a Skydance Productions presentation of a Tom Cruise/Bad Robot production; Dolby; Panavision; Deluxe color; Rated PG-13; 133 minutes; Release date: December 16, 2011

CAST
Ethan Hunt	**Tom Cruise**
Jane Carter	**Paula Patton**
Benji Dunn	**Simon Pegg**
William Brandt	**Jeremy Renner**
Kurt Hendricks	**Michael Nyqvist**
Anatoly Sidorov	**Vladimir Mashkov**
Wistrom	**Samuli Edelmann**
Leonid Lisenker	**Ivan Shvedoff**
Brij Nath	**Anil Kapoor**
Sabine Moreau	**Léa Seydoux**
IMF Secretary	**Tom Wilkinson**
Trevor Hanaway	**Josh Holloway**
Marek Stefanski	**Pavel Kriz**
Bogdan	**Miraj Grbic**
The Fog	**Ilia Volok**
Burly Russian Prisoner	**Goran Navojec**
Prison Guard	**Pavel Bezdek**
Scraggy Tooth	**Vitaliy Kravchenko**
Russian Agent	**Ivo Novák**
Anna Lisenker	**Petra Lustigova**
Alex Lisenker	**Daniel Clarke**
The Fog's Contact	**Andreas Wisniewski**

Ladislav Beran, Jan Filipensky, Jirí Kraus, Ales Putik, Tomás Valik (Control Room Guards), Pavel Cajzl, Randy Hall (Prisoners), Andrey Bestchastney (Kremlin Senate Building Desk Guard), Michael Dopud (Kremlin Subcellar Hallway Guard), Martin Hub (Kremlin Gate Security Guard), Anastasiya Novikova (Russian Hospital Nurse), Marek Dobes, Claudia Vaseková (Russian News Anchors), Brian Caspe (British News Anchor), April Stewart (Swedish Translator), Gina Hirsch (IMF Operator), Ghalib Al Saady (Dock Worker), Mustafa Al Yassri (Doctor Setting Sidorov's Nose), Michael Rys (Russian Sub Captain), Dmitry Chepovetsky (Russian Sub Ensign), Dawn Chubai (San Francisco News Anchor), Nicola Anderson, Keith Blackman Dallas, Tammy Hui, David Stuart, Sabrina Morris (Julia's Friends), Michelle Monaghan (Julia Meade), Ving Rhames (Luther Stickell)

Unjustly accused of a terrorist bombing at the Kremlin, IMF operative Ethan Hunt must find a way to clear himself and his agency members and prevent another attack. Fourth film in the Paramount series following *Mission: Impossible* (1996), *Mission: Impossible II* (2000), and *Mission: Impossible 3* (2006), all of which starred Tom Cruise.

Anil Kapoor

Tom Cruise, Paula Patton, Simon Pegg, Jeremy Renner

Paula Patton, Léa Seydoux

Jeremy Renner, Tom Cruise

Tom Cruise

Michael Nyqvist, Samuli Edelmann

Jeremy Renner © Paramount Pictures

Christopher Plummer, Daniel Craig

Daniel Craig, Christopher Plummer

Daniel Craig

Stellan Skarsgård

Rooney Mara

Rooney Mara, Daniel Craig

THE GIRL WITH THE DRAGON TATTOO

(COLUMBIA/MGM) Producers, Scott Rudin, Ole Søndberg, Søren Stærmose, Ceán Chaffin; Executive Producers, Steven Zaillian, Mikael Wallen, Anni Faurbye Fernandez; Director, David Fincher; Screenplay, Steven Zaillian; Based on the novel by Stieg Larsson; Photography, Jeff Cronenweth; Designer, Donald Graham Burt; Costumes, Trish Summerville; Music, Trent Reznor, Atticus Ross; Editors, Kirk Baxter, Angus Wall; Casting, Laray Mayfield; a Scott Rudin/Yellow Bird production; American-Swedish-British-German; Dolby; Deluxe color; Rated R; 158 minutes; Release date: December 20, 2011

CAST

Mikael Blomkvist	**Daniel Craig**
Lisbeth Salander	**Rooney Mara**
Henrik Vanger	**Christopher Plummer**
Martin Vanger	**Stellan Skarsgård**
Dirch Frode	**Steven Berkoff**
Erika Berger	**Robin Wright**
Nils Bjurman	**Yorick van Wageningen**
Anita Vanger	**Joely Richardson**
Cecilia Vanger	**Geraldine James**
Dragan Armansky	**Goran Visnjic**
Detective Inspector Gustaf Morell	**Donald Sumpter**
Hans-Erik Wennerström	**Ulf Friberg**
Holger Palmgren	**Bengt C.W. Carlsson**
Plague	**Tony Way**
Harald Vanger	**Per Myrberg**
Pernilla Bomkvist	**Josefin Asplund**
Anna Nygren	**Eva Fritjofson**
Harriet Vanger	**Moa Garpendal**
Young Anna	**Maya Hansson-Bergqvist**
Young Cecilia	**Sarah Appleberg**
Young Henrik	**Julian Sands**
Young Isabella	**Anna Björk**
Young Harald	**Gustaf Hammarsten**
Young Martin	**Simon Reithner**
Young Gustaf	**David Dencik**
Young Gunnar Nilsson	**Marcus Johansson**
Young Anita	**Mathilda von Essen**
Young Birger	**Mathias Palmér**

Martin Jarvis (Birger Vanger), Inga Landgré (Isabella Vanger), Reza Dehban (Hussein), Anders Berg (Young Dirch Frode), Mats Andersson (Gunnar Nilsson), Anders Jansson (Doctor), Jürgen Klein (Gottfried), Kalle Josephson (Tech at MacJesus), Sandra Andreis (Photo Editor), Arly Jover (Liv), Pierre Sjö Östergren (Tattoo Artist), Tess Panzer (TV Newscaster), Alastair Duncan (Greger), Alan Dale (Detective Isaksson), Julia Rose (Nurse), Peter Carlberg (Hardware Clerk), Jan Abramson (Forsman), Lena Strömdahl (Mildred), Matthew Wolf (Tech Clerk), Anne-Li Norberg (Lindgren), Leo Bill (Trinity), Marco Albrecht (Junkie), Martina Lotun (Reporter at Vanger), Anna Carlson (FSA Official), Yvonne Åstrand (FSA Reporter), Fredrik Dolk (Wennerström's Lawyer), Christian Heller, Werner Biermeier (Bankers), Christine Adams (Barbados TV Reporter), Peter Hottinger (Zurich TV Reporter), Joyce Giraud (Spain TV Reporter), Bengt Wallgren (Tailor), Elodie Yung (Miriam Wu), Anna Charlotta Gunnarson, Andreas Björklund (Reporters), Embeth Davidtz (Annika Blomkvist Giannini), Joel Kinnaman (Christer Malm), Karen E. Wright (Magda Lovison), Leah Almada Harshaw (Book of Death Victim), George Gerdes (Udevalla Detective)

Disgraced journalist Mikael Blomkvist enlists the aide of punk computer whiz Lisbeth Salander to help him investigate the disappearance and presumed murder of a 16-year-old girl. Remake of the Swedish film that starred Noomi Rapace and Michael Nyqvist.

2011 Academy Award winner for Best Film Editing.

This film received additional Oscar nominations for actress (Rooney Mara), cinematography, sound mixing, and sound editing.

Daniel Craig, Rooney Mara

Daniel Craig, Robin Wright

Rooney Mara, Yorick van Wageningen © Columbia Pictures

THE ADVENTURES OF TINTIN

(PARAMOUNT/COLUMBIA) Producers, Steven Spielberg, Peter Jackson, Kathleen Kennedy; Executive Producers, Ken Kamins, Nick Rodwell, Stephane Sperry; Co-Producers, Carolynne Cunningham, Jason McGatlin; Director, Steven Spielberg; Screenplay, Steven Moffat, Edgar Wright, Joe Cornish; Based on the series of books *The Adventures of Tintin* by Hergé; Music, John Williams; Editor, Michael Kahn; Art Directors, Andrew Jones, Jeff Wisniewski; Animation Supervisor, Jamie Beard; Senior Visual Effects Supervisor, Joe Letteri; Visual Effects Supervisor, Scott E. Anderson; Visual Effects and Animation, Weta Digital Ltd.; Casting, Jina Jay, Victoria Burrows, Scot Boland; an Amblin Entertainment, Wingnut Films, Kennedy/Marshall production, presented in association with Hemisphere Media Capital; American-New Zealand; Dolby; Panavision; Deluxe Color; 3D; Rated PG; 107 minutes; Release date: December 21, 2011

CAST

Tintin	**Jamie Bell**
Captain Haddock/Sir Francis	**Andy Serkis**
Ivanovitch Sakharine/Red Rackham	**Daniel Craig**
Thomson	**Nick Frost**
Thompson	**Simon Pegg**
Pilot	**Cary Elwes**
Silk	**Toby Jones**
Tom/Pirate Flunky #2	**Mackenzie Crook**
Allan/Pirate Flunky #1	**Daniel Mays**
Ben Salaad	**Gad Elmaleh**
Barnaby	**Joe Starr**
Lt. Delcourt	**Tony Curran**
Pedro/1st Mate	**Sebastian Roché**
Afghar Outpost Soldier	**Mark Ivanir**
Bianca Castafiore	**Kim Stengel**
Co-Pilot/French Medic	**Phillip Rhys**
Mr. Crabtree/Nestor	**Enn Reitel**
Old Lady/Lady in the Phonebox	**Jacquie Barnbrook**
Mrs. Finch	**Sonje Fortag**
Sailor/Unicorn Lookout	**Ron Bottitta**
Moroccan Reporter	**Sana Etoile**
Market Artist	**Nathan Meister**
Soldier #4	**Mohamed Ibrahim**

Tintin, an intrepid young reporter, joins forces with Captain Haddock and a pair of bumbling detectives to help decipher the secret behind a model ship tied to a barbaric pirate named Red Rackham.

This film received an Oscar nomination for original score.

Tintin

Thompson, Thomson

Captain Haddock, Tintin

Ivanovitch Sakharine (left)

Tintin, Captain Haddock, Snowy

Thompson, Tintin, Thomson, Snowy, Captain Haddock

Captain Haddock, Tintin, Snowy

Captain Haddock, Tintin, Snowy

Captain Haddock, Snowy, Tintin © Paramount Pictures

Zana Marjanović, Boris Ler

Džana Pinjo, Zana Marjanović

Zana Marjanović, Goran Kostić

IN THE LAND OF BLOOD AND HONEY

(FILMDISTRICT) Producers, Angelina Jolie, Graham King, Tim Headington, Tim Moore; Executive Producers, Holly Goline-Sadowski, Michael Vieira; Director/ Screenplay, Angelina Jolie; Photography, Dean Semler; Designer, Jon Hutman; Costumes, Gabriele Binder; Music, Gabriel Yared; Editor, Patricia Rommel; Casting, Gail Stevens; a GK Films production; Dolby; Super 35 Widescreen; Color; Rated R; 127 minutes; Release date: December 23, 2011

CAST
Ajla	**Zana Marjanovic**
Danijel	**Goran Kostic**
Nebojsa	**Rade Šerbedžija**
Lejla	**Vanesa Glodjo**
Darko	**Nikola Djuricko**
Aleksandar	**Branko Djuric**
Petar	**Fedja Stukan**
Hana	**Alma Terzic**
Esma	**Jelena Jovanova**
Mehmet	**Ermin Bravo**
Tarik	**Boris Ler**

Goran Jevtic (Mitar), Ermin Sijamija (Vuc), Miloš Timotijevic (Durja), Jasna Beri (Mejrema), Aleksandar Djurica (Marko), Džana Pinjo (Nadja), Irena Mulamuhic (Bosnian Woman), Dolya Gavanski (Maida), Levente Törköly (Serbian Officer #2), Dado Jehan (Band Leader), Vladimir Grbic (Police Officer in Club)

An officer in the Bosnian Serb Army must confront his ambiguous feelings about the conflict in his country when he is ordered to evict his former lover and her family from their apartment.

Goran Kostić, Rade Šerbedžija © FilmDistrict

Matt Damon © Twentieth Century Fox

Patrick Fugit, Matt Damon, Scarlett Johansson

Maggie Elizabeth Jones, Scarlett Johansson

Matt Damon, Colin Ford, Thomas Haden Church, Scarlett Johansson, Maggie Elizabeth Jones, Angus Macfadyen, Ben Seeder, Dustin Ybarra, Patrick Fugit, Alice Marie Crowe, Sam Fox

WE BOUGHT A ZOO

(20TH CENTURY FOX) Producers, Julie Yorn, Cameron Crowe, Rick Yorn; Executive Producer, Ilona Herzberg; Co-Producers, Paul Deason, Aldric La'Auli Porter, Marc R. Gordon; Director, Cameron Crowe; Screenplay, Aline Brosh McKenna, Cameron Crowe; Based upon the book by Benjamin Mee; Photography, Rodrigo Prieto; Designer, Clay Griffith; Costumes, Deborah L. Scott; Music, Jonsi; Editor, Mark Livolsi; Visual Effects Supervisor, Paul Graff; Visual Effects, Crazy Horse Effects; Stunts, Thomas Robinson Harper, Doug Seus; Casting, Gail Levin; an LBI Entertainment/Vinyl Films production; Dolby; Super 35 Widescreen; Deluxe color; Rated PG; 124 minutes; Release date: December 23, 2011

CAST

Benjamin Mee	**Matt Damon**
Kelly Foster	**Scarlett Johansson**
Duncan Mee	**Thomas Haden Church**
Robin Jones	**Patrick Fugit**
Dylan Mee	**Colin Ford**
Lily Miska	**Elle Fanning**
Rosie Mee	**Maggie Elizabeth Jones**
Walter Ferris	**John Michael Higgins**
Peter MacCready	**Angus MacFadyen**
Delbert McGinty	**Peter Riegert**
Katherine Mee	**Stephanie Szostak**
Mr. Stevens	**JB Smoove**

Carla Gallo (Rhonda Blair), Desi Lydic (Shea Seger, Lasagna Mom), Dustin Ybarra (Nathan), Mark Hengst (David White), Michael Panes (Principal), Kym Whitley (Cashier), Diamond Nicole Landeen (Donation Girl), Erick Chavarria (Ernesto), Roberto Montesinos (Hugo Chavez), Ben Seeder (Bruce), Cirsty Joy (Jaimie Love), Sam Fox (Alison), Todd Stanton (San Diego Vet), Alice Marie Crowe (Parrot Lady), Michelle Panek (Sarah Tanner, Vet Assistant), Gary D. Robertson (Zookeeper), Nicole Russell, Reid Peters (Volunteers), Benjamin Mee, Ella Mee, Milo Mee, Sammi Yorn (Visiting Family), Steven Lee, Taylor Victoria Cerza, Steve Bessette, Kate Yerves, Hal Alpert, Caroline Hanna, Leslie Trotter, David Lopez (Zoo Patrons), William Crowe, Curtis Crowe (Zoo Kids), Johnny Cicco, Alexia Barroso (Zoo Staff), Bart the Bear (Buster the Bear), Gabriel Escalante (Segundo), Christie Kittelsen, Michelle Glassburn (Zoo Lovers)

Looking to turn his life around after the death of his wife, Benjamin Mee makes the outrageous decision to move his family to a rural property that includes a wild animal park.

Tom Hiddleston, Geoff Bell, Joey, Jeremy Irvine, Peter Mullan

Jeremy Irvine, Joey © DreamWorks

Niels Arestrup, Celine Buckens, Joey

WAR HORSE

(TOUCHSTONE/DREAMWORKS) Producers, Steven Spielberg, Kathleen Kennedy; Executive Producers, Frank Marshall, Revel Guest; Co-Producers, Adam Somner, Tracey Seaward; Director, Steven Spielberg; Screenplay, Lee Hall, Richard Curtis; Based on the novel by Michael Morpurgo; Photography, Janusz Kaminski; Designer, Rick Carter; Costumes, Joanna Johnston; Music, John Williams; Editor, Michael Kahn; Visual Effects Supervisor, Ben Morris; Casting, Jina Jay; a DreamWorks Pictures and Reliance Entertainment presentation of an Amblin Entertainment/Kennedy/Marshall Company production; Distributed by Walt Disney Studios Motion Pictures; Dolby; Super 35 Widescreen; Deluxe color; Rated PG-13; 146 minutes; Release date: December 25, 2011

CAST

Albert Narracott	**Jeremy Irvine**
Ted Narracott	**Peter Mullan**
Rose Narracott	**Emily Watson**
Grandfather	**Niels Arestrup**
Lyons	**David Thewlis**
Capt. James Nicholls	**Tom Hiddleston**
Maj. Jamie Stewart	**Benedict Cumberbatch**
Emilie	**Celine Buckens**
Colin, Geordie Soldier	**Toby Kebbell**
Lt. Charlie Waverly	**Patrick Kennedy**
Pvt. Michael Schröder	**Leonard Carow**
Pvt. Gunther Schröder	**David Kross**
Andrew Easton	**Matt Milne**
David Lyons	**Robert Emms**
Sgt. Fry	**Eddie Marsan**
Friedrich	**Nicolas Bro**
Brandt	**Rainer Bock**
Peter, German Soldier in No Man's Land	**Hinnerk Schönemann**
Si Easton	**Gary Lydon**
Sgt. Sam Perkins	**Geoff Bell**
Army Doctor	**Liam Cunningham**
German Officer at Farm	**Sebastian Hülk**
Market Auctioneer	**Gerard McSorley**
Sgt. Martin	**Tony Pitts**
Sgt. Maj. Singh	**Irfan Hussein**
Maj. Tompkins	**Pip Torrens**
French Auctioneer	**Philippe Nahon**
Butcher	**Jean-Claude Lecas**
Motorbike Rider	**Justin Brett**

Seamus O'Neill, Pat Laffan (Devon Farmers), Michael Ryan, Peter McNeil O'Connor (British Trench Soldiers), Trystan Pütter, Gunnar Cauthery (German Trench Soldiers), Julian Wadham (Trench Captain), Anian Zollner (Senior German Officer), Michael Kranz (Junior German Officer), Hannes Wegener (German Officer), David Dencik (Base Camp Officer), Edward Bennett (Cavalry Recruiting Officer), Johnny Harris (Infantry Recruiting Officer), Philip Hill-Pearson (Wounded Soldier), Tam Dean Burn (Medic in Trench), Alan Williams (Hospital Orderly), Thomas Arnold (Shouting German Soldier), Maximilian Brüeckner (German Artilery Officer), Markus Tomczyk (German Artilery Soldier), Peter Benedict (German Officer on Bridge), Callum Armstrong (Bagpiper), Ray Holder (Fred Goddard), Paul Alexander (Dave Hill), Maggie Ollerenshaw (Narracott's Neighbor), Beth Ogden (David Lyons' Girlfriend), Martin D. Dew (Lyons' Cronie)

As World War I breaks out, the son of struggling farmers is devastated when the family sells the boy's beloved horse Joey to be used in battle by a British cavalry officer.

This film received Oscar nominations for picture, cinematography, art direction, original score, sound mixing, and sound editing.

Jeremy Irvine, Joey

Benedict Cumberbatch, Patrick Kennedy, Tom Hiddleston

David Kross, Leonard Carow

Peter Mullan, Jeremy Irvine, Joey

EXTREMELY LOUD & INCREDIBLY CLOSE

(WARNER BROS.) Producer, Scott Rudin; Executive Producers, Celia Costas, Mark Roybal, Nora Skinner; Director, Stephen Daldry; Screenplay, Eric Roth; Based on the novel by Jonathan Safran Foer; Photography, Chris Menges; Designer, K.K. Barrett; Costumes, Ann Roth; Music, Alexandre Desplat; Editor, Claire Simpson; Casting, Ellen Lewis, Mele Nagler; a Scott Rudin production; Dolby; Widescreen; Deluxe color; Rated PG-13; 129 minutes; Release date: December 25, 2011

Thomas Horn, Stephen McKinley Henderson

CAST

Thomas Schell	Tom Hanks
Linda Schell	Sandra Bullock
Oskar Schell	Thomas Horn
The Renter	Max von Sydow
Abby Black	Viola Davis
Stan the Doorman	John Goodman
William Black	Jeffrey Wright
Oskar's Grandmother	Zoe Caldwell
Minister	Dennis Hearn
Homeless Man	Paul Klementowicz
Deli Waiter	Julian Tepper
Schoolboy	Caleb Reynolds
Walt the Locksmith	Stephen McKinley Henderson
Locksmith Customer	Lorna Guity Pruce
Hazelle Black	Hazelle Goodman
Prayer Group Woman	Bernadette Drayton
Prayer Group Man	David Latham
Piano Man	Marty Krzywonos
Old Mr. Black	Jim Norton
Denise Black	Carmen M. Herlihy
Maris Black	Ryka Dottavio
Stable Girl	Chloe Roe
Fong Black	Diane Cheng
Boris Black	Gregory Korostishevsky
Hector Black	Adrian Martinez
E.S. Black	Marco Verna
Hamlet	Brandon Jeffers
Dick Black	Martin Brens
Richard Black	Gustavo Brens
Astrid Black	Brooke Bloom
Ramos Black	René Ojeda
Alan Black	Madison Arnold

Thomas Horn, Sandra Bullock © Warner Bros.

Henry Morales-Ballet, Bryse Gregory (Deli Customers), William Youmans (Bartender), Kit Flanagan (Cassidy Black), Jenson Smith (Aurelia Black), Ray Iannicelli (Baz Black), Miguel Jarquin-Moreland (B.G. Black), Benjamin McCracken (Benjamin Black), Malachi Weir (Malachi Black), John Joseph Gallagher (Harlan Black), Sam K. Kaufman (Minch), Stephen Kunken (Teacher), Kim Rideout (Business Woman), Chloe Elaine Scharf (Business Woman's Daughter), Eva Kaminsky (Security Guard), Christopher Hardwick (Estate Sale Organizer), Kate Levy (Woman at Estate Sale), Stephanie Kurtzuba (Elaine Black), Catherine Curtin (Leigh-Anne Black), Lola Pashalinski (Mona Black), Clayton James Mackay (Boy), Bailey Grey (Girl)

A boy who has lost his father in the World Trade Center attacks searches throughout the five New York boroughs in hopes of discovering the mystery behind a key found among his father's belongings.

This film received Oscar nominations for picture and supporting actor (Max von Sydow).

Thomas Horn, John Goodman

Max von Sydow, Zoe Caldwell

Thomas Horn, Tom Hanks

Thomas Horn, Max von Sydow

Jeffrey Wright

Thomas Horn, Viola Davis

Tom Hanks, Sandra Bullock

Adepero Oduye, Kim Wayans

Aasha Davis, Adepero Oduye

Pernell Walker

PARIAH

(FOCUS) Producer, Nekisa Cooper; Executive Producers, Spike Lee, Jeff Robinson, Sam Martin, Susan Lewis, Ann Bradley, Joey Carey, Stefan Nowicki, Douglas Eisenberg, Matthew J. Simon, Mary Jane Skalski; Director/Screenplay, Dee Rees; Photography, Bradford Young; Designer, Inbal Weinberg; Costumes, Eniola Dawodu; Editor, Mako Kamitsuna; Casting, Eyde Belasco; a Northstar Pictures and Sundial Pictures presentation in association with Aid+Abet, Chicken & Egg Pictures and MBK Entertainment; Dolby; Super 35 Widescreen; Deluxe Color; Rated R; 86 minutes; Release date: December 28, 2011

CAST
Alike	**Adepero Oduye**
Laura	**Pernell Walker**
Bina	**Aasha Davis**
Arthur	**Charles Parnell**
Sharonda	**Sahra Mellesse**
Audrey	**Kim Wayans**
Candace	**Shamika Cotton**
Mack	**Ray Anthony Thomas**
Mika	**Afton Williamson**
Mrs. Alvarado	**Zabryna Guevara**
Mrs. Singletary	**Kim Sykes**
Sock	**Rob Morgan**

Nina Daniels (Gina, a.k.a. Butch Woman), Jeremie Harris (Bina's Boyfriend), Chanté Lewis, Olithea Anglin (Fast Girls), Joey Auzenne (Math Teacher), Jason Dyer (Cute Boy), Loren Hankin (Laura's Girl), Kymbali Craig, Alaina Dunn, Andrea Smith (Pier Girls), Ozzie Stewart (Laura's Mother), Natalie Carter, Donei Hall (Rowdy Co-Workers), Tamar-Kali (Herself), Thom Loubet (Guitarist), Mark Robohm (Drummer), Jeremiah Hosea (Bass), Maine Anders (Go-Go Dancer)

A 17-year-old black girl living in Brooklyn must deal with her parents' uncomfortable reaction to their daughter's lesbianism.

Kim Wayans, Adepero Oduye © Focus Features

DOMESTIC FILMS B

2011 Releases / January 1–December 31

AMERICATOWN (Mobius Films) Director, Kenneth Price; Screenplay, Jonathan Guggenheim, Kenneth Price, Cory Howard; Designer, Chad Keith; Color; Not rated; 77 minutes; Release date: January 7, 2011. **CAST:** Jonathan Guggenheim (Plymouth Rayban), Cory Howard (Roosevelt Microsoft), Jon Stafford (Mayor John Mercer Maeyer), Barbara Weetman (Ruth)

Cory Howard, Jonathan Guggenheim in *Americatown* © Mobius Films

VIOLENT BLUE (Cinema Epoch) Producers, Gregory Hatanaka, James Avallone, Precious Hilton, Madla Hruza, Silvia Suvadova, Tony T.L. Young; Director, Gregory Hatanaka; Screenplay, Gregory Hatanaka, Tony T.L. Young; Photography, James Avallone, Yasu Tanida, Spike Hasegawa; Designer/Costumes, Madla Hruza; Music, Toshiyuki Hiraoka; Editor, B.N. Lindstrom; Color; Not rated; 129 minutes; Release date: January 7, 2011. **CAST:** Silvia Suvadova (Katarina), Jesse Hlubik (Ondrej), Nick Mancuso (Pietro), Barry O'Rourke (Bolo O'Braonain), Andrea Harrison (Kylie), Garret Sato (Liam), Bogdan Szumilas (Dr. Sobeslav), Anastasia Fontaines (Ms. Dora), Martin William Harris (Zbigniew), Tiffany Bowyer (Helena), Shelli Merrill (Annette), Edwin A. Santos (Toru Von Karajan), Matthew Mahaney (Det. Ichikawa), Mark Motyl (Det. Simek), Luke Y. Thompson (Facemask/Robot Harmon), Meryl Bush (Anika), Shane Ryan (Gustav), Kai Lanette (Katya), Khayyam Kain (Proteus), Reila Aphrodite (Japanese Girl), Kiyomi Fukazawa (Henna), Alexandra Bily (Hanna), Alicia Arden (Cara), Mayka Bily (Libuse), Julia Carpenter (Isadora), Leigh Davis (Arielle), Paul Duke (Fake Ploeg), Douglas Dunning (Lee DeForest), Howard Fong (Raymond Chow), Gregory Hatanaka (Kancha Cheena), Precious Hilton (The Baroness), Nadine Jenson (Allison)

Silvia Suvadova in *Violent Blue* © Cinema Epoch

I'M DANGEROUS WITH LOVE (First Run Features) Producer/Director/ Photography/Editor, Michel Negroponte; Executive Producers, Julie Goldman, Krysanne Katsoolis, Caroline Stevens; Screenplay, Nick Pappas, Joni Wehrli; Music, Brook Williams, Beo Morales; a Blackbridge production in association with Cactus Three; Color; DV; Not rated; 84 minutes; Release date: January 12, 2011. Documentary on the possibility of the illegal hallucinogen ibogaine being used to fight methadone addiction, with Dimitri Mugianis.

Dimitri Mugianis in *I'm Dangerous with Love* © First Run Features

REPO CHICK (Industrial Entertainment) Producers, Alex Cox, Eric Bassett, Daren Hicks, Simon Tams, Benji Kohn, Austin Stark, Bingo Gubelmann; Director/ Screenplay/Editor, Alex Cox; Photography, Steve Fierberg; Designer, Nick Plotquin; Costumes, Alexis Scott; Music, Dan Wool, Kid Carpet; a Collateral Image Project, Industrial Entertainment production, in association with BBC Films, Defilm, Paper Street; American-British; Dolby; Color; Not rated; 85 minutes; Release date: January 14, 2011. **CAST:** Jaclyn Jonet (Repo Chick), Miguel Sandoval (Arizona Gray), Del Zamora (Lorenzo), Alex Feldman (Marco), Chloe Webb (Sister Duncan), Xander Berkeley (Aldrich de la Chasse), Rosanna Arquette (Lola), Robert Beltran (Aguas), Karen Black (Aunt de la Chasse), Zahn McClarnon (Savage Dave), Jenna Zablocki (Eggi), Danny Arroyo (Sixsixsix), Jennifer Balgobin (Nevada), Zander Schloss (Doctor), Angela Sarafyan (Giggli), Eddie Velez (Justice "Two-Strikes" Espinoza), Frances Bay (Grandma de la Chasse), Bennet Guillory (Rogers), Olivia Barash (Railroad Op), Tom Finnegan (Senator Fletcher), Linda Callahan (Rikki Espinoza), Karen E. Wright (Colonel), Cy Carter (Lawyer), Biff Yeager (Golf Course Guard), Kari French (Reporter), Andres Carranza (Journalist), Alex Cox (Professor), Danbert Nobacon (Major), Barney Burman (Captain), Simon Tams (CIA Op), Russell Darling (Homeland Security), Olivia Sandoval (Ad Woman), Rene Carrasco (Tow Truck Driver), Tod Davies, Julie Selberg (Phone Deadbeats), Matt Burch, Kelly Jones, Lyndah Pizarro, Sonia Pizarro, Froylan Tercero (Freddie Mac Offenders), Anthony Ausgang, Bingo Gubelmann (Marina Deadbeats), Erica Getler, Charles Scheinblum (Detroit Deadbeats), Rey Boemi, C.J. Izzo (Cops), Daisy (The Young Dog), Shelley Campbell (Bunker Doorwoman), Vielmehr Klampfe (Bunker Doorman)

Jaclyn Jonet in *Repo Chick* © Industrial Entertainment

DOWN FOR LIFE (Independent Pictures) Producers, Scott William Alvarez, Frank Aragon, Erik Armin, Robert Dolan, Peter Holden; Director, Alan Jacobs; Screenplay, Alan Jacobs, Trina Calderón; Based on the article "Essays in Search of Happy Endings" by Michael Winerip; Photography, Dana Gonzales; Designer, Bernardo Trujillo; Costumes, Paul Simmons; Music, Vito Colapietro, Neely Dinkins Jr.; Editors, Clayton Halsey, Roger Marshall; Casting, Rosalinda Morales; a Slate of Eight Productions presentation; FotoKem Color; Rated R; 92 minutes; Release date: January 14, 2011. **CAST:** Laz Alonso (Officer Barber), Jessica Romero (Rascal), Danny Glover (Mr. Shannon), Snoop Dogg (Mr. Hightower), Kurt Caceres (Rafael), Kate del Castillo (Esther), Cesar Garcia (Flaco), Nicholas Gonzalez (Officer Guttierez), Andres Xavier Sanchez (Sneaky), Iglesias Estefania (Mrs. Rivera), Elizabeth Peña (Mrs. Castro), Emily Rios (Vanessa), Whitney Gamble (Aisha), Isamar Guijarro (Troubles), Sheila Ochoa (Grumpy), Ilene Trujillo (Tiny), Andrea Valenzuela (Babygirl), Art Bonilla (Beto), Carlos Miranda (Trigger), Sergio Candido (Shop Owner, Louis), Luis Alberto Aracena (Tio Juan), Sujata Ray (Melissa), Eddie L. Fauria (Big Creole Dave), Robert "Lil Rob" Flores (Manny), Jamel Gay (Jake), Markevia Lee (Crystal), Dyana Liu (Kathy), Zahn McClarnon (Grim), Luis Moncada (Oso), Stephanie L. Moore (LaToya), Louie Olivos Jr. (Abuelo), Rigo Sanchez (Flaco), Jennifer Siebel (Ms. Hardwicke), Julia Vera (Abuela)

Jessica Romero in *Down for Life* © Independent Pictures

LEMMY (Vantage Media Intl.) Producers/Directors, Greg Olliver, Wes Orshoski; Photography/Editor, Greg Olliver, Wes Orshoski, Karl Schroder, Jeremy Mack, Brian Oliver, Karim Raoul; a Damage Case Films, Three Count Films, and Secret Weapon Films presentation; Dolby; Color; HD; Not rated; 116 minutes; Release date: January 14, 2011. Documentary on Motorhead frontman Lemmy Kilmister; with Lemmy Kilmister, Phil Campbell, Mikkey Dee, Joan Jett, Captain Sensible, David Vanian, Dave Grohl, Ozzy Osbourne, Peter Hook, Billy Bob Thornton, Triple H, Alice Cooper, Mick Jones, James Hetfield, Kirk Hammett, Lars Ulrich, Rob Trujillo, Fast Eddie Clarke, Paul Inder, Henry Rollins, Mike Inez, Slim Jim Phantom, Danny B. Harvey, Geoff Rowley

Lemmy Kilmister in *Lemmy* © Vantage Media

BURNING PALMS (New Films Cinema) Producers, Jason Hewitt, Christopher Landon, Oren Segal; Executive Producers, Naz Jafri, Vince Morella, Tyler Thompson; Director/Screenplay, Christopher Landon; Photography, Seamus Tierney; Designer, Linda Burton; Costumes, Christie Wittenborn; Music, Matthew Margeson; Editor, Gregory Plotkin; Casting, Mary Vernieu, Venus Kanani; a New Films Intl. and Films in Motion presentation; Color; Rated R; 105 minutes; Release date: January 14, 2011. **CAST:** Zoe Saldana (Sarah Cotton), Jamie Chung (Ginny Bai), Rosamund Pike (Dedra Davenport), Lake Bell (Maryjane), Paz Vega (Blanca Juarez), Shannen Doherty (Dr. Shelly), Nick Stahl (Robert Kane), Dylan McDermott (Dennis Marx), Robert Hoffman (Chad Bower), Emily Meade (Chloe Marx), Colleen Camp (Barbara Barish), Victor Webster (Paulo Small), Anson Mount (Tom), Jon Polito (Ned the Pharmacist), Adriana Barraza (Louisa Alvarez), Kate Albrecht (Tammy Lynn), Jason Brooks (Steve), Tom Wright (Maxwell Barron), Jonathan 'Lil J' McDaniel (Trey), Austin Williams (Nicholas Pinter), Peter Macdissi (Geri), Scott Lunsford (Stud), Jake Austin Walker (Trevor Pinter), Dimitri Diatchenko (Bob), Haley Tju (Rose), Victoria Patenaude (Bag Lady), Cherie Thibodeaux (Daphne), Lisa Marie Dupree (Flirty Waitress), Cici Lau (Soon Li), Chandler George Brown (Jeffrey Schneider), Addison Black (Colby Pinter), Tiara McKinney (Mahogany), Aron Coates (Tammy), Naz Jafri (Dr. Pakora), Ross Thomas (Lukas the Waiter), Jim Lau (Tak Bai), Edrick Browne (Medical Center Guard)

Zoe Saldana in *Burning Palms* © New Films Cinema

BREAKING AND ENTERING (Chump Change Productions) Producers, Benjamin Fingerhut, Kelley Maher, Adam Kline, Ashley Nath; Director, Benjamin Fingerhut; Photography, Geoffrey Fingerhut; Music, Andrew Duncan, Todd Taylor; Editor, Ashley Nath; a Red Bag Media presentation; Color; HD; Not rated; 88 minutes; Release date: January 14, 2011. Documentary on people attempting to make it into the Guinness Book of World Records; with Ashrita Furman, George Hood, Diane Kapral, Michal Kapral, Kathy Lewendowski, Denise Spalding, Steve Spalding, Paul Travilla, Zach Warren, Boo McAfee, Zach Warren, Stuart Claxton, Chris Camp, Fr. Jan Piotr Krutewicz, Al Gliniecki, Johnny Rabb, Wilson Casey, Michael Kettman, Robert Speca, Fran Capo, Ed Shelton, Bob Hatch, Ron Sarchian, Narve Laeret, Chao Lu, Todd Taylor, Preston Baccus, Arden Chapman, Cristina Flores, Maureen Kapral, Dr. Moira Kapral, Dr. Raymond Kapral, Eddy Konteil, Dr. Paul Krueger, Ed Spalding, Molly Spalding, Scott Spalding, Warner Tars

Breaking and Entering © Chump Change Prods.

THE HEART SPECIALIST (Freestyle) Producers, David Getachew-Smith, Kristin Overn, Dennis Cooper; Director/Screenplay, Dennis Cooper; Photography, Yasu Tanida; Designer, Alethea Root; Costumes, Tammi Marie-Hicks; Music, Tree Adams, Christopher Faizi; Editor, Jon Schwartz; an Elevate the Game Entertainment and Cooperfly Productions presentation; Dolby; FotoKem color; Rated R; 100 minutes; Release date: January 14, 2011. **CAST:** Wood Harris (Dr. Sidney Zachary), Zoe Saldana (Donna), Brian White (Dr. Ray Howard), Mya (Valerie), Scott Paulin (Dr. Graves), David S. Lee (Dr. Propper), Kenneth Choi (Mitchell Kwan), Irene Tsu (Mrs. Olson), Richard Voigts (Dr. Manson), Tony Perez (Dr. Gutierrez), Brittany Ishibashi (Translator), Kristi Kirk (Nuclear Med Tech), Marla Gibbs (Ms. Overwood), Jasmine Guy (Bit), Jenifer Lewis (Nurse Jackson), Method Man (Lorenzo), Edward Asner (Mr. Olson), Leon (Doctor), Amrapali Ambegaokar (Pakistani Intern), Arthur Roberts (Executive), Samir Younis (Ali), Remy Ryan Hernandez (Hispanic Mother), Christopher Babers (Jamaican Man), Jeanine Jackson (Southern Nurse), Jeffrey Sumner (Ward Secretary), Kathleen Gati (Radiology Technician), Dennis Bailey (Security Guard), Andy Kreiss (University Doctor), Mary Portser (Neurosurgeon), Reena Dutt (Med Student),

Brian White, Zoe Saldana in *The Heart Specialist* © Freestyle Releasing

THE WOODMANS (Lorber Films) Producers, Neil Barrett, Jeff Werner, C. Scott Willis; Director, C. Scott Willis; Photography, Neil Barrett; Art Director, Ekin Akalin; Music, David Lang; Editor, Jeff Werner; Color; Not rated; 82 minutes; Release date: January 19, 2011. Documentary on photographer Francesca Woodman; with Betty Woodman, George Woodman, Charlie Woodman, Patricia Sawin, Edwin Frank, Sloan Rankin, Catherine Chermayeff, Sabina Mirri, Glenn Palmer-Smith, Robert Kushner

George, Betty and Charlie Woodman in *The Woodmans* © Lorber Films

GABI ON THE ROOF IN JULY (Independent) Producers, Sophia Takal, Katherine Fairfax Wright; Director, Lawrence Michael Levine; Screenplay, Lawrence Michael Levine, Kate Kirtz; Photography, Aaron Kovalchik; Art Director, Adam Brustein; Music, Kevin Barker, Currituck Co; Editor, Sophia Takal; a Little Teeth Pictures, Garbled Heritage Production; Color; Not rated; 99 minutes; Release date: January

21, 2011. **CAST:** Sophia Takal (Gabi), Lawrence Michael Levine (Sam), Brooke Bloom (Madeline), Louis Cancelmi (Garrett), Amy Seimetz (Chelsea), Kate Lyn Sheil (Dory), Lena Dunham (Colby), Robert White (Charles), Tarajia Morrell (Astrid), Jay DiPietro (Phil), Andy Albee (Lou), Kevin Barker (Ryan), George Burich (Jorzo), Karen Chamberlain (Olivia), Helga Davis (Robin), Marguerite French (Liz), Chelsea Rodriguez (Franny), Matthew L. Weiss (Daniel)

Lawrence Michael Levine, Sophia Takal in *Gabi on the Roof in July* © Little Teeth

FROM PRADA TO NADA (Lionsgate) Producers, Gigi Pritzker, Linda McDonough, Rossana Arau, Gary Gilbert, Lisa Ellzey; Director, Angel Garcia; Screenplay, Fina Torres, Luis Alfaro, Craig Fernandez; Based on the novel *Sense and Sensibility* by Jane Austen; Photography, Héctor Ortega; Designer, Anthony Rivero Stabley; Costumes, Naomi Crespo; Music, Heitor Pereira; Editor, Bradley McLaughlin; Casting, Victoria Burrows, Scot Boland; an Oddlot Entertainment, Gilbert Films, Lionsgate, Televisa, Hyperion Films production; Dolby; Color; Rated PG-13; 107 minutes; Release date: January 28, 2011. **CAST:** Camilla Belle (Nora Dominguez), Alexa Vega (Mary Dominguez), Wilmer Valderrama (Bruno), Nicholas D'Agosto (Edward), April Bowlby (Olivia), Kuno Becker (Rodrigo), Adriana Barraza (Aunt Aurelia Jimenez), Tina French (Old Librarian), Luis Rosales (Juanito), Pablo Martinez de Velasco (Pablo the Gardener), Alexis Ayala (Gabriel Dominguez Sr.), Norma Reyna (Carmina), Catalina López (Trinita), José Maria Negri (Benjamin Kerensky), Mario Zaragoza (Federico), Pablo Cruz (Gabriel Dominguez Jr.), Begoña Narvaez (Carry Sullivan), Ernesto Arizpe, Diego Mejia, Bernardo Leal (Bad Guys), Joana Brito, Lilian Cruz (Comadres), Romina Peniche (Rosita), Adriana Morales (Chola Leader), Nydia Torres (Chola), Petty Maldonado (Lupe), Jaime Aleman (Car Buyer), Susana Contreras (Elderly Janitor), Aldonza Velez (Angelica Ramirez), Oliverio Gareli (Marco Antonio Ramirez), Geraldine Zinat (Receptionist), Susana Altamirano (Cubicle Head), Harry Porter (Prof. Smith), Diana Bovio (Classmate), Karla Souza (Lucy), Antonio González (Contractor), Alex García (Max Schoeder), Greg Lucas (Richard Pinter), Rosa Maria Soria (Maria Ramirez), Lorena Martinez (Rosalita Ramirez), Nydia Garcia (Esperanza Ramirez), Leticia Fabián (Natalia), Tomas Montemayor (Neighbor Boy), Ersin Pertan (Salesman), Alexander Aguila (Store Guard), Matias Gomez, Carlos Garza, Tony Aguilera, Julian Villarreal, Pavel Cal, Poncho Herrera (Salsa Band)

Alexa Vega in *From Prada to Nada* © Lionsgate

BLACKMAIL BOYS (TLA Releasing) Producers/Directors/Screenplay/Editors, Bernard Shumanski, Richard Shumanski; Executive Producer, Beatrice Carina; Photography, Adam Wingard; Music, Bernard Shumanski; a Shumanski Brothers production; Color; Not rated; 69 minutes; Release date: January 28, 2011. **CAST:** Nathan Adloff (Sam), Taylor Reed (Aaron), Joe Swanberg (Andrew Kenneth Tucker), Danny Rhodes (Dr. Friend), Tamara Fana (Ms. Andrew Kenneth Tucker), Spencer Parsons (Forrest Albernathy), Marc Singletary (John Singulaire)

Nathan Adloff, Taylor Reed in *Blackmail Boys* © TLA Releasing

STRONGMAN (Independent) Director, Zachary Levy; Music, Penny Lang, Heidi Flemming; Editors, Jonathan Oppenheim, Jane Brill, Zachary Levy; Color; Not rated; 113 minutes; Release date: January 28, 2011. Documentary on professional strongman Stan Pleskun (Stanless Steel).

Stanley Pleskun in *Strongman*

TROUBADOURS (Concord Music Group/PBS) Producer, Eddie Schmidt; Executive Producers, Sam Feldman, Michael Gorfaine, Lorna Guess; Director, Morgan Neville; Photography, Nicola Marsh, Arlene Nelson; Editor, Miranda Yousef; a Tremolo Production; Color; Not rated; 91 minutes; Release date: February 2, 2011. Documentary on the golden era (1968-73) of the Troubadour, a West Hollywood nightclub; **WITH:** Lou Adler, Peter Asher, Paul Body, Ursula Britton, Jackson Browne, Tommy Chong, Robert Christgau, David Crosby, Chris Darrow, Richard "Dickie" Davis, Henry Diltz, Craig Doerge, Robert Hilburn, Barney Hoskyns, Elton John, Carole King, Sherry Goffin Kondor, Danny Kortchmar, Kris Kristofferson, Russ Kunkel, Barry Mann, Cheech Marin, Steve Martin, Jim Maxwell, Roger McGuinn, Bonnie Raitt, Leland Sklar, J.D. Souther, Toni Stern, James Taylor, Cynthia Weil

James Taylor, Carole King in *Troubadours* © Concord Music Group

WAITING FOR FOREVER (Freestyle) Producers, Trevor Albert, James Keach; Executive Producers, Forrest S. Baker III, Jane Seymour, Richard Arlook, Tim Nelson, John Papsidera; Screenplay/Co-Producer, Steve Adams; Director, James Keach; Photography, Matthew Irving; Designer, Christopher R. DeMuri; Costumes, Carolyn Leone; Music, Nick Urata; Editor, Pamela March; Casting, John Papsidera; a Trevor Albert/James Keach production in association with Forrest Baker Productions; Dolby; Color; Rated PG-13; 95 minutes; Release date: February 4, 2011. **CAST:** Rachel Bilson (Emma Twist), Tom Sturridge (Will Donner), Scott Mechlowicz (Jim Donner), Richard Jenkins (Richard Twist), Blythe Danner (Miranda Twist), Nikki Blonsky (Dolores), Matthew Davis (Aaron), Jaime King (Susan Donner), Nelson Franklin (Joe), Richard Gant (Albert), Roz Ryan (Dorothy), Jamey Anthony, Christel Edwards (Café Flirts), K.C. Clyde (Dennis), Larry Filion (Larry the Bartender), K. Danor Gerald (Detective #2), Frank Gerrish (Taxi Driver), Christopher K. Hagadone (Skateboarder), Charles Halford (State Trooper), Borzin Mottaghian (Driver), Laura Montoya (Flight Attendant), James C. Morris (Mime – Noh Masque), Ace Olson (Amos, Will's Nephew), Joseph D. Reis (Hopeless Man), Andrew Roach (Stewart), John Ross (Will's Dad), Michelle Sebek (Will's Mother), David Taylor (Dennis)

Tom Sturridge, Scott Mechlowicz in *Waiting for Forever* © Freestyle Releasing

DRESSED (SenArt Films/Jeff Lipsky) Producer/Director/Editor, David Swajeski; Executive Producer, Maryanne Grisz; Photography, Floyd Dean, David Swajeski, Pascal Deickmann; Music, Chris Orazi; a Onerock Moving Pictures production; Dolby; Color; HD; Not rated; 79 minutes; Release date: February 4, 2011. Documentary on fashion designer Nary Manivong; WITH: Nary Manivong, Mickey Boardman, Simon Collins, Simon Doonan, George Furlan, Mary Gehlhar, Anastasia Griffith, Margaret Hayes, Nanette Lepore, Fern Mallis, Janet Mock, Jason Napier, Perrey Reeves, Robert Verdi, Lynn Yaeger.

Nary Manivong in *Dressed* © SenArt Films

COLD WEATHER (Sundance Selects) Producers, Lars Knudsen, Brendan McFadden, Ben Stambler, Jay Van Hoy; Executive Producer, Jack Turner; Director/Screenplay/Editor, Aaron Katz; Story, Aaron Katz, Brendan McFadden, Ben Stambler; Photography, Andrew Reed; Designer, Elliott Glick; Music, Keegan DeWitt; a Parts & Labor Film in association with White Buffalo; Color; HD; Not rated; 97 minutes; Release date: February 4, 2011. **CAST:** Cris Lankenau (Doug), Trieste Kelly Dunn (Gail), Raúl Castillo (Carlos), Robyn Rikoon (Rachel), Jeb Pearson (Jim Warden), Brendan McFadden (Swen), Ben Stambler (Motel Clerk), Katy Rothert (Mom), Paul Rothert (Stepfather), Jerry Moyer (Ice Factory Boss), Virgil L. Howell (Tobacconist), Barry Seltzer (Spencer), Orianna Herrman (Bartender), Elliott Glick (Mike), Joshua Locy (Jose)

Trieste Kelly Dunn, Cris Lankenau in *Cold Weather* © Sundance Selects

THE OTHER WOMAN (IFC Films) formerly *Love and Other Impossible Pursuits*; Producers, Marc Platt, Carol Cuddy; Executive Producers, Natalie Portman, Abby Wolf-Weiss, Rena Ronson, Cassian Elwes; Director/Screenplay, Don Roos; Based on the novel *Love and Other Impossible Pursuits* by Ayelet Waldman; Photography, Steve Yedlin; Designer, Michael Shaw; Costumes, Peggy Schnitzer; Music, John Swihart; Editor, David Codron; Casting, Bernard Telsey; an Incentive Filmed Entertainment presentation of a Marc Platt production in association with Is or Isn't Productions and Handsomecharlie Films; Dolby; Panavision; Technicolor; Rated R; 102 minutes; Release date: February 4, 2011. **CAST:** Natalie Portman (Emilia Greenleaf), Scott Cohen (Jack), Lisa Kudrow (Carolyn), Charlie Tahan (William),

Lauren Ambrose (Mindy), Michael Cristofer (Sheldon), Debra Monk (Laura), Mona Lerche (Sonia), Anthony Rapp (Simon), Kendra Kassebaum (Sharlese), Elizabeth Marvel (Pia), Mary Joy (Marilyn), Maria Dizzia (Jaime Brennan), Ira Hawkins (Businessman), Laura Odeh (Waitress), Nicolette Hart (Stripper), Dave Bradford (Cabby), Daisy Tahan (Emma), Susan Bruce (Volunteer), Lisa LeGuillou (Organizer), Patrick Goodwin, Leslie Kritzer (Paramedics), Nikki Renee Daniels (Nurse Nikki), Jordan Simmons (Mother), Natalia Volkodaeva (Tatiana), Mark Gerrard (Ben), Phil McGlaston, Susan Hogelin-Black (Organizers), Owen Shaw (Skating Boy), Doug Williford (Carolyn's Dentist), Maureen Flynn (Judge)

Natalie Portman, Charlie Tahan in *The Other Woman* © IFC Films

CERTIFIABLY JONATHAN (Area 23a) Producer/Photography, Richard Marshall; Director, Jim Pasternak; Music, Buddy Judge; Editors, Richard Marshall, Robert Pergament; Animation, M. Frank Emanuel; a Film Dada production; Color; HD; Not rated; 79 minutes; Release date: February 11, 2011. Documentary on comedian Jonathan Winters, with a special focus on his art work; **WITH:** Jonathan Winters, Alexis Arquette, David Arquette, Patricia Arquette, Richmond Arquette, Rosanna Arquette, Jim Carrey, Bill Chappelle, Tim Conway, Kevin Dunn, Nora Dunn, Sheena Easton, Steve Edberg, Fabio, Oscar Goodman, Martin Guigui, Clint Holmes, Ivan Karp, Jimmy Kimmel, Robert Klein, Jan Larsen, Howie Mandel, Mary Milton, Gary Owens, David Pieri, Rob Reiner, John Rothman, Joe Shields, Sarah Silverman, Lew Simon, Ryan Stiles, Jeffrey Tambor, Patsy Thompkins, Andrew Weiss, Ed Weston, Robin Williams, Eileen Winters, Lucinda Winters; and Dominic Keating (Nicholas DeBoor), Nikita Ager (Stacy Kaufman), Kyra Groves (Gallery Receptionist), Elan Frank (Man with Gun), Ed Greenberg (Rabbi), Olaf Weidekat (Forger), Charles Pasternak (Michael), Ernie Hudson (Museum Guard), Jim Pasternak (Jim), Michael Bofshever (Michael), Allan Wasserman (Allan)

Jonathan Winters, Kevin Dunn in *Certifiably Jonathan* © Area 23a

MOOZ-LUM (Codeblack) Producers, Samad Davis, Dana Offenbach; Executive Producer, Dana J. Wright; Director/Screenplay, Qasim "Q" Basir; Photography, Ian Dudley; Designer, Joey Ostrander; Music, Misha Segal; Editors, Christopher Scott Cherot; Casting, Aleta Chapel; a Q Productions presentation of a Dana O production in association with Ameena Sky Media, Deep Blue Pictures; Color; Rated PG-13; 99 minutes; Release date: February 11, 2011. **CAST:** Evan Ross (Tariq Mahdi), Nia Long (Safiyah Mahdi), Roger Guenveur Smith (Hassan Mahdi), Summer Bishil (Iman), Dorian Missick (Prof. Jamal), Danny Glover (Dean Francis), Kunal Sharma (Hamza), Michael Simpson (Jason), Kimberely Drummond (Taqua Mahdi), Maryam Basir (Ayanna), Jonathan Smith (Young Tariq), Peter Carey (Dr. Phelps), Molly Paddock (Erin), Lise Lacasse (Mrs. Tyson), Azhar Usman (Brother Hussein), Patricia Yasbeck, Pamela Croydon (Professors), Vladimi Versailles (Cedric), Attika Torrence (Abdul Malik), Stacie Hadgikosti (Crystal), Dredan McFall (Aleem), Jonathan Manganello (Matthew), Atif Hashwi (Muhammad), Wayman Ezell (Brother Dawoud), Devin Scillian (News Anchor), Qasim "Q" Basir (Quincy), Attika Torrence (Abdul Malik), Cher Santiago (Desk Attendant)

Cliff Etheredge in *Carbon Nation* © Clayway Media

Evan Ross in *Mooz-lum* © Codeblack

CARBON NATION (Clayway Media) Producers, Peter Byck, Craig Sieben, Karen Weigert, Artemis Joukowsky, Chrisna Van Zyl; Director/Photography, Peter Byck; Screenplay, Peter Byck, Eric Driscoll, Matt Weinhold, Karen Weigert; Music, Flexi P; Editors, Eric Driscoll, Peter Byck; Narrator, Bill Kurtis; an Earth School Educational Foundation presentation; Color; Not rated; 82 minutes; Release date: February 11, 2011. Documentary on the dangers of global warming; **WITH:** Rohit T. Aggarwala, Jerry M. Allums, Lela Allums, Peter Barnes, Richard Branson, George Bravo, Lester R. Brown, Sean Casten, Ralph Cavanagh, Col. Jim Chevalier, Roger Duncan, Michael Dunham, Cliff Etheredge, David Etheredge, Bob Fox, Greg Franta, Tom Friedman, Eric Gardner, Wayne Gatlin Jr., Sherri Goodman, Eban Goodstein, Stuart Grauer, Denis Hayes, Vickie S. Haynes, Paul Reed Hepperly, Gary Hirshberg, Gwen Holdmann, David Hone, Daryl Horne, Sadhu Johnston, Van Jones, Bernie Karl, James A. Kelly, Kristina Kershner, M. Glen Kertz, Edward Kjaer, Timothy Lasalle, Amory B. Lovins, Joel Makower, Col. Matthew Margotta, Edward Mazria, Kevin McCullough, Michele McGeoy, Jeffrey W. Moyer, Daniel A. Nolan III, Dana Pittard, Reggy Rathmann, Paul Rode, Jim Rogers, Arthur Rosenfeld, John W. Rowe, Lance K. Toyofuku, John Wick, Tom Williams, R. James Woolsey

VIDAL SASSOON THE MOVIE (Phase 4 Films) Producers, Jackie Gilbert Bauer, Michael Gordon; Executive Producer, Jim Czarnecki; Director/Editor, Craig Teper; Screenplay, Heather Campbell Gordon, Craig Teper; Photography, Saul Gittens, Craig Teper; Art Director, Steve Hiett; Music, Steven Griesgraber; Digital Artist/Animator & Visual Effects Supervisor, Yorgo Alexopoulos; a Michael Gordon production; Color/Black and white; Not rated; 94 minutes; Release date: February 11, 2011. Documentary on renowned hairstylist Vidal Vassoon; **WITH:** Vidal Sassoon, Michael Gordon; *London:* Caroline Baker, Richard Blass, Christopher Brooker, Liza Bruce, Richard Buckley, Caroline Cox, Joseph Ettedugui, John Frieda, Joshua Galvin, Tim Hartley, Mark Hayes, Kelly Hoppen, Annie Humphreys, Fumio Kawashima, Elaine Nations, Aitch Peters, Kathy Philips, Mary Quant, Tony Rizzo, John Santilli, Ronnie Sassoon, Anne-Marie Solowij, Etienne Tanaka, Paul Windle, Richard Young; *New York:* Charles Booth, Guido, Christian Hutenbaus, Harold Leighton, Christopher Pluck, Elan Sassoon, Richard Stein, Maurice Tidy; *Los Angeles:* Tony Beckerman, Elgin Charles, William Claxton, Angus Mitchell, Peggy Moffitt, Stephen Moody, Fernando Romero, Ronnie Sassoon, Beverly Sassoon, Eden Sassoon, Laurance Taylor.

Vidal Sassoon in *Vidal Sassoon: The Movie* © Phase 4 Films

LOVERS OF HATE (IFC Films) Producer, Megan Gilbride; Executive Producers, Athina Rachel Tsangari, Jay Duplass, Mark Duplass, Marcy Garriott; Director/Screenplay/Editor, Bryan Poyser; Photography, David Lowery; Designer, Caroline Karlen; Music, Kevin Bewersdorf; an Invisible Kids presentation, in association with Monofonus Press; Color; DV; Not rated; 93 minutes; Release date: February 11, 2011. **CAST:** Chris Doubek (Rudy Lucas), Heather Kafka (Diana Lucas), Alex Karpovsky (Paul Lucas), Zach Green (Dexter), Josh Meyer (Supervisor), Harper Cummings (Girl at Car Wash), Dan Brown (Man at Door), Lana Dieterich (Mrs. Petersen), Garry Peters (Mr. Petersen), Kim LeBlanc (Bookstore Clerk), Eric Moorhead (Convenience Store Clerk)

Chris Doubek in *Lovers of Hate* © IFC Films

ORGASM INC. (First Run Features) Producer/Director/Photography, Liz Canner; Executive Producers, Julie Parker Benello, Wendy Ettinger, Judith Helfand, Marc Weiss; Music, Stephanie Olmanni, Alex Barnett, Don Glasgo; Editors, Linda Canner, Sandra Christie, Jeremiah Zagar; a Chicken and Egg Pictures presentation of an Astrea Media, Inc. production; Stereo; Digibeta; Color; Not rated; 78 minutes; Release date: February 11, 2011. Documentary on the efforts to produce the first Viagara drug for women; **WITH:** Kim Airs, Susan Bennett, Laura Berman, Liz Canner, Andrilla Chakrabarti, Nan Cochran, John Griesemer, Stuart Meloy, Ray Moynihan, Carol Queen, Leonore Tiefert, Kim Wallen, Suzanne Roth

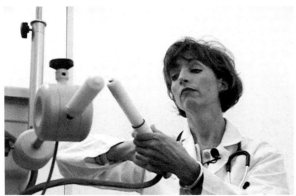

Suzanne Roth in *Orgasm Inc.* © First Run Features

LOVELESS (Streetlight Films) Producer, Shauna Lyon; Line Producer, Julie Christeas; Director/Screenplay, Ramin Serry; Story, Ramin Serry, Shauna Lyon; Photography, Doug Emmett; Music, Ahrin Mishan; Editor, Eric Kahle; Casting, Meredith Tucker; Color; HD; Not rated; 92 minutes; Release date: February 18, 2011. **CAST:** Andrew von Urtz (Andrew), Cindy Chastain (Joanna), Genevieve Hudson-Price (Ava), Gary Wilmes (Tad), Scott Cohen (Ricky), Hannah Beck

(Jane), Kendra Hurley (Kendra), Sabin Streeter (Sabin), Tobias Perse (Tobias), Albert Krause (Albe), Lily Serry (Lily), Shauna Lyon (Shauna), Celene Lee (Bartender), Aziza Dyer (Girlfighter), Liam Cohen (Paul Jr.), Mark Cirnigliaro (Anthony), Paul Romero (Charles), Emma Tapley (Isabella), Kathleen Cholewka (Kathleen), Sylvie Floridis (Sylvie the Dog), Andrew Bradfield (Mike), Tad Floridis (Kevin), Victor Arnold (Paul Sr.), Ethan Basche, Peter Coates, Joy Goodwin, Heidi Goar, Ellen Killoran, Andrea Russell (Party Guests)

8 MURDERS A DAY (One Sheet Studios) Producer/Director, Charlie Minn; Photography, Sam Pool, Malachi Doctor; Music, Kyle Hildenbrand; Editor, Yota Matsuo; J&M Productions; Color; Not rated; 90 minutes; Release date: February 18, 2011. Documentary on how the illegal drug trade has turned Juarez, Mexico into the murder capital of the world; **WITH:** Howard Campbell, Dr. Tony Payan, Diana Washington-Valdez, Daniel Borunda, Charles Bowden, Molly Molloy, Ken Molestina, Darren Hunt, Paul Cicala

8 Murders a Day © One Sheet Studios

THE CHAPERONE (Goldwyn) Producer, Mike Pavone; Executive Producers, David Karl Calloway, Steve Barnettt, Mark Rosman; Director, Stephen Herek; Screenplay, S.J. Roth; Photography, Kenneth Zunder; Designer, Raymond Pumilia; Costumes, Claire Breaux; Music, James Alan Johnston; Editor, Michel Aller; Casting, Denise Chamian Casting; a WWF Studios presentation; Dolby; Color; Rated PG-13; 103 minutes; Release date: February 18, 2011. **CAST:** Paul Levesque (Ray Bradstone), Ariel Winter (Sally). Kevin Corrigan (Phillip Larue), José Zúñiga (Detective Carlos), Kevin Rankin (Goldy), Yeardley Smith (Miss Miller), Enrico Colantoni (Dr. Etman), Israel Broussard (Josh), Jake Austin Walker (Ted), Ashley Taylor (Meredith), Cullen Chaffin (Simon), Darren O'Hare (Augie), Nick Gomez (Nick, the Bus Driver), Annabeth Gish (Lynne), Lucy Webb (Dr. Marjore), Conner Ann Waterman (Tracy), Sean Boyd (CSI Guy), Edrick Browne (Prison Guard), Kim Collins (Mechanic), James DuMont (Stanley), Juliette Enright (Young Sally), J.D. Evermore (Del), Shanna Forrestall (Hijacked Woman), Gary Grubbs (Mr. Mobeleski), Sam Medina (Prison Guy), John Neisler (Mr. Lewis), James Palmer (Roger), Shane Partlow (Manager), Taylor Faye Ruffin (Brenda), Billy Slaughter (Father), Bill Stinchcomb (Sergeant),George Wilson (Cabbie), Kate Adair (Bank Teller), Alec Rayme (Kevin), Dane Rhodes (Dr. Marjorie's Operator), Ethan Hansen (Little Boy), Luke Hawk, Phi-Long Nguyen (Thugs), Samantha Herek (Charlotte), Anita Hemeter (Tour Guide)

Ariel Winter, Paul Levesque in *The Chaperone* © Goldwyn Films

I AM (Paladin) Producer, Dagan Handy; Executive Producers, Jennifer Abbott, Jonathan Watson; Director/Screenplay, Tom Shadyac; Photography, Roko Belic; Editor, Jennifer Abbott; a Flying Eye Productions in association with a Homemade Canvas Production of a Shady Acres Film; Color; Not rated; 76 minutes; Release date: February 18, 2011. Documentary in which filmmaker Tom Shadyac shows how a near-fatal cycling accident left him feeling the need to make our planet better; **WITH:** Tom Shadyac, Desmond Tutu, Howard Zinn, Noam Chomsky, Lynne McTaggart, Coleman Barks, Thom Hartmann, Marc Ian Barasch, John Francis

Tom Shadyac in *I Am* © Paladin Pictures

BROTHERHOOD (Phase 4) Producers, Chris Pollack, Steve Hein, Tim O'Hair, Jason Croft; Director, Will Cannon; Screenplay, Will Cannon, Doug Simon; Photography, Michael Fimognari; Designer, Eric Whitney; Costumes, Leila Heise; Music, Dan Marocco; Editor, Josh Schaeffer; Casting, Michelle Morris Gertz; a Roslyn Productions presentation of a Three Folks Pictures production in association with Hunting Lanes Films and Instinctive Film GmbH; Color; Rated R; 76 minutes; Release date: February 18, 2011. **CAST:** Jon Foster (Frank), Trevor Morgan (Adam Buckley), Arlen Escarpeta (Mike), Lou Taylor Pucci (Kevin), Jesse Steccato (Bean), Jennifer Sipes (Emily), Luke Sexton (Graham), Chad Halbrook (Jackson), Preston Vanderslice (Scott), Tyler Corie (Curtis), Evan Gamble (Tyler), Katherine VanderLinden (Janet), Jeff Gibbs (Officer Jennings), Jack O'Donnell (Dr. Meyers), Matt Phillips (Eric), Ryan Ripple (Brian), Meyer DeLeeuw (Collin),

Jessica Bañuelos (Amber), Lauryn Garner (Amber's Friend), Kirk Griffith (Det. Lewis), Daniel B. Howard (A.J.), Grant James (Old Man), Joshua Moreno (Officer), Randal Scott (Big T), Laurel Whitsett (Nurse), Heather Okun (Freshman Girl), Alan Sather, Andrew Sather (Fraternity Brothers), Omaka Omegah (Sorority Girl)

Arlen Escarpeta in *Brotherhood* © Phase 4 Films

PUTTY HILL (Cinema Guild) Producers, Jordan Mintzer, Steve Holmgren, Joyce Kim, Eric Bannat; Director/ Screenplay, Matt Porterfield; Story, Matt Porterfield, Jordan Mintzer; Photography, Jeremy Saulnier; Art Director, Sophie Toporkoff; Costumes, Sara Gerrish; Editor, Marc Vives; The Hamilton Film Group presentation; Color; HD; Not rated; 85 minutes; Release date: February 18, 2011. **CAST:** Sky Ferreira (Jenny), Cody Ray (Cody), Zoe Vance (Zoe), James Siebor Jr., Dustin Ray, Charles "Spike" Sauers, Catherine Evans, Virginia Heath, Casey Weibust, Drew Harris

Putty Hill © Hamilton Film Group

NOW & LATER (Cinema Libre) Producers, Beth Portello, Philippe Diaz; Director/Screenplay/ Editor, Philippe Diaz; Photography, Denise Brassard; an Imago-Creata production; Stereo; Color; HD; Not rated; 99 minutes; Release date: February 18, 2011. **CAST:** Shari Solanis (Angela), Marcellina Walker (Sally), James Wortham (Bill), Luis Fernandez-Gil (Luis), Adrian Quinonez (Diego), Anas Khalaf, Kenneth Alan James (Clinic Doctors), Antonieta Velasquez (Flower Lady), Heraldo Guiterrez (Eddie), Greg Arrowood, Mark Keeler (Police)

Adrian Quinonez, James Wortham, Shari Solanis in *Now & Later*
© Cinema Libre

Fran Liebowitz in *Public Speaking* © Rialto Pictures

IMMIGRATION TANGO (Roadside Attractions) Producer, Elika Portnoy; Director, David Burton Morris; Screenplay, Martin Kelly, Robert Lee, David Burton Morris, Todd Norwood; Photography, Angel Barroeta; Designers, Jean De Voe, Nichole Ruiz; Music, Dan Wool; Editors, Lee Cipolla, Misha Tenenbaum; a Mutressa Movies presentation; Color; Rated R; 92 minutes; Release date: February 18, 2011. **CAST:** Elika Portnoy (Elena Dubrovnik), McCaleb Burnett (Mike White), Carlos Leon (Carlos Sanchez), Ashley Wolfe (Betty Bristol), Avery Sommers (Ms. Ravencourt), Beth Glover (Jill White), Steve DuMouchel (Harold White), Kristen Dawn McCorkell (Sarah White), Brett Golov (Mr. Geneva), Danielle Lilley (Receptionist), Noelle Conners (Supervisor), Bruce Linser (Pool Buddy), Claudia Buckley (Law Professor), Matt Levine, Larry Zience (INS Agents), Sarah O'Kelly, Alexander Fernandez, Laurel Levey-Giacomino (Prisoners), Omar Caraballo (Guard #1), John Tarpani (Minister), Melinda Lee (Kelly), Jennifer De Castroverde (Immigration Officer), Jimmie Bernal (Bartender), Nelson Reyes (Officer), Ashley Undercuffler, Keri Maletto (Interviewees), Buddha Gonzalez (Cuban Prisoner)

Carlos Leon, Elika Portnoy in *Immigration Tango* © Roadside Attractions

PUBLIC SPEAKING (Rialto Pictures) Producers, Graydon Carter, Fran Lebowitz, Martin Scorsese, Margaret Bodde; Executive Producers, Ted Griffin, John Hayes; Supervising Producer, Jenny Carchman; Director, Martin Scorsese; Photography, Ellen Kuras; a Sikelia Prods. and Consolidated Documentaries production presented by HBO Documentary Films in association with American Express Portraits; Color; Not rated; 82 minutes; Release date: February 23, 2011. Documentary on photographer Fran Lebowitz; **WITH:** Fran Lebowitz, Ivo Juhani. (This film had its premiere on HBO on Nov. 22, 2010).

THE GRACE CARD (Goldwyn) Producers, John Saunders, John Nasraway, Howard A. Klausner; Executive Producers, David Evans, Esther Evans; Director/Story, David Evans; Screenplay, Howard A. Klausner; Photography, John Paul Clark; Designer, Darian Corley; Costumes, Lisa Thomas; Music, Brent Rowan; Editor, Mark Pruett; an Affirm Films and Provident Films in association with Graceworks Pictures and Calvary Pictures production; Dolby; Deluxe Color; Rated PG-13; 101 minutes; Release date: February 25, 2011. **CAST:** Michael Joiner (Bill "Mac" McDonald), Michael Higgenbottom (Sam Wright), Louis Gossett, Jr. (George Wright), Joy Parmer Moore (Sara McDonald), Dawntoya Thomason (Debra Wright), Rob Erickson (Blake McDonald), Kiana McDaniel (Grace Wright), Cindy Holmes Hodge (Dr. Vines), Taylor Ollins (Emily Wright), Stephen Dervan (Officer Mitch Saunders), Chris Thomas (Bob Childers), Brayden Negelein (Tyler McDonald), George Bradshaw (Officer Ken Newman), Chris Johnson (Officer Bob Hunt), Jessica Maharrey (Jenny), Alicia Burton (Young Mother), Wilkes Coleman (Dr. Curry), Bruce Sarratt, Chad Knoor (Undercover Officers), Aaron Buchanan (Teeanger on Bike), Jaylon Walker (Young Rand), James Towles, Lucille Towles (Late for Church), Thom McAdory (Headmaster Ron Penny), Dee Negelein (Advisor Angela Nix), Leroy Jones (Homeless Man), George Jenkins (Judge), Cindy Henshaw, Jim Sarratt (Bartenders), Adrian McQuarter (Suspect with gun), Houston Evans (Young Thug), Joyce Bradshaw (Nurse in Physician's Office), Myrna Smith (Mrs. Bradshaw), Jeremy Lansing (Paramedic), Newmon Goshorn, MD (Dr. Gunther, Surgeon), Taylor Foster (Praying Teen), Ephie Johnson (Church Soloist), Doug Rogers (Associate Pastor), Amisho Lewis (Older Rand), Monica Towles, Antonio Futch (Congregation Members), Anthony Lynn Holmes (Waiting Room Visitor)

Michael Higgenbottom, Louis Gossett Jr. in *The Grace Card* © Goldwyn Films

THE BLEEDING (Anchor Bay) Producers, Michael Tadross Jr., Michael Matthias, Joe Di Maio, Randy Frankel; Executive Producers, Patrick Durham, Randall Emmett, Frank Capra III, George Folsey, Jr.; Director, Charlie Picerni; Screenplay, Lance Lane; Photography, Tom Priestley Jr.; Designer, Steven Legler; Costumes, Leigh Leverett; Music, Justin Burnett; Editors, Brad E. Wilhite, dB Bracamontes; Casting, Kathleen Chopin; an Iron Bull Films production; Color; Rated R; 83 minutes; Release date: February 25, 2011. **CAST:** Vinnie Jones (Cain), Michael Madsen (Father Roy), Armand Assante (Jake Plummer), Katherine von Drachenberg (Vanya), DMX (Tagg), Michael Matthias (Shawn Black), William McNamara (Dan Williams), Pittsburgh Slim (Crash), Rachelle Leah (Lena), Krista Ayne, Monique Zordan (Factory Girls), Tony Schiena (Johnny the Perv), Nancy Young (Nurse), Vanessa Vander Pluym, Rootie Boyd (Cain's Court), Terence J. Rotolo (Bartender), Madison Weidberg (Jenny), Kathy Sue Holtorf (Vampire Victim), Crystal Lonnenberg (Tattooed Vampire), Sindy Espitia (Katya), Robert Capelli Jr. (Jay K), Joe Montanti (Black's Dad), Lucy Spain (Waitress), Jacqueline Martini, Amanda O'Connor, Kendel Colbie Scott (Bloody Victims), Jana Allen (Street Walker), Joe Montanti (Black's Dad), , Fabiano Iha (Mime)), James Seppelfrick (Org)

Michael Matthias, Rachelle Leah in *The Bleeding* © Anchor Bay Films

BEREAVEMENT (Crimson Films) Producer/Director/Screenplay/Music/Editor, Stevan Mena; Executive Producer, Vincent Butta; Photography, Marco Cappetta; Designer, Jack Ryan; Costumes, Charlotte Kruse; Casting, Adrienne Stern; a Crimson Films and Aurilia Arts presentation; Dolby; Color; Rated R; 103 minutes; Release date: March 4, 2011. **CAST:** Alexandra Daddario (Allison Miller), Michael Biehn (Jonathan Miller), Brett Rickaby (Graham Sutter), John Savage (Ted), Nolan Gerard Funk (William), Valentina de Angelis (Melissa), Spencer List (Martin Bristol), Kathryn Meisle (Karen Miller), Peyton List (Wendy Miller), Ashley Wolfe (Katherine), Greg Wood (Teacher), Chase Pechacek (Martin, age 6), Andrea Havens (Agatha), Jamie Farrell (Nurse's Aide), Shannon Lambert-Ryan (Lucy Cardova, Body in Freezer), Miriam A. Hyman (Waitress), Tom McNutt (Clerk in Store), Lynn Mastio Rice (Gym Teacher), Adam Ratcliffe (Officer Jones), Marissa Guill (Victim #1), Sal Domani (Father in Store), Brendan Martinez (Boy in Store)

John Savage in *Bereavement* © Crimson Films

DEAR LEMON LIMA (Phase 4 Films) Producers, Melissa Lee, Jonako Donley; Director/Screenplay, Suzi Yoonessi; Photography, Sarah Levy; Designer, Kay Lee; Costumes, Joy Andrews; Music, Sasha Gordon; Editors, Mara Farrington, Matt Linnell; Casting, Sunday Boling, Meg Morman; a Sanguine Film presentation; Color; Rated PG-13; 88 minutes; Release date: March 4, 2011. **CAST:** Savanah Wiltfong (Vanessa Lemor), Shayne Topp (Philip Georgey), Zane Huett (Hercules Howard), Eleanor Hutchins (Terri Lemor), Meaghan Jette Martin (Megan Kennedy), Vanessa Marano (Samantha Combs), Elaine Hendrix (Coach Roach), Melissa Leo (Mrs. Howard), Beth Grant (Principal Applebomb), Chase Vanek (Jon Mongory), Kari Nissena (Norma), Emma Noelle Roberts (Kellie), Elaine Mani Lee (Mrs. Amigone), Bob McCracken (Mr. Amigone), Jada Morrison (Emmaline Chin), George Bass (Señor Montague), Maia Lee (Madleine "Nothing" Amigone), Michelle Pizzo (Jen), Rick Turner (Mr. Howard), Sheldon Jacobs (Mr. Walters), Jack Gravalis (Marshall), Jesse Michael Salas (Announcer John Sivatuaq), Brian Bloch (Nate), Taylor Finlon (Lynne Chin), Jack Gravalias (Marshall), Emily Oleyer (Erica, WEIO Rep), Brian Goddard (Sean Walsh)

Savanah Wiltfong, Shayne Topp in *Dear Lemon Lima* © Phase 4 Films

CARMEN 3D (RealD) Producer, Phil Streather; Executive Producers, Michael V. Lewis, Joshua Greer, Joseph Peixoto, Robert Mayson, Stephen Michael; Director, Julian Napier; Photography, Sean MacLeod Phillips; Designer, Tanya McCallin; Music, Georges Bizet; Librettists, Henri Meilhac, Ludovic Halévy; Based on the novella by Prosper Mérimée; Choreographer, Arthur Pita; Editors, Julian Napier, Stroo Olofsson; Music Producer, David Groves; Directed for the stage by Francesca Zambello; a RealD and Royal Opera House presentation of a PLF production; American-British; Dolby; 3D; Color; Not rated; 170 minutes; Release date: March 5, 2011. **CAST:** Christine Rice (Carmen), Bryan Hymel (Don José), Aris Argiris (Escamillo), Maija Kovalevska (Micaëla), Dawid Kimberg (Moralès), Nicolas Courjal (Zuniga), Elena Xanthoudakis (Frasquita), Paula Murrihy (Mercédès), Adrian Clarke (Le Dancaïre), Harry Nicoll (Le Remendado)

Bryan Hymel, Christine Rice in *Carmen 3D* © RealD

FOREIGN PARTS (MoMA) Producers/Directors/Photography/Editors, Véréna Paravel, J.P. Sniadecki; a LEF, Harvard Film Study Center, Harvard Sensory Ethnography Lab production; Color; HD; Not rated; 80 minutes; Release date: March 10, 2011. Documentary on the, scrap yards of Willets Point, Queens, New York; **WITH:** Luis Zapiain, Sara Zapiaian,Joe Ardizzone.

Foreign Parts © MoMA

ELEKTRA LUXX (Goldwyn) Producer/Director/Screenplay, Sebastian Gutierrez; Photography, Cale Finot; Designer, Joseph Edelson; Costumes, Denise Wingate; Music, Robyn Hitchcock; Editor, Lisa Bromwell; Casting, Mary Vernieu; a Destination Films presentation of a Gato Nero Films production; Color; HD; Rated R; 97 minutes; Release date: March 11, 2011. **CAST:** Carla Gugino (Elektra Luxx/Celia), Timothy Olyphant (Dellwood Butterworth), Joseph Gordon-Levitt (Bert Rodriguez), Malin Akerman (Trixie), Adrianne Palicki (Holly Rocket), Emmanuelle Chriqui (Bambi Lindberg), Kathleen Quinlan (Rebecca Linbrook), Marley Shelton (Cora), Justin Kirk (Benjamin), Amy Rosoff (Olive Rodriguez), Vincent Kartheiser (Jimmy), Isabella Gutierrez (Charlotte), Ermahn Ospina (Jimmy Cojones), Jake Hames, Patrick Caberty (Thieves), Melissa Stephens (Nadine), Susie Goliti (Maria), Lucy Punch (Dolores), Jesse Garcia (Camilo), John Colella (George), Matt Gerald (Michael Ortiz), Gabriel Gutierrez (The Walton Kid), Tracy Dinwiddie (Madeline), Michael Copon (Lamberto), Christine Lakin (Venus Azucar), Cale Finot (Sy Maplewood), Melissa Ordway (Sabrina Capri), Julianne Moore (Virgin Mary)

Joseph Gordon-Levitt in *Elektra Luxx* © Goldwyn Films

MONOGAMY (Oscilloscope) Producers, Jeffrey Mandel, Tom Heller, Randy Manis, Dana Adam Shapiro; Executive Producers, Chuck Goodgal, Human Loves Human, Tim Duff, Julie Christeas, Jeffrey Prosserman; Director, Dana Adam Shapiro; Screenplay, Dana Adam Shapiro, Evan M. Wiener; Photography, Doug Emmett; Designer, Timothy Whidbee; Costumes, Lisa Grace Hennessy; Music, Jamie Saft; Music Supervisor, Doug Bernheim; Editor, Mollie Goldstein; a Big Leo production in association with Renart Films; Color; HD; Not rated; 96 minutes; Release date: March 11, 2011. **CAST:** Chris Messina (Theo), Rashida Jones (Nat), Meital Dohan (Subgirl), Zak Orth (Quinny), Ivan Martin (Will), Madison Arnold (Mr. Margolin), Sarah Burns (Ella), Paul Diomede (Man), Hannah Gilli (Hannah), Neal Huff (Dr. Gleeman), Adam Pally (Allen), Mason Pettit (Groom), Samantha Sherman (Bride), Gil Rogers (Mr. Lasky), Emily Tremaine (Redhead), Alison Lehman (Flower Girl), Steve Beauchamp (Clerk), Mark Cirnigliaro (Dark Room Developer), Robert C. Kirk (Cop), Leslie Lyles (Yasmine), Jamie Richard (Teenage Brother)

Chris Messina, Rashida Jones in *Monogamy* © Oscilloscope

BONNIE & CLYDE VS. DRACULA (Indican) Producers, Jennifer Friend, Joseph Allen; Director/ Screenplay, Timothy Friend; Photography, Todd Norris; Art Director, Nita Norris; Music, Joseph Allen; Editors, Todd Norris, Timothy Friend; a Big Atom production in association with Outpost Worldwide; Color; Widescreen; HD; rated; 90 minutes; Release date: March 11, 2011. **CAST:** Tiffany Shepis (Bonnie), Trent Haaga (Clyde), Allen Lowman (Dr. Loveless), Jennifer Friend (Annabel), Russell Friend (Dracula), F. Martin Glynn (Henry), T. Max Graham (Jake), Anita Cordell (Liza), Anne Willow (Rosie), Carl Wallace (Ed), Haley Cordell (Fruitstand Girl), Jordan Baranowski (Moonshiner), Katie Barker (Dead Prostitute), Ari Bavel (Older Moonshiner), Alex "Fish" Friend (Moonshine Kid), Thomas Hadden (Corpse), Siouxxsie Harper (Prostitute), Seymour Noone (Farmer), Jared Reck (Horace), Toby Tolbert, Jeff Sisson (Hillbillies), Brook Edward Penca, Michael Friedlander (Cops), Bryan Davis, Donna M. Davis, Penny Harzi, Robert Potter, Sam Hendrix, Audrey Wilson, Chris Carter, Amber Underwood, Kari Paxton, Anthony Paxton, Edward Franklin, Kim Varner, Austin Fraser, Gretchen L. Webster, Emily Foster, Jessica Cooper, Lance Schellhorn, Scott Decker, JoAnn Imre, Ron L. Wilborn Jr. (Vampires)

Trent Haaga, Tiffany Shepis in *Bonnie & Clyde vs. Dracula* © Indican

I WILL FOLLOW (AFFRM) Producers, Denise Sexton, Ava DuVernay, Molly Mayeux; Executive Producer, Howard Barish; Director/Screenplay, Ava DuVernay; Photography, Miguel Bunster; Designer, Jennifer Spence; Music, Kathryn Bostic; Editor, Spencer Averick; Casting, Aisha Coley; The African-American Film Festival Releasing Movement in association with Forward Movement and Kandoo Films presentation; Color; DV; Rated PG-13; 83 minutes; Release date: March 11, 2011. **CAST:** Sally Richardson-Whitfield (Maye), Omari Hardwick (Troy), Michole White (Fran), Dijon Talton (Raven), Tracie Thoms (Tiffany), Damone Roberts, Ramon Leon (Themselves), Blair Underwood (Evan), Beverly Todd (Amanda), Phalana Tiller (Christine), Tony Perez (Tuliau), Royale Watkins (Roy), Owen Smith (Chuck), Robert Silver (Benjamin), Lucas Macfadden (Yard Sale Shopper), J.R. Ramirez (Percy), Kiara Muhammad (Ronda), Scotty Noyd Jr. (Ross), Olivia Alvarado (Fran's Baby), Kiki Walls (Young Amanda)

Salli Richardson-Whitfield, Omari Hardwick in *I Will Follow* © AFFRM

LORD OF THE DANCE IN 3D (SuperVision Media) Producers, Kit Hawkins, Vicki Betihavas; Executive Producers, Michael Flatley, Stephen Marks, Steve Carsey; Director, Marcus Viner; Photography, Nick Wheeler; Music, Ronan Hardiman; Choreographer, Michael Flatley; Editor, Tom Palliser; a Dancelord Intl., Unicorn Entertainment, Supervision Media, Kaleidoscope Film Distribution presentation of a Nineteen Fifteen production in association with ITN Prods.; Dolby; 3D; Color; Rated G; 95 minutes; Release date: March 17, 2011. Documentary of dancer Michael Flatley in performance; **WITH:** Michael Flatley, Tom Cunningham, Bernadette Flynn, Ciara Sexton, Kate Pomfret, Deirdre Shannon, Giada Costenaro, Valerie Gleeson

Michael Flatley in *Lord of the Dance* © SuperVision Media

Os & 1s (You Genius Kinoma) Producer, Michael Shifflett; Director, Eugene Kotlyarenko; Screenplay, Eugene Kotlyarenko, Michael Shifflett, Morgan Krantz; Developed by Andrew Schwartz; Photography, Marcus Gillis; Editors, Drew King, Eugene Kotlyarenko; Color; HD; Not rated; 83 minutes; Release date: March 18, 2011. **CAST:** Morgan Krantz (James Pongo), Jeremy Blackman (Sam), Ryan Reyes (Cole), Matthew Cardarople (Donny), Romy Windsor (Bossy), Eric Sweeney (Brad), Tysen D'Eston (Bucky), Dave Trejo (Diego), Andrew Kozel (Bryan), Sarah Blakely-Cartwright (Sarah), Sara Swain (Kasey), Paul Gellman (Sly Phone Thief), Alexi Wasser (Becky), Ahna O'Reilly (Caitlin), Hannah Hunt (Cassie), Mia Tramz (Meghan), Brandin Halpin (Dean), Mara LaFontaine (Sammy), Nicholas Mongiardo-Cooper (Norm), Marcus Demian (Grandpa), Jed Ochmanek (Jed), Christian Kamongi (Jeremiah), Alex Lewis (Daniel), Jason Shepard (Carroll), J.R. Nutt (Jon), Andi Matheny (Hayden's Mom), John Roderick Davidson (Edwin), Yuri Brown (Sabrina), Ira Gold (Hayden), Terry Peay (Dave), Whitmer Thomas (Corey), Heather Tocquigny (Sabrina's Friend), Bianca Alatoree (Sam's Girlfriend), Marcus Proctor (Patrick)

Os & 1s © You Genius Kinoma

ALABAMA MOON (Faulkner-McLean) Producers, Lee Faulkner, Kenny McLean; Director, Tim McCanlies; Screenplay, James Whittaker, Albert Watkins Key; Based on the novel by Watt Key; Photography, Jimmy Lindsey; Designer, Kelly Curley; Costumes, Dana Embree; Music, Ludek Drizhal; Editor, Mark Coffey; Casting, Mary Jo Slater, Steve Brooksbank; a Faulkner-McLean Entertainment presentation; Dolby; Color; HD; Rated PG; 99 minutes; Release date: March 18, 2011. **CAST:** Jimmy Bennett (Moon Blake), Gabriel Basso (Hal), Uriah Shelton (Kit), Clint Howard (Constable Sanders), John Goodman (Mr. Wellington), J.D. Evermore (Oliver "Pap" Blake), Elizabeth Jackson (Rachael Gene), John McConnell (Mr. Mitchell), Michael Sullivan (Mr. Gene), Kenny McLean (Officer Pete), Lenore Banks (Mrs Broomstead), Mark Adam (Uncle Mike), Walter Breaux (Mr. Carter), Gary Grubbs (Judge Mackin), Peter J. Gabb (George Albroscotto), Cy Thompson, Sean Cunningham (Younger Boys), Chase McDaniel (Older Boy), John Wilmot (Old Man), Shannon Maris (Receptionist), Tammi Arender (TV Reporter), Dixie (Snapper)

Jimmy Bennett in *Alabama Moon* © Faulkner-McLean

MOTHERLAND (Avalon) Producer, Taro Goto; Executive Producers, Doris Yeung, Kenneth Tsang; Director/Screenplay, Doris Yeung; Photography, Christopher Lockett; Designer, Garrett Lowe; Music, Steven Pranoto; Editor, Wayne Yung; an Avalon Films production; Color; HD; Not rated; 90 minutes; Release date: March 18, 2011. **CAST:** Françoise Yip (Raffi Tang), Kenneth Tsang (Stanley Tang), Byron Mann (Michael Wong), Carl Irwin (Attorney Cooper), Shoyi Cheng (Patricia Tang), Leda Lum (Rachel), Diana Caswell (Jaki Tang)

MY PERESTROIKA (Intl. Film Circuit) Producers, Robin Hessman, Rachel Wexler; Director/Photography, Robin Hessman; Music, Lev "Ljova" Zhurbin; Editors, Alla Kovgan, Garret Savage; a Red Square Productions Film; American-British; Stereo; HD; Color; Not rated; 87 minutes; Release date: March 23, 2011. Documentary on five Moscow schoolmates who were raised behind the Iron Curtain and grew up to witness the many changes in the Russian government; **WITH**: Olga Durikova, Boris "Borya" Meyerson, Lyubov "Lyuba" Meyerson, Mark Meyerson, Ruslan Stupin, Andrei Yevgrafov.

My Perestroika © Intl. Film Circuit

DRAWING WITH CHALK (Drawing Chalk Pictures) Executive Producers/Screenplay, Todd Giglio, Christopher Springer; Director/Editor, Todd Giglio; Photography, Michael LaVoie; Music, Six Mile Hill; a Giglio/Springer Film; Dolby; Scope; Color; Not rated; 87 minutes; Release date: March 25, 2011. **CAST:** Todd Giglio (Jay), Christopher Springer (Matt), Pooja Kumar (Jasmin), Brennan Giglio (Bryan), Tom Loughlin (Ray), Debargo Sanyal (Isaac), Kapil Bawa (Dr. Jeyadoss), Susham Bedi (Mrs. Jeyadoss), Tim Berardi (Ron), Michael Gentile (Robert), Devon Goffman (Russ), Pete Hornbeck (Tough Guy at Club), Danni Lang (Bartender), Kenny Sherman (Kenny), Mark A. Smith (Rich), Jimmy Stellato (Jimmy), Bruce Watson (Bruce), Ariel Bailey (Club Patron), Nicholas Cocchetto (Guy with Drink), Chelsea DiNino (Waitress), Tabatha Joy (Girl with Drink), Rich Lundy (Doorman)

SOME DAYS ARE BETTER THAN OTHERS (Palisades Tartan) Producers, Neil Kopp, David Allen Cress; Director/Screenplay, Matt McCormick; Photography, Greg Schmitt; Designer, Ryan Smith; Costumes, Amanda Needham; Music, Matthew Cooper, Matt McCormick; Editor, Chris Jones; Casting, Simon Max Hill; a Rodeo Film Co. presentation; Stereo; Color; DV; Not rated; 93 minutes; Release date: March 25, 2011. **CAST:** Carrie Brownstein (Katrina), James Mercer (Eli), David Wodehouse (Otis), Renee Roman Nose (Camille), Erin McGarry (Chloe), Andrew Dickson (Mr. Bayer), Benjamin Farmer (Noel), Andrew Harris (Mack Johnson), Aubree Bernier-Clark (Aubrey), Todd Robinson (Dale), Joe Von Appen (Bryan), Corrina Repp (Rachel), Anita Lugliani (Dog Shelter Worker), Jennifer Keyser (TSA Worker), Kellie Johnson (Chrissy), Bruce Lawson (Store Manager), Corin Tucker (Soccer Mom), Gabe Nevins (Store Employee), Matt McCormick (Security Guard), Luke Clements (The Single Guy), Cora Benesh (Bachelorette)

James Mercer in *Some Days Are Better Than Others* © Palisades Tartan

PEEP WORLD (IFC Films) Producers, Joe Neurauter, Felipe Marino, Keith Calder; Co-Producer, Paul Davis; Director, Barry W. Blaustein; Screenplay, Peter Himmelstein; Photography, Tobias Datum; Designer, Sue Chan; Costumes, Janicza Bravo; Music, Jeff Cardoni; Editors, Jeff Werner, Evan Schiff, Steve Welch; an Occupant Films presentation; Dolby; Color; DV; Not rated; 89 minutes; Release date: March 25, 2011. **CAST:** Michael C. Hall (Jack Meyerwitz), Sarah Silverman (Cheri Meyerwitz), Rainn Wilson (Joel Meyerwitz), Ben Schwartz (Nathan Meyerwitz), Judy Greer (Laura), Taraji P. Henson (Mary), Kate Mara (Meg), Ron Rifkin (Henry Meyerwitz), Stephen Tobolowsky (Ephraim), Lesley Ann Warren (Marilyn), Alicia Witt (Amy Harrison), Lewis Black (Narrator), Nicholas Hormann (Ted), Michael McDonald (British Director), Troian Avery Bellisario (Film Set P.A.), David Packer (Eli), Danay Garcia (Atractive P.A.), Deborah Pratt (Cassandra Williamson), Michael Cavanaugh (Brad Thompkins), Michael Chinyamurindi (Maduk), Paige Orr (Carly), Octavia Spencer (Alison), Geoffrey Arend (Dr. Novak), Dominic Flores (Salvador), Guillermo Diaz (Jesus), Lester Speight (Wizdom), Jack Plotnick (Bookstore Manager), Kulap Vilaysack (Lily), Emily Kuroda (Nail Salon Owner), Jeff Lam (Chun), Karl Stavem (Paul), David Diaan (Hari), Raja Fenske (Rajeev), Sam Carson (Man in Booth), Armando Molina (Gardener), Tom Katsis (Henry's Friend), Rich Delia (Waiter), Rita Rani (Doctor)

Todd Giglio, Brennan Giglio in *Drawing with Chalk* © Drawing Chalk Pictures

Ben Schwartz, Michael C. Hall, Lesley Ann Warren, Alicia Witt, Stephen Tobolowsky, Sarah Silverman, Rainn Wilson in *Peep World* © IFC Films

THE 5TH QUARTER (Rocky Mountain Pictures) Producer/Director/Screenplay, Rick Bieber; Executive Producers, Alan Cohen, Bob J. McCreary; Photography, Craig Haagensen; Designer, Sofia Mandalana Martinez Moore; Costumes, Deborah Latham Binkley; Music, Andy Mendelson; Editor, Mark Conte; Casting, Monika Mikkelsen, Sheila Jaffe, Tracy Kilpatrick; an Angel City Pictures and McCreary Entertainment presentation; Dolby; Color; Rated PG-13; 97 minutes; Release date: March 25, 2011. **CAST:** Aidan Quinn (Steven Abbate), Andie MacDowell (Maryanne Abbate), Ryan Merriman (Jon Abbate), Michael Harding (Coach Jim Grobe), Stefan Guy (Luke Abbate), Jillian Batherson (Haley Scott), Anessa Ramsey (Lynn Garber), Patrick Stogner (Henry), Bonnie Johnson (Joan Kinsey), William Smith Yelton (Brandon), Maureen Mountcastle (Pam Steele), Andrea Powell (Bonnie), R. Keith Harris (Dr. Phillips), Jon Stafford (Coach Billings), Kristen Nicole LaPrade (Susie Simons), Matt McGrath (Adam Abbate), Kendrick Cross (Fireman), Stacy Earl (Joan Marie), Bradley Evans (Joe Haynes), Mandy Manis (Rachel Abbate), Pastor Brian Bloye, Bob McCreary, Pastor Terry Nelson, Micah Andrews, Steve Uria, Mit Shah (Themselves), Kenny Hinkle (Young Luke Abbate), Josh Smith (Steve Justice), Sammy Nagi Njuguna (Josh Gattis), Rick Meadows (Coach Hines), Patt Noday (ACC Sports TV Reporter), Jason Drago, Heanon Tate (Officers), John Newberg (Coach Hood), Ted Johnson (Bob Kinsey), Capel Kane (Allie), Dave Blamy (Stan Cotten), Justin Smith (Coach Lambert), Sharrin Edwards (Nurse Jean Amato), Alison Lawrence (Sarah Palmer), Earl Guill III (Zack), Colin Womack (Mitchell), Stan Cotten (TV Sports Anchor), Walter Bell (Matt Brim), Madison Clair Knott (Crystal)

Stefan Guy, Ryan Merriman in *The 5th Quarter* © Rocky Mountain Pictures

CAT RUN (Lleju Productions) Producer, William O. Perkins III; Executive Producers, Ram Bergman, Derrick Borte; Director, John Stockwell; Screenplay, Nick Ball, John Niven; Photography, Jean-Francois Hensgens; Designer, Aleksandar Denic; Costumes, Bojana Nikitovic; Music, Devin Powers; Editors, Jeff McEvoy, Ben Callahan; Casting, Mary Vernieu, Venus Kanani; Dolby; Super 35 Widescreen; Color; Rated R; 102 minutes; Release date: April 1, 2011. **CAST:** Paz Vega (Catalina Rona), Janet McTeer (Helen Bingham), Alphonso McAuley (Julian Simms), Scott Mechlowicz (Anthony Hester), Christopher McDonald (Bill Krebb), Karel Roden (Daniel Carver), D.L. Hughley (Dexter), Tony Curran (Sean Moody), Michelle Lombardo (Stephanie), Branko Djuric (Hamilton), Gordan Kicic (Razwell), Jelena Gavrilovic (Grushenka), Albert Pérez (Elpido Rona), Caleb Vela Poquet (Blas Rona), Radik Golovkov (Ryder), Michael Sopko (Shelton), William O. Perkins III (Security Guard), Ana Sakic (Young Russian Woman), Slobodan Boda Ninkovic (Theater Owner), Jean-Christophe Bouvet (Dobber), Milorad Kapor (Hans), Heather Chasen (Bingham's Mum), Kaloian Vodenicarov (Abusive Man), Steve Agnew (US Tourist), Ivanka Bozinovic (Hotel Receptionist), Ken Phillips (Gerry Catch), Pigi Miodrag Radevic (Very Old Man), Neil Nolan (News Anchor), William McBain (Scotsman), Mila Kaladjurdevic (Tall Brunette), Marija Tonic (French Blonde), Biljana Hresnjek (French Redhead Sabina), Benjamin Mustelaj (Gypsy Boy), Dasa Zivkovic (Jieva), Suzana Purkovic (Maid), Ivana Pekovic (Nastusya), Olga Astanaskaja (Abused Woman), Petar Buric (Fit Young Porter), Slobodan Marunic (Sava), Nenad Stefanovic (Masturbating Man), Malique Hawkins (Young Julian), Jovan Krstic (Bahta), Viktor Boroja (Baby Alex), Louis P. Thybulle (Lleju Commando), Stevan Radusinovic (Ivan), Alesandar Tomovic, Dijana Bralovic (Eastern Europeans), Zarko Stanisic (Juggler), Davor Dragojevic, Filip Dzigic, Zoran Dzigic, Risto Kreckovic (Magicians)

Scott Mechlowicz, Alphonso McAuley in *Cat Run* © Lleju Prods.

CIRCO (First Run Features) Producers, Aaron Schock, Jannat Gargi; Director/Photography, Aaron Shock; Screenplay, Aaron Schock, Mark Becker; Music, Joey Burns; Editor, Mark Becker; a Heco a Mano Films and the Independent Television Service production; American-Mexican; Color; Not rated; 75 minutes; Release date: April 1, 2011. Documentary on the Ponce family's circus, which has been in operation throughout Mexico since the 19th century.

Circo © First Run Features

WRECKED (IFC Films) Producer, Kyle Mann; Co-Executive Producers, David Reckzeigel, Jeff Sackman, Patrice Theroux, Adrien Brody, Clay Epstein, Adrian Love, Noah Segal; Co-Producers, Jason Stone, Andrew Mann; Director, Michael Greenspan; Screenplay, Christopher Dodd; Photography, James Liston; Designer, Michael Norman Wong; Costumes, Andrea des Roches; Music, Michael Brook; Editor, Wiebke von Carolsfeld; Casting, Kerry Rock; an Independent Edge production in association with Telefilm Canada and Three-Seven Entertainment; American-Canadian; Dolby; Widescreen; Deluxe Color; Rated R; 90 minutes; American release date: April 1, 2011. **CAST:** Adrien Brody (Man), Caroline Dhavernas (Woman), Ryan Robbins (George Weaver), Adrian Hughes (Raymond Plazzy), Adrian Holmes (Man in the Woods), Lloyd Adams (Eric Stapleton), Jacob Blair (Park Ranger), Mark McConchie (Bank Security Officer)

Adrien Brody in *Wrecked* © IFC Films

TWO GATES OF SLEEP (Factory 25) Producers, Josh Mond, Andrew F. Renzi; Director/ Screenplay, Alistair Banks Griffin; Photography, Jody Lee Lipes; Designer, Kris Moran; Music, Saunder Jurriaans, Daniel Bensi; a BorderLine Films and Andrew F. Renzi presentation; Color; Not rated; 78 minutes; Release date: April 1, 2011. **CAST:** Brady Corbet (Jack), David Call (Louis), Karen Young (Bess), Ross Francis (Hunter), Ritchie Montgomery (Dr. Benjamin), Lindsay Soileau (Dell)

David Call, Brady Corbet in *Two Gates of Sleep* © Factory 25

THE LAST GODFATHER (Roadside Attractions) Producer, Dooho Choi; Director/ Screenplay, Hyung-rae Shim; Photography, Mark Irwin; Designer, Cecilia Montiel; Costumes, Graciela Mazón; Music, John Lissauer; Editor, Jeff Freeman; Casting, Christine Sheaks; a CJ Entertainment presentation of a Younggu Art production; American-South Korean; Dolby; Color; Rated PG-13; 100 minutes; Release date: April 1, 2011. **CAST:** Harvey Keitel (Don Carini), Hyung-rae Shim (Younggu), Michael Rispoli (Tony V), Jason Mewes (Vinnie), Jocelin Donahue (Nancy Bonfante), Jon Polito (Don Bonfante), Blake Clark (Capt. O'Brian), Logan Shea (Little Willie), John Pinette (Macho), Jack Kehler (Cabbie), Paul Hipp (Rocco), Debra Mooney (Sister Theresa), Roger Stoneburner, Mark Alexander Herz, Rahman Dalrymple, Calvin Dean (Carini Wiseguys), Michele Specht (Burlesque Hostess), Michelle Maniscalco (Burlesque Dancer), John Cirigliano (Mangini), Christian Levantino (Tino), Jannette Bloom (Mary), Tristen Bankston (Big Willie), Joshua Rosenthal (Fabrizio), Tom Brangle (Officer Pickett), Gus Lynch (Don Bonfante's Yes-Man), Tristan Bankston (Big Willie)

Hyung-rae Shim, Harvey Keitel in *The Last Godfather* © Roadside Attractions

FAT, SICK & NEARLY DEAD (Reboot Media) Producer, Stacey Offman; Executive Producers, Joe Cross, Shane Hodson, Robert MacDonald; Directors, Joe Cross, Kurt Engfehr; Photography, Daniel Marracino; Music, M.E. Manning; Editors, Alison Amron, Christopher Seward; a Us & Us Media, Fast production; Color; Not rated; 97 minutes; Release date: April 1, 2011. Documentary on how Joe Cross, grossly overweight and suffering from a debilitating autoimmune disease, managed to regain his health; **WITH:** Joe Cross, Amy Badberg, Merv Cross, Virginia Cross, Joel Fuhrman, Tammy Hamlin, Stacy Kennedy, Siong Norte, Prof. Ronald Penny, Mandy Reinking, Phil Riverstone, Austin Staples, Barry "Bear" Staples, Phil Staples, William Staples, Kit Willow Podgornik

Joe Cross in *Fat, Sick & Nearly Dead* © Reboot Media

THE ELEPHANT IN THE LIVING ROOM (NightFly Entertainment) Producer/Director/Screenplay/Photography/Editor, Michael Webber; Executive Producers, Ross Hammer, Elliott Wallach, Russell Muntz; Music, David Russo; a Nightfly Entertainment production in association with Mainsail Prods. and Edify Media; Color; Rated PG; 96 minutes; Release date: April 1, 2011. Documentary about America's who keep dangerous animals in their homes as pets; **WITH:** Terry Brumfield, Russ Clear, Casey Craig, Pat Craig, Tim Harrison, Zuzana Kukol, Raymond Little, Scott Shoemaker, Bill Stiffler

Terry Brumfield in *The Elephant in the Living Room* © NightFly Entertainment

AN AFFIRMATIVE ACT (Take 2 Releasing) Producer/Story/Screenplay, Kenneth Del Vecchio; Executive Producers, Greg Jackson, Rob Moretti, Serge Levin; Director, Jana Mattioli; Photography, Rod Weber, James Houk; Designer, Sarah Schetter; Costumes, Jeffrey Sturdivant; Music, Ramin Kousha; Editor, Rod Weber; Casting, Lawyer Nicholas; a Justice for All productions and Multivisionnaire Pictures presentation of a Kenneth Del Vecchio production; Dolby; Color; Not rated; 100 minutes; Release date: April 1, 2011. **CAST:** Eric Etebari (John DeMine), Candice Holdorf (Terry Succi), Elissa Goldstein (Samantha Succi), Blanche Baker (Lori Belmont), Thomas G. Waites (Samuel "Dixie" Backus), Justin Deas (Gov. Packer Winstroll), Rachael Robbins (Christie DeMine), Jackie Martling (Dutch Holland), Randy Jones (Rollie Handsome), Jeffrey H. Johns (Claude), Robert Clohessy (Lance Lane), Ed Kershen (Judge Nicholas Frier), Rob Moretti (Marty Pearce), Costas Mandylor (Matthew), Charles Durning (The Man in the White Suit), Greg Jackson (Attorney General), Allegra Cohen (Nicole Gallo), Charles Grady (Det. Corwin), Denise Rodell (Barbara Carlyle), Angelo Servidio (Judge Makansas), Mario Del Vecchio (Mario Succi), Julia Weldon (Jennifer), Keith Collins (Manny), Nina Transfeld (Tricia Winstroll), Tope Oni (Brandon), Jacqueline Madden (Kim), Kenneth Del Vecchio (Nick), Francine Del Vecchio (Cassie), Randy Pearce (Rick), Mark Boyland (Stuart), Jennifer Guest (Lydia,

Dixie's Wife), Caitlin Kehoe (Bobbi), Len Annucci (Sal), Jackie Maroney (Lana, John's Secretary), Greg Nutcher (Bailiff), Wynn Van Dusen (Laura Winstroll), Clark Jackson (Dr. Burris), Frank Giglio, John Kerner, James Goral (Uniformed Cops), Anthony Alexander (Officer Grayson), Blair Lewin (Stenographer), Nicole Jaeger (Secretary), James O'Connor (Police Detective), John Mazur (Detective #2), Misti Tindiglia (Court Clerk)

WRETCHES & JABBERERS (Area 23a) Producers, Douglas Biklen, Gerardine Wurzburg; Director, Gerardine Wurzburg; Photography, Gary Griffin; Music, J. Ralph; Editor, Barbara Ballow; a State of the Art, Inc. production; Color; Not rated; 94 minutes; Release date: April 1, 2011. Documentary about two men with autism, Tracy Thresher and Larry Bissonnette; **WITH:** Tracy Thresher, Larry Bissonnette, Naoki Higashida, Pascal Cheng, Harvey Lavoy

Tracy Thresher, Larry Bissonnette in *Wretches & Jabberers* ©Area 23a

BLANK CITY (Insurgent Media) Producers, Aviva Wishnow, Vanessa Roworth; Executive Producers, Josh Braun, Dan Braun, Fisher Stevens, Erik H. Gordon; Director, Celine Danhier; Photography, Ryo Murakami, Peter Szollosi; Music Supervisor, Dan Selzer; Editor, Vanessa Roworth; a Pure Fragment Films production in association with Submarine Entertainment; Color/black & white; HD; Not rated; 94 minutes; Release date: April 6, 2011. Documentary on New York's underground movies of the late 1970's and early '80s; **WITH:** Charlie Ahearn, Patti Astor, Beth B, Scott B, Lizzie Borden, Steve Buscemi, James Chance, Daze, Manuel DeLanda, Vivienne Dick, Sara Driver, Fab5 Freddy, Bette Gordon, Debbie Harry, Tessa Hughes-Freeland, Jim Jarmusch, Becky Johnston, Richard Kern, Lung Leg, Lydia Lunch, John Lurie, Ann Magnuson, Maripol, Michael McClard, Casandra Stark Mele, Eric Mitchell, Thurston Moore, James Nares, Glenn O'Brien, Michael Oblowitz, Kembra Pfahler, Pat Place, Amos Poe, Jack Sargeant, Susan Seidelman, J.G. Thirlwell, Tommy Turner, John Waters, Nick Zedd

Blank City © Insurgent Releasing

THEY'RE OUT OF THE BUSINESS (IFC Films) Producers, Eric Schaeffer, Donal Lardner Ward, Chip Hourihan; Directors/Screenplay, Eric Schaeffer, Donal Lardner Ward; Photography, Marc Blandori; Designer, Alan Bruckner; Editor, Anton Salaks; Casting, Jodi Collins; a Five Minutes Before the Miracle, Clean Slate Pictures presentation of an Outofthebiz production; Color; HD; Not rated; 89 minutes; Release date: April 6, 2011. **CAST:** Eric Schaeffer (Splick), Donal Lardner Ward (Jason), Diane Davis (April), Stefanie Frame (Sarah Jane), Delores McDougal (Splick's Mom), Bill Weeden (Will), Andrée Vermeulen (Amy), Christophe LePage (Tony Robert), Cara Greene (Alex), Alison Carter Thomas (Christie), Joanna Moskwa (Lenka), Bristol Pomeroy (William), Steffi Garrard (Ring Girl Brenda), Kate Nowlin (Meghan), Yury Tsykun (Latchkaya), Nikki Ghisel (Yoga Desk Woman), Matt Oberg (Wally), Steve Witting, Jordan Carlos (Network Executives), Mark Gauthier (Kaheem), Dina Perlman (Registrar), Lisa Kleinman, Maude Burke (Asst. Registrars), Rachel Starr (Porn Star Debbie), Bill Dawes (Porn Star Ed), Mark Ebner (Porn Star Pierre), Rafael Osorio (Sanchez), Tom O'Neill (Café Waiter), Betty Gerena (Housekeeper), John Bianco (Dana), Tom Kemnitz Jr. (Gym Clerk), Olivia Cella (Ellen), Gene Vrlaku (David), David Mandelbaum (Homeless Man), Cara Ann Kirner (Girl in Gym), Karl Ruckdeschel (Guy in Sauna), Nell Casey (Nurse), Allyson Morgan (Yoga Girl)

Donal Lardner Ward, Eric Schaeffer in *They're Out of the Business* © IFC Films

CEREMONY (Magnolia) Producers, Emilio Diez Barroso, Darlene Caamaño Loquet, Polly Johnsen, Matt Spicer; Executive Producers, Jason Reitman, Daniel Dubiecki, Joshua Zeman, Corrie Rothbart, Billy Rovzar, Fernando Rovzar, Jeff Keswin, Alejandro Garcia; Director/ Screenplay, Max Winkler; Photography, William Rexer II; Designer, Inbal Weinberg; Costumes, Heidi Bivens; Music, Eric D. Johnson; Editor, Joe Landauer; Casting, Kerry Barden, Paul Schnee; a Nala Films production in association with Polymorphic Pictures; Dolby; Color; Rated R; 90 minutes; Release date: April 8, 2011. **CAST:** Michael Angarano (Sam Davis), Uma Thurman (Zoe), Reece Thompson (Marshall Schmidt), Lee Pace (Whit Coutell), Jake Johnson (Teddy), Brooke Bloom (Margaret Cornish), Harper Dill (Carol Archer), Rebecca Mader (Esme Ball), Nathalie Love (Blonde Maid), Charlie Moss (Nico Spicer), Lisby Larson (Nina Pileggi), Paul Amodeo (Bruce Singer), Philip Carlson (Butler), Catherine Russell, Jack Koenig (Party Guests), Jerrin Holt (African Man), Von Jeff (Von)

KATI WITH AN I (4th Row Films) Producers, Douglas Tirola, Susan Bedusa, Robert Greene, Sean Price Williams; Director/Editor, Robert Greene; Photography, Sean Price Williams; Music Supervisor, Stuart Wolferman; a Prewar Cinema production; Color; DV; Not rated; 85 minutes; Release date: April 8, 2011. Documentary about high schooler Kati Genthner as she approaches graduation and an uncertain future; **WITH:** Kati Genthner, Brian Genthner, Tomi Genthner, James Holsemback, Meliah Orten, Dalana Parker, Bobby Taylor, Bridgett Taylor

Kati Genthner in *Kati with an I* © 4th Row Films

MEETING SPENCER (Paladin) Producer, George G. Braunstein; Executive Producers, Chien Ya, Natalie Chin; Director, Malcolm Mowbray; Screenplay, Andrew Kole, Andrew Delaplaine, Scott Kasdin; Story, Andrew Kole, Andrew Delaplane; Photography, Paula Huidobro; Designer, Bradd Fillmann; Music, Stephen Coates; Editor, John Travers; a George G. Braunstein production; Color; Rated R; 88 minutes; Release date: April 8, 2011. **CAST:** Jeffrey Tambor (Harris Chappell), Melinda McGraw (Didi Ravenal), Jesse Plemons (Spencer West), Jill Marie Jones (Nikki Ross), Yvonne Zima (Sophia Martinelli), William Morgan Sheppard (Larry Lind), Julian Bailey (Emerson Todd), Caroline Aaron (Nancy Diamond), Marcello Cacioppo (Nicholas), Robert Catrini (Alphonso), Kristen Eck (Candy), Markus Flanagan (Man in Bar), Mark Harelik (David Thiel), Ralph P. Martin (Bart Liebowitz), Brian McGovern (Monte Sobel), Livia Milano (Rose), John Prudhont (Rick), Anthony Russell (Mario), Robert "Sanz" Sanchez (Ricardo), Don Stark (Wolfie), Laura Alcalde (Wolfie's Mother), Izumi (Erika)

Jeffrey Tambor, Ralph P. Martin, Julian Bailey in *Meeting Spencer* © Paladin Pictures

Michael Angarano, Reece Thompson in *Ceremony* © Magnolia Films

HENRY'S CRIME (Moving Pictures Film & Television) Producers, Stephen Hamel, David Mimran, Jordan Schur, Lemore Syvan; Executive Producers, Scott Fischer, Mark Fischer, Cassian Elwes, Lisa Wilson, Alison Palmer, Peter Graham, Stephen Hays, Sacha Gervasi; Director, Malcom Venville; Screenplay, Sacha Gervasi, David White; Story, Stephen Hamel, Sacha Gervasi; Photography, Paul Cameron; Designer, Chris Jones; Costumes, Melissa Toth; Music Supervisor, Blake Leyh; Editor, Curtiss Clayton; Casting, Cindy Tolan; a Mimran Schur Pictures, Parlay Films production of a Company Films and a Mimran Schur Pictures Production in association with Firstar Films and 120dB Films; Dolby; Super 35 Widescreen; Technicolor; Rated R; 108 minutes; Release date: April 8, 2011. **CAST:** Keanu Reeves (Henry Torne), Vera Farmiga (Julie Ivanova), James Caan (Max Saltzman), Peter Stormare (Darek Millodragovic), Judy Greer (Debbie Torne), Fisher Stevens (Eddie Vibes), Danny Hoch (Joe), Bill Duke (Frank), Drew McVety (Detective), Tim Snay (Judge), Carlos Pizarro (Hector), Chris Cardona (Prison Guard), Mark Anthony (Fink), Brian Rogalski, Steve Beauchamp (Other Inmates), Allel Aimiche (Pierre), Currie Graham (Simon), David Costabile (Arnold), Jordan Gelber (Trofimov), Audrey Lynn Weston (Dunyasha), Ken Marks (Gayev), Gideon Banner (Yasha), Julie Ordon (Anya), Paul O'Brien (Head Parole Reviewer), James Hindman (Mr. Tuttle), Jason Fisher (Bruce the Dick), Guy Boyd (Bernie), Peter Appel (Larry), David Bishins (Interrogation Detective)

Keanu Reeves, James Caan in *Henry's Crime* © Moving Pictures

EVIL BONG 3-D: THE WRATH OF BONG (Full Moon Pictures) Producer/Director, Charles Band; Screenplay, August White, Kent Roudebush; Idea, Patrick Klepek; Photography, Terrance Ryker; Designer, Joe Walser; Costumes, Ashley Marie Parker; Editor, Danny Draven; Casting, Jeremiah Lutes; Special Effects Makeup, Cary Ayers, Tom Devlin; Color; 3D; Rated R; 86 minutes; Release date: April 8, 2011. **CAST:** Christina DeRosa (Nurse Hookah), Dena Kollar (Angel Chick), Peter Stickles (Alistair), Robin Sydney (Luann), John Patrick Jordan (Larnell), Irwin Keyes (The Killer), Amy Paffrath (Velicity), Sonny Carl Davis (Rabbit), Mitch Eakins (Bachman), Michelle Mais (Evil Bong Voice), Brian Lloyd (Brett), Circus-Szalewski (Alien Bong Voice), Nina Estes (Graffiti Chick), Jacob Witkin (Gramps), Chrissy Randall (Green Chick), Eden Modiano (Devil Chick), Tara Spadaro (TV Chick)

Evil Bong 3-D © Full Moon Pictures

THE FAMILY JAMS (Factory 25) Producer/Director/Photography/Editor, Kevin Barker; Music, Devendra Banhart, Andy Cabic, Joanna Newsom; an East Gable production; Color; DV; Not rated; 81 minutes; Release date: April 8, 2011. Documentary on the 2004 tour of a traveling acoustic avant garde music group; **WITH:** Alissa Anderson, Devendra Banhart, Meg Baird, Kevin Barker, Andy Cabic, Zach Cowie, Espers, Jim Gaylord, Antony Hegarty, Joanna Newsom, Linda Perhacs, Stacy Nuner

MYSTERIES OF THE JESUS PRAYER (Passion River Films) Producers, John A. McGuckin, David Aslan; Executive Producer/Director, Norris J. Chumley; Screenplay, John A. McGuckin, Norris J. Chumley; Photography, Patrick F. Gallo, Dwight Grimm, John Foster; Music, Richard Devletian; Editor, David Aslan; a Magnetic Arts production; Color; HD; Not rated; 113 minutes; Release date: April 8, 2011. Documentary on Christianity's monastic tradition; WITH: Norris J. Chumley, John McGuckin

Patriarch Kiril in *Mysteries of the Jesus Prayer* © Passion River Films

EXODUS FALL (Oakhurst Pictures) Producers, Sudarshan Kohli, Ankush Kohli; Executive Producers, Kumkum Kohli, Sameer Kohli; Directors, Ankush Kohli, Chad Waterhouse; Screenplay, Chad Waterhouse; Photography, Denis Maloney; Designer, Elizabeth Garner; Costumes, Kerrie Kordowski; Music, Boris Zelkin, Deeji Mincey; Editor, Mitchel Stanley; Casting, Gerald I. Wolff, Christine Joyce; a Gorilla Pictures and Brainstorm Prods. presentation of a Kohli/Waterhouse Film; Color; Super 16; Not rated; 92 minutes; Release date: April 8, 2011. **CAST:** Jesse James (Kenneth Minor), Rosanna Arquette (Marilyn Minor), Devon Graye (Dana Minor), Dee Wallace (Shirley Minor), Christopher Atkins (Wayne Minor), Alexander Carroll (Travis Crawford), Adrien Finkel (Charlotte Minor), Leo Rossi (Ford Ashworth), Duane Whitaker (Marty), Nina Kaczorowski (Lonnie), Jason Ellefson (Dustin), Dale Hersh (Johnny), Lyn Mahler (Mary), Laila Ayad, Sydney Stephenson (Drunk Girls), Richard Burns (Drunk Man, Bob), Jay Duff (Bus Driver), Wil Garret (Grocery Store Clerk), Sunny Malick, Matt Murphy, Larry Varanelli (Police Officers), Aaron Michael McElligott (David), James Quattrochi, Tay Brooks, Mark Sellers (NorCal Officers), Chad Waterhouse (Detective), Alex Petrovitch (Man at Door), Breanne Racano (Biker Bar Bartender)

Jesse James, Adrien Finkel, Devon Graye in *Exodus Fall* © Oakhurst Pictures

FOOTPRINTS (Paladin) Producer, Steven Peros, John Peros; Executive Producer, Saad Al-Enezi; Director/Screenplay, Steven Peros; Photography, Adam Teichman; Costumes, Edgar Revilla; Music, Christopher Caliendo; Editor, Travis Rust; Casting, John Peros; an Our Gal Pictures production; Color; HD; Not rated; 80 minutes; Release date: April 15, 2011. **CAST:** Sybil Temtchine (Our Gal), H.M. Wynant (Victor), Pippa Scott (Genevieve), John Brickner (E-Man), Catherine Bruhier (Cat Woman), Charley Rossman (Mike the Tour Guide), Kirk Bovill (Solitary Stranger), Riley Weston (Super Girl), Joe Roseto (Joe the Auditor), R.J. Cantu (Manny), Jeris Poindexter (Homeless Man), Jim Braswell (Robert), Steve Pacini (Robo-Dude), Jean Iavelli (Grandma), Rita Khrabrovitsky (Lost Russian), Nichole Porges, Stephanie Porges (Teen Girls)

Sybil Temtchine, H.M. Wynant in *Footprints* © Paladin Pictures

PHILLIP THE FOSSIL (American Trash Films) Producers, Garth Donovan, Adam Roffman, Christopher Sachs, Tom Sullivan; Director/Screenplay/Editor, Garth Donovan; Photography, Matt Levin; Music, Adam Sherman, Joe Kowalski; Presented in association with Blackbeet Prods.; Color; HD; Not rated; 72 minutes; Release date: April 15, 2011. **CAST:** Brian Hasenfus (Phillip), Nick Dellarocca (Nick), Ann Palica (Julie), James Killigrew (Sully), Angela Pagliarulo (Summer), William DeCoff (Coach Jenkins), Sarah Nicklin (Julie's Friend), Tom Sullivan (Bones), Dave Neal (Johnny)

Brian Hasenfus in *Phillip the Fossil* © American Trash Films

SQUARE GROUPER (Magnolia) Producers, Alfred Spellman, Billy Corben, Lindsey Snell; Executive Producers, Todd Glaser, Dudley Whitman, Todd Whitman, Robert Kahn; Director, Billy Corben; Photography, Randy Valdes, Matt Staker, Jordy Klein, Ralf Gonzales, Benjamin Rabbers; Music, DJ Le Spam; Editor, Jorge Diaz; a Rakontur & Magnet presentation; Color; HD; Rated R; 100 minutes; Release date: April 15, 2011. Documentary on Marijuana smuggling in Miami during the 1970's and 80's; **WITH:** *The Zion Coptics:* Brother Clifton, Brother Gary, Sister Ilene, Brother Butch, Tony Darwin, Manny Funes, Arthur Tifford, Mark Potter; *The Black Tuna Gang:* Robert Platshorn, Robert Meinster, Lynne Platshorn, Howard Blumin, Harold Copus, Randy Fisher, Dick Moehle, Dennis Cogan, Arthur Tifford, Atlee Wampler; *Everglades City:* Nancy Daffin, Lee "Leebo" Noble, Lewis R. Perry, Naman Coston, L.B. Turner, David Shealy, Dana Masey, Floyd Brown, Shane Daniels, Mark Potter, Kit Johnson, Jimmy Wheeler, Candy Daniels, Frank Chellino, Jack Lloyd

THE IMPERIALISTS ARE STILL ALIVE! (Sundance Selects) Producers, Vanessa Hope, Zeina Durra; Executive Producers, Rami Makhzoumi, Matthew Chausse; Director/Screenplay, Zeina Durra; Photography, Mangela Crosignani; Designer, Jade Healy; Costumes, Ciera Wells; Editor, Michael Taylor; Casting, Sig De Miguel, Stephen Vincent, Manuel Teil; a Hi, Jack Films presentation in association with Corniche Pictures, Goldcrest Films and Tax Credit Finance; Dolby; Color; Not rated; 90 minutes; Release date: April 15, 2011. **CAST:** Élodie Bouchez (Asya), José Maria de Tavira (Javier), Karim Saleh (Karim), Rita Ackerman (Libby), Marianna Kulukundis (Athena), Karolina Muller (Tatiana), Alexis Savino (Luke), Nidal Said (Adaweeya), Joe Donovan (Andrew), Elena Chang, Julie Mun (Pedicurists), Sumy Ahn Lee (Sun-Tae), Vanessa Hope (Alicia), Esosa Edosomwan (African Dancer), Victoria Aitken (Lady in Bathroom), Sophie Auster (Savina), Pierluca Arancio (Marco), Eduardo Constantini (Antonio), Rodrigo Lopresti (Eagle), Henry Kwan (Man in Chinatown Bar), Jackson Ning (Gary), King Wong (Lee), Sebastian Beacon (Eurotrash Boy), Darren "Disco" Copeland (Doorman), Ran Ka (Madame Al-Basha), Munirah Alatas (Suha), Karen Lynn Gorney (Elizabeth), R.N. Rao (John), Arianne Recto (Linda), Mary Maybank (Yvette), Natalia Zisa (Maribelle), Ricky Garcia (Van Driver), Laura Patalano (Sandra), Marilyn McDonald (Hair Lady), Israel Hernandez (Ricky), Robert Chan (Chinese Grocer), Coati Mundi (Officer Lopez), Haythem Noor (Jamal), Foad Attel (Tarek), Neville Aurelius (Bartender), Alexander Wraith (Mohammed), Ted Arcidi (Don), Reza Salazar (Miguel), Kaddur Habari (Arabic Radio Report), Fabien Thelma (French Television News Report), Peter Hilton (English Television News Report), Mona Husami (Asay's Mother's Voice), Saadi Soudavar (Asay's Brother's Voice), Billy Hart, Mike Mikos, Wil Petre, Laine Rettmer, John Robichau, Natalie Thomas, Kristin Warnick (Environmental Dancers), Camilla Webster (American Television News Reporter)

Élodie Bouchez, José Maria de Tavira in T*he Imperialists are Still Alive!* © Sundance Selects

FLY AWAY (New Video) Producers, Janet Grillo, Pavlina Hatoupis; Executive Producers, Catherine Hardwicke, Lee Adhamar G. Feldshon, David F. Schwartz; Director/ Screenplay, Janet Grillo; Photography, Sandra Valde-Hansen; Designer, Katie Byron; Costumes, Trayce Gigi Field; Music, Luke Rothschild; Editor, Danny Daneau; a Cricket Films production; Color; HD; Not rated; 85 minutes; Release date: April 15, 2011. **CAST:** Beth Broderick (Jeanne Cafferty), Ashley Rickards (Mandy), Greg Germann (Tom), J.R. Bourne (Peter), Reno (Liz Howell), Elaine Hall (Ms. Quinlan), Zachariah Palmer (Dylan), Aramazd Stepanian (Mr. Parseghian), Denise Y. Dowse (Susan), Jon Shestack (Samuels), Jay Sincere (Assistant), Peter Binswanger (Kid in Van), Matthew Grillo Russell, Angela Grillo (Elderly Woman), Cannelle Causse (Bartender), Jordan Roberts (Maitre d), Ashley Saunders (O.T. Aide), Ruben Gonzalez, J.B. Popplewell (Cashiers), Peter Blanchett, Lauryn King (Kissing Teens), Enrique Zaldua (Administrator), Charles Larson, Salvatore Camarillo (Groundskeepers), Luke Rothschild (Mr. Lanza), Tamaira Danyluk-Noriega, Fonda Jefferson, Maynor Lopez (Parents at Party), Oscar Ornela Jr., Brooke Star, Michael E. Wise (Kids at Party)

Beth Broderick, Ashley Rickards in *Fly Away* © New Video

THE TENANT (Indican) Producers, Melissa Gruver, Randy Molnar, Jaime Velez-Soto, Jr.; Director/Screenplay, Ric La Monte; Photography, Jose Zambrano Cassella; Designer, Stefan Price; Costumes, Beverly Safier; Music, Stephen E. Cox, Lee Riley; Editors, Drew Koller, Tom Pinnock; a ReelDreams Productions presentation; Color; Rated R; 103 minutes; Release date: April 15, 2011. **CAST:** Michael Berryman (Arthur Delman), J. LaRose (Jeff Thomas), Randy Molnar (Dr. Newman), Bill Cobbs (Jack Rymer), Georgia Chris (Olivia Newman), Sylvia Boykin (Ms. Tinsley), John Kyle (Adam), Justin Smith (Rob), Aerica D'Amaro (Liz Holliman), Ashley Totin (Loni), Christine LaRose (Emma), Haley Boyle (Lydia), Brooke Carroll (Carol), Gabriela Rodriguez (Janet), Travis Ingraham (Justin), Jennifer Sterger (Erin), Kevin O'Neill (Chief Cole), Valensky Sylvain (Sgt. Jackson), Elizabeth Judith (Mary), Louis La Monte (Lt. DiCosta), Robert DiCerbo (Frank Taylor), John Archer Lundgren (Dennis), Amber Freeman (Christie), Amanda Best (Katie), Alyssa Marie Kelly (Kassie, Patient), Ed Donovan (Lt. Malloy), Natalie Ackermann Montealegre (Dr. Alyssa Nichols), Olivia La Monte (Anne, Text Girl), Mike Harbison (Bill), Connor Boyle (Young Adam), Ryan Boyle (Teen Adam), Carrie Drazek (Mrs. Rogers), Brittney Fillon, Anna Lukas (Text Girls), Kenneth Matthews, Eddie Mitchell, Zachary Myerscough, Jaime Velez Soto (Patients), Courtney Paige Kramer (Caroline), Ashley Pinnock (Cassie the Paramedic), Robert Radosti (Police Officer), Hank Stone (Guy Chokin)

DUMBSTRUCK (Truly Indie/Magnolia) Producer, Lindsay Goffman; Executive Producer, Elon Musk; Director/Screenplay, Mark Goffman; Photography, George Reasner; Music, Daniel Licht; Editors, Sven Pape, Doug Blush, Alyssa Clark; a Figures of Speech production in association with Room 9 Entertainment; Color; HD; Rated PG; 85 minutes; Release date: April 15, 2011. Documentary spotlighting five ventriloquists; *WITH:* Bob Ashman, Dylan Burdette, Terry Fator, Dan Horn, Wilma Swartz, Kim Yeager; and Maria Ashman, Robert J. Asgman, Willie Brown, Barry Burdette, Jennifer Burdette, Aileen Carroll, Roger Carroll, Ed Casey, Megan Casey, Michelle Casey, Mark Anthony Ciarlante, Gary Cohen, Marlene Cohen, Sergio Croom, Melinda Fator, Levestia Graham, Marty Hamill, Terry L. Johns, Tom Ladshaw, John McEntee, Jimmy Nelson, Charlie Risner, Jane Risner, Annie Roberts, Michael R. Ruk, Bob Rumba, Tim Selberg, Scott Sibella, Rob Swartz, Lisa Sweasy, Mark Wade.

Terry Fator in *Dumbstruck* © Truly Indie

THE BLEEDING HOUSE (Tribeca Film) Producers, Will Battersby, Tory Tunnell, Per Melita; Executive Producers, Clara Gelatt, Jonathan Gelatt, Peter Askin; Director/Screenplay, Philip Gelatt; Photography, Frederic Fasano; Designer, Jaime Phelps; Costumes, Natasha Noorvash; Music, Hildur Gudnadóttir; a Reno Productions and Safehouse Pictures presentation in association with Cinergy Pictures; Color; HD; Not rated; 86 minutes; Release date: April 20, 2011. **CAST:** Alexandra Chando (Gloria Smith), Patrick Breen (Nick), Richard Bekins (Matt Smith), Charlie Hewson (Quentin Smith), Betsy Aidem (Marilyn Smith), Nina Lisandrello (Lynne), Court Young (Office Schmidt), Henderson Wade (Officer Bayne), Jonathan Gelatt (Jonathan Bell), Per Melita (Mr. Bell), Gretchen McGowan (Mrs. Bell), Victoria Dalpe (Beth)

Alexandra Chandro in *The Bleeding House* © Tribeca Film

WHAT ON EARTH? (Mighty Companions) Producer/Director/Narrator, Suzanne Taylor; Co-Producer/Editor, Mary Duprey; Photography, Gail Bates, Allen Branson, Suzanne Taylor, others; Music, Bruce Hanifan; Color; DV; HD; Not rated; 81 minutes; Release date: April 22, 2011. Documentary on the mystery of crop circles; **WITH:** Suzanne Taylor, Paul Akkerman, Karen Alexander, Francine Blake, Denni Clarke, John Paul DeVierville, Andy Fowlds, Simon Peter Fuller, Bert Janssen, Palden Jenkins, Nick Kollerstrom, Barbara Lamb, John Mack, Charles Mallett, John Martineau, Kerry McKenna, Andreas Müller, Janet Ossebaard, Daniel Pinchbeck, Lucy Pringle, Shawn Randall, Chet Snow, Paul Vigay.

WHEN HARRY TRIES TO MARRY (108 Pics) Producers, Sheetal Vyas, Nayan Padrai, Ritu Ahuja; Director, Nayan Padrai; Screenplay, Ralph Stern, Nayan Padrai; Photography, Nick Taylor; Designer, Jade Gloria Healy; Costumes, Ciera Wells; Editor, Jennifer Lilly; an Ash Pamani presentation of a 108 Production; Dolby; Color; Rated PG-13; 93 minutes; Release date: April 22, 2011. **CAST:** Rahul Rai (Harry Shankar), Stefanie Estes (Theresa), Freishia Bomanbehram (Nita), Osvaldo Hernandez Chavez (Louis), Caitlin Gold (Mary), Tony Mirrcandani (Dev Shankar), Zenobia Shroff (Geeta Shankar), Grant Kretchik (Slick Rick/Sikh/Doctor/TV Host), Kanti Pandya (Pandit Deepak), Actorr Patel (Chotu), Micky Makhija (Commissioner Shah), Lauren LoGuidice (Angela), Kai Chapman (Chinese Blind Date), Gia Crovatin (Waiter), Ivanka Garajova (Stripper #2), Spencer Bazzano, Julia Robles (Love Birds), Fatima Farid (Mrs. Shah), Andrew Gelles (Young Groom in the Park), Kapil Goswami (Arranged Marriage Groom), Kirti Kumar Hati (Priest), Suhel Jagtiani (Holi Party DJ), Pankaj Jhala, Stuti Karani (Sangeet Singers), Yvette Kojic (Gypsy Rose Lady), Kayla Mason (Jaklyn), Dhruv Amrit Mayra (Young Harry), Jena Mroz, Mia Perovetz (Lingerie Models), Megha Nabe (Game Show Bride), Nihaal Nath (Boy on Bike), Ursula Nath (Girl on Bike), Vishaal Pandya (Angry Indian Man), Michael Rosenblum (Prof. Kretchik), Aitan Shachar (Kamal, the Burnout), Eric Tronolone (Gay Student), Nidhi V. Vyas (Young Geeta), Kelly Washington (Young Bride)

Stefanie Estes, Rahul Rai in *When Harry Tries to Marry* © 108 Pics

BEAUTIFUL DARLING (JJay Productions) Producers, Jeremiah Newton, Elisabeth Bentley, Gill Holland; Executive Producer, Michael J. Newman; Director/Screenplay, James Rasin; Photography, Martina Radwan; Music, Gerald Busby, Louis Durra; Editor, Zac Stuart-Pontier; Presented in association with the Sundance Channel, Citi Prods.; Color/Black and white; HD; Not rated; 86 minutes; Release date: April 22, 2011. Documentary on Andy Warhol's transsexual "superstar," Candy Darling; **WITH:** Chloë Sevigny (Voice of Candy Darling), Patton Oswalt (Additional Voices): and George Abagnalo, Paul Ambrose, Penny Arcade, Peter Beard, Bob Colacello, Jayne County, Ron Delsener, Vincent Fremont, Aaron Richard Golub, Pam Green, Pat Hackett, Helen Hanft, Robert Heide, Melba LaRose Jr., Fran Lebowitz, Agosto Machado, Gerard Malanga, Taylor Mead, Paul Morrissey, Julie Newmar, Jeremiah Newton, Glenn O'Brien, Michael J. Pollard, Ruby Lynn Reyner, Geraldine Smith, John Waters, Holly Woodlawn.

Candy Darling, Andy Warhol in *Beautiful Darling* © JJ Prods.

ST. NICK (Beautiful Confusion Films) Producer, James M. Johnston; Executive Producer, Adam Donaghey; Director/Screenplay/Editor, David Lowery; Photography, Clay Liford; Designer, Ellen Weaver; a Zero Trans Fat production; Color; HD; Not rated; 86 minutes; Release date: April 22, 2011. **CAST:** Tucker Sears (The Boy), Savanna Sears (The Girl), Barlow Jacobs (Sam, the Homeowner), Mara Lee Miller (Girl with Guitar), Andy Sensenig (The Father), Laura Stone (The Mother), Richard Olsen (Church Caretaker), Harry Goaz (Detective), Brooke Devenney, Monique Byars (Mean Girls), Adam Donaghey (Police Officer), Cammi Heath (Young Woman), Aven Howell (Aven), Blair Rowan, Chris Gardner, Sandy Staley (Ranchhands), Toby Halbrooks (Convenience Store Clerk), Susan Doke (Mother at Birthday Party)

COUGAR HUNTING (Screen Media) Producers, Robin Blazak, Matt Sinnreich; Director/Screenplay, Robin Blazak; Photography, Dan Stoloff; Designer, Billy Jett; Costumes, Ellen Falguiere; Music, William Goodrum; Editor, Sandy S. Solowitz; Casting, Danny Roth, Dean E. Fronk, Donald Paul Pemrick; an Aspen Entertainment Group production; Color; Rated R; 102 minutes; Release date: April 22, 2011. **CAST:** Matt Prokop (Tyler), Randy Wayne (Dick Richards), Jillian Murray (Penelope), Robin Blazak (Linda), Vanessa Angel (Ursula), Lara Flynn Boyle (Kathy), Jareb Dauplaise (Tom), Frank Drank (Tattoo Artist), Ellen Falguiere (Red Dressed Cougar), Jim Ferraro (Rodger), Bryce Foster (Steve), Ricardo Gil (Ricardo), Laura Leigh (Skyler), Anthony Nuccio (Bill), Jared Petsche (Sad Hot Guy), Gabriel Pimentel (Gabriel), Paul Rohrer (Charlie), Kathryn Saari (Roxy), Matt Sinnreich (Jeremy), Nick Slatkin (Lucas), Kris Wheeler (Garcia), Melissa Wyler (Rhonda), Janice Rust (Bus Driver), David Meeker (Court Cop), Andrew Cader (Man in Tux), Jag Pagnucco (Judge), Kevin Parker (Ben)

Matt Prokop in *Cougar Hunting* © Screen Media Films

EARTHWORK (Shadow Distribution) Producers, Chris Ordal, Brendon Glad, Brad Roszell; Director/Screenplay, Chris Ordal; Photography, Bruce Francis Cole; Designer, Ruben Arana-Downs; Music, David Goodrich; a Hometown Collaboration in association with CO, ink; Color; Rated PG; 93 minutes; Release date: April 29, 2011. **CAST:** John Hawkes (Stan Herd), James McDaniel (Lone Wolf), Zach Grenier (Mayor), Laura Kirk (Jan Herd), Bruce MacVittie (Peter B. Kaplan), Chris Bachand (Ryan), Sam Greenlee (El-Trac), Brendon Glad (Cage), Scott Allegrucci (Andy Weiss), Everett Dexter (DeWayne Herd), Christie Dobson (Nina Kurtz), Tecia Esposito (Kaplan's Cool Chick), Jackson Hoy (Young Stan), Keaton Hoy (Evan Herd), Jon Niccum (Joseph Gerringer), Eleanor Patton (Ginny Breyer), John Pendleton (Pendleton), Patti Broyles Watkins (Delores Herd), Bob Augelli (Uninterested Patron), Matthew Hensley (News Producer), Dragan Ilich (Rental Rep), Ed Kershen (Delivery Man), Jeanne Kisling (News Reporter), Charlotte Kyle (Pregnant Woman), Carol Leighton (Urban Garden Store Clerk), Ashley Miner (News Assistant), Scott Richardson (Arts Patron Rep), Ed Seaman (Surprised Man at Party), Stewart Redwine (News Camera Operator)

Zach Grenier, John Hawkes in *Earthwork* © Shadow Distribution

HOODWINKED TOO! HOOD VS. EVIL (Weinstein Co.) Producers, Maurice Kanbar, Joan Collins Carey; Executive Producers, Bob Weinstein, Harvey Weinstein; Director, Mike Disa; Screenplay Cory Edwards, Todd Edwards, Tony Leech, Mike Disa; Designer/Art Director, Ryan L. Carlson; Music, Murray Gold; Editor, Tom Sanders; Director of Animation/Head of Story, Jeff Siergey; a Kanbar Entertainment presentation; Dolby; Color; 3D; Rated PG; 86 minutes; Release date: April 29, 2011. **VOICE CAST:** Hayden Panettiere (Red Riding Hood), Glenn Close (Granny Puckett), Patrick Warburton (Big Bad Wolf), Joan Cusack (Verushka the Witch), David Ogden Stiers (Nicky Flippers), Bill Hader (Hansel), Amy Poehler (Gretel), Andy Dick (Boingo the Bunny), Martin Short (Kirk the Woodsman), Brad Garrett (The Giant), Cheech Marin (Mad Hog), Tommy Chong (Stone), Heidi Klum (Heidi), Wayne Newton (Jimmy 10-Strings), Cory Edwards (Twitchy), David Alan Grier (Moss the Troll), Phil LaMarr (Wood/Ernesto), Benjy Gaither (Japeth the Goat), Danny Pudi (Little Boy Blue), Debra Wilson Skelton (Iana), Tress MacNeille (Vera/Woman's Voice), Clarissa Jacobson (Flo), Mike Disa (Helmut/Spider/Rhino/ HEA Agents), Rob Paulsen (Johann/Bad Shatner/Bad Kelley), Lance J. Holt (Klaus), Hayley Mills (Queen Azure)

EXPORTING RAYMOND (Goldwyn) Producers, Phil Rosenthal, Jim Czarnecki; Director/Screenplay, Phil Rosenthal; Photography, Geoffrey O'Connor; Music, Rick Marotta; Editors, Brian Singbiel, David Zieff; a Culver Entertainment presentation of a Where's Lunch production, a Full On Service production; Dolby; Color; HD-to-35mm; Rated PG; 86 minutes; Release date: April 29, 2011. Documentary on how the U.S. sitcom *Everybody Loves Raymond* was translated into a Russian television series; **WITH:** Phil Rosenthal, Max Rosenthal, Helen Rosenthal, Eldar Djafarov Arif-Ogli, Elena Stodubtseva, Marina Naumova, Artem Logilov, Sasha Tsyrlin, Jeff Lerner, Stanislav Duzhnikov, Anna Frolovtseva, Boris Klyuev, Konstantin Naumochkin, Aleksandr Zhigalkin

Phil Rosenthal in *Exporting Raymond* © Goldwyn Films

LEBANON, PA. (Truly Indie) Producers, Jason Contino, Ben Hickernell, Charles St. John Smith III; Executive Producer, Sally Fridy; Director/Screenplay/Editor, Ben Hickernell; Photography, Marc Jeff Schirmer; Designer, David Barnes; Costumes, Angeline Zeigler; Music, Matt Pond, Chris Hansen; a Reconstruction Pictures presentation; Color; HD; Rated PG-13; 100 minutes; Release date: April 29, 2011. **CAST:** Josh Hopkins (Will), Samantha Mathis (Vicki), Mary Beth Hurt (Jennette), Rachel Kitson (CJ), Ian Merrill Peakes (Andy), Brea Bee (Secretary), Cecelia Ann Birt (Doctor), Dominick Cicco (Pete's Dad), Tom Cleary (Rosary Man), Tara Copeland (Debbie), Roxie Cotton (Cafeteria Student), Hunter Gallagher (Chase), Josh Hunt (Pete), Christopher Mann (Bartender), James Mount (Craig), Sophia Paulmier (Chase's Girlfriend), Natasha Sattler (Roni), Jason Silvis, Jayson Vance (Bar Guys), Julia Yorks (Lauren), David Howey (Priest), Maureen Torsney-Weir (Counselor), Pete Pryor (Jeff), Lenny Haas (Terrence), Karen Peakes (Liz)

Josh Hopkins, Samantha Mathis in *Lebanon, Pa.* ©Truly Indie

Red Riding Hood in *Hoodwinked Too!* © Weinstein Co.

DYLAN DOG: DEAD OF NIGHT (Freestyle) Producers, Ashok Amritraj, Scott Mitchell Rosenberg, Gilbert Adler; Executive Producers, Christopher Mapp, Matthew Street, David Whealy, Peter D. Graves, Randy Greenberg, Kevin Munroe, Patrick Aiello, Lars Sylvest; Director, Kevin Munroe; Screenplay, Thomas Dean Donnelly, Joshua Oppenheimer; Based on the comic book series created by Tiziano Sclavi; Photography, Geoffrey Hall; Designer, Raymond Pumilia; Costumes, Caroline Eselin-Schaefer; Music, Klaus Badelt; Editor, Paul Hirsch; Visual Effects Supervisor, Olaf Wendt; Special Makeup Effects, Drac Studios; Stunts, Eric Norris; Casting, Elizabeth Coulon; a Hyde Park Entertainment, Platinum Studios Inc. and Omnilab Media Group presentation of an Ashok Amritraj/Platinum Studios production; Dolby; Widescreen; Color; Rated PG-13; 107 minutes; Release date: April 29, 2011. **CAST:** Brandon Routh (Dylan Dog), Sam Huntington (Marcus), Anita Briem (Elizabeth), Taye Diggs (Vargas), Peter Stormare (Gabriel), Kurt Angle (Wolfgang), Kent Jude Bernard (Slake), Mitchell Whitfield (Cecil), Michael Cotter (Phil), Laura Spencer (Zoe), James Hébert (Lorca), Dan Braverman (Big Al), Marco St. John (Borelli), Kyle Russell Clements (Roddy), Douglas M. Griffin (Harkin), Kevin Fisher (Tommy), Garrett Strommen (Josh), Tiffany Reiff (Jade), Brian Steele (Tattooed Zombie), Andrew Sensenig (Rosenberg), Bernard Hocke (Coroner), Kimberly Whalen (Kelly), Randal Reeder (Bob the Mechanic), Courtney J. Clark (Ally), George Wilson (Wino), J. Omar Castro (Bellboy), Dacia Fernandez (Vargas's Girl), Spencer Livingston (Sclavi), John Eyes (Bouncer), Karlee Rosenberg (Frost Stop Zombie), Kendall Rosenberg (Bromer's Cashier), Kelly Ford (Bromer's Shopper)

Brandon Routh, Sam Huntington in *Dylan Dog* © Freestyle Releasing

WE GO WAY BACK (Cyan Pictures) Producers, Peggy Case, Gregg Lachow; Director/Screenplay, Lynn Shelton; Photography, Ben Kasulke; Designer, Tania Kupczak; Music, Laura Veirs; Editors, Lynn Shelton, Michelle Witten; The Film Company production; Color; Not rated; 80 minutes; Release date: April 29, 2011. **CAST:** Ambert Hubert (Kate-at-23), Maggie Brown (Kate-at-13), Robert Hamilton Wright (The Director), Aaron Blakely (Jeff), Basil Harris (Pete), Russell Hodgkinson (Frank), Sullivan Brown (Jeremy), Kate Bayley (Tessa), Alycia Delmore (Felicia), Evan Whitfield (Harry), Nathan Graham Smith (Norwegian Tutor)

Maggie Brown, Amber Hubert in *We Go Way Back* © Cyan Pictures

LORD BYRON (Calponian Films) Producers/Screenplay, Zack Godshall, Ross Brupbacher; Director/Editor/ Photography, Zack Godshall; Costumes, Allisa Brupbacher; Music, Ross Brupbacher; a Zack Godshall/Ross Brupbacher production; Color; Not rated; 91 minutes; Release date: May 6, 2011. **CAST:** Paul Batiste (Byron), Renee King (Ex-Wife), Gwendolyn Spradling (Dancing Daughter), Kayla Lemaire (Laura), Eric Schexnayder (Teddy, the Obnoxious Boyfriend), Bria Hobgood (Girlfriend in Bed), Justin Bickham (Claudius), Katryn Schmidt (Cultured Girlfriend), Rebekah L. Smith (Hitchhiker), Rosco Hall (Drug Dealer)

Paul Batiste, Bria Hobgood in *Lord Byron* ©Calponian Films

PASSION PLAY (Image Entertainment) Producers, Daniel Dubiecki, Megan Ellison, Jonah Hirsch; Executive Producers, Rebecca Wang, Tyler Kwon; Director/Screenplay, Mitch Glazer; Photography, Christopher Doyle; Designer, Waldemar Kalinowski; Costumes, Lisa Jensen-Nye; Music, Dickon Hinchliffe; Editor, Billy Weber; Visual Effects, WhoDoo EFX; Casting, Mary Vernieu, Venus Kanani; a Rebecca Wang Entertainment presentation of an Annapurna Prod. In association with Coridel Prods.; Dolby; Color; Rated R; 94 minutes; Release date: May 6, 2011. **CAST:** Mickey Rourke (Nate Poole), Megan Fox (Lily Luster), Bill Murray (Happy Shannon), Kelly Lynch (Harriet), Rhys Ifans (Sam Adamo), Chuck Liddell (Aldo), Rory Cochrane (Rickey), Solomon Burke, Jimmy Scott (Themselves), Jerry Sawyers (Tommy), Mark Sivertsen (Walt), Frank Bond (Man with Walt), Robert Wisdom (Malcolm), Arron Shiver (Russell), Lora Cunningham (Nurse Kohl), Liezl Carstens (April), Alexandra Essoe (Audrey), Armin Amiri (Bartender), Brian Doyle-Murray (Billy Berg), Marc Miles (Jake), Susan Traylor (Red), Charlie Brown (Kurt), Chris Browning (Cecil), Mike Miller (Drunken Millionaire Singer), Bernardo Gallegos (Father), Marc Mouchet (Bandleader), Bruce McIntosh (Dr. Rosenblum), Andrew McPhee (Donnie), Josh Berry, Alan Blazek (Thugs), Dimitri Dimitrov (Maitre D), Antoinette Antonio (TV Reporter)

Mickey Rourke, Megan Fox in *Passion Play* © Image Entertainment

THE PEOPLE VS. GEORGE LUCAS (Wrekin Hill Entertainment) Producers, Vanessa Philippe, Kerry Deignan Roy, Robert Muratore, Anna Higgs, Alexandre O. Philippe; Director, Alexandre O. Philippe; Photography, Robert Muratore; Music, Jeeve, Jon Hegel; Editor, Chad Herschberger; Animators, Brett Nienburg, Blake Parsons; an Exhibit A Pictures production in association with Quark Films; Color; HD/Video; Not rated; 97 minutes; Release date: May 6, 2011. Documentary on how many of the fans of George Lucas' original *Star Wars* trilogy have turned against the filmmaker because of their displeasure with the second batch of prequels/sequels; **WITH:** Mark A. Altman, John Barger, David Brin, Matt Cohen, Brian Comerford, Michael Cornacchia, Rafik Djoumi, Art Douglas, Jaylin Duffield, Frankie Frain, Boo Friedmann, Neil Gaiman, Berge Garabedian, Peter Gardner, Chris Gore, Peter Hanson, Todd Hanson, Ray Harryhausen, Damian Hess, Phil Hill, John Holderried, Anthony Ingruber, Glenn Kenny, Daniel M. Kimmel, Brandon Kleyla, Ed Kramer, Gary Kurtz, Luis Lecca, Joe Leydon, Jonathan London, Chris Lumb, Richie Mehta, Tony Millionaire, Joe Nussbaum, Tom Payne, Bill Plympton, Dale Pollock, David Prowse, Erick Ramirez, Mark Reilly, Songe Riddle, Kevin Rubio, Richard Sandling, Adrian Sayce, Andrew Semans, Ann Skinner, Eric Stough, Lou Tambone, Howard Tayler, Charles B. Unger, John Venzon, Corey Vidal, Steven S. Vrooman, Chris Waffle, Anthony Waye, Mike White, Nar Williams, Paul Yates,

The People vs. George Lucas © Wrekin Hill Entertainment

VITO BONAFACCI (Cavu Pictures) Producer/Director/Screenplay, John Martoccia; Photography, Patrick Wells; Music, Joseph Prusch; Editors, Patrick Wells, Ingmar Cederstrom; an Anthony Stella production; Color; HD; Not rated; 97 minutes; Release date: May 6, 2011. **CAST:** Paul Borghese (Vito Bonafacci), Tisha Tinsman (Laura Bonafacci), Emelise Aleandri (Mother), William DeMeo (Father La Golbo), Louis Vanaria (The Gardener), Marcantonio Mei (Young Vito), Carin Mei (Marie), Maria Cofano (Sister Grace Vincent), Ercole Ventura (Grandfather), Mike Rizzo (Car Washer), Ralph Squillace (Barber), Rev. Richard Dellos (Himself)

Rip Esselstyn in Forks Over Knives © Monica Beach Media

FORKS OVER KNIVES (Monica Beach Media) Producer, John Corry; Executive Producer, Brian Wendel; Director/Screenplay/Narrator, Lee Fulkerson; Photography, John Orfanopoulos; Music, Ramon Balcazar; Editors, John Orfanopoulos, Brian Crance, Michael Fahey; Dolby; Color; Not rated; 96 minutes; Release date: May 6, 2011. Documentary on the benefits of a plant-based diet over processed and animal-based foods; **WITH:** Joey Acoin, Neal Barnard, Gene Baur, T. Colin Campbell, Junshi Chen, Mac Danzig, Connie B. Diekman, Caldwell B. Esselstyn Jr., Rip Esselstyn, Ruth Heidrich, David Klurfeld, Matthew Lederman, Doug Lisle, Terry Mason, John McDougall, San'Dera Brantley-Nation, Evelyn Oswick, Pam Popper, Alona Pulde, Anthony Yen.

AN INVISIBLE SIGN (IFC Films) Producers, Jana Edelbaum, Lynette Howell, Pamela Falk, Michael Ellis; Director, Marilyn Agrelo; Screenplay, Pamela Falk, Michael Ellis; Based on the book *An Invisible Sign of My Own* by Aimee Bender; Photography, Lisa Rinzler; Designer, Susan Block; Costumes, Sarah Beers; Music, Andrew Hollander; Editor, Sabine Hoffman; Casting, Avy Kaufman; an Ideal Partners presentation in association with 120dB Films, of a Silverwood Films production in association with Sidechop Pictures; Dolby; Color; Not rated; 96 minutes; Release date: May 6, 2011. **CAST:** Jessica Alba (Mona Gray), J.K. Simmons (Mr. Jones), Bailee Madison (Young Mona), Chris Messina (Ben Smith), Sonia Braga (Mom), Blythe Auffarth (Nan), John Shea (Dad), Ashlie Atkinson (Lisa's Aunt), Daniel Pearce (Danny's Dad), Sophie Nyweide (Lisa Venus), Emerald-Angel Young (Rita Williams), Marylouise Burke (Ms. Gelband), Joanna Adler (Lisa's Mom), Jake Siciliano (Elmer Gravlaki), Mackenzie Milone (Ann DiGanno), Ian Colletti (Danny O'Mazzi), Conor Carroll (5th Grader), Daniel Dugan (Attorney), Kevin Fung (Kevin), Crystal Block (Saleswoman), Lilly Hartley (Runner), Marin Gazzaniga (Hostess), Tom Nonnon (Dad's Doctor), Daniel McDonald (First Grader), Stephanie DeBolt (Ellen), Donovan Fowler (Levan Beeze)

Jessica Alba, Chris Messina in An Invisible Sign © IFC Films

UNDER THE BOARDWALK: THE MONOPOLY STORY (Rhino Films) Producers/ Screenplay/Editors, Kevin Tostado, Craig Bentley; Executive Producer, Stephen Nemeth; Director, Kevin Tostado; Photography, Jordan Guzzardo; Music, Larry Groupé; Narrator, Zachary Levi; a Tostie Productions in association with Rhino Films presentation; Color; HD; Rated G; 88 minutes; Release date: May 6, 2011. Documentary on the history of the enduring board game, Monopoly; **WITH:** Hank Azaria, Dale Crabtree, Bjørn Halvard Knappskog, Ken Koury, Richard Marinaccio, Matthew McNally, Domenic Murgo, Phil Orbanes, Tim Vandenberg, Kenneth Brandon Baker, Stephen Balzac, Randolph P. Barton, Lee Bayrd, Mark Bell, Ashley Berry, George Butch, Cory Casoni, Jason Chan, Geoff Christopher, Charles Darrow II, Rob Daviau, John Davis, Geoff Ellis, Stephanie Feeback, Roz Fisher, Merwin Goldsmith, Gary Heller, Bejai Higgins, J. Matthew Horton, Barbora Horváthová, Anthony Jucha, Martin Junghanns, Anthony Kellaris, Oleg Korostelev, Imelda Lasjim, Will Lusby, Jose MacPherson, Helen Martin, W. Eric Martin, John Meyer, Gabe Murgo, Henry Pakkala, Gary Peters, Lara Preister, Adrian Prince, Molly Qerim, Jane Ritson-Parsons, Andrew Shepherd, Shana Targosz, Dave Ulmer, Leon Vanendooren, Tim Walsh, Victor Watson, Craig Way

Under the Boardwalk: The Monopoly Story © Rhino Films

HARVEST (Monterey Media) Producers, Jody Girgenti, Marc Meyers; Director/ Screenplay, Marc Meyers; Photography, Ruben O'Malley; Music, Duncan Sheik, David Poe; Editor, Colleen Sharp; Casting, Stephanie Holbrook; an Ibid Filmworks production in association with Last Light Corp.; Color; HD; Rated R; 102 minutes; Release date: May 6, 2011. **CAST:** Robert Loggia (Siv), Jack T. Carpenter (Josh Winters), Arye Gross (Benny Monopoli), Victoria Clark (Anna Monopoli), Barbara Barrie (Yetta Monopoli), Peter Friedman (Carmine Monopoli), Adriana Sevan (Rosita), Kel O'Neill (Lenny), Christine Evangelista (Tina), Daniel Eric Gold (Seth Winters), Peter Appel (Mario), Rosemary De Angelis (Giuilia), Eileen Lawless (Florence), Jerry Matz (Nathan), Genai Corban (Susie), Daniel Raymont (Dr. Kenneth Noonan), Matt Salinger (Prof. Wickstrom), Peter Randazzo (Frank), Bob Dio (Jeff Winters)

Robert Loggia, Barbara Barrie in *Harvest* © Monterey Media

I'M NOT JESUS MOMMY (FilmDemic) Producer, Bridget McGrath; Director/ Photography/ Editor, Vaughn Juares; Screenplay, Vaughn Juares, Joe Schneider; Designer, Michael Nissen; Music, Karl Preusser; a Fortaleza Filmworks presentation; Technicolor; Rated R; 89 minutes; Release date: May 6, 2011. **CAST:** Charles Hubbell (Dr. Roger Gibson), Bridget McGrath (Dr. Kimberly Gabriel), Joseph Schneider (Bruce Gabriel), Aaron Aoki (Lab Tech), Debbie DeLisi (Roger's Sister), Aja Hale (Rebecca), Rocko Hale (David Gabriel), Ryan Kiser (Government Worker Nissen), Nora Montanez (Esperanza), Erik D. Pakieser (Grocery Store Soldier)

Rocko Hale, Bridget McGrath in *I'm Not Jesus Mommy* © FilmDemic

HEY, BOO: HARPER LEE AND 'TO KILL A MOCKINGBIRD' (First Run Features) Producers, Mary McDonagh, Christopher Seward; Director/Screenplay, Mary McDonagh Murphy; Photography, Rich White; Editors, Christopher Seward, Mary Alfieri, Sean Frechette, Fran Gullo; Narrator, Bob Mayer; HDCAM; Color; Not rated; 82 minutes; Release date: May 13, 2011. Documentary on author Harper Lee and her only novel, the classic *To Kill a Mockingbird*; **WITH:** Mary Badham, Boaty Boatwright, Rick Bragg, Tom Brokaw, Joy Brown, Michael Brown, Rev. Thomas Lane Butts, Rosanne Cash, Mark Childress, Jane Ellen Clark, Allan Gurganus, David Kipen, Wally Lamb, Alice Finch Lee, James McBride, Diane McWhorter, Jon Meacham, James Patterson, Anna Quindlen, Richard Russo, Lizzie Skurnick, Lee Smith, Adriana Trigiani, Mary Tucker, Scott Turow, Oprah Winfrey, Andrew Young; and VOICES: Jennifer Laird White (Tay Hohoff), Jane Beasley (Harper Lee), Bob Mayer (Truman Capote), Christopher Seward (Reporter/Maurice Crain), Donna Coney Island (Idabel Tompkins)

Gregory Peck, Harper Lee in *Hey, Boo* © First Run Features

VIDEO GIRL (Rasha Entertainment) Producers, Datari Turner, Meagan Good, Bennie R. Richburg Jr.; Director, Ty Hodges; Screenplay, Datari Turner; Photography, John Barr; Designer, Robert W. Savina; Costumes, Sandra Algood; Music, Andrew Markus; Editor, Noah Berlow; Casting, Pamela Azmi-Andrew; a Dan Garcia Productions, New Kingdom Pictures and Datari Turner Productions in association with God's Gang Entertainment; Color; Rated R; 100 minutes; Release date: May 13, 2011. **CAST:** Meagan Good (Lorie), Ruby Dee (Grandmother), LisaRaye (Lorie's Boss), Adam Senn (Shark), La'Myia Good (Stacy), Haylie Duff (Khloe), Paul Ben-Victor (Jermaine Stafford), Bun B (CK), Melyssa Ford (La La), Esther Baxter (Bubbles), Edrick Browne (Melvin), Amy Correa (Danielle), Honesty Edwards (Tasha), Leticia Jimenez (Jenna), Carnetta Jones (Mildred), Angela Lola Luv (Jessica), Don Mac (Reverend), Suelyn Medeiros (Taye), Laila Odom (Kandi), Shane Partlow (Gomez), Taylor Faye Ruffin (Morgan), Datari Turner (Jason), Phil Austin (Rehab Counselor), B.G., Lil' Boosie, Guy Broussard, Yung Joc, Jillisa Lynn, Angie Martinez, Webbie (Themselves)

Meagan Good in *Video Girl* © Rasha Entertainment

BROTHER'S JUSTICE (Tribeca Film) Producer, Nate Tuck; Directors, David Palmer, Dax Shepard; Screenplay, Dax Shepard; Photography, David Palmer; Costumes, Abigail Keever; Music, Julian Wass, Jeff Reed; Editor, Dan O'Hara; a Primate Pictures in association with Palmer Productions presentation of a Jeung Guns LLC production; Color; HD; Not rated; 86 minutes; Release date: May 13, 2011. **CAST:** Dax Shepard (Himself/Waylan/Patrick Jeung/Patrick Justice), Tom Arnold (Himself/Mark "Pappy" Jeung), Bradley Cooper (Himself/Dwight Sage), David Koechner (Himself/Senior), Nate Tuck, Greg Siegel, Jon Favreau, James Feldman, Andrew Panay, Ashton Kutcher, Laura Labo, Chevonne Moore, Jordan Morris, Charlie Koechner, Margot Koechner, Steve Tisch, Seth Green (Themselves), David Palmer (Camera Guy), Jess Rowland (Rick), Michael Rosenbaum (Dwayne Sage), Ryan Hansen (Lance Jeung), Josh Temple (Willie), Rome Shadanloo (Waylan's Love)

Dax Shepard in *Brother's Justice* © Tribeca Film

THE BIG BANG (Anchor Bay) Producers, Tony Krantz, Richard Rionda Del Castro, Erik Jendresen; Executive Producers, Gary Howsam, Lewin Webb, Ross Dinerstein, Rich Cowan, Richard Salvatore, Patricia Eberle, Cassian Elwes; Director, Tony Krantz; Screenplay, Erik Jendresen; Photography, Shelly Johnson; Designer, Steve Arnold; Costumes, Debra McGuire; Music, Johnny Marr; Editor, Fred Raskin; Casting, Kelly Barden, Paul Schnee; Hannibal Pictuires presentation of a Big Bang production in association with Flame Ventures and North by Northwest Entertainment, in association with Rollercoaster Entertainment and Blue Rider Pictures; Dolby; Color; Rated R; 101 minutes; Release date: May 13, 2011. **CAST:** Antonio Banderas (Ned Cruz), Thomas Kretschmann (Frizer), William Fichtner (Poley), Sienna Guillory (Julie Kestral/Lexie Persimmon), Autumn Reeser (Fay Neman), Jimmi Simpson (Niels Geck), Bill Duke (Drummer), James Van Der Beek (Adam Nova), Rebecca Mader (Zooey Wigner), Robert Maillet (Anton "The Pro" Protopov), Delroy Lindo (Skeres), Snoop Dogg (Puss), Sam Elliott (Simon Kestral), Robert Ernie Lee (Russell), Rachel Handler (Minkowski's Stripper), Sean Cook (Bartender), Khanh Doan (Mail Carrier), Keith Macgeagh (Sikh), Al Martinez (Janitor), Bill Marlowe (Skinny Faddeev), Devin Barber (Russian Orthodox Priest), John Pritchard, Shane Rice (Porn Stars), Bange (Camera Man), Vincent Aurora (Boom Operator), Reece Pearson (Clapper Guy), Jason Penrod, Tye Scott (Men in White Robes), Robert Martin (LAPD Cop), Brent Schneider, Courtney Yarber (Hospital Interns), Laura Van Der Lind (Kepler's Waitress), Lance Ortega (Sikh in Planck's Café), Paul Hassett (Warden), Brad Hollibaugh (Prison Guard), Chandra Bailey, Janelle Hoffmeister, Kristi Klicker, Katrina Mckinley, Adrienne Thommes (Strippers in Minkowski's), Balkar Singh, Darbara Singh (Sikhs in Collider), Amandeep Kaur (Hindu Woman)

HOW TO LIVE FOREVER (Variance Films) Producer/Director, Mark Wexler; Co-Producer, Mark Luethi; Screenplay, Mark Wexler, Robert DeMaio; Photography, Allan Palmer, Robin Probyn, Sarah Levy; Music, Stephen Thomas Cavit; Editor, Robert DeMaio; a Wexler's World presentation; Color; DV; Not rated; 94 minutes; Release date: May 13, 2011. Documentary on the various methods for prolonging life; **WITH** Gertrude Baines, Dolores Bates, Ray Bradbury, Aubrey de Grey, Brian M. Delaney, Phyllis Diller, Mordecai Finley, Sebastien Gendry, Jonathan Gold, Rathyna Gomer, Brian Harris, Pico Iyer, Marge Jetton, Tanya Jones, Madan Kataria, Ronald Klatz, Tricia Kurunathan, Raymond Kurzweil, Elaine LaLanne, Jack LaLanne, Thomas Lynch, Buster Martin, Shinei Miyagi, Kelly Morton, Al Mott, Samm Mullins, Scott Mullins, Zenei Nakamura, Sherwin Nuland, Kikue Okushima, Ushi Okushima, Don Parker, Edna Parker, John Robbins, Randall Roberts, Linda Salvin, Lisa Schoonerman, Diana Schwarzbein, Willard Scott, Takanori Shibata, Suzanne Somers, Shigeo Tokuda, Ellsworth Wareham, Eleanor Wasson, Craig Willcox, Jessica L. Williams, Marianne Williamson, Tyrus Wong, Heather Yegge, Akimitsu Yokoyama, Robert Young

Marge Jetton in *How to Live Forever* © Variance Films

SKATELAND (Freestyle) Producers/Screenplay, Anthony Burns, Brandon Freeman, Heath Freeman; Executive Producer, Brandon Freeman; Director, Anthony Burns; Screenplay, Anthony Burns, Brandon Freeman, Heath Freeman; Photography, Peter Simonite; Designer, Chris Stull; Costumes, Kari Perkins; Music, Michael Penn; Editor, Robert Hoffman; Casting, Tricia Wood, Jennifer Smith, Deborah Aquila; a Freeman Film production in association with Reversal Films; Dolby; Deluxe color; Super 35 Widescreen; Rated PG-13; 98 minutes; Release date: May 13, 2011. CAST: Shiloh Fernandez (Ritchie Wheeler), Ashley Greene (Michelle Burkham), Heath Freeman (Brent Burkham), Brett Cullen (David Wheeler), Melinda McGraw (Debbie Wheeler), Taylor Handley (Kenny Crawford), Haley Ramm (Mary Wheeler), Ellen Hollman (Deana Trammel), A.J. Buckley (Teddy Tullos), James LeGros (Clive Burkham), Casey LaBow (Candy Boyce), James Hébert (Tommy Dillday), D.W. Moffett (Jimmy Houston, Steakhouse Manager), Anthony Burns (Fireman Burns), David Sullivan (Luther, Super Mart Manager), Joshua Bridgewater (Suit Store Manager), Kent Jude Bernard (Vance "The Man"), Cameron Pierce (Lee), Caroline Horn (Caroline), Rachel Lee Magill (Susan Thompson), Lacie Manshack (Keely), Lanie Taylor (Young Michelle), Caleb Michaelson (Billy Means), Ross Francis (Danny States), Melissa Rude (Jennifer Jones), Morgana Shaw (Myrtle Burkham), Mark Wallace (Jimmy), Lisamaire Lamendola (Doxy Cougar), Brandon Freeman (Fireman Lowery), Christina Bailey (Lulu the Clown), Finch Nissen (Ham-Hocks), Jonathan McClendon (Hunter), Kerrigan Hightower (Pickle Girl), Scott Yarnell (Officer Fullmer), Kendrick Hudson (Chris, Musicland Manager)

Shiloh Fernandez, Ashley Greene in *Skateland* © Freestyle Releasing

VACATION! (Candy Castle Motion Pictures) Producers, Zach Clark, Daryl Pittman, Melodie Sisk; Executive Producer, Elijah Kelley; Director/Screenplay/Editor, Zach Clark; Photography, Daryl Pittman; Costumes, Danielle McIntyre; Music, Fritz Myers; a What's-It Co. presentation of a Gizmo Prods. production in association with This-and-That; Stereo; Widescreen; Color; HDCAM; Not rated; 90 minutes; Release date: May 13, 2011. CAST: Lydia Hyslop (Lorelei), Trieste Kelly Dunn (Donna), Maggie Ross (Sugar), Melodie Sisk (Dee-dee), Michael Abbott Jr. (The Surfer), Tony Greenberg (Infomercial Man), Ellie Nicoll (Infomercial Woman), Tara Everhart (Starla), Martha Stephens (Goth Girl)

Vacation! © Candy Castle Motion Pictures

MAKE BELIEVE (Level 22) Producer, Steven Klein; Executive Producers, Ed Cunningham, Seth Gordon; Director/Editor, J. Clay Tweel; Screenplay, Cleven S. Loham; Photography, Rich Marcus; Music, Lucas Vidal; a Firefly Film; Color; HD; Not rated; 89 minutes; Release date: May 13, 2011. Documentary on teen magicians; WITH: Ed Alonzo, Albert M. Belmont Jr., Gay Blackstone, Eugene Burger, Lance Burton, Joan Caesar, Joe Diamond, Bob Dorian, Kyle Eschen, Siphiwe Fangase, Eric Giliam, Andrew Goldenhersh, William Goodwin, David Gore, Hideo Hara, Hiroki Hara, Mio Hara, Neil Patrick Harris, Mark Kelly, Steve Kline, Matthew Knight, Bill Koch, Christine Koch, Anne Lambert, Krystyn Lambert, Derek McKee, Craig Mitchell, Richard Nakata, Christina Nkonyana, Nkumbuzo Nkonyana, Sean Paranuk, Ben Proudfoot, Aaron Rabkin, Nicholas Saint-Erne, Dustin Seamans, Dylan Seamans, Sharon Seamans, Mike Segal, Joanie Spina, Scarlett Tidy, Luis Villamonte, Becki Wells, Justin Kredible Willman, The Yamagami Brothers, Diana Zimmerman

GO FOR IT! (Lionsgate) Producer/Director/Screenplay, Carmen Marron; Executive Producer, Sid Idris; Photography, Christian Sprenger; Designer, Allessandro Marvelli; Costumes, Rosalind Gene Collection; Music, Kenny Wood; Editors, Carmen Marron, Anthony David, John Coniglio; Choreographers, Kristin Denehy, Rino Nakasone, Alison Faulk; a Pantelon presentation in association with Lionsgate and Sparkhope Productions, a God for It! LLC production; Dolby; Color; Rated PG-13; 105 minutes; Release date: May 18, 2011. CAST: Aimee Garcia (Carmen Salgado), Gina Rodriguez (Gina Esperanza), Al Bandiero (Mr. Martin), Louie Alegria (Pablo Salgado), Derrick Denicola (Jared), David Hernandez (Cuko), Rene Rosado (Nino), Andres Perez-Molina (Jesse Salgado), Jossara Jinaro (Loli), Rino Nakasone (Imported Delight Leader), Maya Chino, Ayodhya "Yoda" Jones, PeiPei Yuan, Mayuko Kitayama, Jeanine Carrillo (Imported Dancers), Ashlee Nino, Jessica Rabone, Diana Carreno, Katie Orr, Marissa Labog, Reina Hidalgo (All-Star Dancers), Katie L. Hall (Miss Simpson), Gustavo Mellado (Luis Salgado), Safia Hannin (Cecy Salgado), Liliana Montenegro (Irene Salgado), Peter Blanchett (Student in Class), Eloisa Garcia (Mrs. Lopez), Hector Garcia (Store Manager), Carlos Pratts (Carols), David Ross Paterson (Richard Hatton), Nicole True Armstrong, Ro Lott, Amy Fernandez, Jeannette Rodriguez (Dancers in Park), Karine Da Silva, Sophie Greene (Girlfighters), Karen Jin Beck (DJ SHY), Daniel Yabut (Danny), Brad Armacost (Jared's Father), Peggy Lee Goss (Jared's Mother), Yomi Perry (Gina's Mother), Alison Faulk, Teresa Espinosa, Lindsey Blaufarb, Keeley Kaukimoce (Beat Freaks), Lisa Roumain (Marina), Gil Menchaca (Juan), Somaya Reece (Somaya), Jennifer Horeni (Woman kissing Jared), Susie Mancini, Kristin Denehy, Sid Idris (Judges)

Aimee Garcia in *Go for It!* © Lionsgate

LOUDER THAN A BOMB (Balcony) Producers/Directors, Greg Jacobs, Jon Siskel; Photography, Stephan Mazurek; Editor, John Farbrother; a Siskel/Jacobs Prods.presentation in association with Own Documentaries; Stereo; Color; DV; Not rated; 100 minutes; Release date: May 18, 2011. Documentary on how students of Chicago's Steinmetz High School managed to compete in the city's annual Louder Than a Bomb teen poetry festival; WITH Novana Venerable, Adam Gottlieb, Nate Marshall, Lamar "The Truth" Jorden, Kevin "KVO" Harris, Jésus "L3" Lark, She'Kira McKnight, Charles "Big C" Smith, James Sloan, Kevin Coval, Peter Kahn, Cody Venerable, Elizabeth Graf, John Hood, Preye Porri, Robbie Q. Telfer

Nate Marshall in *Louder Than a Bomb* © Balcony Releasing

LIFE 2.0 (Andrew Lauren) Producers, Jason Spingarn-Koff, Andrew Lauren, Stephan Paternot; Director/Editor, Jason Spingarn-Koff; Photography, Dan Krauss; Music, Justin Melland; Music Supervisor, Eric Scott Hillebrecht; an Andrew Lauren Prods. and Palmstar Entertainment and OWN: Oprah Winfrey Network in association with Ro*Co Films International presentation; Color; Not rated; 99 minutes; Release date: May 20, 2011. Documentary on Second Life, a virtual online computer program.

LOST BOHEMIA (Impact Partners/This is That) Producers, Jody Shields, Jonathan Ferrantelli; Executive Producers, Abigail Disney, Pierre Hauser, Diana Barrett, Dan Cogan, Anne Carey; Director/Photography, Josef "Birdman" Astor; Music, Lev "Ljova" Zhurbin; Editors, Adam Zucker, Shelby Siegel, Michael Taylor; a Laszlo Pictures production; Color; Not rated; 77 minutes; Release date: May 20, 2011. Documentary about the last days of the Carnegie Hall Studios and the long-time residents who were evicted; **WITH:** Keith Barber, Jeanne Beauvais, Joel Benjamin, Andrew Bergman, Jean Birnkrant, Bill Cunningham, Norma Del Terzo, Clive Gillinson, Wynn Handman, Paul Jordan, Rosemary Lindt, Lucy, Billy Lyons, Frank Mason, Robert Modica, Christine Neubert, Poet, Rodica Prato, Judson Rosebush, Marian Seldes, Editta Sherman, Donald Dr. Shirley, Joe Siegler, Star Szarek, John Turturro, Tod Williams

Editta Sherman in *Lost Bohemia* © Impact Partners

35 AND TICKING (Image Entertainment) Producer, Eric Tomosunas; Executive Producers, Russ Parr, Kym Whitley, Mike Epps; Director/Screenplay, Russ Parr; Photography, Jeff Bollman; Designer, Jim Shaughnessy; Costumes, Roni Burkes; Music, Rico Stars, Ken Lampi; Editor, Dante Wyatt; a One Village Entertainment and Uptoparr Productions in association with Swirl Films presentation; Color; Rated R; 104 minutes; Release date: May 20, 2011. **CAST:** Tamala Jones (Victoria), Nicole Ari Parker (Zenobia), Keith Robinson (Phil), Darius McCrary (Nick West), Dondre Whitfield (Austin), Jill Marie Jones (Coco), Wendy Raquel Robinson (Callise), Kevin Hart (Cleavon), Meagan Good (Falinda), Clifton Powell (Zane), Lunell Campbell (Donya), Nicholas Williams (PJ), Mike Epps (Harold), Karon Joseph Riley (Roderick), Kym Whitley (Shavelle), Mechelle Epps (LaLa), Cametta Jones (Dr. Handcock), Mari Morrow (Toi), Ramsey Moore, Wendell James (Men), Kendrick Redfearne (Grip), Samantha Schacher (Counter Girl), Brett Weinstock (Waiter), Destini Edwards (Young Victoria), Aaron D. Spears (Officer Jones), Reign Edwards (Young Zenobia), Malcolm Ridley (Young Phil), Ethan McDowell (Fan #1), Angelique Bates, Samantha Cha (Gangsta Girls), Justice Smith (Mr. Dangles), John Bryant (TQ)

Nicole Ari Parker, Dondre Whitfield, Tamala Jones in *35 and Ticking* © Image Entertainment

COST OF A SOUL (Rogue) Producers, Sean Kirkpatrick, Edward J. Eberwine III, Jonathan Risinger; Executive Producers, J.P. Mascaro Sr., Sean Kirkpatrick; Director/Screenplay, Sean Kirkpatrick; Photography, Chase Bowman; Designer, Michael Crenshaw; Music, Rodney Whittenberg, Jonathan Risinger; Editor, Jonathan Risinger; an AMC Independent presentation of a Cast Shadow production; Dolby; Color/Black and white; Rated R; 108 minutes; Release date: May 20, 2011. **CAST:** Chris Kerson (Tommy Donahue), Will Blagrove (DD Davis), Mark Borkowski (Jake), Judy Jerome (Faith Donahue), Maddie Morris Jones (Hope Donahue), Gregg Almquist (Charlie "Bernie" Burns), Nakia Dillard (Darnell Davis), Daveed Ramsay (James Davis), Christopher Mann (Carl), Diane M. Johnson (Maybeleen "Mamma" Davis), Buck Schirner (Det. Marlow), Kamal Bostic-Smith (Sha), Franklin Ojeda Smith (Jackie), Todd Ryan Jones (Jon), Matty Shantz (Mickey), John Emanuel (Tre), Steven Johnson (Deke), Michael Kirkpatrick (Faith's Father), James Ritten (Jumbo), Kenneth Roehr (Toolie), Mario Troia (Tony), Yianni Digaletos, Ankit Dogra (Prisoners), Ron Fehmiu, Tim Lahren, Matt Regan, Jae Greene (MI Soldiers)

FLORENT: QUEEN OF THE MEAT MARKET (Magic Lantern) Producers, Trevor Laureence, David Sigal, Laura van Schnedel; Executive Producer, Nick Quested; Director/Photography, David Sigal; Music, Ezekile Honig; Editor, Trevor Laurence; Color; HD; Not rated; 89 miutes; Release date: May 20, 2011. Documentary on gay activist Florent Morellet and his Manhattan restaurant; **WITH:** Florent Morellet, Joseph Arias, Nora Burns, Robin Byrd, Darinka Chase, Christo, Frank DeCaro, Tom Eubanks, James "Tigger!" Ferguson, Murray Hill, Jackie Hoffman, David Ilku, Isaac Mizrahi, Julianne Moore, Lambert Moss, Richard Move, Michael Musto, David Rakoff, Lucy Sexton, Spencer Tunick, Sherry Vine, Diane von Fürstenberg

Florent: Queen of the Meat Market © Magic Lantern

BLOODWORTH (Samuel Goldwyn Films) formerly *Provinces of Night*; Producers, W. Earl Brown, Kenneth Burke, Shane Dax Taylor; Executive Producer, Corky Taylor; Director, Shane Dax Taylor; Screenplay, W. Earl Brown; Based on the novel *Provinces of Night* by William Gay; Photography, Tim Orr; Designer, Brian Stultz; Costumes, Leigh Leverett; Music, Patrick Warren, Randy Scruggs; Executive Music Producer, T Bone Burnett; Editor, Neguine Sanani, Jeffrey Ford; Casting, Mary Vernieu, Venus Kanani; a Buffalo Bulldog Films and Racer Entertainment presentation; Deluxe color; Super 35 Widescreen; Rated R; 105 minutes; Release date: May 20, 2011. **CAST:** Kris Kristofferson (E.F. Bloodworth), Frances Conroy (Julia Bloodworth), Dwight Yoakam (Boyd Bloodworth), Reece Daniel Thompson (Fleming Bloodworth), W. Earl Brown (Brady Bloodworth), Hilarie Burton (Hazel), Sheila Kelley (Louise Halfacre), Val Kilmer (Warren Bloodworth), Hilary Duff (Raven Lee Halfacre), Barry Corbin (Itchy), Brent Briscoe (Colbe), Ben Acland (Clerk), Bear Adkisson (Colt), Robert Beck (The Professor), Claudia Church (Patricia Bloodworth), John Churchill (Patricia's Lover), Gil Gayle (Spivey), Rance Howard (Ira), Mark Jeffrey Miller (Harwood), Travis Nicholson (Steve), Afemo Omilami (Sheriff Bellweather), Elizabeth Omilami (Cora), Michael Proctor (Hunter), Samantha Talbott (Counter Girl), Jilon Ghai (Junkyard Man), Tonya Watts (Bar Singer), Barbara Weetman (Mail Carrier), Hank Williams III (Trigger Lipscomb), David Ferguson (Junior), Brett Gentile (Ronnie), Fred Gill (Gil)

Reece Daniel Thompson, Hilary Duff in *Bloodworth* © Goldwyn Films

SPORK (Underhill Entertainment) Producers, Christopher Racster, Chad Allen, Honey Labrador, Geric Frost; Director/Screenplay, J.D. Ghuman Jr.; Executive Producers, Kevin Frost, Geric Frost; Photography, Bradley Stonesifer; Designer, Nathan Carden; Costumes, Samantha Kuester; Music, Casey James and the Staypuft Kid; Editor, Phillip Bartell; Choreographer, Denise Piane; Casting, Jeremy Gordon; a Last Bastion Entertainment presentation in association with Archer Productions and 11:11 Entertainment; Dolby; Color/black and white; HD; Not rated; 86 minutes; Release date: May 20, 2011. **CAST:** Savannah Stehlin (Spork), Sydney Park (Tootsie Roll), Rachel G. Fox (Betsy Byotch), Michael William Arnold (Charlie), Oana Gregory (Loosie Goosie), Halston Autumn McMurray (Tori), Chad Allen (Loogie), Marcus Bradford (Twix), Yero Brown (Tootsie's Dad), Matthew J. Cates (Donnie), Kevin Chung (Chunk), Keith David (Coach Jenkins), Rodney Eastman (Spit), Beth Grant (Principal Tulip), Odelia Hartl (Jecca), Elaine Hendrix (Felicia), Jenny Koh (Mrs. Chunk), Taaffe O'Connell (Mrs. Byotch), Kelly Park (Mrs. Tootsie Roll), Richard Riehle (Clyde), India Scandrick (Yo-Yo), Sydni Scurlark (Treena), Lili Sepe (JuJu), Yeardley Smith (Ms. Danahy), Francesca Tosti (Candace), Rozie Bala (Muslim Girl), Robert Bradvica (Smart Ass Kid), Tommy the Clown (Booty Ballroom DJ), Alissa Dean (Informercial Girl), Sarah Rochelle Gluzman (Jewish Girl), Donna Hardy (Old Lady), Jarrah Korba (Key Blond Girl), Jenny Phagan (Nerdy Teacher), Ke'Aira "Lil Daisy" Robertson, DeAndra Quarles (Black Street Girls), Rhett Rook (Red Haired Bully), Ali Sepasyar (Spikey Haired Bully), Victoria Strauss (Bunny Girl), Jon Yang (Asian Bus Boy), Jeff Feldman, Sherri Lewandowski (Teachers), Kylia Gray, Anaya Gilliam (Tootsie Roll Crew)

THE ABDUCTION OF ZACK BUTTERFIELD (Thunder Hill Pictures) a.k.a. *The Last Days of April*; Producers/Screenplay, Stephen Ryder, Rick Lancaster; Director, Rick Lancaster; Photography, Aric Jacobson; Designer, Marcia Schunemann; Music, Mark Krench; Editor, Kevin Grossman; a Metropolis Films presentation; Technicolor; HD; Not rated; 91 minutes; Release date: May 27, 2011. **CAST:** Brett Helsham (April McKenna), T.J. Plunkett (Zack Butterfield), Walter Masterson (Mike), Lisa Gunn (Marianne Butterfield), Aaron Letrick (Peter Butterfield), Celine du Tertre (Emily), Domenico D'Ippolito (Chris Briggs), Anthony Ames (Agent Quincannon), Richard Bellmund (Mechanic), Connor Buckley (Travis), James Filardi (Jimmy), Nina Rausch (Cindy Butterfield), Ryan Ward (Gary)

TIED TO A CHAIR (Gotcha Ventures) Producer/Director/Screenplay, Michael Bergmann; Photography, Douglas Underdahl; Designer, Tracy Steele; Costumes, Jenna Nankin; Music, Deborah Mollison; Editor, Jonathan Sloman; Casting, Michele Ortlip; a Process Studio Theater production; Color; Not rated; 94 minutes; Release date: May 27, 2011. CAST: Bonnie Loren (Naomi Holbroke), Richard Franklin (Henry Holbroke), Mario Van Peebles (Billy Rust), Aneta Grenda (Elena), Nicolas Roussiau (Pietro), Pamela Shaw (Ariana Firelli), Jerry Rudes (Jon Singer), Sayed Badreya (Kamal), Joselin Reyes (Det. Rosalie Aragon), Robert Gossett (Det. Peter Farrel), Ali Marsh (Liz), Kim Cristo (Loretta DeMarco), Christine Lawrence (Mrs. Colson), Justin Harris (Clarke Colson), Jerome Domenge (Travel Agent), Jeanne Bournaud, Caroline Le Moing, Victoria Olliqui (Aspiring Actresses), Francois Leroux (Gilles), Alexandre Boussat (Waiter), Didier Nobletz (Hotel Concierge), Doug Underdahl (ATM Man), Roseann Manos ($100 Bill Lady), Frederick Gaston (Taxi Dispatcher), Don Whatley (Naomi's Passenger), Brad Bellamy (Medical Examiner), Tom Stratford (Cop), Mallory Jones Danaher (Ron's Friend), Michele Dotrice (Grace), Jim Bracchitta (Joel), Herbert Rubens (Mordecai), Tony Cucci (Sticky), Garry Pastore (Eddie Foss), John "Cha Cha" Ciarcia (Sticky's Hitman), Mike Murray (Charles Emory, Plant Man), Sinead O'Keefe (Miss Matthews), Alfredo Narciso (Suleiman), Al Nazemian (Farukh), Alexander Wraith (Zac), James Freyes (Zeyn), Charles Santy (Mubarak), Victor Warren (Swat Commander), Frank Piazza (GPS Technician)

!WOMEN ART REVOLUTION (!W.A.R.) (Zeitgeist) Producers, Lynn Hershman Leeson, Kyle Stephan, Alexandra Chowaniec; Executive Producer, Sarah Peter; Director/Screenplay/ Photography/Editor, Lynn Hershman Leeson; Photography, Hiro Narita, Antonio Rossi, others; Music, Carrie Brownstein; Stereo; Color/black and white; Not rated; 83 minutes; Release date: June 1, 2011. Documentary on feminist art; **WITH:** Marina Abramovic, Eleanor Antin, Janine Antoni, Judith Baca,

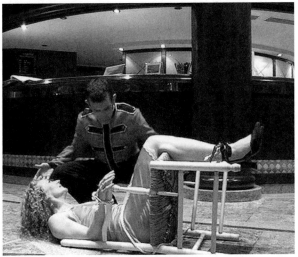

Bonnie Loren in *Tied to a Chair* © Gotcha Ventures

Cornelia Butler, Judy Chicago, Alexandra Chowaniec, Sheila De Bretteville, Mary Beth Edelson, Howard Fox, Susan Grode, Guerrilla Girls, Harmony Hammond, Amelia Jones, Miranda July, Yael Kanarek, Mike Kelley, Joyce Kozloff, Barbara Kruger, Suzanne Lacy, Krista G. Lynes, Yoko Ono, Howardena Pindell, Yvonne Rainer, B. Ruby Rich, Faith Ringgold, Rachel Rosenthal, Martha Rosler, Moira Roth, Miriam Schapiro, Carolee Schneemann, Cindy Sherman, Lowery Stokes Sims, Ingrid Sischy, Silvia Sleigh, Nancy Spero, Marcia Tucker, Camille Utterback, Cecilia Vicuña, Martha Wilson

! Women Art Revolution © Zeitgeist Films

YELLOWBRICKROAD (The Collective/Bloody Disgusting) Producer, Eric Hungerford; Executive Producers, Cassidy Freeman, Clark Freeman; Directors/Screenplay, Andy Mitton, Jesse Holland; Photography, Michael Hardwick; Designer, Joseph Varca; Editors, Judd Resnick, Eric Holland, Andy Mitton; a Points North Film; Color; HD; Rated R; 98 minutes; Release date: June 1, 2011. **CAST:** Cassidy Freeman (Erin Luger), Anessa Ramsey (Melissa Barnes), Laura Heisler (Liv McCann), Clark Freeman (Daryl Luger), Lee Wilkof (Clerk/Usher), Tara Giordano (Jill), Alex Draper (Walter Myrick), Michael Laurino (Teddy Barnes), Sam Elmore (Cy Banbridge)

Yellowbrickroad © The Collective

THE LAST MOUNTAIN (DADA Films) Producers, Clara Bingham, Eric Grunebaum, Bill Haney; Executive Producers, Tim Disney, Sarah Johnson Redlich, Tim Rockwood; Director, Bill Haney; Screenplay, Bill Haney, Peter Rhodes; Photography, Jerry Risius, Stephen McCarthy, Tim Hotchner; Music, Claudio Ragazzi; Editor, Peter Rhodes; Narrator, William Sadler; an Uncommon Productions presentation; Color; Rated PG; 95 minutes; Release date: June 3, 2011. Documentary on the environmental abuses of Big Coal corporations in West Virginia's Coal River Valley; **WITH:** Bill Raney, Bo Webb, Maria Gunnoe, Michael Shnayerson, Joe Lovett, Dr. Allen Hershkowitz, David Aaron Smith, Robert F. Kennedy Jr., Jack Sparado, Dr. Ben Stout III, Jennifer Hall-Massey, Gus Speth, Ed Wiley, Don Blankenship, Chuck Nelson, Lawrence Richmond, Antrim Caskey, Laura von Dohlen, Nick Martin, Joshua Graupera, Amber Nitchman, Joe Manchin, Ron Burris, Devra Davis, Susan Bird, Lorelei Scarbro, Brother Joseph Byron, Gary Gump, Lisa Jackson

The Last Mountain © DADA Films

REJOICE AND SHOUT (Magnolia) Producer, Joe Lauro; Executive Producers, Mark Cuban, Todd Wagner; Director, Don McGlynn; Photography, Stephen Wacks; Editor, Frank Axelson; a Deep River Films production; Color; Rated PG; 115 minutes; Release date: June 3, 2011. Documentary on the history of African-American gospel music; **WITH:** Smokey Robinson, Andrae Crouch, Mavis Staples, Ira Tucker, Marie Knight, Willa Ward, Ira Tucker Jr., Anthony Heilbut, Bill Carpenter, Jacquie Gayles Webb, The Selvy Family, Darrel Petties

Mavis Staples in *Rejoice and Shout* © Magnolia Pictures

LOVE, WEDDING, MARRIAGE (IFC Films) Producer, Michelle Chydzik Sowa; Executive Producers, Michael Arata, Jerry Daigle, Natalia Chydzik, Jeff Abberley, Julia Blackman, Stephen Hays, Peter Graham, Nathalie Marciano, Stefan Jacobs, Gary Raskin, Daniel March; Director, Dermot Mulroney; Screenplay, Caprice Crane, Anouska Chydzik Bryson; Photography, Ottar Gudnason; Designer, Carlos Menendez; Costumes, Antoinette Messam; Music, Blake Neely; Editor, Heather Persons; Casting, Nancy Nayor; a Chydzik Media Group presentation of a Michelle Chydzik Sowa production, a Voodoo Pictures production in association with Scion Films in association with 120dB Films; Dolby; Super 35 Widescreen; Color; Rated PG-13; 91 minutes; Release date: June 3, 2011. **CAST:** Mandy Moore (Ava), Kellan Lutz (Charlie), James Brolin (Bradley), Jane Seymour (Betty), Jessica Szohr (Shelby), Michael Weston (Gerber), Marta Zmuda Trzebiatowska (Kasia), Richard Reid (Ian), Christopher Lloyd (Dr. George), Alexis Denisof (Lloyd), Alyson Hannigan (Courtney), Colleen Camp (Ethel), Andrew Keegan (Jeramiah Stevens), Gabrielle Shuff (Adrianna), Bob Edes Jr. (Minister), Joe Chrest (John), Kim Vu (Amy), Kenneth Brown Jr., Brandi Coleman (Newlyweds), Michael Arata (Cheap Bastard), Mawra Bernstein (Cheap Bastard's Wife), John McConnell (Grateful Husband), Autumn Federici (Jessica), Sarah Lieving (Rachel), Julia Roberts (Voice of Ava's Therapist), Carol Sutton (Matchmaker), Ron Flagge (Voodoo Man), Victor Palacios (Cougar Hunter), Michael Showers (Toothless Man), Douglas M. Griffin (Paramedic), Dean West (Doctor), Gen Teasley (Receptionist)

Jessica Szohr, Mandy Moore, Bob Edes, Jr., Kellan Lutz, Michael Weston in *Love, Wedding, Marriage* © IFC Films

A PROPER VIOLENCE (Cinema Epoch) Producers, Chris Faulisi, Matt Robinson; Director/ Photography/Editor, Chris Faulisi; Screenplay, Matt Robinson, Chris Faulisi, Charlie Baker; Music, Timothy Falzone; a Red Wolf Films presentation; Color; HD; Not rated; 102 minutes; Release date: June 3, 2011. **CAST:** Randy Spence (Morgan Edwards), Justin Morck (Shepard), Shawn Maloney (Rich), Will Brunson (Dustyn), Beverly Lauchner (Lucy), Jeremy Goren (Joe), Joan Roman (Charlie), Tyler Nichols (Tyler), Timothy Selby (Bartender)

Randy Spence in *A Proper Violence* © Cinema Epoch

TURKEY BOWL (Tribeca Film) Producers, Kyle Smith, Stephen Paratore; Director/Screenplay, Kyle Smith; Photography, Jeff Powers; Music Supervisor, Lauren Marie Mikus; Editor, Brian Wessel; Color; HD; Not rated; 64 minutes; Release date: June 3, 2011. **CAST:** Morgan Beck (Morgan), Adam Benic (Adam), Kerry Bishé (Kerry), Troy Buchanan (Troy), Tom DiMenna (Tom), Zeke Hawkins (Zeke), Zoe Perry (Zoe), Jon Schmidt (Jon), Bob Turton (Bob), Sergio Villarreal (Sergio)

Turkey Bowl © Tribeca Film

BEAUTIFUL BOY (Anchor Bay) Producers, Lee Clay, Eric Gozlan; Executive Producers, Mark Moran, Richard Gabai, Richard Iott; Director, Shawn Ku; Screenplay, Michael Armbruster, Shawn Ku; Photography, Michael Fimognari; Designer, Gabor Norman; Costumes, Cynthia Ann Summers; Music, Trevor Morris; Editor, Chad Galster; Casting, Ania Kamieniecki-O'Hare, Tannis Vallely; a Gold Rush Entertainment and First Point Entertainment production in association with Braeburn Entertainment; Dolby; Technicolor; Rated R; 101 minutes; Release date: June 3, 2011. **CAST:** Mario Bello (Kate), Michael Sheen (Bill), Alan Tudyk (Eric), Moon Bloodgood (Trish), Austin Nichols (Cooper), Kyle Gallner (Sammy), Meat Loaf Aday (Motel Clerk), Bruce French (Harry), Cody Wai-Ho Lee (Dylan), Deidrie Henry (Bonnie), Logan South (Young Sammy), Gregory H. Alpert (Baby Shower Carl/Web Reporter Voice), Kelli Kirkland Powers (TV News Reporter), David Lipper (Radio Reporter Voice/Television Ranter), Nigel Gibbs (Police Detective),

Brooke Lyons, Michael Call (TV Reporter Voices), Jessie Usher (Basketball Teen), Davidson Park, Caleb Pearson, Joshua Shannon (Other Basketball Players), Darren O'Hare (Church Pastor), Myra Turley (Grieving Mother Patty), Bella King (Motel Clerk's Daughter), Drake Kemper (Teenage Burglar), Kylie Anderson, Tor Campbell, Judith DiGiacomo, Joe Dioletto, Mary Jane Gibson, Stephen Murano, Josephine Ullrich, Philip Zurfluh (Bill's Co-Workers)

Maria Bello, Michael Sheen in *Beautiful Boy* © Anchor Bay

THE LION OF JUDAH (Animated Family Films) Producers, Phil Cunnigham, Jacqui Cunningham, Sunu Gonera, Daniel Santefort; Directors, Deryck Broom, Roger Hawkins; Screenplay, Brent Dawes; Photography/Designer, Deryck Broom; Music, Greg Sims; a Sunrise production; Color; 3D; Rated PG; 87 minutes; Release date: June 3, 2011. **VOICE CAST:** Ernest Borgnine (Slink), Sandi Patty (Esmay), Anupam Kher (Monty), Michael Madsen (Boss), Georgina Cordova (Judah), Leon Clinghman (Tony), Scott Eastwood (Jack), Asunta D'Urso Fleming (Helda), Roger Hawkins (Hornsby), David Magidoff (Peter), Bruce Marchiano (Jesus), Alphonso McAulley (Drake), Vic Mignogna, Rodney Newman (Ravens), Omar Benson Miller (Horace), Serena Porter (Servant Girl), Matthew Rutherford (Wallace)

Esmay, Slink, Judah, Monty, Horace, Drake in *The Lion of Judah*
© Animated Family Films

ONE LUCKY ELEPHANT (Sandbar/Crossover) Producers, Cristina Colissimo, Jordana Glick-Franzheim; Executive Producers, Greg Little, Elizabeth Zox Friedman; Director, Lisa Leeman; Screenplay, Cristina Colissimo, Lisa Leeman; Photography, Sandra Chandler; Music/Co-Producer, Miriam Cutler; Editors, Kate Amend, Tchavdar Georgiev; a One Lucky Elephant production in association with Sandbar Pictures and Crossover Productions; Color; Not rated; 81 minutes; Release date: June 8, 2011. Documentary about David Balding's efforts to find a home for circus elephant Flora, after she has reached retirement age; **WITH** David Balding, Laura Balding, Scott Blais, Carol Buckley, Gay Bradshaw, Raul Gomez, Ron Magill, Cecil McKinnon, Toni Schamadan, Anouk Schmidt, George Smith, Willie Theison, Randy Tucker

David Balding, Flora in *One Lucky Elephant* © Sandbar

QUEEN OF THE SUN: WHAT ARE THE BEES TELLING US? (Collective Eye) Producers/ Editors, Taggart Siegel, Jon Betz; Director/ Photography, Taggart Siegel; Music, Jami Sieber; Dolby; Color; HD; Not rated; 82 minutes; Release date: June 10, 2011. Documentary on the world's honeybee crisis; **WITH:** Gunther Hauk, Michael Pollan, Vandana Shiva, Raj Patel, Carol Petrini, Horst Kornberger, Jeffrey Smith, Johannes Wirz, May Berenbaum, Michael Thiele, Yvon Achard, Gunther Friedmann, Scott Black, Hugh Wilson, David Heaf, Jacqueline Freeman

JUST LIKE US (Cross Cultural Entertainment) Producers, Taylor Feltner, Matthew Blaine; Director, Ahmed Ahmed; Photography, Taylor Feltner; Music, Omar Fadel; Editors, Benedict X. Kasulis, Veronica Rutledge; Color; Rated R; 72 minutes; Release date: June 10, 2011. Documentary follows a group of comedians as the try out their comic material in various Islamic countries; **WITH:** Ahmed Ahmed, Ted Alexandro, Sherif Azab, Whitney Cummings, Tommy Davidson, Omid Djalili, Erik Griffin, Maz Jobrani, Sebastian Maniscalco, Eman Morgan, Tom Papa, Maria Shehata, Angelo Tsarouchas, Noel Elgrably, Meena Dimian

REVERSION (Lane Street Films) Producers, Mia Trachinger, Rebecca Sonnenshine; Director/Screenplay, Mia Trachinger; Photography, Patti Lee; Designer, Reed Johns; Costumes, Michelle Wang; Music, Jonathan Snipes; Editor, Mischa Liningstone; Casting, Elizabeth Campbell; Color; HD; Not rated; 72 minutes; Release date: June 10, 2011. **CAST:** Leslie Silva (Eva), Jason Olive (Marcus), Tom Maden (Ray), Jason Frost (Ian), Indira Gibson (Midge), Tate Hanyok (Page), Justin Huen (Lee), Jennifer Jalene (Irene), Ed Refuerzo (Surfer Nick), Ina Barron (Stephanie), Dream Kasestatad, Mark Elias (Bad Guys), David Ury (Stranger), Beth Scherr (Darcy), Aly Mawji, George Contreras (Stoners), Rori Cannon (Elfin Girl), Bruno Giannotta (Victim), Lauren Spagnoletti (Wife), Antonia Bath (Beleaguered Wife), Jon Lance Duran, Jim Blum (Policemen), Derek Burke (Husband), Michael Klock (Arguing Husband), Jeremy A. Roberts (Suitor), Adam Briggs (Supermarket Muger), Jose Solomon (Supermarket Manager), Rob Zabrecky, Michelle Wang (Carjackers)

Leslie Silva in *Reversion*
© Lane Street Films

BATTLE FOR BROOKLYN (Rumur Inc.) Producers, Suki Hawley, Michael Galinsky, David Beilinson; Directors, Michael Galinsky, Suki Hawley; Photography, Michael Galinsky; Music, David Reid, Derek Bermel; Editor, Suki Hawley;a co-production of Marshall Curry Productions, LLC, and the Independent Television Service (ITVS); American-British; Color; Not rated; 93 minutes; Release date: June 17, 2011. Documentary on Brooklyn's failed Atlantic Yards development project; **WITH** Daniel Goldstein, Shabnam Merchant, Patti Hagan, Letitia James, Norman Siegel, Marty Markowitz, Bruce Ratner, Michael Bloomberg, Bruce Bender

IF A TREE FALLS: A STORY OF THE EARTH LIBERATION FRONT (Oscilloscope) Producers, Marshall Curry, Sam Cullman; Executive Producers, Nick Fraser, Simon Kilmurry, Sally Jo Fifer, Stephen Bannatyne; Director, Marshall Curry; Co-Director/Photography, Sam Cullman; Screenplay/Editors, Matthew Hamachek, Marshall Curry; Music, James Baxter, The National; a co-production of Marshall Curry Productions, LLC and the Independent Television Service (ITVS); Color; Not rated; 85 minutes; Release date: June 22, 2011. Documentary on the Earth Liberation Front, a band of radical environmentalists who cause destruction of companies accused of destroying the environment; **WITH:** Daniel McGowan, Tim Lewis, Jake Ferguson, Kirk Engdall, Jim Flynn, Lauren Regan (This film received an Oscar nomination for documentary feature).

If a Tree Falls © Oscilloscope Films

THE BEST AND THE BRIGHTEST (Flatiron) Producers, Patricia Weiser, Robert Weiser, Nicholas Simon; Executive Producer, Richard Schiffrin; Co-Producer, Declan Baldwin; Director, Josh Shelov; Screenplay, Josh Shelov, Michael Jaeger; Photography, John Inwood; Designer, Russell Barnes; Costumes, Eden Daniels; Music, Ted Masur; Editor, Peter Iannuccilli; Casting, Suzanne Smith-Crowley, Jessica Kelly; a High Treason Pictures and Wellfleet Phantasy Productions in association with Big Indie Pictures presentation; Color; DV; Rated R; 93 minutes; Release date: June 24, 2011. **CAST:** Neil Patrick Harris (Jeff), Bonnie Somerville (Sam), Amy Sedaris (Sue Lemon), Jenna Stern (Katharine Heilmann), John Hodgman (Henry), Peter Serafinowicz (Clark), Christopher McDonald (The Player), Kate Mulgrew (Player's Wife), Bridget Regan (Robin), Amelia Talbot (Beatrice), Nina Hodoruk (Upper East Side Mom), Michael Elian (Middle Eastern Bag Dealer), Suzanne Savoy (Chapin Headmistress), Jennie Grace (Altoids Mom), Cornelia Guest (Spence Mom), Brea Bee (Grace Church Mom), Kelly Coffield (Cindy Tanaka-Blumstein), Jos Laniado (Luis the Super), Maria Armesto (Consuela), Mets Suber (Abraham), Stephen Park (George Tanaka-Blumstein), Jalen Hoang (Yoshi), Amanda Phillipson (Lucinda), Nina Lisandrello (Bianca), Emily Tremaine (Mica), Richard Schiffrin (Corrupt Nassau Country Lobbyist), Urs Hirschbiegel (Man at Podium)

Neil Patrick Harris, Bonnie Somerville in *The Best and the Brightest* © Flatiron Film Company

A LOVE AFFAIR OF SORTS (Paladin) Producer/Director, David Guy Levy; Executive Producer, Mark Urman; Photography/Story, David Guy Levy, Lili Bordán; Music Supervisor, Howard Paar; Editor, Azazel Jacobs; a Periscope Entertainment production; Color; DV; Not rated; 91 minutes; Release date: June 24, 2011. **CAST:** Lili Bordán (Enci), David Guy Levy (David), Iván Kamarás (Boris), Jonathan Beckerman (Himself)

RAW FAITH (Alive Mind Cinema) Producers, Neil Kopp, Patty Brebner; Executive Producers, Scott MacEachern, Ashley MacEachern; Director/Photography, Peter Wiedensmith; Music, Nathaniel Morgan; Editors, Katie Turinski, Peter Wiedensmith; a Sameboat Prods. presentation of a WKE production in association with Film Action Oregon; Color; HD; Not rated; 86 minutes; Release date: June 24, 2011. Documentary on Unitarian minister Marilyn Sewell; **WITH:** Marilyn Sewell, George Crandall.

CONAN O'BRIEN CAN'T STOP (Abramorama) Producers, Gavin Polone, Rachel Griffin; Executive Producer, Kat Landsberg; Director/Photography/ Editor, Rodman Flender; Music Supervisor, Paul DiFranco; a Pariah production; Color; Rated R; 89 minutes; Release date: June 24, 2011. Documentary on comedian Conan O'Brien's 32-city "Legally Prohibited from Being Funny on Television" tour of 2010; **WITH:** Conan O'Brien, Andy Richter, Jimmy Vivino, Scott Healy, Mike Merritt, James Wormworth, Jerry Vivino, Mark "Love Man" Pender, Richie "La Bamba" Rosenberg, Rachael L. Hollingsworth, Fredericka Meek, José Arroyo, Jack Black, Aaron Bleyaert, Jim Carrey, Margaret Cho, Stephen Colbert, Deon Cole, Andres du Bouchet, Paul Duraso, Alison Flierl, Kyle Gass, Jon Hamm, Michael Kiss, Steve Kroft, Jack McBrayer, Matt O'Brien, Liza Powel O'Brien, Craig Robinson, Jeff Ross, Kristen Schaal, Brian Stack, Jon Stewart, Eddie Vedder, Reggie Watts, Jack White, Kristin Holt.

Conan O'Brien in *Conan O'Brien Can't Stop* © Abramorama

GENERAL ORDERS NO. 9 (Variance) Producer/Editor, Phil Walker; Executive Producer/Director/ Screenplay/Photography, Robert Persons; Music, Chris Hoke; Map Animation/Motion Graphics, Superlux; 3D Animation, Rival Industries; Narrator, William Davidson; a New Rose Window presentation; Color/Black and white; DV; Not rated; 72 minutes; Release date: June 24, 2011. Documentary on loss and change in the American South.

General Orders No. 9 © Variance Films

WITHOUT MEN (Maya Entertainment) Producers, Anthony Moody, Jason Price, Lucas Jarach; Director/Screenplay, Gabriela Tagliavini; Based on the novel *Tales from the Town of Widows* by James Cañon; Photography, Andy Strahorn; Designer, Michael Fitzgerald; Costumes, Oneita Parker; Music, Carlo Siliotto; Casting, Kerry Barden, Paul Schnee, Rich Delia; Presented in association with Tayrona Entertainment Group, an Indalo and Anthony Moody Production in association with Lucas Jarach/Jason Price Productions; Color; Rated R; 86 minutes; Release date: June 29, 2011. **CAST:** Eva Longoria (Rosalba), Christian Slater (Gordon), Kate del Castillo (Cleotilde), Oscar Nuñez (Priest Rafael), Mónica Huarte (Cecilia), Yvette Yates (Virgelina), Maria Conchita Alonso (Lucrecia), Guillermo Díaz (Campo Elias), Paul Rodriguez (Camacho), Camryn Manheim (Boss), Judy Reyes (Magnolia), Fernanda Romero (Ubaldina), Reynaldo Pacheco (Julio), Angel Amaral (John), Douglas Spain (Angel), Augusto Lopez (Suitor), Ray Santiago (Jacinto), Veronica Loren (La Gringa), Albert Polay, Martin Santander, Adam Jona (Guerrilla Rebels)

Christian Slater in *Without Men* © Maya Entertainment

THE PERFECT HOST (Magnolia) Producers, Stacey Testro, Mark Victor; Executive Producer, Martin Zoland; Director/Editor, Nick Tomnay; Screenplay, Nick Tomnay, Krishna Jones; Photography, John Brawley; Designer, Ricardo Jattan; Music, John Swihart; a Stacey Testro Intl. and Mark Victor Prods. presentation; Dolby; Color; HD; Rated R; 93 minutes; Release date: July 1, 2011. **CAST:** David Hyde Pierce (Warwick Wilson), Clayne Crawford (John Taylor), Nathaniel Parker (Detective Morton), Helen Reddy (Cathy Knight), Megahn Perry (Simone De Marchi), Joseph Will (Detective Valdez), Tyrees Allen (Roman), Brooke "Mikey" Anderson (Thief), Cooper Barnes (Rupert), Tracy Britton (News Reporter), Annie Campbell (Chelsea), George Kee Cheung (Storekeeper), Cheryl Francis Harrington (Rental Car Receptionist), Amanda Payton (Girl at Party), Mike Foy (Punk on Car)

David Hyde Pierce in *The Perfect Host* © Magnolia Pictures

CRIME AFTER CRIME (Life Sentence Films) Producer/Director/Editor, Yoav Potash; Consulting Producer, Gail Dolgin; Photography, Yoav Potash, Ben Ferrer; Music, Jaymee Carpenter; an OWN (Oprah Winfrey Network) and OWN/ Documentary Club presentation; Color; Not rated; 93 minutes; Release date: July 1, 2011. Documentary on how Deborah Peagler was unjustly convicted of the 1982 murder of her abusive boyfriend; **WITH:** Deborah Peagler, Joshua Safran, Nadia Costa, Yoav Potash, Bobby Buechler; and Tennille Villagomez (Crystal), Dee Kelly Barrett (Lee Esther), T'Onna Champagne (Debbie Peagler), Tiffany Champagne (Joyce)

Deborah Peagler in *Crime after Crime* © Life Sentence Films

LOVE ETC. (Paladin) Producers, Jil Andresevic; Jeffrey Stewart, Chiemi Karasawa; Executive Producer, Jonathan Tisch; Director, Jill Andresevic; Photography, Luke Geissbuhler; Music, Rob Simonsen; Editors, Alex Israel, Mary Manhardt; a Walnut Hill Media production; Color; Not rated; 94 minutes; Release date: July 1, 2011. Documentary following five New York-based relationships over the course of a year; **WITH:** Albert & Marion ("Lasting Love"), Ethan ("Starting Over"), Chitra & Mahendra ("Getting Married"), Scott ("Single"), Gabriel & Danielle ("First Love")

SEPTIEN (Sundance Selects) Producers, Brooke Bernard, Ryan Zacarias, Brent Stewart; Director/Screenplay, Michael Tully; Story, Michael Tully, Robert Longstreet, Onur Tukel; Photography, Jeremy Saulnier; Designer, Bart Mangrum; Music, Michael Montes; Editor, Marc Vives; a Nomadic Independence Pictures presentation; Color; Super 16-to-HD; Not rated; 79 minutes; Release date: July 6, 2011. **CAST:** Michael Tully (Cornelius Rawilngs), Robert Longstreet (Ezra Rawlings), Onur Tukel (Amos Rawlings), Rachel Korine (Savannah), Mark Darby Robinson (Red "Rooster" Rippington), Jim Willingham (Wilbur Cunningham), John Maringouin (Preacher), Jeffrey T. Williams (Wealthy Golfer)

Michael Tully in *Septien* © Sundance Selects

JOHN CARPENTER'S THE WARD (ARC Entertainment) Producers, Doug Mankoff, Peter Block, Mike Marcus, Andrew Spaulding; Executive Producers, David Rogers, Adam Betteridge, Rich Cowan; Director, John Carpenter; Screenplay, Michael Rasmussen, Shawn Rasmussen; Photography, Yaron Orbach; Designer, Paul Peters; Costumes, Lisa Caryl; Music, Mark Kilian; Editor, Patrick McMahon; Casting, Pam Dixon Mickelson; a Filmnation Entertainment in association with Premiere Picture presentation of an Echo Lake Entertainment production in association with a Bigger Boat; Deluxe Color; Super 35 Widescreen; Rated R; 88 minutes; Release date: July 8, 2011. **CAST:** Amber Heard (Kristen), Mamie Gummer (Emily), Danielle Panabaker (Sarah), Laura-Leigh (Zoey), Lyndsy Fonseca (Iris), Mika Boorem (Alice), Jared Harris (Dr. Stringer), Sydney Sweeney (Young Alice), Dan Anderson (Roy), Susanna Burney (Nurse Lundt), Sean Cook (Jimmy), Mark Chamberlin (Mr. Hudson), Andrea L. Petty (Mrs. Hudson), Jillian Kramer (Ghost Alice), Sali Sayler (Tammy), Tracey Schornick, Kent Kimball (Cops), Joseph O'Shaughnessy (Receptionist), Patrick Treadway (2nd Floor Nurse), Bev Holsclaw (Admitting Nurse)

Amber Heard in *The Ward* © ARC Entertainment

ROMEO AND JULIET IN YIDDISH (Nancy Fishman Releasing) Producers, Lazer Weiss, Mendy Zafir, Eve Annenberg; Director/Screenplay, Eve Annenberg; Photography, Inyoung Choi; Designer, Tricia Peck; Costumes, Jeff Sturdivant; Music, Joel Diamond; Editor, Jack Haigis; a Vilna City Films, DBA, Anatevka Films in association with Stratford Upon the Dnieper and Oscar Productions presentation; Color; Not rated; 92 minutes; Release date: July 8, 2011. **CAST:** Lazer Weiss (Romeo/Lazer), Melissa Weisz (Juliet/Faigie), Mendy Zafir (Benvolio/Mendy), Yoeli "Bubbles" Weiss (Mercutio/Mo), Isaac Schonfeld (Rabbi Lawrence/Isaac), Josef Yossi Friedman (Tybalt/Ty), Melody Beal (Melody), Eve Annenberg (Nurse/Ava), Yelena Schmulenson (Lady Capulet), Solman Wiser (Capulet/Faigie's Father), Aaron Keller (Aaron/Peter), Aaron Genuth (Apothecary), Luzer Twersky (Paris). David Germano (Zalman), Noam Harari (Mohammed), Reyna Schaechter (Juliet's Sister/Rivke), James Rutledge (Attorney), Dennis Wit (Professor), Mayer Kirshner (Montague), Amel Chennoufi (Mohammed's Sister), Samuel Blesofsky (Wedding Chazzan), Brittney Griffith (Massage Girl)

Lazer Weiss, Melissa Weisz in *Romeo and Juliet in Yiddish* © Nancy Fishman Releasing

FARMAGEDDON (Kristin Marie Prods.) Producer/Director, Kristin Canty; Co-Producer, Paul Dewey; Photography, Benjamin Eckstein; Music, Tom Phillips, Tom Martin; Editor, Cob Carlson; Color; HD; Not rated; 90 minutes; Release date: July 8, 2011. Documentary about the government's abusive treatment of this country's farmers; **WITH:** David Acheson, Kevin Brown, Laurie Bucher, Gary Cox, Paula Crossfield, Larry Failace, Linda Failace, Donald Fields, Jason Garnish, David Gumpert, Pete Kennedy, Jack Kittredge, Sarma Melngailis, Mark McAfee, Judith McGeary, Sally Fallon Morell, Annie Novak, Sharon Palmer, Ron Paul, Trina Pilonero, Morse Pitts, Jessica Prentice, Liz Reitzig, Jordan Rubin, Joel Salatin, Mike Seymour, Barbara Smith, Steve Smith, James Stewart, Debbie Stockton, Jackie Stowers, Eric Wagoner, Tim Wichtman, Jessica Ziehm.

Farmageddon © Kristin Marie Prods.

THE LEDGE (IFC Films) Producers, Matthew Chapman, Michael Mailer, Moshe Diamant; Executive Producers, Gregory Walker, Nick Thurlow, Tamara Stuparich de la Barra, Bobby Ranghelov, Tilo Seiffert, Marcus Schöfer, Christian Arnold-Beutel, Ortwin Freyermuth, Steven Saxton, Faisal S.M. Al Saud; Director/Screenplay, Matthew Chapman; Photography, Bobby Bukowski; Designer, Jim Gelarden; Costumes, Jillian Kriener; Music, Nathan Barr; Editors, Anne McCabe, Alex Hall, Jerry Greenberg; Casting, Shannon Makhanian, Avy Kaufman; a Foresight Unlimited presentation of a Mark Damon/Michael Mailer production, aVIP Medienfonds 4 Production in association with Rising Star; Color; Rated R; 100 minutes; Release date: July 8, 2011. **CAST:** Charlie Hunnam (Gavin Nichols), Terrence Howard (Det. Hollis Lucetti), Liv Tyler (Shana Harris), Patrick Wilson (Joe Harris), Jacqueline Fleming (Angela Lucetti), Chris Gorham (Chris), Maxine Greco (Consuela), Geraldine Singer (Doctor), Dean West (Frank), Brianna Dufrene (Gail), Jillian Batherson (Harper), Tyler Humphrey (Jimmy), Mike Pniewski (Lt. Markowitz), Katia Gomez (Selena)

Charlie Hunnam, Terrence Howard in *The Ledge* © IFC Films

FADING OF THE CRIES (Eammon Films) Producers, Karoline Kautz, Thomas Ian Nicholas, Brian A. Metcalf; Director/Screenplay, Brian A. Metcalf; Photography, Brad Rushing; Music, Nathaniel Levisay; Editor, Jeff Smith; a Ratio Pictures production; Color; Widescreen; Rated R; 93 minutes; Release date: July 8, 2011. **CAST:** Brad Dourif (Mathias), Thomas Ian Nicholas (Michael), Elaine Hendrix (Maggie), Mackenzie Rosman (Jill), Hallee Hirsch (Sarah), Julia Whelan (Emily), Jessica Morris (Malyhne), Lateef Crowder (Sylathus), Paul McCarthy-Boyington (John the Drunk), Jordan Matthews (Jacob), Pamela Clay (Jacob's Mother), Ryan Bartley (Anna), Philip J. Silvera, Heidi Shepherd, Scott Lilly, Patrick Hughes, Court Dickert, Diana de Mol, Michael J. Wagner, Marla Rea, Harry Zimm, Stuart Hirsch, Chris Graue, Taylor Thompson, Daniel Kennedy, Daniel Gonzalez, Tom Portanova, Martin R. Mikolajczyk, Mark VanKirk (Creatures)

Fading of the Cries © Eammon Films

SALVATION BOULEVARD (IFC Films) Producers, Cathy Schulman, Peter Fruchtman, Celine Rattray; Executive Producers, Gary Hamilton, Victor Syrmis, Scarlett Lacey, Andrew Sawyer, Neil Katz, Kirk D'Amico; Director, George Ratliff; Screenplay, Doug Max Stone, George Ratliff; Based on the novel by Larry Beinhart; Photography, Tim Orr; Designer, Clark Hunter; Costumes, Lynn Falconer; Music, George S. Clinton; Editor, Michael LaHaie; Casting, Sarah Finn; a Mandalay Vision presentation and production in association with DRO Entertainment, Cineric Inc., 10th Hole Prods. LLC, and Arclight Films International Pty. Ltd.; Dolby; Color; Not rated; 96 minutes; Release date: July 15, 2011. **CAST:** Pierce Brosnan (Dan Day), Jennifer Connelly (Gwen Vanderveer), Ed Harris (Dr. Paul Blaylock), Greg Kinnear (Carl Vanderveer), Marisa Tomei (Honey Foster), Isabelle Fuhrman (Angie Vandermeer), Ciarán Hinds (Joe Hunt), Jim Gaffigan (Jerry Hobson), Yul Vazquez (Jorge Guzman De Vaca), Howard Hesseman (Billy), Mary Callaghan Lynch (Bedelia Hobson), Ele Bardha (Officer Jensen), Cindy Chu (Alisa), Pamela Shaw (Lindsay Moll), Randy Ryan (Duane), Christine Kelly (Tabitha), John Hawkinson (Officer Smith), Mike Eshaq (Ahmad Nazami), Shana Schultz (Nurse), Debora Port (Victoria Day), Michael Maurice (Officer Bill Peale), Sean Scarlett (Orderly), Garrett Fuller (Todd Bowman), Martha Clarke (Anna), Bianca Binno (Laura), Ann Keeble (Mrs. Day), Larry C. Fenn (Father Figure), Josh Carrizales (Jorge's Guard)

Greg Kinnear in *Salvation Boulevard* © IFC Films

GIRLFRIEND (Elephant Eye Films) Producers, Jerad Anderson, Kristina Lauren Anderson, Justin Lerner, Shaun O'Banion; Executive Producers, Jackson Olivier, John Brooks Klingenbeck, Lorne Greenberg; Co-Producers, Sarah Steinberg Heller, Patch Mackenzie, Jackson Rathbone; Director/Screenplay, Justin Lerner; Photography, Quyen Tran; Designers, Seth Chatfield, Harrison Lees; Costumes, June Suepunpuck; Music, 100 Monkeys; Editor, Jeff Castelluccio; Casting, Brad Gilmore; a Make it So Entertainment presentation of a Wayne/Lauren Film Co. production in association with Patchmo Entertainment; Color; HD; Not rated; 94 minutes; Release date: July 15, 2011. **CAST:** Evan Sneider (Evan), Shannon Woodward (Candy), Jackson Rathbone (Russ), Amanda Plummer (Celeste), Jerad Anderson (Kenny), Harrison Lees (Harrison), Seth Chatfield (Jeremy), Joseph Turnbull (Willie Jones), Daniel J. Turnbull (Andy Jones), Nate Krawshuk (Simon), Craig Wesley Divino (Keg Master), Rachel Melvin, Blake Berris (Voices of Television Actors), Darren MacDonald (Darren Jones), Madelyn Welti, Kate Welti, Bette Houston, Nora Welti (Women in Deli), Carole Helman (Janis)

THE UNDEFEATED (Cinedigm Digital Cinema Corp.) Producers, Dan Fleuette, Stephen K. Bannon, Glenn Bracken Evans; Director/Screenplay, Stephen K. Bannon; Inspired by the book *Going Rogue: An American Life* by Sarah Palin; Photography/Editor, Dain Valverde; Music, David Cebert; an ARC Entertainment presentation of a Victory Films production; Color; HD; Rated PG-13; 110 minutes; Release date: July 15, 2011. Documentary on the unfortunate political career of Sarah Palin; **WITH** Andrew Breitbart, Tammy Bruce, Con Bunde, Kristan Cole, Kurt Gibson, Rick Halford, Tom Irwin, Sonnie Johnson, Mark Levin, Kate Obenshain, Judy Patrick, Jamie Radtke, Marty Rutherford, Meghan Stapleton, Gene Therriault, Tom Van Flein

IMPOLEX (Dorset Films) Producer/Director/Screenplay/Editor, Alex Ross Perry; Photography, Sean Price Williams; Designer, Anna Bak-Kvapil; Music, Preston Spurlock; Impolex Productions; Color; Not rated; 73 minutes; Release date: July 15, 2011. **CAST:** Riley O'Bryan (Tyrone S.), Kate Lyn Sheil (Katje), Ben Shapiro (Robinson), Bruno Meyrick Jones (Adrian the Pirate), Roy Berkeley (Lazlo), Brandon Prince (A Stranger), Eugene Mirman (Voice of Octopus)

DAYLIGHT (Cinema Purgatorio) Producers, Jay Van Hoy, Lars Knudsen, Ben Howe; Director, David Barker; Screenplay, David Barker, Alexandra Meierhans, Michael Godere; Photography, Nils Kenaston; Music, Stewart Wallace; Editors, Katie McQuerrey, Lee Percy; a Parts and Labor, Strange Loop, White Buffalo Entertainment; Color; HD; Not rated; 75 minutes; Release date: July 15, 2011. **CAST:** Alexandra Meierhans (Irene), Ivan Martin (Leo), Michael Godere (Renny), Aidan Redmond (Daniel), Brian Bickerstaff (Murph), Kendrick Strauch (Blackstar), Aylam Orian (Husband in Doctor's Office)

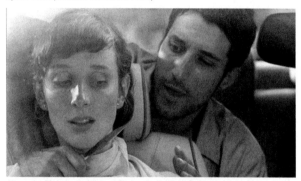

Alexandra Meierhans, Michael Godere in *Daylight* © Cinema Purgatorio

LUCKY (Phase 4) Producers, Caitlin Murney, Gilbert Cates Jr.; Executive Producers, Anthony Gudas, Matthew Chausse; Director, Gil Cates Jr.; Screenplay, Kent Sublette; Photography, Darren Genet; Designer, Frank Zito III; Costumes, Amanda Riley; Music, John Swihart; Editor, Gregor Plotkin; Casting, Barbara Fiorentino, Rebecca Mangieri, Wendy Weidman; a Ten/Four Pictures production in association with Tax Credit Finance; Dolby; Color; Rated R; 103 minutes; Release date: July 15, 2011. **CAST:** Colin Hanks (Ben Keller), Ari Graynor (Lucy St. Martin), Ann-Margret (Pauline Keller), Jeffrey Tambor (Det. Harold Waylon), Mimi Rogers (Ms. Brand), Adam Harrington (Steve Mason), Tom Amandes (Jonathan), Heather Marie Marsden (Allison), Dana Daurey (Wendy), Allison Mackie (Grace), Jason Harris (Radio DJ), Michael Arata (Piña Colada Man), Matt Harwell, Michelle Schrage (Reporters), Bryan McClure (Sandwich Guy), Mark Booker (Physical Therapist), Nic Roewert (Gay Guy), Renee Taglia (Jennifer), Michelle Davidson (Leslie Singer), Elizabeth Uhl (Stephanie), Bennett Wright (Young Ben), Sean Modica (Chip), Leanne Hill Carlson (Shanna), Helen Murray (Aunt Lois), Brett Comstock (Child in Store), Cheri Bloomingdale (Mom), Brent Spencer (Leslie's Father), Olivia Sather (Shannon), Meghan Strange (Woman eating Celery), Samantha Gutstadt (Dark Haired Woman), Eric Kirchberger (Chris, Sunny Mart Clerk), Matt Thompson (Photographer), Jeanne Averill (Saleslady), Jill Carr, Virginia Kincaid (Women), Olivia Johnson (Woman eating Cheese Fingers), Leanne Hill Carlson (Shanna), Thom Sibbitt (Mechanic), Mike Comstock

(Cameraman), Cullen Chollett, Ryle Smith (Men), Patrick Combs, Angelea Jenson (Anchors), Robert W. Baker (Sunny Mart Manager), Bernie Clark (Older Man), Kay Clark (Older Woman), Jeanne Averill (Saleslady), Lena Krussell (8 year-old Lucy), Brent Spencer (Leslie's Father)

Ann-Margret, Colin Hanks in *Lucky* © Phase 4 Films

AUTOEROTIC (IFC Films) Producer, Joe Swanberg; Executive Producer, Kent Osborne; Directors, Adam Wingard, Joe Swanberg; Screenplay, Adam Wingard, Joe Swanberg, Simon Barrett; Photography, Adam Wingard, Chris Hilleke; Music, Lane Hughes; Editor, Adam Wingard; Digital Effects, David Lowery; an IFC Midnight and Swanberry presentation; Color; HD; Not rated; 73 minutes; Release date: July 22, 2011. **CAST:** Kate Lyn Sheil, Amy Seimetz, Lane Hughes, Kris Swanberg, Frank V. Ross, Josephine Decker, Megan Mercier, Joe Swanberg,

Lane Hughes, Amy Seimetz in *Autoerotic* © IFC Films

TRUE ADOLESCENTS (Flatiron Film) Producer, Thomas Woodrow; Executive Producers, Gill Holland, Emanuel Michael; Director/Screenplay, Craig Johnson; Photography, Kat Westergaard; Designer/Costumes, Meg Zeder; Music, Peter Golub; Editor, Jennifer Lee; Casting, Meg Morman, Sunday Boling; The Group Entertainment and Unison Films presentation in association with Lunacy Unlimited of a Furnance Films production; Color; Super 16mm-to-HD; Not rated; 88 minutes; Release date: July 29, 2011. **CAST:** Mark Duplass (Sam Bryant), Bret Loehr (Oliver Mitchell), Carr Thompson (Jake), Melissa Leo (Sharon Mitchell), Emma Noelle Roberts (Cara), Lilly Perreault (Ashley), Linas Phillips (Slater), Davie-Blue (Jericha), Snow Keim (JR), Laura Kai Chen (Amy), Dave Hobbs (Casey), Elizabeth Cook Herron (Waitress), Katie Herron (Jessica Pascal), Erika June Mayfield (Celia), Jennifer Perreault (Candance), Rufus Tureen (Punk Kid #1), The Blakes (The Effort)

Mark Duplass in *True Adolescents* © Flatiron Films

GOLF IN THE KINGDOM (Golf in the Kingdom LLC) Producer, Mindy Affrime; Executive Producer, George Stephanopoulos; Director/Screenplay, Susan Streitfeld; Based on the novel by Michael Murphy; Photography, Arturo D. Smith; Art Director, Matt Karchesky; Costumes, Angela Billows; Music, Dame Evelyn Glennie, Ian Dean; Editor, Kathryn Himoff; a Mindy Affrime production; Color; Widescreen; HD; Rated PG; 86 minutes; Release date: July 29, 2011. **CAST:** David O'Hara (Shivas Irons), Mason Gamble (Michael Murphy), Tony Curran (Adam Greene), Frances Fisher (Eve Greene), Catherine Kellner (Martha McKee), Julian Sands (Peter McNaughton), Jim Turner (Balie MacIver), Joanne Whalley (Agatha McNaughton), Rik Young (Evan Tyree), Malcolm McDowell (Julian Lange)

Mason Gamble in *Golf in the Kingdom* © Golf in the Kingdom LLC

THE HARVEST (Cinema Libre Studio) a.k.a. *La Cosecha*; Producers, U. Roberto Romano, Rory O'Connor; Executive Producers, Alonzo Cantu, Rory O'Connor, Raul Padilla, Eva Longoria, Albie Hecht, Susan MacLauray; Director/Photography, U. Roberto Romano; Music, Wendy Blackstone; Editor, Nicholas Clark; a Shine Global presentation in association with Globalvision; Color; Not rated; 80 minutes; Release date: July 29, 2011. Documentary on the exploitation of child migrant workers; **WITH:** Victor Huapilla, Perla Sanchez, Zulema Lopez

ASSASSINATION GAMES (Samuel Goldwyn Films) Producers, Justin Bursch, Brad Krevoy, Patrick Newall; Director, Ernie Barbarash; Screenplay, Aaron Rahsaan Thomas; Photography, Phil Parmet; Designers, Paul Blanchard, John Welbanks; Costumes, Ioana Coricova; Music, Neal Acree; Editor, Peter Devaney Flanagan; Casting, Carolyn McLeod; a Mediapro Studios, Rodin Entertainment production; Dolby; Color; Rated R; 101 minutes; Release date: July 29, 2011.

CAST: Jean-Claude Van Damme (Vincent Brazil), Scott Adkins (Roland Flint), Kevin Chapman (Culley), Ivan Kaye (Polo Yakur), Valentin Teodosiu (Blanchard), Alin Panc (Kovacs), Serban Celea (Wilson Herrod), Michael Higgs (Godfrey), Kristopher Van Varenberg (Schell), Marija Karan (October), Bianca Van Varenberg (Bianca Bree), Andrew French (Nalbandian), Attila Árpa (Telly), Marioara Sterian (Mrs. Pavlescu), George Remes (Bartok), Iulia Lumânare (Maria Leonte), Florin Busuioc (Gregor Antonescu), Sorin Cristea (Milton Smythe), Ioana Pavelescu (Judge), Anghel Cristian (Bogdan), Salahadine H. Beztout (Max), Relu Poalelungi (Emil Lacroix), Ruxandra Stanciu (Adele Lacroix), Mario Marian (Danzo Yakur), Constantin Viscreanu (Police Officer), Alexandra Apetri (Rodica), Claudiu Trandafir (Doctor), Andrei Finti (Vadim Belsky), Florin Serbanescu (Belsky's Bodyguard), Loredana Groza (Loredana), Catalin Radu Tanase (Reporter), Justin Bursch (Ionescu), Kateryna Zakharchenko (Lena Belskaya)

Jean-Claude Van Damme in *Assassination Games* © Goldwyn Films

FORGED (Maya) Producers, Steven Holtzman, Josh Crook; Executive Producers, Joe Van Wie, David Alcantara; Director/Editor, William Wedig; Screenplay, William Wedig, Manny Perez; Photography, Zeus Morand; Designer, Jaime Whitlock; Music, Evan Wilson; Casting, Donna DeSeta; a Revere Pictures and Stay Tune Vision presentation; Dolby; Color; Not rated; 77 minutes; Release date: July 29, 2011. **CAST:** Manny Perez (Chuco), David Castro (Machito), Margo Martindale (Dianne), Jaime Tirelli (Cesar), Kevin Breznahan (Moose), John Bianco (Frederico), Karen Christie-Ward (Waitress), Steve Cirbus (Stanley), Anthony DeFelice (Parole Board Spokesman), Lanny Flaherty (Tom), Arthur French (Old Man), Robert Haley (Wallace), Christopher Halladay (Foster Father), Laura Heisler (Ashley), Clark Jackson (Bo), Ernestine Jackson (Old Woman), Peter Patrikios (Trucker), Matthew Rios (Young Machito), Tony Ray Rossi (Anthony), Jen Smith (Hot Girl), Dan Teachout (Guy), Joe Van Wie (Billy), April Valvano, Dustin Charles (Parole Board Members)

ALL SHE CAN (Maya) a.k.a. *Benavides Born*; Producers, Daniel Meisel, Susan Kirr; Executive Producers, Hall Wendel, Todd Barnes; Director, Amy Wendel; Screenplay, Amy Wendel, Daniel Meisel; Photography, Rob Hauer; Designer, Jade Healy; Costumes, Amy Maner; Music, Kevin Afflack; Editor, Andres Santamaria; Casting, Toni Cobb Brock, Sally Allen; a Kapok Pictures presentation; Color; Not rated; 91 minutes; Release date: July 29, 2011. **CAST:** Corina Calderon (Luz), Jeremy Ray Valdez (Raynaldo), Joseph Julian Soria (Luis), Julia Vera (Abuela), Julio César Cedillo (Coach Chapa), Julian Works (Carlos), Leticia Magaña (Rosana), Amanda Rivas (Yasmin), Erika Cervantes (Nicole), Jaime Medeles (JM), Gustavo Gomez (Manuel), Manuel Garcia (Sgt. Lopez), Hector Machado (Principal Martinez), Gloria Gutierrez (Gloria Reyes), Rudy Treviño (Head Meet Official), Sonia Acevedo (Mariana – Illegal Immigrant Mother), Thomas Christopher Nieto (Juan), Adalberto Gonazales (Octavio), Cora Cardona (Curandera), Santiago Villalobos (Drug Dealer), Aileen Elizondo (Meet Official), Edmundo B. Garcia, Jr. (Sgt. Marquez), Pedro Garcia (Petey), Pam Garcia (Herself – Monologue), Amparo García (Corina), Consuelo Alvarado (English Teacher), Ruperto Canales III

(Science Teacher), Deborah Leal, Viviana G. Saenz, Andres Elizondo II (Detention Officers), Augustine Garza (Director of Freshman Admissions, University of Texas), Sally Jackson (UT Receptionist), Mayra Guerrero (Coast Bend College Admission Officer), Luis Octavio Gutierrez (Raynaldo's Father), F.H. Canales Jr., Luis Garza (Oil Rig Managers), Junelle Vasquez (Powerlifter), George Luna, Ray Soliz (Powerlifting Coaches), Vidal Conde, Michael Rogge (Powerlifting Judges), Benito Retortillo (Priest), Blanca Villarreal-Gutierrez (AEP Teacher), Sal Hernandez (Police Officer), Kareny Campos (Juvenile Detention Teacher), Amy Gutierrez (National Anthem Singer)

Corina Calderon, Joseph Julian Soria in *All She Can* © Maya Entertainment

WHERE THE ROAD MEETS THE SUN (Maya) Producers, Brett Henenberg, Delon Tio, Yong Mun Chee; Director/Screenplay, Yong Mun Chee; Photography, Gavin Kelly; Designer, Linda Sena; Costumes, Elaine Montalvo; Music, Patrick Kirst; Editor, Azhar Ismon; a Singapore Film Commission and Big Machine Films presentation in association with Nation Pictures; American-Singapore; Color; Not rated; 93 minutes; Release date: July 29, 2011. **CAST:** Eric Mabius (Blake), Laura Ramsey (Sandra), Will Yun Lee (Takashi), Fernando Noriega (Julio), Luke Brandon Field (Guy), Elsa Pataky (Michelle), Emmanuelle Vaugier (Lisa), Erick Avari (Dadi), Jesse Garcia (Jose), Rati Gupta (Yamini), Manuk Aret (Toma), Lina Esco (Natasha), Todd Leigh (Chris), Brois Lee Krutonog (Raffi), Kazumi Aihara (Moshi), Max Bird-Ridnell (Jacob), Edmond Choi (Doctor), Edward Coram-James (Charlie), Rico Devereaux (Giovanni), Leslie Garza (Mom), Carlos Linares (Fernando), Celine Linarte (Misaki), Euriamis Losada (Spikey), Alberto Manquero (Jackie), Adi Marriott (Amir), Mike Moh (Misaki's New Love), Jeff Newman (Big Joe), Peter Nikkos (Armo "The Enforcer"), Deborah Png (Chinese Lady), Mickey Sanchez de Cima (Frankie), Amit Shah (Aamir), Ivan Shulver (Sebastian), Tonje Solheim (Towel Girl), Faradj Vaziri (Ara), Sid Veda (Gupta), Tim Venable (Daron)

Luke Brandon Field, Laura Ramsey in *Where the Road Meets the Sun* © Maya Entertainment

MAGIC TRIP (Magnolia) Producers, Will Clarke, Alex Gibney, Alexandra Johnes; Executive Producers, David McKillop, Molly Thompson, Robert Belau, David Kowitz, Gareth Wiley; Directors/Screenplay, Alex Gibney, Alison Ellwood; Based on the words and recordings of Ken Kesey; Music, David Kahne; Music Supervisor, John McCullough; Editor, Alison Ellwood; Interviewer, Stanley Tucci; a History Films presentation in association with Optimum Releasing, Imaginary Forces and Jigsaw Productions of an Alex Gibney production in association with Phoenix Wiley Ltd.; Dolby; Color; Not rated; 107 minutes; Release date: August 5, 2011. Documentary on author Ken Kesey and his "Merry Band of Pranksters" and their 1964 LSD-fueled road trip to the New York World's Fair.

Timothy Leary, Neal Cassady in *Magic Trip* © Magnolia Pictures

THE PERFECT AGE OF ROCK 'N' ROLL (Redhawk Films) Producers, Joseph White, Scott Rosenbaum, Neil Carter, Michael Ellis; Director, Scott Rosenbaum; Screenplay, Scott Rosenbaum, Jasin Cadic; Photography, Tom Richmond; Editor, Madeleine Gavin; Designer, Sarah Frank; Music, Andrew Hollander; Music Supervisor, Christopher Covert; a Red Hawk Films production; Color; Rated R; 91 minutes; Release date: August 5, 2011. **CAST:** Kevin Zegers (Spyder), Jason Ritter (Eric Genson), Taryn Manning (Rose Atropos), Lukas Haas (Clifton Hangar), Peter Fonda (August West), Lauren Holly (Liza Genson), Kelly Lynch (Maggie), Aimee Teegarden (Annie Genson), Billy Dee Williams (Ace Milestone), Eileen Alana (Warren's Girlfriend), Sugar Blue, Pinetop Perkins, Hubert Sumlin, Willie "Big Eyes" Smith, Robert Stroger (Themselves), Jasin Cadic (Bixx), Ruby Dee (Miss Candy), Martin Erspamer (Bonzo), Keren Gilbert (Teacher), Michael Jeremiah (Lead Vocalist of the Hawks), Scoop Slone (Engineer), Bobbi Jo Kitchen (Bobbi Jo), Billy Morrison (Fashion Jones), James Ransone (Chip Genson), Danielle Simone (Charlie), Craig Snitkoff (Young Eric), Michael Kenneth Williams (Sonnyboy), Ron "Bumblefoot" Thal, Alan Gary, Chris Kiszka, Gary Gray (Hawks), Rodney "Bear" Jackson (Big Bear), Bradley Williams (Brad)

Kevin Zegers in *The Perfect Age of Rock 'n' Roll* © Redhawk Films

FINAL DESTINATION 5 (WB/New Line Cinema) Producers, Craig Perry, Warren Zide; Executive Producers, Richard Brener, Walter Hamada, Dave Neustadter, Erik Holmberg, Sheila Hanahan Taylor; Director, Steven Quale; Screenplay, Eric Heisserer; Based on characters created by Jeffrey Reddick; Photography, Brian Pearson; Designer, David R. Sandefur; Costumes, Jori Woodman; Music, Brian Tyler; Editor, Eric Sears; Visual Effects Supervisor, Ariel Velasco Shaw; Casting, Eyde Belasco; a Practical Pictures/Zide Pictures production; Dolby; Widescreen; Color; 3D; Rated R; 92 minutes; Release date: August 12, 2011. **CAST:** Nicholas D'Agosto (Sam Lawton), Emma Bell (Molly Harper), Miles Fisher (Peter Friedkin), Ellen Wroe (Candice Hooper), Jacqueline MacInnes Wood (Olivia Castle), P.J. Byrne (Isaac Palmer), Arlen Escarpeta (Nathan), David Koechner (Dennis), Courtney B. Vance (Agent Jim Block), Tony Todd (William Bludworth), Brent Stait (Roy), Roman Podhora (John), Jasmin Dring (Cho), Barclay Hope (Dr. Leonetti), Chasty Ballesteros (Spa Receptionist), Mike Dopud (Chef), Tanya Hubbard (Coach), Frank Topol (Federal Agent), Tim Fellingham (Rocker), Blaine Anderson (Crime Scene Tech), Dawn Chubai (Reporter), Ryan Hesp (Mike the Waiter), Ian Thompson (Bus Driver), Andy Nez (Campus Security), Jodi Balfour (Woman), June B. Wilde (FD1 Passenger), Brittany Rogers (Porter), Diana Pavlovská (Flight Attendant), Michael Adamthwaite (Line Cook), Grace Baek (Spa Technician)

Nicholas D'Agosto, Emma Bell, Arlen Escarpeta, Miles Fischer in *Final Destination 5* © New Line Cinema

BAD POSTURE (Armian Pictures) Producers, Lucy Bickerton, Neda Armian; Executive Producers, Malcolm Murray, Megan Baldrige; Director/Photography/Editor, Malcolm Murray; Screenplay, Florian Brozek; Designer, Rich Watts; Music Supervisor, Andrew Chugg; a Rooftop Films production; Color; DV; Not rated; 93 minutes; Release date: August 12, 2011. **CAST:** Florian Brozek (Flo), Trey Cole (Trey), Tabatha Shaun (Marissa), Jason Gutierrez (Jason), Norman Everett (Norm), John Romero (John), Greg Tafoya (Marvel), Joseph Otero (Banks), Mateo Sigwerth (Mateo), Tyrone Trammel (Fly), Joseph Quintana (Booter), W.C. Longacre (W.C.), Manuel Lopez (Manuel), Shangreaux Lagrave (Flo's Boss), Wacey Lee Contant, Joseph Le Compte (Party Guys), Julia Romero (Jessica), Giovanna Hinojosa (Candice), Ximena Araya (Ximena), Amy Archuleta (Amy), Archie Richardson (Archie), Kenneth Ashley (Ken), Joseph Sullivan, Paul Giannini, Melvin Mayes (Graffiti Writers), Jesse Hesch (Marissa's Brother), Brad Jonathan Ramos (Rollerblading Kid), Delwar Alam (Carl Mart Clerk), Hector Alvarado (Food Truck Proprietor), W.M. Miller, Jimmy Martinez (Bus Stop)

LITTLEROCK (Variance) Producers, Fred Thornton, Laura Ragsdale, Sierra Leoni; Executive Producers, Hsin-Fang Li, Denny Densmore; Director/Screenplay, Mike Ott; Story, Mike Ott, Atsuko Okatsuka, Carl McLaughlin; Photography, Carl McLaughlin; Music, The Cave Singers; Editor, David Nordstrom; a Small Form Films production; Dolby; Color; Not rated; 88 minutes; Release date: August 12, 2011. **CAST:** Atsuko Okatsuka (Atsuko Sakamoto), Cory Zacharia (Cory Lawler), Rintaro Sawamoto (Rintaro Sakamoto), Brett L. Tinnes (Jordan Doniel), Roberto

Sanchez (Francisco), Matthew Fling (Garbo), Ryan Dillon (Brody Butler), Markiss McFadden (Marques Wright), Sean Neff (Sean Tippy), Ivy Khan (Tammy), Lee Lynch (Gene), David Nordstrom (Troy Maris), Sarah Tadayon (Sarah), Kathleen Maressa (Guitar Girl)

Littlerock © Variance Films

GLEE: THE 3D CONCERT MOVIE (20th Century Fox) Producers, Ryan Murphy, Dante DiLoreto; Executive Producers, David Nicksay, Ian Brennan, Brad Falchuk; Director, Kevin Tancharoen; Photography, Glen MacPherson; Music Supervisor, P.J. Bloom; Editors, Myron I. Kerstein, Jane Moran, Tatiana S. Regal; a Ryan Murphy production; Dolby; Color; 3D; Rated PG; 84 minutes; Release date: August 12, 2011. The cast of Fox's series *Glee* in concert. **CAST:** Dianna Agron (Quinn Fabray), Lea Michele (Rachel Berry), Gwyneth Paltrow (Holly Holliday), Darren Criss (Blaine Anderson), Chris Colfer (Kurt Hummel), Cory Monteith (Finn Hudson), Heather Morris (Brittany Pierce), Kevin McHale (Artie Abrams), Chord Overstreet (Sam Evans), Mark Salling (Noah "Puck" Puckerman), Naya Rivera (Santana Lopez), Harry Shum Jr. (Mike Chang), Amber Riley (Mercedes Jones), Jenna Ushkowitz (Tina Cohen-Chang), Ashley Fink (Lauren Zizes), Rike Lynch (Jeff), Curt Mega (Nick), Titus Makin Jr. (David), Jaymz Tuaileva (Rebel), Nicholas Jerome Baga, Justin de Vera, Hannah Douglass, Courtney Galiano, Kyle R. Hill, Lexy Hulme, KC Monnie, Brittany Parks, Michael Peter Riccio, Haylee Roderick (Dancers)

Chris Colfer, Amber Riley, Jenna Ushkowitz in *Glee: The 3D Concert Movie* © 20th Century Fox

CORNERSTORE (Global Pictures Studios) Producers, Joe Doughrity, Dwight Patillo, Robert Evangelista; Director/Screenplay, Joe Doughrity; Story, Joe Doughrity, Dwight E. Patillo; Additional Dialouge, Lawrence Lamont; Photography, Dan Love; Designer, Jaclyn Wells; Editors, Shola Akinnuso, Mike Thoroe; Color; Rated PG-13; 94 minutes; Release date: August 12, 2011. **CAST:** Lawrence Lamont (Gerard), Roger Guenveur Smith (Earl), Mike Bonner (Kato), David Ffroot Wells (Derrick), Audrey Beard (Kelly), Bill Hill (Big Jim), Martini Harris (Eddie), Sherzad Sinjari (Nazario), Sky Lee (K.J.), Greg Mathis (Judge Mathis), Trevione Williams (Mykell), Cameron Jones (Corey), Shanie D. (Mrs. Johnson), Paul Elia (Hassan Akrawi), Paul Dean (Rasheed), Rashad Timmons (Leo), Thomas Hearns (Thomas)

Roger Guenveur Smith in *CornerStore* © Global Pictures Studios

DAMN! (Disinformation Co.) Producer, Kristian Almgren; Executive Producers, Aaron Morris Cohen, Gary Baddeley, Robert D. Jacobson; Director/Photography, Aaron Fischer-Cohen; Music, Michael Rosen; Editor, Sam Nalband; a Fantastic Relationship Filmmaking production; Color; HD; Not rated; 73 minutes; Release date: August 12, 2011. Documentary on flamboyant politician Jimmy McMillan's campaign for governor of New York; **WITH:** Jimmy McMillan, Caprice Alves, Vincent Imbesi, Romeo Saltar

Jimmy McMillan in *Damn!* © Disinformation Co.

SUMMER PASTURE (Independent Lens) Producers/Directors, Lynn True, Nelson Walker; Co-Producer/Co-Director, Tsering Perlo; Photography, Nelson Walker; Editor, Lynn True; a True Walker Productions presentation in association with Rabsal; American-Chinese; Color; Not rated; 85 minutes; Release date: August 15, 2011. Documentary following one family of Tibetan nomads; **WITH:** Locho, Yama, Jiatomah.

Summer Pasture © Independent Lens

A HORRIBLE WAY TO DIE (Anchor Bay) Producers, Travis Stevens, Simon Barrett, Kim Sherman; Director/Editor, Adam Wingard; Screenplay, Simon Barrett; Photography, Chris Hilleke, Mark Shelhorse; Art Director, Flynn Thomas Smith; Music, Jasper Justice Leigh; Special Effects, Mike Strain Jr.; a Celluloid Nightmares and Site B presentation of a Two Squirrels/Snowfort Pictures production in association with TTOB Prods. and Arable Entertainment; Color; HD; Rated R; 87 minutes; Release date: August 19, 2011. **CAST:** AJ Bowen (Garrick Turrell), Amy Seimetz (Sarah), Joe Swanberg (Kevin), Brandon Carroll (Rusty), Lane Hughes (Reed), Melissa Boatright (Jessie), Whitney Moore (Daphne), Holly Voges (Carla), Michael J. Wilson (Jones), Steven Buehler (State Trooper), Jen Huemmer (Dark-Haired Woman)

A Horrible Way to Die © Anchor Bay

THE SMELL OF SUCCESS (Initiate Productions) Producers, Ken Johnson, Janet DuBois; Executive Producers, Nick Byassee, Spencer Stander; Director, Larry Smith; Screenplay, Mark Polish, Michael Polish; Photography, M. David Mullen; Designer, Clark Hunter; Costumes, Bic Owen; Music, Stuart Mathewman; Editor, Cary Gries; Casting, Kelly Martin Wagner; a Prohibition Pictures production; Color; Rated PG-13; 96 minutes; Release date: August 19, 2011. **CAST:** Billy Bob Thornton (Patrick), Téa Leoni (Rosemary Rose), Kyle MacLachlan (Jimmy St. James), Ed Helms (Chet Pigford), Mark Polish (Thaddeus Young), Pruitt Taylor Vince (Cleveland Clod), Frances Conroy (Agnes May), Richard Edson (Nelly the Nose), Patrick Bauchau (Mr. Rose), Brent Briscoe (Shotgun Farmer), D.W. Moffett (Agent Chestnut), Aria Alpert (Mrs. Smith), Sean Andrews, Christian Eric Billings, Damian Cecere, Luke Cheeseman, David A. Cooper, Vincent De Paul, Steve Fite, Jeff Gum, Brian A. Gutierrez, Jeffrey Hallman, Ken Johnson, Jeff Joslin, Martin Mathieu, Don McGovern, Jamie Preston, Aaron Skinner, Elizabeth Van Amelsvoort, Liz Van Amelsvoort (Miracle Workers), Michael Arturo (Hot

Dog Vendor), Rachel Winfree, Janet DuBois, Sadie Stratton, Brooke Baumer (Housewives), Scott Michael Campbell (Mr. Diehl), Carole Bardwell (Buyer), Gerald Emerick (Sunflower Farmer), Jon Gries (Early Dunchamp), Steve Hersack (Cook), Valorie Hubbard (Waitress Grace), Derek Johnson, Massi Furlan (Milagro Men), Bryan Law (Bean Farmer), Tony Monsour (FBI Agent), Erin O'Shaughnessy (Mrs. Diehl), David Schroeder (Federal Judge), David Shackleford (Carrot Farmer), Mark Tomesek (Potato Farmer)

Téa Leoni, Billy Bob Thornton in *The Smell of Success* © Initiate Productions

5 DAYS OF WAR (Anchor Bay) Producers, George Lascu, Mirza Papuna Davitaia, Koba Nakopia, Renny Harlin; Executive Producer, Giorgi Gelovani, Cyndy Kuipers, David Imedashvili, Michael Flannigan; Director, Renny Harlin; Screenplay, Mikko Alanne, Based on a screenplay by David Battle; Photography, Checco Varese; Designer, Marc Greville-Masson; Costumes, Elvis Davis; Music, Trevor Rabin; Editor, Brian Berdan; Visual Effects Supervisors, James McQuaide, Vlad Leschinski; a RexMedia presentation of a GIF/Midnight Sun Pictures/ RexMedia production; American-Georgian; Dolby; Color; Rated R; 113 minutes; Release date: August 19, 2011. **CAST:** Rupert Friend (Thomas Anders), Val Kilmer (Dutchman), Andy Garcia (President Mikheil Saakashvili), Dean Cain (Chris Bailot), Emmanuelle Chriqui (Tatia Meddevi), Heather Graham (Miriam Eisner), Mikko Nousiainen (Daniil), Richard Coyle (Sebastian Ganz), Antje Traue (Zoe), Rade Sherbedgia (Col. Alexander Demidov), Mikheil Gomiashvili (Anton Meddevi), Johnathon Schaech (Capt. Rezo Avaliani), Anna Walton (Karin Lange), Luke Albright (Jameson, Satellite Van Technician), Kenneth Cranham (Michael Stilton), Ani Imnadze (Sofi Meddevi), Sergo Shvedkov (Minister Temur Iakobashvili), Alan McKenna (Minister Alexandre Lomaia), Steven Robertson (Minister Davit Kezerashvili), Giorgi Tsaava (Maj. Lavrin), Lasha Kankava, Beka Tabukashvili (Daniil's Men), Lasha Okreshidze (Georgian Lieutenant), Kakha Mikiashvili (Inn Keeper), Natiaa Metreveli (Inn Keeper's Wife), Lile Onilani, Natalia Gularashvili (Inn Keeper's Children), Gia Kusikashvili (Village Man), Lia Suluashvili (Woman shot in Knees), Koka Shanava (Militia Boy), Liako Gogidze (Waitress), Torinke Bziava (Giorgi the Guide), Kakha Gogidze (Priest), Giorgi Kipshidze (Iraqi Taxi Driver), Zura Javaxia (Lasha Tsagareli), Levan Pirtskhalava (Georgian Lieutenant), Zura Ingorokva (Georgian Captain), Rostom Lortkipanidze (Priest), Jino Jiniuzashvili (Oldest Milita Boy), Manana Midelashvili (Disabled Woman), Ruslan Bakradze (Disabled Man), Aleko Gabedava (Rezo's Soldier), Nika Tserediani (Chief of Police), Malkhaz Abuladze (Mayor), Natalia Kipshidze (Girl in Chuch), Dali Doijashvili (Older Village Woman), Nino Jokhadze (Young Village Girl)

THE SCENESTERS (Monterey Media) Producers, Kevin M. Brennan, Jeff Grace, Brett D. Thompson; Executive Producers, Chris R. Sabin, Eric Sherman; Director/ Screenplay, Todd Berger; Photography, Helena Wei; Designer, Eve McCarney; Costumes, Summer Browning; Music, Dan Houlbrook; Editor, Kyle Martin; Casting, Angela Campolla-Sanders; a Johnny Voodoo Prods. presentation in

Emmanuelle Chriqui, Rupert Friend in *5 Days of War* © Anchor Bay

association with Vacationeer Prods. and Midwinter Studios; Color/black and white; DV; Rated R; 102 minutes; Release date: August 19, 2011. **CAST:** Sherilynn Fenn (A.D.A. Barbara Dietrichson), Blaise Miller (Charlie Newton), Suzanne May (Jewell Wright), Jeff Grace (Roger Graham), Kevin M. Brennan (Investigator Henry Muse), Todd Berger (Wallace Cotten), Monika Jolly (Investigator Carlita Travers), James Jolly (Irving Shaw), Summer Perry (Clare), Robert R. Shafer (George Porter), Elizabeth Sandy (Kimberly Rockwell), Joel Stoffer (Hume Wonacott), John Landis (Judge Paxton B. Johnson), Claudia Choi (Dr. Brenda Harper), Brian Huskey (Bill), Juliana Rabe (The Girl in the Blue Dress), Sarah Hall (The Witch), Tony Baker (Officer Breeze), Scott Bird (Investigator Richard Springfield), Tyler Coburn (Niels), Daniel A. Edelman (Officer Alan Moore), Josh Fadem (Mumblecore Josh), Josh Fingerhut (Brian), Andy Forrest (Stanley Cromwell), Kirsten Gronfield (Belinda McHale – Victim #1), Molly Hale (Mumblecore Molly), Marcus Jones (Coroner T. Bird), Sarah Klinger (Wendy Smith), Kyle Martin (Coroner Douglas Luchia), Chris Martins (The Robot), Eve McCarney (Jen Loveworth), Kimberly North (Laura Ortega), Kyoko Okazaki (Berry's Girl), Michael Roach (Dagfinn), Cassiopeia Smith (Tammy Birch), Denver Smith (Mumblecore Denver), Christina Tambakakis (Weegee), Brett D. Thompson (Officer Zachetti), Helena Wei (Mandy Jenkins), Bill Zasadil (Officer Neff), Mikos Zavros (Bailiff Emerson), Heather Bleemers (The Nurse), Chad Brown (Big Baby), Angela Campolla-Sanders (Court Clerk), Mike Dennert (Reporter), Jessica Borden, Laura Fryer (Auditioning Actresses)

The Scenesters © Monterey Media

PROGRAMMING THE NATION? (Intl. Film Circuit/Buzzledom) Producers, Marty Collins, Jeff Warrick; Executive Producer, Lynda Stewart; Director/Screenplay, Jeff Warrick; Photography, Marty Collins; Music, Evan Evans, Robert Macomber; Editors, Jeff Warrick, Stefan Hacker, Catherine Nightingale; an Ignite Productions Film in association with Digital Media Factory; Color/black and white; HD; Not rated; 105 minutes; Release date: August 19, 2011. Documentary on subliminal advertising; **WITH:** Col. John B. Alexander, Richard Beggs, Dr. Nick Begich, August Bullock, Noam Chomsky, Christopher Coppola, David Fricke, Amy Goodman, Hilton A. Green, Andy Johns, Wilson Bryan Key, Dennis Kucinich, Jerry Mander, Mark Crispin Miller, Mark Mothersbaugh, William Poundstone, Douglas Rushkoff, Pastor Joe Schimmel, Howard Shevrin, Ann Simonton, Geoff Tate, Dr. Eldon Taylor, Diane E. Watson, Bill Yousman

Jeff Warrick in *Programming the Nation?* © Intl. Film Circuit

FLYPAPER (IFC Films) Producers, Mark Damon, Peter Safran, Patrick Dempsey, Moshe Diamant; Director, Rob Minkoff; Screenplay, Jon Lucas, Scott Moore; Photography, Steven Poster; Designers, Alec Hammond, Jim Gelarden; Costumes, Mona May; Music, John Swihart; Editor, Tom Finan; Casting, Kerry Barden, Paul Schnee; a Foresight Unlimited presentation of a Safran Films/Foresight Unlimited production in association with Shifting Gears Entertainment, a VIP Medienfonds 4 Production in association with Rising Star; Color; Widescreen; HD; Not rated; 87 minutes; Release date: August 19, 2011. **CAST:** Patrick Dempsey (Tripp Kennedy), Ashley Judd (Kaitlin), Tim Blake Nelson (Billy Ray "Peanut Butter" McCloud), Mekhi Phifer (Darrien), Matt Ryan (Gates), Jeffrey Tambor (Gordon Blythe), John Ventimiglia (Weinstein), Pruitt Taylor Vince (Wyatt "Jelly" Jenkins), Curtis Armstrong (Mitchell Wolf), Rob Huebel (Rex Newbauer), Adrian Martinez (Mr. Clean), Octavia Spencer (Madge Wiggins), Eddie Matthews (Jack Hayes), James DuMont (Detective), Rob Boltin (Credit Manhattan V.P.), Natalia Safran (Swiss Miss), Crystal Kung, Amber Gaiennie, Ashley Braud, Tamara Stuparich de la Barra (Reporters), Thomas C. Daniel (Sgt. Sharpe), Victor Palacios (E.M.T.), Raymond Rivera (Hector the Janitor)

BORN AND BRED (Purebred Films) Producer/Director, Justin Frimmer; Executive Producer, Franklin Rothschild; Photography, Bloski Kurtz; Music, Adam Balazs; Editors, Brad Besser, Guillermo Rodriguez, Justin Frimmer; a 24th Hour Productions presentation; Color; HD; Not rated; 94 minutes; Release date: August 19, 2011. Documentary on the East Los Angeles boxing scene; **WITH:** Teddy Atlas, David Avila, Hector Beccera, Jim Lampley, Robert Luna, Gloria Molina, Javier Molina, Miguel Molina, Oscar Molina, Rodrigo Mosquero, Gabriel Pasillas, Victor Pasillas, Roberto Suro

STRIPPED DOWN (Visualner Entertainment) Producers, Alexandra Norberg, Christo Dimassis, Steven Adams, Bobby Leigh, Alex Norberg; Director/Screenplay, Elana Krausz; Photography, Zoran Popovic; Designer, Deren Abram; Costumes, Oneita Parker; Music, Eric Godal, Mark Fontana; Editor, Aaron I. Yamamoto; a Terra Entertainment and Visualiner presentation; Color; HD; Not rated; 95 minutes;

Javier Molina, Oscar Molina in *Born and Bred* © Purebred Films

Release date: August 26, 2011. **CAST:** Elana Krausz (Lily), Marcus Jean Pirae (Larry), Ian Ziering (Francis), Bre Blair (Wren), Lisa Arturo (Cara), Mitzi Martin (Estella), Shelly Andagan (Runaway Girl), Mel Braxton (Thor), Lou George (IRS Agent), Bill Glass (Joe), Anna Hsieh (Spice), Teri Jaworski (Charlie), Christine Klotz (Susan), April MacKay (May), Alex Norberg (Cami), Christina Romero (Waitress), Harriet Rose (Buffy), Sheri Rosenblum (Barbi), Stasea Rosenblum (Bambi), Steven Shaw (Dan), Ben Watkins (Lee)

REDEMPTION ROAD (Freestyle) Producers, Jeff Balis, Rhoades Rader, Morgan Simpson; Executive Producer, Charlie Poe; Co-Producers, Michael Clarke Duncan, Joel C. High; Director, Mario Van Peebles; Screenplay, Morgan Simpson, George Richards; Story, Morgan Simpson; Photography, Matthew Irving; Designer, Diana "Ruby" Guidara; Costumes, Bega Metzner; Music, Tree Adams; Music Supervisors, Joel C. High, Rebecca Rienks; Editor, Mark Conte; Casting, Kari Kurto, Jo Doster; a Liberty Road Entertainment/Heavy Duty Entertainment production in association with MVP Films; Color; Rated PG-13; 90 minutes; Release date: August 26, 2011. **CAST:** Michael Clarke Duncan (Augy), Morgan Simpson (Jefferson Bailey), Kiele Sanchez (Hannah), Taryn Manning (Jackie), Luke Perry (Boyd), Tom Skerritt (Santa), Melvin Van Peebles (Elmo), Catherine McGoohan (Annie), Linds Edwards (Jimbo), Heather Simpson (Lynn), Jet Jurgensmeyer (Jet), Cassie Jordan (Joy the Grumpy Waitress), Chris Woodson (Bailey's Father), Charlie Poe (Boom Boom), Joshua Heyman, Daniel Heyman (Young Bailey), Weston Poe (Weston), Reegus Flenory (Bailey's Co-Worker), J.K. Hunter (Waitress at Country Music Club), Lee Perkins (Security Guard)

THE FAMILY TREE (Entertainment One) Producers, Allan Jones, J. Todd Harris, Mark Lisson, Kathy Weiss, Mark Lisson; Executive Producers, Robert E. Griffin Jr., Marc Toberoff; Director, Vivi Friedman; Screenplay, Mark Lisson; Photography, Hong-Wei Joplin Wu; Designer, Jesse Benson; Costumes, Kelle Kutsugeras; Editors, Patrick Sheffield, Justine Halliday, Seth Flaum; Casting, Veronica Rooney; a Jones/Harris production; Dolby; Color; HD; Rated R; 87 minutes; Release date: August 26, 2011. **CAST:** Dermot Mulroney (Jack Burnett), Hope Davis (Bunnie Burnett), Chi McBride (Simon Krebbs), Max Thieriot (Eric Burnett), Brittany Robertson (Kelly Burnett), Selma Blair (Ms. Delbo), Keith Carradine (Reverend Diggs), Bow Wow (T-Boy), Gabrielle Anwar (Nina Fouts), John Patrick Amedori (Paul Stukey), Evan Ross (Josh Krebbs), Madeline Zima (Mitzi Steinbacher), Christina Hendricks (Alicia Bouche), Jane Seymour (Grandma Ilene), Rachael Leigh Cook (Rachel Levy), Jermaine Williams (Trey), Steven Grayhm (Andy Porter), Newell Alexander (Dr. Lieberman), Eddie Hassell (Ricky Johnson), Jake Richardson (Roy), Pamela Shaw (Vice Principal Carnes), Jack Kyle (Police Officer #1), Mac Brandt (Young Police Officer), Adrian Alvarado (Uniformed Cop), Peggy Etra (Eunice), Ally Maki (Shauna), Hannah Hodson (Ashley), Colby French (Coach Sutton), Christopher Bradley (Bobby Overmier)

Dermot Mulroney, Hope Davis in *The Family Tree* © Entertainment One

CHASING MADOFF (Cohen Media Group) Producer/Director/Screenplay, Jeff Prosserman; Based on the book *No One Would Listen* by Harry Markopolos; Executive Producers, Jeff Sackman, Anton Nader, Randy Manis; Photography, Julian van Mil; Designer, Harrison Yurkiw; Music, David Fluery; Editors, Jeff Bessner, Garry Tutte; a Jeff Prosserman production; Color/Black and white; Not rated; 90 minutes; Release date: August 26, 2011. Documentary on how Bernie Madoff was responsible for ruining lives with his $18 billion Ponzi scheme; **WITH:** Harry Markopolous, Frank Casey, Neil Chelo, Gaytri Kachroo, Michael Ocrant.

SUING THE DEVIL (RiverRain Prods.) Producers, David Turrell, David Smith, Malcolm McDowell; Director/ Screenplay, Tim Chey; Photography, Tom Gleeson; Designer, Mark Barold; Costumes, Lenya Jones; Music, David Turrell, Daryl Inglis; Casting, Lara Fisher, Douglas White Alisha; a Mouthwatering Productions presentation; Color; Not rated; 95 minutes; Release date: August 26, 2011. **CAST:** Malcolm McDowell (Satan), Shannen Fields (Gwen O'Brien), Corbin Bernsen (Barry Polk), Tom Sizemore (Tony "The Hip" Anzaldo), Bart Bronson (Luke O'Brien), Ros Gentle (Judge Woods), Rebecca St. James (Jasmine Williams), Jennifer Skyler (Cynthia Jones), Jeff Gannon (Mr. Banks), Chad Lammers (Mr. Ice), Annie Lee (Ms. Black), Gabrielle Whittaker (Ms. Scarlett), Gillian Emmett (Ms. Shy), Robin Queree (Mr. Think Tank), Dennis Cole (Murray Fields), Kenny Epps (Mr. Innocent), Gregory Caine (Bailiff), Drew Pearson (Reporter Jk), Rob Walters (Jury Foreman), Melissa Hanes (Juror Kim Thomas), Jessica Saras (Juror Mel Miskell), Linda Mercorella (Juror Carlin Lie), Marina Mercorella (Juror Emma Todd), Bella Blaikock (Juror Raquel Grant), Samantha Clarke (Juror Katie Wilson), Gordon Anderson (Juror Felix Corquet), Michael Grady (Juror Matthew Monaco), Hannah Forsyth (Juror Jayde Maree), Denning James Isles (Juror Dean Given), Shira Van Essen (Juror Kate Foley), Hannah Bath (Melinda Jacobs), Jeff Crabtree (Pastor Matthews), Josh Reid (Oil Executive), Morgan Roy (Michael Ciltern), Jessica Kelly (Librarian), Jayden O'Brien (Gothic Kid), Clara Tsoukaris (Girl Scout), Daniel O'Brien (Boy Scout), Shalane Connors (Law Receptionist), Colin Huxley (Blind Man), Phil Pringle (Pastor Pringle), Peter Rahme (Pastor Scofield), Paul Newsham (Pastor Philips), Erwan Sirvin (French Reporter), Shingo Usami (Japanese Reporter), Sarah Jane Coombe (British Reporter), Lilly McDowell (Jane Douglas)

Malcolm McDowell in *Suing the Devil* © RiverRain Prods.

BUZZKILL (Indican) Producers, Thomas Hanna, Dylan Hundley, Samara Yeshaiek, Barry Shapiro; Director, Steven Kampmann; Screenplay, Steven Kampmann, Matt Smollon; Photography, Stephen Treadway; Designer, Elizabeth Jones; Costumes, Leah Piehl; Editor, Alan Dubin; Casting, Jennifer Euston; a Second City Entertainment presentation; Color; Not rated; 93 minutes; Release date: August 26, 2011. **CAST:** Daniel Raymont (Ray Wyatt), Darrell Hammond (The Karaoke Killer), Krysten Ritter (Nicole), Reiko Aylesworth (Sara), Larry Hankin (Granger), Mike Starr (Agent Brady), Raul Aranas (Dr. Clavell), Judith Kahan (Jill), Lance Kinsey (Dennis), Tony Norris (Tyson Rock), Rose Pasquale (Granger's Girlfriend), Galeit Sehayek (Jamie Moyers), Pamela Shaw (Louise), Asher Grodman (Receptionist), Brian Sacca, Peter Karinen (Cops), Jenna Rae Montgomery (Cowgirl Bartender), Wade Mylius (Bartender), Audrie Neenan (Waitress)

Krysten Ritter, Daniel Raymont in *BuzzKill* © Indican

POLITICS OF LOVE (CodeBlack Entertainment) Producers, Govind Menon, Vikram Singh Lamba, William Sees Keenan; Executive Producer, Rakesh Rathore; Director, William Dear; Screenplay, Gary Goldstein; Photography, Bryan Greenberg; Designer, Rob Howeth; Costumes, Francine Jamison-Tanchuck; Music, Dylan Berry; Editor, Edgar Burcksen; Casting, Michelle Adams; a Davic Holdings presentation of a Nuclear Mango production in association with Split Image Pictures; Color; Not rated; 93 minutes; Release date: August 26, 2011. **CAST:** Brian White (Kyle Franklin), Mallika Sherawat (Aretha Gupta), Loretta Devine (Shirlee Gupta), Gerry Bednob (Vijay Gupta), Ruby Dee (Aretha's Grandmother), Anil Raman (Marvin Gupta), Gabrielle Dennis (Chelsea), Trillionaire (Terrence Miller), Sueann Han (Bianca), Ian Reed Kesler (Brent Murphy), Tracey Walter (Glen), Camille Diebold, Kennerly Diebold (Merry Christian), Carlene Moore (Kathleen), Kevin Anthony Brooks (Kenny the Cameraman), Oliver Dear (Redneck), Marie Lyn Deja (Melinda), Naomi Parmar (Cousin), Michele Specht (Liz Moore), Phillip Agresta (Shirtless Man at Carwash)

Mallika Sherawat, Brian White in *Politics of Love* © Code Black Entertainment

REBIRTH (Oscilloscope) Producers, Jim Whitaker, David Solomon; Director, Jim Whitaker; Photography, Thomas Lappin; Music, Philip Glass; Editors, Kevin Filippini, Brad Fuller; a Project Rebirth presentation in association with Oppenheimer Funds, the Lower Manhattan Development Corp., and the U.S. Department of Housing and Urban Development; Color; Not rated; 106 minutes; Release date: August 31, 2011. Documentary on how several survivors of the World Trade Center attacks of Sept. 11, 2001 have rebuilt their lives; **WITH:** Debbie Almontaser, Tim Brown, Nicholas Chirls, Charles Cook, Larry Courtney, Joseph Keenan, Brian Lyons, Tanya Villanueva Tepper, Ling Young

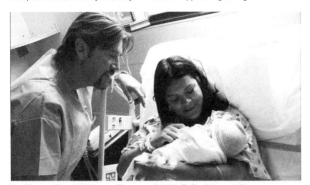

Ray Tepper, Tanya Villanueva Tepper in *Rebirth* © Oscilloscope Pictures

SHARK NIGHT 3D (Rogue Pictures) Producers, Mike Fleiss, Lynette Howell, Chris Briggs; Executive Producers, Ryan Kavanaugh, Tucker Tooley, Douglas Curtis, Nick Meyer, Marc Schaberg, Matthew Rowland, Clint Kisker; Director, David R. Ellis; Screenplay, Will Hayes, Jesse Studenberg; Photography, Gary Capo; Designer, Jaymes Hinkle; Costumes, Magali Guidasci; Editor, Dennis Virkler; Visual Effects Supervisor, Gregor Lakner; Casting, Kelly Martin Wagner; a Rogue, Incentive Filmed Entertainment and Sierra Pictures presentation of a Next Films/Silverwood Films production; Dolby; Color; HD; 3D; Rated PG-13; 91 minutes; Release date: September 2, 2011. **CAST:** Sara Paxton (Sara Palski), Dustin Milligan (Nick), Chris Carmack (Dennis Crim), Katharine McPhee (Beth), Donal Logue (Sheriff Greg Sabin), Joshua Leonard (Red), Joel David Moore (Gordon), Sinqua Walls (Malik), Chris Zylka (Blake), Alyssa Diaz (Maya), Jimmy Lee Jr. (Carl), Damon Lipari (Keith), Christine Quinn (Jess), Kelly Sry (Wonsuk), Tyler Bryan (Kyle), Kyla Pratt (Karla), Ving Rhames (Deputy Fallon)

Sara Paxton, Dustin Milligan in *Shark Night 3D* © Relativity Media

BUTTONS (Factory 25) Producers, The Red Bucket Film Collective; Directors/ Editors/ Photography, Alex Kalman, Josh Safdie, Benny Safdie; Red Bucket Films; Color; DV; Not rated; 91 minutes (including 10 minute countdown intermission); Release date: September 2, 2011. Compilation film of everyday sights and occurrences.

APOLLO 18 (Dimension) Producers, Timur Bekmambetov, Michele Wolkoff; Executive Producers, Bob Weinstein, Harvey Weinstein, Ron Schmidt, Shawn Williamson, Cody Zweig; Director, Gonzalo López-Gallego; Screenplay, Brian Miller; Photography, José David Montero; Designer, Andrew Neskoromny; Costumes, Cynthia Summers; Editor, Patrick Lussier; Visual Effects Supervisors, Dennis Sedov, Terry Hutcheson; a Bekmambetov Projects production; Dolby; Technicolor; Rated PG-13; 86 minutes; Release date: September 2, 2011. **CAST:** Lloyd Owen (Nathan Walker), Warren Christie (Benjamin Anderson), Ryan Robbins (John Grey), Ali Liebert (Nate's Girlfriend), Andrew Airlie (Mission Control), Mike Kopsa (Deputy Secretary of Defense), Kurt Runte, Jan Bos (Lab Techs), Kim Wylie (Laura Anderson), Erica Carroll (John's Fiancée)

Apollo 18 © Dimension Films

RESURRECT DEAD: THE MYSTERY OF THE TOYNBEE TILES (Argot Pictures) Producers/Screenplay, Jon Foy, Colin Smith; Executive Producer, Doug Block; Director/Editor/ Photography/Music, Jon Foy; a Land of Missing Parts presentation; Color; DV; Not rated; 85 minutes; Release date: September 2, 2011. Documentary on the efforts to piece together the meaning behind the many tiled messages popping up in various cities; **WITH:** Justin Duerr, Colin Smith, Steve Weinik.

Justin Duerr in *Resurrect Dead* © Argot Pictures

INSIGHT (Highland Film Group) Producers, Richard Gabai, John Constantine, Larissa Michel; Executive Producers, Elaine J. Constantine, Richard Iott; Director, Richard Gabai; Screenplay, Aaron Ginsburg, Wade McIntyre; Photography, Scott Peck; Designer, Gabor Norman; Costumes, Annalisa Adams; Music, Lisa Gerrard, Marcello De Francisci; Editor, Jeff Murphy; Casting, Billy DaMota; a Braeburn Entertainment and Celco presentation of a G.C. Pix LLC/Check Entertainment production; Color; Rated R; 92 minutes; Release date: September 2, 2011. **CAST:** Sean Patrick Flanery (Det. Peter Rafferty), Natalie Zea (Kaitlyn), Angeline-Rose Troy (Allison), Adam Baldwin (Dr. Graham Brady), Thomas Ian Nicholas (Stephen Geiger), Veronica Cartwright (Patricia), Christopher Lloyd (Shep), Juliet Landau (Dr. Lisa Rosan), Max Perlich (Det. Canto), Lesley-Ann Brandt (Valerie Khoury), Matt Knudsen (Det. Kaz), Rick Overton (Det. Gehrke), Daniel Roebuck (Sgt. Reed), Rance Howard (Cemetery Presider), Jamie Wozny, Diana Busuioc (ER Nurses), Lonnie Henderson, Brent Pope (EMTs), Tim Abell (Head Surgeon), Melissa McCarty (TV Reporter), Ron R. Anantavara (Rooftop Party Goer)

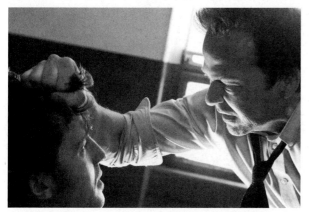

Thomas Ian Nicholas, Sean Patrick Flanery in *InSight* © Highland Film Group

BUCKY LARSON: BORN TO BE A STAR (Columbia) Producers, Adam Sandler, Jack Giarraputo, Allen Covert, Nick Swardson, David Dorfman; Co-Producer, Betsy Danbury; Director, Tom Brady; Screenplay, Adam Sandler, Nick Swardson, Allen Covert; Photography, Michael Barrett; Designer, Dina Lipton; Costumes, Mary Jane Fort; Music, Waddy Wachtel; Editor, Jason Gourson; Casting, Lisa London, Catherine Stroud; a Happy Madison production; Dolby; Deluxe color; Rated R; 96 minutes; Release date: September 9, 2011. **CAST:** Nick Swardson (Bucky Larson), Christina Ricci (Kathy McGee), Don Johnson (Miles Deep), Stephen Dorff (Dick Shadow), Kevin Nealon (Gary), Edward Herrmann (Jeremiah Larson), Miriam Flynn (Debbie Larson), Ido Mosseri (J Day), Mario Joyner (Claudio), Pauly Shore (AFA Emcee), Nick Turturro (Antonio), Tyler Spindel (Jimmy), Meredith Giangrande (Blueberry), Mary Pat Gleason (Marge), Jackie Sandler (Casting Director), Dana Min Goodman (Gretchen), Curtis Armstrong (Clint), Michael O'Connell (Rory), Brandon Hardesty (Lars), Adam Herschman (Dale), Beverly Polcyn (Mrs. Bozobop), Gene Pompa (Tomas), Julia Lea Wolov (Autograph Lady), Brandon Cournoyer (Autograph Man), Jonathan Loughran (Bondage Guy), Keegan Michael Key (Guinness Man), Tembi Locke (Guinness Woman), Owen Benjamin (Production Assistant), Selma Stern (Elderly Woman), Raf Mauro (Chop Restaurant Owner), Henry T. Yamada (Vietnamese Henchman), Kelvin Han Yee (Vietnamese Boss), John Kirk (Commercial Producer), Hans Molenkamp (Bouncer), Kelsey Crane (Hot Sushi Waitress), Peter Dante (Dante), Monty Hoffman (Eddie, Distributor), Pasha Lynchnikoff (Dimitri, Distributor), Joey Coco Diaz (German Guy, Distributor), Payman Benz (Chop Restaurant Valet), J.D. Donaruma (Sound Guy), Shane Ralston (Key Grip), Chris Titone (Prop Guy), Jesse Jane, Kirsten Berman, Robert Harvey, Danni Katz, Danny Abeckaser, Lindsay Gareth, Michael Bernardi, Darrin Lackey, Samantha Schacher, Jennifer Perkins (AFA Presenter), Kevin Brief (Iowa Father), Marcus Demian (Old Man with

Pig), Mario Sellitti (Chewbacca), Rick Williamson (Iowa Farmer), Bryan Anthony, Dominique Kelley (Gay Guys Dancing), Vanessa Nicole Villalovos (Claudio's Girl), Eros Mendoza (J Day's Assistant), Jimmy Fallon (Himself)

Nick Swardson, Stephen Dorff in *Bucky Larson* © Columbia Pictures

PEOPLE V. THE STATE OF ILLUSION (Exalt Films) Producer/Screenplay, Austin Vickers; Director, Scott Cervine; Photography, David Fisher (narrative), Jeff Halperin (interviews); a Movies from the Heart in association with Exalt Films presentation; Color; Not rated; 86 minutes; Release date: September 9, 2011. Drama about the trial and conviction of a single father is dissected by a panel of experts; **WITH:** Austin Vickers, Dr. Joe Dispenza, Debbie Ford, Dr. Michael Vandermark, Dr. Robert Jahn, Dr. Brenda Dunne, Dr. Thomas Moore, Dr. Peter Senge, Dr. Candace Pert; CAST: J.B. Tuttle (Aaron), Michael McCormick (Prison Janitor), Kevin McDonald (The Guard), Tad Jones (Attorney), Melanie Lindahl (Hope), Amy Baklini (Woman in Bar), Ali Agirnas (Officer Parkes), Lauren Dusek (Office Michaels), Lili Dale, Autumn Shields (Forrest Divas), Adam Kurtz (Forrest Wizard), Bill Kurtz, Kristin Kurtz, Olivia Kurtz, Adam Kurtz (Family Dinner)

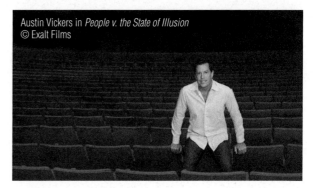

Austin Vickers in *People v. the State of Illusion* © Exalt Films

CREATURE (The Bubble Factory) Producers, Sid Sheinberg, Bill Sheinberg, Jon Sheinberg; Executive Producer, Paul Mason; Director, Fred M. Andrews; Screenplay, Fred M. Andrews, Tracy Morse; Photography, Christopher Faloona; Designer, Jakub Durkoth; Music, Keivn Haskins; Editor, Chris Conlee; Special Effects Makeup, Roland Blancaflor; Casting, Kelly Martin Wagner; Lockjaw Productions; Dolby; Color; Rated R; 93 minutes; Release date: September 9, 2011. **CAST:** Mehcad Brooks (Niles), Serinda Swan (Emily), Dillon Casey (Oscar), Lauren Schneider (Karen), Aaron Hill (Randy), Amanda Fuller (Beth), Pruitt Taylor Vince (Grover), Daniel Bernhardt (Grimley), Sid Haig (Chopper), Wayne Pére (Bud), David Jensen (Jimmy), Rebekah Kennedy (Caroline), Jennifer Lynn Warren (Ophelia), D'Arcy Allen, Ilya Kruger (Villagers)

Lauren Schneider in *Creature*
© The Bubble Factory

Ellen Burstyn, Colin Firth, Patricia Clarkson in *Main Street* © Magnolia Pictures

FORDSON: FAITH, FASTING, FOOTBALL (North Shore Films) Producers, Ash-Har Quraishi, Basma Babar-Quraishi; Executive Producer/Director, Rashid Ghazi; Screenplay, Ruth Leitman; Photography, Mike Shamus; Music Supervisor, Azam Tai; Editor, Ed Pickart; Produced in association with Quraishi Prod.; Color; DV; Not rated; 92 minutes; Release date: September 9, 2011. Documentary on Arab-Americans in Dearborn, Michigan; WITH: Osama Abulhassan, Bilal Abu-Omarah, Ali Baidoun, Imad Fadlallah, Hassan Houssaiky, Baquer Sayed, Fouad Zaban, Yussuf "Big Joe" Berry

Fordson: Faith, Fasting, Football © North Shore Films

MAIN STREET (Magnolia) Producers, Spencer Silna, Megan Ellison, Jonah Hirsch; Executive Producers, Adi Shankar, Douglas Saylor Jr., Ted Schipper; Co-Producer, Yvette Bikoff; Director, John Doyle; Screenplay, Horton Foote; Photography, Donald M. McAlpine; Designer, Christopher Nowak; Costumes, Gary Jones; Music, Patrick Doyle; Editors, Richard Francis Bruce, Neil Farrell, Trudy Ship; Casting, Bernard Telsey; a 1984 Films, Annapurna Productions & Fixed Point Films Productions presentation; Dolby; Panavision; Deluxe color; Rated PG; 93 minutes; Release date: September 9, 2011. **CAST:** Ellen Burstyn (Georgiana Carr), Colin Firth (Gus Leroy), Patricia Clarkson (Willa Jenkins), Orlando Bloom (Harris Parker), Amber Tamblyn (Mary Saunders), Andrew McCarthy (Howard Mercer), Margo Martindale (Myrtle Parker), Victoria Clark (Miriam), Tom Wopat (Frank), Isiah Whitlock Jr. (Mayor), Liam Ferguson (Henry), Martin Thompson (Vaughn Guess), Nadya Simpson (Kate), Christopher Houldsworth (Man in Police Station), Juan Carlos Piedrahita (Jose), Veda Wilson (Shirley), Gezell Fleming (Rebecca), Cheryl McConnell (Lucille), Viktor Hernandez (Estaquio), Ednali Figueroa (Woman at Warehouse), Amy da Luz (Rita) Reid Dalton (Crosby Gage), Michael Fraguada (Other Truck Driver), Cheri Varnadoe (Clara), Thomas Upchurch (Trooper Williams), Stuart Hough (Raymond), Rick Hamilton (Elliott), J.W. Smith (Bill), Luis Lopez (Truck Driver), Andrea Powell (Hostess)

BOBBY FISCHER AGAINST THE WORLD (HBO Films) Producers, Liz Garbus, Stanley Buchthal, Rory Kennedy, Matthew Justus; Director, Liz Garbus; Photography, Robert Chappell; Music, Philip Sheppard; Editors, Karen Schmeer, Michael Levine; an HBO Documentary Films in association with LM Media presentation of a Moxie Firecracker production; American-British; Color; Not rated; 93 minutes; Release date: September 9, 2011. Documentary on enigmatic chess champion Bobby Fischer; **WITH:** Clea Benson, Harry Benson, Dick Cavett, David Edmonds, Larry Evans, Malcolm Gladwell, Fernand Gobet PhD, Asa Hoffman, Garry Kasparov, Henry Kissinger, Nikolai Krogius, Shelby Lyman, Mike Magnusson, Paul Marshall, Fridrick Olafsson, Saemi Palsson, Susan Polgar, Dr. Anthony Saidy, Lothar Schmid, David Shenk, Sam Sloan, Harry Sneider, Boris Spassky, Dr. Kári Stefánsson, Russell Targ, Gudmundur Thorarinsson, (This film debuted on HBO on June 6, 2011).

Boris Spassky, Bobby Fischer in *Bobby Fischer against the World* © HBO Films

TANNER HALL (Anchor Bay) Producers, Julie R. Snyder, Francesca Gregorini, Tatiana von Furstenberg; Executive Producer, Richard L. Bready; Directors/ Screenplay, Francesca Gregorini, Tatiana von Furstenberg; Photography, Brian Rigney Hubbard; Designer, Ray Kluga; Costumes, Karen Baird, Erica Nicotra; Music, Roger Neill; Casting, Amanda Koblin, Amanda Harding; an Islander Films & Royalton Films presentation; Dolby; Technicolor; Rated R; 95 minutes; Release date: September 9, 2011. **CAST:** Rooney Mara (Fernanda), Georgia King (Victoria), Brie Larson (Kate), Amy Ferguson (Lucasta), Tom Everett Scott (Gio), Amy Sedaris (Mrs. Middlewood), Chris Kattan (Mr. Middlewood), Shawn Pyfrom (Hank), Ryan

Rooney Mara, Tom Everett Scott in *Tanner Hall* © Anchor Bay

Schira (Peter), Susie Misner (Roxanne), Tara Subkoff (Gwen), Annika Peterson (Olga), Alaina Steinberg (Margaret), Konstantine Kakanias (Mr. Tependris), Lowry Marshall (Ms. Wallace), Joanne Burk (School Nurse), Alexia Rasmussen (Gretchen), Anne Ramsey (Coffin Vendor), Hayley Goldbach (Student), Alexis Kiernan (Candice), Justin Vogel (Greg), Mark Carter (Attendent), Michael Thayer (Preacher), Russell Steinberg (Father of Dart Girl), Antonia Steinberg (Dart Girl), Collin Brown (Townie), Tom DeNucci (Townie's Friend), Lillian Adams (Victoria's Grandmother), Sydney Neill (Child Victoria), Kate Skye Netto (Child Fernanda), Adriaan Van Zyl, Tatiana von Furstenberg (Voice of Poppet)

ECHOTONE (Reversal Films) Producers, Nathan Christ, Justin A. Gilley, Nicholas K. Jayanty, Victor Moyers, Daniel Perlaky; Director, Nathan Christ; Photography, Robert L. Garza; Editors, Nathan Christ, Robert L. Garza; Produced in association with KNR Prods. and Cobra Music Co.; Color/black and white; Not rated; 88 minutes; Release date: September 9, 2011. Documentary on Austin, Texas's indie music scene; **WITH:** Bill Baird, Dana Falconberry, Black Joe Lewis, Cari Palazzollo, The Apeshits, Belaire, The Black Angels, The Octopus Factory, The Pity Party, Sound Team, Sunset, Ghostland Observatory, Ume, The White White Lights.

INSIDE OUT (Samuel Goldwyn Films) Producer, Mike Pavone; Executive Producer, Lori Lewis; Director, Artie Mandelberg; Screenplay, Dylan Schaffer; Photography, Kenneth Zunder; Designer, Raymond Pumilia; Costumes, Claire Breaux; Music, James Alan Johnston; Music Supervisor, Neil A. Lawi; Editor, Jerry U. Frizell; Casting, Denise Chamian Casting; a WWE Studios presentation; Dolby; Color; Rated PG-13; 93 minutes; Release date: September 9, 2011. **CAST:** Paul Levesque (Arlo "AJ" Jayne), Michael Rapaport (Jack Small), Parker Posey (Claire Small), Julie White (Martha Twiss), Michael Cudlitz (Det. Calgrove), Bruce Dern (Dr. Vic Small), Juliette Goglia (Pepper Small), Jency Griffin (Irena), Mike Agresta (Irate Driver), Allen Boudreaux (Tax Attorney), John Chambers (Store Clerk), James DuMont (Carlo Genova), Danny Epper (Drago), Juli Erickson (Carlo's Mother), J.D. Evermore (Baxter), John P. Fertitta, Lance E. Nichols (Tax Men), Patricia French (Elizabeth), Douglas M. Griffin (Undertaker), Emily D. Haley (Office Accounting), Raymond Hebert (Harbor Police), Grant James (Elizabeth's Father), Anthony Mark Johnson, Leesa Pate (Police Officers), Anthony Morales Jr. (Two Tall), Antonino Paone (Parole Officer), Andy Sims (NOPD Officer), Logan Douglas Smith (Vic Small's Attorney), Timothy A. Vasquez (Parolee), Chris Whetstone (Detective), Don Yesso (IRS Agent)

Paul Levesque, Parker Posey in *Inside Out* © Goldwyn Films

WE WERE HERE (Red Flag Releasing) Producer/Director, David Weissman; Co-Director/ Editor, Bill Weber; Photography, Marsha Kahm; Music, Holcombe Waller; The Film Collaborative; Color; Not rated; 90 minutes; Release date: September 9, 2011. Documentary on the impact the AIDS crisis has had on San Francisco's gay population; **WITH:** Ed Wolf, Paul Boneberg, Daniel Goldstein, Guy Clark, Eileen Glutzer

We Were Here © Red Flag Releasing

AFTER (Girls Gotta Eat Entertainment) Producers, Pieter Gaspersz, Sabrina Gennarino, Rich Angell; Director, Pieter Gaspersz; Screenplay, Sabrina Gennarino; Photography, Jonathan Hall; Art Director, Bill Mancuso; Costumes, Ivan Alvarez, Rosalind Bullard; Music, Jeff Beal; Editor, William Steinkamp; Color; Rated R; 100 minutes; Release date: September 9, 2011. **CAST:** Kathleen Quinlan (Nora Valentino), John Doman (Mitch Valentino), Pablo Schreiber (Christian Valentino), Sabrina Gennarino (Maxine Valentino), Adam Scarimbolo (Nicky Valentino), Diane Neal (Kat), Darrin Dewitt Henson (Andy), Mandy Gonzalez (Molly Valentino), Alexi Maggio (Samantha Valentino), Bruno Gioiello (Elliott), Kim Estes (Brian Blaylock), Joseph Ferrante (Peter Kilborn), Dave Goryl (Eddie), Susan Kwik (Dr. Palmer), Renell Edwards (Marshall), Ralph Ercolano (Tom), Chris Gennarino (Danny), Tracy Howe (Jack Miller), Marcy J. Savastano (Erin), J. Simmons (Greg), Eleanor Vigilante (Megan), Whit Washing (Brad), Pieter Gaspersz (Worker #1)

WHITE WASH (Trespass) Producers, Airrion Copeland, Dan Munger, Ted Woods; Director/ Screenplay/Photography, Ted Woods; Music, The Roots; Editors, Brian Davison, Dan Munger; Narrators, Ben Harper, Tariq "Black Thought" Trotter; a Trespass production; Color/Black and white; Not rated; 78 minutes; Release date: September 9, 2011. Documentary on African-American surfers; **WITH:** Rick Blocker, Sam George, Michael Green, Sal Masekela, James Meredith, "Patrick Quashi" Mitchell, Charles Ross, Bruce Wigo, Billy "Mystic" Wilmot

White Wash © Trespass

ONE FALL (Paladin) Producers, Dean Silvers, Marlen Hecht; Executive Producer, Richard K. Smucker; Director, Marcus Dean Fuller; Screenplay, Marcus Dean Fuller, Richard Greenberg; Photography, Alice Brooks; Designer, Timothy Whidbee; Costumes, Natasha Landau; Music, Ben Toth; Editors, Marlen Hecht, William Henry; Casting, Caroline Sinclair; a Compass Entertainment in association with Marlen Hecht and Dean Silvers production; Color; HD; Rated PG-13; 90 minutes; Release date: September 9, 2011. **CAST:** Marcus Dean Fuller (James Bond/The Janitor), Zoe McClellan (Julie Gardner), Seamus Mulcahy (Tab Barrows/Repeller Boy), James McCaffrey (Werber Bond), Mark La Mura (Cliff Bond), Dominic Fumusa (Tom Schmidt), Mark Margolis (Walter Grigg Sr.), Phyllis Somerville (Mrs. Barrows), LeeAnne Hutchison (Susie Schmidt), Audrey Amey (Nurse Hencheck), Dean Silvers, Maggie Wagner (Security Guards), Sarah Wilson (Claire), Keli Price (Josh), Tyler Silvers (Kyle), Jesse Miller (Jimmy), Charles Techman (Mr. Clarke), Jeff Ames (Luther), Denny Bess, Nick Reece (Guards), Amanda Barron (Victoria Bond), Annie Meisels (Young Nurse), Jan Owen (Mrs. Laysenbee), Nathan Kaufman, Jared Mack (Hunters), Richard Greenberg (Patient), Tijuana Ricks (Moaning Patient)

WHERE SOLDIERS COME FROM (Intl. Film Circuit) Producer/Director, Heather Courtney; Photography, Heather Courtney, Justin Hennard; Music, This Will Destroy You, Alex Chavez, Chad Stocker; Editors, Kyle Henry, Heather Courtney; a Quincy Hill Films/ITVS co-production; Color; Not rated; 90 minutes; Release date: September 9, 2011. Documentary on friends from a small Northern Michigan town who went off to war; **WITH:** Dominic Fredianelli, Cole Smith, Matt "Bodi" Beaudoin, Karim Ahmad, Sgt. Joseph battisfore, Yueh-mei Cheng, Kristin Feeley, Yance Ford, Lt. Nicholas Harrington, 1st Sgt. Robert Jeannottte, Simo Kilmurry, Jeanne Klein, Mickey Klein, Capt. Thomas Lafave, Cara Mertes, Randi Taylor, P.J. Tobia, Win-Sie Tow, Jorge Trelles, Sharon Fredianelli, Brian Fredianelli, Mary Smith, Kevin Smith, Lindsay Smith, Ashley Baker.

Dominic Fredianelli in *Where Soldiers Come From* © Intl. Film Circuit

GRANITO (Intl. Film Circuit) Producer, Paco de Onís; Director, Pamela Yates; Editor, Peter Kinoy; a Skylight Pictures Film; American-Guatemalan-Spanish; Stereo; Color; Not rated; 103 minutes; Release date: September 14, 2011. Documentary on the pursuit of war criminals involved in the Guatemalan Civil War; **WITH:** Rigoberta Menchú, Fredy Peccerelli, Alejandra Garcia, Kate Doyle, Antonio Caba Caba, Almudena Bernabeu, Gustavo Meoño, Naomi Roht-Arriaza

General Benedicto, Lucas Garcia in *Granito* © Intl. Film Circuit

THE WEIRD WORLD OF BLOWFLY (Variance Films) Producer/Director/ Photography, Jonathan Furmanski; Music Supervisor, Doug Bernheim; Editor, Cy Christiansen; a Special Theory Films production; Dolby; Color; HD; Not rated; 89 minutes; Release date: September 16, 2011. Documentary on cult musician Clarence Reid and his bizarre alter ego, Blowfly; **WITH:** Clarence Reid, Steve Alaimo, Die Ärzte, Bela B., Jello Biafra, Tom Bowker, Bo Crane, Chuck D, Norwood Fisher, Joe Galdo, Rodrigo González, Patricia Johnson, Jaime Lowe, Dorothy Martin, Jimmy Maslon, Clarence Reid Jr., Tracy Reid, Otto Van Schirach, Ice-T, Bob Perry.

Clarence Reid in *The Weird World of Blowfly* © Variance Films

PRINCE OF SWINE (Guerilla War Prods.) Producer/Director/Screenplay, Mark Toma; Executive Producer, Danny Collins; Photography, Nick Saglimbeni; Wardrobe, Victoria Kordysh; Music, Gerhard Daum; Editors, Michael Rochford, Richard Codding; Color; Not rated; 100 minutes; Release date: September 16, 2011. **CAST:** Nell Ruttledge (Julie), Mark Toma (Witt), John Klemantaski (Farber), Angel Marin (Alicia), Julian Starks (Biggs), Amber Holley (Kelly), Stanton Schnepp (Goldman), Jeannine Bisignano (Evelyn), Carly Cylinder (Robin), William Knight (Bernie), Heidi Mastrogiovanni (Judge Kimball), David Green (Cameron Casey), Fred Toma (Angry Bartender), Mitchell Moore (Peter), Bernadette Roberts (Bambi Cataldo), Jennifer Johnson (Dancer with a Knife), Michael Mitchell (Tortured Assistant), Jason Frasca (New Age Sensitive Boyfriend), Hawk Younkins (Brute Boyfriend), Sabrina Machado (Chartreuse Ivy), Laura Niles (Mystery Girl), Emil Roco (Goldman's Boytoy), Nicole Armijo (Café Waitress), Sara Irving (Café Girl), Vincent Preziose (Latte Drinker), Danny Collins (Max Weinberg), Rayder Woods (Party Animal), Diana Terranova (Kansas Hating Woman), Justin Burch (Buck Naked)

Nell Ruttledge in *Prince of Swine* © Guerilla War Prods.

BACK DOOR CHANNELS: THE PRICE OF PEACE (Fisher Klingenstein Films) Producers, Matthew Tollin, Arick Wierson; Executive Producer, Donald Tanselle; Director/Editor, Harry Hunkele; Screenplay, Matthew Tollin, Jonathan Hicks, Harry Hunkele, Arick Wierson; Photography, William Fitzgerald; Music, Uri Djemal, Shane Koss; a Channel Production Film; Color; Not rated; 96 minutes; Release date: September 16, 2011. Documentary on the September 1978 peace talks between Egyptian President Anwar el-Sadat and Israeli Prime Minister Menachem Begin; **WITH:** Jimmy Carter, Boutros Boutros-Ghali, Henry Kissinger, Leon Charney, Zbigniew Brzezinski, Wolf Blitzer, Stuart Eizenstat, Samuel Lewis, Robert Lipshutz, William Quandt, Gerald Rafshoon, Patricia Kahane, Nabil Fahmy, Ahmed Maher, Nabil El Araby, Abdel Raouf El Reedy, Mohammed Gohar, Hisham Khalil, Meir Rosenne, Avraham Tamir, David Landau, Shlomo Gazit, Arye Naor, Dan Pattir, Smadar Perry, Yael Dayan, Nabil Shaath, Andre Azoulay

Anwar el-Sadat, Menachem Begin in *Back Door Channels* © Fisher Klingenstein Films

STAY COOL (Initiate Prods.) Producers, Ken Johnson, Janet Dubois, Mark Polish, Michael Polish; Director, Ted Smith (Michael Polish); Screenplay, Mark Polish; Photography, M. David Mullen; Designer, Clark Hunter; Costumes, Christie Wittenborn; Music, Kubilay Uner; Editor, Cary Gries; Casting, Kelly Martin Wagner; a Prohibition Pictures production; Dolby; Color; Rated PG-13; 108 minutes; Release date: September 16, 2011. **CAST:** Mark Polish (Henry McCarthy), Winona Ryder (Scarlet Smith), Sean Astin (Big Girl), Josh Holloway (Wino), Hilary Duff (Shasta O'Neil), Jon Cryer (Javier), Marc Blucas (Brad Nelson), Chevy Chase (Principal Marshall), Frances Conroy (Mrs. Leuchtenberger), Dee Wallace (Mrs. McCarthy), Joanna Cassidy (Mrs. Smith), Michael Gross (Mr. McCarthy), Jessica St. Clair (Darcy Portola), Ken Johnson (Mr. O'Neil), Jessica Schatz (Mrs. O'Neil), Scott Michael Campbell (Officer Bird), Blake Adams (Cop), Catherine Black (Goth Girl), Jenn Shagrin, Josh Sussman (Jungle Journalists), Jane Sheldon (Goth Girl Singer), Clark Hunter (River Village Guard #1), Jack Salvatore Jr. (Student in the Hallway), Nick Thurston (Party Kid), Kelly Wagner (Nurse), Ashley Bell (Valedictorian), David Shackleford (John John), Ryan Best (Disc Jockey), Emily Happe (WRHS TV Host), Bon Ogle (Book Store Employee), Victoria K. Johnson (Student Hollywood Reporter), Max Thieriot (Shasta's Boyfriend), Brian Austin Green (Narrator)

Hilary Duff, Mark Polish in *Stay Cool* © Initiate Prods.

CONNECTED: AN AUTOBIOGRAPHY ABOUT LOVE, DEATH & TECHNOLOGY (Paladin) Producers, Sasha Lewis, Carlton Evans; Director, Tiffany Shlain; Screenplay, Tiffany Shlain, Ken Goldberg, Carlton Evans, Sawyer Steele; Music, Gunnard Doboze; Editors, Tiffany Shlain, Dalan McNabola; Narrator, Peter Coyote; Animation Director, Stefan Nadelman; a Moxie Institute and Impact Partners presentation; Color; Not rated; 80 minutes; Release date: September 16, 2011. Documentary on connections made by the Internet.

Connected © Paladin Pictures

PEARL JAM TWENTY (Abramorama) Producers, Cameron Crowe, Kelly Curtis, Andy Fischer, Morgan Neville; Executive Producer, Michele Anthony; Director/Screenplay, Cameron Crowe; Photography, Nicola B. Marsh; Editors, Chris Perkel, Kevin Klauber; a Vinyl Films production, in association with Monkeywrench, Inc. and Tremolo Prods.; Color; DV; Not rated; 109 minutes; Release date: September 20, 2011. Documentary on Seattle rock group Pearl Jam; **WITH:** Eddie Vedder, Stone Gossard, Mike McCready, Jeff Ament, Matt Cameron, Chris Cornell, Cameron Crowe.

Pearl Jam in *Pearl Jam Twenty* © Abramorama

SHIT YEAR (Cinemad Presents) Producers, Lars Kundsen, Jay Van Hoy; Exdcutive Producers, Ian McGloin, Jamie Mai, Charlie Ledley, Tony Lenosky, Rabinder Sira, Dallas M. Brennan, Chris Gilligan; Director/Screenplay, Cam Archer; Photography, Aaron Platt; Designer, Elizabeth Birkenbuel; Costumes, Stacey Battat, Stephanie Volkmar; Music, Mick Turner; Editor, Madeleine Riley; Casting, Julia Kim; a Parts and Labor production in association with Strange Loop and Wild Invention; Dolby; Black and white/color; Not rated; 95 minutes; Release date: September 21, 2011. **CAST:** Ellen Barkin (Colleen West), Melora Walters (Shelly), Bob Einstein (Rick), Luke Grimes (Harvey West), Theresa Randle (Marion), Josh Blaylock (Not Marcus), Djuna Bel (Girl in Bed), Tiffany Anders (Checkout Girl), Nate Archer (Man with Tractor), Fairuza Balk (Message Voice), Rickie Lee Jones (Narrator), Kevin Keirstead (Voice of Marcus), Anna Moore (Hal's Assistant), Kavita Rao, London Vale (Skin People), David Zellner (Hal Ashland)

Luke Grimes, Ellen Barkin in *Shit Year* © Cinemad

A BIRD OF THE AIR (Paladin) formerly *The Loop*; Producers, Steve Tabakin, Margaret Whitton; Executive Producer, Warren Spector; Director, Margaret Whitton; Screenplay, Roger Towne; Based on the novel *The Loop* by Joe Coomer; Photography, Philippe Rousselot; Designer, Mark Alan Duran; Costumes, Joseph G. Aulisi; Music, David Majzlin; Editor, Sabine Hoffman; Casting, Amanda Mackey, Cathy Sandrich Gelfond; a Tashtego Films presentation; Color; Not rated; 98 minutes; Release date: September 23, 2011. **CAST:** Rachel Nichols (Fiona), Jackson Hurst (Lyman), Linda Emond (Margie), Buck Henry (Duncan Weber), Judith Ivey (Eleanor Reeves), Phyllis Somerville (Ivy Campbell), Anjanette Comer (Mrs. Weber), Erik Jensen (Bearded Man), Kaiulani Lee (Mrs. Blair), Matte Osian (Trucker), Rocco Sisto (Security Guard), Louis Zorich (Stowalski), Jessamyn Blakeslee (Crash Victim), Gary Farmer (Charles Ballard), Carrie Fleming (Reference Librarian), Bernardo P. Saracino (Neil), Stephanie Jones (Dr. Dougherty), Todd La Tourrette (Tom), Juliet Lopez (Dr. Reynosa), Genia Michaela (Amber), Carmela Rappazzo (Prof. Paquet), Kat Sawyer-Young (Billie), Michael Sheets (John), Kevin Skousen (Frank), Jocelyn Towne (Susie), Paul Twitchell (Paul)

Jackson Hurst, Rachel Nichols in *A Bird of the Air* © Paladin Pictures

ART HISTORY (Factory 25)Producer/Director/Editor: Joe Swanberg; Executive Producer, Kent Osborne; Screenplay, Joe Swanberg, Josephine Decker, Kent Osborne; Photography, Adam Wingard, Joe Swanberg; Color; HD; Not rated; 74 minutes; Release date: September 23, 2011. **CAST:** Josephine Decker (Juliette), Joe Swanberg (Sam), Kent Osborne (Eric), Adam Wingard (Bill), Kris Swanberg (Hillary)

FINDING KIND (IndieFlix) Producers, Lauren Parsekian, Molly Stroud; Director/ Screenplay, Lauren Parsekian; Executive Producer, Tom Shadyac; Photography, Christopher Hamilton; Music, Andrew Skrabutenas, Nicole Vaughn; Editor, Vegard H. Sorby; a Kind Campaign production; Color; Not rated; 76 minutes; Release date: September 23, 2011. Documentary about the efforts to stop bullying among girls; **WITH:** Laura Parsekian, Molly Stroud, Jessica Weiner, Rosalind Wiseman, Ken Clark, Tetia Stroud. Debra Parsekian

THUNDER SOUL (Roadside Attractions) Producers, Ketih Calder, Mark Landsman, Jessica Wu; Director, Mark Landsman; Photography, Sandra Chandler; Music, Conrad O. Johnson Sr.; Music Supervisors, Jim Black, Gabe Hilfer; Editor, Claire Didier; Narrator, Jamie Foxx; a Snoot Entertainment production; Dolby; Color; Rated PG; 83 minutes; Release date: September 23, 2011. Documentary on how musician Conrad O. Johnson Sr. transformed the Kashmere High School jazz band into a competitive, award-winning funk band; **WITH:** Conrad O. Johnson Sr., Craig Baldwin, Craig Green, Bruce Middleton, Gaila Mitchell, Reginald Rollins.

Thunder Soul © Roadside Attractions

INCENDIARY: THE WILLINGHAM CASE (Truly Indie) Directors/Producers/ Photography, Steve Mims, Joe Bailey Jr.; Music, Graham Reynolds; Editor, Steve Mims; a Yokel production; Color; HD; Not rated; 102 minutes; Release date: September 23, 2011. Documentary about the unjust conviction and execution of Cameron Todd Willingham for the murders of his three young children; **WITH:** John Lentini, Elizabeth Gilbert, Rick Casey, Dr. Gerald Hurst, David Martin.

MARDI GRAS: SPRING BREAK (Samuel Goldwyn Films) Producers, Armyan Bernstein, Zanne Devine, Peter Jaysen, Gregory Lessans, Charlie Lyons; Director, Phil Dornfeld; Screenplay, Josh Heald; Photography, Thomas E. Ackerman; Designer, Stephen J. Lineweaver; Costumes, Carol Ramsey; Music, Jared Faber; Editor, Mark Scheib; a Holding/Beacon Pictures/Moving Pictures AMG production; Dolby; Color; Rated R; 88 minutes; Release date: September 23, 2011. **CAST:** Nicholas D'Agosto (Mike Morgan), Josh Gad (Bartholomew T. "Bump" Brown), Bret Harrison (Scottie Smith), Arielle Kebbell (Lucy Mills), Danneel Harris (Erica), Carmen Electra (Herself), Regina Hall (Ann Marie), Gary Grubbs (Mr. Duluth), Becky O'Donohue (Cousin Janice), Jessie O'Donohue (Cousin Janine), Charles Shaughnessy (Barry, Chateau Clerk), Jack Betts, Mimi Cozzens (Elderly Couple), Matt Moore (Jonathan), Genevieve Guzchack (Dominique), Eric Paulsen (News Correspondent), J. Patrick McNamara (Prof. Fleischman), Tyler Cross (Penn Dude), Kim Vu, Courtney J. Calrk, Hunter Burke (Penn Students), Stephanie Honore, Melissa Ware, Jack Lineweaver (Bourbon Street People), J. Omar Castro (Hotel Security Guard), Madison Bauer (Tropical Isle Bartender), JT Alexander,

Matt Wool (Tropical Isle Guys), Brandi Coleman (Lucy's Friend), Kevin Gould (Valet), Yohance Myles (Gregory, Hotel Desk Guy), Marcelle Baer, Jessica Heap, Summer Lee (Casamento Girls), Lauren Swinney (Old Lady), Denise Williamson (Samantha), Jennifer Guhlin (Sarah), Mike Mayhall (Jester), Sharon London (Chateau Burgundy Maid), David Joseph Martinez (Chateau Burgundy Security), Dan Levy (Frat House MC), Jon Eyez (Carmen's Bodyguard), Nathaniel Colin Jr. (Geeky Kid), Lauren Fain (Chateau Burgundy Waitress), J.J. Standing (Tommy, Royal Monaco Security), Leon Contavesprie (Carl, Royal Monaco Concierge), Mikki Val (Laura, Royal Monaco Front Desk Girl), Josh Heald (Dude in Crowd)

Nicholas D'Agosto, Josh Gad, Bret Harrison in *Mardi Gras: Spring Break* © Goldwyn Films

LIMELIGHT (Magnolia) Producers, Jen Gatien, Alfred Spellman, Billy Corben; Director, Billy Corben; Executive Producers, Dave Berlin, Jonathan Vinnik; Photography, Ralf Gonzalez, Alexa Harris, Trisha Solyn, Randy Valdes; Music, Brian "Fast" Leiser; Editor, Sam Rega; a Deerjen Films presentation in association with Gulfstream Films of a Rakontur production; Color; Not rated; 103 minutes; Release date: September 23, 2011. Documentary on Manhattan nightclub kingpin Peter Gatien; **WITH:** Peter Gatien, Michael Alig, Benjamin Brafman, Michael Caruso, Sean Kirkham, Edward I. Koch, Steve Lewis, Moby, Frank Owen, Howard Safir

Peter Gatien in *Limelight* © Magnolia Pictures

THE MAN NOBODY KNEW: IN SEARCH OF MY FATHER, CIA SPYMASTER WILLIAM COLBY (First Run Features) Producers, Grace Guggenheim, David Johnson, Carl Colby; Director, Carl Colby; Photography, Gary Steele; Music, Michael Bacon; Editor, Jay Freund; an Act 4 Entertainment production in association with Jedburgh Films; Color/black and white; HD; Not rated; 104 minutes; Release date: September 23, 2011. Documentary on CIA agent William Colby; **WITH:** Dale Andrade, Dr. Zbigniew Brzezinski, Corrado Cantatore, Jonathan Clarke, Carl Colby, Barbara H. Colby, Darren Flitcroft, Donald Gregg, Seymour Hersh, Fisher Howe, Thomas Hughes, Oleg Kalugin, Bob Kerrey, John Langan, James Lilley, Edward Luttwak, Thomas McCoy, Lt. Col. Robert McFarlane, Elizabeth McIntosh, Gen. H.R. McMaster, Hugh Montgomery, Lt. Col. John Nagl, Rufus Phillips, Walter Pincus, Donald H. Rumsfeld, James R. Schlesinger, Daniel Schorr, Gen. Brent Scowcroft, Judge Laurence Silberman, Maj. Gen. John K. Singlaub, Barbara Pindar Smith, Joseph W. Smith, Evan Thomas, Hugh Tovar, Judge William Webster, Tim Weiner, Bob Woodward, Steve Young.

William Colby in *The Man Nobody Knew* © First Run Features

ARCHIE'S FINAL PROJECT (Rocket Releasing/Big Air Studios) formerly *My Suicide*; Producers, David Lee Miller, Larry Janss, Todd Traina, Eric J. Adams; Executive Producers, Michael McDonough, Alana Kagan, Karyn Rachtman, Steven Jay Rubin, Julia Pistor, Karen Dean Fritts, Ken Hertz; Director, David Lee Miller; Screenplay, David Lee Miller, Eric J. Adams, Gabriel Sunday; Story, David Lee Miller, Jordan Miller; Photography, Lisa Wiegand, Angie Hill; Designer, Suzanne Rattigan; Costumes, Amanda Oliver, Caitlin Winn; Music Supervisors, Karyn Rachtman, Bobby LaVelle; Editors, Gabriel Sunday, Jordan Miller; Casting, Laura Corrin; a Regenerate/Archie Films production in association with Red Rover Films, Luminaria Films, Interscope Films; Color; HD; Not rated; 105 minutes; Release date: September 23, 2011. **CAST:** Gabriel Sunday (Archibald Holden Buster "Archie" Williams), Brooke Nevin (Sierra Silver), David Carradine (Jesse Gabriel Vargas), Joe Mantegna (Dr. Gafur Chandrasakar), Mariel Hemingway (Charlotte Silver), Nora Dunn (Gretchen Williams), Zachary Ray Sherman (Corey), Michael Welch (Earl), Vanessa Lengies (Mallory), Tony Hale (Carmelo Peters – LCSW), Sandy Martin (Mrs. Ellis), Tim Halligan (Mr. Silver), Steven Anthony Lawrence, Jack Salvatore Jr. (Brainiacs), Stephen Sowan, Kyle Fisher, Wes Robinson (Stoners), Robert Kurcz (Daryl Williams), Ernie Garrett, Katie Traina (P.E. Teachers), Kurtis Bedford (Mr. Bedford), Jolene Adams (Corey's Mom), Molly Barrow, Jatin Das Gupta (Themselves), Jake Bern (Jason), Michele Clarke, Emily Goglia (Cutters), Vic Dunlop (Salvation), Heather Hershow (Lisa), Tom Lenoci (Pastor), Natalya Oliver (Attention Spree Girl), Jessica Grace Orr (It's Painful Girl), Alex Revan (Brandon), Don Aguilar, Eric Buchow (Policemen), Renee Talbert, Dree Hemingway, Rebecca Adams (Christian Girls), Amanda Thorp (Penelope, Bug Loving Girl), John Everlove, Terry Everett Brown (EMTs), Kristi Flynn (Innocent Girl), Caker Folley (Cheerleader), Steven Christopher Parker (Gamer), Avelawance Phillips (Bro #1)

Gabriel Sunday, Brooke Nevin in *Archie's Final Project* © Rocket Releasing

JOURNEY FROM ZANSKAR (Warrior Films) Producer/Director/Screenplay, Frederick Marx; Photography, Nick Sherman; Music, Michael Fitzpatrick, Adam Schiff; Editors, Joanna Kiernan, Frederick Marx; Narrator, Richard Gere; Color; HD; Not rated; 90 minutes; Release date: September 23, 2011. Documentary on two Buddhist monks' efforts to help 14 children from poor Zanskari villages; **WITH:** Geshe Lobsang Yonten, Lobsang Dhamchoe, The Dalai Lama.

Journey from Zanskar © Warrior Films

IN SEARCH OF GOD (RJ Intl.) Director/Music, Rupam Sarmah; Photography, Suraj Dowerah; Editor, Samuel Markus; Produced in association with Global Media; American-Indian; Color; HD; Not rated; 60 minutes; Release date: September 23, 2011. Documentary on the Indian island sanctuary of Majuli; **WITH:** Kavita Srinivasan, Babu Ram Saikia

COURAGEOUS (TriStar) Producer, Stephen Kendrick; Executive Producers, Michael C. Catt, Jim McBride, Terry Hemmings; Associate Producers, Dennis Wiemer, Larry Frenzel; Director, Alex Kendrick; Screenplay, Alex Kendrick, Stephen Kendrick; Photography, Bob Scott; Designers, Darian Corley, Sheila McBride; Costumes, Terri Catt; Music, Mark Willard; Editors, Alex Kendrick, Stephen Hullfish, Bill Ebel; a Sherwood Pictures presentation in association with Provident Films and Affirm Films of a Kendrick Brothers production; Dolby; Color; Rated PG-13; 129 minutes; Release date: September 30, 2011. **CAST:** Alex Kendrick (Adam Mitchell), Renee Jewell (Victoria Mitchell), Rusty Martin (Dylan Mitchell),

Ken Bevel (Nathan Hayes), Eleanor Brown (Kayla Hayes), Robert Amaya (Javier Martinez), Angelita Nelson (Carmen Martinez), Kevin Downes (Shane Fuller), Ben Davies (David Thomson), T.C. Stallings (T.J.), Rusty Martin Sr. (Frank Tyson), Matt Hardwick (Antonie), Lauren Etchells (Emily Mitchell), Taylor Hutcherson (Jade Hays), Ed Litton (Pastor Hunt), Donald Howze (Derrick), David Milliner (Sgt. Murphy), Christian Dozier (Jordan Hays), Ellie Zapata (Isabel Martinez), Louise Guillebeaux (Clyde Holloman), Daniel Simmons (William Barrett), Evan Zapata (Marcos Martinez), Jose Rodriguez (Jamar Holloman), Kevin Taylor (Deputy), Jessa Duggar, Joy Duggar (Girls at Funeral)

Alex Kendrick, Rusty Martin Jr. in *Courageous* © TriStar

FINDING JOE (Balcony) Producer/Director/Screenplay, Patrick Takaya Solomon; Executive Producers, Patricia Frazier, Patrick Takaya Solomon; Photography, Ezra Migel; Music, Isaac Sprintis; Editor, Paul Forte; a Pat and Pat production; Color; HD-to-35mm; Not rated; 80 minutes; Release date: September 30, 2011. Documentary on mythologist and author Joseph Campbell; **WITH:** Chungliang Al Huang, Rebecca Armstrong, Deepak Chopra, Alan Cohen, Mick Fleetwood, Akiva Goldsman, Laird John Hamilton, Catherine Hardwicke, Tony Hawk, Gay Hendricks, Brian Johnson, Rashida Jones, Lynne Kaufman, David Loy, Joseph Marshall, David Lee Miller, Norman Ollestad, Ken Robinson, Robin Sharma, Robert Walter

Finding Joe © Balcony Releasing

BUNRAKU (ARC Entertainment) Producers, Keith Calder, Jessica Wu, Ram Bergman, Nava Levin; Director/Screenplay, Guy Moshe; Story, Boaz Davidson; Photography, Juan Ruiz-Anchia; Designer, Chris Farmer; Costumes, Donna Zakowska; Music, Terence Blanchard; Editors, Zach Staenberg, Glenn Garland; Visual Effects Supervisor, Oliver Hotz; Fight Choreographer, Larnell Stovall; Casting, Mary Vernieu; an XLrator Media in association with Snoot Entertainment presentation of a Picturesque/Ram Bergman production; Dolby; Super 35 Widescreen; Deluxe Color; Rated R; 121 minutes; Release date: September 30, 2011. **CAST:** Josh Hartnett (The Drifter), Woody Harrelson (The Bartender), Ron Perlman (Nicola), Gackt Camui (Yoshi), Kevin McKidd (Killer #2), Demi Moore (Alexandra), Shun Sugata (Uncle), Jordi Mollà (Valentine), Emily Kaiho (Momoko), Mike Patton (The Narrator), Neil D'Monte (The Pianist), Mark Ivanir (Eddie), Vali Rupita (Gregor), Gabriel Spahiu (Boris Patz), Fernando Chien, Holland Diaz, Razvan Gheorghiu, Yoshio Iizuka, Shahar Sorek, Aaron Toney, Kofi Yiadom, Florian Ciprian (Killers), Andrei Araditz (Croupier), Chris Brewster (Punk Leader), Alin Panc (Card Dealer), Gabi Rauta (Nicola's Assistant Casino), Larnell Stovall (Red Army Commander), George Ivascu (Cab Driver), Linda Manolache (Prostitute), Maria-Antoaneta Tudor (Brass Knuckle Girl), Ciprian Dumitrascu, Doru Firica (Bouncers), Bogdan Uritescu (Mob Office Supervisor), Andreea Padararu (Assistant), Constantin Barbulescu (Absinthe Den Owner), Luminita Stoianovici (Absinthe Den Waitress), Cezara Dafinescu (Lady), Nicolae Predica (Casino Employee), Marcel Iures (Chief of Police), Dorin Zaharia (Ivan), Theodor Danetti (General), Oliver Toderita, Zoltan Butuc (Lowlifes), Samuel Vauramo, Marius Florian, Razvan Calin (Bullies), Emil Hostina, Bogdan Voda (Followers), Ion Lupu (Deputy Mayor), Thayr Harris (League Member), Maxim Esterkin (Nicola Thug #1)

Ron Perlman, Demi Moore in *Bunraku* © ARC Entertainment

FILTH TO ASHES, FLESH TO DUST (Midnight Releasing) Producers, Terry James, Gordon Vasquez; Director/Editor, Paul Morrell; Executive Producer/Screenplay, Armont Casale; Photography, Royce Allen Dudley; Designer, John Nasby; Music, Ken Eberhard; a Jeoa Productions presentation of an Armont Casale production; Color; Not rated; 90 minutes; Release date: September 30, 2011. **CAST:** Meredith Laine (Kimberly), Linda Bella (Caitlin), Allison Ochmanek (Brit), Derrick Bishop (Eric), Anton Troy (Ronan), Teodorico Paul Sajor (Juan), Diana Quezada (Shelly), Bianca Lemaire (Kiara), Eric Lewis (Maxx), Nicholas J. Leinbach (Purge), Christina Iannuzzi (Netty), Dana Chapman (Lisa), Paul Morrell (Missing Person), Stephen Zimpel (Jake), Terry James (Mr. Dowd), Salina Duplessis (Eva), Sophie Gospodarczyk (Roslind Crews), Jodie Gratton, Kirsty Gratton (Pool Girls), Alex Morrell (Orphan)

Filth to Ashes, Flesh to Dust © Midnight Releasing

AMERICAN TEACHER (First Run Features) Producers, Vanessa Roth, Ninive Calegari, Dave Eggers; Director, Vanessa Roth; Co-Director/Editor, Brian McGinn; Based on the book *Teachers Have it Easy: The Big Sacrifices and Small Salaries of America's Teachers* by Daniel Moulthrop, Ninive Calegari and Dave Eggers; Photography, Dan Gold, Steve Milligan, Arthur Yee, Rich White; Music, Thao Nguyen; Narrator, Matt Damon; a Teacher Salary Project production; Color; HD; Not rated; 81 minutes; Release date: September 30, 2011. Documentary on the lack of respect and salary that American teachers deserve; **WITH:** Erik Benner, Linda Darling-Hammond, Jonathan Dearman, Jamie Fidler, Rhena Jasey, Gregory Peters, Rachel Russell, Loran Simon, Zeke Vanderhoek

Jamie Fidler in *American Teacher* © First Run Features

MUNGER ROAD (Freestyle) Producer, Kyle Heller; Executive Producer, Jeffery D. Smith; Director/Screenplay, Nicholas Smith; Photography, Westley Gathright; Designer, Matt Hyland; Costumes, Aly Barohn; Music, Wojciech Golczewski; Editor, Robert Cauble; Casting, Ricki Maslar; an Insomnia Productions Ltd. presentation; Color; Rated PG-13; 90 minutes; Release date: September 30, 2011. **CAST:** Bruce Davison (Chief Kirkhoven), Randall Batinkoff (Deputy Hendricks), Trevor Morgan (Corey LaFayve), Brooke Peoples (Joe Risk), Hallock Beals (Scott Claussen), Lauren Storm (Rachael Donahue), Art Fox (Mayor Swanson), Maggie Henry (Nancy), Bill J. Stevens (Father McCroy), Ron Johnston (Lenny), Judy Proudfoot Schenck (Judy)

SURROGATE VALENTINE (Tiger Industry Films) Producers, Duane Andersen, Dave Boyle; Executive Producer, Gary Chou; Director, Dave Boyle; Screenplay, Dave Boyle, Joel Clark, Goh Nakamura; Photography, Bill Otto; Music/Songs, Goh Nakamura; Editors, Dave Boyle, Michael Lerman, Duane Andersen; a Brainwave Films presentation; Black and white; HD; Not rated; 75 minutes; Release date: September 30, 2011. **CAST:** Goh Nakamura (Himself), Chadd Stoops (Danny Turner), Lynn Chen (Rachel), Mary Cavett (Valerie), Joy Osmanski (Amy), Parry Shen (Bradley), Calpernia Addams (Tammi), Eric M. Levy (Arthur), Josiah Polhemus (Dave Margolis), Dan "Damage" Bjornson (Mark), Di Quon (Emily), Alexandra Fulton (Diane), Natalie Lander (Sarah), Manuela Horn (Mark's Girlfriend), Matthew A. Gallagher, John-Michael Carlton (Fans), Ron Eliot (TV Host)

THE ROAD TO FREEDOM (Creative Freedom) Producer, Tom Proctor; Co-Producer, Blu de Goyler; Executive Producer, Henry Bronson; Director, Brendan Moriarty; Screenplay, Margie Rogers; Photography, David Mun; Designer, David Sandeep Robert; Costumes, Nop Sophorn; Music, Austin Creek; Editors, Sean Halloran, Margie Rogers; a Bajan Vista Productions presentation in association with Madcat Movies; American-Cambodian; Color; Rated R; 93 minutes; Release date: September 30, 2011. **CAST:** Joshua Fredric Smith (Sean Flynn), Scott Maguire (Dana Stone), Tom Proctor (Francias), Kanilen Kang (Mean), Nhem Sokun (Lim Po), Nhem Sokunthol (General), Men Sophak (Lim Po's Wife), Chrem Vutha (Chantha), Thy Wing (Waitress), Kheav Pomsen, Hun Phach, Sean Vandy, Cheun Vuthy, Kheang Ty, Hunh Vitou, Sun Thaiheng, Ong Ritthy, Sem Vuthy (Khmer Rouge)

Joshua Fredric Smith, Scott Maguire in *The Road to Freedom* © Creative Freedom

HELL AND BACK AGAIN (Docurama Films/Impact Partners) Producers, Mike Lerner, Martin Herring, Danfung Denins; Executive Producers, Dan Cogan, Karol Martesko-Fenster, Gernot Schaffler, Thomas Brunner, Maxyne Franklin; Director/Photography, Danfung Dennis; Music, J. Ralph; Editor, Fiona Otway; a Roast Beef production in association with Channel 4 Britdoc Foundation, Sabotage Films and Thought Engine; American-British-Austrian; Stereo; Color; Not rated; 88 minutes; Release date: October 5, 2011. Documentary following U.S. Marine Sgt. Nathan Harris both in combat in Afghanistan and back home; **WITH:** Sgt. Nathan Harris, Ashley Harris, Lt. Col. Christian Cabaniss, Capt. Eric Meador, Lt. Edward Hubbard, Chaplain Terry Roberts, Staff Sgt. Doug Webb, Lt. Cmdr. Robert Gaines, Lt. Cmdr. Matthew Swibe, Sgt. Chris MacDonald. (This film received an Oscar nomination for documentary feature).

Bruce Davison in *Munger Road* © Freestyle Releasing

Ashley Harris, Nathan Harris in *Hell and Back Again* © Docurama Films

GEORGE HARRISON: LIVING IN THE MATERIAL WORLD (HBO) Producers, Martin Scorsese, Olivia Harrison, Nigel Sinclair; Director, Martin Scorsese; Photography, Robert Richardson, Martin Kenzie; Editor, David Tedeschi; a Grove Street Pictures presentation of a Spitfire Pictures/Sikelia Prods. production; Color/black and white; HD; Not rated; 208 minutes; Release date: October 5, 2011 (concurrent with HBO premiere). Documentary on the life and music of Beatle George Harrison; **WITH:** Neil Aspinall, Jane Birkin, Pattie Boyd, Eric Clapton, Ray Cooper, Terry Gilliam, Dhani Harrison, Harold Harrison, Harry Harrison, Louise French Harrison, Olivia Harrison, Peter Harrison, Eric Idle, Jim Keltner, Astrid Kirchherr, Jeff Lynne, George Martin, Paul McCartney, Yoko Ono, Tom Petty, Ken Scott, Ravi Shankar, Phil Spector, Ringo Starr, Jackie Stewart, Joan Taylor, Klaus Voormann

George Harrison in *Living in the Material World* © HBO Films

SUPERHEROES (HBO Documentary Films) Producer, Theodore James; Executive Producers, Doug Blush, Patrick Creadon, Christine O'Malley; Director/ Photography, Michael Barnett; Screenplay, Michael Barnett, Theodore James; Music, Ceiri Torjussen; Editors, Doug Blush, Derek Boonstra, Jeff Chen; a Theodore James Production in association with Freestyle Filmworks and O'Malley Creadon Prods.; Color; HD; Not rated; 82 minutes; Release date: October 7, 2011. Documentary on self-proclaimed, real-life superheroes who patrol cities in costume, hoping to thwart evil; **WITH:** Mr. Xtreme, Stan Lee, Zimmer, Master Legend, Dark Guardian, Robin Rosenberg, Andra Brown. (This film premiered on HBO on Aug. 8, 2011).

Superheroes © HBO Films

THE SONS OF TENNESSEE WILLIAMS (First Run Features) Producer/ Director/ Screenplay, Tim Wolff; Photography, Eric Adkins; Music, Ratty Scurvics; Editors, Tim Wolff, Matt Bucy; a Wolffhouse presentation; Color/black and white; Not rated; 75 minutes; Release date: October 7, 2011. Documentary on Mardi Gras' krewes, or gay social clubs; **WITH:** George Roth, Mike Moreau, Bill Woolley, Jimmy Keyes, Albert Carey, Don Stratton, Wendell Stipelcovich, John Henry Bogie, Tracy Hendrix, Steve Labranche, Freddie Guess, George Patterson, Bill McLemore, Gary de Leaumont, Bill McCarthy, Abram Bowie.

THE ONE (TLA Releasing) Producers, Michael Billy, Aimee Denaro, Caytha Jentis; Executive Producer, Nancie Ellis; Director/Screenplay, Caytha Jentis; Photography, Ben Wolf; Designer, Katherine Whitehead; Music, Kenneth Lampl; Editor, Verne Mattson; Casting, Adrienne Stern; a Fox Meadow Films production; Color; HD; Not rated; 90 minutes; Release date: October 7, 2011. **CAST:** Jon Prescott (Daniel), Ian Novick (Tommy), Margaret Anne Florence (Jen), Natalya Rudakova (Alex), Kelly Coffield Park (Sandy), Christopher Cass (Daniel Sr.), Pierce Forsythe (Jaime), Michael Emery (Luke), Michael Billy (Stephen), David Albiero (Toby), Collin Biddle (Dr. Wilson), Cody Matthew Blymire (GoGo Boy), Aimee Denaro (Janie), Mike DiGiacinto (John), Lateefah Fleming (Fitness Instructor), Lauren Francesca (Jessica), Olivia Gallo (Daniel's Daughter), Rosie Gunther (Martha), Patrick Martin, Anderson Somerselle (Happy Gay Couple), Vincent Pelligrino (Vig 27 Bouncer), Anders Groop, George Psomas, Brendan Ryan (Groomsmen)

Ian Novick, Jon Prescott in *The One* © TLA Releasing

EVERYDAY SUNSHINE: THE STORY OF FISHBONE (Pale Griot Film) Producers/ Directors/Screenplay, Lev Anderson, Chris Metzler; Photography/Editor, Jeff Springer; Music, Norwood Fisher, Jimmy Sloan; Narrator, Laurence Fishburne; Color; HD; Not rated; 104 minutes; Release date: October 7, 2011. Documentary on L.A. band Fishbone; **WITH:** Norwood Fisher, Angelo Moore, Chris Dowd, Walter Kiby II, Kendall Jones, Elaine "Mama Fish" Fisher, Larren Jones, Anna Jones, Dazireen Moore, Cheyenne Moore, Ice-T, Flea, Gwen Stefani, Perry Farrell, David Kahne, Roger Perry, Dallas Austin, Adrian Young, Branford Marsalis, Eugene Hutz, George Clinton, Les Claypool, Mike Watt, Tim Robbins, Vernon Reid, Keith Morris, Tony Kanal, Bob Forrest, ?uestlove, Rocky George, Dre Gipson, John McKnight, John Steward, Phillip "Fish" Fisher, John Bigham, Padre Holmes, Tracey "Spacey T" Singleton, Curtis Storey

Angelo Moore in *Everyday Sunshine* © Pale Griot Film

THE SWELL SEASON (Seventh Art Releasing) Producer, Carlo Mirabella-Davis; Directors/Screenplay, Nick August-Perna, Chris Dapkins, Carlo Mirabella-Davis; Photography, Chris Dapkins; Music, The Swell Season, Iron and Wine; Editor, Nick August-Perna; an Elkcreek Cinema & Overcoat Records presentation; Black and white; HD; Not rated; 90 minutes; Release date: October 7, 2011. Documentary on the tour embarked upon by Glen Hansard and Markéta Inglová that resulted from the success of their film *Once*; **WITH:** Glen Hansard, Markéta Irglová, Colm Mac Con Iomaire, Rob Botchnik, Graham Hopkins, Joe Doyle, Catherine Hansard, Marek Irg, Zuzana Irglová, Jana Irglová, Mark Geary, Sam Beam, Rob Burger, James Morse, Simon Henry, Ben Cohen, Tyler Kennedy, Liz Ross, Fiacre Gaffney, Howard Greynolds, Damien Dempsey, James Hansard.

Glen Hansard, Markéta Irglová in *The Swell Season* © Seventh Art Releasing

TO BE HEARD (ITVS) Producers, Roland Legiardi-Laura, Edwin Martinez, Deborah Shaffer, Amy Sultan, Jill Angelo, Jim Angelo; Directors, Roland Legiardi-Laura, Edwin Martinez, Deborah Shaffer, Amy Sultan; Photography/Editor, Edwin Martinez; Music, Wendy Blackstone; an Odysseus Group Production in co-production with ITVS; Not rated; Color; HD; 87 minutes; Release date: October 12, 2011. Documentary on how three teens from the South Bronx changed their lives by writing poetry; **WITH:** Anthony Pittman, Pearl Quick, Karina Sanchez, Roland Legiardi-Laura, Amy Sultan, Joe Ubiles. (This film premiered on television in 2010.)

To Be Heard © ITVS

AMERICA THE BEAUTIFUL 2: THE THIN COMMANDMENTS (Harley Boy Entertainment) Producers, Darryl Roberts, Eddie Williams III, Harley Decease, Jeff Scheftel; Director/ Screenplay, Darryl Roberts; Photography, David Shawl, Chan Hartman; Music Supervisor, Michael Turner; Editor, Edward Osei-Gyimah; a Gravitas Ventures production presented in association with PMK*BNC; Color; HD; Not rated; 104 minutes; Release date: October 12, 2011. Documentary on America's compulsion to be thin; **WITH:** Darryl Roberts, Linda Bacon, Deepak Chopra, Carolyn Costin, Beverly Johnson, Kathleen Sebilius, Howard Shapiro, Evelyn Tribole, Paul Campos

HAPPY LIFE (Tilt Pocket) Producers, Rachel Fernandes, Spencer Kiernan; Executive Producer, Abel Ferrara; Director/Screenplay, Michael M. Bilandic; Photography, Sean Price Williams; Designer, Matt Walker; Costumes, Linnea Vedder, Meg Browning; Music, Dan Vinci Boi, Hot Hero; Editor, Joseph Saito; Color; HD; Not rated; 73 minutes; Release date: October 14, 2011. **CAST:** Tom McCaffrey (Keith), Amanda Salane (Lil' Tina), Gilles Decamps (DJ Liquidz), Kate Lyn Sheil (Leslie), Alex Ross Perry (Donald), Craig Bugowski (Ron), Jeffrey Cashvan (Amadeus), Nick Catucci (Chaz), Amanda Colbenson (Wendy), Sarah Croce (Patty), Arthur Crossman (Stinkbomb), Aldous Davidson (Roger), Urcella Di Pietro (Emily), Stephen Donovan (Basil), Leah Giblin (Seuss), Lizzie Henney (Strawberry), Angus Hepburn (Marcus), Chris Jacobson (Bud), Jared Kasanofsky (Jit), Spencer Kiernan (Elijah), Terry Lavelle (Frankie J.), Nick Lennen (Seth), Gabriel Lockey (Ian), Liam McMullan (Lance), Isabelle McNally (Mandy), Ben Newman (Marky), Luke Oleksa (Bill), Matt Pinfield (Fred), Miguel Pinzon (Harry), Marc Razo (Juan), Charmaine Reed (Diane), Laura Richard (Melinda), Cliff Samara (Mr. Bill), Peter Sarnoff (Jason), Cecilia Scanlon (Amber), Erin Scanlon (Zoe), Ramy Shedid (Vince), Johnny Skreli (Roy), E. Talley II (Tobias), Timoteo Valero (Andre), Linnea Vedder (Shaista), Sean Price Williams (Evan), Zahir Zahireh (Al the Security Guard), Eric Adolfsen (DJ)

TRESPASS (Millennium) Producers, Irwin Winkler, David Winkler; Executive Producers, Avi Lerner, Danny Dimbort, Trevor Short, Boaz Davidson, John Thompson; Co-Producer, Matthew Leonetti Jr.; Director, Joel Schumacher; Screenplay, Karl Gajdusek; Photography, Andrzej Bartkowiak; Designer, Nathan Amondson; Costumes, Judianna Makovsky; Music, David Buckley; Editor, Bill

Pankow; Casting, Jessica Kelly, Suzanne Smith Crowley; a Nu Image production and a Winkler Films production in association with Saturn Films; Dolby; Hawk Scope; Technicolor; Rated R; 91 minutes; Release date: October 14, 2011. **CAST:** Nicolas Cage (Kyle Miller), Nicole Kidman (Sarah Miller), Ben Mendelsohn (Elias), Cam Gigandet (Jonah), Liana Liberato (Avery Miller), Jordana Spiro (Petal), Dash Mihok (Ty), Emily Meade (Kendra), Nico Tortorella (Jake), Brandon Belknap (Dylan), Terry Milam (Travis), Tina Parker (Security Operator), David Maldonado (Security Guard), Nilo Otero (Mr. Big), Simona Williams (Mrs. Big), Gracie Whitton (Young Avery)

Nicole Kidman, Cam Gigandet in *Trespass* © Millennium Entertainment

BOMBAY BEACH (Focus World) Producers, Boaz Yakin, Alma Har'el; Director/Photography, Alma Har'el; Music, Zach Condon, Beirut, Bob Dylan; Editors, Joe Lindquist, Alma Har'el; Choreographer, Paula Present; Color; Not rated; 80 minutes; Release date: October 14, 2011. Documentary on the residents of the fading Salton Sea community in Southern California; **WITH:** Benny Parrish, Pamela Parrish, Mike Parrish, CeeJay Thompson, Dorran "Red" Forgy.

THE WOMAN (The Collective/Bloody Disgusting) Producers, Andrew van den Houten, Robert Tonino; Executive Producers, Albert Podell, Frank Olsen, Loren Semmens; Director, Lucky McKee; Screenplay, Lucky McKee, Jack Ketchum, based on their novel; Photography, Alex Vendler; Designer, Krista Gall; Costumes, Sandra Alexandre, Michael Bevins; Music, Sean Spillane; Editor, Zach Passero; a Moderncine production; Color; HD; Rated R; 101 minutes; Release date: October 14, 2011. **CAST:** Pollyanna McIntosh (The Woman), Sean Bridgers (Chris Cleek), Angela Bettis (Belle Cleek), Lauren Ashley Carter (Peggy Cleek), Carlee Baker (Genevieve Raton), Marcia Bennett (Deana), Chris Kryzkowski (Roger), Alexa Marcigliano (Socket), Shyla Molhusen (Darlin' Cleek), Frank Olsen (Will Campbell), Lauren Petre (Miss Hindle), Zach Rand (Brian Cleek), Lauren Schroeder (Dorothy), Tommy Nelson (Walter)

PAUL GOODMAN CHANGED MY LIFE (Zeitgeist) Producers, Jonathan Lee, Kimberly Reed; Director, Jonathan Lee; Photography, Benjamin Shapiro; Music, Miriam Cutler; Editor, Kimberly Reed; a JSL Films production; Color/black and white; Not rated; 89 minutes; Release date: October 19, 2011. Documentary about influential New York intellectual, poet and co-founder of Gestalt therapy, Paul Goodman; **WITH:** Epi Bohdi, Noam Chomsky, Jason Epstein, Zeke Finkelstein, Richard Flacks, Frieda Gardner, Geoff Gardner, Daisy Goodman, Naomi Goodman, Sally Goodman, Susan Goodman, Jacqueline Gourevitch, Allen Graubard, Neil Heims, Judith Malina, Deborah Meier, Ed Nevis, Grace Paley, Tom Rodd, Ned Rorem, Michael Rossman, Taylor Stoehr, Jerl Surrat, Nicholas von Hoffman, Michael Walzer, Burton Weiss, Gordon Wheeler, Vera Williams

Grace Paley, Paul Goodman in *Paul Goodman Changed My Life*
© Zeitgeist Films

THE CATECHISM CATACLYSM (IFC) Producers, Megan Griffiths, Lacey Leavitt, David Gordon Green, Jody Hill, Danny McBride, Matt Reilly; Director/Screenplay, Todd Rohal; Photography, Ben Kasulke; Designer, Cassie Miggins; Costumes, Alison Kelly; Music, Joseph Stephens; Editor, Alan Canant; a Littleman, Littleman, Littleman & Biggs presentation of a Rough House Production; Color; Not rated; 81 minutes; Release date: October 19, 2011. **CAST:** Steve Little (Father Billy Smoortser), Robert Longstreet (Robbie Shoemaker), Walter Dalton (Father O'Herlihy), Miki Ann Maddox (Tom Sawyer), Koko Lanham (Huckleberry Finn), Rico (Jim), Joe Ivy (Canoe Shop Owner), Enrique Olguin (Miguel), Barbara Pommer (Milagros Maria), Jay Wesley Cochran (Depressed Businessman), Judy Findlay (Old Lady), Carlos Lopez, Derek Erdman, Ronald McGill (Hoodlums), Alice Bridgforth (Parishioner Linda), Laurel Paxton (Parishioner Gloria), Kevin Seal (Parishioner Kevin), Lynn Shelton (Parishioner Judy), Vinny Smith (Parishioner Teddy), Andy Tribolini (Parishioner Lowery), Sharon Vanderveer (Parishioner Pat), Timothy Watkins (Father Tim), Carol Sparer (Waitress), Garrett Cantrell, Jessica Hutchinson, Brock Hutchinson, Sadie Cantrell (Rest Stop Family), Ernie Joseph (Mr. James Sexmun), Dan Leavitt (Kindly Driver)

Robert Longstreet, Steve Little in *The Catechism Cataclysm* © IFC Films

THE REUNION (Samuel Goldwyn Films) Producers, Mike Pavone, Denise Chamian; Director/Screenplay, Mike Pavone; Photography, Kenneth Zunder; Designer, Raymond Pumilia; Costumes, Claire Breaux; Music, James Alan Johnston; Editor, Marc Pollon; Casting, Denise Chamian Casting; a WWE Studios presentation; Dolby; Super 35 Widescreen; Color; Rated PG-13; 96 minutes; Release date: October 21, 2011. **CAST:** John Cena (Sam Cleary), Ethan Embry (Leo Cleary), Michael Rispoli (Nicholas Canton), Boyd Holbrook (Douglas Cleary), Gregg Henry (Kyle Wills), Lela Loren (Theresa Trujillo), Jack Conley (Jack Nealon), Amy Smart (Nina Cleary), Rio Alexander (Edgar Rodriguez), Josh Berry (Steve Bermutti), Morse Bicknell (Uniformed Officer), Jeremiah Bitsui (Mexican Captain), Luis Bordonada (Actor), Kevin Christopher Brown (FBI Agent), Jacob Browne (Prison Guard), Chad Brummett (Karl), Deborah Chavez (Mrs. Rodriguez), Anthony Escobar (Ricardo), Tait Fletcher (Bodyguard), J.D. Garfield (Verdugo), Gilley Grey (Indian Guide #1), Lynda Halligan (CNN News Anchor), Rafael Herrera (Sixto), Colin Jones (Inmate), Dylan Kenin (Bertram), Lora Martinez-Cunningham (Homeless Woman), David Midthunder (Indian Henchman), Steven Michael Quezada (Col. Ramirez), Grizelda Quintana (Hooker), Ashlee Renz-Hotz (Bar Girl), Kelly Ruble (DEA Agent), Bernardo P. Saracino, Omar Paz Trujillo (Armory Guards), Ryan Schaefer (Red/Blue/Tan Man), River Shields (Janson), Michael Showers (Agent Leon Mailor), Ariana Smythe (Allie), William Sterchi (Mikey)

BOY WONDER (Lightning Entertainment) Producers, John Scaccia, Michael Morrissey; Director/ Screenplay, Michael Morrissey; Photography, Christopher LaVasseur; Designer, Mary Glenn Frederickson; Costumes, Karen Malecki; Music, Irv Johnson; Editors, Douglas Fitch, Ray Hubley; Casting, Adrienne Stern; a Lightning Media, Boy Wonder Productions and Creative Rain Productions presentation; Dolby; Color; Clairmont-Scope; HD; Rated R; 96 minutes; Release date: October 21, 2011. **CAST:** Caleb Steinmeyer (Sean Donovan), Bill Sage (Terry Donovan), Zulay Henao (Teresa Ames), Daniel Stewart Sherman (Gary Stenson), James Russo (Larry Childs), Chuck Cooper (Bill Baldwin), Tracy Middendorf (Mary Donovan), John Sharian (Joe Mancini), Jim Devoti (Firefighter), Nicole Patrick (Amanda), James Chen (Roy), Roberta Wallach (Erin), Kether Donohue (Lizzy), Alex Manette (Mr. Richter), Chris Bert (Tim the Freshman), Suzana Didonna (Linda), Herman Chavez (Tony T), Jeremy Bobb (Artie), Rebecca Kush (Paramedic), Dawn Ressy (Girl on Train), Jake Randazzo (Young Sean), Tom Brangle (Homeless Man on Train), Karl Michael (Tyler Ames), Esther David (Judge), Chaka Desilva (Drug Addict), Marty Garcia (Off-Duty Detective), Leo Kin (Tommy Chen), Monte Bezell (Richard Ames), Kiai Kim (Chinese Mother), Romeo Ballantine (Boyfriend), Angela Garcia (Angel), Leslie C. Nemet (Woman in the Subway), James Morrissey (Firefighter on Train), Wendy Familia (Girlfriend), John John Scaccia (Boy on Train), Joe Thompson (Det. Thompson), Phillip Whitney (Bailiff), Samantha Scaccia, Alexa Morrissey (High School Students)

Caleb Steinmeyer in *Boy Wonder* © Lightning Entertainment

SNOWMEN (ARC Entertainment) Producers, Stephen McEveety, John Shepherd, David Segel; Director/Screenplay, Robert Kirbyson; Executive Producers, Ray Liotta, Diane Hendricks, Tina Segel, Bill O'Kane; Photography, Geno Salvatori; Designer, Christopher R. DeMuri; Costumes, Carolyn Leone; Music, John Debney; Editor, Catherine Kirbyson; Music Supervisor, Randy Jackson; Casting, Joey Paul Jensen; a MPower Pictures production; Dolby; Widescreen; Color; HD; Rated PG; 85 minutes; Release date: October 21, 2011. **CAST:** Bobby Coleman (Billy Kirkfield), Bobb'e J. Thompson (Howard Garvey), Christian Martyn (Lucas Lamb), Josh Flitter (Jason Bound), Doug E. Doug (Leonard Garvey), Christopher Lloyd (The Caretaker), Ray Liotta (Reggie Kirkfield), Demi Peterson (Gwen Nowakowski), Talon G. Ackerman (Cool Kid), Geoff Hansen (The Mayor), Jennifer Klekas (Fiona the Reporter), Chase McKnight (Bully), Darren Fromal (Mayor's Assistant), Johnny Ahn (Mayor's Driver), Carolina Andrus (Sherry), Beverley Mitchell (Mrs. Sherbrook), Hank Pond (Doctor), Terry Wood (Anchorman), Stephen A. Marinaccio II (Dishwasher)

BALLS TO THE WALL (Midwest Movies) Producers, Tara L. Craig, Patrick Rizzotti, Brett Forbes; Director, Penelope Spheeris; Screenplay, Jason Nutt; Photography, Christopher Popp; Designer, Nanci B. Roberts; Costumes, Erica Fyhrie; Music, William Ross; Editor, Thouly Dosios; Choreographer, Jake Mason; Casting, Monika Mikkelsen; an EG Productions, Fortress Features, Midwest Movies, LLC presentation; Color; Rated R: 97 minutes; Release date: October 21, 2011. **CAST:** Joe Hursley (Ben Camelino), Jenna Dewan (Rachel Matthews), Colleen Camp (Maureen), Matthew Felker (Chad), Antonio Sabato Jr. (Uncle Sven), Mimi Rogers (Mrs. Matthews), Christopher McDonald (Mr. Matthews), Dustin Ybarra (Lewis Gardner), Dean Austin (Officer Williams), Mark Adair Rios (Officer Sanchez), Freda Foh Shen (Miss Watson), Logan Hardwick (Li'l Ben), Joy Gohring (Li'l Ben's Mom), John Butterfield (Li'l Ben's Dad), Byron Field (Uncle Ted), Susan Yeagley (Wedding Planner), Raymond O'Connor (Bernie Niles), Gabriel Tigerman (Eddie Niles), Jenica Bergere (Candy Lane), Nic Few (Charlamagne/Iceman), Jorge Ortiz (Stylist), Jennifer Elise Cox (Horny Lady), Brad Williams (Trevor), Nathan Webnar (Oleg), Billy Drago (Belthagor), Krizia Bajos (Anne), Melissa Molinaro (Melissa), Amy Lynn Gruver (Bride-to-Be), Jeff Yesko (Pervy Guy), Norman Deesing (Nicholson Judge), Brooke Forbes (Lady Judge), Ronnie Rodriguez (Depp Judge), Jordan Liddle (Stage Manager), Eric Gores (Poker Player)

Joe Hursley, Colleen Camp in *Balls to the Wall* © Midwest Movies

REVENGE OF THE ELECTRIC CAR (Area 23a) Producers, Jessie Deeter, P.G. Morgan; Executive Producer, Stefano Durdic; Director, Chris Paine; Screenplay, P.G. Morgan, Chris Paine; Photography, Thaddeus Wadleigh; Music, David Robbins; Editor, Chris A. Peterson; Narrator, Tim Robbins; a WestMidWest production; Color; HD; Rated PG-13; 90 minutes; Release date: October 21, 2011. Documentary on the continuing efforts to produce viable electric cars; **WITH:** Greg "Gadget" Abbott, Shai Agassi, Shad Balch, Dave Barthmuss, Bob Boniface,

Gov. Phil Bredesen, Rep. Jason Calacanis, Michael Capuano, Alex Cattelan, Evelyn Chiang, Stephen Colbert, David Cole, Danny DeVito, Martin Eberhard, Bishop Charles H. Ellis III, Jon Favreau, Thomas Friedman, Carlos Ghosn, Adrian Grenier, Charlotte Jackson, Anthony Kiedis, Michelle Krebs, Bob Lutz, Elon Musk, Troy Negaard, Dan Neil, Gavin Newsom, Colette Niazmand, Chris Paine, Talulah Riley, Arnold Schwarzenegger, Jeremy Snyder, Jereme Stafford, J.B. Straubel, Dr. Ian Taras, Alex Taylor, Owen Thomas, Frank Weber, Larry Webster, Ray Wert, Rick Wagoner.

Greg Gadget in *Revenge of the Electric Car* © Area 23a

CARGO (Chameleon Entertainment) Producers, Abigail Honor, Chris Cooper, Yan Vizinberg; Executive Producer, Yuriy Boykiv; Director/Photography, Yan Vizinberg; Screenplay, Yan Vizinberg, Lee Peterkin; Music, Michael Whalen; Editor, Abigail Honor; a Persona Films production; Color; HD; Not rated; 85 minutes; Release date: October 21, 2011. **CAST:** Natasha Rinis (Natasha), Sayed Badreya (Sayed), Philip Willingham (Lukasz), Raoul I Torres (Raul Kidnapper), Misha Kuznetsov (Val), Seth Ruffer (Joe), Darja Schabad (Olga), Alex Trubetskoy (Misha), Vaughn Goland (Tattoo Man), Israel Hernandez (Van Driver), Dave Powers (Driver), Adrian Luke Sinclair (Police Officer), Anita Storr (NYPD Officer)

Natasha Rinis in *Cargo* © Chameleon Entertainment

THE AFFLICTED (Afflicted Picturehouse) Producers, Leslie Easterbrook, Lee Dashiell; Executive Producer, David Hilburn; Director/Screenplay, Jason Stoddard; Photography, Lee Dashiell; Costumes, Erin Rakestraw; Special Effects Make-Up, Dean Jones; Stunts, Kane Hodder; Color; Not rated; 85 minutes; Release date: October 21, 2011. **CAST:** Leslie Easterbrook (Maggie), Kane Hodder (Hank), Daniel Jones (Randy), Michele Grey (Cathy), Constance Collins (Principal), Katie Holland (Carla), J.D. Hart (Cowboy Profit), Anthony Osment (Office Williams), Anthony Garner (Det. Macdonald), Matthew M. Anderson (Officer Salinski), Ron Stafford (Det. Dubose), Cody Allen (Bill),

Leslie Easterbrook in *The Afflicted* © Afflicted Picturehouse

ELEVATE (Variance) Producers, Mark Becker, Anne Buford, Chiemi Karasawa, Victoria Yoffe; Executive Producers, RC Buford, Peter Holt, Robert S. Kaplan, Conor Schell, Daniel Silver; Director, Anne Buford; Photography, Daniel Vecchione; Music, Shawn Lee; Editors, Mark Becker, Chris White; Supervising Editor, Richard Hankin; a Variance Films and ESP Films presentation of a Sharp 7 Production in association with Isotrope Films; Color; Rated PG; 81 minutes; Release date: October 21, 2011. Documentary on four Senegalese basketball players who hope to play in the pros; **WITH:** Dethie Fall, Aziz N'Diaye, Assane Sene, Byago Diouf, Amadou Gallo Fall, Andy Vadnais, Raphael Chillious

ALL'S FAIRE IN LOVE (Hannover House) Producers, Michael Mendelsohn, Ron Singer, Scott Reed, Randy Mendelsohn; Director, Scott Marshall; Screenplay, Scott Marshall, Jeffrey Ray Wine; Photography, Mark Irwin; Designer, John Collins; Costumes, Donna Buckley, Gary Jones; Music, Jeff Cardoni, Julian Jackson; Editors, Josh Muscatine, Tara Timpone; an Eric Parkinson and Fred Shefte in association with Hannover House presentation of a Patriot Pictures/ Kimmel Intl. production; Dolby; Color; Rated PG-13; 108 minutes; Release date: October 28, 2011. **CAST:** Christina Ricci (Kate), Owen Benjamin (Will), Ann-Margret (Mrs. Banks), Matthew Lillard (Crocket), Cedric the Entertainer (Professor Shockworthy), Louise Griffiths (Jo), Sandra Taylor (Princess Jeanette), Martin Klebba (Count Le Petite), Dave Sheridan (Jester Roy/Horny), Chris Wylde (Rank), Bill Engvall (Mr. Mendelson), Tony Stef'Ano (Bubble Butt), Nadine Velasquez (Mathilda), Jonathan Alderman (Cotton), Ewan Bourne (Sleeping Pirate), Corey S. Chabot (Street Walker), Samantha Chase (Emily), Geralyn Clark (Pie Eating Contestant), Mike Dusi (Ticket Scalper), Jason Echols (Wheels), Michael Ellison (Job Candidate), Niki Haze (College Student), Kate Elizabeth Hopkins (Joust Announcer – Mistress of the Lists), Brad Leo Lyon (Football Coach), Michael Mendelsohn (Wall Street Banker), Peter Ransom (General Tso), Brandon Reed (Mitchell), Alexie Schauerte (Fairy), Andrew Thornhill (Mudskipper), Karl Troll (Queen's Guard), Sarana VerLin (Renaissance Fiddler), Francisca Viudes (Tourist at the Fair), Jason Waugh (Biker Dad)

Ann-Margret, Sandra Taylor in *All's Faire in Love* © Hannover House

SILVER BULLETS (Swanberry Prods.) Producers, Joe Swanberg, Amy Seimetz; Director/ Screenplay/Photography/Editor, Joe Swanberg; Music, Orange Mighty Trio; Color; HD; Not rated; 69 minutes; Release date: October 28, 2011. **CAST:** Kate Lyn Sheil (Claire), Ti West (Ben), Amy Seimetz (Charlie), Joe Swanberg (Ethan), Jane Adams (June), Larry Fessenden (Sam)

Joe Swanberg, Kate Lyn Sheil in *Silver Bullets* © Swanberry Prods.

RESTITUTION (Monterey Media) Producers, Mark G. Mathis, Lance K.R. Kawas; Executive Producer/Screenplay, Mark Bierlein; Director, Lance K. R. Kawas; Photography, Edward Gutentag; Designer, Marcie Paul; Music, Misha Segal; Editor, George Artope; Casting, Pamela M. Staton; a Bierlein Entertainment in association with Washington Street Productions presentation; Dolby; Color; Rated R; 101 minutes; Release date: October 28, 2011. **CAST:** Mena Suvari (Heather), Mark Bierlein (Alex Forrester), C. Thomas Howell (John Youngstown), William Sadler (George Youngstown), Tom Arnold (Tom Lipnity), Nancy L. Doetsch (Mrs. Greenberg), Jimmy Doom (Hillbilly), Milica Govich (Real Estate Agent), Shena Adl (Clara's Craft Store Owner), Lance K.R. Kawas (Doctor), Laurie Valko (Mary Thompson), Michael R. Brandon (Frank Lawson), Patrick Moug, Robert Tyrrell, Antonio L. Miller (Waterfront Thugs), Steven Schoomeesters (Mr. Greenberg), Joseph Kathrein (Miles), Dave Davies (Jason), Dean Tyrrell (Driver), Stephen Detherage (Heather's Father), Tiren Jhames (Youngstown Thug), Michael F. Gillespie (Lance Williams), Steve Kosinski (Dr. Pinklady), Dennis North (Chief Winters), Skye LaButte (Young Heather), Tanya LaButte (Heather's Mom)

JANIE JONES (Tribeca) Producers, Keith Kjarval, Eric Bassett; Executive Producers, Ken Meyer, David M. Rosenthal, Matt Luber, Keith Watkins, Aaron L. Gilbert; Director/Screenplay, David M. Rosenthal; Photography, Anastas Michos; Designer, Stephen Altman; Music, Eef Barzelay; Original Songs, Eef Barzelay, Gemma Hayes; Editor, Alan Heim; Casting, Shannon Makhanian; an American Express presentation of a Unified Pictures and Industrial Entertainment presentation of an Eric Bassett/Keith Kjarval production in association with Absurda, a David Lynch company and Media House Capital; Dolby; Color; Not rated; 114 minutes; Release date: October 28, 2011. **CAST:** Abigail Breslin (Janie Jones), Elisabeth Shue (Mary Ann Jones), Alessandro Nivola (Ethan Brand), Brittany Snow (Iris), Peter Stormare (Sloan), Frank Whaley (Chuck), Joel Moore (Dave), Frances Fisher (Lily), Michael Panes (Ulysses), David Lee Smith (Officer Dickerson), Rodney Eastman (Billy), Richard Cotovsky (Club Manager), Adam Shalzi (Creepy Goth Kid), Sam Thakur (Stan), John Turk (Mullet Guy), Douglas Tyler, Ed Flynn (Good Ole Boys), Guy Van Swearingen (Gil), Gene L. Hamilton (Butler), Jessica Joy, Kara Zediker (Girls), Robert Goodwin (Smoking Door Man), Katie Riccio (Brassy Girl), Hillary Watkins (Waitress)

AND THEY'RE OFF (Kinobild Releasing) Producers, Howard Bolter, Alan Grossbard, Pamela Fryman; Director, Rob Schiller; Screenplay, Alan Grossbard; Photography, Ulf Soderqvist; Art Director, Alexa Roman; Costumes, Mark Avery; Music, Lawrence Brown; Editor, Stephen Meyers; Casting, Mark Teschner, Sally Lear; a Scrambled Eggs production; Dolby; Color; Rated PG-13; 90 minutes; Release date: October 28, 2011. **CAST:** Sean Astin (Dusty Sanders), Cheri

Oteri (Dee Johanssen), Martin Mull (Ken Sanders), Mark Moses (Alex Flamm), Gigi Rice (Keri Wannamaker-Flamm), Peter Jacobson (Sebastian McKay), Mo Collins (Tina McKay), James "Lil' JJ" Lewis (Julian Rivers), Kevin Nealon (Mike Bensinger), Luis Chavez (Martin Romero), Susan Yeagley (Molly Bensinger), Alex Rocco (Sol Youngerman), Bob Baffert, Doug O'Neill, Ken Rudulph, Simon Bray, Levar Burton, Martin Garcia, Joe Talamo, Camilla Ball, John Sadler (Themselves), Fred (Sprockets), Jayden Lund (Phil Bloom), Dot Marie Jones (Prom Date), J.T. Sherwood (Student Body President), Jamie Cuzick (Exercise Rider), Greg Cipes (Mark Youngerman), Koji Kataoka (Koji), Amy Lyndon (Caryn), Marcelo Tubert (Mr. Ludel), Zoe Schiller (Daughter at Pony Ride), Matt Adler (Father at Pony Ride), Melissa Weber Bales (Waitress), Freckles (Caveat), Alexandra Ryan (Veterinarian), Alexis Denisof (Father at Accident), Kylie Tyndall (Megan), Keaton Tyndall (Katie), Frank Drank (Biker), Cheryl Bricker (Track Steward), Tyra Colar (Bonnie Rivers), Josh Robert Thompson (Narrator), Dave Zyler (Cameraman Voice), Vic Stauffer (Track Announcer)

INKUBUS (Screen Media) Producers, Chad A. Verdi, Glenn Ciano; Director/ Story, Glenn Ciano; Screenplay, Carl V. Dupré; Photography, Ben DeLuca; Designer, Robert Rotondo Jr.; Music, Mauro Colangelo; Editor, Frank Raposo; Casting, Adrienne Stern; a Woodhaven Production Company production of a Chad A. Verdi production; Color; Rated R; 88 minutes; Release date: October 28, 2011. **CAST:** Robert Englund (Inkubus), William Fosythe (Ret. Det. Gil Diamante), Jonathan Silverman (Officer Tech), Joey Fatone (Det. Tom Caretti), Michelle Ray Smith (Officer Erin Cole), Mike Cerrone (Office Mudge), Jessica Conlan (Jenny), Kevin DeCristofano (Miles), Tom DeNucci (Officer Pax), Dyan Kane (Dr. Emily Winstrom), Aubie Merrylees (David Diamante), Tom Paolino (Officer Meat), Fred Sullivan Jr. (Clinic Psychiatrist), Nicholas John Bilotta, Brinton MacFarland, Corey Jacob Williams (Clinic Orderlies), Chad A. Verdi (Baseball Dad), Sera Verdi (Softball Kid)

Robert Englund in *Inkubus* © Screen Media Films

13 (Anchor Bay) Producers, Rick Schwartz, Valerio Morabito; Executive Producers, Jeanette Buerling, Maggie Monteith, Brian Edwards, Ron Hartenbaum, Douglas Kuber, Géla Babulani, Myles Nestel, Anthony Callie, Caroline Jaczko, Franck Dubarry; Director, Géla Babulani; Screenplay, Géla Babulani, Greg Pruss; Based on the film *13 Tzameti* by Géla Babulani; Photography, Michael McDonough; Designer, Jane Musky; Costumes, Amy Westcott; Music, Alexander Van Bubenheim; Editors, Géla Babulani, David Gray; Casting, Avy Kaufman; an Anchor Bay Films and Barbarian Film Group presentation of an Overnight and Morabito Pictures Company production in association with Magnet Media Group, Oceana Media and Red Dragon Productions; Dolby; Color; Rated R; 90 minutes; Release date: October 28, 2011. **CAST:** Sam Riley (Vince Ferro), Ray Winstone (Ronald Lynn Bagges), Curtis Jackson (Jimmy), Alexander Skarsgård (Jack), Mickey Rourke (Jefferson), Jason Statham (Jasper), Michael Shannon (Henry), Ben Gazzara (Schlondorff), Emmanuelle Chriqui (Aileen), David Zayas

(Det. Larry Mullane), Ronald Guttman (Joe), John Bedford Lloyd (Mark), Alan Davidson (Tony Drizer), Gaby Hoffmann (Clara Ferro), Michael Berry Jr. (William), Daisy Tahan (Jenny Ferro), Chuck Zito (Ted), Wayne Duvall (Mr. Taylor), Stephen Gevedon (Mackinnon), Forrest Griffin (Joey Blarro), Alice Barrett Mitchell (Leanne Ferro), Anthony Chisholm (Mr. Gomez), Chris McKinney (Paul), Darrell Larson (Game Doctor), Rock Kohli (Player #9), Paul Butler (Money Boss), David Conley (Player #16), Gurdeep Singh (Money Man), Stephen Beach (Nick Ferro), Starla Benford (Dr. Anna Cummings), Omar Hernandez (Player #3), Toru Ohno (Mahima), Michael D'Onofrio (Frank), Carlos Reig-Plaza (Warden), John Hoffman (CPS Store Worker), John Fiore, Robert Rizzo, Frank Senger, Jerry Goralnick (Gamblers), Bob Weston (Bookie), Doug Kruse (Rigalowsky), JD Thompson (Trailer Driver), Brad Gallagher (Hans), Gem Jean Marc Danois (Bodyguard), Joseph DeBona (Shed Guard), Ed Bergtold (Cop #1), Ricky Garcia, Doug Torres, Danny Rutigliano (Conductors), Jamison Ernest (Taxi Driver), Temur Babulani (Supervisor), Lars Gerhard, Scott Dillin (Money Men), Don Frye, Nacho Figueras (Handlers), George Feaster (Riley), Jeff Burchfield (Player #14), Peter Figlia (Bartender), Howard Overshown (Police Officer), Paul Lucas (Postman), Glen Trotiner (Deli Counter Man)

Ray Winstone, Sam Riley, Michael Shannon in *13* © Anchor Bay

URBANIZED (Film First) Producer/Director, Gary Hustwit; Photography, Luke Geissbuhler; Music, Kristian Dunn; Editors, Shelby Siegel, Michael Culyba; a Swiss Dots production; American-British; Color; HD; Not rated; 85 minutes; Release date: October 28, 2011. Documentary on urban design; **WITH:** Udo Andriof, Alejandro Aravena, Jon Bird, Amanda Burden, Ricky Burdett, Candy Chang, Yung Ho Chang, Noah Chasin, James Corner, Mark Covington, Joshua David, Ellen Dunham-Jones, Kathryn Ewing, Sir Norman Foster, Grady Gammage Jr., Jan Gehl, Alastair Graham, Robert Hammond, Jacqueline James, Bruce Katz, Tarna Klitzner, Rem Koolhaas, Rahul Mehrotra, Grover Mouton, Oscar Niemeyer, Sicelo Nkohla, Eduardo Paes, Sheela Patel, Enrique Peñalosa, Edgar Pieterse, Ric Scofidio, Michael Sorkin, Gangolf Stocker.

Urbanized © Film First

OCTOBER BABY (Five & Two Pictures) Producers, Dan Atchison, Justin Tolley, Jon Erwin, Andrew Erwin; Directors, Andy Erwin, Cecil Stokes, Jon Erwin; Screenplay, Jon Erwin, Theresa Preston; Story, Jon Erwin, Andrew Erwin, Theresa Preston, Cecil Stokes; Photography, Jon Erwin; Designer, Ed Gurney; Costumes, Anna Redmon; Music, Paul Mills; Editor, Andrew Erwin; Casting, Beverly Holloway; an American Family Studios in association with Provident Films presentation of a Gravitas production; Color; Rated PG-13; 105 minutes; Release date: October 28, 2011. **CAST:** Rachel Hendrix (Hannah), Jason Burkey (Jason), Jasmine Guy (Mary), John Schneider (Jacob), Joy Brunson (Danielle), Carl Maguire (Lance), Tracy Miller (Officer Mitchell), Jennifer Price (Grace), Shari Wiedmann (Cindy Hastings), Chris Sligh (Bmac), Mary Tolley (Julia Armen), Colleen Trusler (Alanna), Robert Amaya (Beach Cop), Maria Atchison (Secretary), Rodney Clark (Priest), Brian Gall (Ren-a-Cop), Lance E. Nichols (Doctor), Don Sandley (Psychiatrist), Corey Winston (Hospital Attendant)

Rachel Hendrix in *October Baby* © Five & Two Pictures

GOD'S LAND (Vindaloo Philm-Wallah) Producer, Jeremiah Kipp; Director/Screenplay, Preston Miller; Photography, Arsenio Assin, Sheldon Smith; Editor, Krishna Kotopelli Anderson; Casting, Wayne Chang; Color; HD; Not rated; 164 minutes; Release date: October 28, 2011. **CAST:** Jodi Lin (Hou "Xiu"), Shing Ka (Hou), Matthew Chiu (Hou Ollie), Wayne Chang (Richard Liu), Jackson Ning (Teacher Chen), Gloria Diaz (Maria Ruiz), John Wu (Wong Hotei), Amy Chiang (Wong Vicki), Brandon Suen (Jesus), Kaitlyn Suen (Buddha), Edmund Suen (Tony), Tony Chiu (Edmund), Carrie Kiamesha (Bijou), Nancy Eng (Dr. Maggie Feng), Ranjit Chowdhry (Raja Chatterjee), Lee Ka (Pastor), Trey Albright (Steve), Jonny Fido (Earl the Grocery Manager), Geeta Citygirl (Sonya), Shui Mak Ka (Granny), Dina Shin (Taiwanese Teacher), Ostaro (Himself), Glenn Kenny (Father Luis Farber), Rob Gorden (Asst. Manager), David Lacombe (Dr. Angel LaColon)

God's Land © Vindaloo Philm-Wallah

5 STAR DAY (Breaking Glass Pictures) Producers, Mike Robertson, Danny Buday, Joel Mendoza; Executive Producer, Mike Robertson; Director/Screenplay, Danny Buday; Photography, Jason Oldak; Designer, Megan Hutchison; Music, Ryan Beveridge; Editor, Curtis Pierce; Casting/Co-Producer, Shannon Makhanian; a Lucid Entertainment presentation of a Virtu Entertainment production; Technicolor; Super 35 Widescreen; Not rated; 97 minutes; Release date: November 2, 2011. **CAST:** Cam Gigandet (Jake Gibson), Jena Malone (Sarah Reynolds), Max Hartman (Wesley Henderson), Brooklyn Sudano (Yvette Montgomery), Will Yun Lee (Samuel Kim), Julianna Guill (Vanessa), Chris J. Johnson (Aaron Greenfield), Nick Chinlund (Prof. Birchbaum), Mark Boone Junior (Homeless Prophet), Richard Riehle (Jim the Plumber), Tad Hilgenbrink (Darren), Patricia Belcher (Patty the Waitress), Yvette Freeman (Social Worker), Reedy Gibbs (Nurse Receptionist), Cesar Garcia (Drug Dealer), Peter Mackenzie (Mr. Peterson), Wendy Haines (Waitress), Kelli Stoner, Sarah Adina (Nurses), Parisa Fakhri (Mr. Peterson's Assistant), Maura Murphy (Wesley's Private Dancer), Alison Moir (Doctor), Bruno Alexander (Apartment Manager), George Ketsios (Bartender), Carl Melius (Bartender), Carl Melius (Yvette's Husband), Christopher Reddick-Johnson (Teenage Thug), Stephen Bowman (Hotel Desk Clerk), Julia Popick (Girl at Diner), Marty Hertzberg (Tavern Bartender), Steve Pandis (Bass Player), Brett Browning (Tyrone), Mark Achilles White (Bouncer), Derek Shipp (TSA Agent #2), Brant J. Cole (Jazz Club Bouncer), Kristin Ornelas (Flight Attendant)

Cam Gigandet in *5 Star Day* © Breaking Glass Pictures

THE OTHER F WORD (Oscilloscope) Producers, Cristan Reilly, Andrea Blaugrund Nevins; Executive Producers, Morgan Spurlock, Jeremy Chilnick; Director/Screenplay, Andrea Blaugrund Nevins; Photography/Editor, Geoffrey Franklin; a Rare Bird Films/Warrior Poets production; Color; DV; Not rated; 97 minutes; Release date: November 2, 2011. Documentary looks at the efforts of various aging punk rockers to adapt to domestic life; **WITH:** Tony Adolescent, Art Alexakis, Rob Chaos, Joe Escalante, Josh Freese, Fat Mike, Flea, Lars Fredricksen, Matt Freeman, Jack Grisham, Brett Gurewitz, Tony Hawk, Greg Hetson, Mark Hoppus, Jim Lindberg, Mike McDermott, Tim McIlrath, Mark Mothersbaugh, Duane Peters, Joe Sib, Ron Reyes, Rick Thorne.

THE LAST RITES OF JOE MAY (Tribeca Film) Producers, Stephanie Striegel, Bill Straus; Executive Producers, Tim Evans, Dennis Mastro; Director/Screenplay, Joe Maggio; Photography, Jay Silver; Designer, Merje Veski; Costumes, Emma Potter; Music, Lindsay Marcus; Editor, Seth Anderson; Casting, Claire Simon; Presented in partnership with American Express, a You're Faded Films and Billy Goat Pictures presentation, in association with Steppenwolf Films; Color; Not rated; 102 minutes; Release date: November 4, 2011. **CAST:** Dennis Farina (Joe May), Jamie Anne Allman (Jenny Rapp), Ian Barford (Stanley Buczkowski), Meredith Droeger (Angelina Rapp), Chelcie Ross (Billy), Gary Cole (Lenny),

Nathan Adloff (Doctor), Mike Bacarella (George), Brian Boland (Scotty May), Jack Bronis (DMV Clerk), Billy Dec (Hipster), Matt DeCaro (Chevy), Hans Fleischmann (Lenny's Sidekick), Justin Palmer (Male Nurse), Roderick Peeples (Butcher Shop Manager), Phil Ridarelli (Landlord)

Meredith Droeger, Dennis Farina in *The Last Rites of Joe May* © Tribeca Film

DRAGONSLAYER (Drag City) Producer, John Baker; Executive Producer, Christine Vachon; Director, Tristan Patterson; Photography, Eric Koretz; Music, T. Griffin; Editors, Jennifer Tiexiera, Lizzy Calhoun; a Killer Films presentation; HD; Color; Not rated; 74 minutes; Release date: November 4, 2011. Documentary on Fullerton, California skateboarding legend Josh "Skreech" Sandoval; **WITH:** Josh "Skreech" Sandoval.

STUCK BETWEEN STATIONS (NECA/Wrekin Hill) Producers, Todd Cobery, Spencer Kiernan, Brady Kiernan, Sam Rosen; Director, Brady Kiernan; Screenplay, Nat Bennett, Sam Rosen; Photography, Bo Hakala; Music, Grant Cutler; Editor, Sam Heyn; an RKB Pictures production; Dolby; Color; Rated R; 85 minutes; Release date: November 4, 2011. **CAST:** Sam Rosen (Casper), Zoe Lister Jones (Becky), Josh Hartnett (Paddy), Michael Imperioli (David), Christiana Clark (Becky's Roommate), Nadia Dajani (Sheila), Brent Doyle (Brent), Casey Greig (Jesse), Sarah Sandusky (Sarah), David Tufford (Brent's Dumb Friend)

A NOVEL ROMANCE (Entertainment One) Producer, Morris S. Levy; Executive Producers, Steve Guttenberg, Brian Stern, Gary Gumowitz, Nathan Hevrony, Peter Bongiorno, Andre Sassoon; Director/Screenplay, Allie Dvorin; Photography, Jon Miguel Delgado; Designer, Joseph Polacik; Costumes, Michael Bevins; Music, Michelangelo Sosnowitz; Editor, Glenn Conte; Casting, Stephanie Holbrook; New Films Intl. presentation of a M.E.G.A. Films production in association with Studio 13; Color; HD; Not rated; 92 minutes; Release date: November 4, 2011. **CAST:** Steve Guttenberg (Nate Shepard), Milena Govich (Jenny Sparks), Shannon Elizabeth (Adi Schwartz), Jay O. Sanders (Walter Evans), Matthew Del Negro (Buddy Andrews), Doug E. Doug (Barry Humfries), Maddie Corman (Alexandra Dumar), Natalya Rudakova (Shelly), Kelly Bishop (Lily Sparks), Matthew Del Negro (Buddy Andrews), Jeffrey Ross (Douglas Silver), Wass Stevens (Sam Steele), Laurence Blum (Larry Love), Audra Blaser (Raines Albright), James A. Stephens (Will Sparks), Peter Bongiorno (Sal), Regina Dvorin (Grace Sparks), Julie Cavaliere (Sarah), Matthew Murumba (Matt), Barry Rohssen (Vic), Mitch Kogen (Mitch), Thomas Michael Sullivan (Bartender)

THE LOVE WE MAKE (Showtime Networks) Producers, Bradley Kaplan, Laura Coxson, Susan Froemke, Ian Markiewicz, Katie Sorohan; Executive Producer, Paul McCartney; Directors, Bradley Kaplan, Albert Maysles; Photography, Albert Maysles; Editor, Ian Markiewicz; a Maysles Films production; Stereo; Black and white/color; 16mm-to-HD; Not rated; 94 minutes; Release date: November 9, 2011. (This film premiered on Showtime Network on September 10, 2011). Documentary on Paul McCartney's concert to benefit the survivors of the fallen

Milena Govich, Steve Guttenberg, Shannon Elizabeth in *A Novel Romance* © Entertainment One

Timothy Gibbs, Michael Landes in *11-11-11* © Rocket Releasing

firemen who perished in the September 11, 2001 terrorist attacks; **WITH:** Paul McCartney, Rusty Anderson, Jon Bon Jovi, David Bowie, Steve Buscemi, Jim Carrey, Eric Clapton, Bill Clinton, Sheryl Crow, Billy Crystal, Leonardo DiCaprio, Gabe Dixon, Harrison Ford, Mick Jagger, Jay-Z, Elton John, Abraham Laboriel Jr., Stella McCartney, Pat O'Reilly, George Pataki, Dan Rather, Brian Ray, Keith Richards, Howard Stern, James Taylor, Pete Townshend, Barbara Walters, Harvey Weinstein, Paul Wickens, Melissa Etheridge, Jimmy Fallon, Will Ferrell, Michael J. Fox, Salma Hayek, Billy Joel, Kid Rock, Richie Sambora, Ozzy Osbourne

GOD'S FIDDLER: JASCHA HEIFETZ (Peter Rosen Prods.) Producer/Director, Peter Rosen; Executive Producers, Carol Colburn Hogel, Lothar Mattner, Bernd Hellthaler; Screenplay, Sara Lukinson; Photography, Peter Rosen, Barry Markowitz; Editors, Joshua Waletzky, Peter Rosen; a WDR, Arte, Euroarts Music Intl. presentation; Color/black and white; HD; Not rated; 87 minutes; Release date: November 11, 2011. Documentary on famed violinist Jascha Heifetz; **WITH:** Ayke Agus, Ivry Gitilis, Ida Haendel, Seymour Lipkin, John Maltese, Bill Van Horn.

Jascha Heifetz in *God's Fiddler* © Peter Rosen Prods.

11-11-11 (Rocket Releasing) Producers, Wayne Allen Rice, Richard Heller, Loris Curci, Christian Molina; Director/Screenplay, Darren Lynn Bousman; Photography, Joseph White; Designer, Mani Martinez; Costumes, Toni Martin; Music, Joseph Bishara; Editor, Martin Hunter; Visual Effects Supervisor, Joseph J. Lawson; a Canonigo Films/Capacity Pictures production, presented in association with Epic Pictures Group; American-Spanish; Color; Rated PG-13; 90 minutes; Release date: November 11, 2011. **CAST:** Timothy Gibbs (Joseph Crone), Michael Landes (Samuel), Denis Rafter (Richard Crone), Wendy Glenn (Sadie), Lluís Soler (Javier), Brendan Price (Grant), Lolo Herrero (Oculto Owner), Montserrat Alcoverro (Celia), Benjamin Cook (Cole), Salomé Jiménez (Sarah), Jesus Cuenca, Pau Trual, Xavi Vara, Alejandro Gil (Demons), Ángela Rosal (Anna)

BARBERSHOP PUNK (This End Up/Monku) Producers, Georgia Sugimura Archer, Kristin Armfield; Executive Producer, Anthony Dominici; Director/ Screenplay, Georgia Sugimura Archer; Co-Director, Kristin Armfield; Photography, Amy Sharp; Music, Peter Golub; Editors, Matt Kregor, José Pulido; a This End Up Films production, Monku Power production in association with Evil Twin Prods.; Color; Not rated; 76 minutes; Release date: November 11, 2011. Documentary on the deregulation and privatization of communication channels in the electronic age; **WITH:** Ian MacKaye, Damian Kulash, Henry Rollins, Janeane Garofalo, John Perry Barlow, Chip Pickering, Marsha Blackburn, Jim Ladd, Mike McCurry, Michele Combs, Rick Carnes, Ted Miller, Jack Burkman, Jonathan Adelstein, Stephen Wildstrom, Scott Cleland, Ben Scott, Markham Erickson, Wes Armstrong, Rick Carnes, Michael Copps, Destiny Topolski, George Ford, Craig Aaron, Michael Bracy, Jason Devitt, Walter McCormick, Judi Topolski, Heidi Topolski, Robb Topolski

Damian Kulash in *Barbershop Punk* © This End Up

LETTERS FROM THE BIG MAN (Antarctic Pictures) Producer/Director/ Screenplay/Editor, Christopher Munch; Executive Producer, Linda Brown; Photography, Rob Sweeney; Music, Ensemble Galilei; Art Director, Ricardo Herrera; Costumes, Kristen Anacker; Special Makeup Effects, Lee Romaire; Casting, Joseph Middleton; Color; HD; Not rated; 104 minutes; Release date: November 11, 2011. **CAST:** Lily Rabe (Sarah), Jason Butler Harner (Sean), Isaac C. Singleton Jr. (The Big Man), Jim Cody Williams (Barney), Fiona Dourif (Penny), Don McManus (Forest Superintendent), Karen Black (Sean's Colleague), Jeri Arredondo (Buffalo Scientist), Skyler Brigmann (Young Sean), Gregory Bennett (Benny Rodriguez), Quinton Fay (Jeff), David Melville (Stephano – *The Tempest*), Bobby Plasencia (Caliban – *The Tempest*), Philip Briggs (Trinculo – *The Tempest*), Jessica Noboa (Storage Attendant), Jim Leske (F.S. General Counsel), Martin William Harris (F.S. Stenographer)

Isaac C. Singleton, Jr. in *Letters from the Big Man* © Antarctic Pictures

THE GREENING OF WHITNEY BROWN (ARC Entertainment) Producers, Charlie Mason, Justin Moore-Lewy; Executive Producers, Ed Fitts, Sue Rathbone; Director, Peter Odiorne; Screenplay, Gail Gilchriest; Photography, James L. Carter; Designer, Caroline Hanania; Costumes, Luellyn Harper; Music, Randy Edelman; Editor, Martin Hunter; Horse Trainer/Stunts, Tommie Turvey; Casting, Kerry Barden, Paul Schnee; a Perfect Weekend production; Dolby; Color; Rated PG; 87 minutes; Release date: November 11, 2011. **CAST:** Sammi Hanratty (Whitney Brown), Brooke Shields (Joan Brown), Aidan Quinn (Henry Brown), Kris Kristofferson (Dusty Brown), Charlotte Matthews (Lindsay), Keith David (Clerk), Slade Pearce (Ben), Anna Colwell (Alicia), Natalia Dyer (Lily), Lily Rashid (Olivia), Kodie Lake (Zack), Cameron Gaskins (Josh), Nicky Buggs (Home-Ec Teacher), Wilbur Fitzgerald (Stanley), Shea Hardy (Sally), Frankie Ingrassia (Interior Designer), Judy Leavell (Mildred), Antje Price (Tennis Coach), Bianca Price (Tennis Player), Morgan Saylor (Annie), India Scandrick (Grace), Wes Wilson (AG Teacher), Gerald Duckworth (Rich man from Philly)

RID OF ME (Phase 4 Films) Producers, Katie O'Grady, James Westby; Director/ Screenplay/ Photography/Editor, James Westby; Executive Producer, Kristin Coleman; Designer, Eric Sellers; Costumes, Alisha Georgianna; Music, Jason Wells; Casting, Lana Veenker; a Submarine Deluxe presentation of an Alcove Moving Pictures production; Color; HD; Not rated; 89 minutes; Release date: November 18, 2011. **CAST:** Katie O'Grady (Meris Canfield), John Keyser (Mitch Canfield), Theresa Russell (Mrs. Lockwood), Storm Large (Briann Lockwood), Orianna Herrman (Trudy), Art Alexakis (Virgil), Ritah Parrish (Dawn), Melik Malkasian (Masud), Betty Moyer (Mrs. Hurbold), John Breen (Bry-Guy), Morgan Hobart (Jeremy Bunquist), Melinda Chilton (Sue Ellen Haggemeyer), Geno Romo (Chris Haggemeyer), Cora Benesh (Freak Girl), Denise Chanterelle DuBois (Sunshine the Barfly), Derek Estes (Pizza Boy), Emily Galash (Alice), Jana Lee Hamblin (Coleen Baumgarden), Christopher D. Harder (Dale Masterson), Brendan Robinson (The Young Man), Angie Rutan (Britney), Joe Spencer (Steve), Danny Taylor (Missy's Boyfriend), Leslie Taylor (Missy), Julie Vhay (Lacy Masterson), Adrienne Vogel (Linda), Kristin Coleman (Softball Player), Paul Ramirez (Softball Pitcher)

THE LIE (Screen Media) Producer, Mary Pat Bentel; Executive Producers, Sriram Das, Mitchell Goldman; Director, Joshua Leonard; Screenplay, Jeff Feuerzeig, Joshua Leonard, Mark Webber, Jess Weixler; Based on the story by T.Coraghessan Boyle; Photography, Benjamin Kasulke; Designer, Thomas S. Hammock; Costumes, Emily Batson; Music, Peter Raeburn; Editor, Greg O'Bryant; a Perception Media Films in association with Das Films presentation; Color; HD; Rated R; 80 minutes; Release date: November 18, 2011. **CAST:** Joshua Leonard (Lonnie), Jess Weixler (Clover), Mark Webber (Tank), Jane Adams (Dr. Bentel), Alia Shawkat (Seven), Kelli Garner (Brianna), Gerry Bednob (Radko), Kirk Baltz (Joel), Tipper Newton (Jeannie), Allison Anders (Allison), Holly Woodlawn (Cherry), James Ransome (Weasel), Matthew Newton (Steve), Kandice Melonakos (Green-Eyed Girl), Germaine Mozel Sims (Diner), Gwyn Fawcett (Mary), Michael McColl (Ted), Violet Long (Baby)

Jess Weixler, Violet Long, Joshua Leonard in *The Lie* © Screen Media Films

BURIED PRAYERS (Historical Media Associates) Producers, Matt Mazer, Steven Meyer, Christopher J. Gambale; Executive Producer, Jean-Pierre Delbecq; Director, Steven Meyer; Screenplay, Douglas K. Dempsey, Matt Mazer; Music, David van Tieghem; Editor, Douglas K. Dempsey; Narrator, Laurie Anderson; a Jean-Pierre Delbecq-Matt Mazer production; American-Polish; Color; Not rated; 82 minutes; Release date: November 18, 2011. Documentary about the efforts to unearth the keepsakes that several prisoners of Poland's Maidanek death camp had buried to ensure they would not be confiscated; **WITH:** Adam Frydman, Tessie Jacob, Ella Prince, Alexander Blank

Adam Frydman in *Buried Prayers* © Historical Media Associates

Katie O'Grady, Orianna Herrman in *Rid of Me* © Phase 4 Films

EAMES: THE ARCHITECT & THE PAINTER (First Run Features) Producers/Directors, Jason Coh, Bill Jersey; Executive Producer, Susan Lacy; Screenplay, Jason Cohn; Music, Michael Bacon; Editor, Don Bernier; Narrator, James Franco; a Quest Productions and Bread and Butter Films production in association with PBS American Masters and Catticus Corp. presentation; Dolby; HD; Color; Not rated; 84 minutes; Release date: November 18, 2011. Documentary on influential designers Charles and Ray Eames; **WITH:** Lucia Eames, Eames Demetrios, Paul Schrader, Richard Saul Wurman, Kevin Roche, Jeannine Oppewall, Deborah Sussman, Gordon Ashby

LAREDOANS SPEAK: VOICES ON IMMIGRATION (Border Town Pictuers) Producers, Victor A. Martinez, Ryan Schafer, Pepe Serna; Directors/Screenplay, Victor A. Martinez, Ryan Schafer; Photography, Victor A. Martinez; Music, Christian Mendoza; Editor, Ryan Schafer; Color; HD; Not rated; 75 minutes; Release date: November 18, 2011. Documentary in which several citizens of Laredo, Texas talk abot immigration; **WITH:** Raul Salinas, Henry Cuellar, Juan Garza, Robert Greenbaum, Richard Pauza Jr., Pepe Serna, Robert Cremo, Jesus Martinez, Smuggler Coyote.

Laredoans Speak: Voices on Immigration © Border Town Pictures

CRAZY WISDOM: THE LIFE & TIMES OF CHOGYAM TRUNGPA RINPOCHE (Alive Mind Cinema) Producers, Johanna Demetrakas, Lisa Leeman; Director, Johanna Demetrakas; Photography, Pablo Bryant; Music, Sean Callery; Editors, Johanna Demetrakas, Kate Amend; Crazy Wisdom Films; Color; Not rated; 86 minutes; Release date: November 25, 2011. Documentary on how Buddhism's "bad boy," Chogyam Trungpa was instrumental in bringing Tibetan Buddhism to America; **WITH:** Pema Chodron, Ram Dass, Diana Mukpo, Gesar Mukpo, Sakyong Mipham Rinpoche, Robert Thurman

Allen Ginsburg, Trungpa Rinpoche in *Crazy Wisdom* © Alive Mind Cinema

A WARRIOR'S HEART (Xenon Pictures) Producers, Steven Istock, Marc Spizzirri, Ed Richardson, Bob Bassett, Tommy Johnson; Executive Producers, Marc Spizzirri, Martin Dugard, James Patterson, James Yount, Robert P. Atwell, Jamie R. Thompson; Director, Mike Sears; Screenplay, Martin Dugard; Story, Martin Dugard, Marc Spizzirri, James Yount; Photography, Thomas L. Callaway; Designer, Brian Livesay; Costumes, Jayme Bohn; Music, Alec Puro; Editor, Ellen Goldwasser; Casting, Donald Paul Pemrick, Dean E. Fronk; a Camelot Entertainment Group presentation of a California Pictures and Family Productions Film; Color; Rated PG; 86 minutes; Release date: December 2, 2011. **CAST:** Ashley Greene (Brooklyn), Kellan Lutz (Conor Sullivan), Gabrielle Anwar (Claire Sullivan), Chord Overstreet (Dupree), Adam Beach (Sgt. Maj. Duke Wayne), William Mapother (David Milligan), Chris Potter (Seamus Sullivan), Aaron Hill (Joe Bryant), Daniel Booko (Powell), Ridge Canipe (Keegan Sullivan), Alex Rose Wiesel (Girls Lacrosse Player #12), Jay Hayden (JP Jones), Bryan Lillis (Riggins), Lauren Minite (Charlie), Basil McCurry (Parent), Diego Acuna (West Coast Referee), Jim Pacitti (Coach Jarvis), Hymnson Chan (Brierfield Player)

Kellan Lutz, Chord Overstreet in *A Warrior's Heart* © Xenon Pictures

ANSWERS TO NOTHING (Roadside Attractions) Producers, Amanda Marshall, Sim Sarina; Executive Producer/Director/Editor, Matthew Leutwyler; Screenplay, Matthew Leutwyler, Gillian Vigman; Photography, David Robert Jones; Designer, Joe Lemmon; Costumes, Keri Smith; Music, Craig Richey; Casting, Michael Testa, Dan Shaner; a Cold Iron Pictures presentation of an Ambush Entertainment production; Dolby; Color; Rated R; 123 minutes; Release date: December 2, 2011. **CAST:** Miranda Bailey (Drew), Julie Benz (Frankie), Dane Cook (Ryan), Zach Gilford (Evan), Kali Hawk (Allegra), Mark Kelly (Carter), Elizabeth Mitchell (Kate), Erik Palladino (Jerry), Vincent Ventresca (Erik), Aja Volkman (Tara), Barbara Hershey (Marilyn), Joel Michaely (Alfonso), Cassius Willis (Det. Grimes), Ric Barbera (Mr. Billick), Andrew Borba (Andy Dillon), Karley Scott Collins (Tina), Nikki Deloach (Georgia), Anthony John Denison (Captain), Jerald Garner (Cop), George Gerdes (Drew's Dad), Greg Germann (Beckworth), John Griffin (Franklin), Erika Hamilton (Volunteer), M.J. Karmi (Claire), Hayes MacArthur (Taylor), Scott MacArthur (Allan), Meghan McLeod (Voice of Radio Psychic), Brian Palermo (Bill), Jacqueline Pinol (Tricia), Leslie Sarna (Lisa), Tiffany Turner (Joan), Troy Williams (Security Guard), Michael Yavnielli (Race Official), Kelvin Han Yee (EMT)

Elizabeth Mitchell, Miranda Bailey in *Answers to Nothing* © Roadside Attractions

SEDUCING CHARLIE BARKER (ARC Entertainment) Producers, Lynn Webb, Maurice Kanbar, Theresa Rebeck; Executive Producer, Maurice Kanbar; Co-Producers, Owen Seitel, Daphne Zuniga, Ned Kopp; Director, Amy Glazer; Screenplay, Theresa Rebeck, based on her play *The Scene*; Photography, Jim Orr; Designer, Doug Freeman; Costumes, Jocelyn Leiser Hernden; Music, Bruce Fowler; Editors, Rick LeCompte, Jordan Cecearelli; a Kanbar Entertainment presentation in association with Bashert Prods.; Color; HD; Rated R; 89 minutes; Release date: December 2, 2011. **CAST:** Daphne Zuniga (Stella), Stephen Barker Turner (Charlie Barker), Heather Gordon (Clea), David Wilson Barnes (Lewis), Steve Cell (Nick), Pamela Gaye Walker (Fiona), Liam Vincent (Lou), Alex Moggridge (Stella's Assistant), Patrick Alparone (Waiter), Elizabeth Fountain (Underling #1), Josh Mendelow (Actor at Audition) , Haley Lasema (Clea's Friend)

Charlie Barker Turner, Heather Gordon in *Seducing Charlie Barker*
© ARC Entertainment

THE BIG FIX (Green Planet Productions) Producer/Co-Director, Rebecca Harrell Tickell; Executive Producers, Peter Fonda, Maggie Wachsberger, Tim Robbins; Director, Josh Tickell; Screenplay, Johnny O'Hara; Photography, Marc Levy; Music, Ryan Demaree; Editors, Sean P. Keenan, Tina Imahara; Color; Not rated; 89 minutes; Release date: December 2, 2011. Documentary on cases of criminal negligence by the Big Oil companies; **WITH:** Josh Tickell, Rebecca Harrell Tickell, Jason Mraz, Jean-Michel Cousteau, Kevin Curole, Margaret Curole, Peter Fonda, Jeff Goodell, Chris Hedges, David Korten, Nomi Prins, Bernie Sanders, Greg Palast, Rikki Ott

Peter Fonda, Jason Mraz in *The Big Fix* © Green Planet Prods.

KINYARWANDA (AFFRM) Producers, Darren Dean, Tommy Oliver, Alrick Brown; Executive Producer, Ishmael Ntihabose; Director/ Screenplay, Alrick Brown; Based on a story by Ishmael Ntihabose; Photography, Danny Vecchione; Designer, Sibomana Omar Mukhtar; Costumes, Emmanuel Ngoye; Music, John Jennings

Boyd; Editor, Tovah Leibowitz; Casting, Simon Rwema; a Visigoth Pictures in association with Cineduc Rwanda presentation; American-French; Color; Not rated; 96 minutes; American release date: December 2, 2011. **CAST:** Cassandra Freeman (Lt. Rose), Hadidja Zaninka (Jean), Cleophas Kabasita (Francine), Marc Gwamaka (Patrique), Edouard Bamporiki (Emmanuel), Mazimpaka Kennedy (Father Pierre), Hassan Kabera (Ismael), Uwimana Abdallah (The Imam), Mutsari Jean (The Mufti of Rwanda), Kena Onyenjekwe (Sgt. Fred), Assumpta Micho (Mayam, The Witch), Ayuub Kasasa Mago (Father Bertrand), Watta Hezekis (Father Jean Claude), Munyantore Bashil (Head Ghanaian Soldier), Ibrahim Kasuiya (Shmael's Father), Farida Uwimana (Shmael's Mother), Ismael Dusengemuanga (Thierry), Ally Majaliwa (Michel, the Husband), Daisy Batamuliza (Delphine)

CAITLIN PLAYS HERSELF (Swanberg) Producer/Director, Joe Swanberg; Screenplay, Joe Swanberg, Caitlin Stainken; Photography, Adam Wingard, Joe Swanberg; Music, Keith Ruggiero; Color; Not rated; 69 minutes; Release date: December 2, 2011. **CAST:** Caitlin Stainken, Joe Swanberg, Kurt Chiang, Megan Mercier, Dean Peterson, Frank V. Ross, Spencer Parsons (Themselves)

I MELT WITH YOU (Magnolia) Producers, Mark Pellington, Norman Reiss, Rob Cowan; Executive Producers, Glenn Porter, Liza Richardson, Rob Lowe, Jason Piette, Sean O'Kelly, Heidi Levitt, Aaron L. Gilbert, Thomas Jane, Neil LaBute, Michael Cowan; Director, Mark Pellington; Screenplay, Glenn Porter; Story, Glenn Porter, Mark Pellington; Photography, Eric Schmidt; Designer, Ian Sebastian Kasnoff; Costumes, Patia Prouty; Music, tomandandy; Editor, Don Broida; Casting, Heidi Levitt; an Iron Hoss Films, Stealth Media Group in association with Media House Capital; Dolby; Color; Rated R; 116 minutes; Release date: December 9, 2011. **CAST:** Thomas Jane (Richard), Jeremy Piven (Ron), Rob Lowe (Jonathan), Christian McKay (Tim), Carla Gugino (Officer Boyde), Tom Bower (Captain Bob), Arielle Kebbel (Randi), Zander Eckhouse (Jonah), Abhi Sinha (Ryan), Sasha Grey (Raven), Joe Reegan (Cole), August Emerson (Ethan), Rebecca Creskoff (Amanda), Melora Hardin (Jane), Melora Walters (Katie), Anne Marie Hunter (Lisa), Anthony Newfield (Restaurant Manager), Tom Donald (Choking Old Man), Emma Friedman (Old Man's Daughter), David Lowe (Officer Stevens), Michael Joseph Stevens (Stevie), Ryan Harry, Alex Solowitz (Pool Players), Natalia Nogalich (Patient), Nico Nicotera (Bartender), Ronnie Rubalcaba (Javier), Shane Roney (Miles), Victoria Bruno (Carrie), Dani Fish (Jody), Isabellla Pellington (Carlie)

Jeremy Piven, Rob Lowe, Christian McKay, Thomas Jane in *I Melt with You*
© Magnolia Pictures

FANNIE, ANNIE & DANNY (CB Films) Producer, Morgan Schmidt-Feng; Executive Producers, Raymond Brown, Judy Brown, Audrey Jackson, Jeff Baker; Director/ Screenplay, Chris Brown; Photography, Gordon Hall; Designer, Judith Jackson; Music, April Campbell; Editor, Ellen Mirsch; a Filmsight Productions presentation; Stereo; Color; HD; Not rated; 82 minutes; Release date: December

9, 2011. **CAST:** Jill Pixley (Fanny), Carlye Pollack (Annie), Jonathan Leveck (Danny), Colette Keen (Edie), George Killingsworth (Ronnie), Nick Frangione (Todd), Anne Darragh (Mrs. Keller), Suzanna Aguayo (Carmen), Nancy Carlin (Stacy), Don Schwartz (Dr. Bob), Esther Mamet (Sheila), Sean Theriault (Alan), Jessica Kitchens (Emily), Cory Bytof (Patient), Russell Ramos (Clerk), T.O.F.U. (Band)

Jill Pixley, Jonathan Leveck in *Fannie, Annie & Danny* © CB Films

RED HOOK BLACK (Land Varied Intl.) Producer/Director/Screenplay, Luis Landivar; Based on the play by José Landivar; Photography, Valentina Caniglia; Designer, Minerva Caicedo; Costumes, Anna Azeglio; Music, Michael Bianco; Editor, Anastasia Cipolla; Dolby; Color; Not rated; 89 minutes; Release date: December 9, 2011. **CAST:** Kyle Fields (Marco), James Jackson (Damian), Danielle Lozeau (Olivia), Victoria Negri (Elizabeth), Keith Walker (Melvin), Cristina Rodlo (Eva), Maria Aparo (Ashley), Penny Bittone (Chester), Stacey Lewis (Mia), Tyler Ham Pong (Danny), Joanna Moskwa (Lara), Sandra M. Schneider (Cassandra), Julius LaMar (Michael Rego), Garry Carbone (Freddy)

Kyle Fields, Victoria Negri in *Red Hook Black* © Land Varied Intl.

CATCH .44 (Anchor Bay) Producers, Randall Emmett, Michael Benaroya, Megan Ellison; Executive Producers, Curtis Jackson, George Furla, Rick Jackson, Robert Ogden Barnum, Stephen Eads, David Willis, Holden Ostrin, Neil Wechsler, Henry M. Karp; Director/ Screenplay, Aaron Harvey; Photography, Jeff Cutter; Designer, Gary Frutkoff; Costumes, Johanna Argan; Editor, Richard Byard; Casting, Shannon Makhanian; an Annapurna production, an Emmett/Furla Films production in association with Benaroya Pictures and Waterfall Media; FotoKem color; Hawk-Scope; Rated R; 94 minutes; Release date: December 9, 2011. **CAST:** Forest Whittaker (Ronny), Bruce Willis (Mel), Malin Akerman (Tes), Nikki Reed (Kara), Deborah Ann Woll (Dawn), Shea Whigham (Billy), Brad Dourif (Sheriff Connors), Michael Rosenbaum (Brandon), Edrick Browne (Devon), Jill Stokesberry (Francine), Jimmy Lee, Jr. (Jesse, Trucker), Reila Aphrodite (Sara),

Kevin Beard (Mel's Driver), Amanda Bosley (Tourist Wife), Ivory Dortch (Waitress), P.J. Marshall (Deputy Elmore), Dan Silver (Businessman David)

Bruce Willis, Malin Akerman in *Catch .44* © Anchor Bay

ADDICTION INCORPORATED (Variance) Producers, Charles Evans Jr., Devorah Devries; Director, Charles Evans, Jr.; Executive Producer, Charmaine Parcero; Line Producer/Recreations, Kate Dean; Photography, Peter Nelson, Igor Martinovic; Story Producer, John Miller-Monzon; Music, Samite Mulondo; Editors, Kristen Huntley, Jay Keuper; an Acappella Pictures presentation of a Dune Road Films production; Dolby; Color; Rated PG-13; 102 minutes; Release date: December 14, 2011. Documentary on how research scientist Victor DeNoble proved that tobacco was addictive; **WITH:** Victor DeNoble, Danny Abel, Phil Barnett, Herbert Barry III, Neal Benowitz, Walter Bogdanich, Joseph M. Bruno, John P. Coale, Greg Connolly, Camela DeNoble, Carol DeNoble, Cliff Douglas, Thomas Doyle, Marc Edell, Sharon Y. Eubanks, William Farone, Jack Henningfield, Russ Herman, Philip J. Hilts, Anne Jeltema, David Kessler, Myron Levin, Gary Light, Paul C. Mele, Michael C. Moore, Matthew L. Myers, Bruce Reed, Joseph Rice, H. Lee Sarokin, William Schultz, Keith Summa, Henry A. Waxman, Ronald Wyden, Steven C. Parrish, Dan Zegart, Mitchell Zeller.

Victor DeNoble in *Addiction Incorporated* © Variance Films

SLEEPLESS NIGHTS STORIES (Jonas Mekas) Director, Jonas Mekas; Photography, Jonas Mekas, Thomas Boujut, Louis Garrel, Jonas Lozoraitis, Benn Northover; Music, Dan Zhu; Editors, Elle Burchill, Jonas Mekas; Color; Not rated; 114 minutes; Release date: December 15, 2011. Pieces of the life of filmmaker Jonas Mekas; **WITH:** Raimund Abraham, Marina Abramovic, Björk Guðmundsdóttir, Thomas Boujut, Louise Bourgeois, Simon Bryant, Phong Bui, Pip Chodorov, Louis Garrel, Flo Jacobs, Ken Jacobs, Harmony Korine, Lefty Korine, Rachel Korine-Simon, Kris Kucinskas, Hopi Lebel, Jean-Jacques Lebel, Diane Lewis, Jonas Lozoraitis, Adolfas Mekas, Oona Mekas, Sebastian Mekas,

DoDo Jin Ming, Dalius Naujokaitis, Benn Northover, Hans Ulrich Obrist, Yoko Ono, Nathlie Provosty, Carolee Schneemann, Patti Smith, Lee Stringer

Jonas Mekas in *Sleepless Night Stories* © Jonas Mekas

THE PILL (Shoot First Entertainment) Producers, J.C. Khoury, Trevor Herrick; Director/ Screenplay/Editor, J.C. Khoury; Photography, Andreas von Scheele; Designer, Anna-Karin Edelbrock; Music, Didier Lean Rachou; Casting, Lindsay Chag; Color; HD; Not rated; 83 minutes; Release date: December 16, 2011. **CAST:** Noah Bean (Fred), Rachel Boston (Mindy), Anna Chlumsky (Nelly), Jean Brassard (Renault), Al Thompson (Jim), Dreama Walker (Rose), Lué McWilliams (Nadine), Rob Yang (Pharmacist), Julia Royter (Belly Dancer), Jack Tartaglia (Alan), Jonathan Berke (Waiter), Mollie O'Rourke (Pregnant Woman), Alan Surchin, Doug Plotz (Dads), Zachary Surchin (Baby), Matthew Plotz, Joseph Plotz (Children)

Rachel Boston, Noah Bean in *The Pill* © Shoot First Entertainment

COOK COUNTY (Hannover House) Producers, David Pomes, Thomas Bickham, Anson Mount, Xander Berkeley, Ryan Donowho, Emily Gerson Saines; Director/ Screenplay, David Pomes; Photography, Brad Rushing; Designer, James Fowler; Costumes, Mirin Soliz; Music, Scott Szabo; Editor, Branan Edgens; an Eric Parkinson, Fred Shefte, Hannover House and Greenwood Films presentation; Color; Not rated; 93 minutes; Release date: December 16, 2011. **CAST:** Anson Mount (Bump), Xander Berkeley (Sonny), Ryan Donowho (Abe), Polly Cole (Lucy), Rutherford Cravens (Fat Earl), Makenna Fitzsimmons (Deandra), Brandon Smith (Wayne), John McClain (Uncle JD), Yankie Grant (Aunt Sally), J.D. Hawkins (Peanut), Gary Chason (Mr. Jimmy), Lisa Williams (Miss Debbie), Toby Lister (Bill Jenkins), Tommy Townsend (Pee Paw), Scott Nankivel (Luke), Anna Megan Raley (Cindy Simpson), Omar Adam (David Damien), Deke Anderson (Officer Crumley), Allison Norman (Phoebe Tims), James Fowler (Officer Simmons)

Xander Berkeley, Ryan Donowho in *Cook County* © Hannover House

THE DARKEST HOUR (Summit) Producers, Tom Jacobson, Timur Bekmambetov; Executive Producers, Arnon Milchan, Monnie Wills; Director, Chris Gorak; Screenplay, Jon Spaihts; Story, Leslie Bohem, M.T. Ahern, Jon Spaihts; Photography, Scott Kevan; Designer, Valeri Viktorov; Costumes, Varya Avdyushko; Music, Tyler Bates; Music Supervisors, Jojo Villanueva, Anastasia Brown; Editors, Priscilla Nedd Friendly, Fernando Villena; Visual Effects Supervisor, Stefen Fangmeier; Casting, Mary Vernieu, Venus Kanani; a Regency Enterprises presentation of a Jacobson Company/Bazelevs/New Regency production; Dolby; Panavision; 3D; Deluxe color; Rated PG-13; 89 minutes; Release date: December 25, 2011. **CAST:** Emile Hirsch (Sean), Olivia Thirlby (Natalie), Max Minghella (Ben), Rachael Taylor (Anne), Joel Kinnaman (Skyler), Veronika Vernadskaya (Vika), Dato Bakhtadze (Sergei), Gosha Kutsenko (Matvei), Nikoloai Efremov (Sasha), Georgy Gromov (Boris), Arthur Smoljaninov (Yuri), Anna Roudakova (Tess), Petr Fedorov (Anton Batkin), Ivan Gromov, Alexsandr Chernyh (Bartenders), Oleg Poddubny, Vasja Fursenko (Policemen), Ilya Ivanov, Sam Vanin (Drunk Russians), Alya Nikulina (Old Woman), Igor Novoselov (Brainy Navy Cadet), Maria Romanova (Russian Flight Attendant), Slava Barkovsky (Hefty Bouncer), Valentina Soboleva (Girl Walking in Club), Louis Leebe (Club DJ), Irina Antanenko (Club Beauty), Katerina Budyakova (Girl at the DJ Booth), Olga Zhuk, Tamara Zhukova, Maria Lavrova (Clubgoers)

Max Minghella, Olivia Thirlby, Emile Hirsch, Rachael Taylor in *The Darkest Hour* © Summit Entertainment

EL SICARIO, ROOM 164 (Icarus) Producers, Serge Lalou, Gianfranco Rosi; Director/ Photography, Gianfranco Rosi; Music, Abraham Spector; Editor, Jacopo Quadri; a co-production of Les Films D'Ici and Robofilms in association with Arte France – La Lucarne; American-French; Color; Not rated; 80 minutes; Release date: December 28, 2011. Documentary on a mysterious, hooded hit man for the Mexican drug cartels.

IF I WANT TO WHISTLE, I WHISTLE

(FILM MOVEMENT) a.k.a. *Eu cand vreau sa fluier, fluier*; Producers, Catalin Mitulescu, Daniel Mitulescu; Co-Produers, Fredrik Zander, Tomas Eskilsson; Executive Producer, Florentina Onea; Director, Florin Serban; Screenplay, Catalin Mitulescu, Florin Serban; Based on the play *Eu cand vreau sa fluier, fluier* by Andreea Valean; Photography, Marius Panduru; Designer, Ana Ioneci; Costumes, Augustina Stanciu; Editors, Catalin F. Cristutiu, Sorin Baican; Casting, Emil Slotea; Celluloid Dreams presentation of a Strada Film (Romania)/Film i Väst and the Chimney Pot (Sweden) production; Romanian-Swedish, 2010; Dolby; Color; Not rated; 94 minutes; American release date: January 5, 2011

CAST
Silviu	**George Pistereanu**
Ana	**Ada Condeescu**
Mother	**Clara Voda**
Penitentiary Director	**Mihai Constantin**
The Brother	**Marian Bratu**

Papan Chilibar (Ursu), Mihai Svoristeanu (Soare), Alexandru Mititelu (Finu), Cristian Dumitru (Blondu), Laurentiu Banescu (Psychologist)

While enduring his final two weeks at a hostile juvenile detention center, Silviu receives news that his delinquent mother has returned to take away the younger brother Silviu had raised like a son.

George Pistereanu, Ada Condeescu © Film Movement

George Pistereanu

Knut Jørgen Skaro, Gard B. Eldsvold, Stellan Skarsgård, Bjørn Floberg

Jannike Kruse, Stellan Skarsgård © Strand Releasing

A SOMEWHAT GENTLE MAN

(STRAND) a.k.a. *En ganske snill mann*; Producers, Stein B. Kvae, Finn Gjerdrum; Director, Hans Petter Moland; Screenplay, Kim Fupzaakeson; Photography, Philip Øgaard; Designers, Handverk by Eivind Stoud Platou, Kaare Martens, Synne Moen Tøften; Costumes, Caroline Sætre; Music, Halfdan E; Editor, Jens Christian Fodstad; Casting, Andrea Eckerbom; a Paradox presentation; Norwegian, 2010; Dolby; Color; Not rated; 103 minutes; American release date: January 14, 2011

CAST
Ulrik	**Stellan Skarsgård**
Rune Jensen	**Bjørn Floberg**
Rolf	**Gard B. Eidsvold**
Karen Margrethe	**Jorunn Kjellsby**
Geir	**Jan Gunnar Røise**
Merete	**Jannike Kruse**

Bjørn Sundquist (Sven) Jon Øigarden (Kristian), Kjersti Holmen (Wenche), Julia Bache Wiig (Silje), Aksel Hennie (Samen), Henrik Mestad (Kenny), Ane H. Røvik Wahlen (Kenny's Wife), Anders Baasmo Christiansen (Junkyard Boss), Per Frisch (Prison Warden), Frank Iversen (Bartender), Lene Kongsvik Johansen (Lady in Bar), Silje Torp Færavaag (Fancy Lady) , Viggo Jønsberg (Warehouse Foreman), Knut Jørgen Skaro (Short Man), Sverre Horgen (Coughing Man), Emil Myhre (Kenny's Son)

Released from prison, gangster Ulrik hopes to live a more peaceful existence only to be ordered by Rune Jensen to kill the man who snitched on him.

Seo Woo, Jeon Do-yeon

Youn Yuh-jung © IFC Films

THE HOUSEMAID

(IFC FILMS) a.k.a. *Hanyo*; Producer, Jason Chae; Executive Producers, Choi Pyung-ho, Seo Bum-seok; Director/Screenplay, Im Sang-soo; Photography, Lee Hyung Deok; Designer, Lee Ha-jun; Costumes, Choi Se-yeon; Editor, Lee Eun-soo; a Sidus FNH-Benex Cinema Fund 1 presentation of a Mirovision Inc. production; South Korean, 2010; Color; Not rated; 106 minutes; American release date: January 21, 2011

CAST
Li Eun-yi	**Jeon Do-yeon**
Hoon	**Lee Jung-jae**
Byung-sik	**Youn Yuh-jung**
Hae-ra	**Seo Woo**
Mi-hee, Hae-ra's Mother	**Park Ji-young**

Ahn Seo-hyeon (Nami), Hwang Jung-min (Eun-yi's Friend), Moon So-ri, Kim Jin-ah (Doctors), Chae Tae-back (Herbal Medicine Shop Doctor), Jeon Shin-hwan (Chief Secretary), Noh Sang-min (Driver), Jang Soon-kyu, Cho Yong-jae (Security), Lim Hyun-kyung (Yoga Instructor), Lee Keum-yun (Old Housemaid), Kim Ji-sun, Han Song-yi (Young Housemaids), Park Ju-sun (Death Leap Girl), Yoon Sun-hye, Seo Ha-young (Nurses), Kim Jae-hyeon (CT Doctor), Woo Hye-sun (Anaesthetist), Kim Eun-ok (Scrub Nurse)

Mi-hee plots revenge when she discovers that her family's new housemaid is sleeping with her husband.

JOHNNY MAD DOG

(IFC FILMS) Producer, Mathieu Kassovitz, Benoît Jaubert; Executive Producer, Elisa Larriere; Director/Screenplay, Jean-Stéphane Sauvaire; Based on the novel by Emmanuel Dongala; Photography, Marc Koninckx; Designer, Alexandre Vivet; Costumes, Karine Nuris; Music, Jackson Tennessee Fourgeaud; Editor, Stéphane Elmadjian; an Explicit Films and Scope Pictures co-production; French-Belgian-Liberian, 2008; Dolby; Color; Not rated; 98 minutes; American release date: January 21, 2011

CAST
Johnny Mad Dog	**Christophe Minie**
Laokolé	**Daisy Victoria Vandy**
No Good Advice	**Dagbeth Tweh**
Small Devil	**Barry Chernoh**
Butterfly	**Mohammed Sesay**
Pussy Cat	**Léo Boyeneh Kote**

Prince Kotie (Young Ma Joi), Nathaniel J. Kapeyou (Nesty Plastic), Joseph Duo (Never Die), Eric Cole (Jungle Rocket), Robert Davies (Fuck Dogo), Prince Doblah (Captain Dust to Dust), Miata Fahnbulleh (Madame Kamara), Papa Jackson (Captain Disrespect), Jimmy Jacobs (Black Cat), Terry Johnson (Joseph), Mohammed Kamara (Disgrunto), Onismus Kamoh (Fofo), Massiata E. Kenneh (Tanya Toyo), Anthony King (Ibrahim's Father), Lawrence King (Ibrahim), Veronica Kollie (Mayama), Jonathan Perry (Sniper), James Ragibo (Scarface), Fanta K. Smith (Ibrahim's Mother), Augustin Tokpa (Tupac), Emmanuel Tozzi (Take it Free), Julius Wood (Quick to Kill), Alexander Zorga (Iron Jacket), Carlos Badawi (Peacekeeper), Maxwell Carter (Mr. Kamara), Gromah Flomo (Pickup Girl)

A vicious teenage rebel militia attempts to overthrow a government stronghold.

© IFC Films

Colin Farrell © Newmarket Films

Saoirse Ronan

Colin Farrell, Ed Harris

THE WAY BACK

(NEWMARKET) Producers, Joni Levin, Peter Weir, Duncan Henderson, Nigel Sinclair; Executive Producers, Keith Clarke, John Ptak, Guy East, Simon Oakes, Tobin Armbrust, Jake Eberts, Mohamed Khalaf, Scott Rudin, Jonathan Schwartz; Co-Producer, Roee Sharon Peled; Co-Executive Producer, Alex Brunner; Director, Peter Weir; Screenplay, Peter Weir, Keith Clarke; Based on the book *The Long Walk: The Story of a Trek to Freedom* by Slavomir Rawicz; Photography, Russell Boyd; Designer, John Stoddart; Costumes, Wendy Stites; Music, Burkhard Dallwitz; Editor, Lee Smith; Visual Effects Supervisors, Tim Crosbie, Dennis Jones; an Exclusive Media Group, National Geographic Entertainment/ImageNation Abu Dhabi presentation of an Exclusive Films production, co-financed by the Polish Film Institute, Monolith Films; British-American-Polish; Dolby; Super 35 Widescreen; Deluxe Color; Rated PG-13; 133 minutes; Los Angeles release date: December 29, 2010; General U.S. release date: January 21, 2011

CAST
Janusz	**Jim Sturgess**
Mr. Smith	**Ed Harris**
Valka	**Colin Farrell**
Irena	**Saoirse Ronan**
Khabarov	**Mark Strong**
Tomasz	**Alexandru Potocean**
Kazik	**Sebastian Urzendowsky**
Voss	**Gustaf Skarsgård**
Zoran	**Dragos Bucur**
Andrei	**Dejan Angelov**
Bohdan	**Igor Gnezdilov**
Lazar	**Mari Grigorov**

Yordan Bikov, Ruslan Kupenov (Garbage Eaters), Sattar Dikambayev (Mongolian Horseman), Sally Edwards (Janusz's Wife – 1939), Nikolay Mutafchiev, Valentin Ganev (Guards), Meglena Karalambova (Jansuz's Wife – 1989), Irinei Konstantinov (Jansuz – 1989), An-Zung Le (Shepherd), Stanislav Pishtalov (Commandant), Stefan Shterev (Cook), Anton Trendafilov (Steam Man), Termirkhan Tursingaliev (Young Mongolian Horseman), Hal Yamanouchi (Official)

The true story of how four prisoners escaped from a Siberian gulag and crossed the Himalayas to freedom.

This film received a 2010 Oscar nomination for makeup.

Jim Sturgess

SANCTUM

(UNIVERSAL) Producer, Andrew Wight; Executive Producers, James Cameron, Ben Browning, Michael Maher, Peter Rawlinson, Ryan Kavanaugh; Co-Producer, Aaron Ryder; Line Producer, Brett Popplewell; Director, Alister Grierson; Screenplay, John Garvin, Andrew Wight; Photography, Jules O'Loughlin; Designer, Nicholas McCallum; Music, David Hirschfelder; Editor, Mark Warner; Casting, Greg Apps; a Relativity Media and Wayfare Entertainment presentation of a Great Wight production; Australian-American; Dolby; HDCAM; 3D; Color; Rated R; 109 minutes; American release date: February 4, 2011

CAST
Frank McGuire	**Richard Roxburgh**
Carl Hurley	**Ioan Gruffudd**
Josh McGuire	**Rhys Wakefield**
Victoria Elaine	**Alice Parkinson**
Crazy George	**Dan Wyllie**
J.D.	**Christopher Baker**
Liz	**Nicole Downs**
Judes	**Allison Cratchley**
Luko	**Cramer Cain**
Dex	**Andre Hansen**
Jim Sergeant	**John Garvin**
Chopper Pilot	**Sean Dennehy**
Kastom Shaman	**Nea Diap**

A diving expedition into a massive cave turns into a life-threatening race against time when Frank and his team find themselves trapped in the underground catacombs.

Rhys Wakefield, Alice Parkinson, Ioan Gruffudd

Rhys Wakefield © Universal Studios

Richard Roxburgh, Rhys Wakefield

Rhys Wakefield

Yun Jung-hee © Kino Intl.

Yun Jung-hee

POETRY

(KINO) a.k.a. *Shi;* Producer, Lee Joon-dong; Executive Producers, Youm Tae-soon, Choi Seong-min; Co-Executive Producer, Michel Saint-Jean, Jung Myung-soo, Lee Seung-ho, Lee Jang-ho; Co-Producer, Lee Dong-ha; Director/Screenplay, Lee Chang-dong; Photography, Kim Hyung-seok; Designer, Sihn Jeom-hui; Editor, Kim Hyun; a Pine House Film production; South Korean, 2010; Dolby; Super 35 Widescreen; Color; Not rated; 139 minutes; American release date: February 11, 2011

CAST
Mija	**Yun Jung-hee**
Wook	**Lee David**
Ki-bum's Father	**Ahn Nae-sang**
Mr. Kang, Old Man	**Kim Hi-ra**
Market Owner	**Kim Gye-sun**
Soon-chang's Father	**Min Bok-gi**
Hee-jin's Mother	**Park Myung-shin**
Park Sang-tae	**Kim Jong-gu**
Kim Yong-tak, Poet	**Kim Yong-taek**
Cho Mi-hye	**Kim Hye-jung**
Park Hee-jin	**Han Su-young**

Lee Jong-yeol (Jong-chul's Father), Park Woo-yeol (Tae-yeol's Father), Park Joong-shin (Byung-jin's Father), Hong Sung-bum (Oh Dong-jin, The Journalist)

Told that she has symptoms of Alzheimer's disease, 66-year-old Mija decides to shake up her mundane existence and take a class in poetry.

CARANCHO

(STRAND) Producer/Director, Pablo Trapero; Executive Producer, Martina Gusman; Screenplay, Alejandro Fadel, Martín Mauregui, Santiago Mitre, Pablo Trapero; Photography, Julián Apezteguia; Art Director, Mercedes Alfonsin; Costumes, Marisa Urroti; Editors, Ezequiel Borovinsky, Pablo Trapero; a Matanza Cine, Finecut, Patagonik, Ad Vitam, L90 with the support of INCAA Programa Ibermedia presentation; Argentine-French-South Korean, 2010; Dolby; Cinemascope; Cinecolor; Not rated; 107 minutes; American release date: February 11, 2011

CAST
Sosa	Ricardo Darín
Luján	Martina Gusman
Fello	Carlos Weber
Casal	José Luis Arias
Pico	Fabio Ronzano

Loren Acuña (Mariana), Gabriel Almirón (Munoz), José Manuel Espeche (Garrido), Francisco Acosta (Pacheco)

A corrupt personal injury lawyer, who specializes in road accidents, falls into an unexpected relationship with an idealistic doctor, only to find his unethical past catching up with him.

Martina Gusman, Ricardo Darin

Ricardo Darin, Martina Gusman © Strand Releasing

Frank Langella, Liam Neeson © Warner Bros.

January Jones, Liam Neeson

Liam Neeson, Diane Kruger

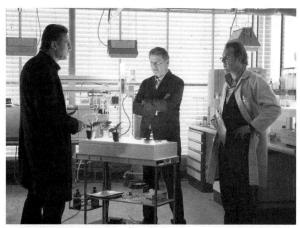

Liam Neeson, Aidan Quinn, Sebastian Koch

UNKNOWN

(WARNER BROS.) Producers, Joel Silver, Leonard Goldberg, Andrew Rona; Executive Producers, Susan Downey, Steve Richards, Sarah Meyer, Peter McAleese; Director, Jaume Collet-Serra; Screenplay, Oliver Butcher, Stephen Cornwell; Based upon the novel *Out of My Head* by Didier Van Cauwelaert; Photography, Flavio Labiano; Designer, Richard Bridgland; Costumes, Ruth Myers; Music, John Ottman, Alexander Rudd; Editor, Tim Alverson; Special Effects Supervisor, Mickey Kirsten; Casting, Lucinda Syson; a Panda production, presented in association with Dark Castle Entertainment; British-German-French; Dolby; Super 35 Widescreen; Technicolor; Rated PG-13; 113 minutes; American release date: February 18, 2011

CAST
Dr. Martin Harris	**Liam Neeson**
Gina	**Diane Kruger**
Elizabeth Harris	**January Jones**
Martin B	**Aidan Quinn**
Ernst Jürgen	**Bruno Ganz**
Rodney Cole	**Frank Langella**
Professor Leo Bressler	**Sebastian Koch**
Smith	**Olivier Schneider**
Jones	**Stipe Erceg**
Herr Strauss	**Rainer Bock**

Mido Hamada (Prince Shada), Clint Dyer (Biko), Karl Markovics (Dr. Farge), Eva Löbau (Nurse Gretchen Erfurt), Helen Wiebensohn (Laurel Bressler), Merle Wiebensohn (Lily Bressler), Adnan Maral (Turkish Taxi Driver), Torsten Michaelis (Airport Taxi Driver), Rainer Sellien, Petra Hartung (Control Room Detectives), Michael Baral (Peter Hoffmann), Sanny Van Heteren (Hotel Adlon Receptionist), Ricardo Dürner (Hotel Adlon Doorman), Marlon Putzke (Hotel Adlon Bellhop), Herbert Olschok (Hans Brandt), Karla Trippel (Hostel Cashier), Petra Schmidt-Schaller (Immigration Officer), Annabelle Mandeng (TV Anchor), Janina Flieger (University Receptionist), Fritz Roth (Taxi Depot Manager), Heike Hanold-Lynch (Anna, Lost & Found Clerk), Matthias Weindehöfer (Hotel Control Room Guard), Kida Khodr Ramadan (Café Owner), Peter Becker (Hotel Guard), Vladimir Pavic (Club Bouncer), Oliver Stolz (River Samaritan), Oliver Lang (Club DJ), Sebastian Stielke (Brandt's Assistant)

Waking up from a four day coma following a car accident, Dr. Martin Harris is shocked to discover that his identity is questioned and that even the woman he is certain is his wife claims not to know him.

Luis Tosar, Gael García Bernal

Gael García Bernal

EVEN THE RAIN

(VITAGRAPH) a.k.a. *También la lluvia*; Producers, Juan Gordon, Eric Altmayer, Monica Lozano, Emma Lustres; Executive Producer, Pilar Benito; Director, Icíar Bollaín; Screenplay, Paul Laverty; Photography, Alex Catalán; Designer, Juan Pedro de Gaspar; Music, Alberto Iglesias; Editor, Ángel Hernandez Zoido; a Morena Films, Vaca Films (Spain)/Mandarin Cinema (France)/Alebrije Cine y Video (Mexico) production with the participation of TVE, Canal Plus; Spanish-French-Mexican, 2010; Dolby; Widescreen; Technicolor; Not rated; 104 minutes; American release date: February 18, 2011

CAST
Costa	**Luis Tosar**
Sebastián	**Gael García Bernal**
Daniel/Hatuey	**Juan Carlos Aduviri**
Antón/Christopher Columbus	**Karra Elejalde**
Alberto/Bartolome de las Casas	**Carlos Santos**
Juan/Antonio de Montesinos	**Raúl Arévalo**
María	**Cassandra Ciangherotti**
Belén/Panuca	**Milena Soliz**
Ona/Sonia	**Sonia Ovando**
Chief of Police	**Luis Bredow**

Leónidas Chiri (Teresa), Ezequiel Diaz (Bruno), Pau Cólera (Actor Captain), Vicente Romero (Actor Comandante), Antonio Mora (Actor Franciscan), Daniel Currás (Galician Soldier), Glenda Rodriguez (Casting Assistant), Jorge Ortiz (Prefect), Bernardo Arancibia (Doctor), Alejandro Lanza (Nurse), Fernando Cervantes (Priest)

A team of filmmakers faces a moral dilemma when they arrive in the Bolivian jungles to shoot a revisionist movie about Columbus, hiring several impoverished locals for bit roles.

Juan Carlos Aduviri © Vitagraph Films

OF GODS AND MEN

(SONY CLASSICS) a.k.a. *Des homes et des dieux*; Line Producer, Martine Cassinelli; Director, Xavier Beauvois; Screenplay, Etienne Comar; Adaptation and Dialogue, Xavier Beauvois, Etienne Comar; Photography, Caroline Champetier; Designer, Michel Barthelemy; Editor, Marie-Julie Maille; Casting, Brigitte Moidon; a Why Not Productions, Armada Films, France 3 Cinema coproduction with the participation of France Télévisions, Canal+, Cinécinéma, Centre National du Cinéma et de l'Image Animée; French; Dolby; Techniscope; Color; Rated PG-13; 120 minutes; American release date: February 25, 2011

CAST
Christian	**Lambert Wilson**
Luc	**Michael Lonsdale**
Christophe	**Olivier Rabourdin**
Célestin	**Philippe Laudenbach**
Amédée	**Jacques Herlin**
Jean-Pierre	**Loïc Pichon**
Michel	**Xavier Maly**
Paul	**Jean-Marie Frin**
Nouredine	**Abdelhafid Metalsi**
Rabbia	**Sabrina Ouazani**
Omar	**Abdallah Moundy**
Bruno	**Olivier Perrier**
Ali Fayattia	**Farid Larbi**

Benaïssa Ahaouari (Sidi Larbi), Idriss Karimi (Hadji), Abdellah Chakiri (Colonel), Goran Kostic (Chief of Shipyard), Stanislas Stanic, Arben Bajraktaraj (Laborers), Zhour Laamri (Sidi Larbi's Woman), Raouya (Villager), Farid Bouslam (Ahmed), Fadia Assal (Nouredine's Woman), Maria Bouslam (Saloua), Soukaïna Bouslam (Saloua's Girl), Adel Bencherif, Rabii Ben Johail, Saïd Naciri, Hamid Aboutaieb (Terrorists), El Alaoui El Hassan (Shepherd)

As Algeria is torn by a civil war, a group of French Cistercian Trappist monks must make a decision on how to deal with the turmoil facing them.

Lambert Wilson, Jean-Marie Frin

Jacques Herlin, Michael Lonsdale

Lambert Wilson, Jacques Herlin, Loïc Pichon, Michael Lonsdale, Philippe Laudenbach; (front row:) Olivier Rabourdin, Jean-Marie Frin, Xavier Maly

Sabrina Ouazani © Sony Classics

HEARTBEATS

(IFC/SUNDANCE SELECTS) a.k.a. *Les amours imaginaires*; Producers, Xavier Dolan, Daniel Morin, Carole Mondello; Director/Executive Producer/Screenplay/Editor/Art Director/Costumes, Xavier Dolan; Photography, Stéphanie Weber-Biron; a Remstar presentation in collaboration with Alliance Vivafilm of a production by Mifilifilms; Canadian-French, 2010; Dolby; Color; Not rated; 95 minutes; American release date: February 25, 2011

CAST
Marie Camille	**Monia Chokri**
Nicolas M.	**Niels Schneider**
Francis Riverëkim	**Xavier Dolan**
Désirée, Nicolas's Mother	**Anne Dorval**

Anne-Elisabeth Bossé, Magalie Lépine Blondeau, Bénédicte Décary (Young Women), Olivier Morin, Éric Bruneau, Gabriel Lessard (Young Men), Jody Hargreaves (Jody), Clara Palardy (Clara), Anthony Huneault (Antonin), Minou Petrowski (Cashier), Perrette Souplex (Hairdresser), Sophie Desmarais (Rockabill), François Bernier, Benoit McGinnis, François Xavier Dufour (Kissers), Louis Garrel (Party Guest)

Marie and her friend Francis both find themselves falling hopelessly in love for a gorgeous and aloof country boy who has just arrived in town.

Xavier Dolan, Niels Schneider, Monika Chokri

Xavier Dolan © Sundance Selects

Wallapa Mongkolprasert © Strand Releasing

UNCLE BOONMEE WHO CAN RECALL HIS PAST LIVES

(STRAND) a.k.a. *Loong Boonmee raleuk chat*; Producers, Simon Field, Keith Griffiths, Charles De Meaux, Apichatpong Weerasethakul; Co-Producers, Hans W. Geissendoerfer, Luis Miñarro, Michael Weber; Director/ Screenplay, Apichatpong Weerasethakul; Photography, Sayombhu Mukdeeprom, Yukontorn Mingmongkon, Charin Pengpanich; Designer, Akekarat Homlaor; Editor, Lee Chatametikool; Casting, Panjai Sirisuvan, Sakda Kaewbuadee; an Illumination Films presentation of a Kick the Machine Films (Thailand) and Illuminations Films Past Lives (UK) production; Thai-British- German-French-Spanish, 2010; Dolby; Color; Not rated; 113 minutes; American release date: March 2, 2011

CAST
Boonmee	**Thanapat Saisaymar**
Jen	**Jenjira Pongpas**
Tong	**Sakda Kaewbuadee**
Huay, Boonmee's Wife	**Natthakarn Aphaiwonk**
Boonsong, Boonmee's Son	**Geerasak Kulhong**

Kanokporn Thongaram (Roong, Jen's Friend in Hotel), Samud Kugasang (Jaai, Boonmee's Chief Worker), Wallapa Mongkolprasert (Princess), Sumit Suebsee (Soldier), Vien Pimdee (Farmer)

As Uncle Boonmee lay dying from acute kidney failure, he is cared for by the spirit of his deceased wife and his long lost son.

William Shimmell © Sundance Selects

Juliette Binoche

William Shimmell, Juliette Binoche

CERTIFIED COPY

(IFC/SUNDANCE SELECTS) a.k.a. *Copie conforme*; Producers, Marin Karmitz, Nathanaël Karmitz, Charles Gillibert, Angelo Barbagallo; Executive Producer, Gaetano Daniele; Director/Screenplay, Abbas Kiarostami; Adaptation, Massoumeh Lahidji; Photography, Luca Bigazzi; Set Designers, Giancarlo Basili, Ludovica Ferrario; Editor, Bahman Kiarostami; an MK2 presentation of a BiBi Film, France 3 Cinema production, in collaboration with Canal Plus, France Télévision, Le Centre National de la Cinematographie; French-Italian-Belgian, 2010; Dolby; Technicolor; HD-to-35mm; Not rated; 106 minutes; American release date: March 11, 2011

CAST
She	Juliette Binoche
James Miller	William Shimell
The Man at the Square	Jean-Claude Carrière
The Woman at the Square	Agathe Natanson
The Café Owner	Gianna Giachetti
The Son	Adrian Moore
The Interpreter	Angelo Barbagallo
The Guide	Andrea Laurenzi
The Bride Groom	Filippo Troiano
The Bride	Manuela Balsimelli

In Tuscany, a British author begins a relationship with a French antique shop owner with whom he adapts the guise of a married couple.

William Shimmell, Juliette Binoche

Michael Fassbender, Imogen Poots

Judi Dench, Mia Wasikowska

Jamie Bell, Holliday Grainger

JANE EYRE

(FOCUS) Producers, Alison Owen, Paul Trijbits; Executive Producers, Christine Langan, Peter Hampden; Co-Producers, Mairi Bett, Faye Ward; Director, Cary Joji Fukunaga; Screenplay, Moira Buffini; Based on the novel by Charlotte Brontë; Photography, Adriano Goldman; Designer, Will Hughes-Jones; Costumes, Michael O'Connor; Music, Dario Marianelli; Editor, Melanie Oliver; Hair/Makeup, Daniel Phillips; Casting, Nina Gold; a Ruby Films production, presented in association with BBC Films; British-American; Dolby; Color; Rated PG-13; 115 minutes; American release date: March 11, 2011

CAST

Jane Eyre	**Mia Wasikowska**
Rochester	**Michael Fassbender**
St. John Rivers	**Jamie Bell**
Mrs. Fairfax	**Judi Dench**
Mrs. Reed	**Sally Hawkins**
Mr. Brocklehurst	**Simon McBurney**
Blanche Ingram	**Imogen Poots**
Lady Ingram	**Sophie Ward**
Adèle Varens	**Romy Settbon Moore**
Young Jane	**Amelia Clarkson**
Bessie	**Jayne Wisener**
Helen Burns	**Freya Parks**

Rosie Cavaliero (Grace Poole), Hayden Phillips (Colonel Dent), Su Elliot (Hannah), Holliday Grainger (Diana Rivers), Tamzin Merchant (Mary Rivers), Craig Roberts (John Reed), Lizzie Hopley (Miss Abbot), Freya Wilson (Eliza Reed), Emily Haigh (Georgiana Reed), Sandy McDade (Miss Scatcherd), Edwina Elek (Miss Temple), Ewart James Walters (John), Georgia Bourke (Leah), Sally Reeve (Martha), Eglantine Rembauville (Sophie), Angela Curran (Undercook), Joe Van Moyland (Lord Ingram), Laura Phillips (Mrs. Dent), Harry Lloyd (Richard Mason), Ned Dennehy (Dr. Carter), Joseph Kloska (Clergyman Wood), Ben Roberts (Briggs), Valentina Cervi (Bertha Mason)

Following an oppressive childhood, Jane Eyre becomes governess at Thornfield Hall, where she toils under the command of the moody, enigmatic Mr. Rochester. Previous theatrical film versions include those made in 1921 (Hodkinson; Mabel Ballin and Norman Trevor), 1934 (Monogram; Virginia Bruce and Colin Clive), 1944 (20th; Joan Fontaine and Orson Welles), and 1996 (Miramax; Charlotte Gainsbourg and William Hurt).

This film received an Oscar nomination for costume design.

Sally Hawkins © Focus Features

BLACK DEATH

(MAGNET) Producers, Robert Bernstein, Jens Meuerer, Douglas Rae, Phil Robertson; Executive Producers, Judy Tossell, Chris Curling, Mark Woolley, Tim Haslam; Director, Christopher Smith; Screenplay, Dario Poloni; Photography, Sebastian Edschmid; Designer, John Frankish; Costumes, Petra Wellenstein; Music, Christian Henson; Editor, Stuart Gazzard; Make-up, Jekaterina Oertel; Casting, Karen Lindsay-Stewart; an Egoli Tossell Film (Germany), Hanway Films (U.K.) & Magnet Releasing presentation, in association with Zephyr Films (U.K.) of an Ecosse Films (U.K.) production; British-German, 2010; Dolby; Hawk Scope; Kodak color; Rated R; 102 minutes; American release date: March 11, 2011

Eddie Redmayne, Sean Bean

CAST
Ulric	**Sean Bean**
Osmund	**Eddie Redmayne**
The Abbot	**David Warner**
Langiva	**Carice van Houten**
Averill	**Kimberley Nixon**
Hob	**Tim McInnerny**
Wolfstan	**John Lynch**
Dalywag	**Andy Nyman**
Mold	**Johnny Harris**
Swire	**Emun Elliott**
Griff	**Jamie Ballard**
Ivo	**Tygo Gernandt**

Marianne Graffam (Suspected Witch), Nike Martens (Elena), Gotthard Lange (Labourer), Ines Westernströer (Bel), Emily Fleischer (Girl in Forest), Daniel Steiner (Monk), Tobias Kasimirowicz (Grimbold), Alex Tondowski (Maldoror), Keith Dunphy (Witch Finder), Thorsten Querner (Fitch, the Torturer), Peter Wolf (Husband)

As the bubonic plague sweeps through Europe, Ulric and his band of mercenary soldiers set out to capture a heretical sorcerer.

Sean Bean, Johnny Harris © Magnet Releasing

John Lynch

Carice van Houten, Eddie Redmayne

WINTER IN WARTIME

(SONY CLASSICS) a.k.a. *Oorlogswinter*; Producers, Els Vandervorst, San Fu Maltha; Co-Producers, Antonio Lombardo, Jasper Van Der Schalie; Line Producer, Niko Post; Director, Martin Koolhoven; Screenplay, Paul Jan Nelissen, Mieke De Jong, Martin Koolhoven; Based on the novel *Oorlogswinter* (*Winter in Wartime*) by Jan Terlouw; Photography, Guido Van Gennep; Designer, Floris Vos; Costumes, Alette Kraan; Music, Pino Donaggio; Editor, Job Ter Burg; Special Effects Supervisor, Darius Cicenas; Casting, Rebecca Van Unen; an Isabella Films & FU Works production in co-production with Prime Time & Max; Dutch, 2008; Dolby; Color; Rated R; 103 minutes; American release date: March 18, 2011

CAST
Michiel van Beusekom	**Martijn Lakemeier**
Uncle Ben	**Yorick van Wageningen**
Jack	**Jamie Campbell Bower**
Johan van Beusekom	**Raymond Thiry**
Erica van Beusekom	**Melody Klaver**
Lia van Beusekom	**Anneke Blok**
Auer	**Dan Husen**
Schafter	**Ad van Klempen**
Dirk	**Mees Peijnenburg**
Bertus van Gelder	**Tygo Gernandt**
Theo	**Jesse van Driel**
Ferryman	**Ben Ramakers**

Tibo Vandenborre, Peter Eberst (German Soldiers), Emile Janesen (Mr. Knopper), Sascha Flengte (Mrs. Knopper), Alja Hoeksema (Aunt Cora), Iris Hadderingh (Janneke), Rolandas Boravskis, Vaidas Lingvinas, Marius Maciulis, Aurimas Zvinys (Dutch Soldiers)

In Nazi-occupied Holland, a thirteen-year-old boy experiences the war around him, when he aids a wounded British paratrooper.

Ad van Klempen, Tygo Gernandt

Melody Klaver, Jamie Campbell Bower

Martijn Lakemeier

Martijn Lakemeier, Raymond Thiry © Sony Classics

MIRAL

Freida Pinto

Vanessa Redgrave, Hiam Abbass, Willem Dafoe

Freida Pinto © Weinstein Co.

(WEINSTEIN CO.) Producer, Jon Kilik; Executive Producers, François-Xavier Decraene, Sonia Raule; Co-Producers, Sebastián Silva, Tarak Ben Ammar, Tabrez Noorani; Director, Julian Schnabel; Screenplay, Rula Jebreal, based on her novel; Photography, Eric Gautier; Designer, Yoel Herzberg; Costumes, Walid Mawed; Editor, Juliette Welfling; Casting, Yael Aviv; a Pathé presentation of a Pathé-ER Productions-Eagle Pictures-India Take One Productions with the participation of Canal+ and CinéCinéma, a Jon Kilik production; French-Israeli-Italian-Indian; Dolby; Techniscope; Color/black and white; Rated R; 112 minutes; American release date: March 25, 2011

CAST
Hind Husseini	**Hiam Abbass**
Miral	**Freida Pinto**
Nadia	**Yasmine Al Massri**
Fatima	**Ruba Blal**
Jamal	**Alexander Siddig**
Hani	**Omar Metwally**
Lisa	**Stella Schnabel**
Eddie	**Willem Dafoe**
Bertha Spafford	**Vanessa Redgrave**

Asma Al Shiukhy, Neemeh Khalil (Women wrapping Body), Jameel Khoury (Brother Amin), Basel Husseini (Brother Khalid), Hanna Shammas, Ibrahim Husseini, Hazem Said (Husseini Brothers), Makram Khoury (Governor Khatib), Wadeeka Khoury (Hind's Mother), Virigina Amsis (Young Girl at Christmas Party), Ansam Qupti (Other Girl at Christmas Party), Fadi Shahen, Raed Said, Jamal Said, Mahmod Debh (Musicians at Christmas Party), Huda Al Imam (Governor's Wife), Butros Copty (Older Guest), Jude Amous (Zeina), Abdallah El-Ackel (Deir Yassin Boy), Miral Hasna (Deir Yassin Girl), Murad Shaheen (Deir Yassin Crying Child), Fatma El-Akel (Deir Yassin Little Girl), Mahmoud Abu Jazi (Teacher Mustafa), Najwa Mubarki (Teacher Nawal), Amjad Barakat (Hotel Director), Juliano Merr Khamis (Sheikh Saabah), Milad Matar (Advisor), Uri Avrahami (Israeli Adoption Officer), Fatma Yahia (Young Tamam), Shmil Ben Ari (Stepfather), Salwa Nakkara (Nadia's Mother), Rami Heuberger (Belly Dance Club Customer), Dov Navon (Yossi), Liron Levo (Man on Bus), Liat Ekta (Wife on Bus), Tsofit Shpan (Prisoner), Muaz Aljubeh (Jordanian Soldier), Adel Abou Raya (Hospital Official), Ana Akwai (Maher), Uri Klauzner (Ticket Man), Hai Maor (Soldier in Cinema), Pini Mittelman (Fatima's Judge), Sanaa Ali (Hawwa), Hind Halabi (Jamal's Mother), Saeed Gazzawi (Wedding Sheik), Ziad Bakri (Helmi), Yolanda El Karam (Young Miral), Samar Qawasmi (Little Leila), Sama Boullata (Little Hadil), Sama Abu-Khadir (Little Rania), Hala Kurd (Little Aziza), Rajaie Khateeb (Tourist Guide), Rana Al Qawasmi (Leila), Frida Elraheb (Hadil), Muataz Welteadi (Boy at Refuge), Mohammad Welteadi (Rami, Kid at Class), Oz Zehavi (Soldier at Refugee Camp), Iman Aoun (Hani's Mother), Faten Khoury (School Secretary), Adrian Tarabshi (Hadil's Uncle), Rozeen Bisharat (Yasmin), Shredy Jabarin (Ali), Ashraf Farah (Ashraf), Hanin Halabi (Girl on Bus), Roy Gurai, Doron Ben-David (Soldiers on Bus), Zohar Shtrauss (Arresting Policeman), Uri Gavriel (Interrogating Officer), Ruth Cats (Torture Woman), Ami Weinberg (Miral's Judge), Yoav Levi (Miral's Prosecutor), Munther Fahmi (Miral's Lawyer), Rawda (Tamam), Doraid Liddwai (Samir), Sharon Alexander (Lisa's Father), Firas Abo Alnor (Soldier at Check Point), Francois Abou Salem-Gasper (DNA Doctor), Abed Zua'bi (Man at Funeral), Amit Bar-am, Ibrahim Firawi, Vito Schnabel (Secret Police at Hotel), Lana Zreik (Sara), François-Xavier Decraene (French Client), Jawhara Baker (Samar Hilal), Anis Nacrour, Nina Burleigh (Journalists at American Colony)

An orphaned Palestinian girl finds herself drawn into the Arab-Israeli conflict.

Catherine Deneuve © Music Box Films

Judith Godrèche, Jérémie Renier, Catherine Deneuve, Karin Viard

POTICHE

(MUSIC BOX FILMS) a.k.a. *Trophy Wife*; Producers, Eric Altmayer, Nicolas Altmayer; Line Producer, Pierre Wallon; Director/Screenplay, François Ozon; Adapted from the play by Pierre Barillet and Jean-Pierre Grédy; Photography, Yorick Le Saux; Designer, Katia Wyszkop; Costumes, Pascaline Chavanne; Music, Philippe Rombi; Editor, Laure Gardette; Casting, Sarah Teper, Leila Fournier (France), Mickael de Nijs (Belgium); a Mandarin Cinema, FOZ, France 2 Cinéma, Mars Films, Wild Bunch (France)/Scope Pictures (Belgium) production, in association with Canal Plus, TPS Star, France Télévisions, Région Wallonne; French-Belgian, 2010; Dolby; Color; Rated R; 103 minutes; American release date: March 25, 2011

Judith Godrèche, Catherine Deneuve

CAST
Suzanne Pujol	**Catherine Deneuve**
Maurice Babin	**Gérard Depardieu**
Robert Pujol	**Fabrice Luchini**
Nadège Dumoulin	**Karin Viard**
Joëlle Pujol	**Judith Godrèche**
Laurent Pujol	**Jérémie Rénier**
Spanish Truck Driver	**Sergi Lopez**
Geneviève Michonneau	**Évelyne Dandry**
André Ferron	**Bruno Lochet**
Young Suzanne	**Elodie Frégé**
Young Babin	**Gauter About**
Young Robert	**Jean-Baptiste Shelmerdine**

Noam Charlier (Flavien), Martin de Myttenaere (Stanilas), Yannick Schmitz (Jean-François), Christine Desodt (Pilar Sanchez), Jean-Louis Leclercq (Doctor), Alexandre Chaidron (Journalist), Anne Carpriau (Mme. Gilberte Pacot), Nathalie Laroche (Nadège's Friend), John Flanders (English Shareholder), Pierre Barilett (2nd Shareholder), Sandrine Laroche, Muriel Hobé (Hostesses), Yvan Coene (Gunnar)

Catherine Deneuve, Gérard Depardieu

A tyrannical businessman's seemingly passive wife shows an unexpected assertiveness when she steps in to negotiate with the striking factory workers who have taken her husband hostage.

William Jøhnk Juel Nielsen, Ulrich Thomsen

Birthe Neumann, Trine Dyrholm © Sony Classics

Markus Rygaard, William Jøhnk Juel Nielsen

Mikael Persbrandt, Trine Dyrholm

IN A BETTER WORLD

(SONY CLASSICS) a.k.a. *Hævnen*; Producer, Sisse Graum Jørgensen; Line Producer, Karen Bentzon; Director, Susanne Bier; Screenplay, Anders Thomas Jensen; Story, Susanna Bier, Anders Thomas Jensen; Photography, Morten Søborg; Designer, Peter Grant; Costumes, Manon Rasmussen; Music, Johan Søderqvist; Editor, Pernille Bech Christensen; a Zentropa Entertainments 16 presentation in co-production with Memfis Film Intl.; Danish, 2010; Dolby; HD Widescreen; Color; Rated R; 113 minutes; American release date: April 1, 2011

CAST
Anton	**Mikael Persbrandt**
Marianne	**Trine Dyrholm**
Claus	**Ulrich Thomsen**
Elias	**Markus Rygaard**
Christian	**William Jøhnk Juel Nielsen**
Headmaster	**Bodil Jørgensen**
Signe	**Elisebeth Steentoft**
Niels	**Martin Buch**
Hanne	**Anette Støvlebæk**
Lars	**Kim Bodnia**
Najeeb	**Wil Johnson**

Eddie Kimani, Mary Nduku Mbai, Preben Harris (Patients), Emily Mulaya, June Waweru (Nurses), Dynah Bereket (Decrepit Woman), Satu Helena Mikkelinen (Hanna), Camila Gottlieb (Eva), Simon Maagaard Holm (Sofus), Emil Nicolai Helms (Sofus' Schoolmate), Toke Lars Bjarke (Morten), Birthe Neumann (Marianne's Colleague), Paw Henriksen, Jesper Lohmann (Policemen), Bodil Jørgensen (Principal), Lucas O. Nyman (Lars' Son), Lars Kaalund (Lars' Colleague), Ondiege Matthew (Big Man), Nancy Akoth (Woman), Camilla Bendix (Løber), Alberte Blichfeldt (Løber's Daughter), Gabriel Muli, Stig Hoffmeyer (Doctors), Rikke Louise Anderson (Lars' Wife), Godfrey Ojiambo (Man), Evans Muthini (Translator)

A Dutch doctor working in Africa hopes to win back his estranged wife and prove a role model for his son, who, back home in Denmark is being bullied in school.

2010 Academy Award Winner for Best Foreign Lanuage Film.

Kevin Kline, Sandrine Bonnaire

Sandrine Bonnaire

Kevin Kline © Zeitgeist Films

QUEEN TO PLAY

(ZEITGEIST) a.k.a. *Joueuse*; Co-Producers, Amelie Latascha, Dominique Besnehard, Michel Feller; Executive Producer, Jean-Philippe Laroche; Director, Caroline Bottaro; Screenplay, Caroline Bottaro, Caroline Maly; Based on the novel *The Chess Player* by Bertina Henrichs; Photography, Jean-Claude Larrieu; Set Designer, Emmanuel de Chauvigny; Costumes, Dorothée Guiraud; Music, Nicola Piovani; Editor, Tina Baz Le Gal; a Mon Voisin Productions (France) and Blueprint Film (Germany) production, in coproduction with Studio Canal+, Canal Horizon, CinéCinéma, Tele München; French-German, 2009; Dolby; Color; Not rated; 96 minutes; American release date: April 1, 2011

CAST
Hélène	**Sandrine Bonnaire**
Dr. Kröger	**Kevin Kline**
Ange	**Francis Renaud**
The American Woman	**Jennifer Beals**
Maria	**Valérie Lagrange**
Lisa	**Alexandra Gentil**
Natalia	**Alice Pol**
Marie-Jeanne	**Elisabeth Vitali**
The American Man	**Dominic Gould**
Chess Club President	**Daniel Martin**

Didier Ferrari (Jacky), Laurence Colussi (Pina), Élisabeth Vitali (Marie-Jeanne), Valérie Tréjean (Nurse), François Orsoni (Journalist), Christine Ambrosini (Woman in Car), Anne-Camille Challier (Fanny), Lionel Tavera (Bus Driver), Gilbert Barbera (Maria's Fiancé)

A French chambermaid's obsession with chess leads her to seek the tutelage of a reclusive American doctor.

Sandrine Bonnaire

HANNA

(FOCUS) Producers, Leslie Holleran, Marty Adelstein, Scott Nemes; Executive Producer, Barbara A. Hall; Director, Joe Wright; Screenplay, Seth Lochhead, David Farr; Story, Seth Lochhead; Photography, Alwin Küchler; Designer, Sarah Greenwood; Music, The Chemical Brothers; Editor, Paul Tothill; Casting, Jina Jay; a Holleran Company production; British-German-American; Dolby; Super 35 Widescreen; Color; Rated PG-13; 111 minutes; Release date: April 8, 2011

Cate Blanchett, Tom Hollander

CAST
Hanna	**Saoirse Ronan**
Erik Heller	**Eric Bana**
Marissa Wiegler	**Cate Blanchett**
Isaacs	**Tom Hollander**
Rachel	**Olivia Williams**
Sebastian	**Jason Flemyng**
Lewis	**John Macmillan**
Walt	**Tim Beckmann**
Johanna Zadek	**Vicky Krieps**
Dr. Burton	**Jamie Beamish**
Sophie	**Jessica Barden**
Miles	**Aldo Maland**

Paris Arrowsmith (CIA Tech #1), Paul Birchard (Bob), Christian Maclolm (Head of Ops), Tom Hodgkins (Monitor), Vincent Montuel, Nathan Nolan (Camp G Doctors), Michelle Dockery (False Marissa), Mohamed Majd (Moroccan Hotel Owner), Sebastian Hülk (Titch), Joel Basman (Razor), Mathias Harrebye-Brandt (Danish Policeman), Álvaro Cervantes (Feliciano), Marc Soto (Feliciano's Brother), Gudrun Ritter (Katrin Zadeck), Martin Wuttke (Knepfler)

Trained by her father to function as a deadly assassin, 16-year-old Hanna finds herself on the run from a determined CIA agent.

Saoirse Ronan

Eric Bana © Focus Features

Jessica Barden, Saoirse Ronan

THE PRINCESS OF MONTPENSIER

(IFC/SUNDANCE SELECTS) Producer, Eric Heumann; Associate Producers, Laurent Brochand, Marc Sillam; Executive Producer, Frédéric Bourboulon; Director, Bertrand Tavernier; Screenplay, Jean Cosmos; Story, Jean Cosmos, François-Olivier Rousseau, Bertrand Tavernier; Photography, Bruno de Keyzer; Designer, Guy-Claude François; Costumes, Caroline de Vivaise; Music, Philippe Sarde; Editor, Sophie Brunet; Casting, Gérard Moulévrier; a Paradis Films, Studio Canal, France 2 Cinéma, France 3 Cinéma, Pandora Filmproduktion co-production; French-German, 2010; Dolby; Panavision; Color; Not rated; 139 minutes; American release date: April 15, 2011

CAST

Princess Marie of Montpensier	**Mélanie Thierry**
Comte de Chabannes	**Lambert Wilson**
Prince of Montpensier	**Grégoire Leprince-Ringuet**
Henri de Guise	**Gaspard Ulliel**
Duc d'Anjou	**Raphaël Personnaz**
Joyeuse	**Anatole de Bodinat**
Quelus	**Eric Rulliat**
La Valette	**Samuel Theis**
Duke of Montpensier	**Michel Vuillermoz**

Judith Chemla (Catherine de Guise), Philippe Magnan (Marquis of Mézières), César Domboy (Mayenne), Jean-Pol Dubois (Cardinal of Lorraine), Florence Thomassin (Marquise of Mézières), Christine Brücher (Duchess of Montpensier), Evelina Meghnagi (Catherine de Médicis), Charles Petit (Nicolas), Joséphine de La Baume (Jeanne), Jean-Yves Roan (The Peddler), Nathalie Krebs (Duenna Marie), Alain Sachs (The Innkeeper), Tomasz Bialkowski (Polish Professor), Jean-Claude Calon (Duke's Stonemason), Olivier Loustau (The Robber), Deborah Grall (Inn Servant), Mathieu Lourdel (Saint-Mégrin), Frédéric Bourboulon (Louvre Noble), Francis Camel (Camel Driver), Frédéric Laforet (Quercy), Romain Vergnaud (Charles), Yann Vaille (Beauvais)

In 16th Century France, Marie of Mézières agrees to marry the Prince of Montpensier despite her obsession with Henri de Guise.

Raphaël Personnaz, Gaspard Ulliel

Mélanie Thierry, Lambert Wilson © Sundance Selects

Gregoire Leprince-Ringuet, Mélanie Thierry, Lambert Wilson

Gaspard Ulliel

Ksenia Rappoport © Goldwyn Films

Ksenia Rappoport, Filippo Timi

Filippo Timi

THE DOUBLE HOUR

(SAMUEL GOLDWYN) a.k.a. *La doppia ora*; Producers, Nicola Giuliano, Francesca Cima; Executive Producer, Viola Prestieri; Director, Giuseppe Capotondi; Screenplay, Alessandro Fabbri, Ludovica Rampoldi, Stefano Sardo; Photography, Tat Radcliffe; Designer, Totoi Santoro; Costumes, Roberto Chiocchi; Music, Pasquale Catalano; Editor, Guido Notari; Casting, Annamaria Sambucco; a Nicola Giuliano, Francesca Cima, Medusa Film presentation of a Medusa Film-Indigo Film production, in collaboration with the Film Commission Torino Piemonte in collaboration with Mercurio Cinematografia; Italian; Dolby; Widescreen; Color; Not rated; 96 minutes; American release date: April 15, 2011

CAST
Sonia	**Ksenia Rappoport**
Guido	**Filippo Timi**
Margherita	**Antonia Truppo**
Riccardo	**Gaetano Bruno**
Bruno	**Fausto Russo Alesi**
Dante	**Michele Di Mauro**
Assistant Hotel Manager	**Lorenzo Gioielli**
Redhead at Speed Date	**Lidia Vitale**

Giampiero Iudica, Roberto Accornero, Diego Gueci, Simone Repetto, Stefano Saccotelli (Men at Speed Date), Lucia Poli (Marisa), Giorgio Colangeli (Priest), Deborah Bernuzzi (Hostess), Barbara Braconi (Receptionist), Federica Cassini, Antonio Sarasso (Nurses), Valentina Gaia (Jewelry Shop Girl), Edoardo La Scala (Marco), Chiara Nicola (Suicidal Girl), Chiara Paoluzzi (Chambermaid), Gilda Postiglione (Doctor), Fabrizio Rizzolo (Hotel Customer), Stefano Sardo (Robber #1), Paolo Maria Serra (Neurologist)

A chambermaid and former cop fall in love after meeting by way of the speed-dating scene, only to find themselves at gunpoint when a burglar disrupts their romantic getaway.

Filippo Timi, Ksenia Rappoport

Mélissa Désormeaux-Poulin, Maxim Gaudette

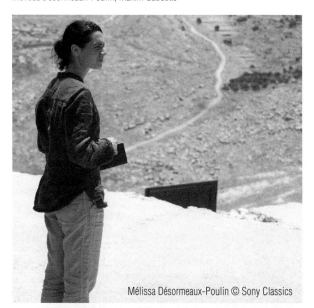

Mélissa Désormeaux-Poulin © Sony Classics

Rémy Girard, Mélissa Désormeaux-Poulin, Maxim Gaudette

Lubna Azabal

INCENDIES

(SONY CLASSICS) Producers, Luc Déry, Kim McCraw; Co-Producers, Miléna Poylo, Gilles Sacuto, Anthony Doncque; Associate Producers, Phoebe Greenberg, Penny Mancuso; Director, Denis Villeneuve; Screenplay, Denis Villeneuve, in collaboration with Valerie Beaugrand-Champagne; Based on the stage play by Wajdi Mouawad; Photography, André Turpin; Designer, André-Line Beauparlant; Costumes, Sophie Lefebvre; Music, Grégoire Hetzel; Editor, Monique Dartonne; Casting, Lucie Robitaille, Lara Atalla, Constance Demontoy; a micro_scope production, in co-production with TS Productions and in association with PHI Group; Canadian-French, 2010; Dolby; Technicolor; Rated R; 130 minutes; American release date: April 22, 2011

CAST
Nawal Marwan	**Lubna Azabal**
Jeanne Marwan	**Mélissa Désormeaux-Poulin**
Simon Marwan	**Maxim Gaudette**
Notary Jean Lebel	**Rémy Girard**
Abou Tarek	**Abdelghafour Elaaziz**
Notary Maddad	**Allen Altman**
Chamseddine	**Mohamed Maid**
Fahim	**Nabil Sawalha**
Maïka	**Baya Belal**

Bader Alami (Nicolas Marwan), Yousef Shuwayhat (Sharif), Karin Babin (Chamseddine's Bodyguard), Mustafa Kamel (Barber of the Militia), Hussein Sami (Nihad), Dominique Briand (Niv Cohen), Frédéric Paquet (Emergency Room Doctor), Hamed Najem (Wahab), Ahmad Massad (Bassem Marwan), Majida Hussein (Nawal's Grandmother), Asriah Nijres (Midwife), John Dunn-Hill (Prof. Saïd Haidar), Nadia Essadiqi (University Secretary), Chaouki Charbal (University Professor), Sumaya Attia (Rafqa), Nabil Koni (Uncle Charbel), Laila Qutub (Nawal's Young Cousin), Raha'a Hikma (Nawal's Aunt), Hayef Majeed Mubarak (Neighbor), Baker Kabbani (Old Berger), Jackie Sawiris (Mother), Fadel Abdel Latif (Grocer), Ali Hussein (Ahmed), Baraka Rahmani (Samia), Rasmeyeh Leftey (Souha), Marwan Dudin (Wajdi), Zalfa Chelhot (Nouchine), Yousef Soufan (Nihad, 15 years), Jabar Risheq (Hamid)

At the reading of their mother's will, Jeanne and Simon Marwan are shocked to discover that their father is still alive and that they have a brother they never knew existed. In order to answer the questions behind these revelations, the siblings travel to the Middle East to dig into their family history.

This movie received an Oscar nomination for foreign language film (2010).

Frank Rautenbach, Neels Van Jaarsveld, Taylor Kitsch, Ryan Phillippe
© Tribeca Productions

THE BANG BANG CLUB

(TRIBECA) Producers, Daniel Iron, Lance Samuels, Adam Friedlander; Executive Producers, Neil Tabatznik, Steven Silver, Patrice Theroux, Laszlo Barna, Chris Ouwinga, Darryn Welch; Director/Screenplay, Steven Silver; based on the book *The Bang-Bang Club: Snapshots from a Hidden War* by Greg Marinovich, Joao Silva; Photography, Miroslaw Baszak; Designer, Emilia Weavind; Costumes, Ruy Filipe; Music, Philip Miller; Music Supervisor, Stacey Horricks; Editor, Ronald Sanders; Stunts, Mick Milligan, Antony Stone; Special Effects Supervisor, Antony Stone; an Entertainment One and Instinctive Film presentation of a Foundry Films, Out of Africa Entertainment production; Canadian-South African; Dolby; Widescreen; Technicolor; Rated R; 109 minutes; American release date: April 22, 2011

CAST
Greg Marinovich	**Ryan Phillippe**
Robin Comley	**Malin Akerman**
Kevin Carter	**Taylor Kitsch**
Ken Oosterbroek	**Frank Rautenbach**
James Natchwey	**Patrick Lyster**
João Silva	**Neels Van Jaarsveld**
Ronald Graham	**Russel Savadier**

Nina Milner (Samantha), Jessica Haines (Allie), Lika Van Den Bergh (Vivian), Kgosi Mongake (Patrick), Patrick Shai (Pegleg), Alf Khumalo (Alf), Craig Palm (Amir), Nick Boraine (Colin), Vusi Kunene (Petrus Maseko), Greg Melvill-Smith (Jacques Hugo), Fiona Ramsey (Margy), Ashley Mulheron (Roxy), Neil Tabatznik (Mladen), Jacques Gombault (Policeman), Ashley Saunders (Sarel), Eloiise Horjus (Sheila), Nats Ramabulawna (Sonny), Mtunzi Mtoyi (Steven), Gabisile Ndebele (Thoko), Julian Rademeyer (Cape Town Reporter), Andy Stead (Durban Reporter), Israel Makoe (Man in White Suit), Geoffrey Sekele, Kate Mbele (Locals)

Four daredevil photojournalists become eyewitnesses to the final days of apartheid in Soweto, South Africa.

13 ASSASSINS

(MAGNET) a.k.a. *Jûsan-nin no shikaku*; Producers, Michihiko Umezawa, Minami Ichikawa, Toichiro Shiraishi, Takahiro Ohno, Hirotsugu Yoshida, Shigeji Maeda; Executive Producers, Toshiaki Nakazawa, Jeremy Thomas, Takashi Hirajo; Co-Producers, Kazuomi Suzaki, Hisashi Usui; Director, Takashi Miike; Screenplay, Daisuke Tengen; Based on a story by Shoichirou Ikemiya and a screenplay by Kaneo Ikegami; Photography, Nobuyasu Kita; Art Director, Yuji Hayashida; Costumes, Kazuhiro Sawataishi; Music, Koji Endo; Editor, Kenji Yamashita; Casting, Yuriko Kitada; a Sedic Intl. (Japan), Recorded Picture Co. (UK) production in association with TV Asahi Corp. (Japan), Toho Co. Dentsu, Sedic Deux & Rakueisha; Japanese-British, 2010; Dolby; Super 35 Widescreen; Color; Rated R; 126 minutes; American release date: April 29, 2011

CAST
Shinzaemon Shimada	**Kôji Yakusho**
Shinrokuro	**Takayuki Yamada**
Koyata	**Yûsuke Iseya**
Lord Naritsugu Matsudaira	**Gorô Inagaki**
Hanbei Kitou	**Masachika Ichimura**
Sir Doi	**Mikijiro Hira**
Kuranaga	**Hiroki Matsukata**
Mitsuhashi	**Ikki Sawamura**
Sahara	**Arata Furuta**
Hirayama	**Tsuyoshi Ihara**

Masataka Kubota (Ogura), Sousuke Takaoka (Hioki), Seiji Rokkaku (Otake), Yûma Ishigaki (Higuchi), Kôen Kondô (Horii), Kazuki Namioka (Ishikzuka), Kazue Fukiishi (Tsuya/Upashi), Koshiro Matsumoto (Yukie Makino), Mitsuki Tanimura (Chise Makino), Takumi Saito (Uneme Makino), Shinnosuke Abe (Genshiro Deguchi), Masaaki Uchino (Zusho Mamiya), Ken Mitsuishi (Asakawa)

Following the suicide of a nobleman whose daughter had been raped, a Shogun official hires a samurai and his team of expert swordsmen to assassinate the man responsible.
Remake of a 1963 Japanese film *The Thirteen Assassins*.

Yûsuke Iseya, Takayuki Yamada © Magnet Releasing

CAVE OF FORGOTTEN DREAMS

(SUNDANCE SELECTS) Producers, Erik Nelson, Adrienne Ciuffo; Executive Producers, Dave Harding, Julian P. Hobbs, David McKillop, Molly Thompson; Co-Producers, Amy Briamonte, Phil Fairclough, Judith Thurman, Nicolas Zunino; Director/Screenplay, Werner Herzog; Photography, Peter Zeitlinger; Music, Ernst Reijseger; Editors, Joe Bini, Maya Hawke; a Sundance Selects, Creative Differences and History Films presentation, in participation with the French Ministry of Culture and Communication, Dept. of Cultural Heritage; Canadian-American-French-German-British, 2010; Dolby; Color; 3D; HD; Rated G; 90 minutes; American release date: April 29, 2011. Documentary in film which filmmaker Werner Herzog is granted access to the oldest known pictorial creation of humankind in the Chauvet caves in Southern France.

WITH
Werner Herzog (and narrator), Dominique Baffier, Jean Clottes, Jean-Michel Geneste, Carole Fritz, Gilles Tosello, Michel Philippe, Julien Monney, Nicholas Conard, Wulf Hein, Maria Malina, Maurice Maurin; and Charles Fathy (Voice of Interpreter)

Wulf Hein, Werner Herzog

© Sundance Selects

Jean-Michel Geneste

Werner Herzog

Nicholas Conard Werner Herzog

Reece Thompson, Kat Dennings © Anchor Bay

DAYDREAM NATION

(ANCHOR BAY) Producers, Christine Haebler, Trish Dolman, Simone Urdl, Jennifer Weiss; Executive Producers, Cameron Lamb, Tim J. Brown, Sam Maydew, Aaron L. Gilbert; Consulting Producers, William G. Santor, Michael Olsen; Director/ Screenplay, Mike Goldbach; Photography, Jon Joffin; Designer, Renée Read; Costumes, Ken Shapkin; Music, Ohad Benchetrit; Editor, Jamie Alain; Casting, Judy K. Lee; a Joker Films presentation of a Screen Siren Pictures and The Film Farm production, in association with Lila 9th Productions; Canadian; Dolby; Deluxe Color; Rated R; 98 minutes; American release date: May 6, 2011

CAST
Caroline Wexler	**Kat Dennings**
Thurston Goldberg	**Reece Thompson**
Barry Anderson	**Josh Lucas**
Enid Goldberg	**Andie MacDowell**
Ms. Budge	**Rachel Blanchard**
Lily Goldberg	**Natasha Calis**
Mr. Wexler	**Ted Whittall**

Quinn Lord (Thomas), Calum Worthy (Craig), Katie Boland (Jenny), Genevieve Buechner (Tina), Luke Camilleri (Rolly), Michele Creber (10-Year-Old Girl), Lauren Robertson (Doomed Cheerleader), Cole Heppell (Teenager), Patricia Isaac (Judy), Laura Jacobs (Laura Lee), Landon Liboiron (Paul), Scott E. Miller (Todd), William Phillips (Killer, White Suit), Jesse Reid (Charles), Ian Robison (Jenny's Dad), Alex Ferris, Connor Stanhope (Kids), Sean Tyson (Police Officer – School), Nadine Wright (Jenny's Mom), Adam Slamang (Party Guy), David Pearson (Man in Suit), Bruce Harwood (Mr. Myers)

A sarcastic teen is appalled by her father's decision to move them to a quirky, dead-end town where she makes it her goal to seduce one of her teachers.

Kat Dennings, Josh Lucas

THE COLORS OF THE MOUNTAIN

(FILM MOVEMENT) a.k.a. *Los colores de la montaña*; Producer, Juan Pablo Tamayo; Executive Producer, Julián Giraldo; Director/Screenplay, Carlos César Arbeláez; Photography, Oscar Jiménez; Art Director, Gonzalo Martínez; Costumes, María Adelaida Olarte; Music, Camilo Montilla; Editors, Felipe Aljure, Andrés Durán; an RCN Cine/e-Nnowa presentation of an El Bus Producciones production; Colombian, 2010; Dolby; Color; Not rated; 88 minutes; American release date: May 6, 2011

CAST
Manuel	**Hernán Ocampo**
Poca Luz	**Genaro Aristizábal**
Julián	**Nolberto Sanchez**

In a mountainous region of war torn Colombia, young Manuel and his friends are anxious to retrieve a soccer ball that has rolled into a minefield, knowing what an essential part of their lives the sport has become.

Hernán Ocampo, Nolberto Sanchez, Genaro Aristizábul

Hernán Ocampo © Film Movement

© Kino Intl.

Gao Yuanyuan, Hideo Nazaizumi

CITY OF LIFE AND DEATH

(KINO) formerly *Nanjing! Nanjing!*; Producers, Han Sanping, Qin Hong, Zhou Li, John Chong, Andy Zhang; Executive Producer/Director/Screenplay, Lu Chuan; Photography, Cao Yu; Designers, Hao Yi, Lin Chaoxiang; Music, Liu Tong; a Beijing Film Stduio/CFGC/Stellar Megamedia/Jiang Su Broadcasting/Media Asia Films/Shanghai Bailiang Investment production; Chinese, 2009; Black and white; Not rated; 133 minutes; American release date: May 11, 2011

CAST
Lu Jianxiong **Liu Ye**
Miss Jiang **Gao Yuanyuan**
Kadokawa **Hideo Nakaizumi**
Mr. Tang **Fan Wei**
Jiang Yiyan (Xiao Jiang), Ryu Kohata (Ida), Liu Bin (Xiaodouzi), John Paisley (John Rabe), Beverly Peckous (Minnie Vautrin), Qin Lan (Mrs. Tang), Sam Voutas (Durdin), Yao Di (Tang Xiaomei), Zhao Yisui (Shunzi)

The true story of Japan's 1937 attack on the Chinese capital of Nanjing.

CAMERAMAN: THE LIFE AND WORK OF JACK CARDIFF

(STRAND) Producer/Director, Craig McCall; Co-Producer, Richard McGill; Executive Producers, Mason Cardiff, Lenny Crooks, Chris Roff, Julie Wililams; Photography, Steven Chivers, Ricardo Coll, Simon Fanthorpe, Nicholas Hoffman, Jonathan Rho, Ian Salvage, John Walker, James Welland, Bob Williams; Music, Mark Sayer-Wade; Editor, Dan Roberts; a Modus Operandi Films and the UK Film Council in association with Smoke & Mirrors presentation; British; Dolby; Panavision; Color; Nor rated; 90 minutes; American release date: May 13, 2011. Documentary on acclaimed cinematographer and director Jack Cardiff

WITH
Jack Cardiff, Martin Scorsese, Kirk Douglas, Lauren Bacall, Charlton Heston, Kim Hunter, John Mills, Alan Parker, Thelma Schoonmaker, Freddie Francis, Raffaella De Laurentiis, Richard Fleischer, Peter Yates, Kathleen Byron, Christopher Challis, Kevin McClory, Ian Christie, Moira Shearer, Craig McCall, Michel Ciment, Peter Handford, George E. Turner, Dustin Hoffman

Jack Cardiff © Strand Releasing

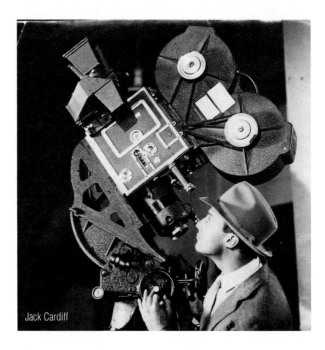

Jack Cardiff

Kamau Mbaya

Oliver Litondo

Oliver Litondo, Naomie Harris © Goldcrest Films

THE FIRST GRADER

(GOLDCREST FILMS) Producers, David M. Thompson, Sam Feuer, Richard Harding; Executive Producers, Joe Oppenheimer, Anant Singh, Norman Merry, Helena Spring; Director, Justin Chadwick; Screenplay, Ann Peacock; Photography, Rob Hardy; Designer, Vittoria Sogno; Costumes, Sophie Oprisano; Music, Alex Heffes; Editor, Paul Knight; Casting, Moonyeenn Lee, Margie Kiundi; a BBC Films and UK Film Council presentation in association with Videovision Entertainment, Lip Sync and ARTE France, a Sixth Sense/Origin Pictures Production; British-American-Kenya, 2010; Dolby; Color; Rated PG-13; 103 minutes; American release date: May 13, 2011

CAST
Jane Obinchu	**Naomie Harris**
Kimani Ng'ang'a Maruge	**Oliver Litondo**
Charles Obinchu	**Tony Kgoroge**
Teacher Alfred	**Alfred Munyua**
Teacher Elizabeth	**Shoki Mokgapa**
Mr. Kipruto	**Vusumuzi Michael Kunene**
Agnes	**Agnes Simaloi**
Kamau Chege	**Kamau Mbaya**

Emily Njoki (Young Maruge's Wife), Lwanda Jawar (Young Maruge), Daniel "Churchill" Ndambuki (DJ Masha), Sam Feuer (American Journalist), Nick Redding (Officer Johnson), John Sibi-Okumu (Chairman of Education), Israel Sipho Makoe (David Chege), Mumbi Kaigwa (Education Secretary), Ainea Ojiambo (Education Officer), Charles Ouda (Adult School Teacher), Melvin Alusa (Mr. Mutahi's Aide), Gilbert Lukhalia (Mr. Mutahi), Lydia Gitachu (CNN Journalist), Abubakar Mwenda (Boie), Peter Marias (Peter), Zingaro Percussions (Mau Mau Warriors), Susan Sisian (Young Mother), Kamau Ndungu (John Gambe), Mary Mbirua, Catherine Njiru (Stall Owners), Rachel Jones (BBC Journalist), Nick Ndichu (Mau Mau Oath Giver), Benta Ochieng (Mother Benta), Paul Mbogo (Mau Mau Leader), Hannah Wacera (Maruge's Daughter), Macharia Kamau (DJ's PA), Rosemary Nyambura (Jacquie – PA to the Chairman), Jackie Musimbi (Village Girl), Mwenga Matilika, Tom Gitau, Shadrack Murimi Gachuhi, Watson Mbirua (Old Codgers), Peter Emera Pious (Jonas), Jeannette Elsworth (Plantation Owner's Wife), John Kimani (Maruge's Baby Son), Irene Kariuki (Mrs. Muthumba), Kathyline Ndogori (Teacher Katherine), Shirlen Wangari (Mother Wanjiku), Joel Rempesa (Joel), Eunice Tekero (Village Woman), Michael Oyier (Newsreader), Kurenda Ole Kureya (Maasai Store Owner)

Maruge, a Mau Mau verteran in his eighties, arrives at a remote mountain top primary school in the Kenyan bush, eager to enroll so that someone can teach him to read.

Vusumuzi Michael Kunene, Oliver Litondo

MIDNIGHT IN PARIS

(SONY CLASSICS) Producers, Letty Aronson, Stephen Tenenbaum, Jaume Roures; Co-Producers, Helen Robin, Raphaël Benoliel; Executive Producer, Javier Méndez; Co-Executive Producer, Jack Rollins; Director/Screenplay, Woody Allen; Photography, Darius Khondji; Designer, Anne Seibel; Costumes, Sonia Grande; Editor, Alisa Lepselter; Casting, Juliet Taylor, Patricia DiCerto, Stéphane Foenkinos; a Mediapro, Versátil Cinema & Gravier production of a Pontchartrain production; Spanish-American; Dolby; Color; Rated PG-13; 100 minutes; American release date: May 20, 2011

CAST

Gertrude Stein	**Kathy Bates**
Salvador Dali	**Adrien Brody**
Museum Guide	**Carla Bruni**
Adriana	**Marion Cotillard**
Inez	**Rachel McAdams**
Paul	**Michael Sheen**
Gil	**Owen Wilson**
Carol	**Nina Arianda**
John	**Kurt Fuller**
F. Scott Fitzgerald	**Tom Hiddleston**
Helen	**Mimi Kennedy**
Zelda Fitzgerald	**Alison Pill**
Gabrielle	**Léa Seydoux**
Ernest Hemingway	**Corey Stoll**
Detective Tisserant	**Gad Elmaleh**
Juan Belmonte	**Daniel Lundh**
Pablo Picasso	**Marcial Di Fonzo Bo**
Luis Buñuel	**Adrien de Van**
Man at Wine Tasting	**Maurice Sonnenberg**
Cole Porter	**Yves Heck**
Joséphine Baker	**Sonia Rolland**
Antiques Dealer	**Laurent Spielvogel**
Alice B. Toklas	**Thérèse Bourou-Rubinsztein**
Djuna Barnes	**Emmanuelle Uzan**
Man Ray	**Tom Cordier**
Detective Duluc	**Serge Bagdassarian**
T.S. Eliot	**David Lowe**
Henri Matisse	**Yves-Antoine Spoto**
Leo Stein	**Laurent Claret**
Henri de Toulouse-Lautrec	**Vincent Menjou Cortes**
Paul Gauguin	**Olivier Rabourdin**
Edgar Degas	**François Rostain**

Thierry Hancisse, Guillaume Gouix, Audrey Fleurot, Marie-Sohne Condé (1920s Partygoers), Sava Lolov, Karine Vanasse (Belle Époque Couple), Catherine Benguigui (Maxim's Hostess), Marianne Basler, Michel Vuillermoz (Versailles Royalty)

A frustrated writer joining his wife on a business trip to Paris is magically transported each night to the 1920's, allowing him to meet his literary idols of the era.

2011 Academy Award winner for Best Original Screenplay.

This film received additional Oscar nominations for picture, director, and art direction.

Michael Sheen, Nina Arianda, Rachel McAdams, Owen Wilson

Carla Bruni, Owen Wilson

Rachel McAdams, Owen Wilson

Léa Seydoux, Owen Wilson

Gad Elmaleh

Owen Wilson, Marion Cotillard © Sony Classics

Kurt Fuller, Mimi Kennedy

Alison Pill, Tom Hiddleston

Corey Stoll, Kathy Bates

Mimi Branescu, Maria Popistasu

Mimi Branescu, Maria Popistasu © Lorber Films

TUESDAY, AFTER CHRISTMAS

(LORBER) a.k.a. *Marti, dupa craciun*; Producer, Dragos Vilcu; Director, Radu Muntean; Screenplay, Alexandru Baciu, Răzvan Rădulescu, Radu Muntean; Photography, Tudor Lucaciu; Set Designer, Sorin Dima; Editor, Alexandra Radu; a Multi Media Est production, with participation of Centrul National al Cinematografie, HBO Romania; Romanian, 2010; Dolby; Widescreen; Color; Not rated; 99 minutes; American release date: May 25, 2011

CAST
Paul Hanganu	**Mimi Brănescu**
Adriana Hanganu	**Mirela Oprişor**
Raluca	**Maria Popistaşu**
Mara Hanganu	**Saşa Paul-Szel**
Cristi	**Dragoş Bucur**

Victor Rebengiuc (Nucu), Dana Dembinski (Raluca's Mother), Silvia Nătase (Ica), Carmen Lopăzan (Cosmina), Adrian Văncică (Mircea Dumbrăveanu), Ioana Blaj (Narcisa)]

Paul Hanganu much chose between his mistress and his wife of ten years.

MR. NICE

(MPI MEDIA GROUP) Producer, Luc Roeg; Executive Producers, Michael Robinson, Andrew Orr, Tim Smith, Paul Brett, David Toso, Linda James, James Perkins, Dan Shepherd, Norman Merry; Director/Screenplay/Photography, Bernard Rose; Based on the book by Howard Marks; Designer, Max Gottlieb; Costumes, Caroline Harris; Music, Philip Glass; Editors, Bernard Rose, Teresa Font; Casting, Alex Johnson; an Independent presentation in association with Prescience, The Wales Creative IP Fund and Lipsync Productions LLP, an Independent Film Production in association with Kanzaman Productions; British-Spanish, 2010; Dolby; Color; Not rated; 121 minutes; American release date: June 3, 2011

CAST
Howard Marks	**Rhys Ifans**
Judy Marks	**Chloë Sevigny**
Jim McCann	**David Thewlis**
Craig Lovato	**Luis Tosár**
Ernie Combs	**Crispin Glover**
Saleem Malik	**Omid Djalili**
Hamilton McMillan	**Christian McKay**

Elsa Pataky (Ilze Kadegis), Jamie Harris (Patrick Lane), Jack Huston (Graham Plinston), Andrew Tiernan (Alan Marcuson), Ania Sowinski (Maureen), Kinsey Packard (Patti Hayes), Ken Russell (Russell Miegs), Craig Stevenson (Webster), Owain Arthur (Albert Hancock), Nathalie Cox (Opium Girl), Emerald Fennell (Rachel), Olivia Grant (Alice), Jay Itzkowitz (Judge James C. Paine), Matthew Jacobs (Eddie Laxton), Rhys McLellan (Bully), Deobia Oparei (Tee Bone Taylor), Ricardo Birnbaum (Miami Cop), Caolan Byrne (Irishman), Daniel Faraldo (Mexican Cop), Eric Loren (Miami District Attorney), Stephen Marzella (Customs Officer), David-Doc O'Connor (US Federal Marshall), Julio Perillán (Parole Examiner), Sara Sugarman (Edna Marks), William Thomas (Dennis Marks), Kal Weber (News Anchor), Ron Forsythe (Gary Lickert), James Jagger (Joshua Macmillan), Howell Evans (George the Scout), Ferdy Roberts (Acid Man), Waris Hussein (Mohammed Durrani), Huw Davies (Donald Nice), David Sibley (Philip Fairweather), Ian Burford (Bank Chairman), Rollo Weeks (Eton Boy), Julian Firth (MIG Duncan), Jams Thomas (James Morris), Thomas Whwatley (John Rogers QC), Mark Tandy (Lord Hitchinson QC), Eric Loren (Miami Prosecutor), Tony Rohr (Landlord)

The true story of notorious Welsh drug dealer Howard Marks.

Rhys Ifans, Chloë Sevigny © MPI Media Group

Craig Roberts, Yasmin Paige

Craig Roberts, Noah Taylor

Sally Hawkins © Weinstein Co.

Craig Roberts

SUBMARINE

(WEINSTEIN CO.) Producers, Mary Burke, Mark Herbert, Andy Stebbing; Executive Producers, Pauline Burt, Peter Carlton, Will Clarke, Paul Higgins, Linda James, Tessa Ross, Ben Stiller, Stuart Cornfeld, Jeremy Kramer,; Director/ Screenplay, Richard Ayoade; Based on the novel by Joe Dunthorne; Photography, Erik Alexander Wilson; Designer, Gary Williamson; Costumes, Charlotte Walter; Music, Andrew Hewitt; Songs, Alex Turner; Editors, Nick Fenton, Chris Dickens; Casting, Karen Lindsay Stewart; a Film4, UK Film Council presentation in association with the Wales Creative IP Fund and the Film Agency for Wales in association with Optimum Releasing and Protagonist Pictures, a Warp Films Production in association with Red Hour Films; British, 2010; Dolby; Deluxe Color; Rated R; 96 minutes; American release date: June 3, 2011

CAST

Oliver Tate	**Craig Roberts**
Jordana Bevan	**Yasmin Paige**
Lloyd Tate	**Noah Taylor**
Graham Purvis	**Paddy Considine**
Jill Tate	**Sally Hawkins**
Chips	**Darren Evans**
Mark Pritchard	**Osian Cai Dulais**
Zoe Preece	**Lily McCann**
Keiron	**Otis Lloyd**
Abby Smuts	**Elinor Crawley**
Mr. Davey	**Steffan Rhodri**
Kim-Lin	**Gemma Chan**
Jude Bevan	**Melanie Walters**

Sion Tudor Owen (Brynn Bevan), Adrienne O'Sullivan (Jackie), Jonny Wier (Malcolm), Lydia Fox (Miss Dutton), Lynne Hunter (Gene), Claire Cage (News Reporter), Edwin Ashcroft (Dafydd), Andrew Phillips (Rhydian Bird), James Alexander Hill, Rikki Hall, Tom Ryan, James Jones (School Boys), Sophy Brady-Halligan, Tanya Brady-Halligan (The Watkins Twins), Sarah Pasquali (Woman Who Looks Nothing Like Jordana), Ben Stiller (Soap Opera Star)

Determined to lose his virginity, fifteen-year-old Oliver Tate sets his sights on classmate Jordana Bevan.

THE TRIP

(IFC FILMS) Producers, Andrew Eaton, Melissa Parmenter; Executive Producers, Henry Normal, Simon Lupton; Director, Michael Winterbottom; Photography, Ben Smithard; Costumes, Celia Yau; Music, Michael Nyman; Editors, Mags Arnold, Paul Monaghan; Casting, Shaheen Baig; a Revolution Films/Baby Cow/Arbie production; British, 2010; Dolby; Color; Not rated; 107 minutes; American release date: June 10, 2011

CAST
Steve	**Steve Coogan**
Rob	**Rob Brydon**
Paul	**Paul Popplewell**
Emma	**Claire Keelan**
Mischa	**Margo Stilley**
Sally	**Rebecca Johnson**
Magda	**Dolya Gavanski**
Steve's US Agent	**Kerry Shale**
York Arms Receptionist	**Mercè Ribot**

Actors Steve Coogan and Rob Brydon bicker and push their friendship to the breaking point as they journey throughout England's Lake District and Yorkshire Dales to review fine restaurants for the *Observer*. This is an edited version of the six-part UK mini-series that ran in 2010.

Steve Coogan, Rob Brydon © IFC Films

Rob Brydon, Steve Coogan

Waldemar Torenstra, Anna Drijver © Music Box Films

Elsie Schaap, Mattijn Hartemink

BRIDE FLIGHT

(MUSIC BOX FILMS) Producers, Anton Smit, Hanneke Niens; Director, Ben Sombogaart; Screenplay, Marieke van der Pol; Photography, Piotr Kukla; Designer, Michel De Graaf; Costumes, Linda Bogers; Music, Jeannot Sanavia; Editor, Herman P. Koerts; Casting, Marina Wijn, Kemna Casting; an IDTV Film, in co-production with Samsa Film & NCRV; Dutch-Luxembourg, 2008; Dolby; Super 35 Widescreen; Color; Rated R; 130 minutes; American release date: June 10, 2011

CAST
Ada	**Karina Smulders**
Marjorie	**Elsie Schaap**
Esther	**Anna Drijver**
Frank	**Waldemar Torenstra**
Old Frank	**Rutger Hauer**
Old Ada	**Pleuni Touw**
Old Marjorie	**Petra Laseur**
Old Esther	**Willeke van Ammelrooy**

Mykola Allen (Bobby), Hannah Banks (Blonde Student), Walter Bart (Leon), Olly Coddington (Kris Moses), Jacques Commandeur (Old Derk), Matt Dwyer (Air Host Wellington), Peter Elliot (Doctor), Benjamin Farry (Esther's Assistant/Lover), Roeland Fernhout (Steward KLM), Frédéric Frenay (Elder), Mattijn Hartemink (Hans), Janine Horsburgh (Mrs. Young), Einarsdottir Hrefna (Stewardess KLM), Micha Hulshof (Derk), Myranda Jongeling (Hannah Doorman), Marc Klein Essink (Bob), Korah Knight (Gynaecologist), Anne Lamsvelt (Hannah Doorman), Marco Lorenzini (Mr. Young), Hans Man in't Veld (Vicar), Linda McFetridge (Air Hostess Wellington), Kelly McKnight (Danny Visser), Rob Mokaraka (Mosie), Debby Mullholland (Nurse), Grayson Neale (Peter Visser), Ann Comfort (Midwife), John Cooper Overstall (Priest), Glynis Paraha (Mosie's Wife), Rawiri Paratene (Old Mosie), Jaap Spijkers (Reporter, London), Gayde Taylor (Julie Visser)

Three young women flee from post-World War II Holland to New Zealand in hopes of finding better lives through marriage.

M'Barka Ben Taleb © Beta Cinema

Fiorello

PASSIONE

(BETA CINEMA) Producers, Alessandra Acciai, Carlo Macchitella, Giorgio Magliulo; Director, John Turturro; Subject/Screenplay, John Turturro, Federico Vacalebre; Based on an idea by Carlo Macchitella; Photography, Marco Pontecorvo; Costumes, Alessandra Gaudioso; Editor, Simona Paggi; Choreography, Giuà; a Skydancers and Squeezed Heart production; Italian-American; Dolby; Color; Not rated; 90 minutes; Release date: June 22, 2011. A look at Neapolitan music and its influences, as heard in 23 songs.

WITH
Mina, Spakka-Neapolis 55, Avion Travel, Misia, Pietra Montecorvino, Massimo Ranieri, Lina Sastri, M'Barka Ben Taleb, Gennaro Cosmo Parlato, Peppe Barra, Angela Luce, Max Casella, Raiz, James Senese, Fausto Cigliano, Fiorello, Fiorenza Calogero, Daniela Fiorentiono, Lorena Tamaggio, Enzo Avitabile, Pino Daniele, John Turturro

BEGINNING OF THE GREAT REVIVAL

(CHINA FILM GROUP) a.k.a. *Jian dang wei ye* and *The Founding of a Party*; Producer, Han Sanping; Executive Producers, Ma Zhengqiang, Gao Chengsheng; Directors, Han Sanping, Huang Jianxin; Screenplay, Dong Zhe, Guo Junli, Huang Xin; Photography, Zhao Xiaoshi; Designers, Yi Zhenzhou, Wang Wenxun; Costumes, Wang Qiuping, Zhang Ling; Music, Shu Nan, Ma Shangyou; Editor, Xu Hongyu; a China Lion Distribution presentation of a China Film Group production; Chinese; Dolby; Color; Widescreen; Not rated; 130 minutes; American release date: June 24, 2011.

CAST
Mao Zedong	**Liu Ye**
Chen Duxiu	**Feng Yuanzheng**
Yuan Shikai	**Chow Yun-fat**
Sun Yat-sen	**Ma Shaohua**
Cai E	**Andy Lau**
Yang Kaihui	**Li Qin**
Li Dazhao	**Zhang Jiayi**

Daniel Wu (Hu Shi), Huang Jue (Lia Da), Tang Guoqiang (Older Mao), Chen Kun (Zhou Enlai), Qi Yuwu (Wang Jinmei), Du Chun (Xu Deheng), Hou Yong (Tang Shaoyi), Leehom Wang (Luo Jialun), Liu Tao (Consort Jin), Chang Chen (Chiang Kai-shek), Zhang Hanyu (Song Jiaoren), He Ping (He Shuheng), Michele Ye (Li Lizhuang), Fan Wei (Li Yuanhong), Alex Fong Chung-sun (Yang Du), Chen Daoming (V.K. Wellington Koo), Li Xuejian (Yang Changii), Dengo Chao (Chen Yi), Dong Jie (Soong Ching-ling), Eric Tsang (Ta Kung Pao, Reporter), Tang Wei (Tao Yi), Angela Yeung Wing (Xiaofengxian), Zhou Jie (Li Hanjun), Wang Xueqi (Cai Yuanpei), John Woo (Lin Shen), Ray Liu (Wu Peifu), Zhao Benshan (Duan Qirui), Feng Gong (Feng Guozhang), Nick Cheung (Liang Qichao), Fan Bingbing (Empress Dowager Longyu), Nie Yuan (Chen Qimei)

A look at the pivotal events in history starting with the October 1911 Wuchang Uprising, that led to the formation of the Chinese Communist Party, ten years later.

Leehom Wang © China Film Group

Sara Forestier, Jacques Gamblin

Sara Forestier © Music Box Films

THE NAMES OF LOVE

(MUSIC BOX FILMS) a.k.a. *Le nom des gens*; Producers, Caroline Adrian, Fabrice Goldstein, Antoine Rein; Director, Michel Leclerc; Screenplay, Baya Kasmi, Michel Leclerc; Photography, Vincent Mathias; Designer, Jean-Marc Tran Tanba; Costumes, Melanie Gauter; Music, Jérôme Bensoussan, David Euverte; Editor, Nathalie Hubert; a co-production of Delante Films-Kare Productions, TF1 Droits Audiovisuels; French, 2010; Dolby; Color; Rated R; 102 minutes; American release date: June 24, 2011

CAST
Baya Benmahmoud **Sara Forestier**
Arthur Martin **Jacques Gamblin**
Cécile Benmahmoud **Carole Franck**
Mohamed Benmahmoud **Zinedine Soualem**
Annette Martin **Michèle Moretti**
Lucien Martin **Jacques Boudet**
Zakariya Gouram (Hassan Hassini), Julia Vaidis-Bogard (Annette at 30), Adrien Stoclet (Adolescent Arthur), Camille Gigot (Infant Arthur), Laura Genovino (Infant Baya), Rose Marit (Infant Annette), Youari Kime (Infant Mohamed), Yann Goven (Pianist), Nabil Massad (Nassim), Cyrille Andrieu-Lacu (David Cohen, Arthur's Grandfather), Cristina Palma Di Figueiredo (Arthur's Grandmother), Camille Chalons (Arthur's First Girlfriend), Joséphine Roplon (Arthur's Second Girlfriend), Lydie Muller (School Director), Nanou Garcia (Civil-State Employee), Thierry Guerrier (TV Journalist)

A free-spirited liberal Algerian woman is surprised to find herself falling in love with an uptight Jewish scientist.

TURTLE: THE INCREDIBLE JOURNEY

(SEAWORLD PARKS/HANNOVER HOUSE) Producers, Sarah Cunliffe, Mike Downey, Sam Taylor; Executive Producers, Chris Clarke, Zorana Piggott, Mike Timms; Co-Producers, Thomas Springer, Helmut G. Weber, Katharina Bogensberger, Helmut Grasser, Solveig Langeland, Beatrix Wesle; Director, Nick Stringer; Screenplay, Melanie Finn; Photography, Rory McGuinness; Music, Henning Lohner; Editors, Richard Wilkinson, Sean Barton; Narrator, Miranda Richardson; a Sola Media (Germany) presentation in association with MTN Movies, Filmsat59 and the Save Our Seas Foundation, supported by Filmstiftung NRW, Austrian Film Institute and ORF – The Austrian Broadcasting Corp., in co-production with Tradewind Pictures, Allegro Film, of a Big Wave and Film & Music Entertainment (U.K.) production; German-British; Dolby; Color; HD-to-35mm; Rated G; 80 minutes; American release date: June 24, 2011. Documentary on the Loggerhead Turtle's treacherous 25 year journey from Florida to Africa and then back again.

© Hannover House

PROJECT NIM

(ROADSIDE ATTRACTIONS/HBO) Producer, Simon Chinn; Executive Producers, John Battsek, Andrew Ruhemann, Jamie Laurenson, Nick Fraser, Hugo Grumbar; Co-Producers, George Chignell, Mauren A. Ryan; Director, James Marsh; Based on the book *Nim Chimpsky: The Chimp Who Would Be Human* by Elizabeth Hess; Photography, Michael Simmonds; Designer, Markus Kirschner; Costumes, Kathryn Nixon; Music, Dickon Hinchliffe; Editor, Jinx Godfrey; Casting, Adine Duron; an HBO Documentary Films, BBC Films and U.K. Film Council of a Red Box Films production in association with Passion Pictures; British; Dolby; Color/ Black and white; HD; Rated PG-13; 93 minutes; American release date: July 8, 2011. Documentary on how scientists taught a chimpanzee they nicknamed "Nim Chimpsky" to communicate via sign language.

WITH
Prof. Herbert Terrace, Stephanie LaFarge, Jenny Lee, Laura-Ann Petitto, Joyce Butler, Bill Tynan, Renee Falitz, Bob Ingersoll, Alyce Moore, Dr. James Mahoney; and Bob Angelini (Lab Tech), Bern Cohen (Dr. William Lemmon), Reagan Leonard (Stephanie LaFarge), Michael LePera (Wer LaFarge)

Nim Chimpsky © Roadside Attractions

Nim Chimpsky, Laura-Ann Petitto

Camille Chalons, Dounia Sichov, Leslie Lipkins

Carla Besnainou © Strand Releasing

THE SLEEPING BEAUTY

(STRAND) a.k.a. *La Belle Endormie*; Producers, Jean-Francois Lepetit, Sylvette Frydman; Director/Screenplay, Catherine Breillat; Photography, Denis Lenoir; Set Deisgner, Francois-Renaud Labarthe; Costumes, Rose-Marie Melka; Editor, Pascale Chavance; a Flach Film Production co-produced with CB Films/Arte France; French; Stereo; Color; Not rated; 82 minutes; American release date: July 8, 2011

CAST
Anastasia	**Carla Besnainou**
Anastasia (age 16)	**Julia Artamonov**
Peter	**Kerian Mayan**
Johan	**David Chausse**

Luna Charpentier (Little Brigande), Rhizlaine El Cohen (Adult Brigande), Delia Bouglione-Romanès (The Gypsy Singer), Diana Rudychenko (Véroutchka), Maricha Lopoukhine (Grandmother), Jean-Philippe Tessé (Father), Dounia Sichov, Leslie Lipkins, Camille Chalons (Fairies), Romane Portail (Snow Queen), Anne-Lise Kedves (Peter's Mother), Rosine Favey (Old Chin-Chin), Dominique Hulin (Giant), Paul Vernet (Prince), Laurine David (Princess), Pierre Estorges (Station Master), Marie Piton (Johan's Mther), Paul Magnard (Paul), Marie Piton (Johan's Mother)

In a twist on the classic fairy tale, Anastasia is put into a 100-year slumber to avoid death, during which she experiences vivid dreams of the possibilities of life.

Li Bingbing, Gianna Jun

Li Bingbing © Fox Searchlight

Hugh Jackman, Vivian Wu

SNOW FLOWER AND THE SECRET FAN

(FOX SEARCHLIGHT) Producers, Wendi Murdoch, Florence Sloan; Executive Producers, Hugo Shong, Ron Bass; Co-Producers, Jessinta Liu, Andrew Loo; Director, Wayne Wang; Screenplay, Angela Workman, Ron Bass, Michael K. Ray; Based on the book by Lisa See; Photography, Richard Wong; Music, Rachel Portman; Editor, Deirdre Slevin; Casting, Leo Tam; a Big Feet production, presented in association with IDG China Creative Media; Chinese-American; Dolby; Color; Rated PG-13; 103 minutes; American release date: July 15, 2011

CAST

Snow Flower/Sophia	**Gianna Jun**
Nina/Lily	**Li Bingbing**
Aunt	**Vivian Wu**
Butcher	**Jiang Wu**
Bank CEO	**Russell Wong**
Anna	**Coco Chiang**
Mrs. Liao	**Hu Jingyun**
Arthur	**Hugh Jackman**
Little Lily	**Guo Congmeng**
Little Snow Flower	**Dai Yan**
Madame Wang	**Tang Ying**

Archie Kao (Sebastian), Yun Hu Qing (Mrs. Liao), Cao Shi Ping (Mr. Wei), Zhang Ruijia (Mrs. Wei), Gong Zhebing (Professor), Zhou Lilia (Nurse), Shen Danping (Lily's Mother), Xu Yulan (Snow Flower's Mother), Wang Shiming (Foot Binder), Xu Shouqin (Lily's Father), Tao Chen (Lang Da), Sun Feihu (Master Lu), Lü Zhong (Lady Lu), Mian Mian (Claire), Lu Yi-Ching (Yong Gang), Fang Zhoubo (Mr. Liao), Ding Xaio Hu (TV News Anchor), Qiang Li (Gao Kao Official), Zhang Li Qiu (Butcher's Mother), Andy Gao (Bartender), Lin Ying (Lotus), Xia Li Hui (Cousin Yan's Mother), Jin Pei (Landlady), Meng Fan Hua (Bathhouse Clerk), Qu Rongyi (Spring Moon, 15 years old)

Businesswoman Nina, distraught that her estranged best friend Sophia has been injured in a bike accident, begins reading the manuscript the latter has been working on, revealing a parallel story about two lifelong companions in 19th Century China.

Li Bingbing, Gianna Jun

LIFE, ABOVE ALL

(SONY CLASSICS) Producer, Oliver Stoltz; Executie Producer, Helge Sasse; Co-Producers, Greig Buckle, Thomas Reisser, Dan Schlanger; Director, Oliver Schmitz; Screenplay, Dennis Foon; Based on the novel *Chanda's Secrets* by Allan Stratton; Photography, Bernhard Jasper; Designers, Christiane Rothe, Tracey Perkins; Costumes, Nadia Kurger; Music, Ali N. Askin; Editor, Dirk Grau; Casting, Moonyeenn Lee; a Bavaria Film Intl. presentation of a Dreamer Joint Venture production in co-production with Senator Film Produktion, Enigma Pictures and Niama Film; South African-German, 2010; Dolby; Color; Widescreen; HD; Rated PG-13; 106 minutes; American release date: July 15, 2011

Khomotso Manyaka, Harriet Manamela

CAST
Chanda	**Khomotso Manyaka**
Esther	**Keaobaka Makanyane**
Lillian	**Lerato Mvelase**
Mrs. Tafa	**Harriet Manamela**
Jonah	**Aubrey Poolo**
Aunt Lizbet	**Tinah Mnumzana**
Iris	**Mapaseka Mathebe**
Soly	**Thato Kgaladi**
Dudu	**Kgomotso Ditshwene**
Aunty Ruth	**Rami Chuene**
Mr. Pheto	**Jerry Marobyane**
Mr. Lesole	**Tshepo Emmanuel Nonyane**
Mrs. Lesole	**Johanna Refilwe Sihlangu**

Vusi Muzi Given Nyathi (Mr. Nylo), Patrick Shai (Dr. Chris Chilume), Nelson Motloung (Mr. Chauke), Ernest Mokoena (Sipho Mandla), Mary Twala (Mrs. Gulubane), Themba Ndaba (Mr. Selalame), Bhekifa Isaac Nyathi (Aunty Ruth's Boyfriend), Foxy Riet (Nurse Nkosi), Solly Meong (Police Officer)

12-year-old Chanda finds herself ostracized by her African village when she stands up for her stricken mother and befriends a prostitute, thereby confronting her community's deep intolerance and fanaticism.

Aubrey Poolo

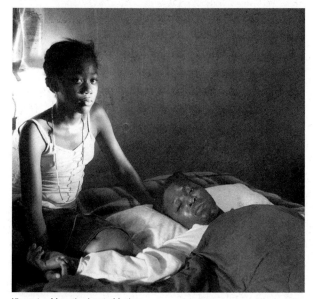

Khomotso Manyaka, Lerato Mvelase

Keaobaka Makanyane, Khomotso Manyaka © Sony Classics

SARAH'S KEY

(WEINSTEIN CO.) a.k.a. *Elle s'appelait Sarah;* Producer, Stéphane Marsil; Director, Gilles Paquet-Brenner; Screenplay, Serge Joncour, Gilles Paquet-Brenner, based on the novel by Tatiana de Rosnay; Photography, Pascal Ridao; Designer, Françoise Dupertuis; Costumes, Eric Perron; Music, Max Richter; Editor, Hervé Schneid; Casting, Gwendale Schmitz; a Hugo Prods. - Studio 37 - TF1 Droits Audiovisules - France 2 Cinéma production with the support of Région Ile-de-France in association with la Sofica A Plus Image; French, 2010; Dolby; Color; DV-to-35mm; Rated PG-13; 111 minutes; American release date: July 22, 2011

Kristin Scott Thomas, Aidan Quinn

CAST

Julia Jarmond	**Kristin Scott Thomas**
Sarah Starzynski	**Mélusine Mayance**
Jules Dufaure	**Niels Arestrup**
Bertrand Tezac	**Frédéric Pierrot**
Édouard Tezac	**Michel Duchaussoy**
Geneviève Dufaure	**Dominique Frot**
William Rainsferd	**Aidan Quinn**
Rykwa Starzynski	**Natasha Mashkevich**
Mamé	**Gisèle Casadesus**
Rachel	**Sarah Ber**
Wladyslaw Starzynski	**Arben Bajraktaraj**
Zoé	**Karina Hin**
Mike Bambers	**James Gerard**
Joshua	**Joe Rezwin**
Alexandra	**Kate Moran**
Michel Strazynski	**Paul Mercier**
Policeman	**Alexandre Le Provost**
Franck Lévy	**Simone Eine**
Concierge	**Serpentine Teyssier**
Vel d'Hiv Woman	**Julie Fournier**
Ornella Harris	**Paige Barr**
Mme. Rainsferd	**Joanna Merlin**
Richard Rainsferd	**George Birt**
Nathalie Dufaure	**Vinciane Millereau**
Bertrand's Mother	**Sylviane Fraval**
Red-Haired Policeman	**Dan Herzberg**
Alice	**Nancy Tate**
Young Richard Rainsferd	**Frédérick Guillaud**
Man playing Violin	**Maurice Lustyk**
Adult Sarah	**Charlotte Poutrel**
Young Édouard Tezac	**Maxim Driesen**
André Tezac	**Xavier Beja**

Arben Bajraktaraj, Mélusine Mayance, Natasha Mashkevich

Jacqueline Noëlle (Old Lady), Jean-Pierre Hutinet (Doctor), Jonathan Kerr (Camp Police Officer), Matthias Kress (German Officer at Farm), Franck Beckmann (German Officer on Train), Nicolas Seconda, François d'Aubigny (Policemen, Vel d'Hiv), Stéphane Charond, José Fumanal, Gilles Louzon (Camp Officers), Céline Caussimon (Nurse, Vel d'Hiv), Claudine Acs (Hysterical Woman, Vel d'Hiv), Mark Fairchild (Bob Rainsferd), Pierre Nahori (Policeman on Train), Robert Rotsztein (Voix 4 Man), Yasmine Ghazarian (Camp Woman), Naëva Lissonnet (Little Girl at Camp), Viktoria Li (Clinic Nurse), Loïc Risser (Nurse), Franck Chailly (Stretcher-Bearer), Marco Florio (Italian Waiter), Alice Erskine (Café Mozart Waitress), Stéphane Gesnel (Young Woman at the Window), Gérard Couchet (Old Man at the Window), Melinda Wade (Young American Woman), Kiley & Brooke Liddell (Baby Sarah)

An American journalist in France discovers that her in-laws benefited from the deportation of a persecuted family during the July 16, 1942 roundup and imprisonment of Parisian Jews.

Mélusine Mayance, Niels Arestrup

Natasha Mashkevich

Kristin Scott Thomas

Kristin Scott Thomas © Weinstein Co.

Mélusine Mayance

Kristin Scott Thomas

Franz Drameh, Alex Esmail, John Boyega, Jodie Whittaker, Leeon Jones

John Boyega, Jodie Whittaker, Luke Treadaway © Screen Gems

Nick Frost, Luke Treadaway

Luke Treadaway, Leeon Jones, John Boyega, Jodie Whittaker, Alex Esmail

ATTACK THE BLOCK

(SCREEN GEMS) Producers, Nira Park, James Wilson; Executive Producers, Matthew Justice, Tessa Ross, Jenny Borgars, Will Clarke, Olivier Courson, Edgar Wright; Director/Screenplay, Joe Cornish; Photography, Tom Townend; Designer, Marcus Rowland; Costumes, Rosa Dias; Music, Steven Price; Editor, Jonathan Amos; Makeup Designer, Jane Walker; Creature Effects, Mike Elizalde, Spectral Motion; Visual Effects, Double Negative; Stunts, Paul Herbert; Casting, Nina Gold; a Studio Canal Features, Film4 and UK Film Council presentation of a Big Talk Pictures production; British-French; Dolby; Super 35 Widesceen; Technicolor; Rated R; 88 minutes; American release date: July 29, 2011

CAST

Sam	**Jodie Whittaker**
Moses	**John Boyega**
Pest	**Alex Esmail**
Dennis	**Franz Drameh**
Jerome	**Leeon Jones**
Biggz	**Simon Howard**
Brewis	**Luke Treadaway**
Hi-Hatz	**Jumayn Hunter**
Ron	**Nick Frost**
Probs	**Sammy Williams**
Mayhem	**Michael Ajao**

Joey Ansah, Adam Leese (Policemen), Flaminia Cinque (Italian Woman), Paige Meade (Dimples), Chris Wilson (Arresting Police Officer), Lee Nicholas Harris (Police Officer —SWAT), Maggie McCarthy (Margaret), Jacey Sallés (Biggz's Mum), Danielle Vitalis (Tia), Terry Notary, Arti Shah, Karl Baumann (Creature Performers), Karl Collins (Dennis' Dad), Stephanie Street (Policewoman), Selom Awadzi (Tonks), Dylan Charles (Police Constable), Yvonne D'Alpra (Pest's Nan), Lee Long (Patrick), Philip Harvey (CO19 Officer), Jermaine Smith (Beats), Natasha Jonas (Gloria), Gina Antwi (Dionne), Paisley Thomas (Roxanne), Haneen Hammou (Bubbles), David Cann (Detective Superintendent)

A group of petty hoodlums turns heroic when their South London tower block is attacked by bloody thirsty aliens.

Ludivine Sagnier, Dominic Cooper

Dominic Cooper, Ludivine Sagnier

THE DEVIL'S DOUBLE

(LIONSGATE) Producers, Paul Breuls, Michael John Fedun, Emjay Rechsteiner, Catherine Vandeleene; Line Producer, Guy Tannahill; Co-Executive Producers, Harm Mulder, Sjef Scholte; Executive Producers, Harris Tulchin, Arjen Terpstra; Director, Lee Tamahori; Screenplay, Michael Thomas; Based on the life story of Latif Yahia; Photography, Sam McCurdy; Designer, Paul Kirby; Costumes, Anna B. Sheppard; Music, Christian Henson; Editor, Luis Carballar; Hair & Make-Up, Jan Sewell; Casting, Amy Hubbard, John Hubbard; a Herrick Entertainment presentation of a Corsan presentation of a Corsan/Corrino/Staccato production in association with FIP Malta Ltd./Tulchin Entertainment/Foreign Media and Film Finance VI; Belgian; Dolby; Super 35 Widescreen; Deluxe Color; Rated R; 108 minutes; American release date: July 29, 2011

Dominic Cooper, Dominic Cooper

CAST

Uday Hussein/Latif Yahia	**Dominic Cooper**
Sarrab	**Ludivine Sagnier**
Munem	**Raad Rawi**
Saddam Hussein/Faoaz	**Philip Quast**
Ali	**Mimoun Oaissa**
Yassem Al-Helou	**Khalid Laith**
Azzam	**Dar Salim**
Latif's Father	**Nasser Memarzia**
Kamel Hannah	**Mem Ferda**
Said	**Pano Masti**
Saad	**Akin Gazi**
Rokan	**Selva Rasalingam**

Stewart Scudamore (Father of School Girl), Amrita Acaria, Elektra Anastasi (School Girls), Amber Rose Revah (Bride), Samson Leguesse (Mercedes Driver), Sarah-Lee Zammit (Amer), Ben Shafik (Kurd), Frank Tanti (Lickspittle), Jamie Harding (Qusay), Marcelle Theuma (Latif's Mother), Tiziana Azzopardi (Gallalha), Manuel Cucciardi (Manservant), Mark Mifsud (Mohammed), Khaled Riani (Republican Guard), Francisco Catania (Captain), Pierre Stafrace (Uday's Doctor), David Leguese (Assassin), Emanuela Ciappara (Munem's Wife), Aiden Aquilina (Rayban Kid), Marwin Allagui (Revolutionary Guard), Frida Cauchi (Sajida), Marama Corlett (Hennahead), Oona Chaplin (Beauty), Rachel Fabri (Abdel Akle), Andre Agius (Kid on Crutches), Stasys Baltakis, Michael Arddt (East German Doctor)

Dominic Cooper © Lionsgate

The true story of how Iraqi army lieutenant Latif Yahia was enlisted to become the "body double" of Saddam Hussein's reckless, sadistic son Uday.

THE GUARD

(SONY CLASSICS) Producers, Chris Clark, Flora Fernandez-Marengo, Ed Guiney, Andrew Lowe; Executive Producers, Martin McDonagh, Don Cheadle, Lenore Zerman, Ralph Kamp, Tim Smith, Paul Brett, David Nash; Line Producer, Paul Myler; Director/ Screenplay, John Michael McDonagh; Photography, Larry Smith; Designer, John Paul Kelly; Costumes, Eimer Ní Mhaoldomhnaigh; Music, Calexico; Music Supervisor, Liz Gallacher; Editor, Chris Gill; Casting, Jin Jay; a Reprisal Films & Element Pictures in association with Prescience, Aegis Film Fund, UK Film Council, Crescendo Productions and Eos Pictures LLP, and with the participation of Bord Scannán na hEireann/The Irish Film Board presentation; Irish; Dolby; Super 35 Widescreen; Technicolor; Rated R; 96 minutes; American release date: July 29, 2011

CAST
Sgt. Gerry Boyle	**Brendan Gleeson**
FBI Agent Wendell Everett	**Don Cheadle**
Francis Sheehy-Skelfington	**Liam Cunningham**
Liam O'Leary	**David Wilmot**
Garda Aidan McBride	**Rory Keenan**
Clive Cornell	**Mark Strong**
Eileen Boyle	**Fionnula Flanagan**
Aoife O'Carroll	**Dominique McElligott**
Sinead Mulligan	**Sarah Greene**
Gabriela McBride	**Katarina Cas**

Ronan Collins, Paraic Nialand, John Patrick Beirne, Liam O'Conghaile, Christopher Kilmartin (Young Men in Car), Declan Mannion (James McCormick), Laurence Kinlan (Photographer), Mícheál Óg Lane (Eugene Moloney), Owen Sharpe (Billy Devaney), Wale Ojo (Doctor Oleyuwo), Mark O'Halloran (Garda No. 1), Gary Lydon (Garda Inspector Gerry Stanton), Darren Healy (Jimmy Moody), Conor Moloney (Detective), Laura Hitchings (Garda), Sharon Kearney (Woman at Bartley's House), David Pearse (Bartley), Dermot Healy (Old Farmer), Eamonn Olwill (Priest), Yuyang Sheilds (Diner Waitress), Pat Shortt (Column Hennessey), Gay McKeon, Mary Corcoran, Colm Gannon, Johnny McDonagh (Musicians), Dominick Hewitt, Giedrius Nagys, Gary Robinson (Henchmen)

When his tiny Irish town becomes the setting for a large drug trafficking investigation, crass Sgt. Gerry Boyle reluctantly teams up with uptight FBI agent Wendell Everett to crack the case.

Brendan Gleeson, Mícheál Óg Lane © Sony Classics

David Wilmot, Liam Cunningham, Mark Strong

Dominique McElligott, Brendan Gleeson, Sarah Greene

Don Cheadle, Brendan Gleeson

Layke Anderson, Benn Northover © Matson Films

HOUSE OF BOYS

(MATSON) Producers, Bob Bellion, Jimmy de Brabant; Executive Producer, Jean-Claude Schlim; Co-Producer, Anita Elsani; Director/Story, Jean-Claude Schlim; Screenplay, Jean-Claude Schlim, Christian Thiry; Photography, Carlo Thiel; Designer, Christina Schaffer; Costumes, Caroline De Viviaise, Francoise Meyer, Isabelle Dickes; Music, Gast Waltzing; Editor, Katharina Schmidt; Casting, Sharon Howard-Field, Monique Durlacher; a Delux, Moonstone Entertainment production in co-production with Elsani Film; German-Luxembourg, 2009; Dolby; Color; Not rated; 117 minutes; American release date: July 29, 2011

CAST
Frank	**Layke Anderson**
Jake	**Benn Northover**
Madame	**Udo Kier**
Emma	**Eleanor David**
Angelo	**Steven Webb**
Dean	**Luke J. Wilkins**
Carole	**Emma Griffiths-Malin**
Dr. Marsh	**Stephen Fry**

Oliver Hoare (Herman), Loïc Peckels (Young Jake), Harry Ferrier (Karl), Michael N. Kuehl (Christopher), Natalie Slevin (Amanda), Gintare Parulyte (Rita), Sascha Ley (Frank's Mother), Chris McHallem (Frank's Father), Jack Kelly (Boyd), Paul Rockenbrod (Paul), Tom Leick (Lisa), Alain Kahn (Penelope), Ross Antony (Rick), David Goldrake (Macho Customer), Jean-Claude Schlim (Snow White), Luc Feit (Dr. Van Linden), Joanna Scanlan (Nurse Suzanne), William Cohn (Johan), Yannick Guedes (Handsome Teenager), Nora König (Jake's Mother), Jules Werner (Jake's Father), Rachid O. (Driss), Elias Comfort, Roya Zargar (Hippies), Mike Furey (Band Singer), Thorunn Egilsdóttir, Runa Egilsdóttir (Angels/Nurses), Claire Johnston (Emergency Nurse), Vicky Krieps (Flower Shop Girl)

In the early 1980s, young Frank escapes from his disapproving parents and journeys to Amsterdam's red light district where he finds employment, love and friendship at a gay nighclub called House of Boys.

POINT BLANK

(MAGNOLIA) a.k.a. *Á bout portant*; Executive Producer, David Giordano; Director, Fred Cavayé; Screenplay, Fred Cavayé, Guillaume Lemans; Photography, Alain Duplantier; Designer, Philippe Chiffre; Costumes, Marie-Laure Lasson; Music, Klaus Badelt; Editor, Benjamin Weil; Casting, Olivier Carbone; an LGM Films, Gaumont, TFI Films Productions, K.R. Productions in association with Nexus Factory and UFund with the participation of Canal+ and TPS Star presentation; French, 2010; Dolby; Super 35 Widescreen; Color; Rated R; 84 minutes; American release date: July 29, 2011

CAST
Samuel Pierret	**Gilles Lellouche**
Hugo Sartet	**Roschdy Zem**
Commandant Patrick Werner	**Gérard Lanvin**
Nadia Pierret	**Elena Anaya**
Commandant Fabre	**Mireille Perrier**
Capitaine Anaïs Susini	**Claire Pérot**
Capitaine Vogel	**Moussa Maaskri**

Pierre Benoist (Capitaine Mercier), Valérie Dashwood (Capitaine Moreau), Virgile Bramly (Capitaine Mansart), Nicky Naude (Capitaine Richert), Adel Bencherif (Luc Sartet), Vincent Colombe (Internal Care), Chems Dahamani, Julie Mouamma (Nurses), Grégoire Bonnet (Jaffart, DPJ Head), Brice Fournier (Marconi), Patrice Guillain (Capitaine Auclert), Max Morel (Max Collet), Diane Stolojan, David Saada (Bus Witnesses), Arnaud Maillard (RATP Agent), Laurence Pollet-Villard (Gynecologist), Bénédicte Dessombz (Hospital Receptionist), Grégoire Guis'hau, Sylvia Amicone (Journalists), Frédéric Kontogom (PC Security Agent), Dorothée Tavernier (Uniformed Policewoman), Bertrand Disset (Policeman on Staircase), Jean-Charles Rousseau, Fred Dessains (Flashball Policemen), Sebastien Vandenberghe, Jean Selesko (Police), Marie-Catherine Soyer (Léa, 7 years old), Léa Philippe (Cousin Léa), Angelo Aybar (Victor Spattoni), Jacques Colliard (Francis Meyer), Frans Boyer (Capitaine Marek), Philippe Couerre (Meyer's Son)

When his pregnant wife is kidnapped, a nurse is forced to aide a gang of criminals who need him to help spring their boss fom the hospital.

Gilles Lellouche © Magnolia Pictures

Rachel Weisz

Vanessa Redgrave © Goldwyn Films

THE WHISTLEBLOWER

(GOLDWYN) Producers, Christina Piovesan, Celine Rattray; Executive Producers, Amy Kaufman, Peter Schafer, Nicolas Chartier; Co-Producers, Benito Mueller, Wolfgang Mueller, Robert Bernacchi; Director, Larysa Kondracki; Screenplay, Eilis Kirwan, Larysa Kondracki; Photography, Kieran McGuigan; Designer, Caroline Foellmer; Costumes, Gersha Phillips; Music, Mychael Danna; Editor, Julian Clarke; Casting, Jenny Lewis, Sara Kay; a Whistleblower (Gen One) Canada, Inc./Barry Films co-production, in association with Sunrise Pictures, Primary Productions, First Generation Films, Mandalay Vision, Indomitable Entertainment; Canadian-German; Dolby; Technicolor; Rated R; 118 minutes; American release date: August 5, 2011

CAST

Kathryn Bolkovac	**Rachel Weisz**
Peter Ward	**David Strathairn**
Jan Van Der Velde	**Nikolaj Lie Kaas**
Zoe	**Anna Anissimova**
Laura Leviani	**Monica Bellucci**
Madeleine Rees	**Vanessa Redgrave**
Bill Hynes	**Liam Cunningham**
Jim Higgins	**Luke Treadaway**
Nick Kaufman	**Benedict Cumberbatch**
Raya	**Roxana Condurache**
Luba	**Paul Schramm**
Viko	**Alexandru Potocean**

William Hope (Blakely), Rayisa Kondracki (Irka), Jeanette Hain (Halyna), David Hewlett (Fred Murray), Coca Bloos (Milena), Anca Androne (Zenia), Sergej Trifunovic (Ivan), Vlad Ivanov (Tanjo), Florin Busuioc (Danik), Alin Panc (Roman), Victoria Raileanu (Julia), Dorotheea Petre (Mara), Rosabell Laurenti Sellers (Erin), Roxana Guttman (Zlata Sehik), Stuart Graham (McVeigh), Catherine McNally (Cop), Geoffrey Pounsett (UN Security Guard), Alexandra Radescu (Tanya), Radu Binzaru (Barman), Zoltan Butuc (Men), Ciprian Dumitrascu (Men), Mihai Ghior (Intern), Sabrina Iaschievici (17-Year-Old Girl), Cristina Cristian (Fadila), Raluca Tataru, Bianca Neagu (Girls), Ion Sapdaru (Border Guard), Ionut Grama (Human Rights Worker), Paul Jerrico (Tim Sebastian), Demetri Goritsas (Kyle), Pilou Asbaek (Bas), Adriana Butoi (Marie), Danny John-Jules (Duke), Bryan Jardine (Judge Twiss), Erwin Simsensohn (Drunk IPTF Officer)

David Strathairn

Monica Bellucci

Nebraska police officer Kathryn Bolkovac accepts a position at the Gender Office in Bosnia where she is shocked to discover that members of the U.N. Human Rights Commission are abetting sex traffickers.

MYSTERIES OF LISBON

(MUSIC BOX FILMS) Producer, Paulo Branco; Director, Raúl Ruiz; Screenplay, Carlos Saboga; Based on the novel *Os Mistérios de Lisboa* by Camilo Castelo Branco; Photography, André Szankowski; Art Director, Isabel Branco; Music, Jorge Arriagada, Luís Freitas Branco; Editors, Valéria Sarmiento, Carlos Madaleno; Casting, Patrícia Vasconcelos; a Clap Filmes with the participation of Alfama Films, ICA/MC, RTP, ARTE France, Cámara Muncipal de Lisboa; Spanish-French, 2010; Color; HD; Not rated; 257 minutes; American release date: August 5, 2011

CAST
Father Dinis	**Adriano Luz**
Ângela de Lima	**Maria João Bastos**
Alberto de Magalhães	**Ricardo Pereira**
Elisa de Montfort	**Clotilde Hesme**
Pedro da Silva	**Afonso Pimentel**
Count of Santa Bárbara	**Albano Jerónimo**
Blanche de Montfort	**Léa Seydoux**
Col. Ernest Lacroze	**Melvil Poupaud**

João Luis Arrais (Pedro as a Child), João Baptista (D. Pedro da Silva), Martin Loizillon (Sebastião de Melo), Julien Alluguette (Benoît de Montfort), Rui Morisson (Marquis of Montezelos), Joana de Verona (Eugénia), Carloto Cotta (D. Álvaro de Albuquerque), Maria João Pinho (Countess of Viso), José Manuel Mendes (Friar Baltaser da Encarnação), Malik Zidi (Viscount of Armagnac), Margarida Vilanova (Marquise of Alfarela), Sofia Aparício (Countess of Penacova), Catarina Wallenstein (Countess of Arosa), Américo Silva (Bailiff), Ana Chagas (Deolinda), André Gomes (Barão de Sá), António Simão (Novelist), Dinarte Branco, Nuno Távora (Dilettantes), Duarte Guimarães (Reigstrar Filipe Vargas – D. Paulo), Helena Coelho (Marquise of Santa Eulália), João Vilas Boas (Butler), José Airosa (Bernardo), Lena Friedrich (Maid), Marcello Urgeghe, Miguel Monteiro (Doctors), Marco D'Almeida (Count of Viso), Paulo Pinto (D. Martinho de Almeida), Pedro Carmo (Gentleman), Vânia Rodrigues (D. Antónia)

A look into the lives of various characters in 19th Century Portugal linked to the destiny of orphan Pedro da Silva.

Léa Seydoux, Julien Alluguette © Music Box Films

Ayrton Senna

Ayrton Senna © Producers Distribution Agency

SENNA

(PRODUCERS DISTRIBUTION AGENCY) Producers, James Gay-Rees, Tim Bevan, Eric Fellner; Executive Producers, Kevin Macdonald, Manish Pandey, Debra Hayward, Liza Chasin; Director, Asif Kapadia; Screenplay, Manish Pandey; Photography, Jake Polonsky; Music, Antonio Pinto; Editors, Gregers Sall, Chris King; a Working Title production in association with Midfield Films, presented in association with ESPN Films; British; Dolby; Technicolor; Rated PG-13; 104 minutes; American release date: August 12, 2011. Documentary on Brazil's racing champion and national sports hero Ayrton Senna, who won the F1 World Championship three times before his untimely death.

WITH
Jean-Marie Balestre, Rubens Barrichello, Gerhard Berger, John Bisignano, Galvão Bueno, Milton da Silva, Ron Dennis, Bernie Ecclestone, Damon Hill, Reginaldo Leme, Luiz Fernando Lima, Nigel Mansell, Riccardo Patrese, Nelson Piquet, Alain Prost, Michael Schumacher, Neyde Senna, Viviane Senna, Jackie Stewart, Prof. Sid Watkins, Frank Williams, Richard Williams

MOZART'S SISTER

(MUSIC BOX FILMS) a.k.a. *Nannerl, la soeur de Mozart*; Producers, René Féret, Fabienne Féret; Director/Screenplay, René Féret; Photography, Benjamin Echazarreta; Set Designer, Veronica Fruhbrodt; Costumes, Dominique Louis; Music, Marie-Jeanne Séréro; Editor, Fabienne Féret; a Les Films Alyne production, with the participation of the Centre National du Cinéma et de l'Image Animée, with the support of Région Ile de France, Région Limousin and in partnership with the Centre National de la Cinéma; French, 2010; Dolby; Color; Not rated; 120 minutes; American release date: August 19, 2011

CAST
Nannerl Mozart	**Marie Féret**
Léopold Mozart	**Marc Barbé**
Anna-Maria Mozart	**Delphine Chuillot**
Wolfgang Mozart	**David Moreau**
The Dauphin	**Clovis Fouin**

Lisa Féret (Louise de France), Adèle Leprêtre (Sophie de France), Valentine Duval (Victoire de France), Dominique Marcas (Mother Abbess), Mona Heftre (Madame Van Eyck), Salomé Stévenin (Isabelle d'Aubusson), Julien Féret (Abbey Music Master), Nicolas Giraud (Versailles Music Master), Arthur Tos (Hugues Le Tourneur), Océane Jubert (Marie-Josèphe de Saxe), René Féret (The Professor of Music)

Forbidden to express herself in music, Wolfgang Mozart's older sister Nannerl seizes her chance to rebel against society's oppression of women when she befriends the offspring of Louis XV.

Lisa Féret, Marie Féret © Music Box Films

David Moreau, Marie Féret

Ryan Kwanten

Ryan Kwanten © Indomina Films

GRIFF THE INVISIBLE

(INDOMINA) Producer, Nicole O'Donohue; Executive Producers, Jan Chapman, Scott Meek; Director/Screenplay, Leon Ford; Photography, Simon Chapman; Designer, Sophie Nash; Costumes, Shareen Beringer; Music, Kids at Risk; Editor, Karen Johnson; Casting, Kristy McGregor; a Screen Australia presentation in association with Screen NSW and FSM of a Green Park Pictures Film; Austalian, 2010; Dolby; Color; Rated PG-13; 90 minutes; American release date: August 19, 2011

CAST
Griff	**Ryan Kwanten**
Melody	**Maeve Dermody**
Tim	**Patrick Brammall**
Tony	**Toby Schmitz**
Benson	**Marshall Napier**
Bronwyn	**Heather Mitchell**

David Webb (Gary), Anthony Phelan (Det. Stone), Kelly Paterniti (Gina), Kate Mulvany (Cecilia), Angela Bauer (Woman in Danger), Patricia Rogan (Woman with Mace), Leon Dobrinski (Cleaner), Joe June (House Owner), Paul-William Mawhinney (Policeman), Karl Beattie (School Boy), Ben Borgia (Large Man), Luke Hobbins (Kid Bully), May Lloyd (Waitress), Ray Carter (Him, Man in Commercial), Sarah Becker (Her, Woman in Commercial), Rhys James (Faceless), Greg Blandy (Stocky), Chan Griffin (Top Hat), Matthew "Chippa" Campbell, Nino Pilla, Kim Fardy, Mark Le Cornu, Neal Horton, Blake Linsdell, Steve Morris (Henchmen)

A timid customer-liaison officer imagines himself an invisible crime fighter.

Carolina Bang

Carlos Areces © Magnet Releasing

THE LAST CIRCUS

(MAGNET) a.k.a. *Balada triste de trompeta*; Producers, Gerardo Herrero, Mariela Besuievsky; Co-Producers, Franck Ribiere, Verane Frediani; Line Producer, Yousaf Bokhari; Director/Screenplay, Alex de la Iglesia; Photography, Kiko de la Rica; Designer, Edou Hydallgo; Costumes, Paco Delgado; Music, Roque Baños; Editor, Alejandro Lázaro; Casting, Camilla-Valentine Isola; a Tornasol Films presentation; Spanish-French, 2010; Dolby; Color; Rated R; 105 minutes; American release date: August 19, 2011

CAST
Javier	**Carlos Areces**
Sergio	**Antonio de la Torre**
Natalia	**Carolina Bang**
Colonel Salcedo	**Sancho Gracia**
Phantom Motorist	**Alejandro Teijeira**
Andres	**Enrique Villén**
Ramiro	**Manuel Tafalle**
Master of Ceremonies	**Manuel Tejada**

Gracia Olayo (Sonsoles), Santiago Segura (Father Stupid Clown), Roberto Alamo (Militian Captain), Fofito (Clown Clever), Sasha Di Benedetto (Javier, Child, 1937), Jorge Clemente (Javier, Young, 1943), Juana Cordero (Children's Mother), Luis Varela (Manuel), Terele Pavez (Dolores), José Manuel Cervino (Secretary), Paco Sagarzazu (Anselmo), Joaquin Climent (Father), Fernando Guillén Cuervo (Militia Captain)

At the end of the Franco regime, Javier, hoping to follow in the steps of his father, joins a circus where he falls in love with an acrobat whom he hopes to rescue from her abusive husband.

THE HEDGEHOG

(NEOCLASSICS FILMS) a.k.a. *Le Hérisson*; Producer, Anne- Dominique Toussaint; Director/Screenplay, Mona Achache; Inspired by the novel *L'Élégance du Hérisson* (*The Elegance of the Hedgehog*) by Muriel Barbery; Photography, Patrick Blossier; Designer, Yves Brover; Costumes, Catherine Bouchard; Music, Gabriel Yared; Editor, Julia Grégory; Casting, Michael Laguens, Sophie Blanvillain; a Les Films des Tournelles, Pathé, France 2 Cinéma, Eagle Pictures, Topaze Bleue production, with the participation of Canal Plus, CinéCinéma, France 2; French, 2009; Dolby; Hawk Scope; Color; Not rated; 98 minutes; American release date: August 19, 2011

CAST
Renée Michel	**Josiane Balasko**
Paloma Josse	**Garance Le Guillermic**
Kakuro Ozu	**Togo Igawa**
Solange Josse	**Anne Brochet**
Manuela Lopez	**Ariane Ascaride**
Paul Josse	**Wladimir Yordanoff**
Colombe Josse	**Sarah Le Picard**

Jean-Luc Porraz (Jean-Pierre), Gisèle Casadesus (Madame de Broglie), Mona Heftre (Madame Meurisse), Samuel Achache (Tibère), Valérie Karsenti (Tibère's Mother), Stéphan Wojtowicz (Tibère's Father), Isabelle Sobelmann (Anna Arthens), Chantal Banlier (Maria Malavoin), Jeanne Candel (Dresser), Miyako Ribola (Yoko), Nao Inazawa (Japanese Cook)

A young girl, intent on ending her life in reaction to the hypocrisy she sees all around her, has second thoughts when she uncovers the secret library of her building's grouchy concierge, and finds an ally.

Garance Le Guillermic, Josiane Balasko

Josiane Balasko, Togo Igawa © Neoclassics

Sam Riley, Andrea Riseborough

Sam Riley © IFC Films

Sam Riley

BRIGHTON ROCK

(IFC FILMS) Producer, Paul Webster; Executive Producers, Jenny Borgars, Will Clarke, Olivier Courson, Ron Halpern, Jamie Laurenson; Co-Producer, Paul Ritchie; Director/Screenplay, Rowan Joffe; Based on the novel by Graham Greene; Photography, John Mathieson; Designer, James Merifield; Costumes, Julian Day; Music, Martin Phipps; Music Supervisor, Ian Neil; Editor, Joe Walker; Stunts, Julian Spencer; Casting, Shaheen Baig; a Studio Canal Features, BBC Films & UK Film Council presentation of a Kudos Pictures production; British, 2010; Dolby; Panavision; Technicolor; Not rated; 111 minutes; American release date: August 26, 2011

CAST
Pinkie Brown	**Sam Riley**
Rose Wilson	**Andrea Riseborough**
Ida	**Helen Mirren**
Phil Corkery	**John Hurt**
Spicer	**Phil Davis**
Dallow	**Nonso Anozie**
Cubitt	**Craig Parkinson**
Colleoni	**Andy Serkis**
Fred Hale	**Sean Harris**
Kite	**Geoff Bell**
Crab	**Steven Robertson**
Chief Inspector	**Maurice Roëves**
Mr. Wilson	**Steve Evets**

Francis Magee (Pavement Photographer), Adrian Schiller (Registrar), Pauline Melville (Mother Superior), Mona Goodwin (Pretty Girl), Kerrie Hayes, Lexy Howe (Borstal Girls), Harry Lloyd-Walker (Child), Dennis Banks (Barman)

A two-bit hoodlum pretends to romance a naïve waitress in order to keep her from blowing the whistle on a gangland murder he carried out. Remake of the 1947 film (which also appeared in the U.S. under the title *Young Scarface*), starring Richard Attenborough.

Helen Mirren John Hurt

CIRCUMSTANCE

(ROADSIDE ATTRACTIONS) a.k.a. *Sharayet*; Producers, Karin Chien, Maryam Keshavarz, Melissa Lee; Executive Producer, Christina Won; Director/Screenplay, Maryam Keshavarz; Photography, Brian Rigney Hubbard; Designer, Natacha Kalfayan; Costumes, Lamia Choucair; Music, Gingger Shankar; Editor, Andrea Chignoli; a Participant Media in association with Marakesh Films, a Space Between, Bago Pictures, Menagerie Pictures and Neon Productions presentation; Iranian-French-American-Lebanese; Dolby; Widescreen; Color; Rated R; 106 minutes; American release date: August 26, 2011

CAST
Atafeh Hakimi	**Nikohl Boosheri**
Shireen Arshadi	**Sarah Kazemy**
Mehran Hakimi	**Reza Sixo Safai**
Firouz Hakimi	**Soheil Parsa**
Azar Hakimi	**Nasrin Pakkho**

Sina Amedson (Hossein), Keon Mohajeri (Joey), Amir Barghashi (Mohammed Mehdi), Fariborz Daftari (Shireen's Uncle), Amir Soleimani (Payam), Siro Fazlian (Shireen's Grandmother), Elie Njeim (Club Drug Dealer), Joseph Fadel (Taxi Merci Driver), Milad Hadchiti (Yusef), Ghina Daou (Party Girl), Hady Tabbal (Molesting Taxi Driver), Rita El-Achkar (Maid), Ele Khater (Young Addict), Amanda Nawfal (Fatima), Paul Bweiz (Good Looking Boy), Layale Harfouche, Nay Harfouche, Neila Salameh (Club Models)

In the underground world of Iranian youth culture, two sixteen year old girls act on their burgeoning sexual interest in one another.

Nikohl Boosheri, Sarah Kazemy © Roadside Attractions

Nikohl Boosheri, Sarah Kazemy

Anna Mougalalis, Eric Elmosnino © Music Box Films

GAINSBOURG: A HEROIC LIFE

(MUSIC BOX) Producers, Marc du Pontavice, Didier Lupfer; Executive Producer, Matthew Gledhill; Director/Screenplay, Joann Sfar; Photography, Guillaume Schiffman; Designer, Christian Marti; Costumes, Pascaline Chavanne; Musical Arrangements, Olivier Daviaud; Special Effects, David Martí, Montse Ribé; Casting, Stéphane Batut; a One World Films, Studio 37, Focus Features Intl., France 2 Cinéma, Lilou Films, Xilam Films production, in association with Uni Etoile 6, with the participation of Canal Plus, France Télévisions, Orange Cinéma Series; French, 2010; Dolby; Super 35 Widescreen; Color; Not rated; 130 minutes; American release date: August 31, 2011

CAST
Serge Gainsbourg	**Eric Elmosnino**
Jane Birkin	**Lucy Gordon**
Brigitte Bardot	**Laetitia Casta**
La Gueule	**Doug Jones**
Juliette Gréco	**Anna Mouglalis**
Bambou	**Mylène Jampanoï**
France Gall	**Sara Forestier**
Lucien Ginsburg	**Kacey Mottet-Klein**
Joseph Ginsburg	**Razvan Vasilescu**
Olga Ginsburg	**Dinara Droukarova**

Philippe Katerine (Boris Vian), Deborah Grall (Elisabeth), Yolande Moreau (Fréhel), Ophélia Kolb (The Model), Claude Chabrol (Gainsbourg's Record Producer), François Morel (Headmaster), Philippe Duquesne (Lucky Sarcelles), Angelo Debarre (Gypsy Guitarist), Grégory Gadebois (Phyphy), Alice Carel (Judith), Le Quatuor (Les Frères Jacques), Roger Mollien (France Gall's Father)

The true story of the personal life and career of provocative, influential French singer Serge Gainsbourg.

LOVE CRIME

(SUNDANCE SELECTS) a.k.a. *Crime d'amour*; Producer, Saïd Ben Saïd; Executive Producer, Frédéric Blum; Director, Alain Corneau; Screenplay, Alain Corneau, Natalie Carter; Photography, Yves Angelo; Designer, Katia Wyszkop; Costumes, Khadija Zeggaï; Music, Pharoah Sanders; Editor, Thierry Derocles; Casting, Gérard Moulevrier; a SBS Films, France 2 Cinéma, Divali Films co-production in association with Sofica UGC 1; French, 2010; Dolby; Color; Not rated; 106 minutes; American release date: September 2, 2011

CAST
Isabelle Guérin	**Ludivine Sagnier**
Christine	**Kristin Scott T homas**
Philippe	**Patrick Mille**
Daniel	**Guillaume Marquet**
Gérard	**Gérald Laroche**
Lawyer	**Julien Rochefort**

Olivier Rabourdin (Judge), Marie Guillard (Claudine), Mike Powers, Matthew Gonder (Bosses), Jean-Pierre Leclerc (Gérard's Assistant), Stéphane Roquet (Fabien), Frédéric Venant (Executive), Stéphane Brel (Isabelle's Neighbor), Marie-Bénédicte Roy (Prison Supervisor), Anne Girouard (Knives Salesgirl), Suzanne Renaud (Claudine's Daughter), Benoît Ferreux (Agitated Executive), Nils Moreau (Maladroit Executive), Fabrice Donnio (Cinema Cashier), Xavier Berlioz (Bureau Employee), Jean-Marie Juan (Jacques), Michel Doré (Cinema Patron)

Isabelle Guérin, a young office assistant, is at first pleased that she is being mentored by a senior executive until she realizes the woman is starting to take credit for Isabelle's ideas, prompting a battle of wills between the two women.

Kristin Scott Thomas

Ludivine Sagnier
© Sundance Selects

Andy Lau © Indomina Films

DETECTIVE DEE AND THE MYSTERY OF THE PHANTOM FLAME

(INDOMINA) a.k.a. *Di renjie zhi tongtian diguo*; Producers, Wang Zhongjun, Wang Zhonglei, Tsui Hark; Executive Producers, Chen Kuofu, Nansun Shi, Peggy Lee,; Director, Tsui Hark; Screenplay, Zhang Jialu; Photography, Chan Chi-ying, Chan Chor-keung; Designer, James Chiu; Costumes, Bruce Yu; Music, Peter Kam; Editor, Yau Chi-wai; Visual Effects Supervisor, Nam Sang-woo, Lee Yong-gi; Action Director, Sammo Hung; Casting, Chai Jin; a Huayi Brothers Media Corporation, Huayi Brothers International Ltd. presentation in association with China Film Co-Production Corporation of a Film Workshop Co. Ltd., Huayi Brothers Media Corp. production; Chinese-Hong Kong, 2010; Dolby; Widescreen; Color; Rated PG-13; 119 minutes; American release date: September 2, 2011

CAST
Detective Dee	**Andy Lau**
Shangguan Jing'er	**Li Bing Bing**
Empress Wu Zetian	**Carina Lau**
Pei Donglai	**Deng Chao**
Shatuo Zhong	**Tony Leung Ka Fai**
General Aspar	**Jean-Michel Casanova**

Sos Haroyan (Assistant to Umayyad Ambassador), Jialin Zhao (Interpreter), Yan Qin (Jia Yi), Jinshan Liu (Xue Yong), Deshun Wang (Xiazi Ling), Shenming He (Prison Officer), Lu Yao (Li Xiao), Yamming Jiang (Undertaker), Huang Yonggang (Zhang Xun), Richard Ng (Wang Lu, Before Face-lift), Teddy Robin (Wang Lu, After Face-lift), Xiao Chen (Lu Li), Liz Veronica Foo (Wife of Jia Yi), Nan Xu (Chamberlain), Jin Chai (Qiu Shenji)

As Wu Zetian is about to take the throne of Empress, she orders Detective Dee released from prison so that he can find out who is responsible for the murder of two high-ranking court officials.

Jackie Chan, Andy Lau © Variance Films

SHAOLIN

(VARIANCE) a.k.a. *Xin Shao Lin Si*; Producers, Albert Lee, Benny Chan; Chief Producer, Shi Yongxin; Executive Producers, Albert Yeung, Han Sanping, Wang Zhongjun, Xue Guizhi, Fu Huayang; Director, Benny Chan; Screenplay, Alan Yuen, Cheung Chi-kwong, Wang Qiuyu, Chan Kam-cheong, Zhang Tan; Photography, Pun Yiu-ming; Designer, Yee Chung-man; Costumes, Stanley Cheung; Music, Nicolas Errera, Anthony Chue; Editor, Yau Chi-wai; Action Choreographers, Vyuen Tak, Li Chung-chi; Action Director, Cory Yuen; an Emperor Classic Films Co Ltd. presentation in association with China Film Group, Huayi Brothers Media Corporation, Beijing Silver Moon Productions, Shaolin Temple Culture Communication Company production; Chinese-Hong Kong; Dolby; Super 35 Widescreen; Color; Not rated; 130 minutes; American release date: September 9, 2011

CAST
Hou Jie	**Andy Lau**
Cao Man	**Nicholas Tse**
Yan Xi	**Fan Bingbing**
Wu Dao, Cook	**Jackie Chan**
Jing Neng	**Wu Jing**
The Abbot	**Yu Hai**
Jing Hai	**Yu Shaoqun**
Suolongtu	**Xiong Xinxin**
Jing Kong	**Xing Yu**
Tian'er	**Bai Bing**

Xiaoliuna (Shengnan), Shi Xiaohong (Song Hu), Hung Yan-yan (Suoxiangtu), Chen Zhihui (Huo Long), Liang Jingke (Song Hu's Wife)

After pillaging the township of Tengfeng, ruthless General Hou Jie attempts to double cross a general who hopes to bring together their children to strengthen their power. When his plan backfires, Hou takes refuge at a monastery where he seeks atonement for his evil ways.

BURKE AND HARE

(IFC FILMS) Producer, Barnaby Thompson; Executive Producers, Nigel Green, James Spring, Tim Smith, Paul Brett, Peter Nichols, James Atherton, Jan Pace; Director, John Landis; Screenplay, Piers Ashworth, Nick Moorcroft; Photography, John Mathieson; Designer, Simon Elliott; Costumes, Deborah Nadoolman; Hair & Makeup Designer, Christine Blundell; Music, Joby Talbot; Editor, Mark Everson; Casting, Danile Hubbard; an Entertainment Film Distributors and Ealing Studios presentation of a Fragile Film in association with Aegis Film Fund, Prescience and Quickfire Films; British, 2010; Dolby; Color; Not rated; 91 minutes; American release date: September 9, 2011

CAST
William Burke	**Simon Pegg**
William Hare	**Andy Serkis**
Ginny Hawkins	**Isla Fisher**
Dr. Robert Knox	**Tom Wilkinson**
Lucky	**Jessica Hynes**
Hangman	**Bill Bailey**
Dr. Monro	**Tim Curry**

Christopher Lee (Old Joseph), Ronnie Corbett (Capt. Tam McLintoch), Michael Smiley (Patterson), David Hayman (Danny McTavish), John Woodvine (Lord Provost), Paul Davis (Patient), Christian Brassington (Charles), Gabrielle Downey (Mad Maggie), Stuart McQuarrie (Magistrate), Mike Goodenough (Aggrieved Customer), Robert Fyfe (Old Donald), Robert Willox (Gravediggers' Bouncer), David Schofield (Fergus), Ciaron Kelly (Private Fox), Reece Shearsmith (Sgt. Mackenzie), Joyce Henderson (Mrs. McFie), Pollyanna McIntosh (Mary), Georgia King (Emma), Amanda Claire (Nicola), Shelley Longworth (Hannah), Allan Corduner (Nicephore), Steve Speirs (McMartin's Doorman), George Potts (Dr. Lister), Duncan Duff (Attendant), Hugh Bonneville (Lord Harrington), Ray Harryhausen, Sir Alan Munroe, Dr. John Gaynor, Michael Wilson, Robert Paynter (Distinguished Doctors), Simon Farnaby (William Wordsworth), Tom Meeten (Samuel Coleridge), Paul Whitehouse (Gentleman Drunk), Michael Winner (Gentleman Passenger), Ella Smith (Barmaid), Janet Whiteside (Old Woman), Jenny Agutter (Lucy), Robert Stone (Miss Clarissa Windsor), Max Landis (Handsome Coachman), Chris Obi (John Martin), Patricia Gibson-Howell (Mrs. John Martin), Michael Billington (Medical Student), Stephen Merchant (Hollyrood Footman), Jacob Edwards (Hollyrood Courtier), Billy Riddoch (Rabble Rouser), Esme Thompson (Nicephore's Girlfriend), Costa-Gavras, Michele Ray Gavras, Romain Gavras, Emmanuel Hamon, Theo Hamon (French Family)

In the 19th Century, a pair of grave robbers earns money by providing corpses for an Edinburgh medical school.

Simon Pegg, Isla Fisher © IFC Films

Charlotte Rampling

Rutger Hauer

© Kino Lorber

Michael York

THE MILL AND THE CROSS

(KINO LORBER) Producer/Director, Lech Majewski; Executive Producer, Angelus Silesius; Line Producers, Malgorzata Domin, Piotr Ledwig; Screenplay, Michael Francis Gibson, Lech Majewski; Inspired by the book by Michael Francis Gibson; Photography, Lech Majewski, Adam Sikora; Designers, Katarzyna Sobańska, Marcel Slawiński; Costumes, Dorota Roqueplo; Music, Lech Majewski, Jósef Skrzek; Editors, Eliot Ems, Norbert Rudzik; Visual Effects, Odeon Film Studio; 3D Animation, Mariusz Skrzypczyński; an Angelus Silesius production, co-produced by Telewizja Polska/Silesia Film/Arkana Studio/Supra Film/Odeon Film Studio/24Media/Bokomotiv; Polish-Swedish; Dolby; HDCAM; Color; Not rated; 92 minutes; American release date: September 14, 2011

CAST

Pieter Breugel	**Rutger Hauer**
Mary	**Charlotte Rampling**
Nicholas Jonghelinck	**Michael York**
Marijken Bruegel	**Joanna Litwin**
Saskia Jonghelinck	**Dorota Lis**
Crucified	**Bartosz Capowicz**
Wheelified	**Mateusz Machnik**
Miller	**Marian Makula**
Netje	**Sylwia Szczerba**
Jan	**Wojciech Mierkulow**
Esther	**Ruta Kubas**
Simon	**Jan Wartak**

Sebastian Cichonski (Peddler), Lucjan Czerny (Bram), Aneta Kiszczak (Magdali), Oskar Hulickza (Horn Player), Adam Kwiatkowski (Traitor), Pawel Kramarz (Pedro De Erazu), Tadeusz Kwak (Rogier De Marke), Andzej Jastrzab (Scharmouille), Josef Barczyk (Thief), Bernadetta Cichon (Miller's Wife), Krzysztof Lelito (Millhand), Jerzy Sucheki (Pitje), Emilia Czartoryska (Beta), Agata Kokosinska (Wero), Tatiana Juszniewska (Magdah), Dariusz Lorek (Josef), Miroslaw Fuchs (Smith), Stanislaw Futek (Wagonner), Grzegorz Kazibudzki (Archer)

Characters from Pieter Breugel's masterwork painting *The Way to Calvary* come to life in this depiction of Christ's Passion, as set in 1564 Flanders under the Spanish occupation.

Sebastian Schipper, Sophie Rois © Strand Releasing

David Striesow, Sebastian Schipper

3

(STRAND) Producer, Stefan Arndt; Director/Screenplay, Tom Tykwer; Photography, Frank Griebe; Designer, Uli Hanisch; Costumes, Polly Matthies; Music, Tom Tykwer, Johnny Klimek, Reinhold Heil, Gabriel Mounsey; Editor, Mathilde Bonnefoy; Casting, Simone Bär; The Match Factory presentation of an X Filme Creative Pool production in coproduction with WDR, ARD Degeto and Arte; German, 2010; Dolby; Color; Not rated; 119 minutes; American release date: September 16, 2011

CAST
Hanna	**Sophie Rois**
Simon	**Sebastian Schipper**
Adam	**David Striesow**
Lotte	**Annedore Kleist**
Hildegard	**Angela Winkler**
Dirk	**Alexander Hörbe**

Winnie Böwe (Petra), Hans-Uwe Bauer (Dr. Wissmer), Michael Dorn (Wedding Official), Cedric Eich (Sven), Hans Hohlbein (Cab Driver), Alexander Scheer (Eupohric Artist), Karl Alexander Seidel (Nick), Hannes Wegener (Jens), Dominique Chiout (Clara), Carina Wiese (Sister Ruth), Marita Hueber (Martha), Edgar M. Böhlke (Simon's Father), Maria Hartmann (Sylvia), Christina Große (Simone), Christian Steyer (Choirmaster), Gertrud Roll (Hanna's Mother), Klaus Hoser (Hanna's Father), Horst Mendroch (Paul)

On the eve of their 20th anniversary together, Hanna and Simon both end up falling in love with a younger man, their desires unbeknownst to one another.

MY AFTERNOONS WITH MARGUERITTE

(COHEN MEDIA GROUP) a.k.a. *La tête en friche*; Producer, Louis Becker; Director, Jean Becker; Screenplay, Jean Becker, Jean-Loup Dabadie; Based on the novel *La tête en friche* by Marie-Sabine Roger; Photography, Arthur Cloquet; Designer, Thérèse Ripaud; Costumes, Annie Perier Bertaux; Music, Laurent Voulzy; Editor, Jacques Witta; Casting, Colomba Falucci; an ICE 3, KJB Production, StudioCanal, France 3 Cinéma, DD Prods. co-production, with the participation of Canal Plus, France Télévisions, CinéCinéma; French, 2010; Dolby; Panavision; Color; Not rated; 82 minutes; American release date: September 16, 2011

CAST
Germain Chazes	**Gérard Depardieu**
Margueritte	**Gisèle Casadesus**
Francine	**Maurane**
Landremont	**Patrick Bouchitey**
Jojo	**Jean-François Stévenin**
Gardini	**François-Xavier Demaison**

Claire Maurier (Mother), Sophie Guillemin (Annette), Mélanie Bernier (Stéphanie), Matthieu Dahan (Julien), Jérôme Deschamps (The Mayor), Gilles Détroit (Dévallée), Régis Laspalès (M. Bayle), Anne Le Guernec, Amandine Chauveau (Young Mothers), Jean-Luc Porraz (The Notary), Bruno Ricci (Marco), Lyès Salem (Youssef), Sylvia Allegre (Shopper), Bernard Bolzinger (Man in Market), Hélène Coulon (Librarian). Guillaume Ferrand (Soldier), Mahé Frot (Computer Woman), Véronique Hervouet (Minimarket Employee), Salah Teskour (Old Arab)

A simple, mother-dominated man meets retiree Margueritte who teaches him literature, thereby opening up a world of possibilities for him.

Gérard Depardieu, Gisèle Casadesus © Cohen Media Group

Tom Cullen, Chris New

Tom Cullen, Chris New

Tom Cullen, Chris New

WEEKEND

(SUNDANCE SELECTS) Producer, Tristan Goligher; Executive Producers, Suzanne Alizart, Anna Seifert-Speck; Line Producer, Rachel Dargavel; Co-Producer, Claire Mundell; Director/Screenplay/Editor, Andrew Haigh; Photography, Ula Pontikos; Designer, Sarah Finlay; Casting, Kahleen Crawford; a Glendale Picture Company Production with The Bureau in co-production with Synchronicity Films in association with EM Media presentation; British; Color; Not rated; 96 minutes; American release date: September 23, 2011

CAST
Russell	**Tom Cullen**
Glen	**Chris New**
Jamie	**Jonathan Race**
Jill	**Laura Freeman**
Johnny	**Jonathan Wright**
Cathy	**Loretto Murray**
Helen	**Sarah Churm**
Damien	**Vauxhall Jermaine**
Justin	**Joe Doherty**
Sam	**Kieran Hardcastle**
Man in Bar	**Mark Devenport**
Paul	**Julius Metson Scott**
Martin	**Martin Arrowsmith**

After what appears to be just another one-night stand, two men begin to wonder if there is the possibility of taking their relationship to a deeper level, despite the fact that one of them is moving to America for a two-year stretch.

Tom Cullen, Chris New

Tom Cullen © Sundance Selects

TOAST

(W2 MEDIA) Producer, Faye Ward; Executive Producers, Alison Owen, Paul Trijbits, Nicole Finnan, Jamie Laurenson; Associate Producers, Eugenio Perez, Hannah Farrell; Director, S.J. Clarkson; Screenplay, Lee Hall; Based on the memoir *Toast: The Story of a Boy's Hunger* by Nigel Slater; Photography, Balazs Bolygo; Designer, Tom Burton; Costumes, Sarah Arthur; Music, Ruth Barrett; Music Supervisor, Matt Biffa; Editor, Liana Del Giudice; Hair & Makeup Designer, Emma Scott; Casting, Rachel Freck; a BBC and Screen WM presentation of a Ruby Film & Television production in association with Lip Sync Productions LLP and K5 International; British, 2010; Dolby; Deluxe color; HD; Not rated; 96 minutes; American release date: September 23, 2011

CAST
Mrs. Potter	**Helena Bonham Carter**
Dad	**Ken Stott**
Mum	**Victoria Hamilton**
Older Nigel Slater	**Freddie Highmore**
Younger Nigel Slater	**Oscar Kennedy**
Stuart	**Ben Aldridge**
Josh	**Matthew McNulty**
Ruby Sturridge	**Selina Cadell**
Mavis	**Clare Higgins**
Percy Salt	**Colin Prockter**
Warrel	**Frasier Huckle**
Gardener	**Roger Walker**

Kia Pegg (Milk Girl), Rielly Newbold (Leonard), Rob Jarvis (Fishmonger), Amy Marston (Primary School Teacher), Louise Mardenborough (Rachel), Corrinne Wicks (Secondary School Teacher), Marion Bailey (Mrs. Adams), Tracey Wilkinson (Sheila), Sarah Middleton (Beany), Nigel Slater (Chef)

A young boy with a passion for cooking strikes up a rivalry with the domestic who has been hired by his widowed dad when he realizes she is trying to win his father's affections with her culinary wizardry.

Victoria Hamilton, Oscar Kennedy

Louise Mardenborough, Freddie Highmore © W2 Media

Helena Bonham Carter, Freddie Highmore

Ken Stott, Helena Bonham Carter, Freddie Highmore

MAMMUTH

(OLIVE FILMS) Producers, Jean-Pierre Guerin, No Money; Executive Producer, Christophe Valette; Directors/Screenplay, Benoît Delépine, Gustave Kervern; Photography, Hugues Poulain; Designer, Paul Chapelle; Costumes, Florence Laforge; Music, Gaëtan Roussel; Editor, Stéphane Elmadjian; a GMT Prods., No Money Prods. Arte France Cinema, DD Prods., Monkey Pack Films production, with the participation of Canal Plus, Banque Postale Image 3, CinéCinéma; French, 2010; Dolby; Color; Super 16-to-35mm; Not rated; 92 minutes; American release date: September 30, 2011

CAST
Serge ("Mammuth")	**Gérard Depardieu**
Catherine	**Yolande Moreau**
The Lost Lover	**Isballe Adjani**
The Competitor	**Benoît Poelvoorde**
Miss Ming	**Miss Ming**
Pernsion Fund Employee	**Blutch**
Director of Retirement Home	**Philippe Nahon**

Bouli Lanners (Recruiting Agent), Anna Mouglalis (Fake Cripple), Albert Delpy (The Cousin), Bruno Lochet, Rémy Roubakha, Joseph Dahan (Restaurant Guests), Gustave Kervern (Delicatessen Employee), Stéphanie Pilonca (Restaurant Waitress), Jawad Enejjax (Judge of Faces), Rémy Kolpa Kopoul (Roundabout Boss), Siné (Wine Grower), Paulo Anarkao (Big Bertha), Céline Richeboeuf (Miss Ming's Friend), Aurélie Brin (Miss Ming's Other Friend), Sophie Seugé (Miss Ming's Accomplice), Bernard Geoffrey (Slaughterhouse Director), Dick Annegarn (The Cemetery Navvy), Marie-Claude Pluviaud (Fish-Shop Customer), Catherine Hosmalin (Catherine's Friend), Eric Monfourny (The Priest), Noël Godin (Le Tartobole), David Pougnaud-Barillon (Supervisor), Serge Nuques (The Crazy Biker), Zoé Weber (The Little Girl on the Phone), Cédric Geoffroy (Slaughterhouse Assistant-Director)

Restless after retirement, dedicated worker Serge takes off on his Mammuth motorbike to track down his former employers, with the intention of settling some paperwork so that he can receive full benefits.

Isabelle Adjani, Gérard Depardieu © Olive Films

Eduardo Noriega
© Magnolia Pictures

Sam Shepard

BLACKTHORN

(MAGNOLIA) Producers, Andrés Santana, Ibon Cormenzana; Director, Mateo Gil; Screenplay, Miguel Barros; Photography, J.A. Ruiz Anchía; Designer, Juan Pedro De Gaspar; Costumes, Clara Bilbao; Music, Lucio Godoy; Editor, David Gallart; Special Effects, Reyes Abades; Casting, Jina Jay; an Ariane Mararía, Arcadia Motion Pictures presentation of a Nix Films, Eter Pictures, Manto Films production, in co-production with Pegaso Producciones, Noodles Prod., in association with Quickfire Films, with the participation of TVE, Canal Plus; Spanish-French-Bolivian-American; Dolby; Widescreen; HD; Color; Rated R; 98 minutes; American release date: October 7, 2011

CAST
James Blackthorn (Butch Cassidy)	**Sam Shepard**
Eduardo Apocada	**Eduardo Noriega**
Mackinley	**Stephen Rea**
Yana	**Magaly Solier**
Young James	**Nicolaj Coster-Waldau**
Sundance Kid	**Padraic Delaney**
Etta Place	**Dominique McElligott**

Daniel Aguirre (Ivan), Luis Bredow (Doctor), Fernando Gamarra (Bank Director), Maria Luque (Tavern Keeper), Cristian Mercado (General of the Bolivian Army)

Thought to have been killed during an ambush, Butch Cassidy takes up residence in a quiet Bolivian village under the name "James Blackthorn," until he decides he's had enough of hiding out and returns to America in hopes of seeing his family one last time.

Sandrine Kiberlain, Fabrice Luchini © Strand Releasing

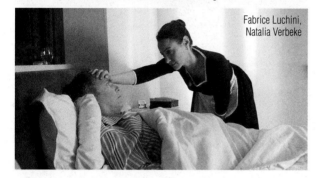

Fabrice Luchini, Natalia Verbeke

THE WOMEN ON THE 6TH FLOOR

(STRAND) a.k.a. *Les femmes du 6ème étage*; Producers, Philippe Rousselet, Etienne Comar; Director, Philippe Le Guay; Screenplay, Philippe Le Guay, Jérôme Tonnerre; Photography, Jean-Claude Larrieu; Set Designer, Pierre-François Limbosch; Costumes, Christian Gasc; Music, Jorge Arriagada; Editor, Monica Coleman; Casting, Tatiana Vialle, Rosa Estevez Ramos; a co-production of Vendôme, France 2 Cinéma, SND with the support of Canal+, CinéCinéma France Télévisions in association with La Banque Postale, Image 4, Cofinova 7, Uni Étoile 8; French; Dolby; Color; Not rated; 104 minutes; American release date: October 7, 2011

CAST
Jean-Louis Joubert	**Fabrice Luchini**
Suzanne Joubert	**Sandrine Kiberlain**
María Gonzalez	**Natalia Verbeke**
Concepción Ramírez	**Carmen Maura**
Carmen	**Lola Dueñas**
Dolores Carbalan	**Berta Ojea**

Nuria Solé (Teresa), Concha Galán (Pilar), Marie Armelle Deguy (Colette de Bergeret), Muriel Solvay (Nicole de Grandcourt), Audrey Fleurot (Bettina de Brossolette), Annie Mercier (Madame Triboulet), Michèle Gleizer (Germaine), Camille Gigot (Bertrand), Jean-Charles Deval (Olivier), Philippe Duquesne (Gérard), Christine Vezinet (Valentine), Jeupeu (Plumber), Vincent Nemeth (Monsieur Armand), Philippe Du Janerand (Piquer), Patrick Bonnel (Goimard), Laurent Claret (Blamond), Thierry Nenez (Fish Merchant), José Etchelus (Priest), Jean-Claude Jay (Pelletier), Joan Massotkleiner (Fernando), Ivan Martin Salan (Miguel)

Jean-Louis's peaceful, bourgeois existence is turned upside down when he and his wife hire a Spanish maid who makes him aware of several other servants sharing the sixth floor quarters, refugees of the Franco regime.

1911

(WELL GO USA ENTERTAINMENT/VARIANCE) a.k.a. *Xinhai geming*; Producers, Wang Zheoin, Jackie Chan; Director, Zhang Li; General Director, Jackie Chan; Screenplay, Wang Xingdong, Chen Baoguang; Photography, Huang Wei; Designer, Chen Minzheng; Music, Ding Wei; Editor, Yang Hongyu; Action Choreographers, Wu Gang, JC Stuntmen; a Well Go USA Entertainment presentation of a Changchun Film Studio Group LLC, Shanghai Film Studio Group Co. Ltd., Shanghai Film Studio Co. Ltd., Beijing Alnair Culture & Media Co. Ltd., Juangsu Broadcasting Corporation, Jackie Chan International Cinema Cultural Holdings Ltd., Xiaoxiang Film Studio Co. Ltd., China City Construction Holding Group Co. Ltd., Hebei Film Studio, Tianjin North Film Group, Media Asia Films Ltd., Huaxia Film Distribution Company presentation; Chinese-Hong Kong; Dolby; Color; Rated R; 118 minutes; American release date: October 7, 2011

CAST
Huang Xing	**Jackie Chan**
Sun Yat-Sen	**Winston Chao**
Xu Zonghan	**Lee Bing Bing**
Empress Dowager Longyu	**Joan Chen**
Zhang Zhenwu	**Jaycee Chan**
Xiong Bingkun	**Dannis Tu**
Li Yuanhong	**Wu Jiang**
Qui Jin	**Ning Jing**

Yu Shaoquin (Wang Jingwei), Ge Hu (Lin Juemin), Winli Jang (Soon Ching-ling), Chun Sun (Yuan Shikal), Ming Hu (Liao Zhongkai), Ya'nan Wang (Yuan Keding)

Revolutionary Huang Xing leads a revolt of oppressed citizens against the powerful army of the Qing Dynasty.

Joan Chen © Variance Films

Antonio Banderas

Antonio Banderas, Elena Anaya

Jan Cornet

Roberto Álamo

Elena Anaya, Roberto Álamo © Sony Classics

Elena Anaya, Antonio Banderas

Elena Anaya, Marisa Paredes

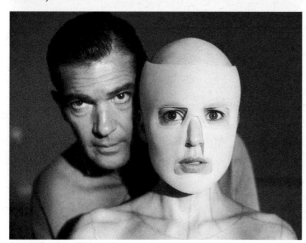

Elena Anaya

Antonio Banderas, Elena Anaya

THE SKIN I LIVE IN

(SONY CLASSICS) a.k.a. *La piel que habito*; Producers, Agustín Almodóvar, Esther García; Director, Pedro Almodóvar; Screenplay, Pedro Almodóvar, Agustín Almodóvar; Based on the novella *Mygale* by Thierry Jonque; Photography, José Luis Alcaine; Art Director, Antxon Gómez; Costumes, Paco Delgado, Jean-Paul Gaultier; Music, Alberto Iglesias; Editor, José Salcedo; an El Deseo presentation; Spanish; Dolby; Super 35 Widescreen; Color; Rated R; 117 minutes; American release date: October 14, 2011

CAST
Dr. Robert Ledgard	**Antonio Banderas**
Vera Cruz	**Elena Anaya**
Marilia	**Marisa Paredes**
Vicente	**Jan Cornet**
Zeca	**Roberto Álamo**
Fulgencio	**Eduard Fernández**
Norma Ledgard	**Blanca Suárez**
Vicente's Mother	**Susi Sánchez**
Cristina	**Bárbara Lennie**
Doctor	**Fernando Cayo**
President of Biotechnology Institute	**José Luis Gómez**
Casilda Efraiz	**Teresa Manresa**
Singer	**Concha Buika**

Ana Mena (Young Norma), Agustín Almodovar (Agustín), Miguel Almodovar (Agustín's Son), Guillermo Carbajo, Sheyla Fariña, David Vila, Jordi Vilaita (Friends), Violaine Estérez (Ledgard's Colleague), Chema Ruiz (Civil Guard), Esther Garcia (Presenter)

Having developed a new skin that might have saved his wife from being burned in a car crash, Dr. Ledgard seeks a human guinea pig on which to test his invention.

Antonio Banderas, Blanca Suárez

JOHNNY ENGLISH REBORN

(UNIVERSAL) Producers, Tim Bevan, Eric Fellner, Chris Clark; Executive Producers, Debra Hayward, Liza Chasin, William Davies; Co-Producer, Ronaldo Vasconcellos; Director, Oliver Parker; Screenplay, Hamish McColl; Story, William Davies; Photography, Danny Cohen; Designer, Jim Clay; Costumes, Beatrix Pasztor; Music, Ilan Eshkeri; Editor, Guy Bensley; Special Effects Supervisor, Mark Holt; Stunts, Paul Herbert; Casting, Lucy Bevan; a Working Title production, presented in association with Studio Canal and Relativity Media; British-American; Dolby; Super 35 Widescreen; Color; Rated PG; 101 minutes; American release date: October 21, 2011

CAST
Johnny English	**Rowan Atkinson**
Simon Ambrose	**Dominic West**
MI7 CEO, Pegasus (Pamela)	**Gillian Anderson**
Kate Sumner	**Rosamund Pike**
Agent Tucker	**Daniel Kaluuya**
Titus Fisher	**Richard Schiff**

Stephen Campbell Moore (Prime Minister), Pik-Sen Lim (Killer Cleaner), Togo Igawa (Master Ting Wang), Roger Barclay (Agent Two), Eric Carte (Agent One), Eleanor Wyld, Mandi Sidhu, Margaret Clunie (Receptionists), Tim McInnerny (Patch Quartermain), Mariella Frostrup (Voice of Royce), Miles Jupp (Technician), Williams Belle (Ling), Paul Carr, Courtney Wu (Chinese Men in Spectacles), Rupert Vansittart (Derek), Isla Blair (Shirley), Emma Vansittart (Margaret), Christina Chong (Barbara), Siu Hun Li (Chinese Susan), Joséphine de La Baume (Madeleine), Wale Ojo (President Chambal), Chris Jarman (Michael Tembe), Andrew Woodall (Foreign Secretary), Burn Gorman (Slater), Isabella Blake-Thomas (Izzie), Janet Whiteside (Pamela's Mother), Maisie Fishbourne (Pamela's Toddler), Mark Ivanir (Karlenko), Gary Kane (Matov), Lobo Chan (Xiang Ping), Clara Paget (Waitress), Richard Syms (Man in Pinstripe), Lily Atkinson (Girl with Crash Helmet), Dave Holland (Man in Wheelchair), Benedict Wong (Chi Han Ly), Ellen Thomas (Tucker's Mum), Ian Shaw (Agent Number Two), Oliver Zheng (Chinese Interpreter)

Disgraced British agent Johnny English is summoned from his monastery retreat to take on a new mission in Hong Kong where he hopes to stop an MI7 mole from stealing a valuable chemical weapon. Sequel to the 2003 film *Johnny English.*

Gillian Anderson, Rowan Atkinson, Daniel Kaluuya © Universal Studios

Emily Watson, David Wenham © Cohen Media

ORANGES AND SUNSHINE

(COHEN MEDIA) Producers, Camilla Bray, Emile Sherman, Iain Canning; Executive Producers, Rebecca O'Brien, Arnab Banerji, Mark Gooder, Sharon Menzies, Suzanne Alizart; Director, Jim Loach; Screenplay, Rona Munro; Based on the book *Empty Cradles* by Margaret Humphreys; Photography, Denson Baker; Designer, Melinda Doring; Costumes, Cappi Ireland; Music, Lisa Gerrard; Editor, Dany Cooper; Visual Effects, Melissa Heagney; Line Producer, Joan Schneider; Casting, Kathleen Crawford, Nikki Barrett; a Screen Australia and Little Gaddesden Productions presentation in association with Fulcrum Media Finance, EM Media, South Australian Film Corporation, Deluxe, Screen NSW and BBC Films of a Sixteen Films/See-Saw Films Production; Australian-British; Dolby; Super 35 Widescreen; Color; Rated R; 105 minutes; Release date: October 21, 2011

CAST
Margaret Humphreys	**Emily Watson**
Len	**David Wenham**
Jack	**Hugo Weaving**
Merv	**Richard Dillane**
Nicky	**Lorraine Ashbourne**
Vera	**Kate Rutter**
Bob	**Greg Stone**

Tara Morice (Pauline), Stuart Wolfenden (Bill), Federay Holmes (Charlotte), Aisling Loftus (Susie), Geoff Morrell(Walter), Russell Dykstra (Dan), Molly Windsor (Rachel), Neil Pigot (James), Kate Box (Radio Studio Receptionist), Marg Downey (Miss Hutchison), Neil Melville (Monsignor Brutin), Adam Morgan (The Intruder), Robert Purdy, Carolina Giammetta (Charity Reps), Tammy Wakefield (Susan), Adam Tedder (Doctor), Jude Henshall (Radio Interviewer), Marie Wheeler-King (Rita), Harvey Scrimshaw (Ben), Hef Lawry (PA to Charity Rep), Alastair Cumming (Australia House Official), Marcus Eyre (Gronom), Eliza Lovell (Hotel Receptionist), Geoff Revell (Syd), Tanya Myers (Joan), Chrissie Page (Betty), Barbara Martin (Mary)

After a confrontation with an emotionally scarred adult, a social worker discovers that there are thousands of such beings who had been illegally deported to Australia from Britain in the 1940s and 50s, who are searching for the truth behind their past.

André Wilms, Blondin Miguel

Pierre Etaix, Kati Outinen

André Wilms, Elina Salo © Janus Films

LE HAVRE

(JANUS) Producers, Aki Kaurismäki, Fabienne Vonier, Reinhard Brundig; Director/Screenplay, Aki Kaurismäki; Photography, Timo Salminen; Designer, Wouter Zoon; Costumes, Fred Cambier; Editor, Timo Linnasalo; Casting, Gilles Charmant; a Sputnik/Pyramide Productions/Pandora Film presentation, in association with Arte France Cinema, ZDF/Arte, with the participation of the Finnish Film Foundation, Canal Plus, Nordisk Film & TV Fond, Le Centre du Cinema et de l'Image Animée, YLE Coproductions, CinéCinéma, Arte France, the Région Haute-Normandie; Finnish-French; Dolby; Color; Not rated; 93 minutes; American release date: October 21, 2011

CAST

Marcel Marx	**André Wilms**
Arletty	**Kati Outinen**
Monet	**Jean-Pierre Darroussin**
Idrissa	**Blondin Miguel**
Denouncer	**Jean-Pierre Léaud**
Claire	**Elina Salo**
Yvette	**Evelyne Didi**
Chang	**Quoc-Dung Nguyen**
Dog	**Laïka**
Grocer	**François Monnié**
Little Bob	**Roberto Piazza**
Dr. Becker	**Pierre Étaix**

In Le Havre, France, a shoeshine man finds meaning to his life when he decides to help a young African stowaway achieve his goal of getting to London.

Laïka, Blondin Miguel

Miriam Stein, Alexander Fehling

Alexander Fehling © Music Box Films

YOUNG GOETHE IN LOVE

(MUSIC BOX FILMS) a.k.a. *Goethe!*; Producers, Christoph Müller, Helge Sasse; Director, Philipp Stölzl; Screenplay, Christoph Müller, Philipp Stöltzl, Alexander Dydyna; Photography, Kolja Brandt; Designer, Udo Kramer; Costumes, Birgit Hutter; Music, Ingo L. Frenzel; Editor, Sven Budelmann; a Beta Cinema presentation of a Senator Film Produktion and Deutschfilm co-production, in associa with Warner Bros. Film Prods. Germany and Seven Pictures; German, 2010; Dolby; Color; Super 35 Widescreen; Not rated; 101 minutes; American release date: November 4, 2011

CAST
Johann Goethe	**Alexander Fehling**
Lotte Buff	**Miriam Stein**
Albert Kestner	**Moritz Bleibtreu**
Wilhelm Jerusalem	**Volker Bruch**
Lotte's Father	**Burghart Klaussner**
Johann's Father	**Henry Hübchen**
Judiciary President Kammermeier	**Hans-Michael Rehberg**
Anna Buff	**Linna Reusse**
Merck	**Stefan Hascke**
Housemaid	**Ann Böttcher**

Sent by his father to a provincial court, in hopes that he will forsake his ambition to be a poet, Johann Goethe falls in love with a woman already betrothed to another man.

INTO THE ABYSS

(SUNDANCE SELECTS) Producer, Erik Nelson; Executive Producers, Dave Harding, Amy Briamonte, Henry Schleiff, Sara Kozak, Lucki Stipetic, Andre Singer; Director, Werner Herzog; Photography, Peter Zeitlinger; Music, Mark Degli Antoni; Editor, Joe Bini; a Creative Differences/Skellig Rock and Investigation Discovery presentation produced in association with More 4/Spring Hill and Werner Herzog Film; German-American-British; Color; HD; Rated PG-13; 107 minutes; American release date: November 11, 2011. Documentary looks at Texas' criminal justice system and some inmates on death-row

WITH
Fred Allen, Lisa Stotler-Balloun, Delbert Burkett, Jason Burkett, Damon Hall, Werner Herzog, Richard Lopez, Michael Perry, Charles Richardson, Jared Talbert, Melyssa Thompson-Burkett, Amanda West

Michael Perry

Jason Burkett © Sundance Selects

Colin Farrell, Keira Knightley

Colin Farrell, Ray Winstone

Colin Farrell © IFC Films

David Thewlis

LONDON BOULEVARD

(IFC FILMS) Producers, Graham King, Tim Headington, Quentin Curtis, William Monahan; Executive Producers, Redmond Morris, Colin Vaines; Director/ Screenplay, William Monahan; Based on the novel by Ken Bruen; Photography, Chris Menges; Designer, Martin Childs; Costumes, Odile Dicks-Mireaux; Music, Sergio Pizzorno; Editors, Dody Dorn, Robb Sullivan; Casting, Nina Gold; a GK Films/Henceforth Pictures/Projection Pictures production; British; Dolby; Deluxe Color; Rated R; 104 minutes; American release date: November 11, 2011

CAST
Mitchel	**Colin Farrell**
Charlotte	**Keira Knightley**
Jordan	**David Thewlis**
Billy Norton	**Ben Chaplin**
Briony	**Anna Friel**
Gant	**Ray Winstone**
D.I. Bailey	**Eddie Marsan**
Dr. Raju	**Sanjeev Bhaskar**
Danny	**Stephen Graham**
Penny	**Ophelia Lovibond**
Whiteboy	**Jamie Campbell Bower**

Velibor Topic (Storbor), Lee Boardman (Lee), Alan Williams (Joe), Jonathan Cullen (Anthony Trent), Robert Willox (Ravaged Guard), Tony Way (Lone Paparazzo), Tim Plester, Jake Abraham (Paparazzi), Damir Koluder (Storbor's Friend), Nick Bartlett (Beaumont), Matt King (Fletcher), Jamie Blackley (The Footballer), Gregory Foreman (Kid with Footballer), Sarah Niles (Hospital Matron), Jonathan Coyne (Heavy One), Bob Mercer (Heavy Two), Elly Fairman (Gant's Wife), Oliver Wood, Jonny Leigh-Wright (Bottom Feeders), Hainsley Lloyd Bennett (Unfortunate Student), Michelle Asante (Woman in Brixton Flat), Julian Littman (Alfons), Sameena Zehra (Indian Woman at Ashmole Estate), Giles Terera (Waiter), Gerald Home (Undertaker)

Following a stint behind bars, Mitchel reluctantly hooks up with low-level hood Billy Norton, which brings him into contact with a troubled movie star who is hoping to escape from the press.

MELANCHOLIA

(MAGNOLIA) Producers, Meta Louise Foldager, Louise Vesth; Executive Producers, Peter Aalbæk, Jensenpeter Garde; Director/Screenplay, Lars von Trier; Photography, Manuel Alberto Claro; Designer, Jette Lehmann; Costumes, Manon Rasmussen; Music Supervisor, Mikkael Maltha; Editor, Molly Malene Stensgaard; Visual Effects Supervisor, Peter Hjorth; a Zentropa Entertainments 27, Film i Vast presentation of a Memfis Film Intl./Zentropa Intl. Köln co-production; Danish-Swedish-French-German; Dolby; Widescreen; Color; HD; Not rated; 135 minutes; American release date: November 11, 2011

CAST
Justine	**Kirsten Dunst**
Claire	**Charlotte Gainsbourg**
John	**Kiefer Sutherland**
Michael	**Alexander Skarsgaard**
Jack	**Stellan Skarsgaard**
Little Father	**Jesper Christensen**
Gaby	**Charlotte Rampling**
Dexter	**John Hurt**
Wedding Planner	**Udo Kier**
Tim	**Brady Corbet**

James Cagnard (Michael's Father), Deborah Fronko (Michael's Mother), Charlotta Miller, Claire Miller (Betty), Gary Whitaker (Limo Driver), Katrine Acheche Sahlstrøm (Girl with Gutiar), Christian Geisnæs (Wedding Photographer)

As a mysterious planet drifts towards Earth, newlywed Justine begins to mentally unravel on her wedding day.

Kiefer Sutherland © Magnolia Pictures

Kirsten Dunst, Alexander Skarsgaard, Kiefer Sutherland, Charlotte Gainsbourg

Kirsten Dunst

John Hurt, Kirsten Dunst

Wagner Moura, Milhem Cortaz © Variance Films

ELITE SQUAD:THE ENEMY WITHIN

(VARIANCE) a.k.a. *Tropa de elite 2: O inimigo agora é outro*; Producers, Marcos Prado, José Padilha; Executive Producers, Leonardo Edde, James D'Arcy; Co-Producers, Wagner Moura, Bráulio Mantovani; Director, José Padilha; Screenplay, Bráulio Mantovani, José Padilha; Photography, Lula Carvalho; Designer, Tiago Marques; Costumes, Cláudia Kopke; Music, Pedro Bromfman; Editor, Daniel Rezende; Visual Effects Supervisor, Andre Waller; Stunts, Keith Woulard; Casting, Maria Fatima Toledo; a Flatiron Film Company, Variance Films, Zazen Producões, Globo Filmes, Feijão Filmes in association with Riofilme presentation; Brazilian, 2010; Dolby; Color; Not rated; 115 minutes; American release date: November 11, 2011

CAST
Lt. Col. Nascimento	**Wagner Moura**
Diogo Fraga	**Irandhir Santos**
Capt. André Matias	**André Ramiro**
Lt. Col. Fábio	**Milhem Cortaz**
Rosane	**Maria Ribeiro**

Seu Jorge (Beirada), Sandro Rocha (Maj. Rocha), Tainá Müller (Clara), André Mattos (Fortunato), Pedro Van-Held (Rafael), Adriano Garib (Guaracy), Julio Adrião (Gov. Gelino), Emilio Orciollo Neto (Valmir), Rodrigo Candelot (Formoso), Charles Fricks (Vermont), Fabrício Boliveira (Marreco), Marcello Gonçalves (Gonçalves), Pierre Santos (Santos), William Vita (Aranha), André Santinho (Maj. Renan), Guilherme Belém (Tatuí), Richard Sodré (Bocão), Marcelo Cavalcanti (Sgt. Gonçalo), Bruno d'Elia (Capt. Azevedo), Cássio Nascimento (Moraes), Francisco Salgado (Pestana), Gabriel Teixeira (Ari), Zé Mário Farias (Felpa), Cadu Fávero (Monitorador Desipe), Vítor Fraga, Johayne Hildefonso (Desipe Agents), Luca Bianchi (Rapé), William J. Shakespeare (Paulinho), Jovem Cerebral (Braço), Chico Melo (Qualé), Deiwis Jamaica (Preso), Ricardo Pavão (Valcir Cunha), Juliana Schlach (Júlia), Rogério Trindade (Delegado Barata), Paulo Giardini (Camelo), Luciano Vidigal (Alexandre)

Promoted to undersecretary of intelligence, riot squad leader Lt. Col. Nascimento finds himself facing corruption within the government as he challenges Col. Fábio's paramilitary death squad.

THE CONQUEST

(MUSIC BOX FILMS) a.k.a. *La conquête*; Producers, Eric Altmayer, Nicolas Altmayer; Director/Adaptation, Xavier Durringer; Screenplay/Dialogues, Patrick Rotman; Photography, Gilles Porte; Art Director, Éric Durringer; Costumes, Jürgen Doering; Music, Nicola Piovani; Editor, Catherine Schwartz; Casting, François Menidrey; a co-production of Mandarin Cinéma, Gaumont with the participation of Canal+, Multithématiques, in association with Manon, Cofimage 22, Cofinova 7, Uni Etoile 8; French; Dolby; Super 35 Widescreen; Color; Not rated; 105 minutes; American release date: November 11, 2011

CAST
Nicolas Sarkozy	**Denis Podalydès**
Céilia Sarkozy	**Florence Pernel**
Jacques Chirac	**Bernard Le Coq**
Claude Guéant	**Hippolyte Girardot**
Dominique de Villepin	**Samuel Labarthe**
Franck Louvrier	**Mathias Mlekuz**
Laurent Solly	**Grégory Fitoussi**

Pierre Cassignard (Frédéric Lefebvre), Saïd Jawad (Rachida Dati), Dominique Besnehard (Pierre Charon), Michèle Moretti (Bernadette Chirac), Emmanuel Noblet (Bruno Le Maire), Michel Bompoil (Henri Guaino), Debré Gérard Chaillou (Jean-Louis), Nicolas Moreau (Pierre Giacometti), Yann Babilée Keogh (Richard Attias), Fabrice Cals (Michaël Darmon), Laurent Olmedo (Philippe Ridet), Bruno López (Jean-François Achilli), Jean-Pierre Léonardini (Bruno Jeudy), Laurent Claret (Philippe Rondot), Dominique Daguier (Jean-Louis Gergorin), Marine Royer (Delphine Byrka), Monica Abularach (Elodie Grégoire)

A look at the five years leading up to Nicolas Sarkozy's election as President of France.

Denis Podalydès, Florence Pernel

Saïd Jawad, Florence Pernel © Music Box Films

Zoé Héran

Jeanne Disson, Zoé Héran © Rocket Releasing

TOMBOY

(ROCKET RELEASING) Producer, Bénédicte Couvreur; Director/Screenplay, Céline Sciamma; Photography, Crystel Fournier; Designer, Thomas Grézaud; Editor, Julien Lacheray; Makeup, Marie Luiset; Casting, Christel Baras; a Hold-Up Films Production in coproduction with ARTE France Cinéma and Lilies Films with the participation of Canal+ and ARTE France with the support of Région Ile-de-France; French; Dolby; Color; Not rated; 82 minutes; American release date: November 16, 2011

CAST
Laure (Michaël)	**Zoé Héran**
Jeanne	**Malonn Lévana**
Lisa	**Jeanne Disson**
Laure's Mother	**Sophie Cattani**
Laure's Father	**Mathieu Demy**
Vince	**Yohan Véro**
Noah	**Noah Véro**

Cheyenne Lainé (Cheyenne), Rayan Boubekri (Rayan), Christel Baras (Lisa's Mother), Valérie Roucher (Rayan's Mother)

After her family moves to a new suburban neighborhood, Laure is mistaken for a boy and decides to pass herself off as such.

KING OF DEVIL'S ISLAND

(FILM MOVEMENT) a.k.a. *Kongen av Bastøy*; Producers, Karin Julsrud, Antoine de Clermont-Tonnerre, Ewa Puszczynska, Mathilde Dedye, Johannes Ahlund; Director, Marius Holst; Screenplay, Dennis Magnusson, Irmelin Wister; Photography, John Andreas Andersen; Set Designer, Janusz Sosnowski; Editor, Michael Leszczylowski; a 4 ½ Film, MACT Productions, Opus Films, St. Paul Film for Euforia Film production; Norwegian, 2010; Dolby; Color; Not rated; 115 minutes; American release date: November 18, 2011

CAST
Governor Bestyreren	**Stellan Skarsgård**
Bråthen	**Kristoffer Joner**
Erling, C-19	**Benjamin Helstad**
Olav, C-1	**Trond Nilssen**
Policeman	**Kimmo Rajala**
Astrid	**Ellen Dorrit Petersen**
Ivar, C-5	**Magnus Langlete**

Morten Løvstad (Ølystein), Daniel Berg (Johan), Odin Gineson Brøderud (Axel), Magnar Botten (Lillegutt), Markus (Brustad), Agnar Jeger Holst (Arne), Tommy Jakob Håland (Terje), Richard Safin (Eirik), Frank-Thomas Andersen (Bjarne), Martin Slaatto (Harald), Ragnhild Vannebo (Committee Chairman), Per Gørvell (Committee Doctor), Kirsti Asskildt (Nurse), Julian Karlsson (Cabin Boy)

Accused of murder, 17-year-old Erling is sentenced to the harsh Bastøy Boys Home correctional facility, where he rebels against the Governor's stern methods of discipline and punishment.

Benjamin Helstad

Stellan Skarsgård, Benjamin Helstad © Film Movement

TYRANNOSAUR

(STRAND) Producer, Diarmid Scrimshaw; Executive Producers, Peter Carlton, Mark Herbert, Katherine Butler, Suzanne Alizart, Hugo Heppell, Will Clarke; Director/Screenplay, Paddy Considine; Photography, Erik Wilson; Designer, Simon Rogers; Costumes, Lance Milligan; Music, Chris Baldwin, Dan Baker; Editor, Pia Di Ciaula; Line Producer, Sarada McDermott; Casting, Des Hamilton; a Film4 and the UK Film Council in association with Screen Yorkshire, EM Media & Optimum Releasing presentation of a Warp X/Inflammable Films production; British; Dolby; Color; Not rated; 91 minutes; American release date: November 18, 2011

CAST
Joseph	**Peter Mullan**
Hannah	**Olivia Colman**
James	**Eddie Marsan**
Tommy	**Ned Dennehy**
Marie	**Sally Carman**
Samuel	**Samuel Bottomley**
Bod	**Paul Popplewell**
Kelly	**Sian Breckin**

Archie Lal (Post Office Cashier), Jag Sanghera (Gurav), Mike Fearnley (Dan), Paul Conway (Terry), Lee Rufford (Paul), Robin Butler (Jack), Fiona Carnegie (Woman in Shop), Julia Mallam (Drunk Woman), Chris Wheat (Wake Singer), Craig Considine (Craig), Robert Haythorne (Rob)

A volatile, unemployed widower, coping with his losses with drink and anger, finds a degree of solace when he meets a woman who is dealing with her own abusive husband.

Olivia Colman
© Strand Releasing

Peter Mullan

Krysten Ritter © ARC Entertainment

KILLING BONO

(ARC ENTERTAINMENT) Producers, Ian Flooks, Nick Hamm, Mark Huffam, Piers Tempest; Executive Producers, Nigel Thomas, Charlotte Walls, Simon Bosanquet, Mark Foligno, Jon Hamm, Deepak Sikka, Ian Hutchinson, Nicholas Myers, Samantha Horley, Cyril Megret, Robert Bevan, Russell Allen, Tommy Moran; Director, Nick Hamm; Screenplay, Dick Clement, Ian La Frenais, Simon Maxwell; Based on the book by Neil McCormick; Photography, Kieran McGuigan; Designer, Tom McCullagh; Costumes, Lorna Marie Mugan; Music, Joe Echo; Music Supervisor, Tarquin Gotch; Editor, Billy Sneddon; Casting, Lucy Bevan, Kelly Hendry; a Greenroom Entertainment, Wasted Talent, The Salt Company, Generator Entertainment in association with Isotope Films, Matador Pictures, Cinema Three, Regent Capital, Molinaire, Silver Reel, Sony Music Entertainment UK, Arri Media and Northern Ireland Screen production; British-Irish; Dolby; Deluxe color; Rated R; 114 minutes; American release date: November 4, 2011

CAST
Neil McCormick	**Ben Barnes**
Ian McCormick	**Robert Sheehan**
Gloria	**Krysten Ritter**
Karl	**Pete Postlethwaite**
Danielle	**Justine Waddell**
Hammond	**Peter Serafinowicz**
Rick	**Luke Treadaway**

Ralph Brown (Leo), Hugh O'Conor (Gary), Martin McCann (Bono), Diarmuid Noyes (Plugger), Lisa McAllister (Erika), Stanley Townsend (Danny Machin), Joni Kamen (Joss), Sam Corry (Paul McGuinness), Jason Byrne (Hotel Receptionist), Frankie McGinty (Doug), Slinky Winfield (Morgan), Mark Griffin (The Edge), David Fennelly (Frankie), Sean Duggan (Liam), Katie Larmour (Doug's Girlfriend), Seán Doyle (Larry Mullen, Jr.), Denis Halligan (Drug Dealer), David Tudor (Adam Clayton), Aoife Holton (Stella McCormick), Joni Kamen (Joss), Thomas Kelly (Hopeless Eric), James Lonergan (Keith), Aidan McArdle (Bill McCormick), Packy Lee (U2 Security Guard), Martin McCloskey (Steve), Ivan McCormick, Neil McCormick (Sleazy Guys), Deirdre O'Kane (Marlene McCormick),

Two Irish brothers, determined to find success as rock musicians, must contend with the fact that their fellow schoolmates have already broken through the big time as U2.

MY WEEK WITH MARILYN

(WEINSTEIN CO.) Producers, David Parfitt, Harvey Weinstein; Executive Producers, Jamie Laurensen, Simon Curtis, Ivan MacTaggart, Christine Langan, Bob Weinstein, Kelly Carmichael; Co-Producer, Mark Cooper; Director, Simon Curtis; Screenplay, Adrian Hodges; Based upon the books *My Week with Marilyn* and *The Prince, the Showgirl and Me* by Colin Clark; Photography, Ben Smithard; Designer, Donal Woods; Costumes, Jill Taylor; Music, Conrad Pope; Music Supervisors, Maggie Rodford, Dana Sano; Marilyn's Theme, Alexandre Desplat; Editor, Adam Recht; Choreographer, Jane Gibson; Casting, Deborah Aquilla, Tricia Wood (US), Nina Gold (UK); a BBC Films presentation in association with Lipsync Productions of a Trademark Films production; British-American; Dolby; Super 35 Widescreen; Technicolor; Rated R; 99 minutes; American release date: November 23, 2011

Eddie Redmayne, Michelle Williams, Dougray Scott

CAST

Marilyn Monroe	**Michelle Williams**
Colin Clark	**Eddie Redmayne**
Sir Laurence Olivier	**Kenneth Branagh**
Vivien Leigh	**Julia Ormond**
Arthur Miller	**Dougray Scott**
Dame Sybil Thorndike	**Judi Dench**
Milton Greene	**Dominic Cooper**
Lucy	**Emma Watson**
Paula Strasberg	**Zoë Wanamaker**
Arthur Jacobs	**Toby Jones**
Sir Owen Morshead	**Derek Jacobi**
Roger Smith	**Philip Jackson**
Lady Jane Clark	**Geraldine Somerville**
Sir Kenneth Clark	**Pip Torrens**
Hugh Perceval	**Michael Kitchen**
Vanessa	**Miranda Raison**
Jack Cardiff	**Karl Moffatt**
Cotes-Preedy	**Simon Russell Beale**
David Orton	**Robert Portal**
Barry	**Jim Carter**
Andy	**Victor McGuire**
Richard Wattis	**Richard Clifford**
Trevor	**Gerard Horan**
Denys Coop	**Alex Lowe**
Rosamund Greenwood	**Georgie Glen**
Jeremy Spenser	**James Clay**
Lucy's Father	**Peter Wight**
Paul Hardwick	**Paul Herzberg**
Waiter	**Richard Shelton**
Senior Policeman	**Des McAleer**
Spectator	**Jem Wall**
Dr. Connell	**David Rintoul**

Richard Attlee, Michael Hobbs, Brooks Livermore, Rod O'Grady (Reporters), Ben Sando, Josh Morris (Schoolboys), Sean Vanderwilt, Adam Perry (Dancers)

Marilyn Monroe arrives in England to film *The Prince and the Showgirl*, indulging in a fling with a young production assistant much to the chagrin of her co-star and director, Laurence Olivier.

This film received Oscar nominations for actress (Michelle Williams) and supporting actor (Kenneth Branagh).

Derek Jacobi

Judi Dench

Zoë Wanamaker, Michelle Williams, Dominic Cooper

Emma Watson

Julia Ormond

Eddie Redmayne

Kenneth Branagh © Weinstein Co.

Sarah Gadon, Michael Fassbender © Sony Classics

Sarah Marecek, Vincent Cassel

A DANGEROUS METHOD

(SONY CLASSICS) Producer, Jeremy Thomas; Executive Producers, Thomas Sterchi, Matthias Zimmermann, Karl Spoerri, Stephan Mallmann, Peter Watson; Associate Producers, Richard Mansell, Tiana Alexandra-Silliphant; Co-Producers, Marco Mehlitz, Martin Katz; Director, David Cronenberg; Screenplay, Christopher Hampton; Based on his stage play *The Talking Cure* and on the book *A Most Dangerous Method* by John Kerr; Photography, Peter Suschitzky; Designer, James McAteer; Costumes, Denise Cronenberg; Music, Howard Shore; Editor, Ronald Sanders; Casting, Deirdre Bowen; a Jeremy Thomas presentation of a co-production of Lago Film, Prospero Pictures, Recorded Picture Company in association with Milbrook Pictures; British-German-Canadian-Swiss; Dolby; Super 35 Widescreen; Deluxe color; Rated R; 99 minutes; American release date: November 23, 2011

CAST
Sabina Spielrein	**Keira Knightley**
Sigmund Freud	**Viggo Mortensen**
Carl Jung	**Michael Fassbender**
Otto Gross	**Vincent Cassel**
Emma Jung	**Sarah Gadon**
Professor Eugen Bleuler	**André M. Hennicke**
Sándor Ferenczi	**Arndt Schwering-Sohnrey**
Jung's Secretary	**Mignon Remé**
Food Nurse	**Mareike Carrière**
Bath Nurse	**Franziska Arndt**

Wladimir Matuchin (Nikolai Spielrein), André Dietz (Medical Policeman), Anna Thalbach (Bathtub Patient), Sarah Marecek (Orchard Nurse), Björn Geske, Markus Haase (Orderlies), Christian Serritiello (Ship's Officer), Clemens Giebel (Ship's Steward), Theo Meller (Karl Abraham), Jost Grix (Leonhard Seif), Severein von Hoensbroech (Johan van Ophuijsen), Torsten Knippertz (Ernest Jones), Dirk S. Greis (Franz Riklin), Katharina Palm (Martha Freud), Nina Azizi (Minna Bernays), Julie Chevalier (Anna Freud), Cynthia Cosima (Sophie Freud), Mirko Guckeisen (Ernst Freud), Julia Mack (Mathilde Freud), Andrea Magro (Jean Freud), Aaron Keller (Oliver Freud), Nadine Salomon (Maid at Freud's House), Naike Jaszczyk (Agathe Jung), Sarah Adams (Gret Jung)

Inspired by his mentor, Sigmund Freud, psychiatrist Carl Jung hopes to use an experimental form of psychoanalysis on a deeply disturbed young woman.

Viggo Mortensen, Michael Fassbender

Keira Knightley, Michael Fassbender

ARTHUR CHRISTMAS

(COLUMBIA) Producers, Peter Lord, David Sproxton, Carla Shelley, Steve Pegram; Co-Producer, Chris Juen; Co-Executive Producer, Peter Baynham; Director, Sarah Smith; Co-Director, Barry Cook; Screenplay, Peter Baynham, Sarah Smith; Designer, Evgeni Tomov; Music, Harry Gregson-Williams; Editors, James Cooper, John Carnochan; Visual Effects Supervisor, Doug Ikeler; Senior Animation Supervisor, Alan Short; Head of Story, Donnie Long; Character Designer, Peter De Sève, Tim Watts; Art Directors, Olivier Adam, Alexei Nechytaylo; Cinematic Designer, Jericca Cleland; 3D Stereoscopic Supervisor, Corey Turner; Casting, Sarah Crowe; a Sony Pictures Animation presentation of an Aardman production; British-American; Dolby; Deluxe color; 3D; Rated PG; 97 minutes; Release date: November 23, 2011

VOICE CAST
Arthur	**James McAvoy**
Steve	**Hugh Laurie**
Grandsanta	**Bill Nighy**
Santa	**Jim Broadbent**
Mrs. Santa	**Imelda Staunton**
Bryony	**Ashley Jensen**
Peter	**Marc Wootton**
North Pole Computer	**Laura Linney**
Chief De Silva	**Eva Longoria**
Gwen	**Ramona Marquez**
Ernie Clicker	**Michael Palin**

Sanjeev Bhaskar, Robbie Coltrane, Joan Cusack, Rhys Darby, Jane Horrocks, Iain McKee, Andy Serkis, Dominic West (Lead Elves), Peter Baynham, Cody Cameron, Kevin Cecil, Kevin Eldon, Rich Fulcher, Bronagh Gallagher, Pete Jack, Danny John-Jules, Emma Kennedy, Stewart Lee, Seamus Malone, Kris Pearn, Alan Short, Sarah Smith, Adam Tandy (Elves), Miggie Donahoe (Pedro), Finlay Duff (French Boy), Rich Hall (Idaho Man), Clint Dyer, Donnie Long (Reporters), Jerry Lambert (N.O.R.A.D.), Deborah Findlay, David Schneider (Generals), Ian Ashpitel, Julia Davis, Kerry Shale (UNFITA OPS)

When the North Pole's efficient operation for delivering Christmas gifts accidentally misses a single child, Arthur Claus comes to the rescue, racing against the clock to rectify the error before Christmas morning.

Bryony, Arthur © Columbia Pictures

Arthur, Steve

Santa

Grandsanta, Arthur

CORIOLANUS

(WEINSTEIN CO.) Producers, Ralph Fiennes, John Logan, Gabrielle Tana, Julia Taylor-Stanley, Colin Vaines; Executive Producers, Marko Miskovic, Will Young, Robert Whitehouse, Christopher Figg, Norman Merry, Christine Langan, Anthony Buckner; Co-Producer, Kevan Van Thompson; Director, Ralph Fiennes; Screenplay, John Logan; Based on the play by William Shakespeare; Photography, Barry Ackroyd; Designer, Ricky Eyres; Costumes, Bojana Nikitovic; Music, Ilan Eshkeri; Editor, Nicolas Gaster; Hair & Makeup Designer, Daniel Parker; Casting, Jina Jay; a Hermetof Pictures, Magna Films and Icon Entertainment Intl. presentation in association with LipSync Prods. LLP, BBC Films of a Kalkronkie production in association with Atlantic Swiss Productions, Artemis Films, Magnoliamae Films, Synchronistic Pictures of a Lonely Dragon production; British; Dolby; Techniscope; Deluxe Color; Rated R; 122 minutes; American release date: December 2, 2011

CAST
Caius Martius Coriolanus	**Ralph Fiennes**
Tullus Aufidius	**Gerard Butler**
Volumnia	**Vanessa Redgrave**
Menenius	**Brian Cox**
Virgilia	**Jessica Chastain**
General Cominius	**John Kani**
Tribune Sicinius	**James Nesbitt**
Tribune Brutus	**Paul Jesson**
First Citizen, Tamora	**Lubna Azabal**
Second Citizen, Cassius	**Ashraf Barhom**

Zoran Čiča, Miloš Dabič, Nicolas Isia, Zoran Miljkovič, Marija Mogbolu, Milan Perovič, Nenad Ristič, Lawrence Stevenson, Marko Stojanović, Tamara Krcunović, Zu Yu Hua, Olivera Viktorović-Đurašković, Danijela Vranješ (Citizens), Slavko Štimac (Volsce Lieutenant), Ivan Đjorđević (Young Roman Soldier), Radovan Vujović, Jovan Belobrković (Soldiers), Dana Tana, Miodrag Milovanov, Andreja Maričić, Svetislav Gonćić (Senators), Dragan Mićanović (Volsce Politician), Radomir Nikolić, Zoran Pajić (Volsce Soldiers), Harry Fenn (Young Martius), Elizabeta Đjorevska (Maid), Dušan Janićijević (Maid), Dušan Janićijević (Old Man in Corioles), Jon Snow (TV Anchorman), David Yelland, Nikki Amuka-Bird (TV Pundits), Uroš Zjdelar (Young Senator), Bora Nenić (Cleaner in Corridor), Slobodan Boda Ninković (War Vet), Mona Hammond (Jamaican Woman), Slodoban Pavelkić (Young Man in Market), Dragoljub Vojnov (Shopkeeper), Kieron Jecchinis (TV War Correspondent), Mirko Pantelić (Camp Barber)

Having triumphed over the Volscians, Caius Martius is appointed to high office in Rome, only to alienate the citizens and find himself in exile.

John Kani, Vanessa Redgrave, Ralph Fiennes, Jessica Chastain, Henry Fenn
© Weinstein Co.

Ralph Fiennes, Vanessa Redgrave

Ralph Fiennes, Jessica Chastain

Ralph Fiennes, Gerard Butler

Emily Browning © IFC Films

SLEEPING BEAUTY

(IFC FILMS) Producer, Jessica Brentnall; Executive Producers, Tim White, Alan Cardy, Jamie Hilton; Director/Screenplay, Julia Leigh; Photography, Geoffrey Simpson; Designer, Annie Beauchamp; Costumes, Shareen Beringer; Music, Ben Frost; Editor, Nick Meyers; Casting, Nikki Barrett; an IFC Films, Screen Australia and Magic Films presentation in association with Screen NSW and Deluxe Australia, Spectrum Films and Big Ears Productions, a Magic Films Production; Australian; Dolby; Deluxe Color; Not rated; 101 minutes; American release date: December 2, 2011

CAST
Lucy	**Emily Browning**
Clara	**Rachael Blake**
Birdmann	**Ewen Leslie**
Man 1	**Peter Carroll**
Man 2	**Chris Haywood**
Man 3	**Hugh Keays-Byrne**

Bridgette Barret, Hannah Bella Bowden, Sarah Kinsella, Stephanie Menere, Lauren Orrell, Natalia Siwek (Waitresses), Les Chantery (Driver), Michael Dorman (Cook), Eden Falk (Thomas), Anni Finsterer (Train Riding Hairdresser), Mirrah Foulkes (Sophie), James Fraser (Guy with Ticket), Robin Goldsworthy, Sarah Snook (Flatmates), Amit Kelkar (Lecturer), Tracy Mann (Waxing Beautician), Henry Nixon (Lucy's Ex-Boyfriend), Justin Smith (Hallelujah Businessman), Pearl Tan (Pedicure Beautician), Jamie Timony (Student Doctor), Daniel Webber (Spy Shop Assistant), Joel Tobeck, Nathan Page (Businessmen), Lizzie Schebesta (Mansion Girl)

A college student takes a job allowing her to submit to the sexual desires of male clients in an utterly passive manner.

LONDON RIVER

(CINEMA LIBRE) Producer, Jean Bréhat; Co-Producers, Bertrand Faivre, Matthieu de Braconier; Director, Rachid Bouchareb; Screenplay, Rachid Bouchareb, Zoe Galeron, Olivier Lorelle; Photography, Jerome Almeras; Designer, Jean Marc Tran Tan Bá; Music, Armand Amar; Editor, Yannick Kergoat; an ARTE (France)/ the Bureau (U.K.)/Tassili (Algeria) production, with the participation of France 3, Region PACA, ACSE, CNC; French-British-Algerian, 2009; DTS; Color; 16-to-35mm; Not rated; 87 minutes; American release date: December 7, 2011

CAST
Elisabeth	**Brenda Blethyn**
Ousmane	**Sotigui Kouyaté**
Butcher	**Roschdy Zem**
Imam	**Sami Bouajila**
Edward	**Marc Baylis**

Francis Magee, Diveen Henry (Inspectors), Bernard Blancan (Forest Worker), Aurélie Eltvedt (Chapel Guide), Gurdepak Chaggar (Travel Agent)

Following the 2005 London bombings, a widower living on an island in the English Channel and an African immigrant both end up traveling to the city in hopes of finding their missing children.

Brenda Blethyn © Cinema Libre

Sotigui Kouyaté, Brenda Blethyn

Michael Fassbender © Fox Searchlight

Carey Mulligan, James Badge Dale, Michael Fassbender

Michael Fassbender

Michael Fassbender, Nicole Behaire

SHAME

(FOX SEARCHLIGHT) Producers, Iain Canning, Emile Sherman; Executive Producers, Tessa Ross, Robert Walak, Peter Hampden, Tim Haslam; Co-Producer, Bergen Swanson; Director, Steve McQueen; Screenplay, Steve McQueen, Abi Morgan; Photography, Sean Bobbitt; Designer, Judy Becker; Costumes, David Robinson; Music, Harry Escott; Music Supervisor, Ian Neil; Editor, Joe Walker; Casting, Avy Kaufman; a Film4 and UK Film Council presentation in association with Momentum Films, Lip Sync Productions and Hanway Films of a See-Saw Films production; British; Dolby; Deluxe color; Rated NC-17; 101 minutes; American release date: December 2, 2011

CAST
Brandon Sullivan	**Michael Fassbender**
Sissy Sullivan	**Carey Mulligan**
David Fisher	**James Badge Dale**
Marianne	**Nicole Behaire**
Woman on Subway Train	**Lucy Walters**
Alexa	**Mari-Ange Ramirez**
Steven	**Alex Manette**
Samantha	**Hannah Ware**
Elizabeth	**Elizabeth Masucci**
Rachel	**Rachel Farrar**
Loren	**Loren Omer**
Hostess	**Lauren Tyrrell**

Marta Milans (Cocktail Waitress), Jake Siciliano (Skype Son), Robert Montano (Waiter), Charisse Merman (Live Chat Woman), Amy Hargreaves (Hotel Lover), Anna Rose Hopkins (Carly), Carl Low (Bouncer), Calamity Chang, DeeDee Luxe (Late Night Lovers), Stanley Mathis (Conductor), Wenne Alton Davis (Police Officer)

A successful Manhattan executive indulges in one sexual encounter after another, basically numbing himself to having any kind of meaningful relationship with a woman.

MY PIECE OF THE PIE

(SUNDANCE SELECTS) a.k.a. *Ma part du gâteau*; Producer, Bruno Levy; Director/Screenplay, Cédric Klapisch; Photography, Christophe Beaucarne; Designer, Marie Cheminal; Costumes, Anne Schotte; Music, Loïk Dury, Christophe "Disco" Minck; Editor, Francine Sandberg; Casting, Jeanne Millet, Sylvie Peyre; a Ce Qui Me Meut, StudioCanal, France 2 Cinema, CRRAV Nord Pas de Calais production with the support of the Nord Pas de Calais Region, in partnership with the CNC with the participation of Canal+, Cinecinema, France Televisions in association with La Banque Postale Image 4; French; Dolby; Hawk Scope; Color; Not rated; 109 minutes; American release date: December 9, 2011

CAST
France	**Karin Viard**
Steve Delarue	**Gilles Lellouche**
Josy	**Audrey Lamy**
JP, Josy's Husband	**Jean-Pierre Martins**
Mélody	**Raphaële Godin**
France's Father	**Fred Ulysse**
Nick	**Kevin Bishop**

Marine Vacth (Tessa), Flavie Bataille (Lucie), Tim Piggott-Smith (Mr. Brown), Philippe Lefebvre (The CEO), Lunis Sakji (Alban), Juliette Navis Bardin (Julie), Camille Zouaoui (Jessica), Adrienne Vereecke (Mallaury), Guillaume Ranson (Jérémie), Xavier Alcan ("Humaniste" Financier), Xavier Mathieu (André), Zinedine Soulaem (Ahmed), Rémi Gillodts (Rémi), Évelyne Dekoninck (The Neighbor), Bernard Debreyne (The Brother-in-Law), Abderrahmane Houfani (Sofiane), Sophie Watrelot (Lucie Companion), Andrew Price (London Waiter), Sandrine Drezen Conchillo (Sandrine, The Union Activist), Michel Masiero (Jean-Claude, Union Activist), Haby Diarra (Jessica Companion), Jean-Benoît Lengeley (JB), Édeline Dufly (Birthday Girl), Husky Kihal (Georges, France's Ex), Alessandro Cecchini (Photographer), Lucie Desclozeaux (Alban's Nursemaid), Suzanne Von Aichinger (Dancer at Party), Mariame N'Diaye (Aminata), Flannan Obé (Caterer)

Following the loss of her factory job, France ends up working as a maid for the stockbroker responsible for her plight.

Karin Viard, Gilles Lellouche © Sundance Selects

Abbie Cornish © Weinstein Co.

W.E.

(WEINSTEIN CO.) Producers, Madonna, Kris Thykier; Executive Producers, Scott Franklin, Donna Gigliotti, Harvey Weinstein; Co-Producers, Colin Vaines, Sara Zambreno; Director, Madonna; Screenplay, Madonna, Alek Keshishian; Photography, Hagen Bogdanski; Designer, Martin Childs; Costumes, Arianne Phillips; Music, Abel Korzeniowski; Music Supervisor, Maggie Rodford; Editor, Danny B. Tull; Make-up and Hair Designer, Jenny Shircore; Visual Effects Supervisor, Sean H. Farrow; Casting, Lucinda Syson, Elaine Grainger; Presented in association with a Semtex Films; British; Dolby; Super 35 Widescreen; Deluxe Color; Rated R; 118 minutes; American release date: December 9, 2011

CAST
Wally Winthrop	**Abbie Cornish**
Wallis Simpson	**Andrea Riseborough**
Edward	**James D'Arcy**
Evgeni	**Oscar Isaac**
William Winthrop	**Richard Coyle**
Ernest	**David Harbour**
King George V	**James Fox**

Judy Parfitt (Queen Mary), Haluk Bilginer (Mohammed Al-Fayed), Geoffrey Palmer (Stanley Baldwin), Natalie Dormer (Elizabeth), Laurence Fox (Bertie), Douglas Reith (Lord Brownlow), Katie McGrath (Lady Thelma), Christina Chong (Tenten), Nick Smithers (Major Fruity Metcalfe), Damien Thomas (George), Liberty Ross (Connie Thaw), Ryan Hayward (Win Spencer), Charlotte Comer (Lady Alexandra), Duane Henry (Dwayne, Security Guard), Anna Skellern (Daphne), Penny Downie (Dr. Vargas), David Redden (Auctioneer), Alberto Vazquez (Victor), Nicole Harvey (Nicola), Daniel André Pageon (Servant), Hywel Morgan (Journalist), Patricia Stark (Newscaster), Annabelle Wallis (Arabella Green), Audrey Brisson (Marie), Emily Denniston (Sotheby's Intern), Suzanne Bertish (Lady Cunard), Ben Willbond (Equerry), Leigh Zimmerman (East Side Woman), David Collins (Guest), Linda Glick (Woman Getting Taxi), Gil Cohen-Alloro (Hotel Clerk), Stephen Jones (Royal Milliner), James McNeill (Sotheby's Staffer), Lisa Gherari (Secretary), Vincent Montuel (Waiter)

When Sotheby's holds an auction of the possessions of the Duke & Duchess of Windsor, Wally Winthrop becomes obsessed with the tale of how their romance rocked the British empire.

This film received an Oscar nomination for costume design.

Gary Oldman, John Hurt

Stephen Graham, Benedict Cumberbatch, Gary Oldman

Gary Oldman, Benedict Cumberbatch

Mark Strong

Kathy Burke

Colin Firth, Gary Oldman, David Dencik, Toby Jones

Svetlana Khodchenkova © Focus Freatures

Ciarán Hinds, Toby Jones

Tom Hardy

TINKER TAILOR SOLDIER SPY

(FOCUS) Producers, Tim Bevan, Eric Fellner, Robyn Slovo; Executive Producers, John le Carré, Peter Morgan, Douglas Urbanski, Debra Hayward, Liza Chasin, Olivier Courson, Ron Halpern; Co-Producer, Alexandra Ferguson; Director, Tomas Alfredson; Screenplay, Bridget O'Connor, Peter Straughan; Based on the novel by John le Carré; Photography, Hoyte van Hoytema; Designer, Maria Djurkovic; Costumes, Jacqueline Durran; Music, Alberto Iglesias; Music Supervisor, Nick Angel; Editor, Dino Jonsäter; Special Effects Supervisor, Mark Holt; Stunts, Andy Bennett; Casting, Jina Jay; a Studio Canal presentation of a Karla Films, Paradis Films, Kinowelt Filmproduktion; co-production with the participation of Canal+ and CinéCinéma of a Working Title production; British-French-German; Dolby; Super 35 Widescreen; Color; Rated R; 128 minutes; Release date: December 9, 2011

CAST

George Smiley	**Gary Oldman**
Connie Sachs	**Kathy Burke**
Peter Guillam	**Benedict Cumberbatch**
Toby Esterhase	**David Dencik**
Bill Haydon	**Colin Firth**
Jerry Westerby	**Stephen Graham**
Ricki Tarr	**Tom Hardy**
Roy Bland	**Ciarán Hinds**
Control	**John Hurt**
Percy Alleline	**Toby Jones**
Irina	**Svetlana Khodchenkova**
Oliver Lacon	**Simon McBurney**
Jim Prideaux	**Mark Strong**
Polyakov	**Konstantin Khabensky**
Magyar	**Zoltán Mucsi**
Mackelvore	**Christian McKay**
Bryant	**Arthur Nightingale**
Mendel	**Roger Lloyd-Pack**
Belinda	**Amanda Fairbank-Hynes**
Fawn	**Peter O'Connor**
Mrs. Pope Graham	**Matyelok Gibbs**
Norman	**Phillip Hill-Pearson**
Spikeley	**Erksine Wylie**
Tufty Thesinger	**Philip Martin Brown**
Mrs. McCraig	**Linda Marlowe**
Kaspar	**Jamie Thomas King**
Jerry Westerby	**Stephen Graham**

Péter Kálloy Molnár (Hungarian Waiter), Ilona Kassai (Woman in Window), Imre Csuja (KGB Agent), Stuart Graham (Minister), Sarah-Jane Robinson (Mary Alleline), Katrina Vasilieva (Ann Smiley), William Haddock (Bill Roach), Tomasz Kowalski (Boris), Alexandra Salafranca (Turkish Mistress), Denis Khoroshko (Ivan), Oleg Dzhabrailov (Sergei), Gillian Steventon (Listening Woman), Nick Hopper (Janitor Alwyn), Laura Carmichael (Sal), Rupert Procter (Guillam's Boyfriend), John le Carré (Christmas Party Guest), Michael Sarne (Voice of Karla), Jean-Claude Jay (French Man at Residency), Tom Stuart (Ben)

George Smiley is called out of retirement to uncover the identity of a mole working at Britain's M16 who is passing information to the Russians.

This film received Osar nominations for actor (Gary Oldman), adapted screenplay, and original score.

WE NEED TO TALK ABOUT KEVIN

(OSCILLOSCOPE) Producers, Luc Roeg, Jennifer Fox, Robert Salerno; Executive Producers, Steven Soderbergh, Christine Langan, Paula Jalfon, Christopher Figg, Robert Whitehouse, Michael Robinson, Andrew Orr, Norman Merry, Lisa Lambert, Lynne Ramsay, Tilda Swinton; Director, Lynne Ramsay; Screenplay, Lynne Ramsay, Rory Stewart Kinnear; Based on the novel by Lionel Shriver; Photography, Seamus McGarvey; Designer, Judy Becker; Costumes, Catherine George; Music, Jonny Greenwood; Editor, Joe Bini; Casting, Billy Hopkins; a Code Red release of a BBC Films and UK Film Council presentation in association with Footprint Investments LLP, Piccadilly Pictures, Lip Sync Productions of an Indepdendent production in association with Artina Films and Rockinghorse Films; British-American; Dolby; Panavision; Deluxe color; Rated R; 112 minutes; American release date: December 9, 2011

Ursula Parker, Ezra Miller

CAST

Eva Khatchadourian	**Tilda Swinton**
Franklin	**John C. Reilly**
Kevin, Teenager	**Ezra Miller**
Wanda	**Siobhan Fallon Hogan**
Lucy	**Ursula Parker**
Kevin, 6-8 Years	**Jasper Newell**
Colin	**Alex Manette**
Celia	**Ashley Gerasimovich**
Kevin, Toddler	**Rock Duer**
Rose	**Erin Darke**
Dr. Goldblatt	**Lauren Fox**
Young Crying Mother	**Suzette Gunn**

Kenneth Franklin (Soweto), James Chen (Dr. Foulkes), Leslie Lyles (Smash Lady), Rebecca Dealy, Louie Rinaldi, Johnson Chong, Kimberly Drummond, Leland Alexander Wheeler, Daniel Farcher, Jennifer Kim, Caitlin Kinnunen (Students), Joseph Melendez (Waiter), Paul Diomede (Al, Corrections Officer), Michael Campbell (Corrections Officer), Aaron Blakely (Concerned Man), Mark Elliot Wilson (Eva's Lawyer), Georgia Lifsher (Checkout Girl), Tah von Allmen (Woman with Birthmark), Blake DeLong, Andy Gershenzon (Young Suited Men), J. Mal McCree (Prison Boy), Michael Pschenichniy (Kevin, Newborn), Kelly Wade (Mother of Little Girl), Jason Shelton (Delivery Guy), Simon MacLean (Mover), Annie O'Sullivan (Waitress), Polly Adams (Mary Woolford), J.J. Kandel (Teacher), Maryann Urbano (School Mother), J.J. Perez (Janitor)

A woman must come to grips with her already ambivalent feelings about her troubled son after he commits a heinous crime.

Tilda Swinton, John C. Reilly

Tilda Swinton

Tilda Swinton, Rock Duer © Oscilloscope

Milla Bankowicz, Robert Wieckiewicz

Benno Fürmann © Sony Classics

Maria Schrader

Kinga Preis

IN DARKNESS

(SONY CLASSICS) Producers, Steffen Reuter, Patrick Knippel, Marc-Daniel Dichant, Leander Carell, Juliusz Machulski, Paul Stephens, Eric Jordan; Executive Producers, Wojciech Danowski, David F. Shamoon, Dr. Carl Woebken, Christoph Fisser; Director, Agnieszka Holland; Screenplay, David F. Shamoon; Based on the book *In the Sewers of Lvov* by Robert Marshall; Photography, Jolanta Dylewska; Designer, Erwin Prib; Costumes, Katarzyna Lewińska, Jagna Janicka; Music, Antoni Komasa-Lazarkiewicz; Editor, Michal Czarnecki; Casting, Weronika Migoń, Heta Mantscheff, John Buchan, Jason Knight; a Beta Cinema presentation of a Schmidt2 Katze Filmolektiv, Studio Filmone Zebra, The Film Works Production; Polish-German-Canadian; Dolby; Color; Rated R; 145 minutes; American release date: December 9, 2011

CAST
Leopold Socha	**Robert Więckiewicz**
Mundek Margulies	**Benno Fürmann**
Klara Keller	**Agnieszka Grochowska**
Paulina Chiger	**Maria Schrader**
Ignacy Chiger	**Herbert Knaup**
Janke Weiss	**Marcin Bosak**
Chaja	**Julia Kijowska**
Jacob Berestycki	**Jerzy Walczak**
Pawel Chiger	**Oliwier Stańczak**
Krystyna Chiger	**Milla Bańkowicz**

Krzysztof Skonieczny (Szczepek), Kinga Preis (Wanda Socha), Olek Mincer (Szlomo Landsberg), Piotr Glowacki (Icek Frenkiel), Maria Semotiuk (Mania Keller), Michal Żurawski (Bortnik), Zosia Pieczyńska (Stefcia Socha), Etel Szyc (Szona Grossman), Weronika Rosati (Young Woman with Child), Andrzej Mastalerz (Sawicki), Ida Łozińska (Teenage Boy Sister), Dorota Liliental (Bystander #1), Maja Bohosiewicz (Girl – Robbery), Vito Hanne (Boy – Robbery), Piotr Nowak (German Soldier), Laura Lo Zito (Irena), Zachariasz Muszyński (Ukranian Militaman), Olena Leonenko, Dorota M. Pacciarelli (Vendors), Jeremias Koschorz (Young German Soldier), Maciej Więckowski (Priest), Alexander Levit (Kovalev), Frank Köbe (Wilhaus), Ireneusz Czop (Janowska SS Man), Anton Levit (Max – Ukranian Officer), Benjamin Höppner (SS Mining Officer), Ryszard Mosingiewicz (Old Man), Filip Garbacz (Teenage Boy), Anielka Nykowska (Anielka), Wolgang Boos (Officer), Benedkit Crisand (Daniel)

The true story of how a petty thief and sewer worker in Nazi-occuppied Lvov, Poland, helped a group of Jews escape death by hiding them in the city's sewers.

This film received an Oscar nomination for foreign language film.

John C. Reilly, Jodie Foster

Christoph Waltz, Kate Winslet

Jodie Foster © Sony Classics

CARNAGE

(SONY CLASSICS) Producers, Saïd Ben Saïd; Co-Producers, Martin Moszkowicz, Oliver Berben, Piotr Reisch, Jaume Roures; Director, Roman Polanski; Screenplay, Yasmina Reza, Roman Polanski; Based on the play *Le Dieu du Carnage (God of Carnage)* by Yasmina Reza, translated by Michael Katims; Photography, Pawel Edelman; Designer, Dean Tavoularis; Costumes, Milena Canonero; Music, Alexandre Desplat; Editor, Hervé de Luze; Casting, Fiona Weir; a Saïd Ben Saïd presentation of a SBS Prods., Constantin Film Produktion, SPI Film Studio, Versatil Cinema, Zanagar Films and France 2 Cinema with the participation of Canal+, Cinecinema, France Télévisions, the Polish Film Institute and Wild Bunch; French-German-Polish-Spanish; Dolby; Super 35 Widescreen; Color; Rated R; 80 minutes; American release date: December 16, 2011

CAST

Penelope Longstreet	**Jodie Foster**
Nancy Cowan	**Kate Winslet**
Alan Cowan	**Christoph Waltz**
Michael Longstreet	**John C. Reilly**
Zachary Cowan	**Elvis Polanski**
Ethan Longstreet	**Eliot Berger**
Telephone Voices:	
Walter	**Joe Rezwin**
Dennis	**Nathan Rippy**
Michael's Mother	**Tanya Lopert**
Secretary	**Julie Adams**

Two couples meet to discuss the altercation between their children and find their initially civil efforts to sort things out escalating into an all-out battle.

John C. Reilly, Jodie Foster, Christoph Waltz, Kate Winslet

Kate Winslet

THE FLOWERS OF WAR

(WREKIN HILL) a.k.a. *Jin líng shí san chai*; Producer, Zhang Weiping; Executive Producers, David Linde, Deng Chaoying, Bill Kong, Leo Shi Young; Director, Zhang Yimou; Screenplay, Liu Heng, Yan Geling; based on the novel *13 Flowers of Nanjing* by Yan Geling; Photography, Zhao Xiaoding; Designer, Yohei Taneda; Costumes, William Chang Suk-ping; Music, Chen Quigang; Editor, Meng Peicong; Presented in association with Row 1 Productions, a New Pictures Film production; Chinese; Dolby; Super 35 Widescreen; HD; Technicolor; Rated R; 146 minutes; American release date: December 21, 2011

CAST
John Miller	**Christian Bale**
Yu Mo	**Ni Ni**
Shu	**Zhang Xinyi**
Maj. Li	**Tong Dawei**
George Chen	**Huang Tianyuan**
Mr. Meng	**Cao Kefan**
Col. Hasegawa	**Atsuro Watabe**
Lt. Kato	**Shigeo Kobayashi**
Yi	**Han Xiting**
Ling	**Zhang Doudou**
Mosquito	**Yuan Yangchunzi**
Hua	**Sun Jia**
Dou	**Li Yuemin**
Lan	**Bai Xue**
Lt. Asakura	**Takashi Yamanaka**
Terry	**Paul Schneider**

During the 1937 Japanese assault on Nanjing, a mortician aides a group of courtesans who have taken refuge in a church.

Ni Ni, Christian Bale © Wrekin Hill

Christian Bale

Christian Bale, Ni Ni

Christian Bale, Ni Ni

ALBERT NOBBS

(ROADSIDE ATTRACTIONS) Producers, Glenn Close, Bonnie Curtis, Julie Lynn, Alan Moloney; Executive Producers, Cami Goff, John C. Goff, Sharon Harel-Cohen, Daryl Roth, David E. Shaw; Co-Executive Producers, Marcia Allen, Theresa Amend, John Amend, John Eger; Director, Rodrigo Garcia; Screenplay, Gabriella Prekop, John Banville, Glenn Close; Based on the short story "The Singular Life of Albert Nobbs" by George Moore; Photography, Michael McDonough; Designer, Patrizia von Brandenstein; Costumes, Pierre-Yves Gayraud; Music, Brian Byrne; Editor, Steven Weisberg; Special Makeup Designer, Matthew W. Mungle; Casting, Amy Hubbard, Priscilla John; an LD Entertainment and Roadside Attractions presentation of a Trillum Productions/Mockingbird Pictures/Parallel Films production in association with Chrysalis Films/Allen & Associates/Westend Films with the participation of Canal+ and Bord Scannán na hÉireann/The Irish Film Board; Irish-British; Dolby; Color; Rated R; 113 minutes; American release date: December 21, 2011

Glenn Close

CAST
Albert Nobbs	**Glenn Close**
Helen Dawes	**Mia Wasikowska**
Joe Macken	**Aaron Johnson**
Dr. Holloran	**Brendan Gleeson**
Hubert Page	**Janet McTeer**
Viscount Yarrell	**Jonathan Rhys Meyers**
Mrs. Baker	**Pauline Collins**
Polly	**Brenda Fricker**
Sean	**Mark Williams**
Mary	**Maria Doyle Kennedy**
Cathleen	**Bronagh Gallagher**
Percy Smythe-Willard	**John Light**
Mrs. Cavendish	**Phyllida Law**
Emmy Keyes	**Antonia Campbell-Hughes**
Patrick	**James Greene**
Viscountess Yarrell	**Phoebe Waller-Bridge**
Mrs. Smythe-Willard	**Emerald Fennell**
Monsieur Pigot	**Kenneth Collard**
Mrs. Amelia Moore	**Serena Brabazon**

Michael McElhatton (Mr. Moore), Angeline Ball (Mrs. Gilligan), Philip O'Sullivan (Mr. Gilligan), Dolores Mullally (Milady), Bonnie McCormack (Miss Shaw), Judy Donovan (Madame Pigot), Daniel Costello (Mr. Sweeney), Katie Ann McDonough, Kathleen Warner Yeates, Cate MacGabhan (Laundry Maids), Katie Long (Young Kitchen Maid), Katie O'Brien (Older Kitchen Maid), Mark Doherty (Porter), Rhys Burke (George Moore), Lauren Kinsella (Milly Moore), Antoinette Healy (Woman on Landau), Annie Starke (Chocolate Shop Waitress), Cathy White (Nanny), Malcolm Blacow (Health Official), Lily Melcher, Lucie Melcher (Country Girls), Raul Riva (Baby), Juno (Polly's Dog)

Glenn Close © Roadside Attractions

In order to survive in the oppressive, male-dominated 19th century Ireland, a woman manages to pass herself off as a man, finding work as a butler over a thirty year period.

This film received Oscar nominations for actress (Glenn Close), supporting actress (Janet McTeer), and makeup.

Aaron Johnson, Glenn Close

Glenn Close

Jonathan Rhys-Meyers, Glenn Close, Pauline Collins

Janet McTeer, Glenn Close

Mia Wasikowska, Aaron Johnson

Mia Wasikowska, Glenn Close

Janet McTeer

Alexandra Roach, Harry Lloyd

SERVICE
QUALITY
VALUE

Alexandra Roach

Meryl Streep

THE IRON LADY

(WEINSTEIN CO.) Producer, Damian Jones; Executive Producers, François Ivernel, Cameron McCracken, Tessa Ross, Adam Kulick; Co-Producers, Anita Overland, Colleen Woodcock; Director, Phyllida Lloyd; Screenplay, Abi Morgan; Photography, Elliot Davis; Designer, Simon Elliott; Costumes, Consolata Boyle; Music, Thomas Newman; Editor, Justine Wright; Casting, Nina Gold; a Yuk Films, Pathé, Film4 and UK Film Council presentation in association with Goldcrest Film Production LLP, of a DJ Films production; British; Dolby; Panavision; Deluxe color; Rated PG-13; 105 minutes; American release date: December 30, 2011

CAST

Margaret Thatcher	**Meryl Streep**
Denis Thatcher	**Jim Broadbent**
Carol Thatcher	**Olivia Colman**
Gordon Reece	**Roger Allam**
June	**Susan Brown**
Jim Prior	**Nick Dunning**
Airey Neave	**Nicholas Farrell**
Alfred Roberts	**Iain Glen**
Michael Heseltine	**Richard E. Grant**
Geoffrey Howe	**Anthony Head**
Young Denis Thatcher	**Harry Lloyd**
Doctor	**Michael Maloney**
Michael Foot	**Michael Pennington**
Young Margaret Thatcher	**Alexandra Roach**
Amanda	**Amanda Root**
Ian Gilmour	**Pip Torrens**
Francis Pym	**Julian Wadham**
Shadow Minister	**David Westhead**
John Nott	**Angus Wright**
Muriel Roberts	**Victoria Bewick**
Edward Heath	**John Sessions**
Susie	**Phoebe Waller-Bridge**
Cleaner	**Alice da Cunha**
Beatrice Roberts	**Emma Dewhurst**
James R	**Clifford Rose**
William	**Michael Cochrane**
James T	**Jeremy Clyde**
Peter	**Michael Simkins**
Young Carol	**Eloise Webb**
Young Mark	**Alexander Beardsley**
House of Commons Speaker	**Richard Syms**

Sylvestra Le Touzel (Hostess, 1949), Michael Culkin (Host, 1949), Stephanie Jacob, Robert Portal, Richard Dixon (Guests, 1949), John Harding, Simon Chandler, Stephen Boxer, Jasper Jacob, Rupert Vansittart, Robin Kermode, Andrew Havill, Michael Elwyn, Peter Pacey, Jeremy Child, James Smith, Hugh Ross, Chris Campbell, Paul Bentley, Martin Wimbush, Simon Slater (Cabinet Ministers), David Cann (TV Interviewer), Christopher Luscombe (Voice Coach), Angela Curran (Crawfie), David Rintoul (Admiral Fieldhouse), Nicholas Jones (Admiral Leach), Richard Goulding (Naval Attaché), Matthew Marsh (Alexander Haig), Willie Jonah (Kenneth Kaunda)

The true story of Margaret Thatcher's journey from grocer's daughter to serving the post of Prime Minister of England for 11 years.

2011 Academy Award winner for Best Actress (Meryl Streep) and Best Makeup.

Meryl Streep

Meryl Streep © Weinstein Co.

Jim Broadbent, Meryl Streep

Meryl Streep (center)

Jim Broadbent

Nichcolas Farrell, Roger Alam

© Sundance Selects

Ditta Miranda Jasjfi

Azusa Seyama, Fabian Prioville (partially hidden)

PINA

(SUNDANCE SELECTS) Producers, Wim Wenders, Gian-Piero Ringel; 3D Producer, Erwin M. Schmidt; Co-Producers, Claudie Ossard, Chris Bolzli; Executive Producer, Jeremy Thomas; Director/Screenplay, Wim Wenders; Photography, Hélène Louvart, Jörg Widmer; Stereographer, Alain Derobe; 3D Supervisor, François Garnier; Music, Thom Hanreich; Editor, Toni Froschhammer; Choreographer, Pina Bausch; a Hanway Films presentation of a Neue Road Movies production in coproduction with Eurowide Filmproduction, ZDF, ZDFtheaterkanal and Arte; German-French; Dolby; Color; 3D; Rated PG; 103 minutes; American release date: December 23, 2011. Documentary on the dance world of choreographer Pina Bausch.

WITH

Regina Advento, Malou Airaudo, Ruth Amarante, Jorge Puerta Armenta, Pina Bausch, Rainer Behr, Andrey Berezin, Damiano Ottavio Bigi, Aleš Cucek, Clémentine Deluy, Josephine Ann Endicott, Lutz Förster, Pablo Aran Gimeno, Mechthild Großmann, Silvia Farias Heredia, Barbara Kaufmann, Nayoung Kim, Daphnis Kokkinos, Ed Kortlandt, Eddie Martinez, Dominique Mercy, Thusnelda Mercy, Ditta Miranda Jasjfi, Cristiana Morganti, Morena Nascimento, Nazareth Panadero, Helena Pikon, Fabien Prioville, Jean-Laurent Sasportes, Franko Schmidt, Azusa Seyama, Julie Shanahan, Julie Anne Stanzak, Michael Strecker, Fernando Suels Mendoza, Aida Vainieri, Anna Wehsarg, Tsai-Chin Yu; in *Le Sacre du printemps:* Alexeider Abad Gonzales, Stephan Brinkmann, Meritxell Checa Esteban, Paul Hess, Rudolf Giglberger, Chrystel Wu Guillebeaud, Mu-Yi Kuo, Szu-Wei Wu, Tomoko Yamashita, Sergey Zhukov, Andy Zondag

This film received an Oscar nomination for feature documentary.

Damiano Ottavio Bigi, Clémentine Deluy

Fabian Prioville, Azusa Seyama

FOREIGN FILMS B

2011 Releases / January 1–December 31

NO ONE KILLED JESSICA (UTV Spot Boy) Producer, Ronnie Screwvala; Creative Producer, Vikas Bahl; Director/Screenplay, Raj Kumar Gupta; Photography, Anay Goswamy; Designer, Sukant Panigrahy; Costumes, Sabyasachi Mukherjee; Music, Amit Trivedi; Lyrics, Amitabh Bhattacharya; Editor, Aarti Bajaj; a UTV Spotboy presentation; India; Color; Not rated; 136 minutes; American release date: January 7, 2011. **CAST:** Vidya Balan (Sabrina Lall), Rani Mukerji (Meera Gaity), Myra Karn (Jessica Lall), Neil Bhoopalam (Vikram Jai Singh), Rajesh Sharma (N.K.), Mohammed Zeeshan Ayyub (Manish Bharadwaj), Bubbles Sabharwal (Mallika Sehgal), Yogendra Tikkus (Sanjit Lall), Geeta Sudan (June Lall), Shireesh Sharma (Pramod Bharadwaj), Samara Chopra (Naina Sehgal), Jasbir Malik (Shyam Tolani), Satyadeep Misra (Meera's Boss), Vintee Bansal, Ashish Goyal (Fighting Couple), Avijit Dutt (BM Bandit)

Vidya Balan in *No One Killed Jessica* © UTV

THE TIME THAT REMAINS (Sundance Selects) Producers, Michael Gentile, Elia Suleiman; Producer, Hani Farsi; Director/Screenplay, Elia Suleiman; Photography, Marc-André Batigne; Designer, Sharif Waked; Costumes, Judy Shrewsbury; Editor, Véronique Lange; a Nazira Films, Artemis Productions, Bim Distribuzione, France 3 Cinema, RTBF (Télévision Belge) and Belgacom co-production, in association with Corniche Pictures, with the participation of MBC Group, France Television, Canal+ and TPS Star; French-Belgian-Italian-British, 2009; Dolby; DTS; Color; Not rated; 109 minutes; American release date: January 7, 2011. **CAST:** Elia Suleiman (E.S), Saleh Bakri (Fuad), Samar Qudha Tanus (Mother, 1970-80), Shafika Bajjali (Mother, Today), Tarek Qubti (The Neighbor), Zuhair Abu Hanna (E.S as a Child), Ayman Espanioli (E.S as a Teenager), Bilal Zidani (Jubran), Leila Mouammar (Thuraya), Yasmine Haj (Nadia), Amer Hlehel (Anis), Nina Jarjoura (Rose), George Khleifi (Mayor), Ali Suliman (Eliza's Boyfriend), Avi Kleinberger (Government Official), Menashe Noy (Taxi Driver), Nati Ravitz (IDF Commander), Ehab Assal (Man with Cell Phone, Tank), Lotuf Neusser (Abu Elias), Alex Bakri (Man Who Shoots Himself), Doraid Liddawi (Ramalla IDF Officer), Ayman Espanioli (ES, Teenager), Isabelle Ramadan (Aunt Olga), Alon Leshem (IDF Officer), Lior Shemesh (Police Officer), Baher Agbariya (Iraqi Soldier), Ziyad Bakri (Jamal), Yaniv Biton (Haganah Soldier), Daniel Bronfman (Policeman at Bridge), Tareq Qobti (Neighbor)

Zuhair Abu Hanna, Samar Qudha Tanus in *The Time That Remains* © Sundance Selects

GO GO TALES (Anthology Film Archives/Independent) Executive Produces, Enrico Coletti, Massimo Cortesi; Director/Screenplay, Abel Ferrara; Photography, Fabio Cianchetti; Designer, Frank De Curtis; Costumes, Gemma Mascagni; Music, Francis Kuipers; Editor, Fabio Nunziata; Casting, Gillian Hawser; a Massimo Gatti presentation of a Bellatrix Media and Go Go Tales production in association with De Nigris Prods.; Italian-American, 2007; Cinecitta Color; Not rated; 105 minutes; American release date: January 7, 2011. **CAST:** Willem Dafoe (Ray Ruby), Bob Hoskins (The Baron), Matthew Modine (Johnie Ruby), Asia Argento (Monroe), Roy Dotrice (Jay), Lou Doillon (French), Riccardo Scamarcio (Dr. Steven), Stefania Rocca (Debby), Bianca Balti (Adrian), Sylvia Miles (Lilian Murray), Burt Young (Murray), Pras Michel (Sandman), Joe Cortese (Danny Cash), Dominot (Anita Finger), Shanyn Leigh (Dolly), Frankie Cee (Luigi), Sammy Pasha (Sam), Nicholas De Cegli (Bobby B.), Johnny Skreli (Junior), Nicky Dee (Bobby B.), Anita Pallenberg (Aunt Sin), Alberto Mangiante (Big Don), Romina Power (Yolanda Vega), Anton Rodgers (The English), Justine Mattera (Sugar), Manuela Zero (Sophie), Sabina Beganovic (Elektra), Selena Khoo (Leila), Chiara Picchi (Ally), Julie McNiven (Madison), Gilda Lepardhaia (Salome), Maria Jurado (Goldie), Julia Mayarchuk (Tania), Aurora Giuliani (Kelly), Mara Adriani (Mara), Leila Virzi (Bonnie), Ray Schnitzer (Upstairs Barman), Elena Vaganova, Irina Vaganova (Murray's Girls), Andy Luotto (Stanley), Danny Quinn (Clark), Lal Nirmal (Nasim), Signh Gurcharnjit (Zoom), Frank De Curtis (DeeJay), Hang Chen Jin (Ling), Sung Uno Cho (Mr. Yamamoto), Shin Yang (Medical Student), Jacopo Lo Faro (The Crab), Francis Pardeilhan, Jay Edward Natelle, Francesco Serina, Donato Antonio Lemmo, Emanuele Carucci Viterbi, Daniele De Martino, Leslie Csuth, Adrian McCourt, Alessandro Demcenko, Daniel Baldock, Marcus J. Cotterell, Joseph Murray, Neri Fiuzzi (Wall Street Brokers)

Willem Dafoe in *Go Go Tales* © Massimo Gatti

PLASTIC PLANET (First Run Features) Producers, Thomas Bogner, Daniel Zuta; Executive Producers, Tom Gläser, Ilann Girard; Director/Screenplay. Werner Boote; Photography, Thomas Kirschner; Music, The Orb; Editors, Ilana Goldschmidt, Cordula Werner, Tom Pohanka; a Neu Sentimental Film Entertainment (Austria)/ Brandstorm Entertainment (Germany)/Cine Cartoon Filmproduktion (Austria); Austrian-German, 2009; Stereo; HD; Color; Not rated; 99 minutes; American release date: January 14, 2011. Documentary on how the abundance of plastic has become a threat to both the environment and our health; **WITH:** John Taylor, Felice Casson, Beatrice Bortolozzo, Susan Jobling-Eastwood, Hiroshi Sagae, Patricia Hunt, Scott Belcher, Theo Colborn, Fred vom Saal, Frederick Corbin, Charles Moore, Peter Frigo, Kurt Scheidl, Margot Wallström, Klaus Rhomberg, Ray Hammond, Gunther von Hagens

Plastic Planet © First Run Features

PETITION (INA) a.k.a. *Petition: La cour des plaignants*; Producer, Sylvie Blum; Director/Photography, Zhao Liang; Editors, Shun Zi, Sylvie Blum, Bruno Barwise, Zhao Liang; an Institut National de l'Audiovisuel, Arte (France)/3 Shadows (China) co-production; Chinese-Swiss-British-French-Belgian-Finnish, 2009; Color; Not rated; 123 minutes; American release date: January 14, 2011. Documentary on China's justice system and the right of the citizens to petition the Government for a redress of grievances; **WITH:** Zhang Weiye, Qi Huaying, Fang Xiaojuan.

Petition © INA

ONG BAK 3 (Magnet Releasing) Producers, Tony Jaa, Panna Rittkrai, Akarapol Techaratanaprasert; Executive Producer, Somsak Techartatanaprasert; Director/Screenplay/Martial Arts Choreographers, Tony Jaa, Panna Rittikrai; Photography, Nattawut Kittkhun; Designer, Chalard Muangjan; Costumes, Chatchai Chaiyon; Music, Banana Record, Terdsak Janpan; Editors, Nattawut Kittkhun, Sarawut Nakajud; Special Effects, Surreal Studio; a Sahamongkolfilm International presentation of an Iyara Film production; Thai, 2010; Dolby; Color; Super 35 Widescreen; Rated R; 94 minutes; American release date: January 14, 2011. **CAST:** Tony Jaa (Tien), Chupong Chungpruk (Bhuti Sanghka, The Crow Demon), Primrata Det-Udom (Pim), Sarunyoo Wongkrachang (Lord Rat-ha-Sei-Na), Nirut Sirichanya (Master Bua), Phetthai Wongkhamlao (Mhen), Sorapong Chatree (Chernung), Chumporn Theppituk (Uncle Mao)

Tony Ja in *Ong Bak 3* © Magnet Releasing

CRIME AND PUNISHMENT (dGenerate Films) a.k.a. *Zui yu fa*; Producers, Sylvie Blum, Nonglux Thongdard; Director/Photography, Zhao Liang; Editors, Zhao Liang, Adam Kerby; a Three Shadows Photography Art Center, Moving Images Studio (China)/Insitut National de l'Audiovisuel (France) presentation; Chinese-French, 2007; Stereo; Color; DigitBeta video; Not rated; 122 minutes; American release date: January 14, 2011. Documentary on the abusive nature of the military police in Northeastern China.

STREET DAYS (Global Film Initiative) a.k.a. *Quichis dgeebi*; Producers, Archil Gelovani, Gia Bazgadze, Levan Korinteli; Executive Producer, Ketevan Machavariani; Director, Levan Koguashvili; Screenplay, Levan Koguashvili, Boris Frumin, Nikoloz Marr; Based on a short story by Mamuka Kherkheulidze; Photography, Archil Akheldiani; Designer, Kote Japaridze; Costumes, Tinatin Kvinikadze; Music, Rezo Kiknadze; Editor, Nodar Nozadze; an Independent Film Project, Moving Pictures and Georgian Public Broadcaster production; Georgian, 2010; Dolby; Color; Not rated; 89 minutes; American release date: January 19, 2011. **CAST:** Guga Kotetishvili (Chekie), Irakli Ramishvili (Ika), Gaga Chikhladze (Gurami), Giorgi Kipshidze (Jaba), Zura Begalishvili (Lado), Zaza Salia (Tengo), Rusiko Kobiashvili (Nini). Eka Chkheidze (Zaza's Wife), Levan Jividze (Vaso), Paata Khetaguri (Ero), Dato Kinghuradze (Maca), Rusiko Kobiashvili (Nini), Zaza Kolelshvili (Sano), Irakli Loladze (Givi), Nikoloz Marri (Nika), Tamriko Melikishvili (Luiza), Zaza Salia (Tengo), Zura Sharia (Zaza Cheishvili), Merab Yolbaia (Dito)

Street Days © Global Film Initiative

EVANGELION: 2.0 YOU CAN (NOT) ADVANCE (Cinema Asia Releasing) a.k.a. *Evangelion shin gekijōban: Ha*; Producers, Toshimichi Otsuki, Hideaki Anno; Directors, Kazuya Tsurumaki, Masauyki Anno, Hideaki Anno; Screenplay, Hideaki Anno; Photography, Tohru Fukushi; Production Designers, Hiroshi Kato, Tatsuya Kushida; Character Designer, Yoshiyuki Sadamoto; Music, Shiro Sagisu; Editor, Hirofumi Okuda; a FUNimation Entertaiment, Gainax, Studio Khara production; Japanese, 2009; Color; Not rated; 112 minutes; American release date: January 21, 2011. **VOICE CAST:** Megumi Ogata (Shinji Ikari), Megumi Hayashibara (Rei Ayanami/Pen Pen/Yui Ikari), Yuko Miyamura (Asuka Shikinami Langley), Maaya Sakamoto (Mari Makinami Illustrious), Kotono Mitsuishi (Misato Katsuragi), Yuriko Yamaguchi (Ritsuko Akagi), Kôichi Yamadrea (Ryoji Kaji), Fumihiko Tachiki (Gendo Ikari), Miki Magasawa (Maya Ibuki), Motomu Kiyokawa (Kouzou Fuyutsuki), Hiro Yuuki (Makoto Hyuga), Takehito Koyasu (Shigeru Aoba), Tetsuya Iwanaga (Kensuke Aida), Tomokazu Seki (Toji Suzuhara), Mugihito (Kiel Lorenz)

Evangelion: 2.0 You Can (Not) Advance © Cinema Asia Releasing

DHOBIT GHAT (MUMBAI DIARIES) (UTV) Producers, Aamir Khan, Kiran Rao; Executive Producer, B. Shrinivas Rao; Director/Screenplay, Kiran Rao; Photography, Tushar Kanti Ray; Designer, Manisha Khandelwal; Costumes, Isha Ahluwalia, Darshan Jalan; Music, Gustavo Santaolalla; Editor, Nishant Radhakrishnan; an Aamir Khan Prods. production in association with Cinema 73; Indian, 2010; Dolby; Color; Not rated; 100 minutes; American release date: January 21, 2011. **CAST:** Aamir Khan (Arun), Prateik Babbar (Munna), Monica Dogra (Shai), Kriti Malhotra (Yasmin), Danish Hussain (Salim), Jehan Manekshaw (Pesi), Kitu Gidwani (Vatsala), Ashok Varma (Yasmin's Husband), Sanjivani Oagle (Neighbor), Aasha Pawar (Latabai), Jyoti Pawar (Vanitha), Babita Sehgal (Munna's Client), Jitendra Shinde (Karim), Nafisa Amin Khan (Amma), Rohit Tiwari (Rakesh), Norma Lobo (Agnes), Homi Mulla (Shai's Father), Sunny Charles (Cabbie), Almas Khan, Jaffar Hussain, Fayaz Shaiyad, Rehan Khan (Street Kids), Sandeep Lokre (Producer), Rashid (Liftman), Rohini Ramanathan (Shai's Friend at Bar), Rubina Shaikh (Girl at Multiplex), Nilesh G. Naik (BMC Man), Abdul Hai (Attarwala)

RAGE (Strand) a.k.a. *Rabia*; Producer, Alvaro Augustín, Rodrigo Guerrero, Eneko Lizarraga, Bertha Navarro, Guillermo del Toro; Director/Screenplay, Sebastián Cordero; Story, Sergio Bizzio; Based on the novel by Sergio Bizzio; Photography, Enrique Chediak; Designer, Eugenio Caballero; Costumes, Eva Arretxe; Music, Lucio Godoy; Editor, David Gallart; WAG in association with Dynamo, Montfort Producciones, Telecino Cinema, Tequila Gang; Mexican-Spanish-Colombian, 2009; Dolby; Color; Not rated; 89 minutes; American release date: January 28, 2011. **CAST:** Gustavo Sánchez Parra (José María), Martina García (Rosa), Concha Velasco (Mrs. Elena Torres), Xavier Elorriaga (Mr. Edmundo Torres), Álex Brendemühl (Alvaro Torres), Iciar Bollain (Marimar Torres), Tania de la Cruz (Viviana), Karlos Aurrekoetxea (Mecánico), Yon González (Adrián), Javier Tolosa (Capataz), Alfonso Torregrosa, Asier Hormaza (Police), Fernando Tielve (Esteban), Anartz Zuazua (Fumigador), Jeremy Xabier Vargas (Joselito)

Gustavo Sánchez Parra, Martina García in *Rage* © Strand Releasing

IP MAN 2 (Variance) a.k.a. *Ip Man 2: Legend of the Grandmaster* and *Yip Man 2*; Producers, Raymond Wong, Li Xin, Ann An; Executive Producers, Zheng Qianghui, Zong Shu Jie, Gao Jun; Director, Yip Wai-Shun; Screenplay, Edmond Wong; Photography, Poon Hang-Sang; Designer, Kenneth Mak; Costumes, Lee Pik-Kwan; Music, Kenji Kawai; Editor, Cheung Ka-Fai; Action Director, Sammo Hung; a Mandarin Films Ltd., He Nan Movie Group Ltd., Beijing Shengshi Huarui Film investment & management ltd., Desen International Media Co. Ltd. presentation of a Mandarin Films Limited production; Chinese, 2010; Dolby; Super 35 Widescreen; Color; Rated R; 108 minutes; American release date: January 28, 2011. **CAST:** Donnie Yen (Ip Man), Lynn Hung (Cheung Wing-sing), Simon Yam (Chow Ching-chuen), Sammo Hung (Master Hung Chun-nam), Huang Xiao-ming (Wong Leung), Xiong Dai-lin (Cheung Wing-sing), Fan Sui-wong (Jin Shanzhao), Kent Cheng (Fatso), Pierre Ngo (Leung Kan), Darren Shahlavi (Taylor "The Twister" Milos), Jiang Daiyan (Bruce Lee), Calvin Chang (Chow Kwong-yiu), Stefan Morawietz (Twister's Coach), To Yue-hong (Cheng Wai-kei), Simon Yam (Chow Ching-chuen), Li Chak (Ip Chun), Charles Mayer (Wallace), Lam Hak-ming (Master Lam), Lo Mang (Master Law), Fung Hak-on (Master Cheng), Brian Thomas Burrell (Emcee)

Sammo Hung, Donnie Yen in *Ip Man 2* © Variance Films

WHEN WE LEAVE (Olive Films) a.k.a. *Die Fremde*; Producers, Feo Aladag, Züli Aladag; Director/Screenplay, Feo Aladag; Photography, Judith Kaufmann; Designer, Silke Buhr; Costumes, Gioia Raspé; Music, Max Richter, Stéphane Moucha; Editor, Andrea Mertens; Casting, Ulrike Müller, Harika Uygur; a Telepol presentation of an Independent Artists film production in co-production with WDR, RBB, ARTE; German, 2010; Dolby: CinemaScope; Not rated; 115 minutes;

American release date: January 28, 2011. **CAST:** Sibel Kekilli (Umay), Settar Tanriögen (Kader, Umay's Father), Derya Alabora (Halime, Umay's Mother), Florian Lukas (Stipe, Umay's Colleague), Tamer Yigit (Mehmet, Umay's Older Brother), Serhad Can (Acar, Umay's Younger Brother), Almila Bagriacik (Rana, Umay's Younger Sister), Alwara Höfels (Atife, Umay's Best Friend), Nursel Köse (Gül, Umay's Boss), Nizam Schiller (Cem, Umay's Son), Ufuk Bayraktar (Kemal, Umay's Husband), Marlon Pulat (Duran, Rana's Fiancé)

Sibel Kekilli in *When We Leave* © Olive Films

INTO ETERNITY (International Film Circuit) Producer, Lise Lense-Møller; Director/ Screenplay, Michael Madsen; Photography, Heikki Färm; Editors, Daniel Dencik, Stefan Sundlöf; a Magic Hour Films production; Danish-Finnish-Swedish, 2010; Color; Not rated; 75 minutes; American release date: February 2, 2011. Documentary on the construction of underground tunnels in Finland to be stored with radioactive waste; **WITH:** Timo Äikäs, Timo Seppälä, Juhani Vira, Esko Ruokola, Wendla Paile, Mikael Jensen, Berit Lundqvist, Peter Wikberg, Carl Reinhold Bråkenhielm, Sami Savonrinne

Into Eternity © Intl. Film Circuit

HOME (20th Century Fox) Producers, Denis Carot, Luc Besson; Director, Yann Arthus-Bertrand; Screenplay, Isabelle Delannoy, Yann Arthus-Bertrand, Denis Carot, Yen Le Van; Photography, Michel Benjamin, Dominique Gentil; Music, Armand Amar; Editor, Yen Le Van; Narrator, Glenn Close; a Europa Corp. production; French, 2009; Dolby; Color; Not rated; 93 minutes; American release date: February 4, 2011. Documentary on the Earth's environmental disasters as seen in 54 countries.

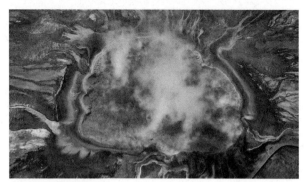

Home © 20th Century Fox

WHAT WOMEN WANT (China Lion) a.k.a. *Wo zhi nu ren xin*; Producers, Dede Nickerson, Chen Daming, Jeffrey Chan; Executive Producer, Chris Liu; Director/ Adaptation, Chen Daming; Based on the motion picture *What Women Want* directed by Nancy Meyers with screenplay by Josh Goldsmith, Cathy Yuspa and story by Josh Goldsmith, Cathy Yuspa and Diane Drake; Photography, Max Wang; Designer, Li Zhuyoi; Costumes, Li Yikai; Music, Christopher O' Young; Editor, Nelson Quan; a Bona Entertainment Co. Ltd., Beijing Bona Film and Cultural Communication Co. Ltd., Focus Films Ltd., Emperor Motion Picture Ltd., CH Entertainment Inc., China Film Group Corp. presentation of a Bona Entertainment Company Ltd. production; Chinese; Dolby; Widescreen; Color; Not rated; 116 minutes; American release date: February 4, 2011. **CAST:** Andy Lau (Sung Zigang), Gong Li (Li Yi-Long), Li Chengru (CEO Dong), Yuan Li (Yanni), Russell Wong (Peter), Hu Jing (Zhao Hong), Wang Deshun (Sun Meisheng), Kelly Hu (Girl in Lotto Commercial), Chau Osric (Chen Er Dong), Chen Daming (Young Sun Meisheng), Zhu Zhu (Secretary to Zigang Sun)

Andy Lau, Gong Li in *What Women Want* © China Lion Films

HOW I ENDED THIS SUMMER (Film Movement) a.k.a. *Kak ya provel etim letom*; Producers, Roman Borisevich, Alexandr Kushayev; Director/Screenplay, Alexei Popogrebsky; Photography, Pavel Kostomarov; Designer, Gennady Popov; Costumes, Svetlana Mikhailova; Music, Dmitry Katkhanov; Editor, Ivan Lebedev; a Bavaria Film Intl., Russia 1 TV Channel presentation; Russian, 2010; Dolby; Color; HD-to-35mm; Not rated; 130 minutes; American release date: February 4, 2011. **CAST:** Grigoriy Dobrygin (Pavel), Sergei Puskepalis (Sergei), Igor Chernevich (Voice of Sofronov), Ilya Sobolev (Voice of Volodya), Artyom Tsukanov (Voice of Stas)

Grigoriy Dobrygin in *How I Ended This Summer* © Film Movement

THE SKY TURNS (New Yorker) a.k.a. *El cielo gira*; Producer, José María Lara; Director, Mercedes Álvarez; Screenplay, Mercedes Álvarez, Arturo Redín; Photography, Alberto Rodríguez; Editors, Sol López, Guadalupe Pérez; a José María Lara, Alokatu production; Spanish, 2005; Dolby; Color; Not rated; 115 minutes; American release date: February 11, 2011. Documentary about a year in the life of the rapidly dying village of Aldealsenor in northwest Spain; **WITH:** Peio Azketa, Hicham Chate, Cirilo Fernández, José Fernández, Josefa García, Román García, Silvano García, Valentina García, Alfredo Jimeno, Crispina Lamata, Antonino Martínez, Blanca Martínez, Áurea Mingo, Milagros Monje, Salah Rafia, Elías Álvarez, Mercedes Alvarez.

The Sky Turns © New Yorker

IN HER SKIN (IFC Films) Producers, Tony Cavanaugh, Thom Mount; Executive Producers, Penny Wolf, John Keating, David Whealy, Matthew Street, Jason Moody, Christopher Mapp, Andy McIntyre, Steve Cooper, Maureen Barron, Catriona Hughes, Leesa Kahn; Director/Screenplay, Simone North; Inspired by the book *Perfect Victim* by Elizabeth Southall & Megan Norris; Photography, Jules O'Loughlin; Designer, Peta Lawson; Costumes, Terry Ryan; Music, Ben Frost, John Butler; Editor, Jane Moran; Casting, Susie Maizels; a Liberty Films International production In association with Screen Queensland; Australian, 2009; Dolby; Super 35 Widescreen; Color; Rated R; 97 minutes; American release date: February 11, 2011. **CAST:** Guy Pearce (Mike Barber), Miranda Otto (Elizabeth Barber), Ruth Bradley (Caroline Reid Robertson), Sam Neill (David Reid), Kate Bell (Rachel Barber), Khan Chittenden (Manni), Graeme Blundell (Ivan), John Butler (Busker), Justine Clarke (Irene), Diane Craig (Joy), Jack Finsterer (Patterson), Rebecca Gibney (Gail), Eugene Gilfedder (DePyle), Jeremy Sims (McLean), Steve Vidler (Drew), Kelley Abbey (Zoe), Melissa Anderson (Janice), Paul Bishop (Doctor), Paul Denny (Paramedic), Damien Garvey (Box Hill Cop),

Stephen Jenkins (Richmond Cop), Claude Minisini (Missing Persons Boss), Veronica Neave (Yvonne), Mia Storey (Mary), Delaware North-Cavanaugh (Cate, 8 years old), Charlie North-Cavanaugh (Mourner), Sally Christie (Ashleigh-Rose, age 11), Amber Ivers (Rachel, age 11), Michael De Marinis (Tony), Grace Silvestri (Rosa), Jacqui Hall (Susan), Karen Price (Shoe Shop Keeper), Jerome Velinsky (Dom), Ross Macrae (Fireman), Patrice Fidgeon (News Reporter), Maya Aleksandra (Skye), Terry Annesley (Thatcher), Andrew Blain (Waddell), Shayler Conder (Chrissy, 13 years old), Amanda Dettrick (Dianne), Taryn Marler (Jenny), Paris Morrissey (Ashleigh-Rose, age 8), Lily Sinclair (Rachel, age 8), Dana Harry (Heather, 5 years old), Tori Forrest (Heather, 9 years old), Karen Pert (Accountant), Dena Kaplan (Pregnant Girl with Pram), Tim Boyle (Policeman #4), Dan Purdey, John Wonnacott (Missing Persons Cops), Deborah Knight (News-reader)

Guy Pearce in *In Her Skin* © IFC Films

ZERO BRIDGE (Joyless Films) Producers, Hilal Ahmed Langoo, Josée Lajoie, Tariq Tapa; Executive Producers, Tyler Brodie, Hunter Gray, Paul Mezey, Calvin Preece, Ed Branstetter; Director/ Screenplay/Photography, Tariq Tapa; Editors, Josée Lajoie, Tariq Tapa; a Joyless Films, Artists Public Domain & Film Desk presentation; Kashmiri-American, 2008; Color; Not rated; 96 minutes; American release date: February 16, 2011. **CAST:** Mohamad Imran Tapa (Dilawar), Taniya Khan (Bani), Ali Mohammad Dar (Uncle Ali), Fahad Banday, Bilal Bhat, Towfig Ahmed Gojri (Cricket Boys), Owaise Qayoom Bhat (Zahoor), Afrooza Langoo (Sister Afrooza), Shaheena Langoo (Sister Shaheena), Shah Nawaz (Zero Bridge Police), Niyaz Ah Patloo (The Musician), Khurshid Ahmad Tarbaji (Bani's Uncle), Sebastian Bergman, Michael McLughan (Tourists), Umar Rashid Dar, Musharraf Khan (Shipping Customers), Hilal Amhed Langoo (Passport Office Clerk), Burhan Qadfir (Processing Officer), Sultan (Passport Dealer Bodyguard), Tawfil (Jewelry Shop Owner), Tiger (Passport Dealer), Mohsin Maqbool Zargar (Motorcycle Thief)

Mohamad Imran Tapa in *Zero Bridge* © Joyless Films

THE EDGE OF DREAMING (Koch Lorber) Producers, Amy Hardie, George Chignell, Doug Block, Lori Cheatle; Director, Amy Hardie; Photography, Amy Hardie, Ian Dodds, Hardie Family; Music, Jim Sutherland; Editor, Ling Lee; Animator, Cameron Duguid; an Amy Hardie Productions, Passion Pictures and Hard Working Movies co-production, with VPRO, More 4, ZDF/Arte and POV; British-Scottish, 2009; Color; Not rated; 73 minutes; American release date: February 16, 2011. Documentary charting a year in Amy Hardie's life, after she has experienced a dream of her own death; **WITH:** Mark Solms, Claudia Goncalves, Phyllida Anam-Aire, Amy Mindell, Arnie Mindell, Irving Weissman

Amy Hardie, Nell Kravitz in *The Edge of Dreaming* © Koch Lorber

THE LAST LIONS (National Geographic Entertainment) Producers, Beverly Joubert, Dereck Joubert, Lisa Truitt, Chris Miller; Executive Producers, Tim Kelly, David Beal, Daniel Battsek, Adam Leipzig; Director/Screenplay/Photography, Dereck Joubert; Music, Alex Wurman; Editor, Susan Scott; Narrator, Jeremy Irons; an NGE presentation in association with Wildlife Films; Botswanan-American; Dolby; Color; HD-to-35mm; Rated PG; 88 minutes; American release date: February 18, 2011. Documentary in which a lioness struggles to keep herself and her cubs alive in the Botswana wetlands.

The Last Lions © National Geographic Entertainment

WE ARE WHAT WE ARE (IFC Films) a.k.a. *Somos lo que hay*; Producer, Nicolás Celis; Executive Producers, Liliana Pardo, Henner Hofmann; Director/Screenplay, Jorge Michel Grau; Photography, Santiago Sánchez; Designer, Alejandro García; Costumes, Fernanda Velez; Music, Enrico Chapela; Editor, Rodrigo Ríos; Casting, April Shannon; a Centro de Capacitación Cinematográfica, Fondo para la Producción Cinematográfica de Calidad Mexico production; Mexican, 2010; Dolby; Panavision; Color; Not rated; 90 minutes; American release date: February 18, 2011. **CAST:** Francisco Barreiro (Alfredo), Alan Chávez (Julián), Paulina Gaitán (Sabina), Carmen Beato (Patricia), Jorge Zárate (Owen), Esteban Soberánes (Octavio), Humberto Yañez (Papá), Adrián Aguirre (Adriana), Miriam Balderas (Sheyla), Juan Carlos Colombo (Funeral Director), Daniel Giménez

Cacho (Tito), Miguel Ángel Hoppe (Gustavo), Raúl Kennedy (Adán), Octavio Michel (Lieutenant)

Alan Chávez, Francisco Barreiro in *We are What We Are* © IFC Films

THE OVER THE HILL BAND (NeoClassics) a.k.a. *Meisjes*; Producers, Jean-Claude Van Rijckeghem, Dries Phlypo; Director, Geoffrey Enthoven; Screenplay, Jean-Claude Van Rijckeghem, Chris Craps; Photography, Gerd Schelfhout; Art Director, Steven Liegeois; Costumes, Tine Verbeurgt; Music, Tom Kestens, Olaf Janssens; Editor, Philippe Ravoet; Casting, Sara de Vries; a Private View, Artémis Productions presentation; Belgian, 2009; Color; Not rated; 93 minutes; American release date: February 25, 2011. **CAST:** Lut Tomsin (Lut), Lea Couzin (Magda), Marilou Mermans (Claire), Jan Van Looveren (Sid), Lucas van den Eynde (Michel), Michel Israel (Artuur), Barbara Sarafian (Pascale), Greg Timmermans (Young Priest), Jurgen Delnaet (Doctor), François Beukelaers (Jean), Robrecht Vanden Thoren (Presenter), Leo Achten (Toon), Claude Musungayi (Jo), Isabel Leybaert (Jessie), Lori Bosmans (Fran), Stefan Declerck (Gerd), Bieke Bosmans (Sarah)

The Over the Hill Band © NeoClassics

A GOOD MAN (Emerging Pictures) Producers, Himman Dhamija, Safina Uberoi, Jenny Day; Executive Producer, David Jowsey; Director, Safina Uberoi; Photography, Himman Dhamija; Music, The Alcohotlicks; Editor, Nicholas Beaumann; a Divana Films production, in association with Screen Australia, Australian Broadcasting Corp. Television, Adelaide Film Festival; Australian, 2009; Color; DigiBeta; Not rated; 78 minutes; American release date: February 25, 2011. Documentary on how Chris Rohrlach went into the prostitution business in order to pay for medical expenses for his quadriplegic wife, Rachel; **WITH:** Chris Rohrlach, Rachel Rohrlach, Trevor Rohrlach, June Rohrlach, Kieron Rohrlach

Rachel Rohrlach, Chris Rohrlach in *A Good Man* © Emerging Pictures

FORGET ME NOT (Cinema Epoch) Producer, Rebecca Long; Directors, Alexander Holt, Lance Roehrig; Screenplay, Mark Underwood; based on a story by Rebecca Long, Steve Spence, Mark Underwood; Photography, Shane Daly; Designer, Anastasia Portas; Costumes, Matthew Price; Music, Michael J. McEvoy; Editor, Kant Pan; Casting, Cara Beckinsale; a Quicksilver Films production; British; Color; HD; Not rated; 92 minutes; American release date: March 4, 2011. **CAST:** Tobias Menzies (Will), Genevieve O'Reilly (Eve), Gemma Jones (Lizzie), John Carlisle (Horace), Nigel Cooke (Jim), Rebecca Cooper (Jackie, Bride-to-Be), Charlie Covell (Carly), Luke de Woolfson (Luke), Ben Farrow (Ben), Laurie Hagen (Ana), Austin Hardiman (Jay), Susie Harriet (Suze), Martina Laird (Doctor), Jessica Lawless (Carly's Best Friend), Rachel Rhodes (Nurse), Badi Uzzaman (Shopkeeper)

Tobias Menzies, Genevieve O'Reilly in *Forget Me Not* © Cinema Epoch

EX DRUMMER (Palisades Tartan) Producers, Eurydice Gysel, Koen Mortier; Executive Producer, Ruben Goots; Director/Screenplay, Koen Mortier; Based on the novel by Herman Brusselmans; Photography, Glynn Speeckaert; Designer, Geert Paredis; Costumes, Catherine Marchand; Music, Millionaire, Arno, Flip Kowlier; Editor, Manu Van Hove; Casting, Kris De Meester; a CCCP production, in association with Czar Group, Quad Prods., Mercurio Cinematografica; Belgian, 2007; Dolby; Color; Super 16-to-35mm; Not rated; 104 minutes; American release date: March 4, 2011. **CAST:** Dries Van Hegen (Dries), Norman Baert (Koen de Geyter), Gunter Lamoot (Jan Verbeek), Sam Louwyck (Ivan Van Dorpe), François Beukelaers (Pa Verbeek), Bernadette Damman (Mother Verbeek), Joris Van Der Speeten (Jan Verbeek, 10 years), Nancy Denijs (Ivan's Wife), Nomie Visser (Ivan's Daughter), Dolores Bouckaert (Lio), Wim Willaert (Jimmy), Barbara Callewaert

(Christine), Jan Hammenecker (Dikke Lul), Vinnie Bonduwe (Friend of Dikke Lul), Chantal Wannyn (Erna), Tristan Versteven (Dorian), Sebastien Dewaele (Stef Vanneste), Hans Claerhout (Fan Dries), Eric Vanrenterghem (Mayor), Flip Kowlier, Frank Dubbe, Kurt Vandemaele, Sophia Theys (Jury Members), Peggy Heyninck (Woman in Parking Lot), Patrick Cronenberg (Bus Driver), Sylviane Aliet (Woman in car), Marcel Deblauwe (Referee), Greta Baert Bruynoghe (Mother Koen)

Dries Van Hegen in *Ex Drummer* © Palisades Tartan

THE HUMAN RESOURCES MANAGER (Film Movement) Producers, Haim Mecklberg, Estee Yacov-Mecklberg, Elie Meirovitz, Thanassis Karanthanos, Karl Baumgartner, Tudor Giurgiu, Talia Kleinhendler; Executive Producers, Moshe Edery, Leon Edery, Ygal Mograbi; Director, Eran Riklis; Screenplay, Noah Stollman: Based on the novel *A Woman in Jerusalem* by A.B. Jehoshua; Photography, Rainer Klausmann; Designers, Dan Toader, Yoel Herzberg; Costumes, Li Alembik, Adina Bucur; Music, Cyril Morin; Editor, Tova Ascher; a 2-Team Productions production, co-produced by Pallas Film, EZ Films, Hai Hui Entertainment, Pie Films; Israeli-German-French-Romanian, 2010; Dolby; Color; Super 16-to-35mm; Not rated; 103 minutes; American release date: March 4, 2011. **CAST:** Mark Ivanir (HR Manager), Gila Almagor (Widow), Guri Alfi (Weasel), Noah Silver (Boy), Rozina Cambos (Consul), Julian Negulesco (Vice Consul), Bogdan Stanoevitch (Ex-Husband), Reymond Amsalem (Divorcee), Irina Petrescu (The Grandmother), Roni Koren (Daughter), Papil Panduru (Driver), Danna Semo (Secretary), Sylwia Drori (Nun), Ofir Weil (Morgue Worker)

Mark Ivanir (center) in *The Human Resources Manager* © Film Movement

I SAW THE DEVIL (Magnet) a.k.a. *Akma-reul bo-at-da*; Producers, Kim Hyun-woo, Jo Seong-won; Executive Producers, Greg Moon, Jeong Hun-you, Kang Dong-seok, Kim Hyun-woo, Rim Ji-hoon, Michelle Park; Co-Executive Producers, Suh Youngjoo, Moon Jae-sik, Cheong Kee-young, Kang Yeong-shin, Kim Kil-soo, Bryan Song, Il Hyung-cho, Kim Byung-ki; Co-Producer, Jo Seong-won; Director/Adaptation, Kim Jee-woon; Screenplay, Park Hoon-jung; Photography, Lee Mogae; Designer, Cho Hwa-sung; Costumes, Kwon Yoo-jin; Music, Mowg; Editor, Nam Na-young; Special Makeup Effects, Kwak Tae-yong; a Softbank Ventures Korea, Showbox/MediaPlex Inc. presentation of a Peppermint & Company production, in association with Siz Entertainment; South Korean, 2010; Dolby; Color; Not rated; 141 minutes; American release date: March 4, 2011. **CAST:** Lee Byung-hun (Kim Soo-hyun), Choi Min-sik (Kyung-chul), Oh San-ha (Ju-yeon), Chun Kook-haun (Capt. Jang), Chun Ho-jin (Detective Oh), Kim Yoon-seo (Se-yeon), Choi Moo-seong (Tae-ju), Kim In-seo (Se-jung)

Lee Byung-hun in *I Saw the Devil* © Magnet Pictures

THE DESERT OF FORBIDDEN ART (Cinema Guild) Producers/Directors/Screenplay, Amanda Pope, Tchavdar Georgiev; Photography, Alexander Dolgin, Gennadi Balitski; Music, Miriam Cutler; Editor, Tchavdar Georgiev; an A. Pope Prods. and Desert of Forbidden Art production, PBS/Independenlens/Films Transit/Cecartslink; Russian-American-Uzbekistan, 2010; Color; HD; Not rated; 80 minutes; American release date: March 11, 2011. Documentary on Uzbekistan's Nukus Museum; **WITH:** the voices of Ben Kingsley (Igor Savitsky), Ed Asner, Sally Field, Igor Paramonov (Artists); and Marinka Babanazarova, Olga Belenikina, John Bowlt, Sergei Efuni, Alla Efuni, Lidia Iovleva, Kalibek Kamalov, Alexei Kandisky, Stephen Kinzer, Irina Korovay, Jildasbek Kuttimuratov, Andrei Sarabianov, Alvina Schpade, Alexander Tereshenko, Lubov Truskova, Alexander Volkov, Maria Volkov, Valery Volkov, Militza Zemskaya

Igor Savitsky in *The Desert of Forbidden Art* © Cinema Guild

CLASH (Indomina Releasing) a.k.a. *Bay rong*; Producers, Jimmy Pham Nghiem, Johnny Tri Nguyen, Ngo Thanh Van; Director, Le Thanh Son; Screenplay, Johnny Tri Nguyen, Le Thahn Son, Ho Quang Hung; Photography, Dominic Pereira; Designer, La Quy Tung; Music, Christopher Wong; Editor, Ham Tran; a Chanh Phuong Films presentation of a Jimmy Pham Nghiem production; Vietnamese, 2009; Color; Rated R; 100 minutes; American release date: March 11, 2011. **CAST:** Johnny Tri Nguyen (Quan), Ngo Thanh Van (Trinh), Hieu Hien (Phong), Lam Minh Thang (Cang), Tran The Vinh (Hawk), Hoang Phuc (Long)

Johnny Tri Nguyen in *Clash* © Indomina Releasing

NOSTALGIA FOR THE LIGHT (Icarus) a.k.a. *Nostalgia de la luz*; Producer, Renate Sachse; Director/Screenplay, Patricio Guzmán; Photography, Katell Djian; Music, Miranda y Tobar; Editors, Patricio Guzmán, Emmanuelle Joly; a coproduction of Atacama Productions S.A.R.L. (France), Blinker Filmproduktion GmbH and WDR (Germany), Cronomedia Lda. Chile; French-German-Chilean; Dolby; Color; Not rated; 90 minutes; American release date: March 17, 2011. Documentary on the Atacama Desert and the astronomers who gather there, 10,000 feet above sea level; **WITH:** Gaspar Galaz, Lautaro Núñez, Luís Henríquez, Miguel, Victor González, Vicky Saaveda, Violeta Berrios, George Preston, Valentina Rodríguez

Nostalgia for the Light © Icarus Films

CRACKS (IFC Films) Producers, Julie Payne, Kwesi Dickson, Andrew Lowe, Rosalie Swedlin, Christine Vachon; Executive Producers, Ricardo García Arrojo, John Wells, Guy Collins, Stephen Margolis, Alain Goldman, Ridley Scott, Tony Scott; Co-Producers, Michael Costigan, Malcolm Reeve, Catherine Morisse, Charles Pugliese; Director, Jordan Scott; Screenplay, Ben Court, Caroline Ip, Jordan Scott; Based on the novel by Sheila Kohler; Photography, John Mathieson; Designer, Ben Scott; Costumes, Alison Byrne; Music, Javier Navarrete; Editor, Valerio Bonelli; Casting, Shaheen Baig; a Scott Free, Industry Entertainment, Killer Films/John Wells production, in association with HandMade Films Intl. and Future Films, in association with Légende and Studio Canal, with the participation of Bord Scannán na hÉireann/Irish Film Board of an Element Pictures (Ireland)

Cracks the Film (U.K.)/Antena 3 Films (Spain) coproduction of; Irish-British-Spanish, 2009; Dolby; Technicolor; Not rated; 107 minutes; American release date: March 18, 2011. **CAST:** Eva Green (Miss G), Juno Temple (Di Radfield), Maria Valverde (Fiamma), Imogen Poots (Poppy), Ellie Nunn (Lily), Adele McCann (Laurel), Zoë Carroll (Rosie), Clemmie Dugdale (Fuzzy), Sinéad Cusack (Miss Nieven), Helen Norton (Matron), Deirdre Donnelly (Miss Lacey), Barbara Adair (Miss Cairns), Alistair Rumble (Ferry Skipper), Kitty McLaughlin-Dunning (Small Dreg), Jonathan White (Shopkeeper)

Eva Green, Juno Temple, Imogen Poots, Ellie Nunn, Adele McCann, Zoë Carroll, Clemmie Dugdale in *Cracks* © IFC Films

THE GIFT TO STALIN (Aldongar) a.k.a. *Pokarok Stalinu*; Producer, Boris Cherdabayev; Director, Rustem Abdrashev; Screenplay, Pavel Finn; Photography, Khasan Kidiraliev; Designer, Alexander Rorokin; Music, Kuat Shildebayev; Editor, Sylvain Coutandin; an Aldongar production, in association with Tor Films, Kazakhfilm; Kazakhstan, 2008; Dolby; Color; Not rated; 95 minutes; American release date: March 18, 2011. **CAST:** Nurjman Ikhtimbayev (Kasym), Bakhtiar Khoja (Bulgabi), Ekaterina Rednikova (Vera/Verka), Dalen Shintemirov (Sashka/Sabyr), Waldemar Szczepaniak (Ezhik)

Dalen Shintemirov in *The Gift to Stalin* © Aldongar

THE BUTCHER, THE CHEF AND THE SWORDSMAN (China Lion Film Distribution) a.k.a. *Dao jiàn xiào*; Producers, Daniel Yu, Tang Xiru; Director, Wuershan; Screenplay, Zhang Jiajia, Tang Que, Ma Luoshan, Wuershan; Based on the short story *The Legend of the Kitchen Knife* by An Changhe; Photography, Michal Tywoniuk; Designer/Costumes, Hao Yi; Music, Gong Geer, Dead J. Miquia; Editor, Huang Zhe; a Fox Intl. Prods., Taihe Universal Film Investment Co., First

Cuts Features, Union Voole Technology Co., Zixuxuanyang Cultural Development Co., Bolong Investment Co. presentation; Hong Kong-Chinese-American; Dolby; Color; Rated PG-13; 95 minutes; American release date: March 18, 2011. **CAST:** Masanobu Andô (Apprentice), Kitty Zhang Yuqi (Madam Mei), You Benchang (Fat Tang), Liu Xiaoye (Chopper), Ashton Xu (Dugu Cheng), Senggerenqqin (Big Beard), Mi Dan (Chef), Xie Ning (Liu)

Masanobu Andô in *The Butcher, the Chef and the Swordsman* © China Lion

DESERT FLOWER (National Geographic) Producer, Peter Herrmann; Co-Producers, Benjamin Herrmann, Danny Krausz; Director/Screenplay, Sherry Hormann; based on the autobiographical novel by Waris Dirie; Photography, Ken Kelsch; Designer, Jamie Leonard; Costumes, Gabriele Binder; Music, Martin Todsharow; Editor, Clara Fabry; The Match Factory presentation of a Desert Flower Filmproductions production in coproduction with Dor Film, Majestic Filmproduktion, BSI Intl., Invest, Bac Films, Mr. Brown Entertainment, MTM West Film & Television, Bayerirscher Rundfunk, ARD/Degeto, with the participation of Backup Films; German-British-Austrian, 2009; Dolby; Color; Rated R; 120 minutes; American release date: March 18, 2011. **CAST:** Liya Kedebe (Waris Dirie), Sally Hawkins (Marylin), Craig Parkinson (Neil), Meera Syal (Pushpa Patel), Anthony Mackie (Harold Jackson), Juliet Stevenson (Lucinda), Timothy Spall (Terry Donaldson), Soraya Omar-Scego (Waris at 12), Teresa Churcher (Nurse Anne), Eckart Friz (Spike), Anna Hilgedieck (Tilda), Prashant Prabhakar (Kami), Matt Kaufman (Burger Bar Manager), Emma Kay (Immigration Officer), Nick Raio (Truck Driver), Robert Robalino (Café Owner), Roun Daher Aïnan (Waris' Mother), Osman Aden Dalieg (Waris' Father)

Liya Kedebe in *Desert Flower* © National Geographic

CATCH ME ... I'M IN LOVE (Star Cinema/Viva Films) Producers, Marizel Samson-Martinez, Vincent Del Rosario, Veronique Del Rosario-Corpus; Executive Producers, Charo Santos-Concio, Malou N. Santos, Vic Del Rosario Jr.; Director, Mae Cruz; Screenplay/Story, Mel Mendoza-Del Rosario; Photography, Manuel Teekhankee; Designer, Nancy Arcega; Music, Francis Concio; Editor, Marya Ignacio; Filipino; Color; Not rated; 106 minutes; American release date: March 23, 2011. **CAST:** Sarah Geronimo (Roan Sanchez), Gerald Anderson (Enrique "Erick" Rodriguez III), Christopher De Leon (President Enrique Rodriguez), Dawn Zulueta (First Lady Elena Rodriguez), Joey Marquez (Mr. Sanchez), Arlene Mulach (Mrs. Sanchez), Matteo Guidicelli (Vitto), Sam Pinto (Nicole Morales), Fred Payawan (PSG), Charee Pineda (Charms), Dino Imperial (Rojie), Janus Del Prado (Dan), Ketchup Eusebio (Jojo), Lito Legaspi (Mr. Morales), Alchris Galura (Paolo), Ian Russell Victor (Girlie), Roden Araneta (NGO Supervisor), Princess Manzon (Cara), Josef Elizalde (Erick's Friend), Erik Santos (Himself)

I TRAVEL BECAUSE I HAVE TO, I COME BACK BECAUSE I LOVE YOU (FiGa Films) a.k.a. *Viajo porque preciso, volto porque te amo*; Producers, Joao Vieira Jr., Daniela Capelato; Executive Producers, Livia de Melo, Nara Aragao; Directors/Screenplay, Marcelo Gomes, Karim Ainouz; Photography, Heloisa Passos; Music, Chambaril; Editor, Karen Harley; a Rec Produtores, Daniela Capelato, Gullane, Petrobras presentation; Brazilian, 2009; Dolby; Color; Super 8, DV, High 8-to-DCP; Not rated; 71 minutes; American release date: March 25, 2011. **CAST:** Irandhir Santos (Jose Renato)

KORKORO (Lorber Films) Producers/Music, Delphine Mantoulet, Tony Gatlif; Director/Screenplay, Tony Gatlif; Photography, Julien Hirsch; Designer, Brigitte Brassart; Costumes, Catherine Rigualt; Editor, Monique Dartonne; a Princes Prod. presentation in co-production with France 3 Cinéma, Rhône-Alpes Cinéma, with the participation of TPS Star, Fracne 3/CinéCinéma, Centre National de la Cinématographie; French, 2010; Dolby; Color; Not rated; 111 minutes; American release date: March 25, 2011. **CAST:** Marc Lavoine (Théodore Rosier), Marie-Josée Croze (Mademoiselle Lundi), James Thiérrée (Félix Taloche), Mathias Laliberté (Petit Claude), Carlo Brandt (Pierre Pentecôte), Rufus (Fernand), Arben Bajraktaraj (Darko), Georges Babluani (Kako), Iljir Selimoski (Chavo), Kevyn Diana (Zanko), Bojana Panic (Tina), Raisa Bielenberg (Puri Dai), Thomas Baumgartner (Tatane), Francis 'Csangalo' Mezei (Tchangalo), Tincuta-Anita Mezei (Marina), Calin-Alin Mezei (Calin), Lena Gorman (Mandra), Gabriel Goman (Calo), Frunza Goman (Cali), Narcissa Stanescu (Piripi), Jacques Sotty (Lucien), Josiane Carle (Mother Radet), Raphaël Simonet, Bernard Villanueva (Militiamen), Jade Teyssier (Jeanne Radet), Alain Besset (Emile Radet), Flavien Tassart (Pierre Lebel), Arno Feffer (Anatole Lebel), Mickaël Furnon, Léonard Bardotti (Villagers)

Marie-Josée Croze in *Korkoro* © Lorber Films

BAL (HONEY) (Olive Films) Producer/Director, Semih Kaplanoglu; Screenplay, Semih Kaplanoglu, Orçun Köksal; Photography, Baris Özbiçer; Art Director, Naz Erayda; Editors, Ayhan Ergürsel, Semih Kaplanoglu, Suzan Hande Güneri; a Kaplan Film production (Turkey)/Heimatfilm (Germany) production, in association with ZDF, Arte; Turkish-German, 2010; Dolby; Color; Not rated; 103 minutes; American release date: March 25, 2011. **CAST:** Bora Altas (Yusuf), Erdal Besikçioglu (Yakup, Father), Tülin Özen (Zehra, Mother), Ayse Altay, Alev Uçarer, Özkan Akcay

Erdal Besikçioglu, Bora Altas in *Bal (Honey)* © Olive Films

MIA AND THE MIGOO (GKids) a.k.a. *Mia et le Migou*; Producers, Jacques-Rémy Girerd, Matthew Modine, Eric Beckman, David Jesteadt; Executive Producer, Emmanuel Bernard; Director, Jacques-Rémy Girerd; Screenplay, Jacques-Remy Girerd, Antoine Lanclaux, Iouri Tcherenkov, Benoît Chieux; Photography, Benoit Razy; Music, Serge Besset; Editor, Herve Guichard; Graphic Design & Storyboards, Benoit Chieux; Head of Design, Gael Brisou; a Folimage, Enarmonia, Gertie-Colourland production; French-Italian, 2008; Dolby; Color; Rated PG; 92 minutes; American release date: March 25, 2011. **VOICE CAST:** John DiMaggio (Jekhide), Whoopi Goldberg (The Sorceress), Matthew Modine (Mr. Houston/ Godfrey), Wallace Shawn (The Migoo), James Woods (Jojo-la-Frite), Amanda Misquez (Mia), Vincent Agnello (Aldrin), Chris Jai Alex (Charlemagne), Jesse Corti (Pedro/Wilford), Marcus DeAnda (Cab Driver/Bus Driver), Andres De Vengoechea (Malakof), Ato Essandoh (Baklava), Hideo Kimura (Mizoguchi), Nancy Linari (Maggie, Jekhide's Mother/Operator), Pasha D. Lynchnikoff (Staravitch), Katilyn Maher, Ruby Modine, Stephanie Sheh (Girls on Bridge), Joaquin Mas (Pablo), Jason Palmer (Johnson/Red Haired Businessman), Vinnie Pena (Gun Shop Dealer), Erika Robledo (Large Angry Woman/Mia's Mother), Michael Sinterniklaas (Poker Buddy), Michael Sorich (Nenesse), Veronica Taylor (Juliette, Aldrin's Mother)

Mia and the Migoo © GKids

MISTS (RC Filmes) a.k.a. *Brumas*; Producer/Director/Photography/Editor, Ricardo Costa; Music, Manu Chao, Nuno Rebelo; Portuguese, 2003; Color; Not rated; 78 minutes; American release date: March 25, 2011. Documentary in which filmmaker Ricardo Costa tracks down the woman who was once his family's maid; **WITH:** Ricardo Costa, Maria José, Maria Velha, Maria Joaquina, Maria Bernardina, Dias Lourenço, Luis C. Peixoto.

ILLEGAL (Film Movement) Producers, Jacques-Henri Bronckart, Olivier Bronckart; Director/Screenplay, Olivier Masset-Depasse; Photography, Tommaso Fiorilli; Designers, Patrick Dechesne, Alain-Pascal Housiaux; Costumes, Magdalena Labuz; Music, André Dziezuk; Editor, Damien Keyeux; a Versus Prod. Production in association with Iris Prods., Dharamsala, Prime Time, RTBF; Belgian-French, 2010; Dolby; Color; Not rated; 95 minutes; American release date: March 25, 2011. **CAST:** Anne Coesens (Tania), Essé Lawson (Aïssa), Gabriela Perez (Maria), Alexandre Gontcharov (Ivan, 14 years), Christelle Cornil (Lieve), Olga Zhdanova (Zina), Tomasz Bialkowski (M. Nowak), Milo Masset-Depasse (Ivan, 6 years), Natalia Belokonskaya (Olga), Denis Dupont (Dimitri), Moktar Belletreche (Man on Bus), David Leclercq (Policemen at Station), Christelle Cornil (Lieve), Olivier Funcken (Guard), Angelo Dello Spedale (Security Agent), Fabienne Mainguet (Carole), Akemi Letelier (Eva), Olga Moiseeva (Russian Bimbo)

ONE HUNDRED MORNINGS (IndiePix) Producer, Katie Holly; Co-Producer, Louise Curran; Director/Screenplay, Conor Horgan; Photography, Suzie Lavelle; Designer, Lucy van Lonkhuyzen; Costumes, Debbie Millington; Music, Chris White; Editor, Frank Reid; Casting, Nick McGinley; a Catalyst Project presentation in association with Blinder Films; Irish, 2010; Color; Not rated; 85 minutes; American release date: March 25, 2011. **CAST:** Ciarán McMenamin (Jonathan), Alex Reid (Hannah), Rory Keenan (Mark), Kelly Campbell (Katie), Paul Ronan (Sgt. Lavelle), Robert O'Mahoney (Tim), Daniel Costello (Oil Tanker Driver), Stephen D'Arcy (Middle Class Man), Damien Dunne (Farmhand), Conor Horgan, Niall Martin (Village Guards), Tony McKenna (Garda), Noel O'Donovan (Farmer), Owen O'Gorman (Gang Leader)

LE QUATTRO VOLTE (THE FOUR TIMES) (Lorber) Producers, Marta Donzelli, Gregorio Paonessa, Susanne Marian, Philippe Bober, Gabriella Manfrè, Elda Guidinetti, Andres Pfaeffli; Director/Screenplay, Michelangelo Frammartino; Photography, Andrea Locatelli; Designer, Matthew Broussard; Costumes, Gabriella Maiolo; Editors, Benni Atria, Maurizio Grillo; a Vivo Film, Essential Filmproduktion, Invisible Film & Ventura Film co-production; Italian-German-Swiss, 2010; Dolby; Color; Not rated; 88 minutes; American Release date: March 30, 2011. **CAST:** Giuseppe Fuda (The Shepherd), Bruno Timpano, Nazareno Timpano (Coal Makers)

Le Quattro Volte © Lorber Films

SHAKTI (Vyjayanthi Movies) Producer, C. Ashwini Dutt; Director, Meher Ramesh; Screenplay, Satyanand; Photography, Sameer Reddy; Art Director, Anand Sai; Music, Mani Sharma; Editor, Martand K. Venaktesh; Indian; Color; Not rated; 165 minutes; American release date: April 1, 2011. **CAST:** N.T.R. Rao Junior (Rudra/Shakti), Prabhu (Mahadevaraya), Ileana (Aishwarya), Pooja Bedi (Rehna), Sonu Sood (Egyptian)

N.T.R. Rao Junior, Ileana in *Shakti* © Vyjayanthi Movies

RUBBER (Magnet) Producers, Gregory Bernard, Julien Berlan; Director/Screenplay/Photography/Editor, Quentin Dupieux; Designer, Pascale Ingrand; Costumes, Jamie Bresnan; Music, Gaspard Augé, Mr. Oizo; Special Effects, Tom Talmon, Valek X. Sykes, Barzolff 814, Milan Jancic, Marco Castilla; Casting, Donna Morong, Andy Henry; a Gregory Bernard presentation of a Realitism Films production with Elle Driver, Arte France Cinema, 1.85 Films, Backup Films, Sindika Dokolo, with the participation of Canal+, Arte France; French, 2010; Dolby; Color; DV-to-35mm; Rated R; 82 minutes; American release date: April 1, 2011. **CAST:** Stephen Spinella (Lt. Chad), Jack Plotnick (Accountant), Wings Hauser (Man in Wheelchair), Roxane Mesquida (Sheila), Ethan Cohn (Film Buff Ethan), Charley Koontz (Film Buff Charley), Daniel Quinn (Dad), Devin Brochu (Son), Hayley Holmes (Teenager Cindy), Haley Ramm (Teenager Fiona), Cecelia Antoinette (Woman), David Bowe (Mr. Hughes), Remy Thorne (Zach), Tara O'Brien (Cleaning Lady), Thomas Duffy (Cop Xavier), Pete Di Cecco (Cop Luke), James Parks (Cop Doug), Courtenay Kellen Taylor (Cop Denise), Blake Robbins (Cop Eric), Michael Ross (Truck Driver), Gaspard Augé (Hitchhiker), Pedro Winter (Tires Burner), Eloy Lara (Paramedic)

Rubber © Magnet Releasing

TO DIE LIKE A MAN (Strand) a.k.a. *Morrer Como um Homem*; Producer/Director, João Pedro Rodrigues; Screenplay, João Pedro Rodrigues, Rui Catalão, João Rui Guerra da Mata; Photography, Rui Poças; Designer, João Rui Geurra da Mata; Costumes, Patrícia Dória; Makeup, Sandra Pinto; Editors, Rui Mourão, João Pedro Rodrigues; a Rosa Filmes (Portugal)/Ad Vitam (France) production; Portuguese-French, 2009; Dolby; Color; Not rated; 133 minutes; American release date: April 8, 2011. **CAST:** Fernando Santos (Tonia), Alexander David (Rosário), Gonçalo Ferreira de Almeida (Maria Bakker), Chandra Malatitch (Zé Maria), Jenny Larrue (Jenny), Cindy Scrash (Irene), Fernando Gomes (Teixeira), Miguel Loureiro (Paula), André Murraças (Dr. Felgueiras), John Jesus Ramão (Mendes), Ivo Barroso (Cardoso), Francisco Peres (Plastic Surgeon), Carloto Cotta (Carlos), Jenny Larrue (Jenny), Gonçalo Mendes (Sergio), Amândio Coroado (Doctor at Hospital)

Fernando Santos in *To Die like a Man* © Strand Releasing

THANK YOU (UTV) Producers, Ronnie Screwvala, Twinkle Khanna; Executive Producer, Ajay Rai; Director, Anees Bazmee; Screenplay, Nisar Akhtar; Story, Anees Bazmee; Photography, Madhu Neelakantan; Designer, Ashok Lokare; Music, Pritam Chakraborty; Lyrics, Amitabh Bhattacharya, Kumaar, Ashish Pandit; Editor, Steven Bernard; Casting, Shahid Hasan; a Hari Om Productions, IBC Motion Pictures production; Indian; Color; Not rated; 125 minutes; American release date: April 8, 2011. **CAST:** Akshay Kumar (Kishan), Bobby Deol (Raj Malhotra), Sonam A. Kapoor (Sanjana Malhotra), Irrfan Khan (Vikram), Rimi Sen (Shivani), Suniel Shetty (Yogi), Celina Jaitley (Maya), Mallika Sherawat (Singer, "Razia" Number), Chahat Khanna (Kuku), Shillpi Sharma (Kammo), Vidya Balan (Kishan's Wife), Manveer Kharaud (Priti Sahota), Jaya Mathur (Kishan's Mom), Akhilendra Mishra (King), Janessa O'Hearn (Crying Banana Girl), Ranjeet (Maya's Dad)

Bobby Deol in *Thank You* © UTV

NO ERES TÚ, SOY YO (Lionsgate) Producer, Matthias Ehrenberg; Executive Producers, Matthias Ehrenberg, Ricardo Kleinbaum, Alejandro Springall; Director, Alejandro Springall; Screenplay, Luis Aura, Alejandro Spingall; Based on the screenplay by Juan Taratuto; Photography, Celiana Cárdenas; Designer, Salvador Parra; Costumes, Mónica Neumaier; Music, Christian Basso; Editor, Jorge Garcia; Casting, Manuel Teil; a Pantelion Films presentation of a Rio Negro, Barracua Films production; Mexican, 2010; Dolby; Color; Rated PG-13; 99 minutes; American release date: April 8, 2011. **CAST:** Eugenio Derbez (Javier), Alejandra Barros (María), Martina Garcia (Julia), Juan Ríos (Martin), Mónica Dionne (Dr. Del Villar), Alberto Estrella (Dr. Carlos), Shaula Vega (Gaby Rincón), Mauricio E. Galaz (Newlywed), Aarón Hernán (Horacio), Mauricio Herrera (Ramiro), Miguel Angel Herrerias (Gay Man), Ricardo Kleinbaum (Veterinarian), Gina Morett (Georgina), Regina Orozco (Indra), Yadira Orozco (Dog Owner), Héctor Ortega (Edmundo), Raquel Pankowsky (Real Estate Agent), Julian Sedgwick (Priest), Blanca Sánchez (Estela), Sharon Zundel (Laura)

Eugenio Derbez in *No Eres Tú, Soy Yo* © Lionsgate

AMERICAN: THE BILL HICKS STORY (Variance) Producers/Directors/Editors, Paul Thomas, Matt Harlock; Photography, Paul Thomas; Animators, Paul Thomas, Matt Harlock, Graham Smith; Music, Bill Hicks, Marblehead Johnson, Kevin Booth; a Jackamo Productions and Halflife Films production, presented in association with Gravitas Ventures; British, 2010; Color/Black and white; Not rated; 101 minutes; American release date: April 8, 2011. Documentary on satirist Bill Hicks; **WITH:** Kevin Booth, Steve Epstein, John Farneti, Lynn Hicks, Mary Hicks, Lynn Hicks, Steve Hicks, Andy Huggins, David Johndrow, James Ladmirault, Dwight Slade.

Bill Hicks in *American: The Bill Hicks Story* ©Variance Films

A SCREAMING MAN (Film Movement) a.k.a. *Un home qui crie*; Producer, Florence Stern; Director/Screenplay, Mahamat-Saleh Haroun; Photography, Laurent Brunet; Designer, Ledoux Madeona; Costumes, Celine Delaire; Music, Wasis Diop; Editor, Marie Hélène Dozo; a Pili Films/Goï-Goï Productions production; Chad-French-Belgian, 2010; Dolby; Color; Not rated; 92 minutes; American release date: April 13, 2011. **CAST:** Youssouf Djaoro (Adam), Diouc Koma (Abdel), Emil Abossolo M'bo (District Chief), Hadjé Fatimé N'goua (Mariam), Marius Yelolo (David), Djénéba Koné (Djeneba), Li Heling (Mrs. Wang), Rémadji Adèle Ngaradoumbaye (Souad), John Mbaiedoum (Etienne), Sylvain Mbaikoubou (The New Cook), Abdou Boukar (The Matire d'Hotel), Fatimé Nguenabaye (The Neighbor), Gérard Ganda Mayoumbila (Noncommissioned Officer), Mahmat Choukou, Tourgoudi Oumar (Soldiers at Roadblock), Hadre Dounia (Young Wounded Soldier)

Youssouf Djaoro in *A Screaming Man* © Film Movement

THE FIRST BEAUTIFUL THING (Palisades Tartan) a.k.a. *La prima cosa bella*; Producers, Fabrizio Donvito, Marco Cohen, Benedetto Habib; Director, Paolo Virzì; Screenplay, Francesco Bruni, Francesco Piccolo, Paolo Virzì; Photography, Nicola Pecorini; Designer, Tonino Zera; Costumes, Gabriella Pescucci; Music, Carlo Virzì; Editor, Simone Manetti; a Medusa Film, Motorino Amaranto, Indiana Production Company production; Italian, 2010; Dolby; Color; Not rated; 122 minutes; American release date: April 15, 2011. **CAST:** Valerio Mastrandrea (Bruno Michelucci – 2009), Micaela Ramazzotti (Anna Nigiotti in Michelucci, 1971-1981), Stefania Sandrelli (Anna Nigiotti in Michelucci – 2009), Claudia Pandolfi (Valeria Michelucci – 2009), Marco Messeri (Nesi), Fabrizia Sacchi (Sandra), Aurora Frasca (Valeria Michelucci – 1970), Giacomo Bibbiani (Bruno Michelucci – Baby), Giulia Burgalassi (Valeria Michelucci – Adolescent), Francesco Rapalino (Bruno – Adolescent), Sergio Albelli (Mario Michelucci), Isabella Cecchi (Zia Leda Nigiotti), Emanuele Barresi (Roberto Lenzi), Dario Ballantini (Avvocato Cenerini), Paolo Ruffini (Cristiano Cenerini), Fabrizio Brandi (Giancarlo – 2009), Jacopo Dini (Giancarlo – 1981), Michel Crestacci (Luciano Valelesi), Bobo Rondelli (Armando Mansani), Alessio Colombini (Anselmo Viani), Paolo Giommarelli (Count Augusto Paoletti), Alessia Innocenti (Contessa Paoletti), Giorgio Algranti (Deputy Mayor), Claudio Marmugi (Announcer, Miss Pancaldi, 1971), Alessandra Cantini (Elena Talini – 1981), Edoardo Ferrari (Andrea Baldacci – 1981), Domenico Cirianni (Andrea Baldacci – 2009), Elena Berardini (Giovane Pharmacist), Isabelle Adriani (Luciana Cenrini), Marcelina Ruocco (Giuliana Cenerini – 2009), Marco Risi (Dino Risi), Diego Salvadori (Aldo), Alessio Silipo (Sergio), Lucilla Serchi (Teacher), Giovanni Rindi (Marcello Mastroianni), Maria Pai Aricó (Chiara), Daniela Carrozzi (Cuoca)

ARMADILLO (Lorber) Producers, Ronnie Fridthjof, Sara Stockmann; Director/Screenplay, Janus Metz; Based on an idea by Kasper Torsting; Photography, Lars Skree; Music, Uno Helmersson; Editor, Per K. Kirkegaard; Danish, 2010; Dolby; Color; HD; Widescreen; Not rated; 100 minutes; American release date: April 15, 2010. Documentary follows a group of Danish soldiers stationed at Armadillo, an army base in the southern Afghan province of Helmand

Francesco Rapalino, Sergio Albelli, Micaela Ramazzotti, Giulia Burgalassi in *The First Beautiful Thing* © Palisades Tartan

THE WARRING STATES (China Lion Film Distribution) a.k.a. *Zhan Guo*; Producer, Lu Zheng; Director, Chen Jin; Screenplay, Shen Jian; Photography, Hyung-Ku Kim; a Beijing Starlit Movie and TV Culture Co. production; Chinese; Color; Not rated; 125 minutes; American release date: April 22, 2011. **CAST:** Sun Honglei (Sun Bin), Jing Tian (Tian Xi), Francis Ng (Pang Juan), Kim Hee-seon (Pang Fei), Kiichi Nakai (King of Qi), Jiang Wu (Tian Ji), Fang Zige (Emperor of Han), Feng Enhe (Emperor of Wei), Hao Hao (Yu Zi), Liao Jingsheng (Emperor of Lu), Ma Jingwu (Prime Minister of Qi), Sun Hao (Pei Feng), Wu Jun (Jia Bo)

Kim Hee-seon, Sun Honglei in *The Warring States* © China Lion

LEGEND OF THE FIST: THE RETURN OF CHEN ZHEN (Variance) a.k.a. *Jingwu fengyun: Chen Zhen*; Producers, Gordon Chan, Andrew Lau; Executive Producers, John Chong, Zhang Zhao, Zhang Guoli; Director, Andrew Lau; Screenplay, Cheung Chi-sing, Gordon Chan, Lui Koon-nam, Frankie Tam; Photography, Andrew Lau, Ng Man-ching; Art Director, Eric Lam; Costumes, Dora Ng; Music, Chan Kwong-wing; Editor, Azrael Chung; Action Director, Donnie Yen; a Media Asia Films, Enlight Pictures, Shanghai Film Media Asia presentation of a Basic Pictures production; Chinese-Hong Kong, 2010; Color/Black and white; Widescreen; Rated R; 106 minutes; American release date: April 22, 2011. **CAST:** Donnie Yen (Chen Zhen/"Qi Tianyuan"), Shu Qi (Kiki/Fang Qing/Yumi Yamaguchi), Anthony Wong (Liu Yutian), Huang Bo (Huang Haolong), Huo Si-yan (Weiwei), Zhou Yang (Qi Zhishan), Kurata Yasuaki (Chikaraishi's Father), Karl Dominik (Vincent), Ryu Kohata (Col. Chikaraishi), Chen Jiajia (Huang Yun/Kumoko), Kohata Ryuichi (Col. Takeshi Chikaraishi), Shawn Yue (General Zeng), Ma Yue (General Zhuo), Ma Su (General Zhou's Wife), Zhang Songwen (Wenzai)

Donnie Yen in *Legend of the Fist* © Variance Films

Sean Rogerson in *Grave Encounters* © Tribeca Film

DUM MAARO DUM (Fox Star Studios) Producer, Ramesh Sippy; Director, Rohan Sippy; Screenplay, Shridhar Raghavan, Purva Naresh; Photography, Amit Roy; Music, Pritam; Lyrics, Anand Bakshi, Jaideep Sahni; Editor, Aarif Sheikh; a Ramesh Sippy Entertainment production; Indian; Color; Rated R; 130 minutes; American release date: April 22, 2011. **CAST:** Abhishek Bachchan (Vishnu Kamath), Rana Daggubati (DJ Joki), Bipasha Basu (Zoe), Aditya Pancholi (Lorsa Biscuita), Prateik Babbar (Lorry), Anaitha Nair (Tani), Govind Namedo (Inspector Rane), Harry Key (DJ Thomas), Bugs Bhargava Krishna (CM Ponda), Muzammil (Mercy), Mariah Pucu Gantois Gomes (Rozana), Hussain Skeikh (Silest), Gulshan Devaiah (Ricky), J. Brandon Hill (Viktor), Emma Brown (Natalya), Megh Varn Pant (Pedro), Ajay Rohilla (Tourism Minister), Deepika Padukone (Singer)

CHILDREN OF HIROSHIMA (BAMcinématek) a.k.a. *Gembaku no ko*; Producer, Kozaburo Yoshimura; Director/Screenplay, Kaneto Shindô; Photography, Takeo Itchi; Art Director, Takashi Marumo; Music, Akira Ifukube; Editor, Zenju Imaizumi; Presented by Benicio Del Toro; Japanese, 1952; Black and white; Not rated; 97 minutes; American release date: April 22, 2011. **CAST:** Nobuko Otowa (Takako Ishikawa), Osamu Takizawa (Iwakichi), Niwa Saito (Natsue Morikawa), Chikako Hosokawa (Setsu), Masao Shimizu (Toshiaki), Yuriko Hanabusa (Oine), Tanie Kitabayashi (Otoyo), Tsutomu Shimomoto (Natsue's Husband)

Deepika Padukone in *Dum Maaro Dum* © Fox Star Studios

Children of Hiroshima © BAMcinémtek

GRAVE ENCOUNTERS (Tribeca Film) Producer, Shawn Angelski; Directors/ Screenplay/ Editors/Visual Effects, The Vicious Brothers; Photography, Tony Mirza; Designer, Paul McCulloch; Costumes, Natalie Simon; Music, Quynne Craddock; a Tribeca Film in association with American Express presentation of a Digital Interference and Twin Engine Films production in association with Darclight; Canadian; Dolby; Color; HD; Not rated; 92 minutes; American release date: April 22, 2011. **CAST:** Sean Rogerson (Lance Preston), Juan Riedinger (Matt White), Ashleigh Gryzko (Sasha Parker), Mackenzie Gray (Houston Gray), Arthur Corber (Dr. Friedkin), Michele Cummins (Ghost), Luis Javier (Gardener), Shawn Macdonald (Morgan Turner), Merwin Mondesir (T.C. Gibson), Bob Rathie (Kenny Sandivol), Ben Wilkinson (Jerry Hartfield), Eva Gifford (Demon Girl)

ZOKKOMON (UTV Communications) Executive Producer, Srila Chatterjee; Director, Satyajit Bhatkal; Screenplay, Lancy Fernandes, Svati Chakravarty Bhatkal, Satyajit Bhatkal; Dialogue, Divy Nidhi Sharma; Photography, Keshav Prakash; Designer, Fali Unwalla; Costumes, Himani Dehlvi; Music, Shankar Mahadevan, Ehsaan Noorani, Loy Mendonca; Lyrics, Javed Akhtar; Choreographers, Raju Sundaram, Shiamak Davar; Editor, Suresh Pai; Casting, Honey Trehan; Co-Produced by Walt Disney Pictures; Presented in association with Highlight Pictures; Indian; Dolby; Panavision; Color; Rated PG; 108 minutes; American release date: April 22, 2011. **CAST:** Darsheel Safary (Kunal/Zokkomon), Anupam Kher (Deshraj), Manjari Fadnis (Kittu), Gargi Datar (Rani), Jai Vyas (Arju), Jayant Gadekar (Master), Tinnu Anand (Shantaram), Sheeba Chaddha (Rajrani)

Darsheel Safary in *Zokkomon* © UTV

DEEP GOLD (Bigfoot Entertainment) Producer, Les Nordhauser; Executive Producer, Kacy Andrews; Director, Michael Gleissner; Screenplay, Michael Gleissner, Frederick Bailey; Photography, Rick Robinson; Designer, John Sabato; Costumes, Oi Mang Wai; Music, Erik Godal; Editors, Kristoffer Villarino, Dave Divehall; a New Cebu Films production; Filipino; Color; 3D; Rated PG-13; 100 minutes; American release date: April 22, 2011. **CAST:** Bebe Pham (Amy Sanchez), Jaymee Ong (Jess Sanchez), Michael Gleissner (Benny Simpson), Laury Prudent (Lulu), Amelia Jackson-Gray (Claire Simpson), Kersten Hui (Chang), Lorenzo Ramos (Ignacio Bautista), Richard Magarey (Frank), Kelsey Adams (Young Amy), Jose Ch. Alvarez (Librarian), Marketa Belonoha (Franziska), Leigh Carcel (Fiona Rabanes), Cutie Del Mar (Rachel Tejano), Raul Del Mar (Mr. Veloso), Ceasar Ditan (Police Chief), Viktoria Hedberg (Claire Simpson), Grace Hutchings (Young Jess), Mon Lacsamana (Henchman Fred), Ian Lim (Sgt. Gabriel), Homer Medici (Bartender), Joe Mercado (Gen. Cordova), John Lawrence Mercado (Col. Diaz), Jude Moore (Frank Townsend), Lj Pineda (Maria), Jack Prinya (Tony dela Cruz), Miguel Ramirez (Henchman Mike), Allan Tercena (Henchman Allan), Joel Torre (Ranulfo Sanchez), Senyo Torres (Mailman) , Thomas Watter (Hans), Lorenzo Ramos (Ignacio Bautista)

Bebe Pham in *Deep Gold* © Bigfoot Entertainment

THE ARBOR (Strand) Producer, Tracy O'Riordan; Executive Producer, Michael Morris; Director/Screenplay, Clio Barnard; Photography, Ole Birkeland; Designer, Matthew Button; Costumes, Matt Price; Music, Harry Escott, Molly Nyman; Editors, Nick Fenton, Daniel Goddard; an Artangel Trust and UK Film Council production in association with Jerwood Charitable Foundation, Arts Council England, More 4; British; Color; Not rated; 90 minutes; American release date: April 27, 2011. Semi-documentary on British playwright Andrea Dunbar as seen through the eyes of her daughter; **WITH:** Christine Bottomley (Lisa), Neil Dudgeon (Steve), Robert Emms (David Dunbar), Natalie Gavin (Andrea Dunbar), Manjinder Virk (Lorraine), Jimi Mistry (Yousaf), Kate Rutter (The Mother)

Jimi Mistry, Natalie Gavin in *The Arbor* © Strand Releasing

THE ROBBER (Kino) a.k.a. *Der Räuber*; Producers, Nikolaus Geyrhalter, Markus Glaser, Michael Kitzberger, Wolfgang Widerhofer, Peter Heilrath; Director, Benjamin Heisenberg; Screenplay, Benjamin Heisenberg, Martin Prinz; Based on the novel by Martin Prinz; Photography, Reinhold Vorschneider; Designer, Renate Schmaderer; Costumes, Stephanie Riess; Music, Lorenz Dangel; Editors, Andrea Wagner, Benjamin Heisenberg; a Nikolaus Geyrhlater Filmproduktion (Austria)/Peter Heilrath Filmproduktion (Germany); Austrian-German, 2010; Dolby; Widescreen; Color; Not rated; 97 minutes; American release date: April 29, 2011. **CAST:** Andreas Lust (Johann Rettenberger), Franziska Weisz (Erika), Markus Schleinzer (Probation Officer), Roman Kettner (Hostel Clerk), Tabea Werich (Young Girl in Supermarket), Hannelore Klauber-Laursen (Bank Cashier), Nina Steiner (Labour Exchange Attendant), Josef Romstorffer (Erika's Colleague), Wolfgang Petrik, Florian Wotruba (Erika's Clients), Johannes Handler (Physiotherapist), Katharina Hülle (Sports Doctor), Tony Nagy (Shoe Salesman), Michaela Christl (Kidnapped Woman), Georg Mlynek (Jogger), Alexander Fennon (Stolen Car Owner), Alex Scheurer, Friedrich Stindl (Strong-Room Employees), Walter Huber (Chasier), Leopold Böhm (Treasurer with weak Attack), Gerda Drabek (Switchboard Operartor without Key), Marcus Bauer (Man at Cash Dispenser), Hannes Ipirotis, Robert Müllner, Christian Buchmayr (Police Unit), Martin Prinz (Leading Marathon Runner), Jürgen Köllner (Nurse), Karin Köllner (First Aid Attendant), Michael Steinbrecher (Fireman), Johann Bednar (Commissioner Lukac), Max Edelbacher (Commissioner Seidl), Michael Welz (Commissioner Welz), Erwin Reichel (Policeman in the Woods), Peter Vilnai (Older Man), Bernd-Christian Althoff, Swintha Gersthofer (Man and Woman at Roadside Parking)

Andreas Lust in *The Robber* © Kino Intl.

RAMMBOCK: BERLIN UNDEAD (The Collective) Producer, Sigrid Hoerner; Director, Marvin Kren; Screenplay, Benjamin Hessler; Photography, Moritz Schultheiß; Designer, Ulrich Frommhold; Music, Marco Dreckkötter, Stefan Will; Costumes, Jennifer Mäurer; Editor, Silke Olthoff; Makeup, Susanne Knebel, Stefan von Essen; a Moneypenny Filmproduktion production; German-Austrian, 2010; Dolby; Color; Rated R; 60 minutes; American release date: May 4, 2011. **CAST:** Michael Fuith (Michael), Anka Graczyk (Gabi), Sebastian Achilles (Kai), Carsten Behrendt (Manni), Melanie Berke (Ina Müller), Emily Cox (Anita), Harald Geil (Thorsten), Jörn Hentschel (Dominik), Brigitte Kren (Frau Bramkamp), Steffen Münster (Klaus), Katelijene Philips-Lebon (Heike), Kaninchen Polly (Flüfli), Katharine Rivilis (Semra), Andreas Schröders (Ulf), Theo Trebs (Harper), Ingrid Beerbaum (Voice of TV Host), Eckehard Hoffmann (Police Spokesman), Arno Kölker (Crafstman), Wolfgang Stegemann (Police Officer), Sabrina Caramanna, Glen Curtis, Jean-Marc Lebon, Nenad Lucic, Florentine Schara, Birgit Smolka, Matthew Hashemian Thomas, Margrit Traupe, Manuel Völlink (Zombies)

Rammbock: Berlin Undead © The Collective

OCTUBRE (New Yorker) a.k.a. *October*; Producers/Directors/Screenplay, Daniel Vega, Diego Vega; Photography, Fergan Chávez-Ferrer; Designer, Guillermo Palacios Pomareda; Music, Oscar Camacho; Editor, Gianfranco Annichini; a Maretazo Cine presentation, in association with Sue Cinema, Comunicacion Fractal; Peruvian-Venezuelan-Spanish, 2010; Dolby; Cinemascope; Deluxe color; Not rated; 83 minutes; American release date: May 6, 2011. **CAST:** Bruno Odar (Clemente), Gabriela Velásquez (Sofía), Carlo Gassols (Don Fico), María Carbajal (Juanita), Sheryl Sánchez Mesco (Milagritos, Baby), Víctor Prada (Julián Gómez), Sofía Palacios (Sabrina), Norma Francisca Villarreal (Rosa), Humberta Trujillo (Julia)

Bruce Odar in *Octubre* © New Yorker Films

CATERPILLAR (Lorber) a.k.a. *Kyatapirā*; Producer/Director, Koji Wakamatsu; Screenplay, Hisako Kurosawa, Deru Deguchi; Photography, Tomohiko Tsuji, Yoshihisa Toda; Art Director, Hiromi Nozawa; Costumes, Masae Miyamoto; Music, Sally Kubota, Yumi Okada; Editor, Shuichi Kakesu; Special Makeup Supervisor, Akiteru Nakada; a Wakamatsu Prod. Inc. and Skhole Corp. production; Japanese, 2010; Dolby; Color; DV-to-35mm; Not rated; 85 minutes; American release date: May 6, 2011. **CAST:** Shinobu Terajima (Shigeko Kurokawa), Shima Onishi (Kyuzo Kurokawa), Ken Yoshizawa (Kenzo Kurokawa), Keigo Kasuya (Tadashi Kurokawa), Emi Masuda (Chiyo Kurokawa), Sabu Kawahara (The Village Chief), Maki Ishikawa (Village Chief's Wife), Gô Jibiki, Arata (Military Officers), Katsuyuki Shinohara (Kuma), Daisuke Iijima (The Headquarters Chief), Ichirô Ogura (Radio Announcer), Sanshirô Kobayashi, Takaaki Kaneko (Village Men), Maria Abe, Mariko Terada, Yasuyo Shiba (Chinese Women), Ryo Mukuta (Japanese Soldier), Taneko (Yayoi), Naoko Orikasa (Toshiko)

Shinobu Terajima in *Caterpillar* © Lorber Films

HOBO WITH A SHOTGUN (Magnet) Producers, Rob Cotterill, Niv Fichman, Frank Siracusa; Executive Producers, Mark Slone, Victor Loewy; Director/Editor, Jason Eisener; Screenplay, John Davies; Photography, Karim Hussain; Designer, Ewen Dickson; Costumes, Sarah Dunsworth; Music, Darius Hobert, Adam T. Burke, Russ Howard III; Casting, Deirdre Bowen, Sheila Lane; an Alliance Films presentation with the participation of Telefilm Canada of a Film Nova Scotia, Rhombus Media, Whizbang Films, Yer Dead Production; Canadian; Dolby; Technicolor; Not Rated; 86 minutes; American release date: May 6, 2011. **CAST:** Rutger Hauer (Hobo), Gregory Smith (Slick), Brian Downey (Drake), Nick Bateman (Ivan/Rip), Robb Wells (Logan), Pasha Ebrahimi (Bumfight Filmmaker), Drew O'Hara (Otis), Molly Dunsworth (Abby), Jeremy Akerman (Chief of Police), Andre Haines (Large Man), Agnes Laan (Prostitute), Duane Patterson (Pimp), Brian Jamieson (Santa), Tim Dunn (Store Clerk), Glen Matthews (Gang Leader), Zach Tovey, Zander Rosborough (Gang Members), George Stroumboulopoulos (TV Host), Mark Owen (Coke Lord), David Brunt (Dirty Cop), Scott Vrooman (Rookie Cop), Juanita Peters (Doctor #1), Peter Simas (Grinder), John Awoods (Doctor with Gun), Scott Owen (Civilian)

Gregory Smith, Rutger Hauer in *Hobo with a Shotgun* © Magnet Releasing

BATTLE OF THE BRIDES (Saiga Films) a.k.a. *Dai Chien*; Producers, Pham Viet Anh Khoa, Ngoc Hiep; Executive Producers, Ngo Thi Bich Hien, Pham Viet Anh Khoa, Nguyen Quang Hai; Director: Victor Vu; Screenplay, Victor Vu, Hong Phuc; Photography, K'Linh Nguyen; Designer, Jose Mari Pamintuan; Music, Pham Huu Tam, Le Xuan Vu; Editor, Nguyen Vi Bao; Casting, Minh Thuan; a Saiga Films and Star Media Group presentation of a Saga Films and Vietnam Studio production, in association with Galaxy Studios, Saigon Movies Media, Phuong Nam Phim and HK Films; Vietnamese; Color; Not rated; 100 minutes; American release date: May 6, 2011. **CAST:** Ngoc Dipe (Linh), Huy Khanh (Thai), Ngan Khanh (Trang), Le Khanh (Quyen), Van Trang (Mai Chau), Phi Thanh Van (Phuong)

Ngoc Diep, Huy Khanh in *Battle of the Brides* © Saiga Films

HAUNTED – 3D (DAR Motion Pictures/BVG) Producers, Vikram Bhatt, Arun Rangachari; Director, Vikram Bhatt; Story, Amin Hajee; Photography, Praveen Bhatt; Music, Chirantan Bhatt; Editor, Kuldeep Mehan; an ASA Production & Enterprises Pvt. Ltd. production; Indian; Dolby; Color; 3D; Not rated; 143 minutes; American release date: May 6, 2011. **CAST:** Mahaakshay Chakraborty (Rehan), Twinkle Bajpai (Meera), Sagar Saikia (Rehan's Father), Achint Kaur (Margaret Malini), Arif Zakaria (Prof. Iyer), Krishna Bhatt (Stevens), Prachi Shah (Mrs. Stevens)

Twinkle Bajpai in *Haunted – 3D* © DAR Motion Pictures

THE TOPP TWINS: UNTOUCHABLE GIRLS (Argot Pictures) Producer, Arani Cuthbert; Director, Leanne Pooley; Photography, Wayne Vinten, Leon Narbey; Music, Lynda Topp, Jools Topp; Editor, Tim Woodhouse; a Diva Films production in association with the New Zealand Film Commission, NZ on Air and Sweeney Vestry; New Zealand, 2009; Dolby; Color; Not rated; 84 minutes; American release date: May 13, 2011. Documentary on comical lesbian singers Lynda and Jools Topp; **WITH:** Jools Topp, Lynda Topp, Billy Bragg, John Clarke, Paul Horan, Charmaine Pountney, Mereana Pittman, Helen Clark, Mark Trevorrow, Don McGlashan, Jean Topp, Peter Topp, Bruce Topp

Lynda Topp, Jools Topp in *The Topp Twins* © Argot Pictures

NEDS (Tribeca Film) Producer, Alain de la Mata, Olivier Delbosc, Marc Missonnier; Executive Producers, Peter Carlton, Carole Sheridan, Brahim Chioua; Co-Producers, Conchita Airoldi, Peter Mullan, Lucinda Van Rie; Director/Screenplay, Peter Mullan; Photography, Roman Osin; Music, Craig Armstrong; Editor, Colin Monie; a Tribeca Film in partnership with American Express presentation of a Film 4, UK Film Council, Scottish Screen and Wild Bunch of a Bluelight, Fidelite Films, Studio Urania production; British-French-Italian, 2010; Dolby; Color; Not rated; 124 minutes; American release date: May 13, 2011. **CAST:** Louise Goodall (Theresa McGill), Gregg Forrest (John McGill, aged 10), Conor McCarron (John McGill, aged 14), Joe Szula (Benny McGill), Gary Miligan (Canta), Richard Mack (Gerr), Christopher Wallace (Wee T), Greg McCreadie (Tora), John Joe Hay (Fergie), Paul Smith (Keyman), Peter Mullan (Mr. McGill), Marianna Palka (Aunt Beth), Mhairi Anderson (Elizabeth McGill), Lee Fanning (Minty), Gary Lewis (Mr. Russell), Steven Robertson (Mr. Bonetti), David McKay (Mr. Holmes), Linda Cuthbert (Mrs. Matheson), Martin Bell (Julian), Joe Cassidy (Janitor), Alex Donald (Mr. Halligan), Paul Donnelly (Mr. Hendry), Robert Findlay (Kelly), John Forrest (McCloskey Boy), Claire Gordon (Louise), Zoe Halliday (Mandy), Chelsey Hanratty (Eileen), Stephen McCole (Mr. McLeod), Marcus Nash (Patrick), Victoria Rose (Carole), Douglas Russell (PC Connelly), Ross Weston (Danny), Ross Greig (Fifey), Wendy Crosby (Mrs. Graham), Stefanie Szula (Linda), Scott Ingram (Casper), Sara MacCallum (Shelagh), Sam Hayman (Jesus), Ryan Walker (Sparra), Peter Lochburn (Headmaster), Leigh Biagi (Mrs. Cassidy), Laurie Ventury (Mr. Gallagher), Khai Nugent (Tam), Kat Murphy (Claire), Jamie Campbell (Desk Sergeant), Gordon Brown (Game Keeper), Gary Hollywood (PC Mark), Frank Miller (Mr. Maloney), Craig Kerr (Rebel), Cameron Fulton (Crystal)

John Joe Hay, Lee Fanning, Joe Szula in *Neds* © Tribeca Film

THE HIGH COST OF LIVING (Tribeca) Producers, Kimberly Berlin, Susan Schneir; Executive Producers, Heidi Levitt, Walter Klymkiw; Director/ Screenplay, Deborah Chow; Photography, Claudine Sauvé; Designer, Susan MacQuarrie; Costumes, Annie Dufort; Music, Normand Corbeil; Editors, Jonathan Alberts, Benjamin Duffield; Casting, Murielle La Ferrière, Claude Brunet, Heidi Levitt; a Filmoption International presentation a Suki Films production; Canadian, 2010; Color; DV; rated; 92 minutes; American release date: May 13, 2011. **CAST:** Zach Braff (Henry Welles), Isabelle Blais (Nathalie), Patrick Labbé (Michel), Aimee Lee (Wai Lin), Julian Lo (Johnny), Pierre Gendron (Det. Lambert), Sean Lu (Kenny), Anick Lemay (Julie), Nicole Braber (Lille), Graham Cuthbertson (Ian), Tony Robinow (Dr. Rosen), Kyle Switzer (Eli), Mylène Savoie (Anna), Paula Jean Hixson (Olivia), Joujou Turenne, Susan Bain (Nurses), Ian Finlay (Paul), Shan Chetty (Martin), Anik Matern (Urban Wife), Victor Andres Trelles Turgeon (Student), Paul-Antoine Taillefer (Medical Resident), Karine Lavergne (Pascale), Mathew Mackay (Gavin), Patrick Costello (Hipster), Nicole Jones (Isabelle), Qamar Abbas (New Father), Valérie Ouimet-Chiriaeff (Sarah), William Phan (Teenage Boy), Richard Robitaille (Urban Bartender), Robert Higden (Urban Husband)

Isabelle Blais, Zach Braff in *The High Cost of Living* © Tribeca Film

L'AMOUR FOU (Sundance Selects) Producers, Kristina Larsen, Hugues Charbonneau; Director, Pierre Thoretton; Screenplay, Pierre Thoretton, Eve Guillou; Photography, Léo Hinstin; Designer, Olivier Guerbois; Music, Côme Aguilar; Editor, Dominique Auvray; a co-production of Les Films du Lendemain, Les Films de Pierre, France 3 Cinéma, with the participation of Canal+ and France Télévisions; French; Dolby; Color; Not rated; 103 minutes; American release date: May 13, 2011. Documentary on French designer Yves Saint Laurent's valuable art collection and his partner Pierre Bergé's decision to auction it off after his lover's death in 2008; **WITH:** Pierre Bergé, Betty Catroux, Loulou De La Falaise, Jack Lang

TRUE LEGEND (Indomina) a.k.a. *Su Qi-Er*; Producers, Bill Kong, Cary Cheng, Wang Tianyun, Xu Jianhai; Executive Producers, Ren Zhonglun, Zhang Zhenyan, Bill Kong, Zhang Qiang; Director, Yuen Woo-ping; Screenplay, Christine To; Photography, Zhao Xiaoding; Designer, Huo Tingxiao; Costumes, Yee Chung Man; Music, Shigeru Umebayashi; Editor, Wenders Li; Action Choreographers, Yuen Cheung Yan, Yuen Shun Yi, Ling Chi Wah; a Focus Features Intl., Grand Plentiful Holdings Group Ltd., Shanghai Film Group, Beijing New Times Film Culture Development Co. Ltd. presentation; Chinese, 2010; Dolby; Widescreen; Color; 3D sequences; Rated R; 116 minutes; American release date: May 13, 2011. **CAST:** Vincent Zhao (Gen. Su Can/Su Qi-Er), Zhou Xun (Ying), Andy On (Yuan), Guo Xiaodong (Ma Qingfeng), Jay Chou (God of Wushu/Drunken God), Michelle Yeoh (Sister Yu), David Carradine (Anton), Xiaogang Feng (Pickpocket), Luxia Jiang (Iron Maiden), Chia Hui Liu (Bearded Man), Leung Ka-yan (Su Wan-kun), Genghong Liu (Iron Lad), Le Cung (Militia Leader), Jacky Heung (General), Conan Stevens (Molotov)

David Carradine in *True Legend* © Indomina

A SERBIAN FILM (Invincible Pictures) a.k.a. *Srpski Film*; Producer/Director, Srdjan Spasojevic; Screenplay, Aleksandar Radivojevic, Srdjan Spasojevic; Photography, Nemanja Jovanov; Designer, Nemanja Petrovic; Costumes, Jasmina Sanader; Music, Sky Wikluh; Editor, Darko Simic; a Contrafilm production; Serbian, 2010; Dolby; Widescreen; Color; Rated NC-17; 99 minutes; American release date: May 13, 2011. **CAST:** Srdjan Todorovic (Milos), Sergej Trifunovic (Vukmir), Jelena Gavrilovic (Marija), Katarina Zutic (Lejla), Slobodan Bestic (Marko), Ana Sakic (Jeca's Mother), Lena Bogdanovic (Doctor), Luka Mijatovic (Stefan), Andjela Nenadovic (Jeca), Nenad Herakovic, Carni Djeric (Guards), Miodrag Krcmarik (Rasa), Lidija Pletl (Jeca's Grandmother), Tanja Divnic (Teacher), Marina Savic (Prostitute), Natasa Miljus (Woman giving Birth)

Jelena Gavrilovic, Srdjan Todorovic in *A Serbian Film* © Invincible Pictures

Yves Saint Laurent in *L'amour Fou* © Sundance Selects

SAVIORS IN THE NIGHT (Menemsha) a.k.a. *Unter Bauern*; Producers, Joachim von Mengershausen, Karl Baumgartner, Werner Wirsing, Pascal Judelewicz; Director, Ludi Boeken; Screenplay, Otto Jägersberg, Imo Moszkowicz, Heidrun Schleef; Based on the book *Retter in der Nacht (Savior in the Night)* by Marga Spiegel; Photography, Dani Schneor; Art Director, Agnette Schlößer; Costumes, Elisabeth Kraus; Music, Martin Meissonnier, Max Raabe; Editor, Suzanne Fenn; Casting, Sabine Schwedhelm; a FilmForm Koln, Pandora Filmproduktion, 3L Filmproduktion (Germany)/Acajou Films (France) production; German-French, 2009; Dolby; Color; Not rated; 100 minutes; American release date: May 13, 2011. **CAST:** Veronica Ferres (Marga Spiegel), Armin Rohde (Siegmund "Menne" Spiegel), Lia Hoensbroech (Anni Aschoff), Martin Horn (Heinrich Aschoff), Margarita Broich (Frau Aschoff), Luisa Mix (Karin Spiegel), Tjard Krusius (Emmerich Aschoff), Kilian Schüler (Florian Aschoff), Marlon Kittel (Klemens Aschoff), Veit Stübner (Pentrop), Daniel Flieger (Erich Reimann), Nicole Unger (Josefa Schwester), Anna Ehrichlandwehr (Großmutter Aschoff), Smadi Wolfman (Frau Albermann), Lina Beckmann (Paula Wacker), Dennis Genske (Foreign Worker Stan), Melanie Reichert (Martha Schwester), Thierry Redler (Foreign Worker Robert), Christiane Niehoff (Frau Dirczus), Patrice Valota (Foreign Worker Witold), Daniela Reichert (Maria Schwester), Heinrich Pachl (Silkenböhmer), Karl Kranzkowski (Father Reimann), Werner Bussmann (Sgt. Nölte), Patrick Edelmann (Soldier Willy), Jörn Kitzelhöfer (Soldier Hecker), Manuel Kern (Young Menne). Jens Görman (Young Hubert), Julian Winter (Heinrich), Sebastian Doeker (Young Hermann)

Lia Hoensbroech, Luisa Mix, Veronica Ferres in *Saviors in the Night*
© Menemsha Films

LOVE U … MR. KALAKAAR! (Rajshri) Producers, Kamal Kumar Barjatya, Rajkumar Barjatya, Ajit Kumar Barjatya; Director/Screenplay, S. Manasvi; Photography, Saurabh Vishwkarma; Music, Sandesh Shandilya; Lyrics, Manoj Muntashir; Editor, Navnita Sen Datta; Rajshri Productions; Indian; Color; Not rated; 155 minutes; American release date: May 13, 2011. **CAST:** Tusshar (Sahil Rastogi), Amrita Rao (Ritu D. Diwan), Ram Kapoor (Deshraj Diwan), Madhoo (Ritu's Aunt), Kiran Kumar (Jayant Singh Chauhan), Prashant Ranyal (Aman), Prem Chopra (Ritu's Grandfather), Snigdha Akolkar (Charu), Jai Kalra (Manohar), Yateen Karyekar (Israni), Kunal Kumar (Hiten)

CHILDREN OF GOD (TLA Releasing) Producers, Trevite Willis, Richard LeMay, Kareem Mortimer; Executive Producer, Jay Gotlieb; Director/Screenplay, Kareem Mortimer; Photography, Ian Bloom; Designer, Margot Bethel; Costumes, Jamillah Moss; Music, Nathan Matthew David; Editor, Maria Cataldo; Casting, Toni Cusumano; a Mercury Rising Media in association with Southern Fried Filmworks presentation; Bahamas, 2010; Color; HD; Not rated; 99 minutes; American release date: May 20, 2011. **CAST:** Johnny Ferro (Johnny Roberts), Sylvia Adams (Grammy Rose), Van Brown (Rev. Clyde Ritchie), Aijalon Coley (Omar Mackey), Mark Ford (Ralph Mackey), Jay Lance Gotlieb (Angry Driver), Margaret Laurena Kemp (Lena Mackaey), Stephen Tyrone Williams (Romeo Fernander), Craig

Amrita Rao in *Love U … Mr. Kalakaar!* © Rajshri

Pinder (Mike Roberts), Jason Elwood Hanna (Purple), Christopher Herrod (Dr. Mark Wells), Juanita Kelly (Lonnette Adderley), Adela Osterloh (Romeo's Mother), Leslie Vanderpool (Rhoda Mackey), Christine Wilson (Anna Ross)

A BEAUTIFUL LIFE (China Lion Film Distribution) a.k.a. *Mei Li Ren Sheng*; Producer/ Director, Andrew Lau; Screenplay, Cindy Tang; Photography, Andrew Lau, Lai Yiu fai; Art Director, Eric Lam; Costumes, Dora Ng; Music, Chan Kwong-wing; Editor, Azrael Chung; Media Asia Films; Chinese-Hong Kong; Dolby; Super 35 Widescreen; Color; Not rated; 124 minutes; American release date: May 20, 2011. **CAST:** Liu Ye (Fang Zhendong) Shu Qi (Li Peiru), Tian Liang (Fang Zhencong), Feng Danying (Xiaowan), Anthony Wong (Zhong), Sa Rina (Xiaowan's Mother), Angelina Yuen Yan Lo (Peiru's Mother)

Liu Ye, Shu Qi in *A Beautiful Life*
© China Lion

WE ARE THE NIGHT (IFC Films) a.k.a. *Wir sind die Nacht*; Producer, Christian Becker; Supervising Producer, Kristina Strohm; Director, Dennis Gansel; Screenplay, Jan Berger; Based on the screenplay *The Dawn* by Dennis Gansel; Photography, Torsten Breuer; Designer, Matthias Müsse; Costumes, Anke Winckler; Music, Heiko Maile; Editor, Ueli Christen; Visual Effects Supervisor, Alex Lemke; Casting, Uta Seibicke; a Constantin Film presentation of a Christian Becker/Rat Pack Film Production in association with Celluloid Dreams; German, 2010; Dolby; Color; Not rated; 95 minutes; American release date: May 27, 2011. **CAST:** Karoline Herfurth (Lena), Nina Hoss (Louise), Jennifer Ulrich (Charlotte), Anna Fischer (Nora), Max Riemelt (Det. Tom Serner), Waléra Kanischtscheff (Wasja), Senta Dorothea Kirschner (Spusi Woman), Arved Birnbaum (Det. Lummer), Steffi Kühnert (Lena's Mother), Ivan Shvedoff (Van Gogh), Jochen Nickel (Lena's Probation Officer), Nic Romm (Olsen), Christian Näthe, Tom Jahn (Watchmen), Neil Belakhdar (Hotel Page), Manou Lubowski (Restaurant Guest), Ruth Glöss (Charlotte's Daughter), Cristina do Rego (Stewardess), Steve Thiese, Bernd Weikert (Rescuers), Thomas Klug (News Moderator)

Jennifer Ulrich, Anna Fischer in *We are the Night* © IFC Films

THE PUZZLE (Sundance Selects) a.k.a. *Rompecabezas*; Producers, Gabriel Pastore, Caroline Dhainaut, Luis Sartor, Natalia Smirnoff; Executive Producer, Gabriel Pastore; Director/Screenplay, Natalia Smirnoff; Photography, Bárbara Álvarez; Art Director, Maria Eugenia Sueiro; Costumes, Julio Suarez; Music, Alejandro Franov; Editor, Natacha Valerga; a Carousel Films, Las Niñas Pictures presentation; Argentine-French, 2009; Dolby; Color; Not rated; 87 minutes; American release date: May 27, 2011. **CAST:** María Onetto (Maria del Carmen), Gabriel Goity (Juna), Arturo Goetz (Roberto), Henny Trailes (Carlotta), Felipe Villanueva (Juan Pablo), Julián Doregger (Iván), Nora Zinsky (Raquel), Marcela Guerty (Susana), Mirta Wons (Graciela), Mercedes Fraile (Carmen), Denis Groesman (Victoria), Jimena Ruiz Echazu (Carla), Pacho Guerty (Pedro), Nestor Caniglia (Ricardo)

Maria Onetto, Arturo Goetz in *The Puzzle* © Sundance Selects

THE WAVE (IFC Films) a.k.a. *Die Welle*; Producer, Christian Becker; Supervising Producer, Anita Schneider; Director, Dennis Gansel; Screenplay, Dennis Gansel, Peter Thorwarth; based on a short story by William Ron Jones and *The Wave* teleplay by Johnny Dawkins, Ron Birnbach; Photography, Torsten Breuer; Designer, Knut Loewe; Costumes, Ivana Milos; Music, Heiko Maile; Editor, Ueli Christen; Casting, Franziska Aigner-Kuhn; a Constantin Film presentation of a Christian Becker production, a Rat Pack Filmproduktion, co-produced by Constantin Film Produktion, Medienfonds GFP I KG & B.A. Produktion; German, 2008; Dolby; Arri Widescreen; Color; Not rated; 106 minutes; American release date: May 27, 2011. **CAST:** Jürgen Vogel (Rainer Wenger), Frederick Lau (Tim Stoltefuss), Max Riemelt (Marco), Jennifer Ulrich (Karo), Christiane Paul (Anke Wenger), Jacob Matschenz (Dennis), Cristina Do Rego (Lisa), Elyas M'Barek (Sinan), Maximilian Vollmar (Bomber), Maximilian Mauff (Kevin), Ferdinand Schmidt-Modrow (Ferdi), Tim Oliver Schultz (Jens), Amelie Kiefer (Mona), Fabian Preger (Kaschi), Odine Johne (Maja), Tino Mewes (Schädel), Karoline Teska (Miri), Marco Bretscher-Coschignano (Dominik), Lennard Bertzbach (Bommel),

Tommy Schwimmer (Maxwell), Joseph M'Barek (Thorben), Jaime Kristo Ferkic (Bobby), Darvin Schmidt (Leon), Leander Hagen (Zecke), Lucas Hardt (Kulle), Maxwell Richter (Faust). Sophie Kurzke (Jens' Girlfriend), Liv Lisa Fries (Laura), Lena Lutz (Leyla), Hendrik Holler, Ilo Gansel (Stallholders), Natascha Paulick (Saleslady), Maren Kroymann (Dr. Kohlhage), Teresa Harder (Mother Karo), Thomas Sarbacher (Father Karo), Hubert Mulzer (Dieter Wieland), Alexander Held (Father Tim), Johanna Gastdorf (Mother Tim), Friederike Wagner (Mother Marco), Dennis Gansel (Hängengebliebener)

Jürgen Vogel in *The Wave* © IFC Films

UNITED RED ARMY (Lorber) a.k.a. *Jitsuroku rengô sekigun: Asam sansô e no michi*; Producer/Director/Editor, Kôji Wakamatsu; Executive Producer, Asako Otomo; Screenplay, Kôji Wakamatsu, Masayuki Kakegawa, Asako Otomo; Based on the novel by Masayuki Kakegawa; Photography, Tomohiko Tsuji, Yoshihisa Toda; Music, Jim O'Rouke; a Wakamatsu production; Japanese, 2008; DTS; Color; Not rated; 190 minutes; American release date: May 27, 2011. **CAST:** Maki Saki (Mieko Toyama), Arata (Hiroshi Sakaguchi), Akie Namiki (Hiroko Nagata), Gô Jibiki (Tsuneo Mori), Anri Ban (Fusako Shigenobu), Shima Ônishi (Kunio Bando), Hideo Nakaizumi (Yasuhiro Uegaki), Toshimitsu Ogito (Michinori Kato), Kaoru Okunuki (Yasuko Muta, Hostage), Tak Sakaguchi (Shiomi Takaya), Yugo Saso (Koichi Teraoka)

Karou Okunuki in *United Red Army* © Lorber Films

FILM SOCIALISME (Lorber) Producers, Ruth Waldburger, Alain Sarde; Director/Screenplay, Jean-Luc Godard; Photography, Fabrice Aragno, Paul Grivas; a Vega Film production, with the participation of Wild Bunch, Canal+, Office Féderal de la Culture, Télévision Suisse-Romande, Fonds Regio Films; Swiss-French, 2010; Dolby; Color; HD/DV-to-35mm; Not rated; 101 minutes; American release date:

June 3, 2011. **CAST:** *Des choses comme ça*: Jean-Marc Stehlé (Otto Goldberg), Agatha Couture (Alissa), Mathias Domahidy (Mathias), Quentin Grosset (Ludovic), Patti Smith, Lenny Kaye, Bernard Maris, Bob Maloubier, Alain Badiou, Elias Sanbar (Themselves), Marie-Christine Bergier (Frieda von Salomon), Nadège Beausson-Diagne (Constance); *Quo vadis Europa*: Catherine Tanvier (Catherine, the Mother), Christian Sinniger (Jean-Jacques Martin, the Father), Marine Battaggia (Florine "Flo" Martin), Gulliver Hecq (Lucien "Lulu" Martin), E. Anzoni (Catherine's Friend), Élisabeth Vltali (France 3 Journalist), Eye Haïdara (France 3 Camerawoman); *Nos humanités*: Blandine Bellavoir, Jean-Michel Féte, Stéphane Henon, Odile Schmitt (Voices)

Patti Smith in *Film Socialisme* © Lorber Films

EMPIRE OF SILVER (NeoClassics Films) a.k.a. *Baiyin diguo*; Producers, Chiao Hsung Ping, Christina Yao; Executive Producer, Jeremy Thomas; Director, Christina Yao; Screenplay, Christina Yao, Cheng Yi; Based on the book *The Silver Valley (Baiyin gu)* by Cheng Yi; Action Choreographer, Stephen Tung Wai; Photography, Anthony Yiu Ming Pun; Designer, Yee Chung Man; Editors, Humphrey Dixon, Liao Ching Song, Tang Hua; a Crystal Clear Pictures and Ocean Pictures production; Hong Kong-Chinese, 2009; Dolby; Widescreen; Color; Not rated; 112 minutes; American release date: June 3, 2011. **CAST:** Aaron Kwok (Third Master), Tie Lin Zhang (Master Kang), Hao Lei (Madame Kang), Jennifer Tilly (Mrs. Landdeck), Ding Zhi Cheng (Manager Qiu), Lei Zhen Yu (Manager Dai), King Shih Chieh (Manager Liu), Hou Tong Jiang (Manager Sun), Tien Niu (Yu Feng), Lu Zhong (Lu Sao), Shi Xiao Man (Lao Xia), Si Da Sheng (First Master), Wang De Shun (Bodyguard Chang You), Chang Lan Tian (Eunuch), Jonathan Kosread (Pastor Landdeck), John Paisley (Dr. Wilson), Hei Zi (Second Master), Lia Yi Xiao (Fourth Mistress), Du Jiang (Fourth Master), Wang Shuang (Third Mistress), Guo Tao (Bandit Head), Wu Fang (San Xi), Chai Jin (Third Master's Page)

REINDEERSPOTTING (GoDigital Media Group) Producers, Jesse Fryckman, Oskari Huttu; Director/Photography, Joonas Neuvonen; Screenplay, Venla Varha; Editor, Sadri Cetinkaya; a Bronson Club presentation; Finnish, 2010; Dolby; Color; Not rated; 86 minutes; American release date: June 8, 2011. Documentary on twenty-year-old junkie Jani.

AGRARIAN UTOPIA (Extra Virgin) a.k.a. *Sawan baan na*; Producer, Pimpaka Towira; Director/Photography/Editor, Uruphong Raksasad; Thai, 2009; Color; HDV; Not rated; 122 minutes; American release date: June 10, 2011. **CAST:** Prayad Jumma, Sai Jumma, Sompong Jumma, Nikorn Mungmeung, Somnuek Mungmeung

VIVA RIVA! (Music Box Films) Producers, Boris Van Gils, Michael Goldberg, Djo Tunda Wa Munga; Director/Screenplay, Djo Tunda Wa Munga; Photography, Antoine Roch; Designer, Philippe Van Herwijnen; Music, Louis Vyncke & Congopunq; Editor, Yves Langlois; a Formosa Production in co-production with MG Productions and Suka! Productions with the participation of Canal+, CineCinema, L'Union Européen; Congo-French-Belgian, 2010; Color; Rated R; 96 minutes; American release date: June 10, 2011. **CAST:** Patsha Bay Mukuna (Riva), Manie Malone (Nora), Hoji Fortuna (César), Alex Herabo (J.M.), Marlene Longange (Commandante), Diplome Amekindra (Azor), Angelique Mbumb

Agrarian Utopia © Extra Virgin

(Malou), Nzita Tumba (Mother Edo), Romain Ndomba (G.O.), Tomas Bie (Jorge), Davly Ilunga (Joaquin)

Patsha Bay Mukuna in *Viva Riva!* © Music Box Films

TROLLHUNTER (Magnet) a.k.a. *Trolljegeren*; Producers, John M. Jacobsen, Sveinung Golimo; Director/ Screenplay, André Øvredal; Photography, Hallvard Bræin; Designer, Martin Gant; Editor, Per Erik Eriksen; Creature Design/Concepts, Håvard S. Johansen, Ivar Rødningen, Rune Spaans; a Filmkameratene As Productions presentation; Norwegian, 2010; Color; Rated PG-13; 103 minutes; American release date: June 10, 2011. **CAST:** Otto Jespersen (Hans, Trollhunter), Glenn Erland Tosterud (Thomas Schølen), Johanna Mørck (Johanna Pedersen), Tomas Alf Larsen (Kalle Stensvik), Urmila Berg-Domaas (Malika Malay-Olsen), Hans Morten Hansen (Finn Haugen), Robert Stoltenberg (Polish Bearhunter), Knut Nærum (Power Company Manager)

Trollhunter © Magnet Releasing

THE CHAMELEON (Lleju Productions) a.k.a. *Le Cameleon*; Producers, Ram Bergman, Marie-Castille Mention-Schaar, Pierre Kubel, Bill Perkins, Cooper Richey; Executive Producer, Dave Pomier; Director, Jean-Paul Salomé; Screenplay, Jean-Paul Salomé, Natalie Carter; Based on the book *Le Cameleon* by Christophe d'Antonio; Photography, Pascal Ridao; Designer, Martina Buckley; Costumes, Susanna Puisto; Music, Jeff Cardoni; Editor, Marie-Pierre Renaud; Casting, Shannon Makhanian; a Lleju Prods. presentation of a Loma Nash/Gordon Street Pictures/Reston's Groupés Productions; Canadian-French-American, 2010; Dolby; Color; Rated R; 100 minutes; American release date: June 10, 2011. **CAST:** Marc-André Grondin (Frédéric Fortin/Nicholas Mark Randall), Famke Janssen (Jennifer Johnson), Ellen Barkin (Kimberly Miller), Emilie de Ravin (Kathy Jansen), Tory Kittles (Dan Price), Brian Geraghty (Brian Jansen), Nick Stahl (Brendan Kerrigan), James DuMont (BR PD Cop A), Ritchie Montgomery (Diner Owner), Lance Nichols (FBI Doctor), Estelle Larrivaz, Xavier Beauvois (Gendarmes), Lindsay Soileau, Katy Preppard (Girls), Nick Chinlund (Mitch), Kent Jude Bernard, Gabe Begneaud (Pool Players), Sergio March (Spanish Policeman), Everett Sifuentes (Superintendent), Josh Gates (Spanish Tattoo Artist), J.D. Evermore (Worker), Gary Grubbs (John Striker), Jean-Paul Salomé (Attorney), Logan Smith (County Sheriff #1), Braden Delee (Young Frédéric)

Nick Stahl, Marc-André Grondin in *The Chameleon* © Lleju Prods.

THE LIPS (Magic Lantern) a.k.a. *Los labios*; Producers, Iván Eibuszyc, Iván Fund, Santiago Loza; Directors/ Screenplay, Iván Fund, Santiago Loza; Photography, María Laura Collaso; Music, Iván Fund, Lisandro Rodriguez; Editor, Lorena Moriconi; a Morocha Films production; Argentine, 2010; Color; Not rated; 100 minutes; American release date: June 13, 2011. **CAST:** Eva Bianco, Raul Lagge, Victoria Raposo, Adela Sanchez

Eva Bianco, Victoria Raposo, Adela Sanchez in *The Lips* © Magic Lantern Films

KIDNAPPED (IFC) a.k.a. *Secuestrados*; Producers, Emma Lustres, Borja Pena; Executive Producer, Borja Pena; Director, Miguel Ángel Vivas; Screenplay, Miguel Ángel Vivas, Javier García; Photography, Pedro J. Márquez; Designer, Miguel Riesco; Costumes, Montse Sancho; Music, Sergio Moure; Editor, José Manuel Jiménez; an IFC Midnight and Filmax International presentation of a Vaca Films production in co-production with Blur, Attic & La Fabrique 2; Spanish, 2010; Dolby; Color; Not rated; 85 minutes; American release date: June 17, 2011. **CAST:** Fernando Cayo (Jaime), Manuela Vellés (Isa), Ana Wagener (Marta), Guillermo Barrientos (Young Criminal), Martijn Kuiper (Albanian Criminal), Dritan Biba (Leader of the Gang), Xoel Yáñez (César), Luisa Iglesia B. (Javier), Pepo Suevos (Security Officer), Eduardo Torroja (Conductor), César Diaz, Eduardo Gómez Bassi (Attendants), Candela Fernández (Cashier),

Manuela Vellés in *Kidnapped* © IFC Films

ANGEL OF EVIL (20th Italia) a.k.a. *Vallanzasc: Angels of Evil* and *Vallanzasca -- Gli angeli del male*; Producer, Elide Melli; Director, Michele Placido; Screenplay, Kim Rossi Stuart, Michele Placido, Antonio Leotti, Toni Trupia, Andrea Leanza, Antonella D'Agostiono; Story, Angelo Pasquini, Andrea Purgatori; Based on the books *Il fiore del male* by Carlo Bonini and Renato Vallanzasca, and *Lettera a Renato* by Renato Vallanzasca and Antonella D'Agostino; Photography, Arnaldo Catinari; Designer, Tonino Zera; Costumes, Roberto Chiocchi; Music, Negramaro; Editor, Consuelo Catucci; a Twentieth Century Fox presentation of a Cosmo Production, Fox Intl. production, in association with Twenty First Century Fox Italy, Babe Film, Mandragora Films; Italian; Dolby; Widescreen; Color; Rated R; 125 minutes; American release date: June 17, 2011. **CAST:** Kim Rossi Stuart (Renato Vallanzasca), Filippo Timi (Enzo), Moritz Bleibtreu (Sergio), Valeria Solarino (Consuelo), Paz Vega (Antonella D'Agostino), Francesco Scianna (Francis Turatello), Gaetano Bruno (Fausto), Nicola Acunzo (Rosario), Stefano Chiodaroli (Armando), Lino Guanciale (Nunzio), Paolo Mazzarelli (Beppe), Giorgio Careccia (Camerlo), Federico Pacifici (Chirugo), Marica Gungui (Maria), Monica Elan Barladeanu (Nicoletta), Lia Gotti (Carmen), Gerardo Amato (Renato's Father), Adriana De Guilmi (Renato's Mother), Lorenzo Gleijeses (Donato), Riccardo Von Hoening Cicogna (Red), Federica Vincenti (Giuliana), Matilde Pezzotta (Serena), Toni Pandolfo (Spaghettino)

Kim Rossi Stuart in *Angel of Evil* © 20th Italia

THE COLORS OF THE PRISM, THE MECHANICS OF TIME (Independent) Producer/ Director, Jacqueline Caux; Screenplay, Daniel Caux; Photography, Claude Garnier, Patrick Ghiringhelli; Editor, Dora Soltani; a Jacqueline Caux production in co-production with le Centre Pompidou; French, 2009; Color; Not rated; 96 minutes; Release date: June 17, 2011. Documentary on minimalist music; **WITH:** Gavin Bryars, John Cage, Philip Glass, Richie Hawtin, Meredith Monk, Pauline Oliveros, Steve Reich, Terry Riley, La Monte Young, Marian Zazeela

R (Olive Films) Producers, René Ezra, Tomas Radoor; Executive Producer, Kim Magnusson; Directors/Screenplay, Tobias Lindholm, Michael Noer; Photography, Magnus Nordenhof Jønck; Costumes, Lotte Stenlev; Editor, Adam Nielsen; Produced by Nodrisk Film Production A/S; Danish, 2010; Dolby; Color; Not rated; 99 minutes; American release date: June 17, 2011. **CAST:** Pilou Asbæk (Rune, "R"), Dulfi Al-Jabouri (Rashid), Roland Møller (The Mason), Jacob Gredsted (Carsten), Kim Winther (Prison Guard Kim), Omar Shargawi (Bazhir), Sune Nørgaard (Sune), Jorg Beutnagel (Prison Guard Bjørn), Lars Jensen (Ladby), Johnny Nielsen (Køkkenchef), Claus Saric Pedersen (Mini), Claus Poulsen (Claus), Helmuth Kristensen (Helmuth), Ali Nehzed (Ali), Lalia Andersson (Grandmother), Mia Maria Back (Kæreste), Bushra Sadaio, Baker Al-Jabouri (Rashid's Brothers)

Pilou Asbæk in *R* © Olive Films

JIG (Screen Media) Producer/Director, Sue Bourne; Executive Producers, Carole Sheridan, Leslie Finlay; Based on an idea by Julie Heekin; Photography, Joe Russell; Music, Patrick Doyle; Editor, Colin Monie; a BBC Scotland and Creative Scotland presentation in association with Head Gear Films and Metrol Technology; Scottish-British; Dolby; Technicolor; HD; Not rated; 93 minutes; American release date: June 17, 2011. Documentary on the 40th Irish Dancing World Championships; **WITH:** Brogan McCay, Julia O'Rourke, Joe Bitter, John Whitehurst, Claire Greaney, Simona Mauriello, Suzanne Coyle, Sandun Verschoor, Ana Kondratyeva, John Carey

VINCENT WANTS TO SEA (Corinth Films) a.k.a. *Vincent will Meer*; Producers, Viola Jäger, Harald Kügler; Director, Ralf Huettner; Screenplay, Florian David Fitz; Photography, Andreas Berger; Designer, Heidi Lüdi; Costumes, Natascha Curtius-Noss; Music, Stevie B-Zet, Ralf Hildenbeutel; Editor, Kai Schroeter; Casting, Nessie Nesslauer; a Corinth Films and BETA Cinema presentation of an Olga Film production; German, 2010; Dolby; Color; Not rated; 96 minutes; American release date: June 24, 2011. **CAST:** Florian David Fitz (Vincent Gellner), Karoline Herfurth (Marie), Heino Ferch (Robert Gellner), Johannes Allmayer (Alexander), Katharina Müller-Elmau (Dr. Rose), Karin Thaler (Monika), Tim Seyfi (Carabiniere), Christoph Zrenner, Butz Ulrich Buse (Gas Station Attendants), Ulrich Boris Pöppl (Priest)

DOUBLE DHAMAAL (Reliance Big Pictures) Producers, Indra Kumar, Ashok Thakeria; Director, Indra Kumar; Screenplay/Story, Tushar Hiranandani; Dialogue, Farhad-Sajid; Photography, Aseem Bajaj; Art Director, Tanushree Sarkar; Music, Anand Raj Anand; Lyrics, Anand Raj Anand, Mauri Puri; Editor, Sanjay Sankla; a Prakash Ja presentation of a Maruti Pictures, Reliance Entertainment production; Indian; Dolby; Super 35 Widescreen; Color; Not rated; 138 minutes; American

release date: June 24, 2011. **CAST:** Sanjay Dutt (Kabir Nayak), Jaaved Jaafery (Nanav Shirvastav/Jojo), Riteish Deshmukh (Deshbandhu Roy/Tukaram), Manav Sherawat (Kamini), Arshad Warsi (Aditya Shrivastav/Ghanta Singh), Ashish Chowdhury (Boman Contractor/Dodo), Kangana Ranaut (Kiya), Satish Kaushik (Bata Bhai), Zakir Hussain (Mohsin Bhai), Prem Chopra (Bose), J. Brandon Hill (Johnny Bonzella)

Arshad Warsi, Jaaved Jaafery, Riteish Deshmukh in *Double Dhamaal* © Reliance Big Pictures

LEAP YEAR (Strand) a.k.a. *Año Bisiesto*; Producers, Edher Campos, Luis Salinas; Director, Michael Rowe; Screenplay, Michael Rowe, Lucía Carreras; Photography, Juan Manuel Sepúlveda; Art Director, Alisarine Ducolomb; Costumes, Adolfo Cruz Mateo; Editor, Óscar Figueroa Jara; a Machete Producciones and Instituto Mexicano de Cinematografía; Mexican, 2010; Dolby; Color; Widescreen; Not rated; 92 minutes; American release date: June 24, 2011. **CAST:** Mónica Del Carmen (Laura), Gustavo Sánchez Parra (Arturo), Marco Zapata (Raúl), Armando Hernández, Diego Chas, Jaime Sierra (Men), Ernesto González, Bertha Mediola (Elderly People), José Juan Meraz (Boyfriend, Novio), Nur Rubio (Cashier), Ireri Solís (Neighbor)

Marco Zapata, Monica del Carmen in *Leap Year* © Strand Releasing

AURORA (Cinema Guild) Producers, Anca Puiu, Bobby Paunescu; Director/ Screenplay, Cristi Puiu; Photography, Viorel Sergovici; Designer, Vali Ighigheanu; Editor, Ion Ioachim Stroe; a Mandragora, Parisienne de Production production in collaboration with Bord Cadre Films, Essential Filmproduktion, ARTE France Cinéma, ZDF/ARTE, Societatea Romana de Televiziune, TSR/SSR, HBO Romania; Romanian, 2010; Dolby; Color; Not rated; 181 minutes; American release date:

June 29, 2011. **CAST:** Cristi Puiu (Viorel), Clara Voda (Gina Filip), Catrinel Dumitresu (Mrs. Livinski), Luminita Gheorghiu (Mioara Avram), Valentin Popescu (Stoian), Valeria Seciu (Pusa), Gelu Colceag (Mr. Livinski), Anthony Correa (Doctor), Alina Grigore (Vanzatoare)

POLYTECHNIQUE (Remstar Media Partners) Producers, Maxime Rémillard, Don Carmody; Director, Denis Villeneuve; Screenplay, Jacques Davidts, Denis Villeneuve, Éric Leca; Photography, Pierre Gill; Designer, Roger Martin; Costumes, Annie Dufort; Music, Benoît Charest; Editor, Richard Comeau; an Alliance Films, Wild Bunch production; Canadian, 2009; Dolby; Black and white; Not rated; 77 minutes; American release date: June 29, 2011. **CAST:** Sébastien Huberdeau (Jean-François), Maxim Gaudette (The Killer), Karine Vanasse (Valérie), Evelyne Brochu (Stéphanie), Pierre-Yves Cardinal (Éric), Johanne-Marie Tremblay (Jean-François' Mother), Pierre Leblanc (Mr. Martineau), Francesca Barcenas (Injured Student at Copier), Ève Duranceau (Student with the Ear Injury), Mathieu Ledoux, Nathalie Giard (Injured Students), Adam Kosh (Killer's Roommate), Larissa Corriveau (Killer's Neighbor), Manon Lapointe (Killer's Mother), Chantale Bilodeau (Physiotherapist), Mireille Brullemans (Admissions Office Secretary), Jorge Bustos-Estefan (Laughing Student), Jonathan Dubsky (Frightened Student), Emmanuelle Girard, Anne Trudel (Students Behind Speakers), Pierre-Xavier Martel (Security Agent)

Evelyne Brochu, Karine Vanasse in *Polytechnique* © Remstar Media Partners

SMALL TOWN MURDER SONGS (Monterey Media) Producers, Lee Kim, Ed Gass-Donnelly; Director/Screenplay/Editor, Ed Gass-Donnelly; Photography, Brendan Steacy; Designer, Rachel Ford; Costumes, Laura Montgomery; Music, Bruce Peninsula; Casting, Jenny Lewis, Sara Kay; a Kinosmith presentation of a 3 Legged Dog Films and Resolute Films and Entertainment Production; Canadian; Dolby; Panavision; Deluxe color; Rated R; 75 minutes; Release date: July 1, 2011. **CAST:** Peter Stormare (Walter), Martha Plimpton (Sam), Jill Hennessy (Rita), Ari Cohen (Washington), Jackie Burroughs (Olive), Alexandria Benoit (Sarah), Eric McIntyre (Steve), Aaron Poole (Jim), Alyssa Mariano (Cindy), Amy Rutherford (Ava), Trent McMullen (Officer Kevin), Ann Holloway (Greta), Stuart Hughes (Billy), Heather Allin (Mrs. West), John Stead (David), Jessica Clement (Deb), Kat Germain (Jenny), Timm Zemanek (Wilson), Vladimir Bondarenko (Deacon), Erin Brandenburg (Officer Michelle), Herm Dick (Walter's Father), Andrew Penner, Alan Penner (Workers), Colin Burrowes (Police Constable), Sean Eaton (Morgue Attendant), Mark Snowdon (Frank)

DELHI BELLY (UTV Motion Pictures) Producers, Aamir Khan, Kiran Rao, Ronnie Screwval; Director, Abhinay Deo; Screenplay, Akshat Verma; Photography, Jason West; Costumes, Niharika Khan; Music, Ram Sampath; Editor, Huzefa Lokhandwala; Indian; Color; Not rated; 103 minutes; American release date: July 1, 2011. **CAST:** Imran Khan (Tashi Malhotra/Tashi Dorjee Lhaloo), Kunaal Roy Kapur (Nitin), Vir Das (Arup), Shenaz Treasury (Sonia), Poorna Jagannathan (Menaka), Kim Bodnia (Vladimir Dragunsky), Paresh Ganatra (Manish Chand Jain), Vijay Raaz (Cowboy), Ashraf-Ul-Haque (Titoo), Nikita Bhatt (Leena), Neville Dadachanji (Keval Maharaj), Nayani Dixit (Ambika), Gabriel John (Lucky), Janet Hookway (Louise Eggen), Lushin Dubey (Sonia's Mother), Dharmendar Singh (Bunty), Rahul Singh (Rajiv), Michael Terry (Frank Eggen)

RAPT (Lorber) Producers, Patrick Sobelman, Diana Elbaum, Sebastian Delloy; Director/Screenplay, Lucas Belvaux; Photography, Pierre Milon; Art Director, Frédérique Belvaux; Costumes, Nathalie Raoul; Editor, Danielle Anezin; Casting, Brigitte Moidon, Gersa Diddens; an Agat Films/France 3 Cinema/Entre Chien & Loup/RTBF/Ateliers de Baere production; French-Belgian, 2009; Dolby; Color; Not rated; 125 minutes; American release date: July 6, 2011. **CAST:** Yvan Attal (Stanislas Graff), Anne Consigny (Francoise Graff), André Marcon (Andre Peyrac), Francoise Fabian (Marjorie), Akex Descas (Walser), Michel Voita (Commissioner Paoli), Gerard Meylan (Le Marseillais), Maxime Lefrançois (Bertaux), Christophe Kourotchkine (Jean-Jacques Garnier), Sarah Messens (Véronique), Julia Kaye (Martine), Patrick Descamps (Massart), Betrand Constant (Captain Verne), Marc Rioufol (Commander Chenut), Richard Sammut (Lt. Grazziani), Tania Torrens (Madame Keller), Elef Zack (Le Chatelain), Vincent Nemeth (Judge), Jean-Baptiste Malartre (Minister), Nicolas Pignon (Prefect of Police), Olivier Darimont (Mahoux), Pierre Rochefort (Fostier), Olivier Ythier (Montrouveau), Philippe Toussaint (La Chassagne), Circe Lethem (Maid), Swan Scalabre (Graff's Mistress)

Yvan Attal in *Rapt* © Lorber Films

COLD FISH (The Collective) a.k.a. *Tsumetai nettaigyo*; Producers, Yoshinori Chiba, Toshiki Kimura; Director, Sion Sono; Screenplay, Sion Sono, Yoshiki Takahashi; Photography, Shinya Kimura; Designer, Takashi Matsuzuka; Costumes, Satoe Araki; Music, Tomohide Harada; Editor, Junichi Ito; Special Effects Supervisor, Yoshihiro Nishimura; a Bloody Distgusting and Nikkatsu presentation; Japanese; Color; Not rated; 144 minutes; American release date: July 6, 2011. CAST: Mitsuru Fukikoshi (Nobuyuki Syamoto), Denden (Yukio Murata), Asuka Kurosawa (Aiko Murata), Megumi Kagurazaka (Taeko), Hikari Kajiwara (Mitsuko Syamoto), Testu Watanabe (Takayasu)

FLYING FISH (MoMA) a.k.a. *Igillena maluwo*; Producer/Director/Story, Sanjeewa Pushpakumara; Screenplay, Sanjeewa Pushpakumara, Chinthana Dharamadasa; Photography, Vishwajith Karunarathna; Designer/Costumes, Bimala Dushmantha; Music, Tharindu Priyankara; Editor, Ajith Ramanayake; an Asia Digital Entertainment, Sapushpa Expressions presentation; Sri Lanka; Dolby; Color; Not rated; 124 minutes; American release date: July 7, 2011. **CAST:** Chaminda Sampath Jayaweera, Gayesha Perera, Rathnayaka Marsinghe, Siththi Mariyam, Sanjeewa Dissanayake, Sumathy Sivamohan, Kaushalya Fernando, Nilanka Dahanayake, Thissa Bandaranayaka, Wasanthy Ranwala, Mohammed Ali Rajabdeen

IRONCLAD (ARC Entertainment) Producers, Rick Benattar, Andrew Curtis, Jonathan English; Director, Jonathan English; Screenplay, Stephen McDool, Jonathan English, Erick Kastel; Photography, David Eggby; Designer, Joseph Nemec III; Costumes, Beatrix Aruna Pasztor: Music, Lorne Balfe; Editor, Peter Amundson; Special Effects Supervisor, Richard van den Bergh; Casting, Kelly Valentine Hendry, Robyn Owen; an ARC Entertainment and XLRator Media presentation of a VIP Medienfonds 4 production, in association with Rising

Start, Silver Reel, Premiere Picture, The Wales Creative IP Fund, Contentfilm International and Molinare Perpetual Media Captial presentation of a Mythic International Entertainment production; British-American-German; Dolby; Panavision; Color; Rated R; 120 minutes; American release date: July 8, 2011. **CAST:** James Purefoy (Marshal), Brian Cox (Albany), Kate Mara (Lady Isabel), Derek Jacobi (Cornhill), Paul Giamatti (King John), Charles Dance (Archbishop Langton), Jason Flemyng (Becket), Jamie Foreman (Coteral), Mackenzie Crook (Marks), Rhys Parry Jones (Wulfstan), Aneurin Barnard (Squire), Vladimir Kulich (Tiberius), Annabelle Apsion (Maddy), Bree Condon (Agnes), Guy Siner (Captain Oaks), Steffan Rhodri (Cooper), Daniel O'Meara (Phipps), Bree Condon (Agnes), Guy Siner (Oaks), David Melville (Baron Darnay), Marcus Hoyland (Abbott Marcus), John Pierce Jones (Cook), Jeff Jones (Head Clerk), Wyn Bowen Harries, Dewi Williams (Barons), John Weldon (Castle Darnay Sentry), Laura Sibbick (Castle Servant Girl), Steve Purbrick (Tavern Landlord)

Paul Giamatti in *Ironclad* © ARC Entertainment

SUMMER OF GOLIATH (FiGa Films) a.k.a. *Verano de Goliat*; Producer/Director/ Screenplay/ Editor/Designer, Nicolás Pereda; Photography, Alejandro Coronado; a Santas Producciones, En Chinga Films production; Mexican-Canadian-Dutch; Color; HD; Not rated; 75 minutes; American release date: July 8, 2011. Docu-drama looks at some of the people of Huilotepec, Mexico; WITH: Gabino Rodríguez, Teresa Sánchez, Juana Rodríguez, Harold Torres, Oscar Saavedra Miranda, NIco Saavedra Miranda, Amalio Saavedra Miranda

Oscar Saavedra Miranda in *Summer of Goliath* © FiGa Films

ANITA (Menemsha) Producer/Director, Marcos Carnevale; Screenplay, Marcos Carnevale, Marcela Guerty, Lily Ann Martin; Photography, Guillermo Zappino; Art Director, Adriana Slemenson; Music, Lito Vitale; Editor, Pablo Barbieri Carrera; Casting, Sabrina Kirzner; a Shazam S.A. production; Argentine, 2009; Dolby; Color; Not rated; 104 minutes; American release date: July 8, 2011. **CAST:** Norma Aleandro (Dora Feldman), Luis Luque (Felix), Leonor Manso (Nora), Peto Menahem (Ariel), Alejandra Manzo (Anita Feldman)

PHASE 7 (Salient Media) a.k.a. *Fase 7*; Producer, Stebastian Aloi; Director/ Screenplay, Nicolás Goldbart; Photography, Lucio Bonelli; Art Director, Mariela Ripdoas; Music, Guillermo Guareschi; Editors, Pablo Barbieri Carrera, Nicolás Godlbart; Special Effects Coordinator, Franco Burattini; an Aeroplano Cine production in association with Televisión Federal (Telefe); Argentine; Dolby; Cinecolor; Not rated; 95 minutes; American release date: July 13, 2011. **CAST:** Daniel Hendler (Coco), Jazmín Stuart (Pipi), Yayo Guridi (Horacio), Federico Luppi (Zanutto), Carlos Bermejo (Guglierini), Abian Vainstein (Lange)

Phase 7 © Salient Media

MURDER 2 (Eros) Producer, Mukesh Bhatt; Director, Mohit Suri; Screenplay, Mahesh Bhatt, Shagufta Rafique; Photography, Ravi Walia; Music, Sangeet Haldipur, Siddharth Haldipur, Mithun Sharma; Editor, Devendra Murdeshwar; a Vishesh Films production; Indian; Color; Not rated; 127 minutes; American release date: July 15, 2011. **CAST:** Jacqueline Fernandes (Priya), Yana Gupta (Jyoti), Emraan Hashmi (Arjun V. Bhaagwat), Amardeep Jha (Reshma's Mom), Bikramjeet Kanwarpal (Senior Police Official), Prashant Narayanan (Dheeraj Pandey), Sudhanshu Pandey (Sada), Sulagna Panigrahi (Reshma)

Jacqueline Fernandes, Emraan Hasmi in *Murder 2* © Eros

GUNLESS (Alliance Films) Producers, Niv Fichman, Steven Hegyes, Shawn Williamson; Director/Screenplay, William Phillips; Photography, Gregory Middleton; Designer, Matthew Budgeon; Music, Greg Keelor; Editor, Susan Maggi; a Rhombus Media, Brightlight Pictures production; Canadian, 2010; Color; Super 35 Widescreen; Not rated; 89 minutes; American release date: July 15, 2011. **CAST:** Paul Gross (The Montana Kid), Sienna Guillory (Jane Taylor), Dustin Milligan (Cpl. Jonathan Kent), Tyler Mane (Jack), Callum Keith Rennie (Ben Cutler), Graham Greene (N'Kwala), Jay Brazeau (Dr. Angus Schiffron), Michael Eklund (Larry), Alex Zahara (Jon), Jody Racicot (Paul), Shawn Campbell (Carl), Paul Coeur (Claude), Melody Choi (Adell), Tseng Chang (Mr. Kwon), Laura Bertram (Miss Alice), Glynis Davies (Beth), Bronwen Smith (Beatrice), Teach Grant (Ringo), Dave Leader (Posse Dave), Quentin Schneider (Posse Q), Grace Fatkin (Mrs. Kwon), Edward Vincenzo Phillips (Edwin), Donavon Stinson (Constable Hughes), Gerald Paetz, Brent Connolly (Constables), Warren Choi (Railway Worker), Barbara Choi (Railway Worker's Wife), Michael Choi (Railway Worker's Son), Aieisha Li (Chinese Lady with Glasses), Raymond Yu (Chinese TNT Guy)

Paul Gross in *Gunless* © Alliance Films

THE TREE (Zeitgeist) a.k.a. *L'arbe*; Producers, Sue Taylor, Yael Fogiel; Director/Screenplay, Julie Bertuccelli; Based on the novel *Our Father Who Art in the Tree* by Judy Pascoe; Photography, Nigel Bluck; Set Designer, Steven Jones-Evans; Costumes, Joanna Mae Park; Music, Grégoire Hetzel; Editor, François Gédigier; Casting, Nikki Barrett; a Taylor Media and Les Films du Poisson production, with the participation of Canal+ and ARTE France; French-Australian, 2010; Dolby; Color; Not rated; 100 minutes; American release date: July 15, 2011. **CAST:** Charlotte Gainsbourg (Dawn O'Neil), Marton Csokas (George Elrick), Morgana Davies (Simone O'Neil), Aden Young (Peter O'Neil), Gillian Jones (Vonnie), Penne Hackforth-Jones (Mrs. Johnson), Christian Byers (Tim O'Neil), Tom Russell (Lou O'Neil), Gabriel Gotting (Charlie O'Neil), Zoe Boe (Megane Lu), Bob MacKay (Ab), Ryan Potter (Tree Lopper), Murray Shoring (Council Inspector), Taren Stewart, Robert Joseph Stewart, Wencis Burns (Lou's Friends), Margaret Foote, Betty Cartmill (Mackenzie Twins), Patrick Boe (Mr. Lu), Arthur Dignam (Uncle Jack), Wendy Playfair (Aunt Harriet), Jackie Kelleher (Aunt Jacqueline), Benita Collings (Aunt Mary)

ZINDAGI NA MILEGI DOBARA (Eros) Producers, Farhan Akhtar, Ritesh Sidhwani; Director, Zoya Akhtar; Screenplay, Zoya Akhtar, Reema Kagti, Farhan Akhtar; Photography, Carlos Catalan; Designer, Susanne Caplan Merwanji; Costumes, Arjun Bhasin; Music, Shankar Mahadevan, Loy Mendonsa, Ehsaan Noorani, Tubby; Lyrics, Javed Akhtar; Choreographers, Bosco-Caesar, Vaibhavi Merchant; Editor, Anand Subaya; an Eros. Intl, Excel Entertainment presentation; Indian; Dolby; Widescreen; Color; Not rated; 150 minutes; American release date: July 15, 2011. **CAST:** Abhay Deol (Kabir Dhiman), Kalki Koechlin (Natasha), Hrithik Roshan (Arjun), Katrina Kaif (Laila), Farhan Akhtar (Imran Habib), Ariadna Cabrol (Nuria), Lolo Herrero (Tattooed Guy), Deepti Naval (Rehna Habib), Mandi Sidhu (Rohini), Naseeruddin Shah (Salman Habib)

THE WOMAN WITH THE 5 ELEPHANTS (Cinema Guild) a.k.a. *La femme aux 5 éléphants*; Producers, Hercli Bundi, Vadim Jendreyko, Thomas Tielsch; Director/Screenplay, Vadim Jendreyko; Photography, Niels Bolbrinker, Stéphane Kuthy; Music, Daniel Almada, Martin Iannaccone; Editor, Gisela Castronari-Jaensch; a Mira Film GmbH/Filmtank GmbH production; Swiss-German, 2010; Dolby; Color; Not rated; 93 minutes; American release date: July 20, 2011. Documentary on Svetlana Geier, thought to be the greatest translator of Russian literature; **WITH:** Svetlana Geier, Anna Götte, Hannelore Hagen, Jürgen Klodt.

FIRE IN BABYLON (Tribeca) Producers, Charles Steel, John Battsek; Executive Producers, Ben Goldsmith, Ben Elliott; Director/Screenplay, Stevan Riley; Photography, Stuart Bentley; Editor, Peter Haddon; an E&G Productions in association with Hargitay & Hargitay Pictures in Motion presentation of a Cowboys Films/Passion Pictures production; British; Color; HD; Not rated; 88 minutes; American release date: July 22, 2011. Documentary on how the West Indies cricketers triumphed over racism to become one of the most gifted sports teams in history; **WITH:** Vivivan Richards, Clive Lloyd, Joel Garner, Gordon Greenidge, Colin Croft, Michael Holding, Desmond Haynes, Deryk Murray, Andy Roberts, Bunny Wailer, Frank I, Colin Cumberbatch, Hilary Beckles.

SINGHAM (Reliance Big Pictures) Producer, Rohit Chaudhury; Director, Rohit Shetty; Screenplay, Yunus Sajawal; Dialogue, Sajid-Farhad; Photography, Dudley; Art Director, Narendra Rahurikar; Costumes, Vkiram Phadnis, Kavin Shetty; Music, Ajay-atul; Lyrics, Swanand Kirkire; Editor, Steven H. Bernard; a Reliance Entertainment production; Indian; Dolby; Widescreen; Color; Not rated; 143 minutes; American release date: July 22, 2011. **CAST:** Ajay Devgan (Inspector Bajirao M. Singham), Kajal Agarwal (Kavya G. Bhosle), Prakash Raj (Jaykant Shikre), Sonali Kulkarni (Megha Kadam), Sachin Khedekar (Gautam Bhosle), Sudhanshu Pandey (Inspector Rakesh Kadam), Ravindra Berde (Chandrakant), Suhasini Deshpande (Mrs. Bhosle), Agasthya Dhanorkar (Nitin Kadam), Anant Jog (Minister Anant Narvekar), Govind Namdeo (Manikrao Singham), Vijay Patkar (Havaldar Kelar), Ashok Samarth (Shiva Nayak)

Ajay Devgan in *Singham* © Reliance Big Pictures

Morgana Davies, Charlotte Gainsbourg in *The Tree* © Zeitgeist Film

EL BULLI: COOKING IN PROGRESS (Alive Mind Cinema) Producer, Ingo Fliess; Director, Gereon Wetzel; Screenplay, Anna Gnestí Rosell, Gereon Wetzel; Photography, Josef Mayerhofer; Food Photography, Francesc Guillamet; Music, Stephane Diethelm; Editor, Anja Pohl; an if ... Productions film; German, 2010; Dolby; Color; HD; Not rated; 108 minutes; American release date: July 27, 2011. Documentary on how chef Ferran Adrià closes his restaurant El Bulli for half a year in order to create a new menu for the upcoming season; **WITH:** Ferran Adrià, Oriol Castro, Eduard Xatruch, Eugeni de Diego, Aitor Lozano

Eduard Xatruch in *El Bulli* © Alive Mind Cinema

GOOD NEIGHBORS (Magnolia) Producer, Kevin Tierney; Executive Producers, Kirk D'Amico, Joe Iacono; Director/Screenplay, Jacob Tierney; Based on the novel *Chère voisine* by Chrystine Brouillet; Photography, Guy Dufaux; Designer, Anne Pritchard; Costumes, Francesca Chamberland; Casting, Rosina Bucci; Editor, Arthur Tarnowski; a Myriad Pictures presentation of a Park Ex Picutres production; Canadian; Dolby; Color; Rated R; 96 minutes; American release date: July 29, 2011. **CAST:** Jay Baruchel (Victor), Scott Speedman (Spencer), Emily Hampshire (Louise), Ann-Marie Cadieux (Valérie Langlois), Micheline Lanctôt (Mme Gauthier), Gary Farmer (Brandt), Pat Kiely (Bilodeau), Kaniehtiio Horn (Johanne), Diane D'Aquila (Miss Van Ilen), Clara Furey (Nathalie), Xavier Dolan (Jean-Marc), Sean Lu (Mr. Chou), Kevin Tierney (Jerome Langlois), Nathalie Girard (Nightclub Waitress)

LIFE IN A DAY (National Geographic Entertainment) Producer, Liza Marshall; Executive Producers, Ridley Scott, Tony Scott; Co-Producers, Jack Arbuthnott, Tim Partridge; Director, Kevin Macdonald, YouTube Contributors; Photography, YouTube Contributors; Music, Harry Gregson-Williams; Music & Song, Matthew Herbert; Editor, Joe Walker; Visual Effects Supervisor, Stefan Drury; a YouTube/ Ridley Scott & Tony Scott presentation of a Scott Free Films production; British-American; Stereo; Technicolor/Black and white; DV; Rated PG-13; 95 minutes; American release date: July 29, 2011. Documentary in which people all over the world contributed footage they shot on a single day, July 24, 2010; **WITH:** Cindy Baer, Mojca Brecelj, Caryn Waechter, Hiroaki Aikawa, Drake Shannon, Christopher Brian Heerdt, David Jacques, Bob Liginski Jr., Ester Brym Ortiz Guillen, Ranja Kamal, Boris Grishevich, Ashley Meeks, Cec Marquez, Ayman El Gazwy, Shahin Najafipour, Arsen Grigoryan, Lilit Movsisyan, Fredeik Boje Mortensen, Jane Haubrich, Shir Decker, Jennifer M. Howd, Teagan Bentley, Catherine Liginski, Ildikó Zöldi, Amelie Sara Kukucska, Jack C. Marquez

SLEEP FURIOUSLY (Microcinema International) Producers, Margaret Matheson, Gideon Koppel; Executive Producers, Mike Figgis, Serge Lalou; Director/Photography, Gideon Koppel; Music, Aphex Twin; Editor, Mari Battistel; a Bard Entertainments, Van Film production; British, 2009; Color; Not rated; 94 minutes; Release date: July 29, 2011. Documentary on the Welsh farming community of Trefeurig.

THE MOUTH OF THE WOLF (MoMA) a.k.a. *La bocca del lupo*; Producers, Nicola Giuliano, Francesca Cima, Dario Zonta; Director/Screenplay/Photography, Pietro Marcello; Music, ERA; Editor, Sara Fgaier; Narrator, Franco Leo; a Fondazione San Marcellino Onlus presentation of an Indigo Films, L'Avventurosa

Film production, in association with RAI Cinema, Babe Films; Italian, 2009; Color/black and white; DigiBeta; Not rated; 67 minutes; American release date: August 4, 2011. Documentary on an imprisoned felon and his transsexual lover; **WITH:** Vincenzo Motta, Mary Monaco, Andrea Cambi, Stefano Carappa, Claudio Coppola, Domenico Fertini, Michela Jugovich, Anita Lee, Anna Massa, Antonio Micheletti, Roberto Polloni, Adriano Rossi, Manuela Rossi, Ursula Salvo, Sara Trombetti

Vincenzo Motta in *The Mouth of the Wolf* © MoMA

PROTEKTOR (Film Movement) Producers, Milan Kuchynka, Pavel Strnad; Director, Marek Najbrt; Screenplay, Benjamin Tucek, Robert Geisler, Marek Najbrt; Photography, Miloslav Holman; Designer, Ondřej Nekvasil; Costumes, Andrea Králová; Music, Midi Lidi; Editor, Pavel Hrdlička; Casting, Kateřina Oujezdská; a Negativ presentation, in co-production with Czech Television/UPP/ Soundsquare; Czech, 2009; Dolby; Color/black and white; Not rated; 100 minutes; American release date: August 5, 2011. **CAST:** Marek Daniel (Emil Vrbata), Jana Plodková (Hana Vrbatová), Klára Melíšková (Věra), Richard Stanke (Tomek), Tomáš Měcháček (Petr), Jan Budař (Colleague), Jiři Ornest (Fantl), Sandra Nováková (Krista), Martin Myšička (Franta), Josef Polášek (Producer), Simon Schwarz (Gestapo Officer), Tomáš Žatečka (Jindra), Adam Kubišta (Jenda), Cyril Drozda (Dr. Kouba, PhD), Leoš Noha (Worker), Eduard Jenický (Czech Army Officer), Philipp Schenker (Non-Commissioned Officer), Roman Slovák (Policeman), Roman Vejdovec, Thomas Zielinsky (Gestapo Officers), David Máj, Jan Jankovský (Interrogation Thugs), Ondřej Matějka (Reinhard Heydrich), Petra Nesavačilová, Dana Marková (Groupies)

Tomás Mechácek, Jana Plodková in *Protektor* © Film Movement

HABERMANN (Corinth Films) Co-Producers, Pavel Kovy, Jan Kudela, Veit Heiduschka, Lucki Stipetic, Kai Grueneke; Director, Juraj Herz; Screenplay, Wolfgang Limmer; Based on the novel *Habermann's Mill* by Josef Urban; Photography, Alexander Surkala; Designer, Petr Fort; Costumes, Simona Rybakova; Music, Elia Cmiral; Editor, Melanie Werwie; Casting, Ingrid Graber, Zdenka Munzarova; a production of Karel Dirka and Art-Oko Film, GmbH & Co. Filmproduktions KG; German-Austrian-Czech, 2010; Dolby; Color; Not rated; 104 minutes; American release date: August 5, 2011. **CAST:** Mark Waschke (August Habermann), Karel Roden (Jan Brezina), Hannah Herzsprung (Jana Habermann), Wilson Gonzalez-Ochesenknecht (Hans Habermann), Andrej Hryc (Bürgermeister Jan Hartl), Ben Becker (Major Kurt Koslowski), Wilson Gonzalez Ochsenknecht (Hans Habermann), Franziska Weisz (Martha Brezina), Radek Holub (Masek), Zuzana Krónerová (Eliska Masek), Jan Hrusinský (Vaclav Pespichal), Oldrich Kaiser (Brichta), Jaromír Dulava(Buchhalter Hora), Andrej Hryc (Bürgermeister Jan Hartl)

Hannah Herzsprung in *Habermann* © Corinth Films

OVER YOUR CITIES GRASS WILL GROW (Kino Lorber) Producers, Sophie Fiennes, Kees Kasander, Emilie Blezat; Director, Sophie Fiennes; Photography, Remko Schnorr; Music, Freie Stucke Fur; Editor, Ethel Shepherd; Interviewer, Klaus Dermutz; an Amoeba Film, Kasander, Sciapoda production; French-British-Dutch, 2010; Dolby; Super 35 Widescreen; Color; Not rated; 105 minutes; American release date: August 10, 2011. Documentary on how artist Anselm Kiefer constructed a series of elaborate installations at a derelict silk factory near Barjac. **WITH:** Anselm Kiefer.

SCHEHERAZADE TELL ME A STORY (ArtMattan) a.k.a. *Ehky ya Scheherazade*; Producer, Kamel Abou Ali; Director, Yousry Nasrallah; Screenplay, Wahid Hamed; Photography, Samir Bahzan; Designer, Mohamed Atteya; Costumes, Dina Nadeem; Music, Tamer Karawan; Editor, Mona Rabei; a Misr Cinema production; Egyptian, 2009; Dolby; Color; Not rated; 135 minutes; American release date: August 12, 2011. **CAST:** Mona Zakki (Hebba Younis), Mahmoud Hemida (Adham), Hassan El Raddad (Karim), Sawsan Badr (Amani), Rihab El Gamal (Safaa), Nesrine Amin (Wafaa), Nahed El Sebaï (Hanaa), Mohamed Ramadan (Saïd), Sanaa Akroud (Nahed), Hussein El Imam (Ahmed Fadlallah), Ahmed Fouad Selim (Karim's Boss), Shady Khalaf (Roshdy)

AARAKSHAN (Reliance Big Pictures) Director, Prakash Jha; Screenplay, Prakash Jha, Anjum Rajabali; Photography, Sachin Krishn; Art Director, Jayant Deshmukh; Costumes, Priyanka Mundada; Music, Shankar Ehsaan Loy; Background Music, Wayne Sharp; Lyrics, Prasoon Joshi; Choreographer, Jayesh Pradhan; Editor, Santosh Mandal; Action Director, Prem Sharma; a Base Industries Group production; Indian; Color; Not rated; 165 minutes; American release date: August 12, 2011. **CAST:** Amitabh Bachchan (Prabhakar Anand), Saif Ali Khan (Deepak Kumar), Deepika Padukone (Poorbi Anand), Manoj Bajpayee (Mithilesh Singh), Prateik Babbar (Sushant Seth), Manish Kapoor (Ravi Anand), Shradda Thakur

Hassan El Raddad, Mona Zakki in *Scheherazade Tell Me a Story* © ArtMattan

(Ishika Sahani), Tanvi Azmi (Kavita P. Anand), Hema Malini (Shakuntala Thakral), Saurabh Shukla (Mantri Baburao), Darshan Jariwala (Anirudh), Yashpal Sharma (Shambhu), Mukesh Tiwari (Police Inspector), Rajeev Verma (Damodar), S.M. Zaheer (Retired Professor), Vinay Apte (Neta Bhishamber), Anita Kanwar (Mrs. Kantaprasad), Aanchal Munjal (Muniya S. Yadav), Saurabh Shukla (Education Minister)

Saif Ali Khan, Deepika Padukone in *Aarakshan* © Reliance Big Pictures

3-D SEX AND ZEN: EXTREME ECSTASY (China Lion) Producers, Stephen Shiu, Stephen Shiu Jr.; Director, Christopher Sun; Screenplay, Mark Wu, Stephen Shiu, Stephen Shiu Jr.; Based on the ancient text *The Carnal Prayer Mat*; Photography, Jimmy Wong; Art Director, Tony Yu; Costumes, Cindy Cheung; Music, Raymond Wong; Editors, Asrael Chung, Mathew Hui; a One Dollar Production, Ltd.; Hong Kong; Dolby; Color; Not rated; 129 minutes; American release date: August 12, 2011. **CAST:** Hiro Hayama (Wei Yangsheng), Leni Lan (Tie Yuxiang), Vonnie Lui (The Elder of Bliss), Saori Hara (Ruizhu), Suou Yukiko (Dongmei), Tony Ho (Prince of Ning), Kirt Kishita (Quan Laoshi), Jason lu (Scholar Shangguan Shun), Carina Chen (Maid Xian Lan), Justin Cheung (Mr. Lam), Mark Wu (Tiancam), Tenky Tai Man Tin (Dique), Wong Shu Tong (Monk Budai), Lau Shek Yin (Mayor)

THE JOURNALS OF MUSAN (Finecut) Producer, Lee Jinuk; Director/Screenplay, Park Jungbum; Photography, Kim Jongsun; Designer, Eun Heesang; Costumes, Lee Arong; Editor, Jo Hyunjoo; a Secondwind Film presentation in association with Jinjin Pictures; North Koreanm, 2010; Color; Not rated; 127 minutes; American release date: August 17, 2011. **CAST:** Park Jung-bum (Jeon Seung-chul), Jin Yonguk (Kyung-chul), Kang Eunjin (Sook-young), Baek-gu

Park Jung-bum (right) in *The Journals of Musan* © Finecut

ATROCIOUS (Bloody Disgusting/The Collective) Producers, Jessica Villegas, David Sanz; Director/Screenplay/Editor, Fernando Barreda Luna; Photography, Ferrán Castera; Visual Effects Supervisor, Luis Tinoco; a Nabu Films, Silencio Rodamos Producciones production; Spanish-Mexican, 2010; Dolby; Color; Rated R; 75 minutes; American release date: August 17, 2011. **CAST:** Cristian Valencia (Cristian), Clara Moraleda (July), Chus Pereiro (Debora), Sergi Martin (Jose), Xavi Doz (Santiago), Jose Masegosa (Carlos), Sammy Gad (David)

Atrocious © The Collective

IRON CROWS (C&Docs/CreativEast) Producer, Kim Min-chul; Director, Park Bong-nam; Screenplay, Park Bong-nam, Moon Ye-won; Photography, Seo Yeon-taek; Editor, Lee Chang-kyun; an FNS production; South Korean; Color; HD; Not rated; 93 minutes; American release date: August 24, 2011. Documentary on "ship breaking" along the coastline of Bangladesh.

Iron Crows © C& Docs

SHUT UP LITTLE MAN! AN AUDIO MISADVENTURE (Tribeca) Producers, Sophie Hyde, Michael Bate; Executive Producers, Stephen Cleary, Julie Ryan; Director/Screenplay, Matthew Bate; Photography/Editor, Bryan Mason; Designer, Tony Cronin; Music, Jonny Elk Walsh; a Filmlab presentation of a Closer production in association with South Australian Film Corp. and Adelaide Film Festival; Australian; Color; HD; Not rated; 90 minutes; Release date: August 26, 2011. Documentary on how two San Franciscans began recording the explosive verbal battles between the two older men who lived next door; **WITH:** Ivan Brunetti, Daniel Clowes, Mitch Deprey, Patrick Frost, Eddie Guerriero, Gregg Gibbs, Mark Gunderson, Mike Mitchell, Tony Newton, David Riesen, Henry S. Rosenthal, Doug Wiggins, Eddie Lee Sausage, Peter Haskett, Raymond Huffman.

SWINGING WITH THE FINKELS (Freestyle) Producer, Deepak Nayar; Executive Producers, Thomas Augsberger, David Mutch, Philip von Alvensleben; Director/Screenplay, Jonathan Newman; Photography, Dirk Nel; Designer, James Lewis; Costumes, Annie Hardinge; Music, Mark Thomas; Editor, Eddie Hamilton; an ICAP Media and Freestyle Releasing presentation of a Reliance Big Pictures and Starlight Film Partners production in association with Kintop Pictures and Filmaka; British; Dolby; Color; Rated R; 85 minutes; American release date: August 26, 2011. **CAST:** Martin Freeman (Alvin Finkel), Mandy Moore (Sarah Finkel), Melissa George (Janet), Jonathan Silverman (Peter), Jerry Stiller (Mr. Winters), Angus Deayton (Richard), Edward Akrout (Andrew), Louie Spence (Juan Carlos), Daisy Beaumont (Clementine), Tim Beckmann (Jim), Michael Burgess (Pee Man), Paul Chowdhry (Henry), Alec Christie (Italian Waiter), Ed Coleman (Shop Assistant), Kenneth Collard (Toe Jam Man), Elizabeth Tan (Pedicurist), Graham Bohea (Dustbin Man), Carolyn Tomkinson (Toe Jam Woman), Sarah Edwardson (Jenny), Beverley Klein (Mrs. Winters), Ian Midlane (Bondgage Man), Will Norris (Bob), Mario Vernazza (Jewish Man), Tracy Wiles (Bondage Woman), Haruka Kuroda (Japanese Woman)

Mandy Moore, Martin Freeman in *Swinging with the Finkels* © Freestyle

TALES FROM THE GOLDEN AGE (IFC Films) a.k.a. *Amintiri din epoca de aur*, Producers, Oleg Mutu, Cristian Mungiu; Directors, Ioana Uricaru, Hanno Hoefer, Razvan Marculescu, Constantin Popescu, Cristian Mungiu; Screenplay, Cristian Mungiu; Photography, Oleg Mutu, Alex Sterian, Liviu Marghidan; Designers, Cezara Armasu, Mihaela Poenaru, Dana Istrate, Simona Paduretu; Costumes, Dana Istrate, Brandusa Ioan, Luminita Mihai, Ana Ioneci; Music, Hanno Hoefer, Laco Jimi; Editors, Dana Bunescu, Theodora Penciu, Ioana Uricaru; Casting, Catalin Dordea; a Mobra Films production, with the support of Why Not Prods.; Romanian, 2009; Dolby; Color; Not rated; 155 minutes; American release date: August 26, 2011. **CAST:** *The Legend of the Official Visit:* Alexandru Potocean (The Secretary), Teodor Corban (The Mayor), Emanuel Pirvu (The Party Inspector); *The Legend of the Party Photographer:* Avram Birau (The Photographer), Paul Dunca (The Photographer's Assistant), Viorel Comanici (The Party Secretary); *The Legend of the Chicken Driver:* Vlad Ivanov (Girgore), Tania Popa (Camelia),

Liliana Mocanu (Marusia); *The Legend of the Greedy Policeman:* Ion Sapdaru (Policeman Alexa), Virginia Mirea (Policeman's Wife), Gabriel Spahiu (Neighbor); *The Legend of the Air Sellers:* Diana Cavallioti (Crina), Radu Iacoban (Bughi); *The Legend of the Zealous Activist:* Calin Chirilia (The Party Activist), Romeo Tudor (The Shepherd)

Tales from the Golden Age © IFC Films

SPECIAL TREATMENT (First Run Features) a.k.a. *Sans queue ni tête;* Producer, Jani Thiltges; Executive Producer, Serge Zeitoun; Director, Jeanne Labrune; Screenplay, Jeanne Labrune, Richard Debuisne; Photography, Virginie Saint-Martin; Set Decorator, Régine Constant; Costumes, Claire Fraïssé; Music, André Mergenthaler; Editor, Anja Lüdcke; a Liaison Cinematographique, Art-Light Prods., Samsa Film, Artemis prods. presentation and production; French-Luxembourg-Belgian, 2010; Dolby; Color; Not rated; 95 minutes; American release date: August 26, 2011. **CAST:** Isabelle Huppert (Alice Bergerac), Bouli Lanners (Xavier Demestre), Richard Debuisne (Pierre Cassagne), Sabila Moussadek (Juliette), Valérie Dréville (Hélène Demestre), Mathieu Carriére (Robert Masse), Didier Bezace (The Happy and Sad Man), Frédéric Longbois (The Transvestite), Christophe Odent (The Pipe Collector), Jean-François Wolff (The Pedophile Client), Gilles Cohen (The Elegant Athlete), Frédéric Pierrot (François Briand), Karim Keklou (Bruno), Christophe Lambert (Olive), Valérie Bodson (Elisabeth), Serge Hutry (The Auctioneer), Patricia Miroy (Salesgirl), Anne Fournier (Teller), Hélêne Moor (Concierge), Nicole Legros (Béatrice), Nathalie Kutzner (Psychiatrist), Mohamed Ouachen (Milkman), Marcos Adamantiadis (Guide), Fabienne Mainguet (Hospital Secretary), Paolo Signorini (Torch Man)

THE CALLER (Samuel Goldwyn Films) Producers, Amina Dasmal, Robin Fox, Piers Tempest, Luillo Ruiz; Executive Producers, Phil Hunt, Compton Ross, Robert Bevan, Cyril Megret; Director, Matthew Parkhill; Screenplay, Sergio Casci; Photography, Alexander Melman; Designer, Guifre Tort; Music, Unkle, Aidan Lavelle; Editor, Gabriel Coss; Special Effects Coordinator, Charlie Bonilla; Casting, Sharon Howard-Field; a Pimienta Film Co., the Salt Co., Alcove Entertainment in association with Head Gear Films, Metrol Technology presentation; British-Puerto Rican; Dolby; Color; HD; Rated R; 92 minutes; American release date: August 26, 2011. **CAST:** Rachelle Lefevre (Mary Kee), Stephen Moyer (John Guidi), Luis Guzmán (George), Ed Quinn (Steven), Lorna Raver (Rose), Marisé Alvarez (Nurse), Alfredo De Quesada (Attorney Davies), Cordelia González (Judge), Brian Tester (Attorney Kirkby), Aris Mejias (Young Woman), Gladys Rodríguez (Mrs. Guidi), Grace Connelly (Dr. Hain), Jose Cotte (Social Services Clerk), Leonardo Castro (Fire Dancer), Johnathan R. Santiago (Creepy Student), Abimael Linares (Young Man), Wilfred Perez (Young Guy), David Rittenhouse (Real Estate Agent)

Rachelle Lefevre in *The Caller* © Goldwyn Films

LITTLE GIRL (First Run Features) a.k.a. *La Pivellina;* Producer/Photography, Rainer Frimmel; Directors, Tizza Covi, Rainer Frimmel; Screenplay/Editor, Tizza Covi; a Vento Film production; Austrian-Italian, 2009; Stereo; Color; HDCAM; Not rated; 100 minutes; American release date: August 31, 2011. **CAST:** Patrizia Gerardi (Patty), Asia Crippa (Asia), Tairo Caroli (Tairo), Walter Saabel (Walter), Pierino Atzeni (Farmer), Tailor Intruglio (Fiancee), Fabrizio Borri, Marco Gerani (Policemen), Roberto Caroli (Father), Donald Crippa (Baby), Gigliola Crippa (Donna), Mirco Crippa (Zio), Tania Crippa (Mother), Evelyn Freirejimenez, Juan Freirejimenez, Andres Quezada, David Quezada (Friends), Lucia Rado Maria (Lucia), Luciano Salgado (Luciano), Alfredo Parri (News Dealer), Donato Prina (Popo), Claudio Carbonari (Cugino), Pathan Zahid Khan (Magician)

BODYGUARD (Reliance Entertainment) Producers, Alvira Agnihotri, Atul Agnihotri; Director, Siddique; Screenplay, Siddique, J.P. Chowksey, Kiran Kotrial; Photography, Sejal Shah; Art Director, Angelica Monica Bhowmick; Costumes, Alvira Agnihotri, Ashley Rebello, Manish Malhotra; Music, Sandeep Shirodkar, Himesh Reshammiya; Lyrics, Shabbir Ahmed, Neelesh Misra; Editor, Sanjay Sankla; a Reel Life Prod. production; Indian; Dolby; Super 35 Widescreen; Color; Not rated; 131 minutes; American release date: August 31, 2011. **CAST:** Salman Khan (Lovely B. Singh), Kareena Kapoor (Divya S. Rana), Raj Babbar (Sartaj Rana), Asrani (Shekhar), Vidhya Sinha (Mrs. Rana), Hazel Keech (Maya), Chetan Hansraj (Mhatre), Mohammad Faizan (Sartaj L. Singh), Rajat Rawail (Tsunami Singh), Aditya Pancholi (Vikrant Mahtre), Mahesh Manjrekar (Ranjan Mhatre), Sharat Saxena (Bindra)

Jean-François Wolff, Isabelle Huppert in *Special Treatment* © First Run Features

LOVE EXPOSURE (Olive Films) a.k.a. *Ai no mukidashi*; Producers, Toyoyuki Yokohama, Shinya Kawai; Director/Screenplay, Sion Sono; Photography, Sôhei Tanikawa; Designer, Takashi Matsuzuka; Music, Tomohide Harada; Editor, Junichi Itô; an Omega Project Entertainment, Studio Three Co. production; Japanese, 2009; Dolby; Color; HD-to-35mm; Widescreen; Not rated; 237 minutes; American release date: September 2, 2011. **CAST:** Takahiro Nishijima (Yû), Hikari Mitsushima (Yôko), Sakura Andô (Koike), Yutaka Shimizu (Yûji), Hiroyuki Onoue (Takahiro), Tasuku Nagaoka (Senpai), Sô Hirosawa (Kumi), Yûko Genkaku (Keiko), Mami Nakamura (Yû no Haha), Arata Yamanaka (Roido no Deshi A), Junya Iwamoto (Roido no Deshi B), Motoki Ochiai (Koike no Sukina Otoko), Sango (DJ), Atsushi Yamanaka (Tannin no sensei), Kôichi Koshimura (Kyôtô), Shingo Tanaka (Bakudan Otoko)

Hikari Mitsushima in *Love Exposure* © Olive Films

SAVING PRIVATE PEREZ (Patelion) a.k.a. *Salvando al Soldado Pérez*; Producers, Billy Rovzar, Fernando Rovzar, Alex García, Walter von Borstel, Alexis Fridman; Executive Producers, Billy Rovzar, Fernando Rovzar, Mariano Menéndez, Anwar Safa, Alejandro Safa, Alex García; Director, Beto Gómez; Screenplay, Beto Gómez, Francisco Payó González; Photography, Danny Jacobs; Designer, Raymundo Cabrera; Costumes, Marylin Fitoussi; Music, Mark Mothersbaugh; Editor, Mario Sandoval; Casting, Manuel Teil; a Lemon Films production in coproduction with Fidecine and Via Media and in association with Terregal Films; Mexican; Dolby; Widescreen; Color; Rated PG-13; 103 minutes; American release date: September 2, 2011. **CAST:** Miguel Rodarte (Julian Pérez), Adal Ramones (Benito García), Jaime Camil (Eladio), Jesús Ochoa (Chema Díaz), Gerardo Taracena (Carmelo Benavides), Joaquín Cosio (Rosalio Medoza), Isela Vega (Doña Elvira de Pérez), Rodrigo Oviedo (Pumita), Marius Biegai (Sasha Boginski), Claudia Salinas (Chayito), Roberto Espejo (Lucio), Alexander Minchenko (Yuri), Gerardo Ott (Pascual), Kaven Parmas (Amhed Kubba), Guillermo Quintanilla (Delfino), John Gerald Randall (Daily), Wililam Raymond (Willis), Randy Vasquez (Lt. Diaz). Juan Carlos Flores (Juan Pérez Nomel)

I'M GLAD MY MOTHER IS ALIVE (Strand) a.k.a. *Je suis heureux que ma mère soit vivante*; Producer, Jean-Louis Livi; Directors/Adaptation & Dialogue, Claude Miller, Nathan Miller; Screenplay, Alain Le Henry; Based on an article by Emmanuel Carrere; Photography, Aurélien Devaux; Designer, Jean-Pierre Kohut-Svelko; Costumes, Elsa Gies; Music, Vincent Segal; Editor, Morgane Spacagna; a Jean-Louis Livi and Jacques Audiard presentation of a co-production of F Comme Film, Orly Films, France 3 Cinéma and Page 114, with the participation of Canal+, TPS Star, France 3 with the support of Ile-de-France Région; French, 2009; Dolby; Color; Not rated; 91 minutes; American release date: September 2, 2011. **CAST:** Vincent Rottiers (Thomas Jouvet, 20 years), Sophie Cattani (Julie Martino), Christine Citti (Annie Jouvet), Yves Verhoeven (Yves Jouvet), Maxime Renard (Thomas, 12 years), Olivier Guéritée (Patrick/François, 17 years), Ludo Harlay (Patrick/François, 9 years), Gabin Lefebvre (Tommy, 4 years), Quentin Gonzalez (Frédéric), Chantal Banlier (Chantal Duronnet, the Neighbor), Thomas Momplot (Mathieu), Alberto Actis (The Shredder), Dominique Hulin (The Taulier from the Hotel Lux), Samir Guesmi (Employer), Sabrina Ouazani (Cinema Cashier), Célia Granier-Deferre (Police Employee), Bruno Chiche (Frédéric's Father), Carole Franck (Orphanage Director), Françoise Gazio (Doctor), Virginie Emane-Balu (Patricia), Iria Loureiro Dos Santos (Schoolgirl), Jacqueline Woelffel (The Headmaster), Louis Czajkowski, Gabriel Czajkowski (Patrick, 2 years), Rémy Robakha (Chief), Clémence Boué (Florist), Bruno Duron (Candy Seller), Florence Huige (Mother), Xavier Thiam (Man in the White Shirt), Raphaël Beauville (Usher), Lionel Robert (Internship Professor), Christophe Désenclos (Hotel Detective), Grégoire Roger (Nude Man), Gilles Demurger (Auto Accident), Laura Schiffman (Servant), Lyzéa Chevereau-Martin, Lucy Chevereau-Martin (Patrick, 8 months)

THAT GIRL IN YELLOW BOOTS (IndiePix) Producer/Director, Anurag Kashyap; Screenplay, Anurag Kashyap, Kalki Koechlin; Photography, Rajeev Ravi; Designer, Wasiq Khan; Costumes, Shubhra gupta; Music, Naren Chandavarkar; Editor, Shweta Venkat Mathew; a Tipping Point Films presentation of an Anurag Kashyap Films production in association with National Film Development Corp., Sikhya Entertainment; Indian; Color; Widescreen; HD; Not rated; 103 minutes; American release date: September 2, 2011. **CAST:** Kalki Koechlin (Ruth), Naseeruddin Shah (Divakar), Prashant Prakash (Prashant), Gulshan Devaiah (Chittiappa), Puja Sarup (Maya), Kumud Mishra (Lynn), Kartik Krishnan (Main Cop – Bribe/At Ruth's House), Shlok Sharma (Wrangler Boy), Shiv Subramanian (Peter), Divya Jagdale (Divya), Somrita Nandy (Lynn's House Caretaker), Pradeep Dalvi (Muchhad, at Fro), Murai (Rude Man, at Fro), Deepak Damie (Sleazy Man, at Fro), Mushtaq Khan (Superintendent), Anubhuti Kashyap (Maa Anubhuti), Piyush Mishra (Rickshaw Driver), Thani (Thani), Sankalp Acharekar (Sankalp), Jai Mehta (Shy Boy for Shag), Kashyap Das (Susu Boy), Ronit Roy (Cop at Versova Police Station), Makrand Deshpande (Postmaster), Rajat Kapoor (Man in Elevator)

Kaliki Koechlin in *That Girl in Yellow Boots* © IndiePix

Miguel Rodarte, Gerardo Taracena, Rodrigo Oviedo, Joaquín Cosio, Jesús Ochoa in *Saving Private Perez* © Patelion Films

THE BLACK POWER MIXTAPE 1967-1975 (Sundance Selects) Producer, Annika Rogell; Executive Producer, Tobias Janson; Co-Producers, Joslyn Barnes, Danny Glover, Axel Arnö; Director/Screenplay, Göran Hugo Olsson; Music, Om'Mas Keith, Ahmir Questlove Thompson; Executive Music Producer, Corey Smyth; Editors, Göran Hugo Olsson, Hanna Lejonqvist; a Story AB, Louverture Films, Sveriges Television AB, Blacksmith Corp. production; Swedish; Black and white/color; Not rated; 100 minutes; American release date: September 9, 2011. Documentary on the Black Power movement; **WITH:** Stokely Carmichael, Eldridge Cleaver, Kathleen Cleaver, Bobby Seale, Huey P. Newton, Emile de Antonio, William Kunstler, Angela Davis; Commentary by: Erykah Badu, Harry Belafonte, John Forté, Kenny Gamble, Robin Kelley, Talib Kweli, Abiodun Oyewole, Melvin Van Peebles, Sonia Sanchez, Ahmir Questlove Thompson

Angela Davis in *The Black Power Mixtape* © Sundance Selects

THE WHALE (Paladin) Producer, Suzanne Chisholm; Executive Producers, Ryan Reynolds, Scarlett Johansson, Eric Desatnik; Directors/Photography, Suzanne Chisholm, Michael Parfit; Screenplay/Editor, Michael Parfit; Music, David Parfit, Tobin Stokes; Narrator, Ryan Reynolds; a Telefilm Canada through the Theatrical Documentary Program presentation of a Mountainside Films production in association with CBC News Network; Canadian; Color; HD; Rated G; 85 minutes; American release date: September 9, 2011. Documentary on how a baby whale from Puget Sound ended up 200 miles away in Canada.

The Whale © Paladin Pictures

MY KINGDOM (China Lion) a.k.a. *Da wu sheng*; Producers, André Morgan, Zoë Chen; Executive Producer, Ross Alan Pollack; Director, Gao Xiaosong; Screenplay, Zou Jingzhi, Gao Xiaosong; Photography, Kwong Ting Wo; Designer, Yang Yaoyu; Costumes, Gino Xie; Music, Joachim Horsley; Editor, Christopher Blunden; Action Director, Sammo Hung; a Celestial Pictures, DW Films Ltd., Skyland Films; Chinese; Dolby; Color; Not rated; 108 minutes; American release date: September 9, 2011. CAST: Wu Chun (Guan Yilong), Han Geng (Meng Erkui), Barbie Hsu (Xi Mulang), Louis Liu (General Lu), Yuen Biao (Master Yu Shengying), Yu Rongguang (Master Yue)

Barbie Hsu in *My Kingdom* © China Lion

LOVE IN SPACE (China Lion/Fox Intl.) a.k.a. *Quan qiu re lian*; Producer, Fruit Chan; Directors, Wing Shya, Tony Chan; Screenplay, Tony Chan, Lucretia Ho; Photography, Bartek Kaczmarek, Michael Tywoniuk; Designer/Costumes, Sean Kunjambu; Music, Eddie Chung; Editor, Wenders Li; a Huayi Brothers, Sundream Motion Pictures production; Chinese-Hong Kong; Dolby; Color; Not rated; 103 minutes; American release date: September 9, 2011. **CAST:** Aaron Kwok (Michael), Eason Chan (Johnny), René Liu (Rose), Gwei Lun Mei (Lily), Xu Fan (Mary), Angelababy (Peony), Jing Boran (Wen Feng), Grace Huang (Bunny)

THE AUTOBIOGRAPHY OF NICOLAE CEAUȘESCU (Film Desk) Producer, Velvet Moraru; Director/Screenplay, Andrei Ujică; Editor, Dana Bunescu; an Icon Production in association with Societatea Română de Televiziune; Romanian-German, 2010; Dolby; Color/black and white; Not rated; 180 minutes; American release date: September 9, 2011. Documentary on Romanian dictator Nicolae Ceaușescu.

THE INHERITORS (Icarus) a.k.a. *Los Herederos*; Producer/Director/Photography/Editor, Eugenio Polgovsky; Music, Banda Mixe de Oaxaca; a Tecolote Films production; Mexican, 2008; Color; DV; Not rated; 90 minutes; American release date: September 9, 2011. Documentary on the rural poor of Mexico.

A KISS AND A PROMISE (Lab4 Prods.) Producers, Lenny Bitondo, Mike Guzzo; Director, Phillip Guzman; Screenplay, Mick Rossi, Phillip Guzman; Photography/Editor, Philip Roy; Art Director, Meredith Woodley; Music, David M. Frost; Produced in association with Rozman Pictures; Canadian; Dolby; Color; HD; Rated R; 90 minutes; American release date: September 9, 2011. **CAST:** Mick Rossi (David Beck), Natasha Gregson Wagner (Samantha Beck), Sean Power (Charlie Matthews), Patrick Bergin (Det. Anthony Dolan), Robert Miano (Det. Joseph Bello), Sile Bermingham (Rose Miller), Danielle Watling (Mary Miller), Brian Foyster (Ian Brin), Lisa Ciara (Lily Turner), Samantha Farrow (Angel), Aaron Gallagher (Sparky), Cathy Giannone (Mrs. Wyman), Steve Boyer (John Miller), Manny Barbosa (Alex), George Ghali (Yari Patel), David Schaap (Ed), Laura Adamo (Joyce), Joan Massiah (Mrs. O), Nick Ballie (Brian), Jullian Tassielli, Dan Fox (Officers), Marc Trottier (Uniformed Officer)

Natasha Gregson Wagner, Mick Rossi in *A Kiss and a Promise* © Lab4 Prods.

POSITION AMONG THE STARS (HBO Films) a.k.a. *Stand van de sterren*; Producer, Hetty Naaijkens-Retel Helmrich; Director, Leonard Retel Helmrich; Screenplay, Hetty Naaijkens-Retel Helmrich, Leonard Retel Helmrich; Photography, Ismail Fahmi Lubish, Leonard Retel Helmrich; Music, Danang Faturahman, Fahmy Al-Attas; Editor, Jasper Naaijkens, ; a Scarabeefilms, Human Broadcasting presentation; Dutch, 2010; Color; HD; Not rated; 109 minutes; American release date: September 15, 2011. Documentary following the Indonesian working class Sjamsuddin family; **WITH:** Rumidjah Sjamsuddin, Theresia Untari, Bachtiar Becker, Sriwyati, Dwikomarisah, Bagus Nur Alam, Tumisah (Third in a trilogy following *The Eye of the Day* in 2001 and *Shape of the Moon* in 2004).

Position among the Stars © HBO Films

THE TREASURE HUNTER (Eleven Arts) a.k.a. *Ci Ling*; Executive Producer, Du Yang; Director, Chu Yen-ping; Music, Ricky Ho; Stunts, Ching Siu-tung; a Yen Ping Films production; Taiwanese, 2009; Dolby; Color; Not rated; minutes; American release date: September 15, 2011. **CAST:** Jay Chou (Qiao Fei), Lin Chiling (Lan Ting), Eric Tsang (Chop), Chen Daoming (Master Hua), Chen Chu-he (Desert Eagle), Will Liu (Friday), Miao Pu (Swords Thirteen), Ian Powers (Russian Smuggler), Kenneth Tsang (Tu Lao-dai)

Chiling Lin, Jay Chou in *The Treasure Hunter*
© Eleven Arts

SILENT SOULS (Shadow) a.k.a. *Ovsyanki*; Producers, Igor Mishin, Mary Nazari; Director, Aleksei Fedorchenko; Screenplay, Denis Osokin; Based on the novel *Ovsyanki* by Aist Sergeyev; Photography, Mikhail Krichman; Designer, Andrey Ponckratov; Costumes, Anna Barthuly; Music, Andrei Karasyov; Editor, Sergei Ivanov; a Media Mir Foundation/February 29 Film Company/April MIG Pictures Films Company production; Russian, 2010; Dolby; Widescreen; Color; Not rated; 75 minutes; American release date: September 16, 2011. **CAST:** Igor Sergeyev (Aist), Yuriy Tsurilo (Miron), Yuliya Aug (Tanya), Ivan Tushkin (Little Aist), Viktor Sukhorukov (Vesa), Olga Dobrina (Yulya), Leisan Sitdikova (Rimma), Yulia Tushina (Aist's Mother), Vyacheslav Melechov (Bird Seller), Sergey Yarmolyuk (STSI Inspector)

Olga Dobrina, Yuliya Aug in *Silent Souls* © Shadow Distribution

SOUND IT OUT (Glimmer Films) Producer/Director/Photography, Jeanie Finlay; Executive Producer, Dunstan Bruce; Music Supervisor, Graham Langley; Editor, Barbara Zosel; a Glimmer Films in association with Sideshow presentation; British; Stereo; Color; Not rated; 74 minutes; American release date: September 16, 2011. Documentary on the last surviving vinyl record shop in Teesside, North East England. **WITH:** Tom Butchart, David Laybourne, Becky Jones

BERLIN '36 (Corinth Films) Producer, Gerhard Schmidt; Executive Producer, Tim Rostock; Director, Kaspar Heidelbach; Screenplay, Lothar Kurzawa; Based on an idea by Eric Friedler; Photography, Achim Poulheim; Designer, Götz Weidner; Costumes, Lucia Faust; Music, Arno Steffen; Editor, Hedy Altschiller; Casting, Anja Dihrberg; a Gemini Film Eyeworks Production in co-production with NDR Degeto Film and Beta Film; German, 2009; Dolby; Color; Not rated; 100 minutes; American release date: September 16, 2011. **CAST:** Karoline Herfurth (Gretel Bergmann), Sebastian Urzendowsky (Marie Ketteler), Axel Prahl (Hans Waldmann),

Tom Butchart in *Sound it Out* © Glimmer Films

Rick Okon, Maximilian Befort in *Romeos* © Strand Releasing

August Zirner (Edwin Bergmann), Maria Happel (Paula Bergmann), Franz Dinda (Rudolph Bergmann), Leon Seidel (Walter Bergmann), Thomas Thieme (Hans von Tschammer), Johann von Bülow (Karl Ritter von Halt), Julien Engelbrecht (Elisabeth "Lilly" Vogt), Klara Manzel (Thea Walden), Robert Gallinowski (Sigfrid Kulmbach), Elena Uhlig (Frau Vogel), Otto Tausig (Leo Löwenstein), John Keogh (Avery Brundage), Harvey Friedman (Jackson), Tomas Spencer (Nigel), Adrian Zwicker (Heinz), Marita Breuer (Eleonore Ketteler)

JANE'S JOURNEY (First Run Features) Producers, Philipp Schall, Michael Halberstadt, Philipp Wundt; Director/Screenplay, Lorenz Knauer; Photography, Richard Ladkani; Music, Wolfgang Netzer; Editors, Corina Dietz, Patricia Rommel; a NEOS Film GmbH & Co. KG, CC Medien GmbH & Co. KG, Sphnix Media production; German-Tanzanian, 2010; Dolby; Color; HD; Not rated; 111 minutes; American release date: September 16, 2011. Documentary on famed primatologist Jane Goodall; **WITH:** Jane Goodall, Mary Lewis, Angelina Jolie, Pierce Brosnan, Hugo Eric Louis van Lawick, Dale Peterson, Judy Waters, Anthony Collins, Peter Whitemountain, Tom Mangelsen, Patricia Hamond

Sebastian Urzendowsky, Karoline Herfurth in *Berlin '36* © Corinth Films

Jane Goodall in *Jane's Journey* © First Run Features

ROMEOS (Strand) Producers, Kristina Löbbert, Janna Velber; Director/Screenplay, Sabine Bernardi; Photography, Moritz Schultheiß; Costumes, Verena Reuter; Music, Roland Appel; Editor, Renata Salazar Ivancan; Casting, Laura Solbach; a Boogiefilm, Das Kleine Femsehspiel (ZDF), Enigma Film production; German; Dolby; Color; HD; Not rated; 94 minutes; American release date: September 16, 2011. **CAST:** Rick Okon (Lukas), Maximilian Befort (Fabio), Liv Lisa Fries (Ine), Felix Brocke (Sven), Silke Geertz (Annette), Gilles Tschudi (Mr. Boeken), Sigrid Burkholder (Luka's Mother), Johannes Schwab (Luka's Father), Tessa Lukat (Leila), Ben Gageik (Sven's Friend), Katrin Heß (Nurse Jessy), Mira H. Benser, Lilli Lorenz (Nurses), Julia Schäfle (Blondie), Juliane Knoppek (Jaqueline), Michael Neupert (Betrunkener), Peter Foyse (Zivi Marcus), Daniel Rodic (Massimo), Rolf Döring (Old Man), Luciana Cagliotti (Fabio's Mother), Antonio Baiuncol (Fabio's Father)

HAPPY, HAPPY (Magnolia) Producer, Synnøve Hørsdal; Director, Anne Sewitsky; Screenplay, Ragnhild Tronvoll; Art Director, Camilla Lindbråten; Costumes, Ellen Dæhlie Ystehede; Music, Stein Berge Svendsen; Editor, Christoffer Heie; a Maipo AS presentation; Norwegian; Color; Rated R; 88 minues; American release date: September 16, 2011. **CAST:** Agnes Kittelsen (Kaia), Joachim Rafaelsen (Eirik), Maibritt Saerens (Elisabeth), Henrik Rafaelsen (Sigve), Oskar Hernæs Brandsø (Theodor), Ram Shihab Ebedy (Noa), Heine Totland (Choral Director)

SECTOR 7 (CJ Entertainment) a.k.a. *7 gwanggu*; Director, Kim Ji-hun; Screenplay, Yun Je-gyun; a JK Film, Polygon Entertainment production; Japanese; Color; Not rated; 112 minutes; American release date: September 16, 2011. **CAST:** Ha Ji-won (Cha/Hae-jun), Ahn Sung-Kee (Jeong Man), Oh Ji-ho (Kim/Dong-soo), Cha Ae-ryeon (Scientist Kim), Lee Han-wi (Medic), Park Cheol-min, Song Sae-Byeok (Crew), Park Jeong-hak (Unit Head)

Agnes Kittlesen,
Henrik Rafaelson
in *Happy, Happy*
© Magnolia Pictures

Oh Ji-ho, Ha Ji-won in *Sector 7* © CJ Entertainment

DOOKUDU (Ficus) Producers, Anil Sunkara, Gopichand Achanta, Ram Achanta, G. Ramesh Babu; Director, Sreenu Vaitla; Screenplay, Kona Venkat; Story, Gopimohan; Photography, K.V. Guhan, Prasad Murella; Art Director, A.S. Prakash; Costumes, Roopa Vaitla; Music, Thaman S.; Editor, M.R. Varma; 14 Reels Entertainment and Krisha Productions; Indian; Dolby; Color; Not rated; 170 minutes; American release date: September 23, 2011. **CAST:** Mahesh Babu (G. Ajay Kumar), Prakash Raj (Shankar Narayana), Samantha Ruth Prabhu (Prashanthi), Sonu Sood (Nayak), Srinivasa Rao Kota (Mallesh Goud), Rajeev Kanakala (Satyam), Brahmanandam (Padmasri), Abhimanyu Singh (Bunty), Pragathi (Padma), Supreeth (Amberpet Ganesh), Sudha (Janaki), Parvati Melton (Guest), Brahmaji (Prakash), Chandramohan (Tulsi)

Mahesh Babu in *Dookudu*
© Ficus Films

THERE WAS ONCE ... (Gabor Kalman/Cinema-Film) a.k.a. *Egyzer volt*; Producers, Gabor Kalman, Gabor Garami; Director, Gabor Kalman; Photography, Zsolt Tóth, John Dunham; Music, Mark So; Editors, Kate Amend, Susan Metzger; a Gabor Kalman, Cinema-Film co-production; Hungarian-American; Color; HD; Not rated; 104 minutes; American release date: September 23, 2011. Documentary on Hungarian teacher Gyongi Mago's campaign to honor the Jewish population of her hometown who were murdered in the Holocaust; **WITH:** Gyongi Mago, Torak Gusztav Andor, Gabor Kalman, Thomas Kertesz, Eva Toth.

YOU DON'T LIKE THE TRUTH: 4 DAYS INSIDE GUANTÁNAMO (Films Transit) Producers/Directors/Screenplay/Photography, Luc Côté, Patricio Henriquez; Editor, Andrea Henriquez; a Les Films Adobe production in association with D; Canadian-Australian; Dolby; Color; HD; Not rated; 100 minutes; American release date: September 28, 2011. Documentary on the abusive interrogation suspected terrorist Omar Khadr was subjected to in Guantanamo; **WITH:** Omar Ahmed Khadr, Moazzam Begg, Mamdouh Habib, Ruhal Ahmed, Dr. Raul Berdichevsky, Damien Corsetti, Omar Deghayes, Bill Graham, Lt. Cmdr. William Kuebler, Michelle Shephard, Richard Belmar, Dr. Stephen Xenakis, Craig Mokhiber, Gar Pardy, Nathan Withling, Dennis Edney, Maha Elsamnah, Zaynab Khadr

MY JOY (Kino Lorber) a.k.a. *Schastye moe*; Producers, Heino Deckert, Oleg Kokhan; Executive Producers, Olena Yershova, Od Howell; Director/ Screenplay, Sergei Loznitsa; Photography, Oleg Mutu; Designer, Kirill Shuvalov; Costumes, Mare Raidma; Editor, Danielius Kokanauskis; a Maj.de.Fiction, Sota Cinema Group, Lemming Film, ZDF, Arte production; German-Ukranian-Dutch, 2010; Dolby; Color; Not rated; 127 minutes; American release date: September 30, 2011. **CAST:** Viktor Nemets (Georgy), Vladimir Golovin (Old Man), Alexey Vertkov (Young Lieutenant), Dmitriy Gotsdiner (Commander), Olga Shuvalova (Young Prostitute), Maria Varsami (Maria, Gypsy Woman), Boris Kamorzin (Truck Driver), Vlad Ivanov (Major from Moscow), Olga Kogut (The Major's Wife), Yuriy Sviridenko (One-Armed Man), Konstantin Shelestun (Teacher)

Olga Shuvalova, Viktor Nemets in *My Joy* © Kino Lorber

SARAH PALIN: YOU BETCHA! (Freestyle Releasing) Producer, Marc Hoeferlin; Executive Producers, Shani Hinton, Sophie Watts, Gregory Unruh; Directors, Nick Broomfield, Joan Churchill; Photography, Joan Churchill; Music, Jamie Muhoberac; Editor, Michael X. Flores; a Channel 4 in association with Awakening Films presentation; British; Color; DV; Not rated; 91 minutes; American release date: September 30, 2011. Documentary on Sarah Palin's incompetence as a politician; **WITH:** Nick Broomfield, Howard Bess, John Bitney, Laura Chase, Colleen Cottle, Lyda Green, Chuck Heath, Sally Heath, Walt Moneghan, Mike Wooten.

FORCE (Fox Star Studios) Producer, Vipul Amrutlal Shah; Executive Producer, Aashin A. Shah; Director, Nishikant Kamat; Screenplay, Ritesh Shah; Photography, Ayanaka Bose; Music, Harris Jayaraj, Lalit Pandit; Editor, Aarif Sheikh; a Sunshine Pictures production; Indian; Color; Rated R; 137 minutes; American release date: September 30, 2011. **CAST:** John Abraham (ACP Yashvardhan), Genelia D'Souza (Maya), Vidyut Jammwal (Vishnu), Mohnish Bahl (Atul), Raj Babbar (Minister),

Kamlesh Sawant (Inspector Kamlesh), Anaitha Nair (Rachna M. Pandey), Mukesh Rishi (Vasu Anna Reddy)

TUCKER AND DALE VS EVIL (Magnet) Producers, Albert Klychak, Rosanne Milliken, Morgan Jurgenson, Deepak Nayar; Executive Producers, Mark Ryan, Thomas Augsberger; Director, Eli Craig; Screenplay, Eli Craig, Morgan Jurgenson; Photography, David Geddes; Designer, John Blackie; Costumes, Mary Hyde-Kerr; Music, Mike Shields; Editor, Bridget Durnford; Casting, Sean Milliken; a Reliance Big Pictures and Loubyloo Productions presentation in association with Eden Rock Media, Gynormous Pictures of an Urban Island in association with the Government of Alberta and the Alberta Film Development Program; Canadian-American; Dolby; Color; Rated R; 88 minutes; Release date: September 30, 2011. **CAST:** Tyler Labine (Dale Dobson), Alan Tudyk (Tucker), Katrina Bowden (Allison), Jesse Moss (Chad), Philip Granger (Sheriff), Brandon McLaren (Jason), Christie Laing (Naomi), Chelan Simmons (Chloe), Travis Nelson (Chuck), Alexander Arsenault (Todd), Adam Beauchesne (Mitch), Joseph Sutherland (Mike), Mitchell Verigin, Angela DeCorte (College Kids), Karen Reigh (Cheryl), Tye Evans (Dad), Dave Brown (Clerk), Bill Baska (BJ Bald Hillbilly), Mark Allard, Shaun Tisdale (Killer Hillbillies), Myles Pollard (Hillbilly Kid), Eli Craig (Billy, Cameraman), Sasha Craig (News Reporter), Weezer (Jangers the Dog), Bryn Bass, Conner Bass, Lara Milliken (Bowling Kids)

Tyler Labine, Alan Tudyk in *Tucker and Dale vs Evil* © Magnet Releasing

BENDA BILILI! (National Geographic Cinema Ventures) Producers, Yves Chanvillard, Nadim Cheikrouha, Florent de La Tullaye, Renaud Barret; Directors/Screenplay/Photography, Renaud Barret, Florent de La Tullaye; Music, Staff Benda Bilili; Editor, Jean-Christophe Hym; a Screenrunner, La Belle Kinoise presentation; French, 2010; Dolby; Color; DV-to-35mm; Rated PG-13; 86 minutes; American release date: September 30, 2011. Documentary on several paraplegic street musicians from Kinshasa in the Democratic Republic of the Congo; **WITH:** Waroma "Santu Papa" Abi-Ngoma, Maria Barli Djongo, Cubain Kabeya, Kabanba Kabose Kasungo, Roger Landu, Leon "Ricky" Likabu, Paulin "Cavalier" Kiara-Maigi, Claude Kinunu Montana, Theo "Coude" Nsituvuidi, Makembo Nzale, Zadis Mbulu Nzungu, Djuana Tanga-Suele, Coco Ngambali Yakala

Benda Bilili! © National Geographic

SAHEB BIWI AUR GANGSTER (UTV Motion Pictures) Producer, Rahul Mittra; Director, Tigmanshu Dhulia; Screenplay, Tigmanshu Dhulia, Sanjay Chouhan; Photography, Assem Mishra; Editor, Rahul Srivastava; a Bohra Bros Productions, Brandsmith Motion Pictures and Tigmanshu Dhulia Films production; Indian; Color; Not rated; 120 minutes; American release date: September 30, 2011. **CAST:** Randeep Hooda (Babloo/Lalit), Jimmy Shergill (Aditya Pratap Singh), Mahie Gill (Begum), Vipin Sharma (Gainda Singh), Deepal Shah (Suman), Shreya Narayan (Mahua), Deep Raj Rana (Kanhaiya), Sonal Joshi (Rukma)

Mahie Gill, Randeep Hooda in *Saheb Biwi aur Gangster* © UTV

THE NINE MUSES (Icarus Films) Producers, Lina Gopaul, David Lawson; Director/Screenplay, John Akomfrah; Photography, Dewald Aukema; Costumes, Jackie Vernon; Music, Trevor Mathison; Editor, Miikka Leskinen; a UK Film Council/the Arts Council of England/Soul Rebel Pictures presentation in association with Creation Rebel Films/BBC English Regions/Naxos Audio Books/A Made in England Initiative of a Smoking Dogs Films production; British; Dolby; Technicolor/black and white; HD; Not rated; 96 minutes; American release date: October 7, 2011. Documentary/collage on Alaskan immigrants in England from 1960 onwards; **WITH:** John Akomfrah, David Lawson, Trevor Mathison.

JOSÉ AND PILAR (Outsider Pictures) Producers, Miguel Gonçalves Mendes, Agustin Almodóvar, Fernando Meirelles; Director/Screenplay, Miguel Gonçalves Mendes; Photography, Daniel Neves; Editor, Cláudia Rita Oliveira; a JumpCut production; Spanish-Brazilian-Portuguese; Stereo; Color; Not rated; 117 minutes; American release date: October 7, 2011. Documentary on Portugeuse artist José Saramango and his wife Pilar; **WITH:** José Saramango, Pilar del Río, Gael García Bernal, Fernando Merielles

THE HUMAN CENTIPEDE II (FULL SEQUENCE) (IFC) Producers, Ilona Six, Tom Six; Director/Screenplay, Tom Six; Photography, David Meadows; Designer, Thomas Stefan; Music, James Edward Barker; Editor, Nigel De Hond; Special Prosthetics Supervisor, John Schoonraad; an IFC Midnight presentation of a Six Entertainment Company production; British; Black and white; Not rated; 88 minutes; American release date: October 7, 2011. **CAST:** Ashlynn Yennie (Miss Yennie), Laurence R. Harvey (Martin), Vivien Bridson (Misses Lomax), Bill Hutchens (Dr. Sebring), Maddi Black (Candy), Kandace Caine (Karrie), Dominic Borrelli (Paul), Lucas Hansen (Ian), Lee Nicholas Harris (Dick), Dan Burman (Greg), Daniel Jude Gennis (Tim), Georgia Goodrick (Valerie), Emma Lock (Kim), Katherine Templar (Rachel), Peter Blankenstein (Alan), Peter Charlton (Jake), Daniel De'sioye (Baby)

Laurence R. Harvey in *The Human Centipede II* © IFC Films

WAR OF THE ARROWS (CJ Entertainment) a.k.a. *Choi-jong-byeong-gi Hwal*; Producers, Jang Won-seok, Kim Sung-hwan; Director/Screenplay, Kim Han-min; Photography, Kim Tae-seong; Designer, Jang Chun-seob; Music, Kim Tae-seong; Editors, Kim Chang-ju, Steve Choi; a Lotte Entertainment production; South Korean; Color; Not rated; 122 minutes; American release date: October 7, 2011. **CAST:** Park Hae-il (Nam-Yi), Moon Chae-won (Jan-In), Ryoo Seung-yong (Jyu Shin-Ta), Kim Mu-Yeol (Seo-Goon), Lee Han-wi (Gap-Yong), Lee Kyeong-yeong (Kim Moo-Sun), Park gi-woong (Doreukon), Rye Hei Otani (Nogami), Kim Gu-taek (Kang-Doo), Eunjin Kang (Eun-Yi), Lee Seung-joon (Wan-Han), Lee Jae-goo (Hoo-Man), Park No-shik (Jang-Soon), Lee Da-wit (Nam-Yi, young), Jeon Min-seo (Ja-In, young)

Moon Chae-won in *War of the Arrows* © CJ Entertainment

RASCALS (Eros) Producers, Sanjay Dutt, Sanjay Ahluwali, Vinay Choksey; Director, David Dhawan; Screenplay, Sanjay Chhel, Yunus Sajawal; Photography, Vikas Sivaraman; Designer, Sailesh Mahadik; Music, Atul Raninga, Sanjay Wandrekar; Songs, Vishal & Shekhar; Editor, Nitin Rokade; Sanjay Dutt Productions, M/s Rupali Aum Entertainment; Indian; Color; Not rated; 128 minutes; American release date: October 7, 2011. **CAST:** Ajay Devgan (Bhagat Bhosle), Sanjay Dutt (Chetan Chouhan), Kangana Ranaut (Khushi), Lisa Haydon (Dolly), Arjun Rampal (Anthony Gonsalves), Satish Kaushik (Father Pascal), Hiten Paintal (Nano), Chunky Pandey (Bhagat Bholabhai Chaganmal), Bharati Achrekar (Rosy Gonsalves), Anil Dhawan (Police Inspector), Mushtaq Khan (Usmann)

NO OTHER WOMAN (Viva/Star Cinema) Producers, Vincent del Rosario. Veronique Del Rosario-Corpus; Executive Producers, Charo Santos-Concio, Malou S. Santos, Vic Del Rosario Jr.; Director, Ruel Santos Bayani; Screenplay, Kriz G. Gazmen, Jay Fernando; Story, Jay Fernando, Kriz G. Gazmen; Photography, Charlie S. Peralta; Designer, Nancy Arcega; Music, Raul Mitra; Editor, Vito Cajili; a Viva Films, Star Cinema production; Philippines; Color; Not rated; 110 minutes; American release date: October 7, 2011. **CAST:** Anne Curtis (Kara Zalderiaga), Derek Ramsey (Ramses Escaler), Cristine Reyes (Charmaine Escaler), Niña Dolino (Marian), Ricci Chan (Raymond), Tirso Cruz III (Fernando Zalderiaga), Carmi Martin (Babygirl Dela Costa), John Arcilla (Mario Dela Costa), Mariann Flores (Violet Dela Costa), Ron Morales (Victor), Matt Evans (Jake Escaler), Johnny Revilla (Jaime Escaler), Kitkat Bañas (Mimi), Kat Alano (Michelle), Peter Serrano, Fred Payawan (Sales Team Staff), Melvin Lee (Ito Dela Cruz), Paul Jake Castillo (Architect), Malou Crisologo (Torch Receptionist), Alphonso Deza (Ram's Lolo), Via Antonio, Antonette Garcia (Charmaine's Friends), Drew Rivera (Kate's Date at Torch), Veronica Columna (Charmaine's Maid), Barbie Salvador (Mario's Mistress), Marnie Lapuz (Costa Luz Manager), Renan Evangelista, Rodrigo Oliveira (Brazilian Guys at Beach)

Derek Ramsay in *No Other Woman* © Viva Films

THE DEAD (Global Cinema) Producer, Howard J. Ford; Directors/Screenplay, Howard J. Ford, Jon Ford; Photography, Jon Ford; Designer, Daniel Gomme; Music, Imran Ahmad; Special Makeup Effects Artist, Max Van De Banks; Indelible Productions; British; Color; Not rated; 105 minutes; American release date: October 7, 2011. **CAST:** Rob Freeman (Lt. Brian Murphy), Prince David Osei (Sgt. Daniel Dembele), David Dontoh (The Chief), Stephen Asare Amaning, Kwsi Asmah, Edward Bruce, Frank Owusu Darko, Chamberlain Dembele, Joseph Sakey (The Dead), Mark Chapman, Nelson E. Ward (Pilots), Ben Crowe (Mercenary Leader), Anne Davaud (Doctor), Fae Ford-Brister (Murphy's Daughter), Sergho Dak Jean Gustaphe (Survival Camp Leader), Amir Moallemi (Father on Plane), Kerry Moallemi (Mother on Plane), Kian Moallemi (Baby on Plane), Dan Morgan (James), Katy Richardson (Murphy's Wife), Julia Scott-Russell (James' Fiance), Laura Jane Stephens (Drowning Woman), Amanda Ford, Alicia Reilly (Women on Plane), John Reilly (Man on Plane), Elizabeth Akingbade, Benjamin C. Akpa, Anthony Arinze, Genardo Campbell, Ofuya Elias, Baiden Kweku, Basil Senior (Survivors), Benjamin James Elliot, Michael Kuper, Mark Loberg, Glenn Salvage (Mercenaries)

LABIOS ROJOS (Lionsgate) Producer, Jorge Aguirre; Director/Screenplay/Editor, Rafa Lara; Photography, Germán Lammers; Art Directors, Laiza Dorcé, Hector Iruegas; Mexican, 2009; Color; Rated R; 93 minutes; American release date: October 14, 2011. CAST: Jorge Salinas (Ricardo), Jesús Ochoa (Inspector Gorráez), Silvia Navarro (Blanca), Jorge Zárate (Ayudante Pérez), Diana García

(Violeta), Fernando Luján (Don Luis Covarrubias), Guillermo Iván (Miguel), Sophie Alexander (Lorena), Gloria Izaguirre (Cosmetologist), Antonio Merlano (Fabián), Luis Romano (Young Ricardo), Carmen Salinas (Señorita Claudia)

Guillermo Ivan in *Labios Rojos* © Lionsgate

MY FRIEND PINTO (UTV Motion Pictues/SLB Films) Producers, Sanjay Leela Bhansali, Ronnie Screwvala; Director, Raaghav Dar; Screenplay, Raaghav Dar, Arun Sukumar; Photography, Gargey Trivedi; Costumes, Shabina Khan, Darshan Jalan; Music, Hitesh Sonik; Editors, Shan Mohammed, Dipika Kalra; a Sanjay Leela Bhansali Films production; Indian; Color; Not rated; 115 minutes; American release date: October 14, 2011. **CAST:** Prateik Babbar (Michael Pinto), Arjun Mathur (Sameer Sharma), Kalki Koechlin (Maggie), Divya Dutta (Reshma Shergill), Makrand Deshpande (Don), Rajendranath Zutshi (Mac), Shakeel khan (Asif), Aseem Hattangadi (Bhargav), Faisal Rashid (Abhay), Shikha Talsania (Neha), Asif Basra (Joe, Maggie's Uncle)

AZAAN (JMJ Entertainment) Executive Producer, M.R. Shahjahan; Director, Prashant Chadha; Screenplay, Prashant Chadha, Heeraz Marfatia, Shubhra Swarup; Photography, Axel Fischer; Costumes, Roopa Chadha; Dreamaker Productions; Indian; Color; Not rated; 128 minutes; American release date: October 14, 2011. **CAST:** Sachiin Joshi (Azaan Khan), Candice Boucher (Afreen), Arya Babbar (Imaad), Sarita Choudhury (Menon), Samy Gharbi (Malak), Vijayendra Ghatge (Home Minister), Sajid hasan (Doctor), Alyy Khan (Sam Sharma), Sachin Khedekar (Home Minister Manohar Kamat), Ravi Kissen (Pandey), Neet Nohan (Aman Khan), Amber Rose Revah (Sofiya), Dalip Tahil (Mahfouz)

CHALET GIRL (IFC Films) Producers, Pippa Cross, Harriet Rees, Dietmar Güntsche, Wolfgang Behr; Director, Phil Traill; Screenplay, Tom Williams; Photography, Ed Wild; Designer, Benedkit Herforth; Costumes, Leonie Hartard; Music, Christian Henson; Editor, Robin Sales; Casting, Dan Hubbard; a U.K. Film Council presentation; British-Austrian-German; Dolby; Color; Not rated; 97 minutes; American release date: October 14, 2011. **CAST:** Felicity Jones (Kim), Ed Westwick (Jonny), Bill Nighy (Richard Madsen), Brooke Shields (Caroline), Tamsin Egerton (Georgie), Ken Duken (Mikki), Billy Bailey (Bill), Tara Dakides (Tara), Gregor Bloeb (Bernhardt), Sophia Bush (Chloe), Adam Bousdoukos (Willy), Georgia King (Jules), Rebecca Lacey (Thea), Chandra Ruegg (Trace), Tom Goodman-Hill (Les), Jo Martin (Lexi)

THE GREATEST MIRACLE (Dos Corazones Films) a.k.a. *El Gran Milagro*; Producer, Pablo Jose Barroso; Director, Bruce Morris; Screenplay, Luis De Velasco; Animation Director, Patricia Garcia Pena; Music, Mark McKenzie; a Dos Corazones Films production; Mexican; Color; Rated PG; 70 minutes; American release date: October 14, 2011. **VOICE CAST:** JB Blanc (Don Chema), Bryan Brems (Melvin), Mari Devon (Trini), Richard Epcar (Locksmith), Dorothy Fahn (Monica), Erin Fitzgerald (Mrs. Jones/Lady/Confessional), Barbara Goodson (Dona Cata), Jay Kasten (Walla), Chris Marlowe (Christ), Dave Miles (Man), Ethan Murray (Father), Jaime Seibert (Fernando), Richard Smallberries Jr. (All Angels), Michael Sorich (Old Priest), Owen Zingus (Diego)

Ken Duken, Tamsin Egerton, Georgia King in *Chalet Girl* © IFC Films

KLITSCHKO (Corinth Films) Producer, Leopold Hoesch; Director, Sebastian Dehnhardt; Photography, Johannes Imdahl; Music, Stefan Ziethen; Editor, Lars Roland; a Broadview Pictures production; German; Colro; HD; Not rated; 116 minutes; American release date: October 21, 2011. Documentary on sibling Ukranian world heavyweight champions Vitali and Wladimir Klitschko; **WITH:** Vitali Klitschko, Wladimir Klitschko, Fritz Sdunek, Emmanuel Steward, Wladimir Klitschko Sr., Nadeschda Uljanowna Klitschko, Bernd Bonte, Lamon Brewster, Lennox Lewis, Chris Byrd, Dr. Pearlman Hicks, Natalia Klitschko, Klaus-Peter Kohl, Larry Merchant, Falk Nebiger, Dan Rafael, Hartmut Scherzer, Andrej Schistow, Anna Starostenko, Emanuel Steward, Wladimir Zolotarew

Vitali Klitschko, Wladimir Klitscko in *Klitschko* © Corinth Films

SIDEWALLS (Sundance Selects) a.k.a. *Medianeras*; Producers, Natacha Cervi, Hern án Musalupi, Christoph Friedel, Luis Miñaro, Luis Sartor; Director/ Screenplay, Gustavo Taretto; Photography, Leandro Martinez; Designers, Luciana Quartaruolo, Romeo Fasce; Costumes, Flavia Gaitán; Music, Gabriel Chwojnik; Editors, Pablo Mari, Rosario Suárez; Argentine-German-Spanish; Color; Not rated; 92 minutes; American release date: October 26, 2011. **CAST:** Pilar López de Ayala (Mariana), Javier Drolas (Martín), Inés Efrón (Ana), Carla Peterson (Marcela), Rafa Fero (Rafa), Adri án Navaro (Lucas)

RA.ONE (Eros) Producer, Gauri Khan; Director, Anubhav Sinha; Screenplay, Kanika Dhillon, David Beullo, Mushtaq Sheikh, Anubhav Sinha; Photography, Nicola Pecorini; Designers, Sabu Cyril, Marcus Wookey; Music, Vishal and Shekhar; Editors, Martin Walsh, Sanjay Sharma; Indian; Dolby; Color; Not rated; 155 minutes; American release date: October 26, 2011. **CAST:** Shah Rukh Khan (Shekhar Subramaniam/G.One), Kareena Kapoor (Sonia S. Subramanium), Arjun Rampal (Ra.One), Armaan Verma (Prateek), Shahana Goswami (Jenny Nayar), Priyanka Chopra (Khalnayak's Girlfriend), Satish Shah (Iyer), Dalip Tahil (Barron),

Suresh Menon (Taxi Driver), Sanjay Dutt (Khalnayak), Rajnikanth (Chitti), Joe Egan (The Daddy), Ben Hawkey (Billy)

MY REINCARNATION (Long Shot Factory) Producer/Director/Photography, Jennifer Fox; Music, Jan Tilman Shcade, Moe Jaksch; Editor, Sabine Krayenbuhl; a Zohe Film Prods., ZDF-Arte, RSI-Televisione Svizzera, Buddhist Broadcasting Foundation, Lightbuck Film, Ventura Film and Vivo Film production; Swiss-Dutch-Finnish; Stereo; Color; DV-to-HD; Not rated; 100 minutes; American release date: October 28, 2011. Documentary on Tibetan spiritual master Chögyal Namkhai Norbu Rinpoche and his Italian-born son Yeshi; **WITH:** Cheogyal Namkhai Norbu Rinpoche, Yeshi Namkhai.

Yeshi Rinpoche in *My Reincarnation* © Long Shot Factory

HIPSTERS (Leisure Time Features) a.k.a. *Stilyagi*; Producers, Leonid Lebedev, Leonid Yarmolnik, Vadim Goryainov, Valery Todorovsky; Director, Valery Todorovsky; Screenplay, Yuri Korotkov, based on his book *Boogie Bones*; Photography, Roman Vasyanov; Art Director, Vladimir Gudilin; Costumes, Alexander Ospiov; Music, Konstantin Meladze; Libretto, Valery Todorovsky, Evgeny Margulis; Editor, Alexey Bobrov; Russian; Dolby; Color; CinemaScope; Not rated; 130 minutes; American release date: October 28, 2011. **CAST:** Anton Shagin (Mels), Oksana Akinshina (Polly), Evgenia Brik (Katya), Maksim Matveev (Fred), Igor Voynarovsky (Bob), Ekaterina Vilkova (Betsi), Konstantin Balakirev (Dryn), Aleksandr Stefantsov (Nolik), Georgiy Sivokhin (Kim), Olga Smirnova (Sherri), Yanina Buiko (Liza), Irina Rozanova (Mat Polzy), Sergey Garmash (Otets Melsa), Oleg Yankovskiy (Otets Freda), Aleksey Gorhunov (Labukh)

Anton Shagin, Maksim Matveev, Igor Voynarovsky in *Hipsters*
© Leisure Time Features

CHERKESS (Sindika) Producer/Director/Screenplay, Mohy Quandour; Photography, Nikolay Troukhin; Art Director, Jamil Awwad; Music, Waleed Al Hasheem; Editor, Anas Shabsagh; Jordanian, 2010; Color; Not rated; 114 minutes; American release date: November 4, 2011. **CAST:** Mohamad al Abadi (Ab Aziz), Mohadeen Komakhov (Temur), Azamat Bekov (Nart), Sahar Bishara (Hind), Ruslan Firov (Kazbolat)

Mohadeen Komakhov in *Cherkess* © Sindika

THE LOOK (Kino Lorber) Executive Producer, Michael Trabitsch; Producers, Gerd Haag, Serge Lalou, Charlotte Uzu; Director/Screenplay, Angelina Maccarone; Photography, Bernd Meiners, Judith Kaufmann; Music, Jakob Hansonis, Alex de Silva; Editor, Bettina Böhler; a Tag/Traum Filmproduktion/ Prounen Film, Les films d'ici production; German-French; Dolby; Color; HD-to-35mm; Not rated; 94 minutes; American release date: November 4, 2011. Documentary on British actress Charlotte Rampling; **WITH:** Charlotte Rampling, Paul Auster, Franckie Diago, Cynthia Fleury, Joy Fleury, Peter Lindbergh, Anthony Palliser, Frederick Seidel, Barnaby Southcombe, Juergen Teller

Anthony Palliser, Charlotte Rampling in *The Look* © Kino Lorber

PIANOMANIA (First Run Features) a.k.a. *Pianomania: Die suche nach dem perfekten Klang*; Producer, Robert Cibis; Directors, Lilian Franck, Robert Cibis; Photography, Jerzy Palacz; Music, Matthias Petsche; Editor, Michelle Barbin; an Oval Filmemacher, Wildart Film production; Austrian-German, 2009; Color; Not rated; 93 minutes; American release date: November 4, 2011. Documentary on piano tuner Stefan Knüpfer and the attention paid in choosing the right keyboard for some of the great virtuosos of the world: WITH: Stefan Knüpfer, Pierre-Laurent Aimard, Ian Bostridge, Alfred Brendel, Rudolf Buchbinder, Christoph Claßen, Julius Drake, Till Fellner, Aleksey Igudesman, Christoph Koller, Richard Hyung-Ki Joo, Lang Lang, Tobias Lehmann, Marita Prohmann

A MOTHER'S STORY (Star Cinema) Director, John-D J. Lazatin; Screenplay/Story, Senedy Que; Photography, Shayne Sarte; a Filipino Channel production; Filipino; Color; Not rated; 120 minutes; American release date: November 6, 2011. **CAST:** Pokwang (Meldy), Xyriel Manabat (Queenie), Rayver Cruz (King), Nonie Buencamino (Gerry), Beth Tamayo (Helen), Daria Ramirez (Choleng),

DOG SWEAT (Indiexpix) a.k.a. *Aragh sagee*; Producers, Hossein Keshavaraz, Maryam Azadi, Alan Oxman; Director/Screenplay/Editor, Hossein Keshavarz; Photography, Ehsan Karimi; Designer, Rezal Farhadi; Costumes, Bahereh Azadi; Music, Simon Taufique; Editors, Hossein Keshavar, Mollie Goldstein; a Deluxe Art Films presentation; Iranian, 2010; Color; HD; Not rated; 90 minutes; American release date: November 11, 2011. **CAST:** Sara Esfahani (Katherine), Tahereh Azadi (Katie), Shakrokhi Taslimi (Massoud), Ahmad Akbarzadeh (Dawood), Rahim Zamani (Hooshang), Bagher Forohar (Hooman), Maryam Mousavi (Mahsa), Tahereh Esfahani (Nicki)

INSIDE HANA'S SUITCASE (Menemesha) Producers, Rudolf Biermann, Jessica Daniel, Larry Weinstein; Director, Larry Weinstein; Screenplay, Thomas Wallner; Photography, Horst Zeidler; Music, Alexina Louie, Alex Pauk; Editor, David New; Canadian-Czech Republic, 2009; Color; Not rated; 88 minutes; American release date: November 11, 2011. Documentary and part dramatic recreation of the story behind a suitcase in the Holocaust Museum with the name Hana Brady painted on it; WITH: George Brady, Lara Brady, Fumiko Ishioka.

Hana Brady, George Brady in *Inside Hana's Suitcase* © Menemsha

ROCKSTAR (Eros) Producer, Shree Ashtavinayak; Director/Story, Imtiaz Ali; Photography, Anil Mehta; Music, A.R. Rahman; Editor, Aarti Bajaj; a Cine Vision Ltd. Production; Indian; Color; Not rated; 159 minutes; American release date: November 11, 2011. **CAST:** Ranbir Kapoor (Janardhan Jakhar), Nargis Fakhri (Heer Kaul), Shammi Kapoor (Ustad Jameel Khan), Aditi Rao Hydari (Sheena), Moufid Aziz (Jai), Kumud Mishra (Khatana), Piyush Mishra (Dhingra), Shernaz Patel (Neena Kaul), Shika Jain (Meena), Paritosh Sand (Doctor), Mandy (Herself)

INNI (Cinema Purgatorio) Producers, John Best, Dean O'Connor; Director, Vincent Morisset; Photography, Rob Hardy; Music, Sigur Ros; Editor, Nick Fenton; a Klikk Film presentation; Canadian-Icelandic-British; Black and white/color; HD; Not rated; 75 minutes; American release date: November 11, 2011. Documentary concert of Icelandic band Sigur Ros; WITH: Jon Thor Birgisson, Orri Pall Dyrason, George Holm, Kjartan Sveinsson

UNDER FIRE: JOURNALISTS IN COMBAT (JUF Pictures) Producers, Martyn Burke, Anthony Feinstein; Director/Screenplay, Martyn Burke; Vombat Diary Footage, Finbarr O'Reilly, Paul Watson; Music, Mark Korven; Editor, Chris McEnroe; Presented in association with Documentary Channel; Canadian; Color; Not rated; 90 minutes; American release date: November 11, 2011. Documentary about the psychological damage inflicted upon journalists covering wars.

DZI CROQUETTES (Tria Prods.) Producers, Tatiana Issa, Raphael Alvarez, Bob Cline; Directors/Screenplay/Photography, Tatiana Issa, Raphael Alvarez; Art Director, Carolina Vaz; Editor, Raphael Alvarez; Narrator, Tatiana Issa; a Tria Prods., Canal Brasil production; Brazilian, 2009; Color/black and white; HD; Not rated; 111 minutes; American release date: November 18, 2011. Documentary on Brazilian drag act Dzi Croquettes; **WITH:** Ciro Barcelos, Norma Bengell, Maria Zilda Bethlem, Patrice Calmettes, Pedro Cardoso, Rogerio de Poly, Jean-Marc Dugas, Miguel Falabella, Betty Faria, Jorge Fernando, Gilberto Gil, Benedictus Lacerda, Ron Lewis, Elke Maravilha, Ney Matogrosso, Luis Carlos Miele, Liza Minnelli, Nelson Motta, José Possi Neto, Marilia Pêra, Claudia Raia, Bayard Tonelli, Claudio Tovar, Nega Vilma

LARGO WINCH (Music Box Films) a.k.a. *The Heir Apparent*; Producer, Nathalie Gastaldo; Executive Producer, Eric Zaouali; Director, Jérôme Salle; Screenplay, Julien Rappeneau, Jérôme Salle; Based on the graphic novel series *Largo Winch* by Van Hamme and Philippe Francq; Photography, Denis Rouden; Designer, Michael Barthelemy; Costumes, Khadija Zeggaï; Music, Alexandre Desplat; Editor, Richard Marizy; Casting, Gigi Akoka; a coproduction of Pan-Européenne – Wild Bunch – TF1 Films Production – Casa Productions; French-Belgian, 2008; Dolby; Super 35 Widescreen; Color; Not rated; 108 minutes; American release date: November 18, 2011. **CAST:** Tomer Sisley (Largo Winch), Kristin Scott Thomas (Ann Ferguson), Miki Manojlovic (Nerio Winch), Mélanie Thierry (Léa/Naomi), Gilbert Melki (Freddy), Anne Consigny (Hannah), Karel Roden (Mikhaïl Korsky), Steve Waddington (Stephan Marcus), Radivoje Bukvic (Goran), Nicolas Vaude (Gauthier), Bojana Panic (Melina), Benjamin Siksou (Teenage Largo), Benedict Wong (William Kwan), Gérard Watkins (Cattaneo), Wolfgang Pissors (Attinger), Ted Thomas (Greenfield), David Gasman (Alexander Meyer), Elizabeth Bennet (Miss Pennywinkle), Eddy Ko (Tattouer), Ivan Marevich (Josip), André Oumansky (Jacques Wallenberg), Digger Mesch (Police Officer), Emmanuel Avena (Hicham), Micaelle Mee-Sook (Rebecca)

Tomer Sisley in *Largo Winch* © Music Box Films

Ranbir Kapoor in *Rockstar* © Eros

GARBO: THE SPY (First Run Features) a.k.a. *Garbo: El espia*; Producers, Edmon Roch, Sandra Hermida, Belén Bernuy; Director, Edmon Roch; Screenplay, Edmon Roch, Isaki Lacuesta, María Hervera; Photography, Bet Rourich, Gabriel Guerra, Joachin Bergamin; Music, Fernando Velázquez; an Ikiru Films presentation in co-production with Colosé Producciones, Centuria Films in association with Olek Film, Televisión de Catalunya; Spanish, 2009; Dolby; Color/black and white; Not rated; 87 minutes; American release date: November 18, 2011. Documentary on World War II double agent Juan Pujol; **WITH:** Nigel West, Mark Seaman, Xavier Vinader, Stan Vranckx, Aline Griffith, José Antonio Escoriza, Juan Kreisler, Joan Pujol

Juan Pujol in *Garbo: The Spy* © First Run Features

IN HEAVEN UNDERGROUND: THE WEISSENSEE JEWISH CEMETERY (Seventh Art) a.k.a. *Im Himmel, unter der Erde – Der Jüdische Friedhof Weißensee*; Producers, Britta Wauer, Hans-Günther Brüske, Birgit Mehler, Dagmar Mielke; Director/Screenplay, Britta Wauer; Photography, Kaspar Köpke; Music, Karim Sebastian Elias; Editor, Berthold Baule; a Britzka Film, RBB, SR production in collaboration with Arte; German; Color; Not rated; 95 minutes; American release date: November 18, 2011. Documentary on the Weissensee Jewish Cemetery of Berlin, the largest active Jewish burial ground in Europe; **WITH:** Rabbi William Wolff, Harry Kindermann, Baruch Bernard Epstein, Daniel Hakarem, Gabriella Naidu, Reinhard Maenne, Klaus Lorenz, Hannah Lickert, Hermann Simon, Benny Epstein, Alfred Etzold, Ronnie Golz, Robert Dietrich, Rainer Altenkamp, Gesine Sturm, Lev Tabachnik

In Heaven Underground © Seventh Art

DESI BOYZ (Eros) Producers, Krishika Lulla, Vijay Ahuja, Jyoti Deshpande, Akshay Kumar; Director/Screenplay, Rohit Dhawan; Photography, Najan Subramaniam; Music, Pritam, Sandeep Shirodkar; a Next Generation Pictures production; Indian; Dolby; Color; Not rated; 122 minutes; American release date:

November 25, 2011. CAST: Akshay Kumar (Jignesh Patel/Jerry/Rocco), John Abraham (Nikhil Mathur/Nick/Hunter), Deepika Padukone (Radhika Awasthi), Chitrangda Singh (Tanya), Omi Vaidya (Ajay Bapat), Sartaj Garewal (Menon), Ashwin Mushran (Defense Lawyer), Anupam Kher (Suresh Awasthi), Shraman Jain (Rohan), Mohnish Behl (Social Activist), Master Virej Desai (Veer), Rajat Barmecha (Sameer), Shekhar Bassi (Mall Manager), Bruna Abdalah (Rocco's Client), Peter Brown (Mr. Smith), Sanjay Dutt (Boss), Shaun Lucas (School Teacher), Gabriela Montaraz (Housemaid)

Deepika Padukone, John Abraham in *Desi Boyz* © Eros

ROMANTICS ANONYMOUS (Tribeca) a.k.a. *Les émotifs anonymes*; Producers, Nathalie Gastaldo, Philippe Godeau; Director, Jean-Pierre Améris; Screenplay, Jean-Pierre Améris, Philippe Blasband; Photography, Gérard Simon; Set Designer, Sylvie Olivé; Costumes, Nathalie du Roscoat; Music, Pierre Adenot; Editor, Philippe Bourgueil; Casting, Tatiana Vialle; a Pan-Européenne Production in association with StudioCanal; French, 2010; Dolby; Color; Not rated; 80 minutes; American release date: November 25, 2011. CAST: Benoît Poelvoorde (Jean-René), Isabelle Carré (Angélique), Lorella Cravotta (Magda), Lise Lamétrie (Suzanne), Swann Arlaud (Antoine), Pierre Niney (Ludo), Stéphan Wojtowicz (Psychologist), Jacques Boudet (Rémi), Céline Duhamel (Mimi), Grégoire Ludig (Julien), Philippe Fretun (Maxime), Alice Pol (Adèle), Philippe Gaulé (Philippe), Joëlle Sechaud (Joëlle), Isabelle Gruault (Sylviane), Claude Aufaure (Mr. Mercier), Philippe Laudenbach (Head of the Jury), Marie-Christine Demarest (Madame Legrand), Pascal Ternisien (Waiter), Jean-Yves Chatelais (Receptionist), Christiane Millet (Angélique's Mother), Vincent Paillier (Franck)

A BRIGHTER SUMMER DAY (Central Motion Picture Corp.) a.k.a. *Gu ling jie shao nian sha ren shi jian*; Director, Edward Yang; Screenplay, Edward Yang, Yan Hangya, Yang Shunqing, Lai Mingtang; Photography, Zhang Huigong, Li Longyu; Set Designers, Yu Welyan, Edward Yang; a Yang and His Gang Filmmakers production; Taiwan, 1991; Color; Not rated; 237 minutes; American release date: November 25, 2011. CAST: Zhang Zhen (Xiao Si'r), Lisa Yang (Ming), Zhang Guozhu (Zhang Ju), Elaine Jin (Mrs. Zhang), Wang Juan (Elder Sister), Han Zhang (Elder Brother), Chang Kuo-chu (Father), Lawrence Ko (Airplane), Tan Zhigang (Ma), Lin Hongming (Honey), Chiang Hsiu-chiang (Middle Sister), Lai Fanyun (Youngest Sister), Wang Qizan (Cat), Mingxin (Underpants), Rong Junlong (Sex Bomb), Zhou Huiguo (Tiger), Liu Qingqi (Hefty)

HOUSE OF PLEASURES (IFC Midnight) a.k.a. *L'Apollonide: Souvenirs de la maison close* and *House of Tolerance*; Executive Producers, Kristina Larsen, Betrand Bonello; Director/Screenplay/ Music, Bertrand Bonello; Photography, Josée Deshaies; Set Decorator, Alain Guffroy; Costumes, Anaïs Romand; Editor, Fabrice Rouaud; a Les Films du Lendemain and My New Picture presentation, co-produced with ARTE France Cinema; French; Dolby; Color; Not rated; 125 minutes; American release date: November 25, 2011. CAST: Hafsia Herzi (Samira), Céline Sallette (Clotilde), Jasmine Trinca (Julie), Adèle Haenel (Léa),

Alice Barnole (Madeline), Iliana Zabeth (Pauline), Noémie Lvovsky (Marie-France), Judith Lou Levy, Anaïs Thomas, Pauline Jacquard, Maïa Sandoz, Joanna Grudzinska, Esther Garrel, Xavier Beauvois, Louis-Do de Lencquesaing, Jacques Nolot, Laurent Lacotte

Maïa Sandoz, Alice Barnole, Jasmine Trinca in *House of Pleasures* © IFC Midnight

KHODORKOVSKY (Kino Lorber) Creative Producers, Yelena Durden-Smith, Thomas Schmidt; Producer/Director/Photography, Cyril Tuschi; Music, Arvo Part; Editors, Claudia Simonesci, Salome Machaidze, Cyril Tuschi; Narrators, Jean-Marc Barr, Harvey Friedman; a Rezo Films, Farbfilm Verleih Berlin presentation of a Lala Films production in association with LeVision, Bayerischer Rundfunk; German; Dolby; Color; Not rated; 111 minutes; American release date: November 30, 2011. Documentary on Russian Mikhail Khodorkovsky's transformation from socialist to capitalist; **WITH:** Mikhail Khodorkovsky, Pavel Khodorkovsky, Marina Khodorkovskaya, Lena Khodorkovskaya, Anton Drel, Joschka Fischer, Anatoliy Chubays, Grigoriy Yavlinskiy, Nina Kravets, Maksim Valetzky, Leonid Nevzlin, Mikhail Brudno, Christian Michel, Evgeny Saburov, Aleksey Kondaurov, Dmitry Gololobov, Andrei V. Vasilyev, Boris Nemtsov, Ben Aris, Igor Yurgens, Alexander Temerko, Boris Ponomariov, Milan Horacek, Ilya Yashin

Mikhail Khodorkovsky in *Khodorkovsky* © Kino Lorber

THE YELLOW SEA (Wellmade Star M/Popcorn Film) a.k.a. *Hwanghae* and *The Murderer*; Producer, Han Sung-goo; Executive Producers, Byun Jong-eun, You Jung-hoon; Director/ Screenplay, Na Hong-jin; Photography, Lee Sung-je; Designer, Lee Hwo-kyoung; Costumes, Chae Kyung-hwa; Music, Jang Young-gyu, Lee Byung-hoon; Editor, Kim Sun-min; a Wellmade Star M, Popcorn Films, Showbox/Mediaplex production; South Korean, 2010; Dolby; Color; Rated R;

139 minutes; American release date: December 2, 2011. **CAST:** Ha Jung-woo (Gu-nam), Kim Yun-seok (Myun-ga), Cho Seong-ha (Tae-won), Kim Seung-hyun (Kwak Byoung-kyu)

LADS & JOCKEYS (Music Box Films) Producer, Daniel Marquet; Director, Benjamin Marquet; Photography, Sebastien Buchmann, Laurent Chalet, Benjamin Marquet; Music, Les Nature Boys (Damien Dassaradanayadou, Ezecheil Pailhes); Editors, Isabelle Devinck, Emmanuelle Joly; a Groupe Deux presentation with the participation of Leo Vision – Jean-Louis Burgat; French, 2008; Dolby; Color; Not rated; 100 minutes; American release date: December 2, 2011. Documentary follows a group of 14-year-olds as they train to become jockeys; **WITH:** Flavien Masse, Steve Le Guern, Florian Basquet, Andre Pmmier.

REDLINE (Manga Entertainment) Producers, Kentarō Yoshida, Yukiko Koike; Director, Takeshi Koike; Screenplay, Katsuhito Ishii, Yōji Enokido, Yoshiki Sakurai; Story, Katsuhito Ishii; Photography, Riuu Takizawa; Music, James Shimoji; Editors, Akira Terauti, Naoki Kawanishi; a Madhouse, Gastonia production; Japanese, 2010; Dolby; Color; Not rated; 102 minutes; American release date: December 2, 2011. **VOICE CAST:** Takuya Kimura (JP), Yū Aoi (Sonoshee), Tadanobu Asano (Frisbee), Ken'yū Horiuchi (Titan), Yoshiyuki Morishita (Shinkai), Kanji Tsuda (Trava)

JP in *Redline* © Manga Entertainment

I AM SINGH (Reliance Big Pictures) Producers Sardar Peshaura Singh Thind, Sardar Dalbir Singh Thind; Director/Screenplay, Puneet Issar; Photography, W.B. Rao, Raja Ratnam; Art Director, Narendra Rahurikar; Music, Surender Sodhi; Editor, Sanjay Verma; a K.R. Films Hollywood production; Indian-American; Dolby; Color; Not rated; 127 minutes; American release date: December 2, 2011. **CAST:** Gulzar Chahal (Ranveer Singh), Amy Rasimas (Amy Washington), Brooke Johnston (Amelia White), Rizwan Haider (Rizwan), Puneet Issar (Fateh Singh), Nathan Bush (Deputy Frank Holland), Gary Castro Churchwell (Deputy John Davis), Paul Clark (Greg Vaughn), Andrew Constantini (Officer Paretti), Inder Dadlani (Amit Bansal), Khan Dally (Anwar), David Dhillon (Waqar Hassan), Sunita Dhir (Ranveer's Mother), Stephanie Drapeay (Dr. Armstrong), John Gammon (FBI Interrogator), Joseph Gatt (Leif Lungren), Paul Harika (Balvir Singh Sodhi), Benny Harris (Mr. Simon Cooper), Kristen Herbert (Talk Show Host), Yusuf Hussain (Hasan, Sara's Father), Holly Jeanne (Judge), Tulip Joshi (Sara), Kaka (Veer), Pramod Kumar (Mr. Patel), Alison Lees-Taylor (Mrs. Melissa Cooper), Neetha Monhindra (Simra), Rahul Nath (Vidor), Elliot Pasentino (Kiplinger), Pauli Pettit (Deputy Ida Powell), Aaron Zachary Philips (Adria Cooper), Jeff Prewett (Sodi Killer, Neo Nazi), Michael Raif (Prosecuting Attorney), Kavi Raz (Ranveer's Father), Daniel Robaire (Agent James Callahn), Arsh Singh (Shariff Mohammad), Mike Singh (Ajit Singh), Albert Stroth (Sheriff Ivan Fredrick), Sunny Vachher (Sunny), Chacko Vadaketh (Muslim Community Leader), Luke Vexler (Neo-Nazxi Harry Karst), Alex Wexo (FBI Agent Kevin Johnson), Sewell Whitney (Mr. Foreman)

FORCE OF NATURE (Shadow) Producers, Yves J. Ma, Janice Tufford, Sturla Gunnarsson; Director, Sturla Gunnarsson; Photography, Tony Westman; Designer, Dany Lyne; Editor, Nick Hector; an Entertainment One presentation in association with Telefilm Canada and the Rogues Group of Funds through the Theatrical Documentary Program; Canadian, 2010; Dolby; Color; Not rated; 93 minutes; American release date: December 2, 2011. Documentary on environmentalist David Suzuki; **WITH:** David Suzuki, Dr. Tara Cullis, Severn Cullis-Suzuki, Ann-Marie MacDonald, Miles Richardson, Ruby Wilkerson

David Suzuki in *Force of Nature* © Shadow Distribution

OUTRAGE (Magnet) a.k.a. *Autoreiji*; Producers, Masayuki Mori, Takio Yoshida; Director/Screenplay/Editor, Takeshi Kitano; Photography, Katsumi Yanagijima; Designer, Norihiro Isoda; Costumes, Kazuko Kurosawa, Yohji Yamamoto; Music, Keiichi Suzuki; a Bandai Visuals, TV Tokyo, Omnibus Japan and Office Kitano presentation; Japanese, 2010; Dolby; Kowa Scope; Color; Rated R; 109 minutes; American release date: December 2, 2011. **CAST:** Beat Takeshi (Otomo), Kippei Shiina (Mizuno), Ryo Kase (Ishihara), Tomokazu Miura (Kato), Jun Kunimura (Ikemoto), Tetta Sugimoto (Ozawa), Takashi Tsukamoto (Iizuka), Hideo Nakano (Kimura), Renji Ishibashi (Murase), Fumiyo Kohinata (Det. Kataoka), Soichiro Kitamura (Mr. Chairman)

Beat Takeshi in *Outrage* © Magnet Releasing

UNDER CONTROL (Credofilm) Producers, Susann Schimk, Jörg Trentmann; Directors/Idea, Volker Sattel, Stefan Stefanescu; Photography, Volker Sattel; Editors, Stephan Krumbiegel, Jutta Krug, Sabine Rollberg; a co-production with WDR, ARTE; German; Dolby; Color; Not rated; 98 minutes; American release date: December 2, 2011. Documentary on German nuclear plants.

Under Control © Credofilm

PASTORELA (Lionsgate) Producer, Rodrigo Herranz Fanjul; Director/Screenplay, Emilio Portes; Photography, Damian Garcia; Designer, Alejandro García; Editors, Emilio Portes, Rodrigo Rios; Casting, Genaro Hernandez; from Pantelion Films; Mexican; Rated R; 88 minutes; American release date: December 2, 2011. **CAST:** Joaquín Cosío (Agent Jesús Juárez), Carlos Cobos (Father Mundo Posadas), Melissa Bahnsen (Magdalena), Eduardo España (Godfather Vulmaro), Dagoberto Gama (Comandante), Ernesto Yáñez (God/El Monaguillo), Héctor Jiménez (Muchacho Poseido), Ana Serradilla (Monja) , Eduardo Manzano (Cardinal), Jose Sefami (Tuerto), Rubén Cristiany (Bishop), Silverio Palacios (Dr. Godinez), María Aura (Reporter), Omar Ayala (Agent)

Eduardo España in *Pastorela* © Lionsgate

THE LADY (Cohen Media Group) Producers, Virginie Besson-Silla, Andy Harries; Director, Luc Besson; Screenplay, Rebecca Frayn; Photography, Thierry Arbogast; Designer, Hughes Tissandier; Costumes, Olivier Beriot; Music, Eric Serra; Editor, Julien Rey; Casting, Fiona Weir, Raweeporn "Non" Jungmeier; a EuropaCorp, Left Bank Pictures, France 2 Cinema co-production with the participation of Canal+ and France Televisions; French-British; Dolby; Widescreen; Technicolor; Rated R; 132 minutes; American release date: December 2, 2011. **CAST:** Michelle Yeoh (Aung San Suu Kyi), David Thewlis (Michael Aris), Jonathan Raggett (Kim Aris), Jonathan Woodhouse (Alexander Aris), Susan Wooldridge (Lucinda Philips), Benedict Wong (Karma Phuntsho), Flint Bangkok (Nyo Ohn Myint), Guy Barwell (Military Policeman), Sahajak Boonthanakit (Leo Nichols), Antony Hickling (Voice of BBC Journalist), William Hope (James Baker), Teerawat Mulvilai (Soldier, Bad News), Agga Poechit (Tan Shwe), Victoria Sanvalli (Ma Then), Nay Myo Thant

(Win Thein), Danny Toeng (Col. Than Tun), Dujdao Vadhanapakorn (Nita May), Frank Walmsley (BBC Journalist), Marian Yu (Daw Khin Yi)

Michelle Yeoh in *The Lady* © Cohen Media Group

MAGIC TO WIN (China Lion) a.k.a. *Hoi sam mo fa* and *Happy Magic*; Producer, Wong Bak-King; Executive Producer/Screenplay, Edmond Wong; Director, Wilson Yip; Photography, Man Po Cheung; Editor, Cheung Ka-Fai; a Pegasus Motion Pictures, Huyai Brothers production; Hong Kong-Chinese; Dolby; Color; Not rated; 100 minutes; American release date: December 9, 2011. **CAST:** Tonny Jan (Charlie), Wu Chun (Ling Feng), Wong Bak-Ming (Professor Hong), Raymond Wong (Kang), Louis Koo (Gu Xin Yue), Karena Ng (Macy Cheng), Jacky Wu (Bi Ye Wu), Yan Ni (Volleyball Coach)

Wu Chun in *Magic to Win* © China Lion

KNUCKLE (ARC Entertainment) Producers, Teddy Leifer, Ian Palmer; Executive Producers, Nick Fraser, Alan Maher; Director, Ian Palmer; Photography, Michael Doyle, Ian Palmer; Music, Ilan Eshkeri; Editor, Ollie Huddleston; a Rise Films presentation in association with Seafield Films and Bord Scannán na hÉireann/ the Irish Film Board; Irish; Color; Rated R; 96 minutes; American release date: December 9, 2011. Documentary on the frequent fights that have taken place between the feuding McDonagh and Joyce families; **WITH:** James Quinn McDonagh, Paddy Quinn McDonagh, Michael Quinn McDonagh, Big Joe Joyce, Ian Palmer, Davey Nevin, Christy Nevin, Thomas Nevin.

Jack McDonagh, David Nevin in *Knuckle* © ARC Entertainment

LADIES VS. RICKY BAHL (Yash Raj Films) Producer, Aditya Chopra; Director, Maneesh Sharma; Screenplay, Devika Bhagat; Dialogue, Habib Faisal; Story, Aditya Chopa; Photography, Asseem Mishra; Designer, Wasiq Khan; Costumes, Aki Narula, Arun Chauhan, Ayesha Khanna; Music, Salim Sulaiman; Lyrics, Amibtabh Bhattacharya; Editor, Namrata Rao; a Yash Raj production; Indian; Dolby; Widescreen; Color; Not rated; 139 minutes; American release date: December 9, 2011. **CAST:** Ranveer Singh (Ricky Bahl/Vikram/Sunny/Iqbal/ Deven), Anushka Sharma (Ishika Desai/Ishika Patel), Parineeti Chopra (Dimple Chaddha), Dipannita Sharma Atwal (Raina Parulekar), Aditi Sharma (Saira Rashid), Shireesh Sharma (Mr. Chaddha)

DON 2 (Reliance Entertainment) Producers, Ritesh Sidhwani, Shahrukh Khan, Farhan Akhtar; Executive Producer, Arunima Roy; Director, Farhan Akhtar; Screenplay/Story, Farhan Akhtar, Ameet Mehta, Amrish Shah; Photography, Jason West; Designer, T.P. Abid; Costumes, Jaimal Odedra; Choreographer, Vaibhavi Merchant; Music, Shankar Ehsaan Loy; Lyrics, Javed Akhtar; Editor, Anand Subaya; Casting, Aardore Mukherjee; an Excel Entertainment production; Indian; Dolby; 3D; Color; Not rated; 145 minutes; American release date: December 23, 2011. **CAST:** Shah Rukh Khan (Don), Priyanka Chopra (Roma), Boman Irani (Vardhaan), Om Puri (Vishal Malik), Kunal Kapoor (Sameer Ali), Alyy Khan (J.K. Diwan), Rike Schmid (Yana), Nawwab Shah (Jabar), Sahil Shroff (Arjun), Florian Lukas (Det. Jens Berkel), Lara Dutta (Ayesha), Wolfgang Stegemann (Karl), Bianca Karsten (Sophie Kohl), Frank Christian Marx, Senta Dorothea Kirschner, Hermann Eppert (Hostages), Hans-Eckart Eckhardt (President of Court), Rajesh Khattar (Singhania)

Shah Rukh Khan in *Don 2* © Reliance Big

MISS MINOES (Music Box Films) a.k.a. *Minoes* and *Undercover Kitty*; Producers, Burny Bos; Executive Producer, Michiel de Rooij; Director, Vincent Bal; Screenplay, Tamara Bos, Burny Bos, Vincent Bal; Based on the novel *Minoes* by Annie M.G. Schmidt; Photography, Walther Vanden Ende; Designer, Vincent de Pater; Costumes, Bernadette Corstens; Music, Peter Vermeersch; Editor, Peter Alderliesten; a Bos Bros. Film-TV Productions presentation; Dutch, 2001; Color; Rated PG; 92 minutes; American release date: December 23, 2011. **CAST:** Carice van Houten (Minoes), Theo Maassen (Tibbe), Sarah Bannier (Bibi), Pierre Bokma (Mr. Ellemeet), Hans Kesting (Harrie de Haringman), Kees Hulst (Mr. van Dam), Olga Zuiderhoek (Mrs. van Dam), Marisa van Eylen (Mrs. Ellemeet), Lineke Rijxman (Newspaper Editor), Jack Wouterse (Burgermeester van Weezel)

Carice van Houten, Sarah Bannier in *Miss Minoes* © Music Box Films

PORCO ROSSO (GKids) a.k.a. *Kurenai no buta* and *Crimson Pig*; Producers, Rick Dempsey, Toshio Suzuki; Director/Screenplay, Hayao Miyazaki; Designers, Hayao Miyazaki, Takeshi Seyama; Music, Joe Hisaishi; Japanese, 1992; Rated PG; 94 minutes; American release date: December 23, 2011. (English) **VOICE CAST:** Michael Keaton (Porco Rosso), Susan Egan (Gina), Cary Elwes (Curtis), Brad Garrett (Mamma Aiuto Boss), Kimberly Williams-Paisley (Fio), David Ogden Stiers (Grandpa Piccolo), Bradley Pierce (Gas Boy), Bill Fagerbakke, Kevin Michael Richardson, Frank Welker (Mamma Aiuto Gang)

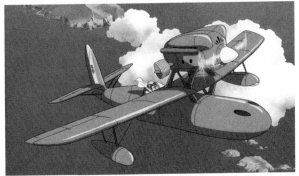

Porco in *Porco Rosso* © GKids

PRINCE OF THE HIMALAYAS (Independent/Rubin Museum of Art) Producers, Sherwood Hu, Jianhua Yin; Director, Sherwood Hu; Screenplay, Sherwood Hu, Trashidawa, Dorje Tsering; Based on the play *Hamlet* by William Shakespeare; Photography, Hou Yong; Designer, Suyalatu; Editor, Mu Yu; a Shanghai Film Group, Shanghai Film Studios, Hus Entertainment presentation; Tibetan, 2006; Technicolor; Not rated; 108 minutes; American release date: December 23, 2011.

CAST: Purba Rgyal (Prince Lhamoklodan), Sonamdolgar (Odsaluyang), Trashi (Lessar), Zomskyid (Nanm), Lobzangchopel (King Tsanpo), Lobden (Po-iha-nyisse), Dobrgyal (Kulo-ngam), Oma (Achessergyal), Ciringdongrub (Horshu), Dechendolma (Mochangki), Da Wa Pian Duo (Minister), Jia Zeng Da Jie (Ma Sang Ah Yi), Luo Sang De Ji (A Xi Su Jie)

BATTLE ROYALE (Anchor Bay) Producers, Masao Sato, Masumi Okada, Teruo Kamaya, Tetsu Kayama; Director, Kinji Fukasaku; Screenplay, Kenta Fukasaku; Based on the novel by Koushun Takami; Photography, Katsumi Yanagishima; Music, Masamichi Amano; Editor, Hirohide Abe; a Toei Company production; Japanese, 2000; Color; Not rated; 114 minutes; American release date: December 24, 2011. **CAST:** Tatsuya Fujiwara (Shuya Nanahara), Aki Maeda (Noriko Nakagawa), Taro Yamamoto (Shogo Kawada), Takeshi Kitano (Kitano), Masanobu Andô (Kazuo Kiriyama), Kô Shibasaki (Mitsuko Souma), Takashi Tsukamoto (Shinji Mimura), Sosuke Takaoka (Hiroki Suigmura), Yukihiro Kotani (Yoshitoki Kuninobu), Chiaki Kuriyama (Takako Chigusa), Eri Ishikawa (Yukie Utsumi), Sayaka Kamiya (Satomi Noda), Aki Inoue (Fumiyo Fujiyoshi), Takayo Mimura (Kayoko Kotohiki), Yutaka Shimada (Yutaka Seto), Ren Matsuzawa (Keita Iijima), Hirohito Honda (Kazushi Nida), Ryou Nitta (Kyoichi Motobuchi), Sayaka Ikeda (Megumi Eto), Anna Nagata (Hirono Shimuzu), Yukari Kanasawa (Yukiko Kitano)

LE PÈRE NOËL EST UNE ORDURE (G.E.F.) Producer, Yves Rousset-Rouard; Director, Jean-Marie Poiré; Screenplay, Jean-Marie Poiré, Marie-Anne Chazel, Josiane Balasko, Thierry Lhermitte, Christian Clavier, Gérard Jugnot, Bruno Moynot; Photography, Robert Alazraki; Designers, Marc Frédérix, Willy Holt; Costumes, Cécile Magnan; Music, Vladimir Cosma; Editor, Catherine Kelber; a Trinacra Films production; French, 1982; Color; Not rated; 88 minutes; American release date: December 28, 2011. **CAST:** Anémone (Thérèse), Josiane Balasko (Madame Musquin), Marie-Anne Chazel (Zézette), Christian Clavier (Katia), Gérard Jugnot (Félix), Thierry Lhermitte (Pierre Mortez), Bruno Moynot (Zadko Preskovic), Martin Lamotte (Mr. Leble), Jacques François (Pharmacist), Claire Magnin (Madame Leble), Michel Blanc (Telephone Voice)

ANGELS CREST (Magnolia) Producedrs, Shirley Vercruysse, Leslie Cowan; Executive Producers, Tim Perell, William Mulroy; Director, Gaby Dellal; Screenplay, Catherine Trieschmann; Based on the book by Leslie Schwartz; Photography, David Johnson; Designer, Louise Middleton; Costumes, Christine Thomson; Music, Stephen Warbeck; Editors, Mick Audsley, Giles Bury; Casting, Steve Vincent, Sig De Miguel; a Process presentation of a Harrow Films production; British-Canadian; Dolby; Widescreen; Color; Rated R; 96 minutes; Release date: December 30, 2011. **CAST:** Thomas Dekker (Ethan), Lynn Collins (Cindy), Elizabeth McGovern (Jane), Joseph Morgan (Rusty), Jeremy Piven (Jack), Mira Sorvino (Angie), Kate Walsh (Roxanne), Barbara Williams (Cindy's Mother), Ameko Eks Mass Carroll (Nate), Emma MacGillivary (Rosie), Dave Brown (Frank), Colin Campbell (Paul), Greg Lawson (Bill), Marty Antonini (Charlie), Chris Ippolito (Will), Jonathan Lachlan Stewart (Kyle), Mathieu Bourassa (Clerk), Christianne Hirt (Yvette), Lindsay Burns (Donna), Aedan Tomney (Travis), Gillian Carfra (Celina Cervantes), Rachel Clentworth (Melody), Julian Domingues (George), Mallory Minerson (Saleswoman), Douglas Hinds (Barber), Rachael Stewart (Rachel), Wally Houn (Judge McKay)

Thomas Dekker in *Angels Crest* © Magnolia Pictures

Nina Arianda (*Higher Ground, Midnight in Paris, Tower Heist, Win Win*)

Joel Courtney (*Super 8*)

Jessica Chastain (*Coriolanus, The Debt, The Help, Take Shelter, Texas Killing Fields, The Tree of Life*)

Chris Hemsworth (*Thor*)

Tom Hiddleston (*Midnight in Paris, Thor, War Horse*)

Felicity Jones (*Chalet Girl, Like Crazy*)

Adepero Oduye (*Pariah*)

Thomas Horn (*Extremely Loud & Incredibly Close*)

Jeremy Irvine (*War Horse*)

Elizabeth Olsen (*Martha Marcy May Marlene*)

Andrea Riseborough (*Brighton Rock, W.E.*)

Chris New (*Weekend*)

ACADEMY AWARDS

Winners and Nominees 2011

BEST PICTURE

THE ARTIST

(WEINSTEIN CO.) Producer, Thomas Langmann; Executive Producers, Daniel Delume, Antoine De Cazotte, Richard Middleton; Associate Producer, Emmanuel Montamat; Director/ Screenplay, Michel Hazanavicius; Photography, Guillaume Schiffman; Designer, Laurence Bennett; Costumes, Mark Bridges; Music, Ludovic Bource; Editors, Anne-Sophie Bion, Michel Hazanavicius; Choreographer, Fabrien Ruiz; Casting, Heidi Levitt; a La Petite Rein and Thomas Langmann presentation of a Studio 37, La Classe Americaine, JD Prod, France 3 Cinéma, Jouror Productions, Ufilm co-production; French; Black and white; Rated PG-13; 100 minutes; American release date: November 25, 2011

John Goodman

CAST

George Valentin	**Jean Dujardin**
Peppy Miller	**Bérénice Bejo**
Al Zimmer	**John Goodman**
Clifton	**James Cromwell**
Doris	**Penelope Ann Miller**
Constance	**Missi Pyle**
The Dog	**Uggie**
Peppy's Maid	**Beth Grant**
Peppy's Butler	**Ed Lauter**
Policeman, Fire	**Joel Murray**
Norma	**Bitsie Tulloch**
Pawnbroker	**Ken Davitian**
The Butler	**Malcolm McDowell**
Auctioneer	**Basil Hoffman**
Policeman, Tuxedo	**Bill Fagerbakke**
Admiring Woman	**Nina Siemaszko**
Set Assistant	**Stephen Mendillo**
Peppy's Boyfriends	**Dash Pomerantz, Beau Nelson**
Guards	**Alex Holliday, Wiley Picket**
Audition Casting Assistant	**Ben Kurland**
Audition Dancers	**Katie Nisa, Katie Wallick**
Napoleon	**Hal Landon, Jr.**
Set Technician	**Cleto Augusto**
Laughing Dancers	**Sarah Karges, Sarah Scott**
Shouting Dancer	**Maize Olinger**
Journalists	**Ezra Buzzington, Fred Bishop**
Director #1 (Restaurant)	**Stuart Pankin**
Director #2	**Andy Milder**
Director #3 (Finale)	**David Cluck**

Kristian Falkenstein (Actor in "The Brunette"), Matt Skollar (Peppy's Assistant), Annie O'Donnell (Woman with Policeman), Patrick Mapel (Assistant with Newspaper), Matthew Albrecht (Tennis Player), Harvey Alperin (Doctor), Lily Knight (Nurse at Peppy's House), Clement Blake (Beggar), Tasso Feldman, Chris Ashe (Zimmer's Assistants), Adria Tennor (Zimmer's Secretary), Cletus Young (Bartender), J. Mark Donaldson, Brian Williams (Thugs), Andrew Ross Wynn (Big Dancer, Restaurant), Jen Lilley, Brian Chenoweth (Onlookers), Tim De Zarn (Soldier), Niko Novick (Producer), Vincent De Paul (Restaurant Manager), Mohamed Dione (African), Kevin Michael Hoffman (Peppy's Dance Partner)

Bérénice Bejo

As the end of the silent movie era approaches, one of Hollywood's reigning stars faces an uncertain future in this story told without dialogue.

2011 Academy Award winner for Best Picture, Best Actor (Jean Dujardin), Best Director, Best Costume Design, and Best Original Score.

This film received additional Oscar nominations for supporting actress (Bérénice Bejo), screenplay, art direction, cinematography, and editing.

James Cromwell

Jean Dujardin

Uggie, Bérénice Bejo

Penelope Ann Miller

Bérénice Bejo, Malcolm McDowell

Jean Dujardin, Missi Pyle

Jean Dujadrin, Bérénice Bejo © Weinstein Co

Rango

Mariachi Owls

Balthazar, Jedidiah

Spoons, Rango, Elgin, Buford

Priscilla

Rattlesnake Jake

Rango, Roadkill

Spoons

Rango, Wounded Bird

Rango, Beans © Paramount Pictures

The Mayor

BEST ANIMATED FEATURE

RANGO

(PARAMOUNT) Producers, Gore Verbinski, Graham King, John B. Carls; Executive Producer, Tim Headington; Co-Producers, Shari Hanson, Adam Cramer, David Shannon; Director, Gore Verbinski; Screenplay, John Logan; Story, John Logan, Gore Verbinski, James Ward Byrkit; Designer, Mark "Crash" McCreery; Music, Hans Zimmer; Editor, Craig Wood; Animation Director, Hal Hickel; Visual Effects Supervisors, Tim Alexander, John Knoll; Feature Animation, Industrial Light & Magic; a Nickelodeon Movies presentation of a BlindWink/GK Films production; Dolby; Widescreen; Deluxe color; Rated PG; 105 minutes; Release date: March 4, 2011

VOICE CAST

Rango/Lars	**Johnny Depp**
Beans	**Isla Fisher**
Priscilla	**Abigail Breslin**
Mayor	**Ned Beatty**
Roadkill	**Alfred Molina**
Rattlesnake Jake	**Bill Nighy**
Doc/Merrimack/Mr. Snuggles	**Stephen Root**
Balthazar	**Harry Dean Stanton**
Spirit of the West	**Timothy Olyphant**
Bad Bill	**Ray Winstone**
Ambrose	**Ian Abercrombie**
Wounded Bird	**Gil Birmingham**
Waffles/Gordy Papa/Joad/ Cousin Murt/Curlie/Knife Attacker/Rodent Kid	**James Ward Byrkit**
Angelique	**Claudia Black**
Buford	**Blake Clark**
Elgin	**John Cothran**
Delilah/Maybelle	**Patrika Darbo**
Señor Flan – Mariachi Accordion	**George Del Hoyo**
Lucky	**Maile Flanagan**
Elbows	**Charles Fleischer**
Bonnie	**Beth Grant**
Jedidiah	**Ryan Hurst**
Ezekiel/Lasso Rodent	**Vincent Kartheiser**
Chorizo	**Hemky Madera**
Spoons	**Alex Manugian**
Parsons	**Mark "Crash" McCreery**
Rock-Eye	**Joseph A. Nuñez**

Chris Parson (Hazel Moats/Kinski/Stump/Clinker/Lenny/ Boseefus/Dirt Kid), Lew Temple (Furgus/Hitch), Alanna Ubach (Boo/Cletus/Fresca/Miss Daisy), Gore Verbinski (Sergeant Turley/Crevice/Slim/Lupe – Mariachi Violin), Kym Whitley (Melonee), Keith Campbell (Sod Buster)

A lizard passing himself off as a great gunfighter is enlisted by the citizens of the dying town of Dirt to help them battle their corrupt mayor and save them from the mysterious drought that has brought them to the brink of ruin.

2011 Academy Award winner for Best Animated Feature.

BEST FOREIGN LANGUAGE FILM

A SEPARATION

(SONY CLASSICS) a.k.a. *Jodaeiye Nader az Simin*; Producer/Director/
Screenplay, Asghar Farhadi; Executive Producer, Negar Eskandarfar;
Photography, Mahmood Kalari; Set Designer/Costumes, Keyvan Moghadam;
Editor, Hayedeh Safiyari; an Asghar Farhadi production, Memento Films
International with the participation of Dreamlab Films; Iranian; Dolby; Color;
Rated PG-13; 123 minutes; American release date: December 30, 2011

CAST

Simin	**Leila Hatami**
Nader	**Peyman Moadi**
Hodjat	**Shahab Hosseini**
Razieh	**Sareh Bayat**
Termeh	**Sarina Farhadi**
Judge	**Babak Karimi**
Nader's Father	**Ali-Ashgar Shahbazi**
Simin's Mother	**Shirin Yazdanbakhsh**
Somayeh	**Kimia Hosseini**
Ms. Ghahraei	**Merila Zarei**

Sahabanu Zolghadr (Azam), Mohammadhasan Asghari, Hamid Dadju,
Manuchehr Mohammadzade, Nosratollah Seyfizade (Creditors), Shirin
Azimiyannezhad (Woman on the Bus), Mohammad Ebrahimian (Judge), Samad
Farhang (Interrogator's Office Manager), Ali Fattahi, Hamid Janane, Seyyd
Hamid Mirshams (Soldiers), Nafise Ghodrati (School Teacher), Roya Hosseini,
Mazdak Mohaymeni (Police Officers), Seyyed Jamshid Hosseini, Majid Nameni
(Accused Men), Sahar Kaye (Neighbor Woman), Ali Nazari (Satelite Receiver
Operator), Farhad Nosrati (Piano Dlivery Man), Mahmoud Rafi'i (Interrogator's
Secretary), Bahare Riyahi (Hospital Receptionist), Peyman Sadeghi (Doctor),
Mohammad Saffari (Shoemaker), Bahare Shahbazi (Neighbor Girl), Khodarahm
Soleymannezhad (School Janitor), Maria Tehranchi (School Principal), Armine
Zeytounchian (Mrs. Kalanni)

Determined to leave Iran, Simin sues her husband for divorce when he refuses to
abandon his Alzheimer-suffering father.

2011 Academy Award winner for Best Foreign Language Film.

This movie received an additional Oscar nomination for original screenplay.

Leila Hatami

Peyman Moadi, Sarina Farhadi

Shahab Hosseini (center)

Shahab Hosseini © Sony Classics

ACADEMY AWARD FOR BEST ACTOR: Jean Dujardin in *The Artist*

ACADEMY AWARD FOR BEST ACTRESS: Meryl Streep in *The Iron Lady*

ACADEMY AWARD FOR BEST SUPPORTING ACTOR: Christopher Plummer in *Beginners*

ACADEMY AWARD FOR BEST SUPPORTING ACTRESS: Octavia Spencer in *The Help*

ACADEMY AWARD NOMINEES FOR BEST ACTOR

Demián Bichir in *A Better Life*

George Clooney in *The Descendants*

Gary Oldman in *Tinker Tailor Soldier Spy*

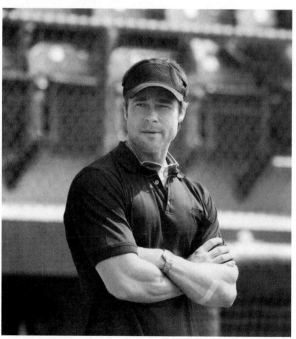

Brad Pitt in *Moneyball*

ACADEMY AWARD NOMINEES FOR BEST ACTRESS

Glenn Close in *Albert Nobbs*

Viola Davis in *The Help*

Rooney Mara in *The Girl with the Dragon Tattoo*

Michelle Williams in *My Week with Marilyn*

ACADEMY AWARD NOMINEES FOR BEST SUPPORTING ACTOR

Kenneth Branagh in *My Week with Marilyn*

Jonah Hill in *Moneyball*

Nick Nolte in *Warrior*

Max von Sydow in *Extremely Loud & Incredibly Close*

ACADEMY AWARD NOMINEES FOR BEST SUPPORTING ACTRESS

Bérénice Bejo in *The Artist*

Jessica Chastain in *The Help*

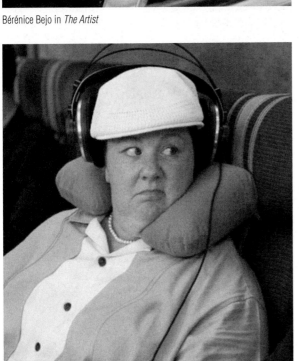

Melissa McCarthy in *Bridesmaids*

Janet McTeer in *Albert Nobbs*

TOP BOX OFFICE

Stars and Films 2011

1

TOP
BOX OFFICE
STARS OF 2011

1. Brad Pitt
2. George Clooney
3. Johnny Depp
4. Leonardo DiCaprio
5. Matt Damon
6. Sandra Bullock
7. Bradley Cooper
8. Robert Downey, Jr.
9. Meryl Streep
10. Ben Stiller

2

3

4

5

6

7

8

9

10

2011 BOX OFFICE FILMS

1. Harry Potter and the Deathly Hallows Part 2 (WB) — $381,100,000
2. Transformers: Dark of the Moon (Paramount) — $352,390,000
3. Breaking Dawn Part 1 (Summit) — $281,290,000
4. The Hangover Part II (WB) — $253,470,000
5. Pirates of the Caribbean: On Stranger Tides (Disney) — $241,100,000
6. Fast Five (Universal) — $209,840,000
7. Mission: Impossible – Ghost Protocol (Paramount) — $209,370,000
8. Cars 2 (Disney) — $190,460,000
9. Sherlock Holmes: A Game of Shadows (WB) — $186,770,000
10. Thor (Paramount) — $181,100,000
11. Rise of the Planet of the Apes (20th) — $176,750,000
12. Captain America (Paramount) — $176,660,000
13. The Help (BV/DreamWorks) — $169,710,000
14. Bridesmaids (Universal) — $169,110,000
15. Kung Fu Panda 2 (DreamWorks/Paramount) — $164,250,000
16. Puss in Boots (DW/Paramount) — $149,240,000
17. X-Men: First Class (20th) — $146,410,000
18. Rio (20th) — $143,620,000
19. The Smurfs (Columbia) — $142,620,000
20. Alvin and the Chipmunks: Chipwrecked (20th) — $133,000,000
21. Super 8 (Paramount) — $127,100,000
22. Rango (Paramount) — $123,260,000
23. Horrible Bosses (WB) — $117,540,000
24. Green Lantern (WB) — $116,610,000
25. Hop (Universal) — $108,100,000
26. Just Go with It (Columbia) — $103,100,000

Gonzo in *The Muppets*

Asa Butterfield, Sacha Baron Cohen in *Hugo*

Chris Evans, Hayley Atwell in *Captain America*

Ralph Fiennes in *Harry Potter and the Deathly Hallows Part 2*

Emma Stone, Viola Davis in *The Help*

Owen Wilson, Rachel McAdams in *Midnight in Paris*

27. Paranormal Activity 3 (Paramount)	$102,920,000	55. The Adjustment Bureau (Universal)	$62,500,000
28. The Girl with the Dragon Tattoo (Columbia)	$101,710,000	56. Happy Feet Two (WB)	$60,820,000
29. Bad Teacher (Columbia)	$100,300,000	57. Water for Elephants (20th)	$58,710,000
30. Cowboys & Aliens (Universal)	$100,250,000	58. The Lincoln Lawyer (Lionsgate)	$58,100,000
31. Gnomeo& Juliet (Disney)	$99,970,000	59. Midnight in Paris (Sony Classics)	$56,730,000
32. The Green Hornet (Columbia)	$98,790,000	60. Friends with Benefits (Screen Gems)	$55,810,000
33. The Lion King (Disney) (3D reissue)	$94,230,000	61. I am Number Four (BV)	$55,100,000
34. The Muppets (Disney)	$88,610,000	62. Source Code (Summit)	$54,720,000
35. Real Steel (Disney)	$85,470,000	63. New Year's Eve (New Line/WB)	$54,550,000
36. Crazy, Stupid. Love. (WB)	$84,360,000	64. Insidious (Film District)	$54,100,000
37. Battle Los Angeles (Columbia)	$83,560,000	65. Madea's Big Happy Family (Lionsgate)	$53,350,000
38. Immortals (Relativity Media)	$83,460,000	66. Diary of a Wimpy Kid: Rodrick Rules (20th)	$52,700,000
39. The Descendants (Fox Searchlight)	$82,280,000	67. Footloose (Paramount)	$51,500,000
40. Zookeeper (Columbia)	$80,370,000	68. The Dilemma (Universal)	$48,480,000
41. War Horse (Disney/DW)	$79,890,000	69. Arthur Christmas (Columbia)	$46,470,000
42. Limitless (Relativity)	$79,250,000	70. Hall Pass (WB)	$45,100,000
43. Tower Heist (Universal)	$78,100,000	71. The Artist (Miramax)	$44,680,000
44. The Adventures of Tintin (Paramount)	$77,560,000	72. Soul Surfer (TriStar)	$43,860,000
45. Contagion (WB)	$75,660,000	73. Final Destination 5 (New Line/WB)	$41,590,000
46. Moneyball (Columbia)	$75,610,000	74. The Ides of March (Columbia)	$40,970,000
47. We Bought a Zoo (20th)	$75,590,000	75. Hanna (Focus)	$40,260,000
48. Jack and Jill (Columbia)	$74,160,000	76. Something Borrowed (WB)	$39,100,000
49. Hugo (Paramount)	$73,830,000	77. Spy Kids: All the Time in the World (Dimension)	$38,530,000
50. Justin Bieber: Never Say Never (Paramount)	$73,100,000	78. Big Mommas: Like Father, Like Son (20th)	$37,910,000
51. Dolphin Tale (WB)	$72,290,000	79. Red Riding Hood (WB)	$37,670,000
52. No Strings Attached (Paramount)	$70,670,000	80. In Time (20th)	$37,530,000
53. Mr. Popper's Penguins (20th)	$68,230,000	81. Paul (Universal)	$37,420,000
54. Unknown (WB)	$63,690,000	82. J. Edgar (WB)	$37,320,000

83. The Roommate (Screen Gems)	$37,310,000	92. 50/50 (Summit)	$35,100,000
84. Jumping the Broom (TriStar)	$37,300,000	93. A Very Harold & Kumar 3D Christmas (New Line)	$35,000,000
85. Scream 4 (Dimension)	$37,190,000	94. Courageous (TriStar)	$34,200,000
86. The Change-Up (Universal)	$37,110,000	95. Arthur (WB)	$33,100,000
87. 30: Minutes or Less (Columbia)	$37,100,000	96. The Rite (NL/WB)	$33,100,000
88. Colombiana (Screen Gems)	$36,670,000	97. Extremely Loud & Incredibly Close (WB)	$31,840,000
89. Sucker Punch (WB)	$36,400,000	98. The Debt (Focus)	$31,180,000
90. Larry Crowne (Universal)	$35,610,000	99. The Sitter (20ᵗʰ)	$30,330,000
91. Drive (Filmdistrict)	$35,110,000	100. The Iron Lady (Miramax)	$30,100,000

Morgan Freeman in *Dolphin Tale*

Armie Hammer, Leonardo DiCaprio, Stephen Root in *J. Edgar*

Thomas Horn in *Extremely Loud & Incredibly Close*

OBITUARIES

2011

Ray Aghayan

Tom Aldredge

Pedro Armendáriz, Jr.

James Arness

George Baker

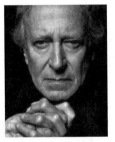

John Barry

Roberts Blossom

Joseph Brooks

Leslie Brooks

Alfred Burke

Michael Cacoyannis

Charlie Callas

William Campbell

Linda Christian

Diane Cilento

Jeff Conaway

Jackie Cooper

John Howard Davies

John Dye

Robert Easton

RAY AGHAYAN, 83, Iranian-born costume designer, who received Oscar nominations for his work on *Gaily Gaily, Lady Sings the Blues,* and *Funny Lady,* died in Los Angeles on October 10, 2011. His other film credits include *Father Goose, The Art of Love, Do Not Disturb, The Glass Bottom Boat, Our Man Flint, Caprice, Doctor Dolittle* (1967), and *Hannie Caulder.* Survived by his partner, designer Bob Mackie.

THEONI V. ALDREDGE (TheoniAsanathiou), 88, Greece-born costume designer, who won the Academy Award for her creations for the 1974 film *The Great Gatsby,* died of cardiac arrest in Stamford, CT, on January 21, 2011. Her other movies include *Never on Sunday* (Oscar nomination), *Phaedra* (Oscar nomination), *You're a Big Boy Now, Last Summer, Harry and Walter Go to New York, Network, Semi-Tough, The Rose, Can't Stop the Music, Rich and Famous, Annie, Ghost Busters, Moonstruck, Other People's Money, The First Wives Club,* and *The Mirror Has Two Faces.* She was survived by her husband of 57 years, actor Tom Aldredge.

TOM ALDREDGE, 83, Ohio-born character actor, known for his roles on Broadway in such shows as *Sticks and Bones, On Golden Pond* and *Into the Woods,* died in Tampa, FL, on July 22, 2011, after a battle with lymphoma. His movies include *The Mouse on the Moon, Who Killed Teddy Bear, The Boston Strangler, The Rain People, *batteries not included, See You in the Morning, Other People's Money, The Adventures of Huck Finn, Lawn Dogs, Rounders, Intolerable Cruelty,* and *Cold Mountain.* His wife of 57 years, designer Theoni V. Aldredge predeceased him by 6 months.

KAY ARMEN (Armenuhi Manoogian), 95, Chicago-born singer-actress-songwriter died in New York City on Oct. 3, 2011 following a brief illness. She was seen in the films *Hit the Deck; Hey, Let's Twist!;* and *Paternity.*

PEDRO ARMENDÁRIZ, JR. (Pedro Armendáriz Bohr), 71, Mexican character actor died of cancer on December 26, 2011 in New York City. His movies include *Guns for San Sebastian, The Undefeated* (1969), *Macho Callahan, Chosen Survivors, The Dogs of War, Walker, License to Kill, Tombstone, Amistad, The Mask of Zorro, The Mexican, The Crime of Father Amaro,* and *Once Upon a Time in Mexico.* Survived by several children.

JAMES ARNESS (James Aurness), 88, Minneapolis-born actor, best known for playing Marshal Matt Dillon for twenty seasons on the western television series *Gunsmoke,* died on June 3, 2011 at his home in Los Angeles. He appeared in such motion pictures as *The Farmer's Daughter* (1947), *Battleground, Wagon Master, Stars in My Crown, The People vs. O'Hara, The Thing from Another World* (in the title role), *Carbine Williams, Big Jim McLain, Horizons West, Island in the Sky, Hondo, Them!, Her Twelve Men, Many Rivers to Cross, The Sea Chase, The First Traveling Saleslady,* and *Alias Jesse James.* He is survived by his second wife, a son, six grandchildren, and a great-grandchild. His younger brother, actor Peter Graves, died in March of 2010.

DOE AVEDON (Dorcas Nowell), 86, Westbury, NY-born model-turned-actress died in Los Angeles on December 18, 2011. Discovered by photographer Richard Avedon (who became her first husband), she would go on to act in five theatrical features: *Jigsaw* (1949), *The High and the Mighty, Deep in My Heart, The Boss,* and *Love Streams.* She is survived by four children from her marriage to director Don Siegel; her stepson, actor Kristoffer Tabori; her companion; seven grandchildren; and five great-grandchildren.

GEORGE BAKER, 80, Bulgaria-born U.K. actor died of pneumonia in West Lavington, Wiltshire, England, on October 7, 2011 after a recent stroke. His theatrical films include *The Dam Busters, Hell in Korea, Sword of Lancelot, Goodbye Mr. Chips* (1969), *On Her Majesty's Secret Service, A Warm December, The Spy Who Loved Me, The Thirty Nine Steps* (1980), *ffolkes,* and *For Queen and Country.* On British television he was best known for the *Ruth Rendell Mysteries,* appearing opposite his third wife, Louie Ramsey. He is survived by five daughters and several grandchildren.

JOHN BARRY (John Barry Prendergast), 77, British composer, who won two Academy Awards for the music and title song from the film *Born Free,* and who composed the scores for 11 James Bond movies, died of a heart attack in New York on January 30, 2011. He earned three additional Oscars, for *The Lion in Winter, Out of Africa,* and *Dances with Wolves,* plus nominations for *Mary, Queen of Scots* and *Chaplin.* His many other scores include *Never Let Go, Séance on a Wet Afternoon, Zulu, Goldfinger, The Ipcress File, The Knack … and How to Get It, The Wrong Box, The Whisperers, You Only Live Twice, They Might Be Giants, The Tamarind Seed, The Day of the Locust, Robin and Marian, The Deep, The Black Hole, Somewhere in Time, Frances, Jagged Edge, Peggy Sue Got Married, Indecent Proposal,* and *Playing by Heart.* He is survived by his third wife, four children, and five grandchildren.

DORIS BELACK, 85, New York City-born character actress died of natural causes in Manhattan on October 4, 2011. Among her movie credits are *The Black Marble, Hanky Panky, Tootsie, Fast Forward, *batteries not included, The Luckiest Man in the World, She-Devil, What about Bob?, Naked Gun 33 1/3: The Final Insult, Krippendorf's Tribe,* and *Prime.* Her husband of 65 years, theater producer Philip Rose, had died four months earlier.

ROBERTS BLOSSOM, 87, Connecticut-born character actor died in Santa Monica, CA, on July 8, 2011. His movie credits include *The Hospital, Slaughterhouse-Five, Deranged, The Great Gatsby, Handle with Care (Citizens Band), Close Encounters of the Third Kind, Escape from Alcatraz, Resurrection, Christine, Reuben Reuben, The Last Temptation of Christ, Home Alone, Doc Hollywood,* and *The Quick and the Dead.* Survived by a daughter and a son.

EVE BRENT (Jean Ewers), 82, Houston-born actress died on August 27, 2011 in Sun Valley CA, of natural causes. Her movies include *The Garment Jungle, Forty Guns, Tarzan and the Trappers, Tarzan's Fight for Life* (in the last two as Jane), *Mara of the Wilderness, A Guide for the Married Man, Coogan's Bluff, The Happy Ending, Airport, The Barefoot Executive, Racing with the Moon, The Green Mile,* and *Garfield.* Survivors include her son.

PATRICIA BRESLIN, 80, New York City-born actress, who starred opposite Jackie Cooper in the 1950s series *The People's Choice,* died in Baltimore on October 12, 2011. Although principally seen on television she also appeared in the movies *Go, Man, Go!, Andy Hardy Comes Home, Homicidal,* and *I Saw What You Did.* Survived by her husband, two sons, and six grandchildren.

JOSEPH BROOKS, 73, New York City-born songwriter-filmmaker, who won an Academy Award for writing the song "You Light Up My Life," committed suicide in his Manhattan apartment on May 22, 2011. He had been awaiting trial for suspicion of rape. He served as director-producer-writer-actor-songwriter on such films as *You Light Up My Life* and *If Ever I See You Again.* Survived by three children.

LESLIE BROOKS (Virginia Leslie Gettman), 89, Nebraska-born actress of the 1940s, died in Sherman Oaks, CA, on July 1, 2011. Her movies include *You Were Never Lovelier, Cover Girl, Tonight and Every Night, It's Great to Be Young, The Corpse Came C.O.D., Romance on the High Seas,* and *Blonde Ice.* She retired from the business in 1949. She is survived by her second husband and three children.

ALFRED BURKE, 92, London-born character actor died on Feb. 16, 2011. His movies include *Law and Disorder* (1958), *The Angry Silence, The Small World of Sammy Lee, Children of the Damned, The Nanny, One Day in the Life of Ivan Denisovich,* and *Harry Potter and the Chamber of Secrets.* Survivors include his wife and two sets of twins.

MICHAEL CACOYANNIS (Mihalis Kakogiannis), 89, Cyprus-born filmmaker, who earned 3 Oscar nominations as director, producer, and co-writer of the 1964 movie *Zorba the Greek,* died on July 25, 2011 in Athens, of complications from a heart attack. His other credits include *Electra, The Day the Fish Came Out, The Trojan Women, Iphigenia,* and *The Cherry Orchard.* Survived by two sisters.

CHARLIE CALLAS, 86, Brooklyn-born comedian, famous for his bizarre vocal effects, died in Las Vegas on January 27, 2011. His movie credits include *The Big Mouth, Silent Movie, Pete's Dragon* (as the voice of the dragon), *Hysterical,* and *Dracula: Dead and Loving It.* Survived by two sons and two grandchildren.

WILLIAM CAMPBELL, 84, Newark-born actor died on April 28, 2011 in Woodland Hills, CA, following a long illness. His movies include *The Breaking Point, Inside the Walls of Folsom Prison, The People Against O'Hara, Holiday for Sinners, Escape from Fort Bravo, The High and the Mighty, Battle Cry, Man without a Star, The Naked and the Dead, The Young Racers, Dementia 13; Hush ... Hush, Sweet Charlotte; Pretty Maids All in a Row,* and *Black Gunn.* Survived by his third wife.

GILBERT CATES (Gilbert Lewis Katz), 77, New York City-born director-producer died on October 31, 2011 after collapsing in a parking lot on the campus of UCLA. He had recently undergone heart surgery. His theatrical directing credits include *I Never Sang for My Father, Summer Wishes Winter Dreams, The Promise,* and *The Last Married Couple in America.* On television, in addition to directing and producing several movies, he served as producer of 14 Oscar ceremonies over an 18-year period (1990-2008). Survived by his wife; three sons; two stepdaughters; and five grandchildren.

LINDA CHRISTIAN (Blanca Rose Henrietta Stella Welter Vorhauer), 87, Mexico-born actress died in Palm Springs, CA, on July 22, 2011, after suffering from colon cancer. Her movies include *Holiday in Mexico, Green Dolphin Street, Tarzan and the Mermaids, The Happy Time, Athena, The House of the Seven Hawks,* and *The V.I.P.s.* She was married and divorced from actors Tyrone Power and Edmund Purdom. Her two daughters from her marriage to the former survive her along with 8 grandchildren.

DIANE CILENTO, 78, Australia-born actress, who earned an Oscar nomination playing the slatternly Molly in the 1963 Academy Award-winner *Tom Jones,* died in Cairns, Queensland, Australia on October 6, 2011. Her other movies include *Stop Me before I Kill!, The Naked Edge, I Thank a Fool, The Third Secret, Rattle of a Simple Man, The Agony and the Ecstasy, Hombre, Negatives, Z.P.G., Hitler: The Last Ten Days,* and *The Wicker Man* (1973; later marrying its writer, Anthony Shaffer). Survivors include her daughter from her first marriage, and her son, actor Jason Connery, from her second marriage, to actor Sean Connery.

JEFF CONAWAY, 60, New York City-born actor, best remembered for playing Kenickie in the hit musical film *Grease,* died on May 26, 2011 in Encino, CA, nine days after being put into a medically induced coma. He had been found unconscious on May 11, after an apparent overdose of painkillers. He had been suffering from heart problems. His other films include *The Eagle Has Landed, I Never Promised You a Rose Garden, Pete's Dragon,* and *Elvira Mistress of the Dark.* On television he was featured in the series *Taxi.* He is survived by his second wife; two sisters; and a stepson.

GEORGINA COOKSON, 92, British actress died on October 1, 2011 in Sydney, Australia. She was seen in such movies as *Your Past is Showing* (*The Naked Truth*), *Five Golden Hours, Darling, Your Money or Your Wife, The Woman Who Wouldn't Die* (*Catacombs*), and *The Counterfeit Constable.* Survived by her son and daughter from her second marriage.

JACKIE COOPER (John Cooper, Jr.), 88, Los Angeles-born actor-director-producer-executive, who holds the record as the youngest performer nominated for a leading Oscar, for *Skippy,* receiving the honor when he was only 9, died on May 3, 2011 in Los Angeles after a brief illness. In addition to appearing in several *Our Gang* shorts, he was seen in such features as *The Champ* (1931), *The Bowery, Treasure Island* (1934), *Peck's Bad Boy* (1934), *Dinky, O'Shaughnessy's Boy, The Devil is a Sissy, Boy of the Streets, White Banners, That Certain Age, Newsboys' Home, The Spirit of Culver, What a Life, Seventeen, The Return of Frank James, Ziegfeld Girl, Glamour Boy, The Navy Comes Through, Kilroy Was Here, Everything's Ducky, The Love Machine, Stand Up and Be Counted* (also director), *Chosen Survivors, Superman* (as Perry White, a role he repeated in 3 sequels), and *Surrender.* From 1964 to 1969 he was a production executive for Screen Gems Television, and then a frequent director of episodic television, winning 2 Emmys for his work on *M*A*S*H.* Survived by his two sons.

NORMAN CORWIN, 101, Boston-born writer, known as radio's "poet laureate" for his many scripts written for that medium, died at his home in Los Angeles on October 18, 2011. His screenplays include *Forever and a Day, The Blue Veil,*

Lust for Life (Oscar nomination), *The Story of Ruth,* and *Madison Avenue.* He is survived by his daughter and his son.

JOHN HOWARD DAVIES, 72, London-born former child actor-turned-television producer/director, best known for playing the title role in David Lean's 1948 version of *Oliver Twist* (released in the U.S. in 1951), died of cancer on August 22, 2011 at his home in Blewbury, England. After appearing in 3 more films, *The Rocking Horse Winner, Tom Brown's Schooldays,* and *The Magic Box,* he later worked behind the scenes on such U.K. series as *Monty Python's Flying Circus, Steptoe and Son, Fawlty Towers,* and *Law and Disorder.* He also held several executive positions at BBC, EMI and ITV television. Survived by his wife; his son; and his daughter.

DENISE DARCEL (Denise Billecard), 87, Paris-born actress who appeared exclusively in English-language product, died on December 23, 2011 in Los Angeles following complications from emergency surgery to repair a ruptured aneurysm. Following her 1948 debut in *To the Victor,* she was seen in such pictures as *Battleground, Tarzan and the Slave Girl, Westward the Women, Dangerous When Wet, Vera Cruz,* and *Seven Women from Hell.* She retired from the business in 1963. Survived by two sons.

SHELAGH DELANEY, 71, British writer, best known for her breakthrough play, *A Taste of Honey,* produced in the West End when she was only 19 years old, died of cancer on November 20, 2011 in Suffolk, England. In addition to adapting *Honey* to the screen in 1961, her other film credits include *Charlie Bubbles* and *Dance with a Stranger.* Survived by her daughter and three grandchildren.

DON DIAMOND, 90, Brooklyn-born character actor, best remembered for his role of Crazy Cat on the TV sitcom *F Troop,* died on June 19, 2011 in Los Angeles. He could be seen in such motion pictures as *The Old Man and the Sea, The Story of Ruth, Irma La Douce, How Sweet it Is!, Viva Max, Mrs. Pollifax – Spy, Breezy,* and *Herbie Goes Bananas.* He is survived by his wife and three daughters.

MARION DOUGHERTY, 88, Pennsylvania-born casting director died on December 4, 2011 in New York City. Her many credits include *The World of Henry Orient, Hawaii, The Heart is a Lonely Hunter, Midnight Cowboy, The Owl and the Pussycat, The Anderson Tapes, Slaughterhouse Five, The Paper Chase, The Sting, Pretty Baby, Escape from Alcatraz, The World According to Garp, The Killing Fields, The Lost Boys, Nuts, Batman* (1989), *The Man without a Face,* and *Conspiracy Theory.* Survived by two sisters.

WILLIAM DUELL (George William Duell), 88, New York-born character actor, whose many roles include playing one of the inmates, Sefelt, in the 1975 Oscar-winner *One Flew Over the Cuckoo's Nest,* died of respiratory failure at his Manhattan home on Dec. 22, 2011. His other movies include *The Hustler, 1776, The Happy Hooker, King of the Gypsies, Grace Quigley, The Pope of Greenwich Village, Mrs. Soffel, Ironweed, In & Out, Cradle Will Rock,* and *How to Lose a Guy in 10 Days.* Survived by his wife.

JOHN DYE, 47, Mississippi-born actor, best known for playing "Andrew" the Angel of Death on the series *Touched by an Angel,* died of heart failure at his San Francisco home on January 10, 2011. He was also seen in such films as *Making the Grade, Modern Girls, Campus Man, Best of the Best,* and *The Perfect Weapon.* Survived by his parents.

ROBERT EASTON (Robert Easton Burke), 81, Milwaukee-born actor, better known in Hollywood as a dialect teacher for countless performers, died in Toluca Lake, CA, on Dec. 16, 2011. His motion pictures include *The Red Badge of Courage, Cause for Alarm!, Comin' Round the Mountain, Somebody Up There Likes Me, Voyage to the Bottom of the Sea, The War Lover, Come Fly with Me, The Loved One, Paint Your Wagon, Pete's Dragon, When You Comin' Back Red Ryder?, Working Girl, Needful Things, Primary Colors,* and *Gods and Generals.*

PETER FALK, 83, New York-born actor, who received back-to-back Oscar nominations for his performances in *Murder, Inc.* and *Pocketful of Miracles,* died at his home in Beverly Hills, CA, on June 23, 2011. He had been suffering from Alzheimer's disease. His other films include *Wind Across the Everglades* (debut, 1958), *Pretty Boy Floyd, Pressure Point, The Balcony, It's a Mad Mad Mad Mad*

Peter Falk

Edith Fellows

Anne Francis

Dolores Fuller

Betty Garrett

Annie Girardot

Susan Gordon

Michael Gough

Farley Granger

Edward Hardwicke

Jill Haworth

Charles Jarrott

Miriam Karlin

Aron Kincaid

Sidney Lumet

Kenneth Mars

Hugh Martin

Anna Massey

Bill McKinney

Sid Melton

World, Robin and the 7 Hoods, The Great Race, Penelope, Luv, Anzio, Machine Gun McCain, Castle Keep, Husbands, A Woman under the Influence, Murder by Death, Mikey and Nicky, The Cheap Detective, The Brink's Job, The In-Laws (1979), *The Great Muppet Caper, … All the Marbles, Wings of Desire, Happy New Year, The Princess Bride, Cookie, In the Spirit, Tune in Tomorrow…, Roommates, Lake Boat, Made, Checking Out,* and *Next.* On television he was best known for his starring role on the series *Columbo* for which he won 4 Emmys.He is survived by his second wife and two daughters from his previous marriage.

EDITH FELLOWS, 88, Boston-born child actress, who appeared opposite Bing Crosby in the 1936 musical *Pennies from Heaven,* died on June 26, 2011. Her other pictures include *Emma* (1932), *Jane Eyre* (1934; as Adele), *Mrs. Wiggs of the Cabbage Patch* (1934), *She Married Her Boss, Five Little Peppers and How They Grew* (and two sequels), *Girls' Town, Lilith,* and *In the Mood.* She is survived by her daughter.

MARGARET FIELD (Margaret Morlan), 89, Houston-born screen and television actress, died on November 6, 2011 at her Malibu, CA, home following a long battle with cancer. Among her movie credits were *The Big Clock, Beyond Glory, Night Has a Thousand Eyes, My Friend Irma, The Man from Planet X, The Dakota Kid, The Story of Will Rogers, The Raiders, So This is Love, Slim Carter,* and *Desire in the Dust.* She is survived by her two daughters, one of whom is actress Sally Field; her son; seven grandchildren; and eight great-grandchildren.

ANNE FRANCIS (Ann Marvak), 80, New York-born actress, who starred in such notable 1950s films as *Blackboard Jungle, Bad Day at Black Rock* and *Forbidden Planet,* died in Santa Barbara, CA, on January 2, 2011, of complications of pancreatic cancer. Her other film credits include *Portrait of Jennie, So Young So Bad, The Whistle at Eaton Falls, Elopement, Lydia Bailey, Dreamboat, A Lion is in the Streets, Susan Slept Here, Rogue Cop, The Rocket Man, Battle Cry, The Scarlet Coat, The Rack, The Great American Pastime, Don't Go Near the Water, The Crowded Sky, The Satan Bug, Brainstorm* (1965), *Funny Girl, Hook Line and Sinker, The Love God?,* and *Born Again.* She is survived by two daughters and a grandson.

DAN FRAZER, 90, New York City-born character actor, who appeared as Capt. Frank McNeil on the series *Kojack,* died of cardiac arrest at his Manhattan home on December 18, 2011. His movies include *Lilies of the Field, Lord Love a Duck, Take the Money and Run, …tick…tick…tick…, Bananas, Fuzz, Cleopatra Jones,* and *Deconstructing Harry.* Survived by his daughter.

DAVID F. FRIEDMAN, 87, Alabama-born exploitation film producer died on February 14, 2011 in Anniston, AL, of heart failure. His movies include *Blood Feast, Goldilocks and the Three Bares, Scum of the Earth, Two Thousand Maniacs!, Color Me Blood Red, She Freak,* and *Ilsa: She Wolf of the SS.* No reported survivors.

ALAN FUDGE, 77, Wichita-born character actor died on October 10, 2011 in Los Angeles, of lung and liver cancer. His motion picture credits include *Two People, Airport 1975, Capricorn One, Chapter Two, The Border, Brainstorm* (1983), *The Natural, Breaking In, Edward Scissorhands,* and *The Man Who Wasn't There* (2001). He is survived by his wife; a son; two daughters; and a grandson.

DOLORES FULLER (Dolores Agnes Eble), 88, Indiana-born actress-songwriter, best known for her collaborations with filmmaker Edward D. Wood Jr., including *Glen or Glenda* and *Bride of the Monster,* died on May 9, 2011 at her home in Las Vegas, following a long illness. She also wrote songs for several Elvis Presley movies including *Blue Hawaii* and *Roustabout.* Survived by her husband; her son; three grandchildren; and numerous stepchildren and step-grandchildren.

BETTY GARRETT, 91, Missouri-born actress, who played cabbie Brunhilde Esterhazy in the classic musical *On the Town,* died in Los Angeles of an aortic aneurysm on February 12, 2011. Her other movies include *The Big City* (debut, 1948), *Words and Music, Take Me Out to the Ball Game, Neptune's Daughter, My Sister Eileen* (1955), and *Shadow on the Window.* On television she was a series regular on *All in the Family* and *Laverne & Shirley.* She is survived by two sons from her marriage to actor Larry Parks (who died in 1975) and a granddaughter.

ANNIE GIRARDOT, 79, French actress died on February 28, 2011 in Paris after a long battle with Alzheimer's disease. Among her films released in the United States are *Inspector Maigret, Rocco and His Brothers, Love and the Frenchwoman, La Bonne Soupe, The Organizer, The Dirty Game, Live for Life, The Witches* (1968), *Story of a Woman, Love is a Funny Thing, Dear Detective* (*Dear Inspector*), *Run after Me Until I Catch You, Traffic Jam, All Night Long* (1981), *La vie continue, Les Miserables* (1995), *The Piano Teacher,* and *Cache.* Survived by her daughter.

DAVID ZELAG GOODMAN, 81, New York City-born screenwriter, who earned an Oscar nomination for co-scripting *Lovers and Other Strangers,* died in Oakland, CA, on September 26, 2011 of progressive supranuclear palsy. His other credits include *Monte Walsh, Straw Dogs* (1971), *Farewell My Lovely, Logan's Run, Eyes of Laura Mars,* and *Man Woman and Child.* Survived by his wife of 61 years, his sister, and a daughter.

BRUCE GORDON, 94, Massachusetts-born character actor, who specialized in playing thugs and gangsters, died on January 20, 2011 in Santa Fe, NM following a long illness. Although he was seen more frequently on television and stage, his movies include *Love Happy, The Buccaneer* (1958), *Key Witness, Tower of London* (1962), *Hello Down There,* and *Piranha* (1978). Survived by his wife.

SUSAN GORDON, 62, Minnesota-born child actress, who appeared in four motion pictures directed by her father, B-moviemaker Bert I. Gordon, died of thyroid cancer in Teaneck, NJ on December 11, 2011. In addition to her many television appearances, she was seen in six feature films: *Attack of the Puppet People, Man in the Net, The Five Pennies, The Boy and the Pirates, Tormented,* and *Picture Mommy Dead.* Survived by her father; her mother; her sister; her husband; her six children; and five grandchildren.

MICHAEL GOUGH, 94, India-born British character actor, who had leading roles in such horror films as *Horrors of the Black Museum, Konga,* and *Black Zoo* and who played the butler Alfred in four *Batman* movies, died on March 17, 2011 at his home in London. His other pictures include *Anna Karenina* (1948), *The Man in the White Suit, Rob Roy: The Highland Rogue, Richard III, Horror of Dracula, The Horse's Mouth, I Like Money* (*Mr. Topaze*), *No Place like Homicide!, The Phantom of the Opera* (1962), *Berserk, Women in Love, A Walk with Love and Death, Trog, The Go-Between, Savage Messiah, The Boys from Brazil, The Dresser, Top Secret!, Out of Africa, Let Him Have It, The Age of Innocence* (1993), *Sleepy Hollow,* and *Alice in Wonderland* (voice of the Dodo; 2010). He is survived by his wife, two sons, and a daughter.

FARLEY GRANGER, 85, San Jose-born actor, who starred in such notable films of the late-1940's/early 1950's as *They Live by Night* and *Strangers on a Train,* died of natural causes at his Manhattan home on March 27, 2011. Following his 1943 debut in *The North Star,* he was seen in such other movies as *The Purple Heart, Rope, Roseanna McCoy, Side Street, Edge of Doom, Our Very Own, O. Henry's Full House, Hans Christian Andersen, The Story of Three Loves, Small Town Girl* (1953), *Senso, The Girl in the Red Velvet Swing, They Call Me Trinity, Arnold, The Prowler,* and *The Imagemaker.* No reported survivors.

ROSS HAGEN (Leland Lando Lilly), 72, Arizona-born character actor died of cancer on May 7, 2011 in Los Angeles. He acted in such pictures as *The Mini-Skirt Mob, Speedway, The Hellcats, The Organization, Angels' Wild Women, Melinda,* and *Angel,* and directed-wrote movies like *The Glove* and *B.O.R.N.* Survived by his partner; his son and his daughter.

PETER HAMMOND (Peter Charles Hammond Hill), 87, British actor-turned director died in London on Oct. 12, 2011. He appeared in such movies as *Waterloo Road, Holiday Camp* (and the subsequent "Huggett" series), *Operation Disaster,* and *Fortune in Diamonds.* He later directed episodes of such programs as *The Avengers* and the *Sherlock Holmes* mysteries. His wife of 57 years, actress Maureen Glynne died in 2005. Their five children survive Hammond.

EDWARD HARDWICKE, 78, British actor, best known for playing Dr. Watson on *The Return of Sherlock Holmes* series, died of cancer on May 16, 2011 in Chichester, England. The son of actor Cedric Hardwicke, his motion pictures include *A Guy Named Joe, Hell Above Zero, Othello* (1965; as Montano), *A Flea in Her Ear, Otley, The Day of the Jackal, Baby: Secret of the Lost Legend, Let Him*

Mary Murphy

David Nelson

John Neville

Paul Picerni

Marie-France Pisier

Alice Playten

Pete Postlethwaite

Peggy Rea

Cliff Robertson

Jane Russell

Ken Russell

Michael Sarrazin

Maria Schneider

Bubba Smith

G.D. Spradlin

Elaine Stewart

Elizabeth Taylor

Sada Thompson

Margaret Tyzack

Yvette Vickers

Have It, Shadowlands, Richard III (1995; as Lord Thomas Stanley), *Elizabeth, Love Actually,* and *Oliver Twist* (2005; as Mr. Brownlow), He is survived by his second wife and his two daughters from his first marriage.

JILL HAWORTH (Valeria Jill Haworth), 65, British actress, best known for creating the role of Sally Bowles in the original Broadway production of *Cabaret,* died of natural causes at her Manhattan home on January 3, 2011. Her motion pictures include *Exodus, The Cardinal, In Harm's Way, It!,* and *The Mutations.* No determined survivors.

DAVID HESS, 75, New York City-born songwriter-actor, who starred in Wes Craven's 1972 horror film *The Last House on the Left,* died of a heart attack on October 8, 2011. Among his other movies are *The Swiss Conspiracy, Avalanche Express, Swamp Thing,* and *Let's Get Harry.* He is survived by his wife, brother, two sisters, three sons, and a daughter.

TIM HETHERINGTON, 40, co-director of the Oscar-nominated documentary *Restrepo* was killed by mortar fire while documenting rebel fighting in Misrata, Libya on April 20, 2011. He also photographed the documentary *The Devil Came on Horseback.* Survived by his parents, his sister and brother.

HAROLD HOPKINS, 67, Australian actor died in Sydney on December 11, 2011 from asbestos-related cancer mesothelioma. His movies include *Age of Consent, Adam's Woman, Don's Party, The Picture Show Man,* and *Gallipoli.* Survived by his twin brother and five other siblings.

BILL HUNTER, 81, Australian character actor died of cancer on May 21, 2011 in Melbourne. His movie credits include *Ned Kelly* (1970), *Newsfront, Gallipoli, The Hit, Rikky and Pete, Strictly Ballroom, The Adventures of Priscilla – Queen of the Desert, Muriel's Wedding, Kangaroo Jack, Finding Nemo* (voice), and *The Square.* He is survived by his son and his brother and sister.

FERLIN HUSKY, 85, Missouri-born country singer, best known for his 1956 hit "Gone," died at his home in Hendersonville, TX, on March 17, 2011. He had been suffering from various health problems in recent years. He was seen in such movies as *Mister Rock and Roll, Country Music Holiday, The Las Vegas Hillbillys,* and *Hillbillys in a Haunted House.* He is survived by his companion, country singer Leona Williams; six daughters; and 11 grandchildren.

GUALTIERO JACOPETTI, 91, Italian filmmaker, best known for the "shockumentary" *Mondo Cane,* died on August 17, 2011. His other movies include *Women of the World, Mondo Cane 2, Goodbye Uncle Tom,* and *Africa Addio.* Survived by his daughter.

KEVIN JARRE, 56, Detroit born screenwriter who wrote the 1989 Civil War film *Glory,* died of heart failure at his home in Santa Monica, CA, on April 3, 2011. His other credits include *Tombstone, The Devil's Own,* and *The Mummy* (1999; also executive producer). Survivors include his aunt.

CHARLES JARROTT, 83, London-born director, best known for helming the 1969 Oscar nominated film *Anne of the Thousand Days,* died in Woodland Hills, CA, on March 4, 2011 of prostate cancer. His other movies include *Mary - Queen of Scots, Lost Horizon* (1973), *The Dove, The Other Side of Midnight, Condorman,* and *The Amateur.* Survived by a brother and three stepchildren.

SYBIL JASON, 83, South African former 1930's child actress died on August 23 2011 in Northridge, CA, of chronic obstructive pulmonary disease. Her movies include *Little Big Shot, I Found Stella Parish, The Singing Kid, The Little Princess,* and *The Blue Bird* (1940). Survived by her daughter and a grandson.

HAL KANTER, 92, Savannah-born writer-producer-director died of pneumonia on November 6, 2011 in Encino, CA. He directed *Loving You* (also writer), *I Married a Woman,* and *Once Upon a Horse* (also writer, producer), and wrote such films as *Two Tickets to Broadway, Road to Bali, Off Limits, Casanova's Big Night, About Mrs. Leslie, The Rose Tattoo, Mardi Gras, Blue Hawaii, Move Over Darling,* and *Dear Brigitte.* On television he was known for such series as *The George Gobel Show* and *Julia,* as well as writing for the Academy Awards, which brought him two Emmys. He is survived by his wife of 70 years; 3 daughters; his sister; and a granddaughter.

MIRIAM KARLIN (Miriam Samuels), 85, London-born actress, perhaps best known to U.S. audiences as the "Cat Lady" murdered by Malcolm McDowell in *A Clockwork Orange,* died on June 3, 2011 in London. Her other movies include *The Deep Blue Sea* (1955), *Room at the Top, The Entertainer, The Millionairess, Hand in Hand, The Phantom of the Opera* (1962), *The Small World of Sammy Lee, Heavens Above!, Mahler,* and *Children of Men.* On British television she starred in the series *The Rag Trade.* No reported survivors.

LEONARD KASTLE, 82, Bronx born composer-filmmaker died on May 18, 2011 at his home in Westerloo, NY. He directed and wrote only one movie, *The Honeymoon Killers,* which became a cult favorite. Survived by his sister.

BARBARA KENT (Barbara Cloutman), 103, Canadian-born silent film actress died on October 13, 2011 in Palm Desert, CA. Her credits include *Flesh and the Devil, Prowlers of the Night, The Drop Kick, No Man's Law, The Small Bachelor, Stop That Man, Lonesome, Welcome Danger, Feet First, Chinatown after Dark, Emma, Vanity Fair* (1932), *Oliver Twist* (1933), *Her Forgotten Past, Old Man Rhythm,* and her last, *Guard That Girl,* in 1936, after which she retired from acting. No immediate survivors.

ARON KINCAID (Norman Neale Williams III), 70, Los Angeles-born actor died in L.A. on January 6, 2011 of heart-related complications. He appeared in such movies as *The Girls on the Beach, Ski Party, Beach Ball, The Ghost in the Invisible Bikini,* and *Cannonball!,* while also maintaining separate careers as a model and an artist. No reported survivors.

WYATT KNIGHT, 56, actor best known for playing Tommy Turner in the hit 1982 comedy *Porky's* and its two sequels was found dead outside his home in Maui, Hawaii on Oct. 26, 2011, an apparent suicide. He had been suffering from cancer. He is survived by his third wife and two children from his second marriage.

ANDREW LASZLO, 85, Yugoslavia-born cinematographer died on October 10, 2011 in Montana. His credits include *One Potato Two Potato, You're a Big Boy Now, The Night They Raided Minsky's, The Out of Towners, Lovers and Other Strangers, The Owl and the Pussycat, Thieves, The Warriors, Southern Comfort, First Blood, Remo Williams: The Adventure Begins, Innerspace,* and *Newsies.* Survived by his wife, three sons, and a daughter.

ARTHUR LAURENTS, 93, New York City-born writer-director, best known for his librettos for the musicals *West Side Story* and *Gypsy,* died of complications of pneumonia on May 5, 2011 at his Manhattan home. His motion picture scripts include *Rope, Anastasia* (1956), *Bonjour Tristese, The Way We Were,* and *The Turning Point* (1977; also producer); Oscars nominations for screenplay and picture). He won Tonys for writing *Hallelujah Baby!* and for directing *La Cage aux Folles.* Survived by a niece and nephew.

LEN LESSER, 88, New York City-born character actor died on February 16, 2011 in Burbank, CA, of pneumonia and cancer. His movies include *Shack Out on 101, I Want to Live!, Bells are Ringing, How to Stuff a Wild Bikini, Kelly's Heroes, Papillon, The Outlaw Josey Wales, Take This Job and Shove It,* and *Baadasssss!* No reported survivors.

SUE LLOYD, 72, British actress died of cancer on October 20, 2011 in London. Her credits include *The Ipcress File, Hysteria, Where's Jack?, Percy, Revenge of the Pink Panther, The Bitch, Rough Cut,* and *Eat the Rich.* On British television she was best known for the series *Crossroads.* No reported survivors.

TERENCE LONGDON, 88, British actor died on April 23, 2011. His movies include *Mr. Arkadin, Helen of Troy, The Man Who Never Was, Another Time Another Place, Ben-Hur* (1959), *The Return of Mr. Moto,* and *The Sea Wolves.* Survived by his second wife.

PHYLLIS LOVE, 85, Des Moines-born actress, who portrayed Gary Cooper's Quaker daughter, Mattie Birdwell, in *Friendly Persuasion,* died at her home in Meinfee, California, on Oct. 30, 2011. She had been suffering from Alzheimer's disease. Her other theatrical films are *So Young So Bad* and *The Young Doctors.* Survivors include her second husband.

SIDNEY LUMET, 86, Philadelphia-born director, who earned Oscar nominations for his work on *Twelve Angry Men* (his debut feature, in 1957), *Dog Day Afternoon, Network,* and *The Verdict* (1982), died at his home in Manhattan on April 9, 2011. He had lymphoma. His other credits include *Stage Struck, That Kind of Woman, The Fugitive Kind, A View from the Bridge, Long Day's Journey into Night, Fail-Safe, The Pawnbroker, The Hill, The Group, Bye Bye Braverman, The Seagull, Last of the Mobile Hot-Shots, The Anderson Tapes, The Offence, Child's Play, Serpico, Lovin' Molly, Murder on the Orient Express, Equus, The Wiz, Prince of the City* (also co-writer), *Deathtrap, Daniel, Garbo Talks, The Morning After, Running on Empty, Q&A, Guilty as Sin, Night Falls on Manhattan, Find Me Guilty,* and *Before the Devil Knows You're Dead.* In 2004 he was presented with a special Academy Award. He is survived by his fourth wife; two daughters from his third marriage, one of whom is screenwriter Jenny Lumet; two stepdaughters; nine grandchildren; and a step-son.

JOHN MACKENZIE, 83, Edinburgh-born director of the British crime drama *The Long Good Friday* died in London on June 8, 2011. Among his other movies are *Unman, Wittering and Zigo; Beyond the Limit, The Fourth Protocol,* and *Ruby* (1992). Survived by three daughters.

KENNETH MARS, 75, Chicago-born character actor, best known for his comical roles in the Mel Brooks films *The Producers* (as the Nazi playwright Franz Liebkind) and *Young Frankenstein* (as the one-armed Inspector Kemp), died of pancreatic cancer at his home in Granada Hills, CA, on February 12, 2011. His other movies include *The April Fools, Viva Max, Desperate Characters, What's Up Doc?, The Parallax View, Night Moves, Yellowbeard, Protocol, Fletch, Radio Days, The Little Mermaid* (as the voice of Triton), *Shadows and Fog,* and *Citizen Ruth.* He is survived by two daughters and six grandchildren.

HUGH MARTIN, 96, Alabama-born songwriter, who, in collaboration with Ralph Blaine, received Oscar nominations for "The Trolley Song" (from *Meet Me in St. Louis*) and "Pass That Peace Pipe" (from *Good News*), died of natural causes at his home in Encinitas, CA, on March 11, 2011. His songs were heard in such other movies as *Best Foot Forward, Thousands Cheer, Broadway Rhythm, Ziegfeld Follies, Bud Abbott and Lou Costello in Hollywood,* and *The Girl Most Likely.* Another selection from *Meet Me in St. Louis*, "Have Yourself a Merry Little Christmas," became his most enduring song. Survivors include his brother.

ARTHUR MARX, 89, New York City-born writer died at his home in Los Angeles on April 14, 2011, of natural causes. The son of comedian Groucho Marx he wrote two memoirs about his relationship with his father, *Life with Groucho* and *Son of Groucho,* as well as collaborating on the Marx Brothers musical *Minnie's Boys.* His screenplays include *Blondie in the Dough, A Global Affair, Eight on the Lam,* and *Cancel My Reservation.* He is survived by his second wife; two sons; a stepdaughter; two sisters; and four grandchildren.

ANNA MASSEY, 73, British actress died at her home in London on July 3, 2011 from cancer. The daughter of actor Raymond Massey and younger sister of actor Daniel Massey, she made her movie debut in 1958 in *Gideon of Scotland Yard,* then later appeared in such features as *Peeping Tom, Bunny Lake is Missing, Frenzy, A Doll's House, A Little Romance, Another Country, The Little Drummer Girl, The Tall Guy, Mountains of the Moon, Impromptu, Angels & Insects, The Importance of Being Earnest* (2002; as Miss Prism), *The Machinist,* and *Mrs. Palfrey at the Claremont.* She is survived by her second husband and two sons from her first marriage.

BILL McKINNEY, 80, Chattanooga-born actor, who played the crazed hillbilly who assaulted Ned Beatty in the film *Deliverance,* died on December 1, 2011 of cancer of the esophagus. Among his other movies are *Junior Bonner, The Life and Times of Judge Roy Bean, Cleopatra Jones, Thunderbolt and Lightfoot, The Outlaw Josey Wales, The Shootist, The Gauntlet, Every Which Way but Loose, First Blood, Against All Odds,* and *The Green Mile.* Survivors include his son.

ADOLFAS MEKAS, 85, Lithuanian-born filmmaker, best known for the 1963 avant-garde work *Hallelujah the Hills!,* died of heart failure in Poughkeepsie, NY, on May 31, 2011. His other movies include *Windflowers* and *Going Home.* Survived by his wife, a son, and a brother.

SID MELTON (Sidney Meltzer), 94, Brooklyn-born character actor, most recognizable for his recurring roles on the series *The Danny Thomas Show* as Uncle Charley Halper and *Green Acres,* as Alf Monroe, died of pneumonia on November 2, 2011 in Burbank, CA. His movies include *Kilroy Was Here, Knock on Any Door, White Heat, Always Leave Them Laughing, On the Town, The Steel Helmet, The Lemon Drop Kid* (1951), *Lost Continent, Beau James, The Joker is Wild, The Geisha Boy, The Rise and Fall of Legs Diamond, Why Must I Die?, Lady Sings the Blues,* and *Sheila Levine is Dead and Living in New York.* He is survived by two nephews.

HARRY MORGAN (Harry Bratsburg), 96, Detroit-born character actor, whose long list of film credits included *The Ox-Bow Incident, The Glenn Miller Story,* and *Inherit the Wind,* died on December 7, 2011 at his Los Angeles home, of pneumonia. Launching his movie career in 1942 as "Henry Morgan," he was seen in such movies as *To the Shores of Tripoli, Happy Land, A Bell for Adano, Dragonwyck, The Big Clock, All My Sons, Yellow Sky, Down to the Sea in Ships, Holiday Affair, Madame Bovary, The Blue Veil, Scandal Sheet, Bend of the River, High Noon, Torch Song, About Mrs. Leslie, The Far Country, Not as a Stranger,* and *The Teahouse of the August Moon;* under the name "Harry" his films include *It Started with a Kiss, The Mountain Road, How the West Was Won* (as Ulysses S. Grant), *Frankie and Johnnie, What Did You Do in the War Daddy?, The Flim-Flam Man, Support Your Local Sheriff!, Viva Max!, The Barefoot Executive, The Apple Dumpling Gang, The Shootist,* and *Dragnet* (1987). His many series on television included *December Bride, Dragnet,* and, most notably, *M*A*S*H,* which brought him an Emmy Award. He is survived by his second wife; three sons from his first marriage; and eight grandchildren.

DOROTHY MORRIS, 89, Los Angeles-born actress, who appeared mainly for MGM in the 1940s, died on Nov. 20, 2011. Her credits include *Down in San Diego, This Time for Keeps, The War against Mrs. Hadley, The Human Comedy, Cry Havoc, I Dood It, Thirty Seconds over Tokyo, Our Vines Have Tender Grapes, Macabre,* and *Seconds.* Survived by her sister, actress Caren Marsh.

MARY MURPHY, 80, Washington, D.C.-born actress, best known for her role opposite Marlon Brandon in the 1953 motorcycle drama *The Wild One,* died at her home in Beverly Hills, CA, on May 4, 2011 of heart disease. Her other movies include *Off Limits* (1953), *Main Street to Broadway, Beachhead, The Mad Magician, Sitting Bull, The Desperate Hours, The Maverick Queen, Finger of Guilt, Crime & Punishment USA, 40 Pounds of Trouble,* and *Junior Bonner,* She is survived by her daughter.

CHARLES NAPIER, 75, Kentucky-born character actor died in Bakersfield, CA, on October 5, 2011 after collapsing in his home two days earlier. His movies include *Supervixens, Handle with Care, The Blues Brothers, Melvin and Howard, Swing Shift, Something Wild, Married to the Mob, Ernest Goes to Jail, Miami Blues, The Grifters, The Silence of the Lambs, National Lampoon's Loaded Weapon 1, Philadelphia, The Cable Guy, Austin Powers: International Man of Mystery, Lords of Dogtown,* and *The Goods.* Survived by his second wife and three children.

SILVIO NARIZZANO, 84, Montreal-born director, best known for helming the classic 1966 British film *Georgy Girl,* died on July 26, 2011. His other theatrical features include *Die! Die! My Darling* (*Fanatic*), *Blue, Loot, Why Shoot the Teacher?,*and *The Class of Miss MacMichael.* He is survived by two sisters and a brother.

MARILYN NASH, 84, Michigan-born actress, who appeared opposite Charles Chaplin in his 1947 black comedy *Monsieur Verdoux,* died on October 6, 2011 in Oroville, California. Her only other theatrical release was *Unknown World.* She later worked as a casting director and at various other jobs outside the industry. Survived by four sons and six grandchildren.

DAVID NELSON, 74, New York City-born actor, who played a version of himself on his family's long-running sitcom, *The Adventures of Ozzie and Harriet,* died on January 11, 2011 at his Century City, CA, home of complications from colon cancer. He was also seen in such movies as *Here Come the Nelsons, Peyton Place, The Remarkable Mr. Pennypacker, The Big Circus, -30-, The Big Show, Up*

Nicol Williamson

Googie Withers

John Wood

Dana Wynter

Peter Yates

Susannah York

in *Smoke*, and *Cry-Baby*. He is survived by his second wife; four sons; a daughter; and seven grandchildren.

JOHN NEVILLE, 86, British actor died on November 19, 2011 in Toronto. He had been suffering from Alzheimer's disease. Among his films are *Oscar Wilde, I Like Money* (*Mr. Topaze*), *Billy Budd, A Study in Terror* (as Sherlock Holmes), *The Adventures of Baron Munchhausen, The Road to Wellville, Little Women* (1994), *Dangerous Minds, High School High, The Fifth Element, Sunshine* (1999), *Spider*, and *The Statement*. After moving to Canada in 1972 he became a mainstay in theater there. Survived by his wife of 62 years, their six children, and six grandchildren.

LENA NYMAN, 66, Swedish actress who starred in the controversial 1969 film *I am Curious (Yellow)*, died in Stockholm on February 4, 2011, following a long illness. Among her other films to receive U.S. distribution were *491, I am Curious (Blue), The White Wall, Autumn Sonata*, and *Ronja Robbersdaughter*.

RICHARD PEARSON, 93, Wales-born character actor died in London on Aug. 2, 2011, one day after his birthday. His movies include *A Christmas Carol* (1951), *Libel, The Yellow Rolls-Royce, How I Won the War, Charlie Bubbles, Macbeth* (1971), *Sunday Bloody Sunday, Pope Joan, Tess, The Mirror Crack'd*, and *Pirates*. He is survived by his wife, two sons, and two grandchildren.

DON PETERMAN, 79, Los Angeles-born cinematographer, who earned Oscar nominations for *Flashdance* and *Star Trek IV: The Voyage Home*, died on February 5, 2011 at his home in Paolo Verdes Estates, CA, of complications from myelodysplastic syndrome. His other credits include *Splash, Cocoon, She's Having a Baby, Point Break, Addams Family Values, Mr. Saturday Night, Get Shorty*, and *How the Grinch Stole Christmas*. Survived by his wife of 54 years; a daughter and three sons; and 10 grandchildren.

ROLAND PETIT, 87, French choreographer-dancer died in Geneva on July 10, 2011. Creator of Les Ballets des champs-Elysees and Ballets de Paris, he contributed choreography to such movies as *Hans Christian Andersen* (also dancer), *Daddy Long Legs* (1955), *The Glass Slipper, Anything Goes* (1956), and *Black Tights* (also dancer). He is survived by his wife of 57 years, dancer Zizi Jeanmaire, and his daughter, dancer Valentine Petit.

PAUL PICERNI, 88, New York City-born actor, best remembered for his role as Agent Lee Hobson on the hit series *The Untouchables*, died of a heart attack on January 12, 2011 at his home in Llano near Palmdale, CA. He was also seen in such movies as *Operation Pacific, I Was a Communist for the FBI, Inside the Walls of Folsom Prison, Cattle Town, She's Back on Broadway, Mara Maru, House of Wax* (1953), *To Hell and Back, Miracle in the Rain, Operation Mad Ball, The Brothers Rico, Marjorie Morningstar, Torpedo Run, The Young Philadelphians, Strangers When We Meet, The Scalphunters, Airport, Kotch*, and *Capricorn One*. He is survived by his wife of 63 years, six children, and ten grandchildren.

MARIE-FRANCE PISIER, 66, Vietnam-born French actress, best known in America for her roles in *Cousin Cuisine* and *The Other Side of Midnight*, was found dead in her swimming pool at her home in St. Cyr sur Mer in the South of

France on April 24, 2011. Her other U.S.-released films include *Love at 20, Stolen Kisses, Celine and Julie Go Boating, Phantom of Liberty, French Provincial, Love on the Run, French Postcards*. She is survived by her second husband; a sister, a brother, a son, and a daughter.

POLLY PLATT, 72, Illinois-born production designer-producer died of Lou Gehrig's disease on July 27, 2011 at her Brooklyn home. Her production design credits include *Targets* (for which she also provided the story), *The Last Picture Show, What's Up Doc?, Paper Moon, A Star is Born* (1976), *The Man with Two Brains, Terms of Endearment* (Oscar nomination), and *The Witches of Eastwick*, while her producing credits include *Pretty Baby* (also writer), *Broadcast News, Say Anything … * (also actress), and *The War of the Roses*. She is survived by her brother; her two daughters from her marriage to director Peter Bogdanovich; two stepchildren from her second marriage; and three grandsons.

ALICE PLAYTEN (Alice Plotkin), 63, New York City-born actress died of heart failure on June 25, 2011 in Manhattan. Her movies include *Ladybug Ladybug, Who Killed Mary What'sername?, California Dreaming, Legend, For Love or Money* (1993), and *I.Q.* Survived by her husband and a brother.

PETE POSTLETHWAITE, 64, British actor, who earned an Oscar nomination for playing the wrongly imprisoned Giuseppe Conlon in the 1993 film *In the Name of the Father*, died in Shropshire, England, on January 2, 2011 following a long battle with cancer. His other movies include *A Private Function, Distant Voices Still Lives, Hamlet* (1990, as the Player King), *Waterland, The Last of the Mohicans, The Usual Suspects, James and the Giant Peach, DragonHeart, Romeo + Juliet* (as Father Laurence), *Brassed Off, Jurassic Park: The Lost World, Amistad, Among Giants, The Shipping News, The Constant Gardener, Clash of the Titans* (2010), *Inception*, and *The Town*. He is survived by his wife, his son, and his daughter.

DAVID RAYFIEL, 87, New York-born screenwriter, who worked mainly with director Sydney Pollack on several projects (both credited and uncredited), died of congestive heart failure in Manhattan on June 22, 2011. Among those movies on which he received credit were *Valdez is Coming, Three Days of the Condor, Lipstick, 'Round Midnight, Havana, The Firm, Intersection*, and *Sabrina*. Survived by his third wife; a daughter; two stepchildren; a brother; and two grandchildren.

PEGGY REA, 89, Los Angeles-born character actress died of complications from congestive heart failure at her home in Toluca Lake, CA on Feb. 5, 2011. Her movies include *7 Faces of Dr. Lao, Walk Don't Run, Valley of the Dolls, The Learning Tree, Cold Turkey, What's the Matter with Helen?, In Country, Love Field*, and *Devil in a Blue Dress*. No immediate survivors.

BETTY JANE RHODES, 90, Illinois-born singer-actress died on December 25, 2011. Her brief movie career found her appearing in such pictures as *Jungle Jim, Stage Door; Oh, Johnny, How You Can Love* (singing the title song), *The Fleet's In, Sweater Girl, Star Spangled Rhythm*, and *You Can't Ration Love*. Survived by one child and three stepchildren.

CLIFF ROBERTSON (Clifford Parker Robertson III), 88, La Jolla-born actor, who won the Academy Award for his portrayal of a mentally handicapped man who temporarily becomes a genius in the 1968 movie *Charly*, died in Stony Brook, NY, of natural causes on September 10, 2011, one day after his birthday. Following his 1955 film debut in *Picnic*, he was seen in such other pictures as *Autumn Leaves, The Girl Most Likely, The Naked and the Dead, Gidget, The Big Show, All in a Night's Work, Underworld U.S.A., The Interns, PT 109* (as John F. Kennedy), *Sunday in New York, The Best Man, 633 Squadron, Masquerade, The Honey Pot, The Devil's Brigade, Too Late the Hero, J.W. Coop* (which he also directed, produced, and wrote), *The Great Northfield Minnesota Raid, Ace Eli and Rodger of the Skies, Man on a Swing, Three Days of the Condor, Midway, Obsession, The Pilot* (also director, writer), *Star 80, Class, Brainstorm* (1983), *Wild Hearts Can't Be Broken, Wind, Renaissance Man, Escape from L.A., 13th Child* (also writer), and *Spider-Man*. He is survived by his daughter from his first marriage and a granddaughter.

JANE RUSSELL (Ernestine Jane Geraldine Russell), 89, Minnesota-born actress, who starred in such hit films as *The Paleface* and *Gentlemen Prefer Blondes*, died of a respiratory-related illness at her home in Santa Maria, CA, on February 28, 2011. After becoming famous for her controversial appearance in the western *The Outlaw*, she was seen in such other movies as *His Kind of Woman, Double Dynamite, The Las Vegas Story, Son of Paleface, Montana Belle, The French Line, Underwater!, The Tall Men, The Revolt of Mamie Stover, The Fuzzy Pink Nightgown, Fate is the Hunter, Waco, The Born Losers,* and *Darker Than Amber*. She is survived by her 3 children, 8 grandchildren, and 10 great-grandchildren.

KEN RUSSELL (Henry Kenneth Alfred Russell), 84, British filmmaker, whose controversial, daring directorial style could be seen in such major 1970s films as *Women in Love* (for which he earned an Oscar nomination for directing) and *Tommy* (which he also adapted from the Who's rock opera and produced), died on November 27, 2011 in London, following a series of strokes. His other credits as director (and often as writer and producer) include *Billion Dollar Brain, The Music Lovers, The Devils, The Boy Friend, Savage Messiah, Mahler, Lisztomania, Valentino* (1977), *Altered States, Crimes of Passion, Gothic, Salome's Last Dance, The Lair of the White Worm, The Rainbow,* and *Whore*. He is survived by his fourth wife and his 6 children.

JIMMY SANGSTER, 83, Welsh-born filmmaker, known for his long and varied association with Hammer Studios, died on August 19, 2011 in London. As writer his credits include *The Curse of Frankenstein, Horror of Dracula, The Revenge of Frankenstein, The Crawling Eye, Jack the Ripper, The Mummy* (1959), *The Brides of Dracula, The Nanny, Dracula: Prince of Darkness, The Anniversary* (also producer), *The Horror of Frankenstein* (also director), *Whoever Slew Auntie Roo?,* and *Fear in the Night* (also director). Survived by his wife, actress Mary Peach; a son from a previous marriage; and two grandchildren.

MICHAEL SARRAZIN (Jacques Michel André Sarrazin), 70, Quebec-born actor, best known for starring opposite Jane Fonda in the 1969 Depression-era drama *They Shoot Horses, Don't They?,* died in Montreal on April 17, 2011, following a battle with cancer. His other movies include *The Flim Flam Man, Gunfight in Abilene, The Sweet Ride, Eye of the Cat, In Search of Gregory, The Pursuit of Happiness, Sometimes a Great Notion, The Life and Times of Judge Roy Bean, Harry in Your Pocket, For Pete's Sake, The Reincarnation of Peter Proud, The Gumball Rally, Caravans, Joshua Then and Now, Malarek,* and *FeardotCom*. Survived by his brother, producer Pierre Sarrazin, and his two daughters.

TURA SATANA (Tura Luna Pascual Yamaguchi), 75, Japan-born actress, best known for her leading role in Russ Meyer's cult film *Faster, Pussycat! Kill! Kill!* died of heart failure on February 4, 2011 in Reno, NV. Her other movies include *Irma La Douce, Our Man Flint,* and *The Astro-Zombies.* Survived by two daughters and two sisters.

BERT SCHNEIDER, 78, New York City-born producer, whose production company Raybert, was responsible for such counter-culture classics as *Easy Rider* and *Five Easy Pieces*, died in Los Angeles on December 12, 2011. His other credits include *Head; Drive, He Said; The Last Picture Show, Hearts and Minds* (for which he won the Academy Award), and *Days of Heaven*. He is survived by his daughter and his son from his first marriage and four grandchildren.

MARIA SCHNEIDER (Marie Christine Gélin), 58, Paris-born actress, who created a stir when she starred opposite Marlon Brando in the X-rated film *Last Tango in Paris*, died of cancer in Paris on February 3, 2011. Her other movies released in the U.S. include *The Passenger, The Conviction,* and *Jane Eyre* (1996). No reported survivors.

RONALD SEARLE, 91, Cambridge-born cartoonist-illustrator, best known for creating the *St. Trinian's* characters, died in his sleep on December 30, 2011 in Draguignan, France, after a brief illness. In addition to his illustrations appearing in four movie adaptations of the "St. Trinian's" works, they were also seen in *Those Magnificent Men in Their Flying Machines* and *Scrooge*. Survivors include his son; his daughter; and a grandson.

BUBBA SMITH (Charles Aaron Smith), 66, Texas-born former NFL football player-turned-actor was found dead at his Los Angeles home on Aug. 3, 2011, of acute drug intoxication. He also suffered from heart disease and high-blood pressure. His movies include *Police Academy*, and its many sequels; *Stroker Ace,* and *Black Moon Rising*. No reported survivors.

PATRICIA SMITH, 80, New Haven-born actress died of heart failure on January 2, 2011 in Los Angeles. Among her movie credits are *The Bachelor Party, The Spirit of St. Louis, Save the Tiger,* and *Mad City*. Survivors include two sons.

G.D. SPRADLIN (Gervase Duan Spradlin), 90, Oklahoma-born character actor died of natural causes at his home in San Luis Obispo, CA, on July 24, 2011. A former oil company producer, he turned to acting in his 40's, appearing in such pictures as *Will Penny, Monte Walsh, The Godfather Part II, One on One, MacArthur, North Dallas Forty, Apocalypse Now, The Formula, Wrong is Right, The Lords of Discipline, Tank, The War of the Roses, Ed Wood, Canadian Bacon, The Long Kiss Goodnight,* and *Dick*. He is survived by his second wife; his two daughters from his first marriage; and five grandchildren.

LEONARD STERN, 88, New York City-born producer-writer-director, who won Emmys for his work on *The Phil Silvers Show* and *Get Smart*, died at his home in Los Angeles on June 7, 2011. Although he worked principally on television, he wrote such motion pictures as *Ma and Pa Kettle Go to Town, Abbott and Costello in the Foreign Legion, The Milkman, Lost in Alaska, Three for the Show, Just You and Me Kid* (which he also directed), and *The Nude Bomb*. He is survived by his wife; a son and a daughter; two grand-children; and a great-grand-daughter.

KAYE STEVENS (Catherine Louise Stevens), 79, Pittsburgh-born singer-actress died on Dec. 28, 2011 in The Villages, FL, after battling breast cancer and blood clots. Her four theatrical releases were *The Interns, The Man from the Diner's Club, The New Interns,* and *Jaws 3D*. No reported survivors.

MARGOT STEVENSON (Margaret Helen Stevenson), 98, Manhattan-born actress died on January 2, 2011 at her home in New York. Her movies include *Invisible Stripes, Granny Get Your Gun, Castle on the Hudson, Valley of the Dolls, Rabbit Run,* and *Going in Style*. Survived by her daughter.

ELAINE STEWART (Elsy Steinberg), 82, New Jersey-born actress, died on June 27, 2011 in Beverly Hills after a long illness. Her movies include *Singin' in the Rain, Sky Full of Moon, The Bad and the Beautiful, Young Bess* (as Anne Boleyn), *Brigadoon, The Tattered Dress, Night Passage,* and *The Rise and Fall of Legs Diamond*. Survived by her husband, producer Merrill Heatter, and two children.

LEONARD STONE, 88, Oregon-born character actor died after a brief bout with cancer on November 2, 2011, one day before his 89th birthday. His movie credits include *Toys in the Attic, Shock Treatment, The Big Mouth, Angel in My Pocket, Getting Straight, Willy Wonka & the Chocolate Factory, Soylent Green, Mame,* and *Hardly Working*. He is survived by his wife; three daughters; a son; and eight grandchildren.

BARBARA STUART (Barbara Ann McNeese), 76, Illinois-born actress died at her home in St. George, UT, on May 15, 2011. Although mostly seen guest starring on countless television episodes, she also popped up in a handful of movies including *Marines, Let's Go;Hellfighters, Dreamer, Airplane!,*and *Bachelor Party.* Survived by a brother and three stepchildren.

ALAN SUES, 85, California-born actor, one of the ensemble cast members of the hit comedy series *Rowan & Martin's Laugh-In,* died at his West Hollywood home on December 1, 2011, an apparent heart attack. His movie credits include *The Helen Morgan Story, The Wheeler Dealers, Move over Darling, The Americanization of Emily,* and *Oh Heavenly Dog.* Survived by his sister-in-law.

HERB TANNEY, 80, New Jersey-born actor died of congestive heart failure in San Diego, CA on June 28, 2011. A licensed Endocrinologist, he was called on by one of his patients, director-writer Blake Edwards, to appear in several of his movies, using fake first names, notably *Victor Victoria,*as the private investigator (billed as "SherloqueTanney"). Among the other Edwards films were *Darling Lili, Wild Rovers, The Return of the Pink Panther, 10, S.O.B., Blind Date, Skin Deep,* and *Switch.* Survived by his wife and two children.

ELIZABETH TAYLOR, 79, London-born actress, who won Academy Awards for her performances in *BUtterfield 8* and *Who's Afraid of Virginia Woolf?,*and became one of the most famous celebrities in the world, died in Los Angeles on March 23, 2011 of congestive heart failure. She received additional Oscar nominations for *Raintree County, Cat on a Hot Tin Roof,* and *Suddenly, Last Summer.* Following her debut in 1942 in *There's One Born Every Minute,* she became a star with *National Velvet.* Her other movies include *Lassie Come Home, The White Cliffs of Dover, Jane Eyre* (1944), *Life with Father, A Date with Judy, Julia Misbehaves, Little Women* (1949), *Conspirator, Father of the Bride* (1950), *A Place in the Sun, Ivanhoe, The Girl Who Had Everything, Beau Brummel, Elephant Walk, The Last Time I Saw Paris, Giant, Cleopatra* (1963; the first of several with her fifth and sixth husband, actor Richard Burton), *The VIPs, The Sandpiper, The Taming of the Shrew* (1967), *Reflections in a Golden Eye, The Comedians, Doctor Faustus, Boom, The Only Game in Town, XY & Zee, Hammersmith is Out!, Ash Wednesday, The Blue Bird* (1976), *A Little Night Music, The Mirror Crack'd,* and *The Flintstones.* She also received the Jean Hersholt Humanitarian Award for raising millions to fight against AIDS; the American Film Institute Lifetime Achievement Award and the Kennedy Center Honors. She is survived by her two sons, from her marriage to actor Michael Wilding; her daughter from her marriage to producer Mike Todd; her adopted daughter; and 10 grandchildren, and 4 great-granchildren.

SADA THOMPSON, 81, Des Moines-born actress, who won a Tony for her performance in *Twigs* and an Emmy for her role on the series *Family,* died of lung disease in Danbury, CT, on May 4, 2011. She appeared in the films *The Pursuit of Happiness, Desperate Characters,* and *Pollock.* Survived by her husband, her daughter, and a brother.

MICHAEL TOLAN (Seymour Tuchow), 85, Detroit-born actor died of heart disease and renal failure on January 31, 2011 in Hudson, NY. His movies include *The Enforcer* (1950, as Lawrence Tolan), *The Savage, Julius Caesar* (1953), *The Greatest Story Ever Told, Hour of the Gun, John and Mary, All That Jazz,* and *Presumed Innocent.* He was one of the founders of the American Place Theater in New York. Survivors include his companion; a daughter from his first marriage, to actress Rosemary Forsyth; and two daughters from his second marriage.

GORDON TOOTOOSIS, 69, Saskatchewan-born actor died of pneumonia on July 5, 2011 in Saskatoon, Canada. His movie credits include *Alien Thunder, Black Robe, Leaving Normal, Legends of the Fall, Pocahontas* (voice), *Lone Star* (1996), *Alaska, The Edge, Reindeer Games,* and *Open Season* (voice). He was also a member of the National Indian Brotherhood and served as vice president of the Federation of Saskatchewan Indian Nations. Survived by his wife, four children, and grandchildren.

MARGARET TYZACK, 79,British actress died in London on June 25, 2011 after a brief battle with cancer. Her motion pictures include *The Whisperers, 2001: A Space Odyssey, Thank You All Very Much, A Clockwork Orange, The Legacy, Prick Up Your Ears, Mrs. Dalloway, Bright Young Things,* and *Match Point.* On television she was known for her roles in *The Forsyte Saga* and *Claudius,* and won a Tony for appearing on Broadway in *Lettice and Lovage.* Survived by her husband and son.

THEADORA VAN RUNKLE (Dorothy Schweppe), 83, Pittsburgh-born costume designer, who received Oscar nominations for her work in *Bonnie and Clyde, The Godfather Part II,* and *Peggy Sue Got Married,* died of lung cancer on November 4, 2011 in Los Angeles. Her other credits include *I Love You Alice B. Toklas!, The Reivers, Mame, Nickelodeon, New York New York, Same Time Next Year, The Jerk, S.O.B., The Best Little Whorehouse in Texas, Everybody's All-American, Stella* (1990), and *Leap of Faith.* She is survived by her son and daughter; and her grandson.

YVETTE VICKERS (Yvette Vedder), 82, Kansas City-born actress, best known for appearing in such "B" thrillers as *Attack of the 50 Ft. Woman* and *Attack of the Giant Leeches,* was found dead in her Benedict Canyon, CA, home on April 27, 2011. She had died of heart disease. Her badly decomposed body and reports of last sightings by neighbors suggested she had been dead for several months. Her other movies include *Sunset Blvd., Reform School Girl, Short Cut to Hell, The Sad Sack, I Mobster, Hud, What's the Matter with Helen?,* and *Evil Spirits.* Survived by a brother.

GARY WINICK, 49,New York City-born filmmaker died of brain cancer on February 27, 2011 in Manhattan. He directed such movies as *Tadpole, 13 Going on 30, Charlotte's Web* (2006), *Bride Wars,* and *Letters to Juliet,* and served as producer on films like *Tape, Chelsea Walls, Pieces of April,* and *Lonesome Jim.* He is survived by his parents; his fiancée; his stepmother; and his stepfather.

GOOGIE WITHERS (Georgette Lizette Withers), 94, India-born British actress, who appeared in such notable 1940s U.K. films as *One of Our Aircraft is Missing, Dead of Night,*and *It Always Rains on Sunday,* died in Sydney, Australia on July 15, 2011 of natural causes. Her other movies include *The Lady Vanishes* (1938), *The Amazing Mr. Forrest* (*The Gang's All Here*), *They Came to a City, On Approval, Miranda, The Loves of Joanna Godden, Night and the City* (1950), *White Corridors, The Magic Box, Country Life,* and *Shine.* Her second husband (whom she married in 1948) was actor John McCullum, who died in 2010. Their three children survive.

JOHN WOOD, 81, British character actor died in his sleep on August 6, 2011 in Gloucestershire, England. His films include *Two Way Stretch, Love is a Ball, The Mouse on the Moon, Which Way to the Front?, Nicholas and Alexandra, WarGames, The Purple Rose of Cairo, Ladyhawke, Lady Jane, Heartburn, Jumpin' Jack Flash, Shadowlands, The Madness of King George, Richard III* (1995), *Sabrina* (1995), *Jane Eyre* (1996), *Metroland, An Ideal Husband* (1999), *The Little Vampire,* and *The White Countess.* On Broadway he won a Tony for his performance in *Travesties.* Survived by his wife and four children.

DANA WYNTER (Dagmar Wynter), 79, Germany-born British actress, best remembered for her starring role in the 1956 sci-fi classic *Invasion of the Body Snatchers,* died of congestive heart failure in Ojai, CA, on May 5, 2011. She was seen in such other pictures as *The Crimson Pirate, The View from Pompey's Head, D-Day the Sixth of June, Something of Value, Shake Hands with the Devil, Sink the Bismarck!, On the Double, The List of Adrian Messenger,* and *Airport.* Survived by her son.

PETER YATES, 81, British filmmaker, who earned directing and producing Oscar nominations for *Breaking Away* and *The Dresser,* died in London on January 9, 2011 after a long illness. His other credits as director include *Summer Holiday, One Way Pendulum, Robbery* (also writer), *Bullitt, John and Mary, Murphy's War, The Hot Rock, The Friends of Eddie Coyle, For Pete's Sake, The Deep, Suspect,* and *Roommates,* while he was director-producer on such other pictures as *Mother, Jugs & Speed; Eyewitness; The House on Carroll Street; Year of the Comet;*and *The Run of the Country.* He is survived by his wife, a son and a daughter.

SUSANNAH YORK (Susannah Yolande Fletcher), 72, London-born actress who appeared in the Oscar-winning films *Tom Jones* (as Sophie Western) and *A Man for All Seasons* (as Thomas More's daughter, Margaret), died of cancer on January 15, 2011 in London. Her other motion picture credits include *Tunes of Glory, Loss of Innocence, Freud, The 7th Dawn, Kaleidoscope, Sebastian, Duffy, The Killing of Sister George, Oh! What a Lovely War, Battle of Britain, They Shoot Horses Don't They?* (Oscar nomination for supporting actress), *Brotherly Love* (*Country Dance*), *Happy Birthday Wanda June, X Y & Zee, The Maids, The Shout, Superman, The Silent Partner, The Awakening, Loophole, Yellowbeard,* and *A Summer Story.* She is survived by a son, actor Orlando Wells; a daughter; and grandchildren.

ROSEL ZECH, 69, German actress who played the title role in the 1982 Rainer Werner Fassbinder movie *Veronika Voss,* died on August 31, 2011. Among her other titles released in the U.S. were *Salmonberries,* and *Aimee & Jaguar.* Survived by her mother.

LAURA ZISKIN, 61, California-born producer of such films as *Pretty Woman* and *Spider-Man* died of breast cancer at her home in Los Angeles on June 12, 2011. Her other credits include *Eyes of Laura Mars, Murphy's Romance, No Way Out* (1987), *Everybody's All-American, What about Bob?* (also story), *The Doctor, Hero* (1992; also story), *To Die For, As Good as it Gets,* and the posthumously released *The Amazing Spider-Man.* She is survived by her companion of many years, writer Alvin Sargent, and her daughter.

Index